Butterworths International Insolvency Laws

Butterworths International Insolvency Laws

Edited by

Philip Wood
Partner, Allen & Overy

Peter G Totty
Partner, Allen & Overy

Translation Editor

Martin G Bates BA (HONS) (OXON)
Solicitor of the Supreme Court
Associate with Allen & Overy

Butterworths
London, Dublin, Edinburgh
1994

United Kingdom	Butterworth & Co (Publishers) Ltd, Halsbury House, 35 Chancery Lane, LONDON WC2A 1EL and 4 Hill Street, EDINBURGH EH2 3JZ
Australia	Butterworths, SYDNEY, MELBOURNE, BRISBANE, ADELAIDE, PERTH, CANBERRA and HOBART
Canada	Butterworths Canada Ltd, TORONTO and VANCOUVER
Ireland	Butterworth (Ireland) Ltd, DUBLIN
Malaysia	Malayan Law Journal Sdn Bhd, KUALA LUMPUR
New Zealand	Butterworths of New Zealand Ltd, WELLINGTON and AUCKLAND
Puerto Rico	Butterworths of Puerto Rico, Inc, SAN JUAN
Singapore	Butterworths Asia, SINGAPORE
South Africa	Butterworth Publishers (Pty) Ltd, DURBAN
USA	Butterworth Legal Publishers, CARLSBAD, California, and SALEM, New Hampshire

Note: The translations included in this volume are not recognised as official translations.

The publishers would like to thank EIBUN-HOREI-SHA, INC, Tokyo, Japan, for their permission to publish their English translations of the Civil Code of Japan, Corporate Reorganisation Law, and Bankruptcy Law of Japan.

The publishers are grateful to the relevant authorities in Switzerland, Luxembourg and Spain for granting permission to publish the translations of their country's laws contained within this volume.

A CIP Catalogue record for this book is available from the British Library.

ISBN 0 406 00085 9

Typeset by Doublestruck Limited, London
Printed by Mackays of Chatham PLC, Chatham, Kent

Preface

This book contains translations of nine non-English insolvency laws from some of the most commercially important jurisdictions in the world.

The growing international dimension of insolvency cases leads to the result that English-speaking lawyers now need to do more than merely refer the foreign element of their cases to foreign correspondents, and in doing more, they need to be able to read the texts of the foreign insolvency laws. The object of this work is to enable foreign lawyers' advice to be put in context and thus enable the English-speaking lawyer to better comprehend the foreign insolvency regime.

There are no real equivalents for legal terms in other languages and so sometimes the translation may be an approximation only. Nevertheless, I believe the effort was worthwhile and the greater understanding of the differences and similarities between some of the world's more important insolvency laws will be of real benefit to insolvency lawyers in whatever jurisdiction they may practice.

We are particularly grateful to the translation editor, Martin Bates, whose energy and determination brought this work to fruition, and to the many lawyers in our firm and abroad who laboured with such commitment to improve and review the translations.

Philip Wood
Peter Totty
Allen & Overy
1 New Change
London EC4

Translation Editor's Note

With the exception of Japan, which was given to us, and of the Netherlands, which was the work of an official court translator who also works for our associated firm in the Netherlands, Loeff Claeys Verbeke, these translations are primarily the work of lawyers with Allen & Overy – trainees, assistants and partners – and done entirely voluntarily, over the last three years. The basic instruction to them was: if in doubt be literal. Once they had completed the first draft, this was reviewed in most cases by a bilingual, or near bilingual, associate within the firm, in some cases on secondment from the relevant foreign jurisdiction, in conjunction with myself. We would look for errors and inconsistencies and at the same time work the text into the more natural flow of the English language. Finally, the text would be sent to a friendly foreign lawyer, usually an insolvency specialist, in the relevant jurisdiction who, again voluntarily, would rework the text, correct errors and discuss and resolve with me in detail any difficult points still outstanding. In this way, we have endeavoured to avoid errors and inconsistencies. For any that may remain, however, I accept full responsibility. I have mentioned already that these translations have been prepared over a period of time and we recommend that practitioners check the exact status of the legislation with their correspondent lawyer. That said, I hope that, used with these limitations in mind, the work will fulfil a need for direct access by English speaking lawyers to these foreign texts. The team, without whose help this could never have happened is:

Belgium	Initial work:	Adrian Hockridge, Matthew Jansen, Bianca Henry, Rod Cork
	Review:	Pru Mitchell
	Belgian lawyer:	Eric Cusas
France	Initial work:	Martin Bates
	Review:	Claire Bijon, Pru Mitchell
	French lawyer:	Pascal Alix
Germany	Initial work:	Candida Otto-Jones, Chris Warncke, Natalie Burn, Sally Prest, Ian Rose, Martin Hedemann-Robinson
	Review:	Susanne Perker, Martin Bates
	German lawyer:	Dr. iur. Matthias Benecke

Italy	Initial work:	Michael Reynolds, Natalie da Gama Rose, Anne-Claude May
	Review:	Martin Bates
	Italian lawyer:	Eugenio Grippo
Luxembourg	Initial work:	Deborah Jackson, Lola Grange, Carol Swaffer, Peter Lewis, James Dakin
	Review:	Pru Mitchell
Netherlands		Friso Meeter, Peter Stuijt, Joke Duinhouwer, all of Loeff Claeys Verbeke in Rotterdam
Switzerland	Initial work:	Matthew Lindsay, Adrian Hockridge, Deborah Jackson, Patrick Martensson, Mark Whitehouse, Matthew Jansen, Joanne Gray
	Review:	Martin Bates
	Swiss lawyer:	Richard Pease
Spain	Initial work:	Catriona Smith, Sarah Berwick, Isaac Felberbaum, Jacqui Kerr, Susie Lane
	Review:	Catriona Smith
	Spanish lawyer:	Alfonso Lopez-Ibor

I thank them one and all. Special mention must be made of the overseas lawyers who gave so very freely of their time: Eugenio Grippo of Studio avv. Grippo, Milan, Peter Stuijt of Loeff Claeys Verbeke in Rotterdam, Eric Cusas of Loeff Claeys Verbeke in Brussels, Richard Pease of Lenz & Staehelin in Geneva, Philippe Dupont of Arendt & Medernach in Luxembourg, Pascal Alix of Gide Loyretteg Nouel in Paris, Matthias Benecke of Bruckhaus Westrick & Stegemann and Susanne Perker in Hamburg.

Martin Bates

CONTENTS

BELGIUM

Belgian insolvency law is contained in Book III of the Commercial Code, and the Decree of 25th September 1946 which consolidates the previously enacted scheme of arrangement provisions of the Laws of 29th June 1887 and 10th August 1946. The assignment of property chapter of the Civil Code is included since it deals with the surrender of assets by debtors. The translation is of the law as it was on 1st January 1992.

Book III is set out in four parts or titles. Part I deals with the whole of the bankruptcy laws, as described in the chapter headings. All the chapters are procedural except for chapter II (the effect of bankruptcy) and chapter VII (creditors' rights). Part II deals with bankruptcy offences, Part III with discharge, and Part IV with the suspension of payments provisions. The Decree, which contains the scheme of arrangement provisions, is entirely procedural.

CHAPTER ONE

Belgian Insolvency Laws

TABLE OF CONTENTS

COMMERCIAL CODE

BOOK III. BANKRUPTCY, FRAUDULENT BANKRUPTCY AND SUSPENSION OF PAYMENTS

General provisions

437. Any trader who ceases making payments and whose credit is unsound is in a state of bankruptcy.

Any person who has ceased trading may be declared bankrupt if he had ceased making payments at a time when he was still trading.

A trader may be declared bankrupt after his death if he had ceased making payments by the time of his death.

438. Bankruptcy is designated as non-fraudulent bankruptcy and will be punished by a fine if the bankrupt trader's act or omission is within one of the categories of serious misdemeanour contained in chapter I of part II.

Bankruptcy is designated as fraudulent bankruptcy and will be punished as a crime if the bankrupt trader's act or omission is within one of the categories of fraud contained in chapter II of part II.

439. Applications for suspension of payments will be presented and determined in accordance with the provisions of part IV.

PART I. BANKRUPTCY

Chapter I: Admission and declaration of bankruptcy, and cessation of payments

440. Any person who is bankrupt must make an admission at the registry of the district commercial court for the area in which he resides within three days of cessation of payments. The three day period includes the day on which he ceased making payments.

In the case of a bankrupt partnership, the admission will contain the name and address of each of the partners who is jointly liable; it will be made at the registry of the district commercial court for the area in which the principal office of the partnership is situated.

Where a limited company has been declared bankrupt, the proceedings will be brought against the directors, who, whenever so requested will appear before, and provide all required information to, the bankruptcy judge and the trustees.

441. The following documents will be attached to the admission:

(1) a balance sheet of the bankrupt's business or a memorandum explaining the reasons why this cannot be filed;

(2) the registers required to be kept by chapter I of the law relating to accounting and annual accounts of businesses; these registers will be closed by the clerk of the court who will make a record of the state in which he finds them.

The balance sheet will contain a list and valuation of all the real and personal property of the debtor, a list of assets and liabilities, the profit and loss account, and a schedule of expenses; the balance sheet will be certified as correct, dated and signed by the debtor.

At the foot of the bankrupt's admission and any attached documents the clerk of the court will certify the date on which they were received at the registry and, if required, provide a receipt.

Delivery to the registry of all other documents relating to the bankruptcy will be recorded in the same manner, but it will not be necessary to file any other document at the court.

442. Bankruptcy is declared by judgment of the district commercial court upon either the bankrupt's admission or on the petition of one or more creditors, or on its own motion.

By the same judgment or by a later judgment made on the report of the bankruptcy judge, the district commercial court will determine the time at which the bankrupt ceased making payments either on its own motion or on request by any interested party.

Except as provided by article 613, the time at which payments ceased to be made may not be fixed at a date which precedes the declaratory judgment of bankruptcy by more than six months.

Unless specifically determined otherwise, the cessation of payments will be presumed to have occurred with effect from the time when the judgment of bankruptcy is declared or, where the bankruptcy is declared after the death of the bankrupt, with effect from the date of death.

Without prejudice to the appeal procedure available to interested parties under article 473, no application for the date of cessation of payments to be fixed at a time other than that which would have been established by the declaration of bankruptcy or by a later judgment, will be admissible after the day appointed for the close of proceedings for the verification of claims.

443. During the first ten days of each month, the registration office will send a list of protests against bills of exchange accepted and promissory notes registered in the previous month to the president of the district commercial court for the area in which the protest was made. This list will contain: (1) the date of the protest; (2) the name, first names, occupation and address of the drawer or the beneficiary of the bill; (3) the name, first names, occupation and address of the issuer of the promissory note or acceptor of the bill of exchange; (4) the date of maturity; (5) the amount of the bill; (6) a record of the amount paid; and (7) the response made to the protest.

A similar list will be sent to the president of the district commercial court within whose judicial district the issuer of the promissory note or the acceptor of the bill of exchange resides; if this is in Belgium, the list must be sent to a judicial district other than that where payment is to be made.

These lists will remain on file and open for inspection at the respective registries of the above-mentioned courts.

Chapter II: The effect of bankruptcy

444. From the date of declaration of the judgment of bankruptcy, the bankrupt ceases at law to have control over his entire estate, including any property which becomes his during his bankruptcy.

All payments, transactions and legal documents made by the bankrupt and all payments made to the bankrupt after the judgment has been declared are void at law.

445. The following transactions are void and without legal effect in so far as they relate to the bankruptcy estate if performed by the debtor after the time fixed by the court as the time of cessation of payments or within the previous ten days.

All gratuitous transfers of personal or real property, as well as legal documents, transactions, barter agreements or contracts for valuable consideration, if the value of that which was given by the bankrupt is substantially greater than the value received by him in return.

All payments, whether in cash, by assignment, sale, set-off or otherwise for any debt whether due or not and all payments made otherwise than in cash or by bill of exchange.

All contractual or judicial mortgages, and all rights under assignments by way of security of income from real property, or security taken over the assets of the debtor for previously contracted debts.

446. All other payments made by the debtor on debts accrued due and all other transactions entered into by him for value by him after cessation of payments and before the declaration of bankruptcy may be avoided if those who received value from the debtor or who contracted with him, were aware that the debtor had ceased to pay his debts.

447. Rights validly acquired under a mortgage or charge may be registered up to the date of declaration of bankruptcy.

Nevertheless, registrations made within ten days before the cessation of payments, or after, may be declared void if registration of the mortgage or preferential right takes place more than fifteen days after its creation.

448. All transactions or payments made with intent to defraud creditors are void, irrespective of the date or when they were made.

449. Where payment under a bill of exchange has been made after the date fixed as the time of cessation of payments and before the declaration of bankruptcy, proceedings to recover the payment may only be brought against the person for whose benefit the bill was issued; in the case of a promissory note the proceedings may only be brought against the first endorser.

In each case, it is necessary to prove that the person from whom recovery is sought was aware of cessation of payments at the time of issue of the bill or note.

450. A judgment by way of declaration of bankruptcy accelerates any debts of the bankrupt which are not yet due and payable. If the bankrupt is the issuer of a promissory note, the acceptor of a bill of exchange or the drawer in the case of dishonour, the other obligors will be obliged to provide a guarantee for payment on maturity unless they prefer to pay immediately.

However debts not accrued due which do not carry interest and which are due to expire in more than one year will not be admitted as a liability without deduction of the legal interest calculated from the declaration of bankruptcy up to maturity.

If one co-obligor makes immediate payment under a promissory note or a non-interest bearing bill of exchange which has not yet accrued due, the payment will be subject to deduction of the legal interest for the period remaining until expiry.

451. Interest is suspended as regards the bankruptcy estate only, from the time of the declaration of bankruptcy, on all claims which are not secured by pledge, mortgage or other preferential right or lien.

Interest on secured claims may only be claimed on the proceeds of sale of assets which are pledged or mortgaged or charged with some other preferential right.

452. From the time of declaration of bankruptcy, actions and enforcement proceedings against the bankrupt's personal and real property may only be continued, instituted or exercised against the trustees of the bankruptcy estate.

The court may nevertheless admit the bankrupt as an intervening party.

453. A judgment by way of declaration of bankruptcy terminates any distraint proceedings brought by unsecured and unpreferred creditors over the bankrupt's personal and real property.

If, before this judgment, the date for the compulsory sale of any distrained real or personal property has already been fixed and officially published, the sale will take place on behalf of the bankruptcy estate.

Nevertheless, if the interests of the bankruptcy estate so require, the court may, at the request of the trustees, authorise rescheduling of the sale to another time.

454. All enforcement proceedings against personal property forming part of the bankruptcy estate to obtain payment of preferred claims are suspended until close of proceedings for the verification of claims without prejudice to any protective and legal measures available to a landlord for the repossession of rented properties.

In the latter case, suspension of enforcement procedures under the present article ceases as a matter of law in favour of the landlord.

Chapter III: Administration and liquidation of the bankruptcy estate

Section I: General provisions

455. Upon the recommendation of the relevant appeal courts, sworn liquidators may be appointed by order of the State to particular areas served by the district commercial courts if the number and importance of bankruptcies renders this necessary.

456. The trustees of the bankruptcy estate will be appointed from among the sworn liquidators who are established in the district unless a different choice is required for reasons of distance, kinship, conflict of interest, or on other legitimate grounds, or for the proper administration of the bankruptcy estate.

If there are no sworn liquidators, and in such cases where, in accordance with the previous paragraph, the court believes it ought to make another choice, the trustees of the bankruptcy estate will be appointed from those having the highest reputation for intelligence and honesty as administrators.

These trustees will have the same rights and powers and will be subject to the same control and duties as if they have been appointed from amongst the sworn liquidators.

457. The number of sworn liquidators will be determined by Royal Decree on the advice of the Court of Appeal and the district commercial court according to the requirements of the service.

They are appointed by Royal Decree from two lists in duplicate put forward by these same bodies.

458. The sworn liquidators are appointed for five years and retain this function, in all cases, until their successors are sworn in. They may be reappointed.

A sworn liquidator, who is not reappointed, will nevertheless conclude all the operations entrusted to him and the liquidation of the bankruptcy estate for which he had been appointed trustee.

459. The sworn liquidators are under the supervisory control of the district commercial court. They may be removed from the office by Royal Decree.

460. Within fifteen days of their appointment, the liquidators will make oath, at an open session of the district commercial court, to properly and faithfully fulfil their duties as trustees in bankruptcy.

461. The district commercial court will determine the fees of the trustees, depending on the nature and size of the bankruptcy, and in accordance with the scale established by Royal Decree.

462. The district commercial court may, at any time, replace the bankruptcy judge for a particular bankruptcy by another of its members, and may also remove one or more of the trustees from the office, replace them or increase their number.

Any trustee who has been removed from office will first be given a hearing before the court in chambers. The decision will be announced in public.

463. The bankruptcy judge is specifically empowered to expedite and control the operations, management and liquidation of the bankruptcy estate; he will make a report in public on all disputes arising from it; he will order any urgent measures necessary for the security and preservation of the assets of the bankruptcy estate and will preside at creditors' meetings.

The bankruptcy judge may take any action within his competence outside his district if he considers the circumstances urgent or serious enough to require it.

Orders of the bankruptcy judge are provisionally enforceable. Any appeal against these orders will be brought before the district commercial court.

464. The public prosecutor may intervene in any of the operations of the bankruptcy, inspect the books and papers of the bankrupt, assess his financial position and obtain from the trustees any information he considers useful.

465. All orders made in relation to the bankruptcy are provisionally enforceable; the normal time limit for appeals is fifteen days from notification of the order.

The following decisions may not be contested, and are not open to appeal, or to review by the Supreme Court on a question of law:

(1) Decisions relating to the appointment or replacement of the bankruptcy judge or to the appointment or dismissal of trustees;
(2) Decisions concerning applications for assistance for the bankrupt and his family;
(3) Decisions authorising the sale of personal effects or goods forming part of the bankruptcy estate, or, in accordance with article 453, paragraph 3, postponement of the sale of any distrained items;
(4) Decisions which suspend any judicial scheme of arrangement;
(5) Decisions on appeal from orders issued by the bankruptcy judge and made within his competence.

Section II: Formalities relating to the declaration of bankruptcy and initial provisions concerning the bankrupt and his property

466. In the same judgment as the declaration of bankruptcy, the district commercial court will appoint the bankruptcy judge and order the affixing of seals. The court will appoint one or more trustees, depending on the size of the bankruptcy. The court will order the bankrupt's creditors to declare their claims at the registry within a period not exceeding twenty days from the date of the judgment declaring the bankruptcy and will indicate, in accordance with article 472, the journals in which this order and the order determining the date of cessation of payments will be published.

The same order will also designate the times and dates for the close of the official record of proceedings for the verification of claims with the court and for the hearing in court of any disputes arising from the verification. These dates will be arranged so that there will be not less than five or more than twenty days between expiry of the time limit fixed for the declaration of claims and the time limit for the filing of the official record of the verification of claims, and a similar interval between then and the date fixed for the hearing of any disputes.

In the same order the court may instruct the bankruptcy judge to exercise all the powers conferred on local court judges under this Bankruptcy Code.

467. Repealed.

468. If the court considers that an inventory of the assets of the estate may be drawn up in one day, it will order the inventory to be made immediately in the presence of the bankruptcy judge and without first affixing the seals.

469. The clerk of the district commercial court will immediately give the public prosecutor and the trustees notice of the provisions of the order for the fixing of the seals and the appointment of the trustees.

Only in cases where the debtor has either absconded or dissipated all or part of his assets, may the local court judge affix the seals before issue of the order, either of his own motion or on the application of one or more creditors.

470. The appointed trustees will begin their duties immediately after the declaration of bankruptcy; if they have not been chosen from amongst the sworn liquidators, they will first swear before the bankruptcy judge properly and faithfully to fulfil the functions entrusted to them; they will manage the bankruptcy estate with due diligence and in good faith under the supervision of the bankruptcy judge, and they will, if necessary, order the seals to be affixed immediately.

The seals will be affixed to the shops, counters, tills, portfolios, books, documents, furniture and personal effects of the bankrupt.

In the case of a bankrupt partnership or limited partnership, the seals will be affixed in the residence of each of the jointly liable partners as well as in the principal office of the partnership.

In every case, the local court judge will immediately inform the president of the district commercial court and the trustee appointed over the bankruptcy estate, that the seals have been affixed by him.

471. The following items will not be sealed, or, if a seal is affixed, the items will be removed and handed over to the trustees:

(1) The bankrupt's books, once they have been closed by the local court judge, who will record in his report the state in which he finds them;

(2) Short-term bills or bills capable of immediate acceptance, or requiring protective measures: a schedule of these will be provided to the bankruptcy judge;
(3) Items which may perish or depreciate in the immediate future;
(4) Items used in the running of a business in the circumstances provided in article 475;
(5) Items included in the list referred to in article 476.

An inventory of the items referred to in this article will be drawn up by the trustees in the presence of the local court judge, who will sign the memorandum.

472. At the instigation of the trustees and within five days of the date on which they were issued, extracts of the declaration of bankruptcy and the order which finally determined the date of cessation of payments will be published in the journals printed in the areas or towns closest to where the bankrupt has his residence or business premises and designated by the district commercial court, and in the Belgian Official Gazette.

These extracts will contain:

(1) the names, first names, place and date of birth together with the address and registration number at the bankrupt's local trade registry; and, in the case of a commercial company, the name or trading name and the registered office:
(2) the date of the declaration of bankruptcy and the court which pronounced it;
(3) if necessary, the date of the order determining the cessation of payments and the date of cessation;
(4) the name, first names and address of the trustee(s).

The journals containing the extracts are proof of their publication.

473. The declaration of bankruptcy and order determining the date of cessation of payments may be contested by interested persons who were not parties to the relevant orders.

Opposition is only permissible if made by the bankrupt within eight days, and, by all other interested persons, within fifteen days, of publication of the orders in the journals mentioned in article 472 printed in the place nearest to their residence.

474. If a debtor, who has admitted his bankruptcy, has declared that his assets are more than sufficient to pay all his debts, and has requested a stay of execution, the district commercial court may, without halting the progress of bankruptcy, order an immediate appraisal of the state of his affairs by one or more experts; and if, after the result of this appraisal, the court agrees that the assets of the debtor exceed his liabilities, it will order an immediate meeting of creditors and the matter will proceed as provided in part IV.

475. In the case provided in the preceding article, and in every case where the bankrupt has requested a judicial scheme of arrangement, and if required in the interests of the creditors, the court may, following the report of the bankruptcy judge, and having heard the trustees, order that the commercial operations of the bankrupt be continued provisionally by them or by a third party under their supervision. The court may also, following the report of the bankruptcy judge and having heard the trustees, modify or revoke this order.

476. On the authorisation of the bankruptcy judge, the trustees may deliver to the bankrupt and his family, suits, clothes, linen, furniture and personal effects necessary for their personal use. The trustees will draw up a list of these items.

Furthermore, the bankrupt may obtain maintenance for himself and his family at a level determined by the court on the recommendation of the trustees and following the report of the bankruptcy judge.

477. On the authority of the bankruptcy judge, the trustees may sell immediately any items liable to perish or depreciate in the immediate future.

Before rejection of a judicial scheme of arrangement, other items may only be sold with the authority of the court; the court will determine the manner and conditions of sale following the report of the bankruptcy judge and after having duly called or heard the bankrupt.

478. Letters addressed to the bankrupt will be handed over to the trustees who will open them; if the bankrupt is available, he will be present when the letters are opened.

479. The trustees will pursue and recover against receipt all claims or sums due to the bankrupt and issue a receipt. The proceeds of sale and recoveries by the trustees will be deposited at the office of the public trustee within eight days of receipt after deduction of any amounts required by the bankruptcy judge. If deposit is delayed, and without prejudice to the application of articles 459 and 462, the trustees will owe commercial interest on any amounts not deposited.

480. Payment of any amounts attributable to the creditors under the bankruptcy is effected directly by the clerk of the Public Trustee Office upon examination of a copy of the distribution schedule signed by the trustees and endorsed by the bankruptcy judge; this copy will provide all the information required by the clerk of the Public Trustee Office to enable him to proceed with issuing transfer orders or postal cheques for the benefit of interested parties.

The amount of the fees and disbursements owed to the trustees is entered at the head of the list of creditors and payment is made according to the procedure provided for in relation to creditors.

481. Repealed.

482. The bankrupt may only absent himself on the authority of the bankruptcy judge. He is obliged to attend all meetings called either by the bankruptcy judge or by the trustees.

483. The trustees will summon the bankrupt in order to close and draw up the books and accounts in his presence.

484. The trustees will proceed immediately to verify and correct the balance sheet. If it has not already been filed, they will draw up the balance sheet with the aid of the bankrupt's books and documents and any other information which they may obtain, and will file it at the registry of the district commercial court.

485. The bankruptcy judge is authorised to summon the bankrupt, his book-keepers and employees and any other person to be heard before him, either in relation to the

verification or the drawing up of the balance sheet, or in connection with the causes or circumstances of the bankruptcy.

486. Where a trader has been declared bankrupt after his death or, where the bankrupt has died after filing an admission of bankruptcy, his widow, children or heirs may present themselves or send a representative to fulfil the role which the bankrupt would have had in the production of the balance sheet or in any other stage of the bankruptcy.

487. From the moment when the trustees assume office, they are personally liable to ensure that everything necessary is done to preserve the rights of the bankrupt as against his debtors.

They are also obliged to require registration of any mortgages over the properties of the bankrupt's debtors if the bankrupt has not himself required this to be done; registration by the trustees will be in the name of the bankruptcy estate, the trustees will attach to their memorandum a certificate of the clerk of the court in support of their appointment.

Further, they are obliged to ensure that any real property of the bankrupt of which they are aware is registered in the name of the creditors as a group. Registration is made on a short memorandum recording that a bankruptcy has occurred and showing the date of the order appointing the trustees.

488. Within three days of assuming office, the trustees will if necessary demand removal of the seals and proceed to draw-up an inventory of the bankrupt's assets in the bankrupt's presence or after he has been duly summoned.

On the authority of the bankruptcy judge, the trustees may request the assistance of any person they think suitable to draw up the inventory and value the relevant items.

489. Whenever seals are removed from an item, it will be included in the inventory drawn up by the trustees; the bankruptcy judge will attend and attest each removal; a record will be deposited at the registry within twenty four hours of final completion of the inventory. The trustees may take copies free of charge and against reimbursement of their travelling expenses.

In accordance with article 471, items which have not been placed under seal or from which the seal has been removed and which have been entered in the inventory will be placed in the custody of the trustees.

490. Where bankruptcy is declared after death, and where an inventory has not been drawn up before this declaration or where the bankrupt dies before an inventory has been commenced, an inventory will be drawn up immediately in the manner prescribed in the preceding article, in the presence of the heirs or after they have been duly summoned.

491. Once the inventory has been completed, the goods, money, current title deeds and bills of exchange, assets, furniture and personal effects of the debtor will be returned to the trustees who will make a note to that effect at the foot of the inventory.

492. On the authority of the bankruptcy judge, and after the bankrupt has been duly summoned, the trustees may settle all disputes relating to the estate, including disputes concerning shares and real property rights.

If the settlement relates to real property rights or if the subject matter of the settlement is of undetermined value or exceeds 10,000 Francs, it will only be enforceable after its approval has been confirmed in the report of the bankruptcy judge.

The bankrupt will be summoned to attend the approval of any such settlement; in every case he will have the opportunity to dispute the settlement. If the object of the settlement is real property, opposition by the bankrupt will suffice to block the settlement.

On the authority of the district commercial court and after the bankrupt has been duly summoned, the trustees may also give their sworn support to the opposing parties in the determination of any disputes arising from the bankruptcy.

493. The trustees may employ the bankrupt to facilitate and clarify any matter arising from their administration. The bankruptcy judge will decide the conditions of his employment.

494. In every bankruptcy, and within fifteen days of assuming office, the trustees must provide the bankruptcy judge with a memorandum or summary of the apparent state of the bankruptcy, giving its main causes, apparent features and circumstances.

The bankruptcy judge will immediately send the memorandum with his observations to the public prosecutor. If it has not been sent within the prescribed time limit, he will inform the public prosecutor and provide reasons for the delay.

495. If proceedings against the bankrupt are brought for simple or fraudulent bankruptcy and if an order to appear or warrant for arrest has been issued against him, the public prosecutor will notify the bankruptcy judge without delay.

Chapter IV: Declaration and verification of claims

496. The bankrupt's creditors are required to file a declaration of claims at the registry of the district commercial court together with proof of title within the time limit fixed in the declaration of bankruptcy. The clerk will retain the declaration of claims and issue a receipt.

The creditors will receive notice to this effect in the publications prescribed in article 472. They will also be advised by a registered circular letter which the trustees will send to them as and when their existence becomes known to the trustees.

This circular will set out the time and dates fixed for the close of proceedings for the verification of claims and for hearing any disputes arising from the verification.

Certificate of posting will be annexed to, and will remain annexed to, a memorandum of the circular which will be endorsed by the bankruptcy judge.

497. If there are any creditors residing or domiciled outside the kingdom of Belgium for whom the time limit fixed by the declaration of bankruptcy is too short, the bankruptcy judge may extend it for their benefit according to the circumstances; any such extension will be referred to in the circulars addressed to the creditors in accordance with article 496.

498. The declaration of claims of each creditor will contain his surname, first names, occupation and address, the amount and grounds for his claim, any preferential rights, mortgages or pledges relevant to it and the documents evidencing the claim.

The declaration will end with an affirmation in the following terms:

'I swear in honour and good faith that this claim is sincere and true.'

The declaration will be signed by the creditor or by his attorney in his name; in that event, the power of attorney will be annexed to the declaration, and will state the amount of the claim and contain the affirmation prescribed by this article.

499. The declaration of claims of any creditor not domiciled in the district where the commercial court is situated will contain an election of domicile in that district.

In the absence of an election of domicile, all notices and information may be left at the court registry.

500. The trustees will verify the claims as and when the declarations of claim are filed at the registry; verification will take place in the presence of the bankruptcy judge and also the bankrupt who is entitled to intervene, or after the bankrupt has been duly summoned. The documents evidencing the claim will be checked against the accounts and records of the bankrupt.

The trustees' claims will be verified by the bankruptcy judge.

A report on the progress of the bankruptcy will be drawn up by the trustees and signed at each meeting by them and the bankruptcy judge. It will contain the addresses of the creditors and their attorneys. It will contain a summary description of the documents provided, refer to any additions, deletions and omissions, and state whether the claim is admitted or denied.

If the claim is denied or if it does not appear fully justified, the trustees will adjourn their decision until the close of proceedings for the verification of claims and if the creditor is not present in person or represented by his attorney at the time of this adjournment, they will notify him immediately by registered letter.

501. On his own motion or otherwise, after each claim has been declared and up until the date fixed for the hearing of any disputes which may have arisen regarding it, the bankruptcy judge may order the creditor or his attorney or any person who could provide information to appear in person. He will draw up a report of their statements. He may also order production of the creditor's books or demand by order for discovery that a transcript be made of them by the local judge.

502. At the meeting fixed in order to close the proceedings for the verification of claims, submissions from both sides will be heard in respect of all declared claims which are disputed or which have not yet been admitted. The trustees will endorse the document evidencing each of the admitted and uncontested claims with a declaration in the following terms:

> 'Admitted as a liability in the bankruptcy of .... in the amount of .... dated ....'

The bankruptcy judge will sign the declaration; he will refer all disputes relating to disputed claims to the court.

503. The bankrupt and any creditors whose claims have been verified or entered on the balance sheet may attend the verification of claims meeting and object to any verifications which have been made or remain outstanding. After close of the proceedings for the verification of claims, any objections to verifications made and contained in the official record must, at the risk of being declared void, be formally served in writing on

the creditors who have declared their claims and must be filed at the registry together with the relevant evidence of title two days before the date fixed for the hearing of the disputed claims.

Objections to verifications made after close of the proceedings for the verification of claims will, also at the risk of being declared void, be served within ten days after admission of the disputed claim. However, as regards creditors admitted after this period, the time limit will only run from the date of verification of their claims.

504. The bankruptcy judge will submit his report on the day fixed for the hearing of disputed claims in the declaration of bankruptcy. Once the court has received the report, it will, as a matter of urgency, suspend all other business, and, if possible in a single judgment, proceed to settle all the disputes relating to the verification of claims without prior summons and without awaiting expiry of any time limits which have been extended under article 497. This judgment will be made after having heard all the submissions of the trustees, the bankrupt and any admitted or objecting creditors who have attended the hearing.

The hearing of any disputes which cannot be settled immediately will be adjourned. The court may nevertheless make an interim order that the disputed creditors will be admitted up to a sum specified in the same order for the purpose of participating in the discussions on the preparation of any judicial scheme of arrangement. If the court does not make a decision to this effect, the disputed creditors may not take any part in the administration of the bankruptcy until the dispute has been decided.

No appeal lies against the order made under this article, or against any judgment at a later stage on any disputes which have been postponed. Furthermore, no appeal or appeal on a point of law lies against an interim order provisionally admitting disputed creditors.

505. Repealed.

506. Until judgment is pronounced on the disputes, all declarations of claims, documents produced in support and all deeds, reports, objections and applications relating to them will remain on file at the registry and will be made available to interested parties on request.

507. For every bankruptcy, the clerk of the court will keep a schedule divided into columns and containing the following information for each declared claim:

(1) The reference number;
(2) The surname, first names, occupation and address of the creditor filing his declaration of claim, together with evidence of his title to the claim;
(3) The date of filing;
(4) The amount of the declared claim;
(5) A summary of the assets or items over which a mortgage or other preferential charge is claimed;
(6) Whether the claim is included in the liabilities of the bankruptcy or if it has been rejected by the trustees;
(7) The date of the admission or rejection;
(8) The objections to the claim;
(9) The names of those objecting;
(10) The dates of the objections;
(11) The date of close of proceedings for the verification of claims;

(12) The date of commencement of the hearing of submissions on disputed claims;
(13) A summary of the final decision;
(14) The date of this decision;
(15) Other information which could be useful to interested parties.

This schedule will be drawn up by the clerk of the court; the prescribed information will be entered on a day-to-day basis as and when the facts and circumstances to which the information relates come to light; it will be made available to any interested party on request.

508. Any person, known or unknown, who fails to declare or affirm his claim within the time limit fixed by the declaration of bankruptcy as extended under article 497, will not be included in the distributions. However, such persons may declare and affirm their claims up to and including the last distribution of proceeds. Their declarations will not suspend distributions which have already been ordered; however, if new distributions are ordered after such declarations, they shall be included up to an amount which will be fixed provisionally by the bankruptcy judge and will be held in reserve until their claims have been admitted. In each case, any expenses incurred in the verification and admission of such claims will the creditor's responsibility and may not be reclaimed from the distributions ordered before their declarations; if they can prove that it was impossible for them to make their declaration and affirmation within the prescribed time limit, they will have the right to draw on any undistributed assets for the dividends attributable to their claims in the first distributions.

Chapter V: Judicial scheme of arrangement

Section I: Creditors' meeting

509. The parties will proceed with the formation of the scheme of arrangement immediately after issue of the judgment in accordance with article 504 and without waiting for expiry of the time limits allowed under article 497.

To this end, the bankruptcy judge will summon a meeting of creditors and fix the place, date and time of the meeting.

The date of the meeting will be arranged so that it takes place within fifteen days of the judgment issued under article 504 and so that, between receiving notice of the meeting and the date of the meeting, a period of two days increased by one day for each five myriameters between his actual residence and the place of meeting is allowed for each creditor.

510. Notice of the meeting will be given to creditors within five days of the summons of the bankruptcy judge; will be given under the direction of the trustees by publication and by circular letter individually addressed to the creditors whose claims have been definitively or provisionally admitted, all in accordance with the manner and form prescribed by articles 472 and 496.

511. The meeting will take place under the chairmanship of the bankruptcy judge at the place, date and time fixed by him. Only creditors admitted definitively or provisionally or their attorneys will be permitted to attend.

The bankrupt will be summoned to the meeting; he may send a representative only if he has valid reasons which have been approved by the bankruptcy judge.

The bankruptcy judge will verify the powers of those attending the meeting under power of attorney. The trustees will report on the progress of the bankruptcy, on the formalities carried out and any steps already taken, and on the probable outcome of the liquidation. The bankrupt will be accorded a hearing. The trustee's report will be signed and given to the bankruptcy judge who will draw up a report on what has been discussed and decided at the meeting.

Section II: Formation of the scheme of arrangement

512. Except as provided under article 520, no agreement may be made between the creditors determining the matter and the bankrupt debtor until the formalities prescribed above have been fulfilled.

An agreement by way of scheme of arrangement may only be made by a majority in number of those creditors who represent three-quarters of the total claims which have been definitively or provisionally admitted in accordance with chapter IV: if these conditions are not fulfilled the agreement is void.

513. Creditors with registered mortgages or other preferential rights or who are secured under pledges may not vote in respect of these secured claims on any business relating to a scheme of arrangement, and their votes will not be counted unless they surrender their mortgages, preferential rights or pledges.

This surrender will arise by operation of law if a secured creditor votes on the scheme of arrangement; if the scheme of arrangement is not accepted the surrender will be of no effect.

A secured creditor may only vote on the scheme of arrangement by surrendering his preferential right, mortgage or pledge to the extent of the equivalent of at least half of the amount of his claim. In this event, the claim will only be counted to that extent in any matters relating to the scheme of arrangement.

514. There will be no scheme of arrangement if the bankrupt is within article 495 or if he has been convicted of fraudulent bankruptcy.

When article 495 applies, creditors called to the meeting to discuss the scheme of arrangement may vote in the same majorities prescribed by article 512 to postpone their decision until after proceedings have been issued. Rejection of any motion to postpone will result in rejection of the scheme of arrangement.

515. The scheme of arrangement will be signed while the meeting is in session or may otherwise be declared void. The meeting will be postponed for eight days if only a majority in number or a majority of three quarters of the total claims agree the scheme of arrangement. In this instance, any resolutions made or agreement concluded at the time of the first meeting will be of no effect.

516. Any creditor entitled to take part in agreeing the scheme of arrangement, or who would have been so entitled after it has been agreed, may object to it.

Reasons for the objection will be given and should be notified to the trustees and the bankrupt within five days following the scheme of arrangement, failing which the objection may be declared void. Within five days of this notification, the trustees and the bankrupt may give notice of their application in reply to the objection and file it at the registry together with any documents on which they rely.

Immediately after this period of time and without any other formalities or proceedings, the bankruptcy judge will report on the bankruptcy, and on the acceptability of the scheme of arrangement, and the court will issue in a single judgment a decision ratifying the scheme of arrangement and any objections to it. Nevertheless, the parties may appear or be represented at the meeting to present a summary of any evidence in support of their submissions.

If only one trustee has been appointed and he opposes the scheme of arrangement, he must arrange for another trustee to be appointed in order to fulfil the requirements of this article.

If the judgment on the objections involves decisions on issues outside the competence of the district commercial court because of the subject matter concerned, the court will defer judgment until after these issues have been resolved.

517. If the above provisions are not observed, or if the scheme of arrangement is not in the public interest or in the interests of the creditors, the court will refuse to ratify it. In such cases the scheme of arrangement is deemed to be set aside as regards all interested parties.

518. Ratification of the scheme of arrangement renders it binding on all creditors, proven or unproven, whether or not they are listed on the balance sheet, including those creditors referred to in article 497, together with all those who would have been admitted to the discussions by virtue of article 504 whatever amount is ultimately awarded to them in the final judgment. It will preserve for the benefit of each of the creditors the mortgage registered in accordance with the last paragraph of article 487 over the bankrupt's real property. To this end, and unless the scheme of arrangement provides otherwise, the trustees will register the ratifying judgment on the mortgages.

Following the report submitted by the bankruptcy judge, the court may authorise the former trustees or, failing them, a trustee specially appointed for this purpose by the court, to delete the registration made in accordance with this article and also the registration made under article 487.

519. The trustees' duties terminate as soon as the judgment ratifying the scheme of arrangement has become final.

The trustees will present their final account to the bankrupt in the presence of the bankruptcy judge; the account will be completed following discussion. The trustees will return the whole of his assets to the bankrupt, including books, documents and personal effects; the bankrupt will provide a receipt for these items, and the bankruptcy judge will draw up a comprehensive report.

Any objection will be settled by the district commercial court following the report of the bankruptcy judge.

520. Repealed.

Section III: Cancellation and dissolution of the scheme of arrangement

521. The scheme of arrangement will be void at law if the bankrupt is convicted of fraudulent bankruptcy after ratification of the scheme.

If, after ratification of the scheme of arrangement, proceedings for fraudulent bankruptcy are brought against the bankrupt, or a warrant of arrest, or an order to prevent him absconding is issued against him, the district commercial court may make any appropriate protective orders following the report of the bankruptcy judge. These orders will cease to take effect at law from the date of a declaration that there are no grounds to proceed or when the case is dismissed or the bankrupt is acquitted.

522. After the scheme has been ratified, no action may be brought to have it declared void except for reasons of fraud discovered after the ratification and taking the form of either concealment of assets or the exaggeration of liabilities.

The setting aside of the scheme of arrangement either for fraud or following conviction for fraudulent bankruptcy operates at law as of right even as regards the guarantors.

523. If the conditions of the scheme of arrangement are not fulfilled by the bankrupt, an action to rescind the scheme may be brought against him before the district commercial court in the presence of the guarantors, if any, or after the guarantors have been duly summoned.

Rescission of the scheme of arrangement does not release any guarantors who intervened to guarantee its total or partial implementation.

524. In the judgment ordering either the setting aside or rescission of the scheme of arrangement, or in the cases provided under article 521, the district commercial court may, by a judgment made on the application of one or more creditors, or even of its own motion following the report of the bankruptcy judge, instruct the previously nominated trustees to take up their duties or instruct new trustees and order the persons who have becomes creditors of the bankrupt since notification of the scheme of arrangement to declare their claims within the time limit fixed under article 466.

The provisions of articles 469 and 472 will be followed with respect to this judgment. A notice containing the following information will be published:

(1) The bankrupt's name, first names, place and date of birth and also his address and registration number at the Companies Registry; if it is a commercial company, the name or trading name and its registered office;
(2) the date of the judgment ordering either the setting aside, rescission or nullity at law of the scheme of arrangement and the court which issued the relevant order;
(3) the name, first names and address of the trustee(s).

The journals containing the above notices are proof of publication of the notices.

The trustees may have seals affixed. Without delay and with the help of the bankruptcy judge, the trustees will proceed on the basis of the original inventory, taking any securities, shares and bills into safe custody and if necessary drawing up a supplementary inventory. They will prepare a supplementary balance sheet and send the circular letter referred to in article 496 to the new creditors.

525. Any new claims must be declared, affirmed and proved in accordance with the provisions of chapter IV.

No new proof of the claims already admitted as liabilities is necessary, but this will nevertheless not affect the rejection or reduction of those which have since been extinguished in whole or part.

526. Those transactions referred to in article 445 and made by the bankrupt after the judgment ratifying the scheme of arrangement and before it has been set aside or rescinded are void and of no effect. Other transactions of the bankrupt during this period will only be set aside if they were made with the intention of prejudicing performance of the scheme of arrangement or of defrauding the creditors.

527. Those who were already creditors before the scheme of arrangement will retain all their rights as against the bankrupt himself; but their participation rights in the bankruptcy estate are only as follows:

If they have not received any dividend, the whole of their claim; if they have received part of their dividend, that part of their initial claim which corresponds to the proportion of the promised dividend which has not been received.

The provisions of this article apply in cases where a second bankruptcy has begun without prior setting aside or rescission of the scheme of arrangement.

Chapter VI: Liquidation of the bankruptcy estate

528. If no scheme of arrangement is agreed, the trustees will continue to represent the creditors as a whole and will proceed with the liquidation of the bankruptcy estate: they will arrange for the sale of any real property, goods and personal effects and the payment of debts owed to and by the bankrupt; the whole procedure will be under the supervision of the bankruptcy judge in accordance with the provisions of articles 479 and 480 and without any need for the bankrupt to appear in person before the court.

They may compromise any of the rights of the bankrupt in the manner prescribed by article 492 notwithstanding any objections by him.

529. Nevertheless, the creditors may authorise either the trustees or a third party under the trustees' supervision to continue using the available assets for the benefit of the estate.

The decision conferring this authority will also determine its scope and duration and fix the amount which the trustees may retain to cover their costs and expenses; the decision must be taken in the presence of the bankruptcy judge immediately after rejection of the scheme of arrangement and by the majority in number and amount provided under article 512.

The bankrupt and any objecting creditors may challenge this decision, but this will not suspend execution.

If the transactions of the trustees, or of those duly authorised, result in liabilities which exceed the available assets, only those creditors who authorised these liabilities will be personally liable over and above their share in the assets, but only up to the limits of the authority granted by them. Their contributions will be pro rata to their proven claims.

530. Where a partnership is in bankruptcy, the creditors may only enter into a scheme of arrangement with one or more of the partners; in such cases the whole of the partnership's assets remain subject to the bankruptcy; the personal assets of those with whom the scheme of arrangement has been agreed will be excluded, and the particular agreement concluded with them may only include an obligation to make a payment relating to those assets which are outside the partnership assets.

A partner who has agreed a special scheme of arrangement will be discharged from joint liability.

531. Immediately following the rejection of a scheme of arrangement, the creditors will be consulted in meeting as regards the continuation of maintenance provided in accordance with article 476 or of whatever maintenance may ultimately be available to the bankrupt and his family from the assets of the bankruptcy. With the agreement of the majority of creditors present, maintenance will be granted or allowed to continue. The trustees will propose an amount which will be agreed by the bankruptcy judge and may only be appealed by the trustees to the district commercial court.

532. After the scheme of arrangement has been set aside or rejected, the bankruptcy judge may summon the creditors if he considers this is necessary.

By simple majority vote and with the authorisation of the court after the bankrupt has been duly summoned, the creditors in meeting may instruct the trustees to forfeit and dispose of all or part of any unrealised rights or causes of action.

533. When the liquidation has been completed the creditors will be summoned by the bankruptcy judge. He may order the trustees' report of the liquidation to be annexed to the summons.

The report will be discussed at this meeting, with the bankrupt in attendance or after he has been duly summoned. The final distribution will be made from the balance shown in the report.

If any objection is made, the procedure set out in article 519 paragraph 3 will be followed.

At the same meeting, the creditors will give their opinion on whether the bankrupt should be released from further liability. A minute of the meeting will be drawn up in which each creditor may record his statements and observations.

534. The bankruptcy judge will present the court in chambers with the decision of the creditors as regards the release of the bankrupt and will report to the court in chambers on the characteristics and circumstances of the bankruptcy. The court will decide whether or not the bankrupt should be released.

No release will be granted to the following persons:

Fraudulent bankrupts of whatever kind, persons convicted for theft, forgery, extortion, deceit or breach of trust, and bailees, guardians, administrators or other persons liable to account who have not submitted and balanced their accounts.

535. No trader who is a debtor will be allowed to petition for his release on the grounds of assignment of his assets.

If the bankrupt is declared released, he will also be released from the warrant of arrest as regards the creditors of his bankruptcy, and except as provided in particular statutes, proceedings may be brought by them only against his assets.

If he is not declared released, the creditors retain the right to take individual action either against the bankrupt personally or against his assets.

536. If at any time before the creditors are summoned to discuss the scheme of arrangement, it becomes clear that there will be insufficient assets to pay for the estimated administration and liquidation costs, the district commercial court may, even of its own motion, and following the report of the bankruptcy judge pronounce termination of the bankruptcy proceedings. In such cases the creditors retain the right to take individual action against the bankrupt personally and against his assets.

In the same judgment the court may issue its decision on the release of the bankrupt.

Implementation of a judgment pronouncing termination of the bankruptcy proceedings is suspended for one month.

At any time the bankrupt or any other interested person may restore the proceedings before the district commercial court by proving that sufficient funds exist to cover the bankruptcy proceedings or by depositing a sufficient sum with the Public Trustee. The costs of proceedings brought under this article must in any event be paid in advance.

Chapter VII: Different categories of creditors and their rights

Section I: Co-obligors and guarantors

537. A creditor entitled to performance of any obligation underwritten, endorsed or guaranteed jointly by the bankrupt and other bankrupt co-obligors, will participate in

distributions from each bankruptcy estate and will participate for the full nominal value of his claim until full and final payment.

538. Recourse by one co-obligor against another for dividends which have been paid is only available where the total dividends from these bankruptcies exceed the amount of the principal claim plus interest in which case the excess will be distributed to those obligors who are guaranteed by the other obligors according to the priority of their obligations.

539. If a creditor entitled to performance of obligations owed jointly by the bankrupt and other co-obligors or obligations secured by guarantee, has received a partial payment for his debt before the bankruptcy, he will only be included in the estate after deduction of this payment and only retain his rights against the co-obligors or the guarantor for what remains due to him.

540. Any amount which a co-obligor or guarantor making a part payment has paid to discharge the bankrupt will be taken into account.

541. Notwithstanding any scheme of arrangement, creditors will retain their rights to the whole of their claim against the co-obligors of the bankrupt.

Section II: Creditors secured by pledges, and creditors secured by charges or other preferential rights and charges over personal property

542. Account of the bankrupt's creditors who are validly secured by pledges will only be taken for the record.

543. At any time, and on the authority of the bankruptcy judge, the trustees may release pledges in favour of the bankruptcy estate by repaying the debt owed by it.

544. If a pledge is not released by the trustees and if the pledged item is sold by the creditor for a price which exceeds the claim, any surplus will be recovered by the trustees. If the price is less than the claim, the secured creditor will be entitled to claim for the shortfall against the estate as an ordinary creditor.

545. In favour of those workers referred to in article 1 of the law relating to the protection of workers' remuneration, the remuneration as defined by article 2 of the said law and the indemnities included in such remuneration and which are due to the same persons by reason of the breach of their contract of employment, are, without regard to the fact that the breach took place before or after the declaration of bankruptcy, entered as a preferred claim with the same priority and up to the same amounts as the preference afforded to such persons by article 19, paragraph 3(2) of the law of 16th December 1851 relating to mortgages and charges.

546. The preferential right and right of claim established by article 2102, paragraph 4, of the Civil Code in favour of a vendor of chattels and also the right of rescission, are not available in cases of bankruptcy.

This preferential right will nevertheless continue to exist for five years from delivery in favour of suppliers of machines, equipment, tools and other items of professional equipment used in industrial, commercial or craft businesses.

It will only be effective if, within fifteen days of delivery, a copy of the invoice certified as true by the vendor, even if not accepted by the buyer, or any other document evidencing the sale, is filed at the registry of the commercial court for the district in which the debtor is domiciled or, failing which, is resident. The clerk will endorse a certificate of deposit on the the copy. The copies are filed together in one volume and an index is drawn up on a daily basis showing the names of the purchasers. Once the identity of the purchaser has been indicated to him, the clerk must send a copy to any person who requests it.

The preferential right is available even where the machines, equipment, tools and other items of equipment have become real property by virtue of their intended use or by incorporation.

Subject to proof to the contrary, delivery is evidenced by the vendors' accounts.

Where the bankruptcy of a debtor is declared before expiry of the five years preference period, the preferential right will continue to exist until after liquidation of the bankruptcy estate.

547. The trustees will present the bankruptcy judge with a list of those creditors claiming preferential rights or other charges over the personal property within the bankruptcy estate and the bankruptcy judge will, if necessary, authorise payment of such creditors from the first proceeds recovered.

If a preferential right is disputed, the court will settle the dispute.

Section III: The rights of creditors with mortgages or preferential rights or other charges over real property

548. Where the proceeds of sale of real property are distributed before the proceeds of sale of personal property, or at the same time, creditors with charges or mortgages which have not been satisfied by the proceeds of sale of real property will compete with the unsecured creditors for the amount which remains due to them, and will be paid from the proceeds allocated to the unsecured creditors, provided however that their claims have been affirmed and approved according to the procedure described above.

549. If other distributions are made before the proceeds of sale of real property are distributed, the creditors with charges or mortgages over real property will compete in these distributions in proportion to their total claims and without, in that event, allowing for deductions calculated in accordance with the following provisions.

550. After sale of the real property and final arrangement of the order of priority between creditors with mortgages and other preferential rights and charges, those who have priority in the proceeds of sale of real property up to the total amount of their claim, will not receive the amount to which they are entitled under their mortgage ranking until after deduction of any amounts received by them from the unsecured estate.

Such deducted amounts do not continue to form part of the mortgaged estate, but go to the unsecured estate for the benefit of which the deduction was effected.

551. As regards those mortgaged creditors who rank only partially in the distribution of the proceeds from real property, the procedure will be as follows: Their rights over the unsecured estate will be finally determined according to the sums for which they remain creditors after the prior ranking secured creditors have been satisfied, and the proceeds of sale received by them from the preceding distribution in excess of the amount of their unsecured claim will be retained from the amount received by them as secured creditors and held for the unsecured creditors.

552. Mortgage creditors without effective priority will be considered as unsecured creditors and subject as such to the terms of the scheme of arrangement and to all dealings in the unsecured estate.

Section IV: The effects of bankruptcy of a married person with regard to his or her spouse

553. It is not necessary for the trustee to obtain prior agreement from the spouse of a bankrupt person or the authority required by articles 215, paragraph 1, 1418 and 1420 of the Civil Code, in order to sell the real and personal property belonging to the personal estate of the bankrupt's spouse or to their joint estate.

554. If the marriage is dissolved after the bankruptcy has been declared and before its termination, neither the bankrupt's spouse nor the trustee may benefit from the marriage contract.

555. Payment of joint debts incurred by the bankrupt in the performance of his occupation and which are not settled through the liquidation of the bankruptcy estate, may not be made from the estate of the bankrupt's spouse.

556–560. Repealed.

Chapter VIII: Distribution among creditors

561. After the costs and expenses of the administration of the bankruptcy, the maintenance granted to the bankrupt or his family and the sums paid to preferred creditors have been set aside, the amount of the bankrupt's liquid assets will be distributed among all the creditors in proportion to their declared and verified claims.

To this end, the trustees will provide the bankruptcy judge every month with a report on the position of the bankruptcy and a statement of the proceeds deposited with the Public Trustee; the bankruptcy judge will, if necessary, order a distribution to be made to the creditors in an amount determined by him.

The creditors will be advised of the decisions of the bankruptcy judge and of the commencement of the distribution by circular letter sent by post in the manner provided in article 496.

562. If there are any creditors with claims not admitted to proof and for whom the time limit as extended under article 497 has not yet expired, or creditors whose claims, which were declared within the prescribed time limit, have given rise to objections which have not yet been determined, no distribution will be made until after an amount equal to the dividend to which they would be entitled has been put in reserve. In the former case the amount will be the amount entered on the balance sheet; in the latter case the amount will be the amount declared and affirmed.

Where claims of creditors domiciled or resident outside the Kingdom of Belgium, for which the time limit has been extended in accordance with article 498, have not been entered on the balance sheet in an exact manner, the bankruptcy judge may decide that the reserve be increased. The trustees may dispute this decision before the district commercial court.

563. No payment may be made by the trustees without production of the document evidencing the claim.

The trustees will enter on the document the sum paid or authorised in accordance with article 480. Where it is not possible to produce the document, the bankruptcy judge may authorise payment after having regard to the official record of the verification of claims. In every case, the creditor must acknowledge receipt in the margin of the distribution statement.

Chapter IX: The sale of real property belonging to the bankrupt

564. If proceedings for the compulsory purchase of real property have not been commenced before the rejection or setting aside of a scheme of arrangement, the trustees alone may proceed with a sale of real property. They must do so within eight days, on the authority of the bankruptcy judge and in accordance with the method prescribed in the fourth part of part IV, chapter IV, of the Judicial Code.

On the authority of the district commercial court, and after summoning the bankrupt, the trustees may stay any proceedings which have been commenced at any time, by proceeding in accordance with the same method with the sale of any real property which has been attached.

In this case the trustees must notify the creditor who has brought proceedings and the debtor at least eight days prior to the sale, of the place, date and time at which the sale will take place.

A similar notification will be made within the same period of time to all creditors who are registered at their chosen place of domicile in the document registering their debt.

The foregoing provisions are not applicable to a creditor who is secured by a first mortgage who may, in any case, proceed to have the property subject to the mortgage sold in accordance with the provisions of articles 1560–1626 of the Judicial Code.

565. Repealed.

Chapter X: Action for repossession

566. An action for repossession in the event of bankruptcy may be brought with respect to negotiable instruments and other unpaid instruments of title which were still in that form in the bankrupt's possession at the date of the judgment declaring the debtor's bankruptcy. Such an action may be brought where delivery of the instrument has been made by an owner duly authorised to recover sums due under the instrument and to retain the amount at the disposal of the creditor, or where the instrument has been specially appropriated to particular payments.

567. An action for repossession may also be brought in respect of any goods consigned to the debtor by way of bailment or for him to sell on behalf of the shipper so long as they remain in their original state, either as a whole or in part.

An action may also be brought for the price or for any part of the price of these goods which has not been paid or settled in some other way, or for which monies have been paid into a current account between the bankrupt and the purchaser.

568. An action for repossession may also be brought in respect of goods sent to the bankrupt, so long as passing of property in the goods did not occur in the bankrupt's shops or to those of an agent responsible for selling the goods on behalf of the bankrupt.

Nevertheless this action for repossession will not be allowed if, prior to their arrival, the goods have been lawfully sold against invoices, bills of lading or waybills signed by the shipper of the goods.

A person seeking to bring an action for repossession must respect the rights of a secured creditor relying on a bill of lading or waybill.

569. A person bringing an action for repossession is obliged to reimburse the creditors with any amount which he has received, together with the balance of any advances of freight or consignment costs, commission, insurance or other expenses, and to pay any such sums which may be due for these items.

570. The vendor may retain any goods sold but not yet delivered to the bankrupt or which have not yet been sent, either to the bankrupt or to any third party on the account of the bankrupt.

571. In the cases referred to in articles 568 and 570, and on the authority of the bankruptcy judge, the trustees have the power to require delivery of the goods by paying to the vendor the price agreed between the vendor and the bankrupt.

572. The trustees may, with the approval of the bankruptcy judge, admit applications for repossession, and if these are disputed, the court will decide the issue on its merits on the basis of a report prepared by the bankruptcy judge.

PART II. NON-FRAUDULENT AND FRAUDULENT BANKRUPTCY

Chapter I: Non-fraudulent bankruptcy

573. A bankrupt trader will be declared a non-fraudulent bankrupt in the following cases:

(1) If his personal or household expenses are judged excessive;
(2) If he has spent large sums on gambling, or on deals of pure chance, or on fictitious trading on the stock exchange or in the commodity markets;
(3) If, with intent to delay his bankruptcy, he has bought goods with a view to resale below the market price, or if, with the same intention, he has taken out loans, endorsed negotiable instruments or used other onerous methods of procuring funds;
(4) If he fabricated fictitious expenses or losses, or if he cannot prove the existence or use of any assets appearing in his latest stock inventory or of any cash, securities, furniture and personal effects of any nature whatsoever received after the date of the latest stock inventory;
(5) If, after he ceased to make payments, he has made a payment to or has preferred any creditor to the prejudice of his general creditors.

574. A trader may be declared a non-fraudulent bankrupt in the following situations:

(1) If, without receiving value in exchange, he has undertaken on behalf of any third party, obligations which are too great considering his situation at the time he undertook these obligations;

(2) If he is declared bankrupt for a second time, without having satisfied his obligations under a previous scheme of arrangement;
(3) If, being married with a dowry or without joint sharing of property, he has not complied with article 69;
(4) If he has not admitted his inability to make payments within the time limits prescribed by article 440; if this admission does not contain the names of all his jointly liable partners; if in making this admission he has not supplied the information and explanations required by article 441 or if such information and explanations are inaccurate;
(5) If he absconds without the authority of the bankruptcy judge or if, without a legitimate excuse, he has not attended hearings in person on the summons of the bankruptcy judge or the trustees;
(6) Repealed.

575. The following persons will be ordered to pay fines for non-fraudulent bankruptcy without prejudice, if appropriate, to the application of article 578:

(1) Those who, in the interests of the debtor, have taken possession of, hidden or knowingly received all or part of the assets (whether fixed or moveable) of the debtor;
(2) Those who have fraudulently claimed in the debtor's bankruptcy and have claimed, either in their own name or by third parties, fictitious or exaggerated debts;
(3) A creditor who has obtained for himself, either with the debtor or with other persons, any particular advantages by reason of his vote at any meetings concerning the bankruptcy or who has entered into a particular agreement by which he has obtained an advantage over the assets of the bankrupt;
(4) A trustee who is found guilty of a misappropriation of funds.

Any person found so liable, will in addition, be ordered to pay a fine equal to the value of the illegal advantages which he has obtained or to make restitution and pay damages with interest to the general body of creditors in a sum of not less than one hundred francs.

576. The directors of limited liability companies who have not supplied the information requested of them, either by the bankruptcy judge or by the trustees, or who have given inaccurate information, may also be liable to be ordered to pay fines for non-fraudulent bankruptcy.

This also applies to those persons who, without a legitimate excuse, have not appeared before the bankruptcy judge or the trustee when so requested.

Chapter II: Fraudulent bankruptcy

577. A bankrupt trader will be guilty of fraudulent bankruptcy in any of the following situations:

(1) If he has removed in whole or in part the accounts books and documents referred to in chapter I of the law relating to company accounts and annual returns, or if he has fraudulently removed, erased or altered the contents of such books and documents;
(2) If he has diverted or concealed any part of his assets;

(3) If, in any written document, whether public or private, or in the balance sheet of his business he has fraudulently purported to be a debtor for sums which he does not owe.

578. Those persons who, by one of the means indicated in article 60 of the Penal Code, have instigated any of the situations referred to in the preceding article or have given instructions to do so, and those who have knowingly helped the fraudulent bankrupt in his plans or have facilitated his bankruptcy, or have assisted in the circumstances which give rise to it, will be held to be accomplices in fraudulent bankruptcy.

Chapter III: General provisions

579. In the cases referred to in articles 575, 577 and 578 and even if a party is acquitted the court hearing the case will:

(1) of its own motion order any assets, rights or actions which have been fraudulently removed to be restored to the general creditors;
(2) decide on any award sought for damages and interest and granted in any order or decree.

Contractual agreements will, in addition, be declared void with regard to all persons including the bankrupt.

A creditor will be obliged to account to the person entitled for money or securities received from any agreement declare void.

580. Where the avoidance of the fraudulent deeds or agreements referred to in articles 575 and 577 is sought under civil law, proceedings will be brought before the commercial court in the judicial district in which the bankruptcy proceedings were commenced.

581. Costs arising in fraudulent or non-fraudulent bankruptcy proceedings will only be borne by the general creditors when the accused is acquitted and the trustees authorised by a majority of the creditors present have also brought proceedings for civil compensation in the criminal proceedings.

582. In the event of a scheme of arrangement, the Treasury may only recover costs from the bankrupt after completion of the conditions agreed in the scheme.

583. Any judgments or convictions under articles 573–578 which order publication by way of advertisement, at the expense of the guilty party, of the judgment or conviction, will be published in the Belgian Official Gazette and also in journals selected and printed in the places or towns which are nearest to the residence of the guilty party or the places where he carries on business.

These advertisements will contain:

(1) The full names, place and date of birth as well as the address and registration number of the business of the guilty parties and if relevant the business name and registered address of any bankrupt commercial companies of which they are the directors or managers;
(2) The date of the judgment or conviction and the judicial district in which it was made;

(3) The criminal acts or omissions which have given rise to the conviction and the fines which have been awarded; when, in the interests of simplicity, a single fine has been awarded for non-fraudulent bankruptcy or fraudulent bankruptcy or other criminal acts or omissions, the text will mention all the criminal acts or omissions which have been punished by this single fine.

Chapter IV: The administration of assets in fraudulent and non-fraudulent bankruptcy

584. In all proceedings and convictions for fraudulent or non-fraudulent bankruptcy, civil actions, other than those referred to in article 579, remain separate, and all provisions relating to assets forming part of the bankruptcy will be implemented without being applied to, or invoked in, the criminal courts or the assize court.

585. However, trustees in bankruptcy are obliged to deliver to the public prosecutor all documents, documents of title, papers and information requested of them. During the proceedings these documents, deeds and papers will be held, and made available if required, by the clerk of the court. They will be delivered at the request of the trustees who will be able to take extracts for use in the civil courts or require copies to be delivered to them free of expense by the clerk of the court. Any documents, documents of title and papers which have not been officially filed on the instructions of the court will, after the order or judgment has been issued, be returned to the trustees who will give a receipt for them.

PART III. DISCHARGE

586. A bankrupt who has paid all of the principal amount, interest and expenses which he owes in full, may obtain his discharge.

He will not obtain a discharge if he is jointly liable as a partner in a trading company which is bankrupt until he can prove that all the debts of the company have been paid in full as to principal, interest and expenses, even though a special scheme of arrangement has been agreed with him and the company.

A bankrupt may be discharged after his death.

587. All applications for discharge will be sent to the appeal court in the judicial district in which the bankrupt is resident. The person making the application will attach to his application all receipts and other supporting documents. The Director of Public Prosecutions at the court of appeal, acting on the application submitted to him, will send certified copies to the public prosecutor and to the president of the commercial court in which the person making the application is resident and if there has been a change of residence since the bankruptcy, the papers will be sent to the Public Prosecutor at the court and to the president of the commercial court for the area where the bankruptcy took place, requesting them to obtain all available information on the truth of the facts as now disclosed.

To this effect, on the request of the public prosecutor, a copy of the application will be displayed for a period of two months both in the civil and commercial courts, and at the stock exchange and in the town hall, and will be inserted by way of extract in the official journals.

588. Any creditor whose debt has not been fully paid as to the principal amount, interest and expenses, and any other interested party, may, during the period while

the application is on display, oppose the discharge by filing a notice at the court registry accompanied by supporting documents. A creditor opposing the petition for discharge will never become a party to the proceedings relating to the discharge.

589. After the expiry of two months the public prosecutor and the president of the commercial court will send, separately, to the Director of Public Prosecutions at the court of appeal, the information which they have collected and any opposing statements which have been made. They will also add their recommendation on the petition for discharge.

The Director of public prosecutions at the court of appeal will pronounce judgment by way of acceptance or rejection of the petition for discharge. If the petition is rejected, a further petition may not be made until the expiry of one year.

590. The judgment granting a discharge will be sent both to the public prosecutor and to the president of each of the courts to which the application has been submitted. The judgment will be read aloud in the courts and a transcript will be recorded in their registers.

591. The following will not be discharged from bankruptcy: fraudulent bankrupts of whatever kind, persons convicted of theft, forgery, extortion, deceit or breach of trust, bailees, guardians, administrators or other persons liable to account who have not submitted and balanced their accounts.

A non-fraudulent bankrupt who has suffered the penalty to which he was sentenced may be discharged from bankruptcy.

592. No bankrupt trader may deal on the stock exchange or act as adviser or represent parties at the commercial court unless he has obtained his discharge.

PART IV. SUSPENSION OF PAYMENTS

593. Suspension of payments is only granted to a trader who, as a consequence of extraordinary and unforeseen events, is obliged temporarily to cease payments but who also, after due verification of his balance sheet, has assets or means sufficient to satisfy all his creditors both as to principal and interest.

In the event of death of a trader, suspension of payment of his debts may be granted to his successors for the reasons and on the conditions mentioned in the previous paragraph.

594. The debtor will apply simultaneously to the commercial court in the area in which he is resident and to the court of appeal in that judicial district. He will annex to his application:

(1) A summary of the events on which he bases his application;
(2) A detailed list of his assets and liabilities together with an estimate;
(3) A list of the names and addresses of his creditors indicating the amount of his debts to them.

The application addressed to the court of appeal will be notified by the senior president of the court to the Director of Public Prosecutions. It must be signed by a lawyer attached to that particular court.

595. The application addressed to the commercial court will be delivered to the clerk of the court who will give a good receipt without drawing up a formal deed of deposit for it.

Following this application, the court will appoint the place, date and time on which, within fifteen days, the creditors will be summoned to appear.

The court, if necessary in extraordinary session, will appoint one or more experts who will proceed with the verification of the debtor's state of affairs and will appoint one of its judges to supervise the case.

The court may either immediately or during the course of the proceedings grant the debtor a provisional suspension of payments.

In this event, the court will appoint one or more administrators who will be responsible for supervising and controlling the debtor's business transactions throughout the whole of the suspension period.

596. The creditors will be summoned individually by the bankruptcy judge by registered letter posted at least eight days before the date of the meeting. This summons will, in addition, be inserted on three different occasions in the Belgian Official Gazette, and also in journals selected by the bankruptcy judge.

One copy of the journals carrying the summons will be filed at the court registry before the creditor's meeting.

The debtor will deposit the sum considered necessary to cover the expenses of the summons and insertions with the clerk of the court responsible for these arrangements.

597. On the appointed day, the bankruptcy judge will report to the court in the presence of the creditors or their authorised representatives.

The creditors or their authorised representatives will be heard in argument against the debtor. They will declare individually the amount of their claims, and whether they agree or not with the debtor's application.

A detailed minute of the meeting will be made to which will be attached any documents produced by the creditors and by the debtors.

The court will attach its reasoned opinion to this minute.

598. The court's opinion, together with all the documents relating to the application, will be sent within three days to the Director of Public Prosecutions at the court of appeal who will submit them, with his conclusions, to the senior president. The latter will nominate an adviser, and the court will issue its decision on the basis of his report within eight months of receipt of the documents.

599. The court may not grant a suspension of payments, even though the assets exceed the liabilities, unless the majority of creditors whose claims represent three quarters of all sums due, have expressed their agreement with the application.

The majority by number of creditors and amount of claims will be established without counting the claims of creditors who have not appeared at the hearing, whose residence is abroad and too far away from the place of the meeting for them to be present physically or represented on the date specified.

Those claims which are declared as preferred claims under article 605 and the persons to whom such claims are owed, will not count either in the calculation.

600. The court may grant the suspension of payments for a period not exceeding twelve months.

The court will appoint one or more administrators who will be responsible for supervising and controlling the debtor's business transactions throughout the whole of the suspension period.

The suspension of payments may be extended. No extension may be granted for more than 12 months. The same debtor may not benefit from either provisional or final suspension of payments for more than two years.

Nevertheless a final extension of one year at the most may be granted to a debtor who can prove he has discharged at least 60% of his liabilities during the previous suspensions.

Any extension of the suspension of payments must be preceded by an announcement made in the manner prescribed in article 594 and the following articles.

At law, rejection of the application entails revocation of the provisional suspension of payments.

Successors of the debtor do not benefit from a suspension of payments granted to a debtor unless they accept the succession on terms that liability does not exceed the value of the assets inherited.

601. An order granting a provisional suspension or the decree granting a final suspension of payments will, within five days of its date, be published at the request of the administrator by way of announcement in the Belgian Official Gazette and in journals selected by the judge in accordance with article 596.

This announcement will contain:

(1) The full name, place and date of birth as well as the address and registration number at the trade registry of the beneficiary, and also, in the case of a commercial company, the objects, designation and registered office of the company;
(2) The date of the order or decree granting suspension of payments and the court which gave it;
(3) The duration of the suspension of payments;
(4) The full names and address of the administrators responsible for supervising and controlling the business operations of the debtor during the period of the suspension of payments.

A copy of the pages of the journal in which the announcements appear will be sufficient evidence of their publication.

602. Experts and commissioners will be chosen from persons resident in the debtor's area.

Before taking up their appointments, the experts will swear on oath before the judge faithfully and properly to carry out their duties.

The commissioners will also swear the same oath before the president of the commercial court.

Their fees will be taxed by the commercial court in accordance with the nature and importance of the debtor's business. Their fees and disbursements will be paid in priority to other debts.

Any creditor of the debtor appointed as a commissioner will not be paid a fee.

603. Payment of claims existing at the time of the application may not be made by instalments throughout the period of the suspension of payments, unless all the creditors are finally paid pro rata according to the amount of their claims.

When claims are contested, article 562 of this Code will apply.

Without the authority of the supervising commissioners, the debtor may not transfer, charge, or mortgage his property, whether real or personal, settle or attempt to settle, or, borrow or receive any sum or make any payment or make himself available for any act of administration.

The commercial court will determine any dispute.

604. During the period of the suspension of payments, no execution may be made against the debtor's person or property. Distraints and attachments made before the suspension of payments will remain in force but the court may, depending on the circumstances, lift such measures after hearing submissions from the debtor, the creditor and the supervising administrators.

Suspension of payments does not suspend proceedings which have been commenced nor the bringing of new actions against the debtor unless these actions are solely aimed at obtaining payment of a debt which is not in dispute.

However, it is not possible during a provisional or final suspension of payments, to register any mortgage on the debtor's real property arising as a result of any orders of the court issued during that time.

605. Suspension of payments only applies to obligations contracted prior to the grant of the suspension. It does not apply in favour of co-debtors, or any guarantors who have renounced the benefit of preliminary proceedings. It does not apply in relation to:

(1) Taxes or other public charges, and contributions for canals and dams;
(2) Preferred claims or claims secured by mortgages or other charges;
(3) Claims for maintenance;
(4) Claims for the supply of necessaries to the debtor and his family during a period of six months preceding the suspension of payments.

606. During the suspension of payments, the secured or preferred creditors may not proceed to have any buildings or fixtures used in the course of the profession or business of the debtor, attached or sold, provided that any interest due on the secured claims is paid in full and promptly.

607. Revocation of the suspension of payments may be demanded by one or more creditors, or by the administrators, if the debtor has been found guilty of fraud or of acting in bad faith, if he is in breach of article 603, or if it appears that his assets no longer cover all his debts in full.

The application to revoke the suspension of payments will be made to the commercial court, which, after hearing the debtor's submissions, will give a decision, if the provisional suspension of payments is in issue, or will issue its opinion, if a final suspension of payments is in issue.

Any decree or judgment relating to the revocation of the suspension of payments will be published in the manner prescribed under article 601.

The announcement will contain:

(1) The full name, place and date of birth as well as the address and registration number at the trade registry of the person who is the subject of the decree to revoke the suspension of payments. If it is a commercial company, the objects, name and registered address of the company;
(2) The date of the judgment or decree revoking the suspension of payments.

A copy of the pages of the journal in which the announcements appear will be sufficient evidence of their publication.

608. Any withdrawal of an application for suspension of payments will be sent both to the court of appeal and to the commercial court.

It will be put into effect on the production of proof that a notice announcing the application to withdraw has already been published in the form prescribed in article 595.

609. A judgment which grants, refuses or revokes a provisional suspension of payments will not be open to challenge or appeal.

A debtor may however oppose a judgment which revokes a provisional suspension of payments if he has been legitimately prevented from attending the hearing.

Any decree ordering suspension of payments may be referred to the Supreme Court.

610. Any instruments, documents or other written material which might assist the court and the court of appeal to reach a view on the request for a suspension of payments may be produced and filed by the debtor, the creditors or the supervising administrators and without any need to have them formally stamped or registered.

Judgments relating to the grant, extension or revocation of provisional suspensions of payments will be registered against a fixed rate fee of three francs.

611. The debtor is subject to the same penalties as a non-fraudulent bankrupt:

(1) If, in order to determine or to facilitate the grant of a suspension of payments, he has in any manner whatsoever voluntarily concealed a part of his liabilities or exaggerated his assets;
(2) If the debtor has caused or allowed one or more fictitious creditors or creditors whose claims have been exaggerated to appear in any meetings relating to his application for a suspension of payments.

612. Any person who, without being a creditor, has taken part in meetings relating to the application for the suspension of payments or who, being a creditor, has fraudulently exaggerated the claims entitling him to take part in these meetings, will be liable to the same penalty.

613. In the event of bankruptcy of a debtor within six months following expiry of the period of suspension of payments, the date of cessation of payments, by way of derogation from article 422, will, as a matter of law, be deemed to be the date of the application for the suspension of payments.

In addition to the void transactions referred to in article 445, all transactions entered into by the debtor without the authority of the administrators, where authorisation was required, are void and of no legal effect.

614. Suspension of payments is available to owners of industrial properties who are not considered as traders at law.

All the provisions of this part IV apply to a suspension of payments of this type with the exception of article 613.

If, on expiry of the period of suspension of payments, there is a liquidation or sale of assets, mortgages effected pursuant to judgments rendered during this period, and also all transactions entered into by the debtor without the authority of the administrators, where authorisation was required, will be void and of no legal effect.

DECREE ISSUED BY THE REGENT ON 25TH SEPTEMBER 1946

CONSOLIDATED LAWS ON JUDICIAL SCHEMES OF ARRANGEMENT

1. A debtor who is a trader may avoid a declaration of bankruptcy, if he obtains a judicial scheme of arrangement from his creditors in the form and on the terms prescribed by this law.

This scheme of arrangement may also be granted after the debtor's death.

2. (1) This type of scheme of arrangement will only arise if the majority of creditors, represented by uncontested claims or claims provisionally admitted in accordance with article 22, and representing two-thirds of all sums due, have accepted the debtor's application.

However, creditors of those who have not taken part in the vote, or whose vote did not arrive, will not be included for the purposes of calculation of the majorities.

Votes of creditors who have expressed their wish in a qualified or doubtful way will not be counted.

The scheme of arrangement will only take effect after it has been approved by the commercial court.

This approval will only be granted in favour of a debtor who has suffered misfortune and who has acted in good faith.

(2) Approval of a scheme of arrangement requested by a public company, or a limited partnership or a cooperative company may not be refused by the court on the grounds of transactions undertaken by one or more directors or managers, unless these transactions were undertaken with the approval or consent of the company or partnership in general meeting and, at the time, the general meeting was aware of the nature of these transactions or that they were of such of kind as to taint the whole activity of the company or partnership with bad faith.

3. The debtor will address his application by petition to the commercial court where he is resident. He will attach to his petition:

(1) a summary of the events on which he bases his application;
(2) a detailed list and estimated account of his assets with a general summary of that part of the assets charged by way of mortgage, pledge or other preferential right, and an indication of the amount of his liabilities;
(3) a list of the names of his creditors, acknowledged or presumed, with their addresses and the amount of their claims;
(4) the proposals for a scheme of arrangement.

The debtor will deposit at the court registry the amount considered necessary to cover the cost of the proceedings for the grant of a scheme of arrangement.

4. The petition will be delivered to the court registry and entered in a special list. The public accounts clerk or the clerk of the court will give a receipt for the petition without charge or other formality.

Within twenty-four hours, the clerk of the court will notify the public prosecutor of the petition. The public prosecutor will be able to assist in the scheme of arrangement, examine the debtor's books and verify at all times the state of the debtor's business.

5. As a matter of law, the filing of the petition will give rise to a provisional suspension of payments in favour of the debtor which will affect all subsequent executory measures and all declarations of bankruptcy, except for the possible application of article 24.

A provisional suspension of payments will not benefit co-debtors or guarantors who have renounced the opportunity for negotiation.

An extract of the petition will be published at the instigation of the public accounts clerk or the clerk of the court in the Belgian Official Gazette within three days of the filing.

6. Before considering whether it is appropriate to proceed with the petition the court in chambers will appoint in all cases one or more judges to report on the application and, if the need arises, also on the debtor's financial position.

7. The court in chambers will decide within one week whether it is competent to hear the petition, whether the petition is presented in the form stipulated in article 3 and, if appropriate, whether the persons who have filed the petition are competent to make the application in the name of the debtor.

The judge will report in chambers. The debtor will be summoned to appear by registered letter.

The debtor may comment on the judge's report.

It may arise that the court will decide it is not a competent forum, or will hold the petition inadmissible and in both cases it will give its reasons for its decision.

8. If the court accepts that it has jurisdiction to deal with the application, the judge appointed will report to the court on the debtor's position to enable the court to issue its decision at the latest within two weeks from the date of the judgment.

The report will be made to the court in chambers.

The debtor will be summoned to appear by registered letter.

The debtor may comment on the report.

If the court considers at that stage that the conditions required for the grant of a scheme of arrangement have not been fulfilled, it will reject the petition by giving a reasoned decision.

If the court decides that proceedings for the grant of a scheme of arrangement may be continued, it will determine the place and time at which the creditors will be summoned to appear and will designate one or more journals, in addition to the Belgian Official Gazette, in which the notice of the hearing will be announced within three days of this decision.

The judge will be appointed chairman of the creditors' meeting. He will supervise the progress of the scheme of arrangement.

If the number of creditors is such that it is impossible for the meeting referred to in paragraph 6 to take place within the relevant court room, the court may decide, in a judgment to that effect, that the creditors will not be summoned to appear in person and that the vote will be taken by delivery or despatch of a voting paper to the court registry.

The court in this case may decide that, by way of derogation from the provisions of article 13, the creditors will not be summoned to appear individually and that they will not be notified of the proposals for the scheme of arrangement except by means of publication which will be determined in accordance with article 13.

9. Judgments rendered in accordance with articles 7 and 8 may not be contested.

No appeal lies against a judgment which declares an application inadmissible.

The debtor may appeal against a judgment by which the court declares itself incompetent to hear the matter.

Similarly the debtor may appeal against any judgment made under article 8, paragraph 5.

Notice of appeal must be given within one week from the date of announcement of the judgment.

In both cases the delegated authority given to one of the judges will be maintained until expiry of the appeal period and, in the event of an appeal, until this has been determined by the court.

In any event, this delegated authority will terminate if the court declares the debtor bankrupt after holding the application inadmissible or rejecting it.

10. Repealed.

11. During proceedings for a scheme of arrangement, the debtor may not dispose of, mortgage or otherwise deal with his property, without the authority of the judge.

12. Either immediately, or before his report to the court, or during the examination of the debtor, the appointed judge may appoint one or more experts who, after having sworn on oath to carry out their duty in good faith, will proceed to verify the state of the debtor's affairs.

Their fees will be taxed by the court. These fees together with their disbursements will be paid in priority to other claims.

13. Unless the court decides that in accordance with article 8, paragraph 8, there will not be a creditors' meeting, the appointed judge will summon a creditors' meeting by registered letter delivered by post at least fifteen days before the date fixed for the meeting.

This letter will contain the proposals for the scheme of arrangement. It will reproduce the text of articles 2 and 15.

Creditors living abroad may be summoned by registered telegram indicating the subject matter of the meeting but without the need to include the proposals.

One copy of a journal carrying the notice of meeting and a memorandum of the letter and telegram sent to creditors and a summary of the recommendations will be filed at the court registry before the creditors' meeting.

If, because of the large number of creditors, the court decides that there will not be a creditors' meeting, the court will determine whatever methods of announcement are to be used, with a view to making known to the creditors the proposals for a scheme of arrangement, the period within which their votes must be recorded in order to be eligible, and the precise address of the office of the clerk of the court to which the voting papers should be sent.

This announcement will have annexed to it the appointed judge's summary report and will reproduce the text of article 15.

This announcement will be published in the Belgian Official Gazette, in at least four Belgian journals of which two will be in the French language and the other two in Dutch, and, in the event that there are numerous foreign creditors, also in one or two journals in the country or countries to which these creditors belong.

14. On the date appointed for the creditors' meeting, the judge will make his report on the debtor's state of affairs.

The debtor, or an authorised representative, will put forward his proposals. The creditors, either in person or through their authorised representatives, will declare in writing the amount of their claims and state whether or not they assent to the arrangement.

Any persons who claim to be creditors and who have not been summoned will be allowed to make their declarations of claim. Each declaration may be contested by the debtor or by the creditors.

Before the ballot is taken, the appointed judge will read article 15 aloud to the meeting.

15. Creditors secured by a mortgage, lien or other charge or preferential right, will only be able to vote in respect of their claims in the scheme of arrangement if they surrender their security.

Any creditor voting in the scheme of arrangement renounces his security as a matter of law. This surrender will not take effect if the scheme of arrangement between creditors is not accepted.

These creditors may however vote in the scheme of arrangement without renouncing their liens, mortgages or other charges or preferential rights, but only for an amount equivalent to one half of their claims. In this event, these claims will only be counted for this pro-rata amount in the scheme of arrangement.

16. The appointed judge is entitled to adjourn the creditors' meeting. He may also adjourn the meeting to take place at the latest within fifteen days from the date of this decision. Any adjournment will be noted in the minutes. In the event of adjournment, the creditors will be summoned again to the meeting in accordance with articles 8 and 13.

17. The minutes of the creditors' meeting will include:

(1) A list of creditors attending the meeting, either upon summons or voluntarily, with details of the amount and the nature of their claims;
(2) Any objections raised, in particular regarding the existence and amount of the claims;
(3) The definitive proposals put forward by the debtor;
(4) The result of the ballot on these proposals, and completion of the formality prescribed by paragraph 4 of article 14;
(5) The date on which the appointed judge will report to the court, and when the court will be requested to rule on the objections and on the ratification of the arrangement. If the minutes are not signed during the meeting they will be void.

Any documents produced by the debtor and the creditors will be annexed to the minutes.

18. The minutes of the creditors' meeting, drawn-up in accordance with article 17 and the documents annexed thereto, will immediately be filed at the registry of the commercial court for inspection by interested parties.

19. During the week following this meeting, any claim may be filed at the court registry together with the supporting documents by any of the creditors referred to in the list delivered by the debtor to the court in accordance with article 3.

Creditors who do not appear on the above list and who do not appear voluntarily at the meeting may also produce proof of any claim at the court registry, as long as it is supported by the original deed or by good documentary evidence.

Any documents supporting the claim will be put on file.

Any new claim will be submitted with an indication of its acceptance or refusal under the scheme of arrangement.

If no creditors' meeting has taken place, a creditor who does not appear on the list of creditors described in paragraph 1 may vote at the court registry as provided in paragraphs 2 and 3.

This vote must be taken at the latest at the date fixed by the judgment delivered in accordance with article 13, paragraph 5.

20. If no creditors' meeting has taken place, the appointed judge will draw up a minute confirming completion of the voting formalities, the conditions in which the ballot will be taken, the result of the ballot, and any objections which have been made. The judge will appoint the date on which the court will be asked to decide on the objections and on the ratification.

This report will immediately be filed at the court registry for inspection by interested parties.

21. On the date appointed in accordance with article 17, paragraph 5, the judge will read his report in open court. The creditors and the debtor, or their authorised representatives, may be heard and the court will then in a single judgment issue its ruling on any objections and on the ratification of the scheme of arrangement.

22. The decision of the court with regard to contested claims will not turn on the substance of the objection but will merely govern the admission of creditors, for the whole or part of their contested claims, to meetings in connection with the formation of the scheme of arrangement.

23. If these provisions are not observed or if the scheme of arrangement is unable to proceed on grounds relating to public interest or to the interests of creditors, the court will refuse to ratify the scheme of arrangement.

24. From the date of the first report made by the judge pursuant to article 7 and until ratification of the scheme of arrangement by the court, the court may, if it considers that the debtor is not acting in good faith, at any moment declare the debtor bankrupt after hearing the debtor's explanations or after summoning the debtor by registered letter.

In the event of a declaration of bankruptcy, either following the rejection of the application for a scheme of arrangement in accordance with article 7 or article 8, or under the preceding paragraph, the date of the cessation of payments may be backdated to six months before the filing of the petition.

25. The judgment ratifying the scheme of arrangement will be published on the instructions of the judge in the form of an extract of the judgment in the journals referred to, as appropriate, in articles 8 or 13. The extract will contain:

(1) The full name, place and date of birth as well as the address and registration number at the trade registry of the beneficiary, and also, in the case of a commercial company, the objects, designation and registered office of the company;

(2) The date of the judgment ratifying the arrangement between creditors;
(3) The settlement proposals;
(4) The full names and addresses of the administrators or liquidators appointed.

A copy of the pages of the journal in which the announcements appear will be sufficient evidence of their publication.

26. This judgment may not be contested except by creditors who were not summoned to the meeting, who did not present themselves voluntarily at the creditors' meeting, or who have not made use of the right provided under article 19.

This opposition, which does not suspend execution of the decision, must be supported by written submissions and notified to the debtor within a week, starting from the date of publication in the journals, and must be accompanied by a writ requesting the debtor's appearance before the commercial court. Only one day's delay in appearance will be permitted. The court will rule on all matters pending before it.

The judgment ratifying the scheme of arrangement may only be revoked if the court considers there has been bad faith on the part of the debtor.

27. The judgment is open to appeal by the debtor, or by any creditors who were not summoned to appear at the meeting, or who voted against adoption of the scheme of arrangement, or whose claims have been rejected in whole or in part.

An appeal does not suspend execution of the judgment.

As regards creditors, it must be made within one week running from the date of the publications referred to in article 25, and as regards the debtor, the date of issue of the judgment.

The provisions of paragraph 1 of article 10 apply to this appeal procedure.

Furthermore, an appeal made by the creditors will be notified to the debtor with a writ requesting the debtor to appear before the court of appeal within four clear days.

The case will come before the court at one of the earliest hearings. The court will rule on all matters pending before it. The public prosecutor will be heard by the court.

All creditors who have made their rights known before the commercial court may intervene in the appeal; intervention is made by a simple petition, notified to the appeal bailiff. It cannot delay the hearing.

The judgment of the court of appeal will be published in accordance with article 25.

28. The decrees determining ratification of the scheme may be referred to the Supreme Court of Appeal.

The appeal must be formally constituted in the official bulletin of the court of appeal.

29. Ratification of the scheme of arrangement by the court is binding on all creditors; it only applies to obligations contracted prior to ratification by the court. When these are contested claims, the procedure for application of the provisions of article 562 of the law of 18th April 1851 should be followed.

Neither co-debtors nor joint guarantors may benefit from a scheme of arrangement. It is without effect as regards:

(1) Taxes and other public charges, and also contributions for canals and dams;
(2) Claims secured by liens, mortgages or other charges or preferential rights;
(3) Claims due by way of alimony.

30. In the event of an arrangement by way of surrender of all assets, any ratifying judgment must appoint one or more liquidators. In other cases it must appoint one or more commissioners.

If the proposals for a scheme of arrangement submitted to the court include the appointment of one or more liquidators, the court may also add one or more liquidators.

The powers of liquidators are subject to the supervision of the appointed judge.

On the request of the judge, the powers provided under article 32 may be modified by the court.

Any commissioners appointed by the court in arrangements which do not include the surrender of all assets, have a supervisory power exercisable with the approval of the appointed judge.

31. Upon a reasoned petition presented by any interested party, the court may revoke the appointment of all or any of the liquidators, whether appointed by the court or by the creditor.

The court will not order revocation of the appointment of a liquidator until the liquidator or liquidators, who may be assisted by counsel, have been heard in chambers.

The court may, if appropriate, replace any one or more liquidators whose appointment has been revoked.

32. The liquidators are responsible for selling the real and personal property which constitute the total assets to be surrendered.

The appointed judge will determine the method and conditions of sale.

Real property may be sold by private contract.

The liquidators act in the name of and for and on behalf of the general creditors, and both for them as well as for the debtor, since only he is entitled to sue in tort.

The filing of the application for a scheme of arrangement is deemed to be an irrevocable mandate to this effect.

The liquidators may intervene in all legal proceedings to which the debtor is a party.

32B. When liquidation of the scheme of arrangement by way of surrender of all assets is terminated, the creditors will be summoned before the appointed judge. The judge may order that the liquidators' account be annexed to this summons.

The liquidator's account will be debated at this hearing, the debtor being present or duly summoned.

In the event of a dispute, the commercial court will issue its decision after hearing the report of the appointed judge.

33. The court will fix the fees of the liquidators and administrators. These fees, together with the disbursements are paid by way of priority over the amounts available for distribution to creditors. If the creditors appoint a commissioner the latter does not have a right to any remuneration.

34. A debtor who has been granted a scheme of arrangement must, where his circumstances have improved, pay his creditors in full.

35. Guarantors and other creditors bound by the scheme of arrangement may request its dissolution if a conviction for non-fraudulent or fraudulent bankruptcy is made after the ratification by the court of the arrangement between creditors, or if fraud arising either from dissipation of the debtor's assets or from exaggeration of his liabilities is discovered after the date of the scheme of arrangement.

In these two cases the court may also, following the report of the appointed judge and after hearing the debtor and the guarantors, or once these have been duly called, rescind the arrangement and declare the debtor bankrupt.

A setting aside of a scheme of arrangement releases any guarantor as of right.

36. In the event of non-performance of the scheme of arrangement, an application to dissolve it may be heard in the presence of the guarantors, or after these have been duly summoned if they have guaranteed total or partial performance of the arrangement. Dissolution of the arrangement will not release these guarantors.

37. At least every three months and each time as ordered by the court, the appointed judge must examine the state of financial affairs of the debtor subject to the scheme of arrangement with, if he considers this would be useful, the assistance of experts in accordance with article 12.

The appointed judge will report to the court, which, after hearing the debtor and the guarantors or having duly summoned them, may order dissolution of the scheme of arrangement and declare the debtor bankrupt.

38. In the event of bankruptcy of the debtor within the six months which follow dissolution of the scheme of arrangement, the time when cessation of payments occurs may, by derogation from article 442 of the law of 18th April 1851, be put back to the date when the application was made for the scheme of arrangement. Independently of the nullity provided under article 445 of this law, all transactions effected by the debtor without the authority of the judge where this is required, are void and without legal effect.

39. Article 527, paragraph 1, of the law of 18th April 1851 applies where bankruptcy is declared after the court has ratified the scheme of arrangement.

40. The debtor is subject to the same penalty as for non-fraudulent bankruptcy:

(1) If in order to determine or facilitate the agreement for a scheme of arrangement he has, in any manner whatsoever, voluntarily dissipated part of his assets or exaggerated his assets;
(2) If he has made or knowingly permitted one or more fictitious creditors or creditors whose claims have been exaggerated to intervene in the meetings;
(3) If he has knowingly omitted one or more creditors from the list of creditors.

41. All persons who, not being creditors, have fraudulently taken part in meetings concerning the scheme of arrangement, or, being creditors, have exaggerated their claims, and those persons who have either with the debtor or with other persons obtained a preferential position arising out of the use of their vote in scheme of arrangement meetings or who have concluded a special agreement resulting in a preferential position with regard to the debtor's assets will be subject to the fine set out in article 490 of the Penal Code.

42–43. Repealed.

44. Article 520 of the law of 18th April 1851 and the law of 20th June 1883 is repealed.

45. This law comes into force on the day of its publication in the Belgian Official Gazette. It applies to all proceedings for obtaining a scheme of arrangement which have not been terminated by a final judicial decision.

46. The decree issued by the Regent on 12th February 1946 concerning judicial schemes of arrangement is repealed.

EXTRACT FROM THE CIVIL CODE

5. Assignments of property

1265. An assignment of property is the surrender a debtor makes of all his assets to his creditors when he is not in a position to pay his debts.

1266. An assignment of property may be voluntary or by judicial order.

1267. A voluntary assignment of property is an assignment which the creditors accept voluntarily and has the effect of a contract between the creditors and the debtor.

1268. A judicial assignment is a benefit which the law accords to a debtor acting in good faith who has suffered misfortune and who is allowed, in order to avoid imprisonment, to surrender all his property to his creditors notwithstanding any provision to the contrary.

1269. A judicial assignment does not transfer ownership to the creditors, it only gives them the right to sell the property for their benefit and to collect the sale proceeds of that property.

1270. The creditors may not refuse a judicial assignment if it is not within the cases excepted by law.

An assignment precludes the imprisonment of the debtor for non-payment of his debts.

In addition, it only releases the debtor up to the value of the property surrendered by him; and, when this is insufficient to cover his debts, if he receives further property, he is obliged to surrender it until his debts have been paid in full.

FRANCE

French business insolvency law is contained in Law No 85-98 of 25th January 1985 and Decree No 85-1388 of 27th December 1985. The translated texts are of the law as amended up to 1st January 1992.

They have in common, as their title, the judicial reconstruction and compulsory liquidation of businesses. The three articles of Decree No 85-1387 contain administrative provisions relating to the Law of 25th January 1985. The translated texts do not include the further provisions relating to the court officers charged with the administration of the insolvency procedures which are contained in Law No 85-99 of 25th January 1985 and Decree No 85-1389 of 27th December 1985.

The first two articles of Law No 85-98 of 25th January 1985 are introductory and describe the objective and scope of the law. Generally, the law contains the substantive provisions, leaving administration and procedure to the Decree. Since, however, the law is itself described in procedural terms as a regime, much of the law is not directly concerned with purely substantive measures. It is divided into eight parts or titles, with Part I containing more than half of the whole law and setting out the main features of the regime. Three eventualities are considered: survival, sale or compulsory liquidation. Chapter I deals with the preliminary six-month observation period and includes, in articles 46 to 60, important substantive provisions regarding creditors' rights. Chapter II deals with the plans for survival or sale of the business; chapter III contains further detailed provisions regarding creditors' rights, here described in terms of the assets and liabilities of the business, and the following whole chapter, chapter IV, is dedicated to employees' claims. Part II sets out a summary procedure for small businesses; part III sets out the compulsory liquidation measures, and part IV contains the appeals provisions. Part V contains special provisions for companies and directors; parts VI and VII deal with offences and part VIII with consequential amendments to other laws, repeals, EC harmonisation and transitional measures. The eight parts or titles of the decree generally mirror the sequence of the law. Their content is wholly administrative or procedural.

Since preparation of these translations for printing, amending legislation has been introduced with effect from 21st October 1994 (Law No 94-475 of 10th June 1994/ Decree No 94-910 of 21st October 1994). The basic principles and framework of the 1985 legislation are not altered, but preventive procedures have been improved by extending these to businesses which, although technically solvent, are in financial difficulties, and the position of creditors has been slightly improved by the introduction of immediate liquidation without the observation and investigatory phases in situations where trading has ceased and rescue is clearly impossible. The position of secured creditors has been significantly improved. These now rank ahead of creditors who provided financing during the observation and investigatory phases. In addition, legislation in 1994 has permitted the netting of contracts on insolvency in certain markets. There are also many technical procedural changes.

The Publishers will be producing a Supplement to this title which will provide a translation of the text of the French amending legislation. The ISBN number of the Supplement will be 0 406 05345 6. The price is yet to be fixed.

Customers wishing to purchase a copy or obtain further details should contact Customer Services at the following address, and quote the ISBN number 0 406 05345 6:

Customer Services
Butterworth & Co (Publishers Ltd)
Borough Green
Sevenoaks
Kent
TN15 8PH
Tel: 0732 884567
Fax: 0732 884079

CHAPTER TWO

French Insolvency Laws

TABLE OF CONTENTS

LAW NO. 85–98 OF 25TH JANUARY 1985 RELATING TO THE JUDICIAL RECONSTRUCTION AND COMPULSORY LIQUIDATION OF BUSINESSES

Preparatory work

National Assembly:

Bill No. 1578, and private bill nos. 74 and 1048;
Mr. Gouzes' report, issued by the law commission, no. 1872;
Debated 5th, 6th, 9th and 10th April 1984;
Adopted 10th April 1984.

Senate:

Bill adopted by the National Assembly, no. 261 (1983/1984);
Mr. Thyraud's report issued by the law commission, no. 332 (1983/84);
Opinion issued by the social affairs commission, no. 328 (1983/84);
Debated 5th, 6th, 7th, 8th and 12th June 1984; Adopted 12th June 1984.

National Assembly:

Law project, modified by the Senate, no. 2186;
Mr. Gerard Gouzes' report, issued by the law commission, no. 2349;
Debated and adopted 15th October 1984.

Senate:

Bill adopted with modifications by the National Assembly, upon second reading, no. 27 (1984/85);
Mr. Thyraud's report, issued by the law commission, no. 54 (1984/85);
Debated and adopted 6th November 1984.

National Assembly:

Bill modified by the Senate upon second reading no. 2411;
Mr. Gouzes' report, issued by the joint round table commission, no. 2471;
Debated and adopted 6th December 1984.

Senate:

Bill adopted by the National Assembly (1984–85);
Mr. Thyraud's report, issued by the joint round table commission, no. 98 (1984/85);
Debated and adopted 12th December 1984.

Constitutional Council:

Decision no. 84-183 DC of 18th January 1985.

LAW NO. 85–98 OF 25TH JANUARY 1985 RELATING TO THE JUDICIAL RECONSTRUCTION AND COMPULSORY LIQUIDATION OF BUSINESSES[1]

(Official Gazette of 26th January 1985)

The National Assembly and the Senate having adopted the law, and the Constitutional Council having declared the law to be in conformity with the Constitution, the President of the Republic promulgates the following law:

Article 1

A procedure for judicial reconstruction is hereby established with the objective of permitting the survival of businesses, the preservation of employees and employment, and the discharge of their liabilities.

Judicial reconstruction is implemented according to a plan approved by the court following a period of observation. This plan provides for either the survival or the sale of the business. When neither of these solutions appears possible, compulsory liquidation will be ordered.

Article 2

Judicial reconstruction applies to any trader, artisan, farmer or body incorporated under private law.

It applies to any person who has taken advantage of the procedure for out-of-court settlement provided under law no. 84-148 of 1st March 1984 relating to the out-of-court settlement of difficulties relating to businesses, and who is in breach of financial undertakings given under a binding arrangement with his creditors.

Individuals or bodies corporate employing up to 50 employees and having a pre-tax turnover which is below a threshold fixed by decree of the Council of State are subject to the simplified procedure set out in part II of this law.

1 Modified by law no. 85–1407 of 30th December 1985 (Official Gazette of 31st December 1985).

PART I
GENERAL REGIME OF JUDICIAL RECONSTRUCTION

CHAPTER I. PROCEEDINGS FOR JUDICIAL OBSERVATION

Section I: Commencement of proceedings

Sub-section 1 – Jurisdiction of the court and its decision

Article 3

Proceedings for judicial reconstruction are available to any business referred to in article 2, which is unable to meet its current liabilities from its liquid assets.

Commencement of proceedings must be requested by the debtor at the latest within fifteen days after cessation of payments as defined in the preceding paragraph.

Article 4

Proceedings may also be commenced upon the application by summons of a creditor, regardless of the nature of his claim.

However, subject to articles 16 and 17, proceedings may only be commenced against an unincorporated farming business if the president of the civil court of first instance has first been served with a request for the appointment of a mediator in accordance with article 23 of law no. 88-1202 of 30th December 1988 relating to the adjustment of farming business within its economic and social environment.

In addition, the court may commence proceedings of its own motion or at the instigation of the public prosecutor.

The works council of the business or, failing which, the delegates of the work force may communicate to the president of the court or to the public prosecutor all facts evidencing cessation of payments by the business.

Article 5

In the event of non-performance of binding financial obligations in the context of an out-of-court agreement under either article 37 of law no. 84-148 of 1st March 1984 or article 27 of law no. 88-1202 of 30th December 1988 relating to the adjustment of farming business within its economic and social environment, proceedings are commenced by the court, or at the request of the public prosecutor, the debtor, or a creditor who is a party to the out-of-court arrangement. The court will order the termination of the out-of-court arrangement. The creditors will recover the whole of their claims and security after deduction of any amounts already received.

Article 6

The court will order the commencement of proceedings, having heard or duly summoned before a judge in chambers the debtor and the representatives of the works council or, failing which, the delegates of the work force.

The court may also hear any person who appears to the court to be able to make a useful contribution.

In the circumstances described in article 5, the court will make an order after hearing or duly summoning the mediator in whose presence the out-of-court arrangement was concluded.

Article 7

The commercial court has jurisdiction where the debtor is a trader or an artisan; In all other cases the civil court of first instance has jurisdiction. If it appears that one or more persons should be joined to the original proceedings, the court in which the proceedings were commenced remains the competent court.

A decree of the Council of State determines in each department which court or courts has jurisdiction in proceedings for judicial reconstruction applicable to persons other than those mentioned in the third paragraph of article 2, as well as the jurisdictional area in which these courts will exercise the powers assigned to them.

When justified by the interests represented before the court, the Court of Appeal, upon the application of the president of the competent court or the director of public prosecutions, may decide to refer the matter to another court of the same nature in the same jurisdictional area and which also has jurisdiction in judicial reconstruction in accordance with the preceding paragraph.

Article 8

An order for judicial reconstruction operates to commence a period of observation for the purpose of preparing an analysis of the economic and social position of the business and proposals for the survival or sale of the business. When neither of these solutions appears possible, the court will order compulsory liquidation.

The period of observation is limited to six months, renewable once by the court at the request of the administrator, the debtor, the public prosecutor, or on the court's own motion. In exceptional circumstances, the period may be further extended by the court for a period not exceeding six months at the request of the public prosecutor.

The court will approve the plan or order compulsory liquidation before expiry of the period of observation fixed by it.

Article 9

If necessary the court will determine the date of cessation of payments. In the absence of determination of this date, cessation of payments is deemed to have occurred on the date of the order confirming cessation of payments. The date may be modified one or more times but no further back than eighteen months before the order commencing proceedings.

This is ordered upon the court's own motion, or at the request of either the administrator, the creditors' representative, the liquidator or the public prosecutor. The request to modify the date must be made to the court before expiry of the period of fifteen days after the filing of either the report provided in article 18, or the draft reconstruction plan provided in article 145, or the list of creditors provided in article 103 if compulsory liquidation has been ordered.

Sub-section 2 – Organs of the court

Article 10

In the order commencing proceedings, the court will appoint the bankruptcy judge and two officers of the court, namely the administrator and the creditors' representative. The court will invite the works council or, if none, the delegates of the work force, or, if none, the employees, to appoint a representative of their number. The employees elect their representative by secret uninominal ballot.

The administrator may request the appointment of one or more experts.

No relative up to and including the fourth degree of the head of the business or of its officers in the case of bodies corporate, may be appointed to hold any of the positions referred to in this article.

Article 11

The employees' representative as well as the employees who elected the representative, must not have been convicted of any of the offences provided under articles L.5 and L.6 of the electoral code. The employees' representative must be over eighteen years old.

Disputes relating to the appointment of the employees' representative are within the jurisdiction of the district court, from which no appeal lies.

Article 12

The court may either of its own motion, or on the invitation of the bankruptcy judge or at the request of the public prosecutor, arrange for the replacement of the administrator, the expert, or the creditors' representative. In the same way it may add one or more administrators to the one already nominated.

The administrator and the creditors' representative may request the bankruptcy judge to approach the court for that purpose. In the same way, the debtor may request the replacement of the administrator or the expert. The creditors may request replacement of their own representative.

Only the works council, or, failing which, the delegates of the work force, or, failing which, the employees of the business, may replace the employees' representative.

Article 13

The administrator and the creditors' representative will keep the bankruptcy judge and the public prosecutor informed of the progress of the proceedings. The bankruptcy judge and the public prosecutor may at any time require disclosure to them of all acts or documents relating to the proceedings.

The public prosecutor will disclose to the bankruptcy judge on his own initiative or at the request of the bankruptcy judge, notwithstanding any provision of any law to the contrary, all information in his possession which may assist the proceedings.

Article 14

The bankruptcy judge is responsible for ensuring the rapid progress of the proceedings and for protecting the interests of the parties to the proceedings.

Article 15

Either one or two inspectors selected from amongst the creditors may be appointed by order of the bankruptcy judge.

No relative up to and including the fourth degree of the head of the business or of the officers of a body corporate may be appointed inspector or representative of a body corporate appointed as an inspector.

The inspectors will assist the creditors' representative in his functions and the bankruptcy judge in his task of supervising the management of the business. They may require to have disclosed to them all the documents distributed to the administrator and the creditors' representative.

The inspectors will receive no remuneration for their work which must be carried out by them in person. Their appointment may be revoked by the court at the instance of the bankruptcy judge or the creditors' representative. They will only be personally liable for their own gross negligence.

Sub-section 3 – Particular cases

Article 16

When a trader, artisan or farmer dies following cessation of payments, proceedings will be commenced within a period of a year from the date of death, upon notice from an heir or upon summons from a creditor.

Within the same period the court may commence proceedings either of its own motion or on the request of the public prosecutor upon hearing the known heirs or upon their being duly summoned before the court.

Article 17

Proceedings may only be commenced within a period of a year from one of the following events and only when this occurs after the cessation of payments by the debtor:

- striking off from the Register of Commerce and Companies; in the event of a body corporate the period runs from the striking off which follows official publication of the termination of liquidation;
- cessation of the activity if an artisan or farmer is concerned;
- official publication of the completion of liquidation if a non-registrable incorporated body is concerned.

With respect to a person, member or partner of a body corporate with unlimited liability, proceedings may only be commenced within a period of a year from notice of his deletion from the register of commerce and companies when cessation of payments by the body corporate occurs before this deletion.

In each of these cases the court may be requested to commence proceedings or do so of its own motion in the circumstances provided in article 4.

Section II: Preparation of an analysis of the economic and social position of the business and the reconstruction plan

Article 18

The administrator, with the co-operation of the debtor and the assistance if required of one or more experts, is responsible for drawing up an analysis of the economic and social position of the business. Based on this analysis, the administrator will propose either reconstruction or compulsory liquidation.

This analysis will set out the origin, importance and nature of the problems faced by the business.

The reconstruction plan will set out the prospects for reconstruction and how they will be achieved, the state of the market and the available means of financing.

It will identify the steps to be taken to discharge the liabilities of the business and the guarantees to be given by the head of the business in order to ensure implementation of the reconstruction plan.

This reconstruction plan will describe and justify the level of, and future prospects for, employment, and also the labour and welfare conditions envisaged for the future operation of the business. When the reconstruction plan provides for redundancies, it will record measures already taken and define action to be taken with a view to the rehabilitation and compensation of employees whose employment is threatened.

Article 19

Notwithstanding any law or regulation to the contrary, the bankruptcy judge may require disclosure of information from statutory auditors, members and representatives of the workforce, public bodies and authorities, state and private insurance organisations and social security agencies, banks, as well as the authorities responsible for controlling bank exposure and bad debts to enable him to compile an accurate picture of the economic and financial state of the business.

Article 20

The administrator will receive from the bankruptcy judge all information and documents necessary to assist him and the experts in the performance of their respective tasks.

When proceedings are commenced under article 5, the experts' report referred to in article 36 of law no. 84-148 of 1st March 1984 will be disclosed to the administrator or, as the case may be, the experts' report and the account referred to in articles 24 and 27 of law no. 88-1202 of 30th December 1988.

The administrator will consult the debtor and the creditors' representative and will hear every person likely to provide information on the state of the business and its restructuring prospects, the steps to be taken to discharge its liabilities and the labour and welfare conditions under which the business operated.

The administrator will keep the debtor, the creditors' representative and the works council, or, failing which, the delegates of the workforce, informed of the progress of his work. He will consult them regarding the measures he plans to propose in the light of information and offers received.

Article 21

As from the commencement of proceedings, third parties may submit offers to the administrator which have as their objective the survival of the the business in accordance with one or more of the methods defined in chapter II of this part.

An offer so submitted cannot be modified or withdrawn after the date of filing of the administrator's report. The offeror remains bound by his offer until the decision of the court responsible for approving the reconstruction plan, provided this decision is taken during the month following the filing of the report. Unless the offeror consents, he is not bound beyond that time, particularly in the event of an appeal.

The offers are analysed by the administrator and annexed to his report.

Article 22

When the administrator considers proposing to the court a reconstruction plan for the survival of the business based on a reorganisation of its capital, he will request the board of directors or managers, as the case may be, to hold an extraordinary general meeting or a meeting of the partners of the business. If necessary the administrator himself may call the meeting. The meeting is subject to the formalities and timings provided by decree issued by the Council of State.

If, by reason of the losses disclosed in the accounts, the capital of the business amounts to less than half the authorised capital, the meeting will first be asked to inject capital into the business up to the amount proposed by the administrator and which cannot be less than half the authorised capital. The meeting may also be asked to determine the reduction or increase in capital in the interests of one or more persons who undertake to carry out the reconstruction plan.

Performance of the obligations undertaken by the shareholders or partners or by new subscribers is subject to the approval of the reconstruction plan by the court.

Articles designed to secure in advance the shareholders' consent to the proposals of the partners or officers of the body corporate are void.

Article 23

When such action is required in order to ensure survival of the business, the court may, at the request of the administrator or the public prosecutor or of its own motion, make the implementation of the reconstruction plan dependent upon the replacement of one or more of the officers or managers of the business.

When necessary and in the same way as above, the court may declare non-transferable the shares, stock or voting certificates held by one or more of the officers or managers, whether he holds office at law or in fact, paid or unpaid, and may rule that the voting rights attaching thereto will be exercised during a fixed period by an officer of the court appointed for that purpose. The court may also order the sale of those stocks or shares, the price to be fixed by an expert.

For the purposes of this article, the officers or managers of the business and members of the works council or, failing which, the delegates of the work force, may be heard or duly summoned before the court.

Article 24

The administrator will disclose proposals for the discharge of debts progressively as and when they are prepared and under the supervision of the bankruptcy judge, to the creditors' representative, the inspectors and the works council or, failing which, to the delegates of the workforce.

The creditors' representative will obtain either individually or all at the same time the agreement of each creditor who has lodged a declaration of debt in accordance with article 50 below to the deferral and writing-off of his debts proposed to him by the administrator or debtor. In the case of a written request, failure to reply within thirty days of receipt of the letter from the creditors' representative will be deemed to constitute acceptance by the creditor. These provisions apply to the institutions described in article L.143-11-4 of the employment code in respect of amounts advanced in conformity with the third paragraph of article 50 of this law, even though their claim may not have been declared.

In the case of debts owed to the Treasury, the state and private insurance organisations, and the social security agencies, compromises may be agreed subject to the conditions set out by decree of the Council of State. The same applies to the alteration of the priority of a claim or mortgage or to the surrender of these interests.

The creditors' representative will draw up a statement of the replies given by the creditors. This statement is addressed to the administrator so as to enable him to proceed with the preparation of his report.

Article 25

The debtor, the works council, or, failing which, the delegates of the workforce and the creditors' representative will be kept informed and consulted regarding the report delivered to them by the administrator.

This report is addressed at the same time to the competent administrative authority responsible for employment law. The minutes of the meeting, for which the agenda recorded the consultation with the representatives of the workforce, will be distributed to the court and also to the administrative authority mentioned above.

At his request, the public prosecutor will receive a copy of the report.

Section III: Conduct of the business during the observation period

Sub-section 1 – Conservatory measures

Article 26

As from the time of his taking office, the administrator is bound, as the case may be, either to require the head of the business to do, or to do himself, everything necessary to ensure the protection of the rights of the business against its debtors and the preservation of its production capacity.

The administrator is empowered to register on behalf of the business all mortgages, other security, pledges or preferential rights, which the head of the business may have neglected to effect or renew.

Article 27

The bankruptcy judge may direct seals to be affixed and an inventory prepared of the assets of the business.

Article 28

From the order commencing proceedings, any disposal of stock or shares or certificates of investment or of voting rights representing their rights as shareholders of the company which is the subject of the order commencing proceedings and made by the officers of the company whether they hold office in law or in fact, paid or unpaid, is voidable unless otherwise ordered by the court.

The shares and certificates of investment or of voting rights are transferred into a special blocked account opened by the administrator in the name of the holder, and held by the company or the stakeholder bank as the case may be. No transfer may be effected under this account without the authority of the bankruptcy judge.

If appropriate, the administrator will note on the register of a body corporate the non-transferability of any shares owned by its officers.

Article 29

During the observation period, the bankruptcy judge may order letters addressed to the debtor to be delivered to the administrator.

Following notice of this, the debtor may be present at the opening of letters.

However the administrator must immediately return all personal letters to the debtor.

Article 30

The bankruptcy judge will determine the remuneration of the head of the business or the officers of the body corporate.

In the absence of remuneration, the persons referred to in the preceding paragraph may use the business assets to draw advances as determined by the bankruptcy judge in favour of themselves or their families.

Sub-section 2 – Management of the business

PARAGRAPH I – ADMINISTRATION OF THE BUSINESS

Article 31

In addition to the powers conferred under this law, the powers and duties of the administrator or administrators are determined by the court.

The court will require them, either jointly or individually:

1. To supervise the management operations; or
2. To assist the debtor in all or some of the matters concerning the management of the business; or
3. To take charge themselves of the whole or part of the management of the business.

In the course of performing his duties, the administrator must honour the legal or contractual obligations of the head of the business.

At any time the court may modify the administrator's powers and duties at the request of either the administrator himself, or the creditors' representative or the public prosecutor, or of its own motion.

The administrator has power to sign the bank and post office accounts held by the debtor if the debtor is subject to the sanctions set out in articles 65-2 and 68, third paragraph, of the decree of 30th October 1935 unifying the law relating to cheques.

Article 32

The debtor will continue to perform acts of sale and management over the property and to deal with those rights and claims which are not within the powers and duties of the administrator.

In addition, save as excepted under articles 33 and 37 below, the acts of management in the ordinary course of business of the debtor are deemed to be valid as against third parties acting in good faith.

Article 33

The order commencing proceedings automatically prohibits the payment of any claim arising before the order commencing proceedings.

The bankruptcy judge may authorise the head of the business or the administrator either to make a disposal outside the ordinary course of the business, or to grant a mortgage or other security or to compromise or compound a claim.

The bankruptcy judge may also authorise the head of the business or the administrator either to pay claims arising before the date of the order so as to discharge a pledge or to release a valid lien provided that these acts are necessary for the survival of the business.

Every act or payment made in breach of the provisions of this article is voidable at the request of any interested party made within three years from the conclusion of the act or the payment of the claim. When the relevant act is subject to advertising requirements, the period runs from the date of publication.

Article 34

In the event of the sale of an asset charged with a security or mortgage, that proportion of the sale proceeds equal to the sum secured by these charges is transferred to a deposit account at the Central Deposit and Savings Bank. Upon implementation of the reconstruction plan or in the event of compulsory liquidation, the creditors entitled to these securities or entitled to statutory rights are paid out of the sale proceeds in accordance with the order of priority amongst themselves and, when subject to delays in the plan for survival of the business, in conformity with article 78.

The debtor or the administrator may propose to the creditors the substitution of equivalent security to the security held by them. In the absence of agreement, the bankruptcy judge may order substitution. Appeal against this order will be heard by the Court of Appeal.

PARAGRAPH 2 — MAINTENANCE OF THE BUSINESS

Article 35

The business will be maintained during the observation period subject to the following provisions.

Article 36

The court may at any time, at the request of the administrator, the creditors' representative, the debtor, the public prosecutor, or of its own motion, and upon the report of the bankruptcy judge, order the business to be wholly or partially shut down, or may order compulsory liquidation.

The court will give its ruling after having heard or duly summoned before it in chambers each of the debtor, the administrator, the creditors' representative and the representatives of the works council or, failing which, the delegates of the work force.

If the court orders compulsory liquidation, this terminates the observation period and the powers and duties of the administrator.

Article 37

Only the administrator has the power to require performance of existing contracts. This is effected by performing the agreed promise given to the person who has contracted with the debtor.

This other contracting party must perform his obligations in spite of the breach on the part of the debtor in the performance of contractual obligations arising before the order commencing proceedings. Breach on the part of the debtor does not give rise to any rights in favour of the creditors other than to add the claim to the debtor's liabilities.

Disclaimer of continued performance of the contract is presumed after one month without reply from the administrator following the service of a formal notice on the administrator by the other party. Before expiry of this period, the bankruptcy judge may however impose a shorter period for the administrator's reply, or may grant him an extension.

Failure by the administrator to adopt the contract may give rise to a claim for damages in a sum which will be added to the claim of the other contracting party. The other contracting party may nevertheless postpone repayment of any amount paid in excess by the debtor in the course of performance of the contract until judgment on his claim for damages.

Notwithstanding any provision of law or contractual clause, no frustration or termination of the contract may arise solely by reason of the commencement of proceedings for judicial reconstruction.

The provisions of this article do not apply to employment contracts.

Article 38

A lessor may only commence or continue an action for termination of the lease of real property used in the activity of the business on the grounds of default in the payment of rent where such payments have been due for more than three months after commencement of proceedings for judicial reconstruction.

Notwithstanding any contractual provision, failure to continue with the business during the observation period in any one or more properties leased by the business does not give rise to termination of the lease.

Article 39

In the event of judicial reconstruction, the lessor may only claim priority for arrears for the two years before the order commencing proceedings.

If the lessor does terminate the lease, he may in addition claim priority for the current year, for any claim relating to the performance of the obligations under the lease and for damages which may be awarded in his favour by the courts.

If the lessor does not terminate the lease, he may not demand payment of future rent if security granted in his favour at the time the lease was made remains in effect, or if security granted to him following the order commencing proceedings is deemed to be sufficient.

The bankruptcy judge may authorise the debtor or the administrator, as the case may be, to sell movable items of equipment in the rented premises which are liable to rapid deterioration or depreciation, or expensive to maintain, or the disposal of which does not affect either the existence of the business or the maintenance of sufficient security for the lessor.

Article 40

Claims arising in the ordinary course of business after the order commencing proceedings are payable as they fall due so long as the business continues. In the event of sale of the whole business or liquidation, or if, in the event of continuation, these claims are not paid as they fall due, they will be paid in priority to all other claims whether privileged or secured, except for claims protected by articles L.143-10, L.143-11, L.742-6 and L.751-15 of the employment code.

Such claims will be paid in the following order:

1. Wages which were not advanced by way of loan under articles L.143-11-1 to L.143-11-3 of the employment code;

2. Legal expenses;
3. Loans granted by the banks and claims arising from the performance of contracts carried out in accordance with the provisions of article 37, and where the other contracting party has agreed to accept deferred payment; these loans and deferred payments will be authorised by the bankruptcy judge up to the level necessary to enable trading to continue during the observation period, and are subject to official publicity requirements;
4. Sums advanced by way of a loan under paragraph no. 3 of article L.143-11-1 of the employment code;
5. All other claims according to their priority.

Article 41

Every sum received by the administrator or the creditors' representative for the purpose of continuing the business which is not recorded in the debtor's accounts at the bank or the post office must be transferred immediately into a deposit account with the Central Deposit and Savings Bank.

Where there is delay on the part of the administrator or the creditors' representative in transferring such sums they are personally liable for interest on those sums at a rate equal to the legal rate of interest plus five points.

Article 42

When the failure of the business would be sufficiently important to cause serious interference with the national or regional economy, and at the request of the public prosecutor and after consultation with the works council, or, failing which, the delegates of the work force, the court may, during the observation period, authorise conclusion of a lease management contract notwithstanding the existence of any clause to the contrary in particular in the lease of the business premises.

The contract will be of a maximum duration of two years. The duration of the observation period is extended to the end of the contract period.

The provisions of articles 4, 5 and 8 of law no. 56-277 of 20th March 1956 relating to the contract management of businesses and artisan establishments do not apply.

Article 43

The administrator will supervise the contractual obligations entered into by the lease manager.

If the lease manager performs an act which may prejudice the assets leased under the lease-management, or if he reduces the value of any security given, the court may order termination of the lease-management either of its own motion, or at the request of the administrator, the creditors' representative or the public prosecutor after consultation with the works council or, failing which, with the representatives of the work force.

Sub-section 3 – Employees' position

Article 44

The creditors' representative will submit the list of claims resulting from employment contracts for verification to the employees' representative referred to in article 10. The creditors' representative must disclose to him all relevant documents and information. In the event of difficulties, the employees' representative may approach the administrator, and, if necessary, apply to the bankruptcy judge. The employees' representative is bound by the confidentiality requirement referred to in article L.432-7 of the employment code. Time spent in the exercise of his task, as determined by the bankruptcy judge, is automatically deemed to be time lawfully engaged at work and is paid for by the employer, the administrator, or the liquidator, as the case may be, on the normal due date.

Article 45

When dismissals for redundancy are urgent, inevitable and necessary during the observation period, the administrator may be authorised by the bankruptcy judge to effect these redundancies. Prior to the administrator's request to the bankruptcy judge, the administrator will inform and consult both the works council or, failing which, the delegates of the work force, and the administrative authority competent in matters of employment law as laid down in articles L.321-7, second paragraph, and L.321-10 of the employment code. In support of his request to the bankruptcy judge, the administrator will annexe opinions received and the grounds for his action with a view to facilitating the compensation and rehabilitation of the employees.

Sub-section 4 – Creditors' position

PARAGRAPH 1 – REPRESENTATION OF THE CREDITORS

Article 46

Only the creditors' representative appointed by the court has capacity to act in the name of and in the interests of the creditors.

The sums recovered as a result of proceedings taken by the creditors' representative are credited to the debtor's estate and, in the event of continuation of the business, are dealt with in accordance with the methods prescribed for the discharge of the liabilities of the business.

PARAGRAPH 2 – DISCONTINUANCE OF INDIVIDUAL ACTIONS

Article 47

The order commencing proceedings stays or prevents the commencement of all legal proceedings on behalf of every creditor whose claim arises before the date of the order, and which have as their objective:

- enforcement of a monetary award against the debtor;
- termination of a contract on the grounds of default in payment of a sum of money.

In addition the order prevents or suspends all executory measures on the part of such creditors against the moveable or immoveable property of the debtor.

Time limits resulting in forfeiture or loss of rights are therefore suspended.

Article 48

Subject to the provisions of article 124, proceedings already instituted are stayed until the plaintiff creditor has declared his claim. The proceedings are then automatically reinstated, the creditors' representative and, if necessary, the administrator being duly summoned, but with the object only of the admission of the claims and the establishment of their amount.

Article 49

Court actions and executory measures against the debtor, other than those referred to in article 47, will be pursued during the observation period after joinder of the administrator and the creditors' representative in the proceedings or after revival at their instigation.

PARAGRAPH 3 – DECLARATION OF CLAIMS

Article 50

With effect from the date of publication of the order, all creditors whose claims had arisen before the order commencing proceedings, with the exception of employees, must file a declaration of their claims with the creditors' representative. Creditors whose security has been officially published will be notified personally and, if necessary, at their address for service.

The declaration of claims must be made even if the claims may not have been evidenced. The claims of the Treasury and the state insurance and social security agencies which have not been made the subject of a writ of execution at the time of declaration will be admitted provisionally on the basis of the sum declared. Whatever the circumstances, the Treasury and the social security agencies declarations are always made subject to tax and any other claims which may not have been determined at the date of declaration.

The institutions referred to in article L.143-11-4 of the employment code are subject to the provisions of this article in respect of sums advanced by them and reimbursed to them under the conditions providing for claims arising before the date of the order commencing proceedings.

Article 51

The declaration will show the total amount claimed as owing at the date of the order commencing proceedings and will indicate sums falling due in the future together with due dates. It will set out the nature of any preferential right or security attached to a claim.

When a claim is expressed in foreign currency, the amount is converted into French francs at the exchange rate current at the date of the order commencing proceedings.

Save when a claim is executory, any claim declared for an amount exceeding a figure fixed by decree will be certified fair and correct by the creditor. The creditor's statutory auditor, or failing which, his accountant, if any, will certify the declaration after establishing the existence of the claim on the basis of the documents to which he has access. The decision to refuse to certify must be justified by the creditor's auditor.

Article 52

The debtor will deliver the certified list of his creditors and of the total amount of his debts to the creditors' representative.

Article 53

In the event of failure to declare a claim within the period fixed by decree of the Council of State, the creditors will not be entitled to share in distributions and dividends unless disbarred by the bankruptcy judge upon their establishing that the failure is not due to their act or omission. In that event they may only compete for distributions made after the date of their demand.

Application for disbarment relief may only be made within a period of a year from the order commencing proceedings or, in the case of the institutions referred to in article L.143-11-4 of the employment code, from expiry of the period during which claims resulting from employment contracts are guaranteed by those institutions.

Claims which have not been admitted and are not entitled to disbarment relief are void.

Article 54

If a dispute arises in respect of all or part of a claim other than the claims referred to in articles 106 and 123, the creditors' representative will notify the interested creditor and invite him to make known his views. Failure to reply within thirty days operates to prevent any further opposition to the proposal submitted by the creditors' representative.

PARAGRAPH 4 – SUSPENSION OF THE RUNNING OF INTEREST AND THE CIRCUMSTANCES IN WHICH TERMS PROVIDING FOR ACCELERATION ARE RENDERED INEFFECTIVE

Article 55

The order commencing proceedings for judicial reconstruction suspends the accrual of statutory and contractual interest as well as all default or compound interest, except in the case of interest arising from loan agreements providing for repayment following a period equal to or exceeding one year, or arising from contracts providing for payment to be deferred over a period of a year or more.

Article 56

The order commencing proceedings for judicial reconstruction does not cause claims not due at the date of issue of the order to become immediately payable. Any clause to the contrary is deemed void.

PARAGRAPH 5 – PROHIBITION OF REGISTRATION

Article 57

Mortgages, charges over intangible and moveable assets, preferential rights as well as judicial acts and decisions transferring or creating rights in rem may not be registered after the date of the order commencing proceedings for judicial reconstruction.

However, the Treasury retains its preferential right for claims which it was not obliged to register on the date of the order commencing proceedings, and in respect of claims asserted after that date if the claims are declared in accordance with article 50.

Notwithstanding the provisions of the first paragraph of this article, the seller of the assets and goodwill of the business may register his preferential right.

Paragraph 6 – Sureties and joint obligors

Article 58

A creditor holding contractual undertakings underwritten, endorsed or guaranteed jointly by two or more joint obligors subject to proceedings for judicial reconstruction may officially declare his claim in the face value of the security in each of the proceedings.

Article 59

Joint obligors subject to proceedings for judicial reconstruction have no mutual recourse for payments already made unless the sums paid in the course of each proceeding exceed in total the amount of the principal and other sums owing under the claim, in which event the excess is paid over to those of the joint obligors who are guaranteed by the others, in accordance with the order in which these became contractually committed.

Article 60

If a creditor holding contractual undertakings, which are jointly underwritten by a debtor subject to judicial reconstruction and other joint obligors, has received an instalment payment on account of his claim before the commencement of proceedings, he may only declare his claim after deduction of this payment, retaining his rights to claim the balance due to him from the joint obligor or surety.

The joint obligor or surety who has made the partial payment may declare his claim in the whole amount paid by him towards discharge of the indebtedness owed by the debtor.

CHAPTER II. THE PLAN FOR SURVIVAL OR SALE OF THE BUSINESS

Section I: The order approving the scheme

Article 61

After hearing or duly summoning the debtor, the administrator, the creditors' representative and also the representatives of the works council or, failing which, of the delegates of the workforce, the court will give its ruling after taking into account the report of the administrator, and will approve a plan for reconstruction or will order liquidation.

This plan will provide for either the survival of the business or its sale or for its partial survival and partial sale.

The plan providing for total or partial disposal of the business may include a period of lease management for all or part of the assets and goodwill of the business. In that event, the contract of lease management will include an undertaking to purchase upon expiry.

Article 62

The plan will designate the persons responsible for putting the plan into effect and will refer to the totality of the undertakings entered into by them and which are required for the reconstruction of the business. These undertakings will relate to the future activity and the means of maintaining and financing the business, the settling of liabilities of the business arising before the order commencing proceedings, and also, if necessary, any guarantees provided in order to ensure implementation of the plan.

The plan will describe and justify the level of, and future prospects for, employment as well as the social conditions envisaged for the continued activity of the business.

Save as provided in articles 22, 72, 86, 89 and 93, the persons appointed to put the plan into effect, even in the capacity of partners, will not be subjected to any personal responsibilities other than those undertaken in the course of preparation of the plan.

Article 63

When the plan proposes redundancies, it will not be approved by the court until the works council or, failing which, the delegates of the workforce, as well as the competent administrative authority, have been informed and consulted in accordance with the provisions of articles L.321-7 second paragraph, and L.321-10 of the employment code.

The plan will in particular define whatever redundancies are required to take place within the period of one month following the order. In this period redundancies will take place upon ordinary notification by the administrator but without prejudice to rights of notice available at law, or under the labour conventions or collective agreements.

Article 64

The order approving the plan renders its provisions valid as against the whole world.

Nevertheless joint sureties and joint obligors may not take advantage of the plan for their own benefit.

Article 65

Without prejudice to the application of the provisions of article 74, the duration of the plan will be fixed by the court. This may be extended in due course by the period set out in article 97 below.

Article 66

The court will prescribe the administrator's duties and grant him the powers necessary to put the plan into operation.

The creditors' representative will remain in office for such time as is necessary for the verification of creditors' claims.

Article 67

The court will appoint a commissioner responsible for supervising implementation of the plan. The appointment of the commissioner will be for the period fixed under article 65 as extended in due course by the period set out in article 97 below. The administrator or the creditors' representative may be appointed to this office. The commissioner may be replaced by the court either of its own motion, or on the request of the public prosecutor.

Actions commenced by either the administrator or the creditors' representative before the order approving the plan will be continued by the commissioner.

The commissioner may require the production to him of all documents and information relevant to his duties.

He will account to the president of the court and to the public prosecutor for any failure to execute the plan. He will keep the works council informed of any such failure or, failing which, the delegates of the work force.

Article 68

Substantial modification to the objectives and terms and conditions of the plan may only be approved by the court upon the application of the head of the business and following the report of the commissioner.

The court will give its decision after hearing or duly summoning the parties, the representatives of the works council or, failing which, the delegates of the work force, and any other interested person.

Nevertheless, save as provided in the second paragraph of article 98, upon the sale of the business, the price fixed in the order approving the plan will not be modified.

Section II: Survival of the business

Article 69

Following the report of the administrator, the court will decide in favour of survival of the business where there exists a serious possibility for the reconstruction of the business and the payment of its liabilities.

This decision will be taken at the same time, if necessary, as the decision to stop, add to, merge or sell particular parts of its activities. Disposals carried out under this article are subject to the provisions of articles 82–93 (second paragraph) below.

Article 70

In the order approving or modifying the plan, the court may decide that assets which it considers vital for the survival of the business should not be disposed for a fixed period without the authority of the court.

Official publicity of the temporary prohibition of disposal will be effected, in the case of real estate in accordance with the provisions of article 28 of decree no. 55-22 of 4th January 1955 relating to the reform of the publication of notice of interests in real estate, and, in the case of works equipment belonging to the business, by filing notice at the court registry under the circumstances set down by decree of the Council of State.

Any act done in breach of the provisions of the first paragraph of this article is voidable at the request of any interested party made within a period of three years from the date of the relevant act. When the act is subject to official publicity requirements, the period runs from the date of publication.

Sub-section 1 – Amendment of the articles of incorporation of bodies corporate

Article 71

The plan will refer to any amendment to the articles of incorporation necessary to the survival of the business.

Article 72

The order approving the plan will authorise the administrator to call a meeting in accordance with the formalities and time limits fixed by the Council of State. The meeting will be competent to bring into force the amendments envisaged by the plan.

Article 73

New associates or shareholders are required immediately to pay up any capital subscribed by them in full. They are however entitled to set-off to the extent of their admitted claims but subject to the abatement to which their claims are subject under the plan in the form of discounts or deferments.

Sub-section 2 – Methods of discharge of liabilities

Article 74

The court will place on record the deferrals and compromises accepted by creditors in the circumstances set out in the second and third paragraphs of article 24. These deferrals and compromises may, if appropriate, be reduced by the court. As regards other creditors, the court will impose uniform deferral of payment periods with the exception, in the case of term loan creditors, of longer repayment periods agreed between the parties before the commencement of proceedings.

The repayment periods may exceed the duration of the plan.

Article 75

The plan may give creditors a choice of repayment in shorter equal periods but subject to a proportional reduction in the amount of their claims.

In that event, the repayment periods will not exceed the duration of the plan.

The abatement of a claim only becomes final after payment at the due date of the last instalment in accordance with the plan.

Article 76

By way of exception to the provisions of articles 74 and 75, the following claims will not be discounted or deferred:

1. Claims protected by the preferential right established under articles L.143-10, L.143-11, L.742-6 and L.751-15 of the employment code;
2. Claims arising from a contract of employment protected by the preferential rights set out in the 4th paragraph of article 2101 and in the 2nd paragraph of article 2104 of the civil code if the amount claimed has not been advanced by way of loan by the institutions referred to in article L.143-11-4 of the employment code or has not been subrogated.

Up to a limit of 5 per cent of the estimated total liabilities of the business, the smallest claims, ranking by ascending order of magnitude, and subject to their not exceeding an amount fixed by decree, will be repaid without abatement or deferral. This provision does not apply when the aggregate of the debt owed to the same person exceeds one tenth of the percentage referred to above, or where subrogation has been agreed or a third party payment has been effected.

Article 77

Registration of a claim within the plan and the agreement to deferrals or abatements by the creditor will not prejudice the final admission to proof of the claim as a liability of the business.

Distributions relating to litigated claims will only be paid after final admission of the claim as a liability of the business. However, the court which has jurisdiction over the relevant litigation may decide whether the creditor will participate on a provisional basis, in whole or in part, in distributions made before final admission of the claim.

Unless otherwise provided by law or by the plan, payments set out in the plan are collectable without further process from the address for service of the business.

Article 78

In the event of the sale of an asset charged with a lien or other prior right or mortgage, the creditors entitled to those securities, or to a general preferential right, will be paid out of the sale proceeds after the payment of claims protected by the preferential right established under articles L.143-10, L.143-11, L.742-6 and L.751-15 of the employment code.

These creditors will receive the dividends which would have become due to them under the plan, discounted to take into account payment in advance, in the order of priority existing between themselves.

If an asset is charged with a lien or other prior right or mortgage, alternative security of equivalent value may be substituted if necessary. Any dispute will be determined by the court.

Article 79

In the event of partial sale of assets, the proceeds are paid to the business subject to the application of article 78.

Article 80

If the debtor fails to perform his financial undertakings within the time limits set out in the plan, a creditor or group of creditors representing at least 15 per cent of the total amount claimed may, after informing the commissioner, apply to the court for termination of the plan and the commencement of proceedings for judicial reconstruction with the sole objective of sale or compulsory liquidation.

The court may also apply to the public prosecutor or the commissioner.

Creditors subject to the plan will submit a declaration for the full amount of their claims and securities after deduction of sums received.

Section III: Sale of the business

Sub-section 1 – General provisions

Article 81

Following examination of the report prepared by the administrator, the court may order sale of the business.

The objective of sale is to ensure the preservation of any activity susceptible to commercial exploitation and the employment of all or part of the labour force attached to it, and to discharge the liabilities of the business.

The sale may be in whole or in part. If the sale is in part, it will deal with homogenous units of commercial exploitation which form one or more complete and autonomous areas of business activity.

In the absence of a plan for survival of the business, assets not included in the sale plan will be sold in accordance with the terms and conditions set out in part III.

Sub-section 2 – Terms and conditions of sale

Article 82

A sale may only be ordered by the court if it relates to one or more of the units within the meaning of article 81.

The court will determine the composition of these business units.

When a unit essentially consists of a farming lease, the court may, subject to the tenant's rights of indemnity which arise notwithstanding other provisions of agricultural law to the contrary, either authorise the lessor, his spouse or his heirs to take the business back into exploitation, or to grant the farming lease to another tenant proposed by the lessor or, failing which, to any other tenant whose offer has been received in accordance with the conditions set out in articles 83, 84 and 85. However, when several offers have been received, the court will have regard to the provisions contained in the paragraphs numbered 1, 2, 3 and 4 of article 188-5 of the rural code. In every case, the provisions relating to the supervision of agricultural organisations do not apply.

Article 83

Every offer for the business must be received by the administrator within the time fixed by him and contain the following details:

1. Proposals for future activity and financial forecast for the business.
2. Sale price and settlement terms and conditions.
3. Sale completion date.
4. Level of employmet, and future employment prospects, justified by the proposed activity.
5. Guarantees to be given by the transferee as security for completion of the transaction.

The bankruptcy judge may request further details.

Article 84

The administrator will provide the court with all possible information to enable the serious nature of the offer to be verified.

Article 85

The court will choose the offer which, under the best conditions, affords the most stable employment prospects for the business unit to be sold, and the payment of creditors.

Article 86

The court will decide which contracts for leasing, hire or supply of goods or services are necessary to keep the business going having regard to the views of the debtor's suppliers as reported by the administrator.

The order approving the plan operates to assign these contracts even though the assignment may be preceded by the lease management referred to in article 94.

These contracts must be performed on the terms and conditions in force at the time of commencement of the proceedings notwithstanding any provision to the contrary save for any deferred payment terms which the court, after hearing or duly summoning the contracting party, may impose in order to ensure the continued activity of the business.

Article 87

In carrying out the plan approved by the court, the administrator may enter into any contract necessary for completion of the sale.

Pending completion, the administrator may, on his own responsibility, allow the purchaser to manage the business which is the subject of the sale.

Article 88

By way of exception to article 67, the appointment of the commissioner will continue up to payment in full of the sale price.

Sub-section 3 – Obligations of the purchaser

Article 89

So long as any part of the sale price is outstanding, the purchaser may not, save in the case of stock, dispose of, or arrange for the lease management of, the tangible or intangible assets acquired by him.

Total or partial sale of these assets, or charging them by way of security, or their hire or lease management may be authorised by the court upon the report of the commissioner who must first consult the works council or, failing which, the delegates of the work force. The court must take into account any guarantees offered by the purchaser.

Any act in breach of the provisions of this article is voidable at the request of any interested party made within a period of three years from the date of the relevant act. When the act is subject to official publicity requirements, the period runs from the date of publication.

Article 90

In the event of default in the payment of the sale price, the court may of its own motion, or following the request of the administrator or the public prosecutor or any interested party, appoint an ad hoc commissioner to act in accordance with terms of reference determined by the court.

Sub-section 4 – The effect of the sale on creditors

Article 91

The order approving the plan for sale of the business as a whole accelerates any debts which have not accrued due.

Article 92

In the event of sale of the business as a whole, the court will, of its own motion, order termination of the proceedings after the performance of everything necessary for completion of the sale.

The sale price will be distributed by the commissioner among the creditors according to their priority ranking.

After the order of termination of proceedings, the creditors will regain their individual rights of action subject to the limits set out in article 169.

Article 93

If assets charged with a lien or prior charge or a mortgage are included in the sale, a proportion of the sale price is assigned by the court to each relevant asset for the purpose of the proper distribution of the sale price in accordance with the relevant preferential right.

However, the burden of the prior charge which secures in favour of the seller or the lender the purchase price for the tools of the business or its other professional equipment will pass to the purchaser. The purchaser will then be bound to honour payments due to the seller or lender and outstanding after the transfer of title or, in the case of lease management, of the right of possession, subject to any deferred payment terms imposed under the conditions provided in the third paragraph of article 86.

Up to the time of completion of payment of the price, whereupon charges registered against the assets subject to the transfer will be deleted, creditors entitled to a right to trace may only exercise this right in the event of sale by the purchaser of the transferred asset.

Sub-section 5 – Lease management

Article 94

In the order approving the plan the court may authorise a lease management of the business to be concluded on the conditions provided in article 61, notwithstanding any provision to the contrary in particular in the lease of the business premises. This contract will be concluded in favour of the person who has submitted the offer to acquire the business which affords the best conditions for the preservation of the most stable employment prospects and for the payment of the creditors.

Article 95

The commissioner may require the lease manager to disclose all documents and information relevant to his role. The commissioner will account to the court for any damage suffered by the business units subject to lease management and for any default by the lease manager in the performance of his obligations.

The court may of its own motion, or on the application of the commissioner or the public prosecutor, order rescission of the lease management contract and termination of the plan.

Termination of the plan involves the commencement of new proceedings for judicial reconstruction with respect to the grantor of the contract. Creditors participating in the distribution of the sale price will recover their claims and securities in full after deduction of any sums already received.

Article 96

The provisions of articles 4, 5 and 8 of law no. 56-277 of 20th March 1956 referred to earlier do not apply.

Article 97

In the event of lease management, the business should effectively be transferred within two years of the order approving the plan.

Article 98

If the lease manager fails to perform his purchase obligation under the conditions and within the time limits fixed by the plan, proceedings for judicial reconstruction will be commenced in relation to the contract manager at the request of the commissioner, the public prosecutor or any other interested person without the need to establish cessation of payments.

However, if the lease manager is able to justify his failure to purchase upon the original conditions on grounds not attributable to him, he may request the court to modify these conditions at any time before expiry of the lease and after seeking the opinion of the commissioner.

CHAPTER III. THE BUSINESS ASSETS AND LIABILITIES

Section I: The verification and admission of claims to proof

Article 99

In the event of sale or compulsory liquidation, the court will not proceed with the verification of unsecured claims if it is apparent that the proceeds of sale of the assets will be entirely absorbed by the legal expenses and the preferred claims, unless, in the case of a body corporate, it is appropriate in accordance with article 180 below to hold the officers of the body corporate, in law or in fact, paid or unpaid, responsible for all or part of the liabilities.

Article 100

After hearing the comments of the debtor, the creditors' representative will draw up one or more lists of declared claims together with his proposals for their admission to proof, rejection or re-submission before the competent court. He will deliver these lists to the bankruptcy judge as and when drawn up.

Article 101

Following consideration of the proposals of the creditors' representative, the bankruptcy judge will determine the admission to proof or rejection of the claims, or will establish whether proceedings have been commenced, or if the dispute is not within his competence.

The bankruptcy judge may not reject a claim in whole or in part or declare himself incompetent to hear the claim until he has heard or duly summoned the creditor, the debtor, the administrator (when administration of the business is within his duties), and the creditors' representative.

Article 102

If the matter is within the competence of the court which dealt with commencement of the proceedings for judicial reconstruction, an appeal from the decision of the bankruptcy judge lies to the Court of Appeal at the instance of the creditor, the debtor, the administrator (when administration of the business is within his duties), and the creditors' representative.

However, a creditor whose claim is disputed in whole or in part and who has not replied to the creditors' representative within the time limit provided in article 54 may not appeal the decision of the bankruptcy judge if it confirms the proposal of the creditors' representative.

If the matter is within the competence of another court, notice of the decision of denying competence of the bankruptcy judge operates to start a period of two months within which the claimant must commence proceedings in a competent court, failing which his claim will be time barred.

Article 103

The decisions of the bankruptcy judge to admit claims to proof or to reject them, or as to the court's competence to hear particular claims, are recorded on a statement filed with the court registry. Any interested party with the exception of those referred to in article 102 may have access to this statement and may formulate an objection within the time limit fixed by decree of the Council of State.

The bankruptcy judge will give his ruling on the objection after hearing or duly summoning before him the creditors' representative and the other interested parties.

Appeal against the bankruptcy judge's ruling on the objection lies to the Court of Appeal.

Article 104

The decision made by the court with jurisdiction under the conditions set out in the third paragraph of article 102 will be recorded on the statement referred to in the preceding article. Third parties may only dispute this decision within the period of one month following report of the decision on the statement filed with the court registry.

Article 105

Decisions of the bankruptcy judge are not appealable in the cases described in this section if the value of the principal amount of the claim is within the maximum limit in respect of which the decisions of the court where proceedings were commenced are final.

Article 106

Claims under the general tax code or under the customs code may only be disputed in accordance with the conditions provided in those codes. Such claims will be admitted to proof as a matter of right.

Section II: Voidability of certain acts

Article 107

The following acts are void if done by the debtor after the date of cessation of payments:

1. All voluntary acts by way of transfer of real estate or moveable property;
2. All contracts in which the debtor's obligations substantially exceed those of the other contracting party;
3. Any payment of whatever kind of debts maturing after the date of payment;
4. Any payment of due debts made otherwise than by cash, negotiable instrument, bank transfer, or certificate of transfer, as provided under law no. 81-1 of 2nd January 1981 for the promotion of business credit, or any other method of payment commonly accepted in commercial relationships;
5. Any deposit and any transfer of monies effected in accordance with article 2075-1 of the civil code without a court decision having the force of res judicata;
6. Any contractual mortgage, judicial mortgage or statutory marriage mortgage, and any prior right secured on the assets of the debtor in respect of pre-existing debts;
7. Any conservatory measure unless it took place or was registered before the date of cessation of payments. The court may in addition declare void a gift of the kind referred to in paragraph 1 of this article made within six months before the date of cessation of payments.

The court may in addition declare void a gift of the kind referred to in paragraph 1 of this article made within six months before the date of cessation of payments.

Article 108

Payment of due debts made after the date of cessation of payments, and the performance of onerous acts after that date, may be avoided if those dealing with the debtor knew of the cessation of payments.

Article 109

The provisions of articles 107 and 108 do not affect the validity of payment under a bill of exchange, promissory note or cheque.

Nevertheless, the administrator or the creditors' representative may bring an action for recovery against the drawer of the bill of exchange or, in the case of a drawing on an account, against the issuer of the order, and also against the payee of a cheque and the first indorser of a promissory note, if it is proved that they knew of the cessation of payments.

Article 110

Proceedings for avoidance are commenced by the administrator, the creditors' representative, the liquidator, or the commissioner. The effect of these proceedings is to reconstitute the debtor's assets.

Section III: Rights of the debtor's spouse

Article 111

The spouse of a debtor under judicial reconstruction is required to establish the constituent elements of his or her personal assets in accordance with the rules of matrimonial law.

Article 112

On proving with whatever evidence is available that the assets claimed to have been acquired by the debtor's spouse have in fact been acquired for consideration provided by the debtor, the creditors' representative or the administrator may request that assets thus acquired be restored to the debtor's estate.

Article 113

Restorations made in accordance with article 111 may only be effected after allowing for the debts and mortgages lawfully attaching to the relevant assets.

Article 114

The spouse of a debtor who was a trader, artisan or farmer at the time of his marriage or who became a trader or artisan within a year of his marriage may not bring proceedings in the judicial reconstruction on the grounds of benefits granted by one spouse to the other either under the marriage contract or in the course of the marriage; by the same token the creditors may not take advantage of these benefits for themselves.

Section IV: Rights of the seller of moveable property and actions for recovery

Article 115

Proceedings for recovery of moveable property may only be instituted after a period of three months from the date of the order commencing proceedings for judicial reconstruction.

Article 116

The preferential right, the action for rescission and the right of recovery conferred under the 4th paragraph of article 2102 of the civil code for the benefit of the seller of moveable property may only be exercised in accordance with the following provisions.

Article 117

Goods may be recovered either through the court or by operation of a condition subsequent if they still physically exist, either in whole or in part, when the contract for their sale has been rescinded before the order commencing proceedings for judicial reconstruction.

The recovery must also be admitted, even though rescission of the sale may have been ordered or confirmed through the court after the order commencing proceedings for judicial reconstruction, when the action for recovery or rescission has been commenced by the seller before the order commencing proceedings on grounds other than default in the payment of the purchase price.

Article 118

Goods despatched to the debtor may be recovered as long as the transfer did not take place in his warehouses or in warehouses belonging to an agent selling the goods on behalf of the debtor.

Nevertheless, recovery may not be sought if, before the arrival of the goods, they have been resold without fraud on the basis of normal commercial invoices or consignment notes.

Article 119

Goods may be retained by the seller which have not been delivered to, or despatched to, the debtor, or to a third party acting on his behalf.

Article 120

Provided they still remain in the debtor's hands, bills of exchange or other unpaid commercial instruments may be recovered which have been remitted by their owners for redemption or appropriation against specific payments.

Article 121

Goods may be recovered provided they still physically exist which have been consigned to the debtor either by way of deposit or in order to be sold on behalf of the owner.

Goods which have been sold on condition that transfer of title is dependent upon payment of the price in full may also be recovered if they still physically exist, provided that this condition was agreed between the parties in writing at the latest upon delivery. However, recovery is not available if the price is paid immediately or, if payment is guaranteed by the administrator, at the latest following the initial observation period and the time fixed by the bankruptcy judge.

Article 122

The price, or that part of the price, of the goods referred to in article 121 may be recovered which has not been paid, and for which neither value nor set-off on current account have been given between the debtor and the buyer.

CHAPTER IV. SETTLEMENT OF CLAIMS ARISING OUT OF THE CONTRACT OF EMPLOYMENT

Section I: Verification of claims

Article 123

After verification, and upon hearing or duly summoning the debtor, the creditors' representative will draw up within the time limits provided in article L.143-11-7 of the employment code the schedules of claims arising from a contract of employment. The schedules of claims will be submitted to the employees' representative in the circumstances provided in article 44. The schedules are certified by the bankruptcy judge, filed with the court registry and are subject to official publicity under the conditions fixed by decree of the Council of State.

Any employee whose claim is not set out in full or in part on such a schedule may apply to the relevant conciliation tribunal within a period of two months from the date of the publicity referred to in the previous paragraph, failing which this right will be time barred. He may require the employees' representative to assist him or to represent him before the conciliation tribunal.

The creditors' representative who appeared before the conciliation tribunal or, failing which, the plaintiff, will summon the institutions referred to in article L.143-11-4 of the employment code to appear before this tribunal. Either the debtor or the administrator, when the administration of the business is within his duties, will be joined in the action.

Article 124

With effect from the date of the order commencing proceedings for judicial reconstruction, the hearings before the conciliation tribunal will take place in the presence of the creditors' representative and the administrator, when the administration of the business is within his duties, or after both of these persons have been duly summoned.

The creditors' representative will inform the tribunal seized with the matter and the employees who are parties to it within ten days of the commencement of proceedings for judicial reconstruction.

The institutions referred to in article L.143-11-4 of the employment code are joined by the creditors' representative or, failing which, the claimant employees, within ten days of the order commencing proceedings for judicial reconstruction.

Article 125

If the institutions referred to in article L.143-11-4 of the employment code refuse for whatever reason to pay a claim stated in a schedule of claims arising out of a contract of employment, they will notify their rejection of the claim to the creditors' representative who will immediately inform the employees' representative and the employee concerned.

The employee may apply to the conciliation tribunal. The creditors' representative, the head of the business or the administrator when the administration of the business is within his duties will be joined in the matter.

The employee may ask the employees' representative to assist him or represent him before the conciliation tribunal.

Article 126

Disputes submitted to the conciliation tribunal in accordance with articles 123 and 125 are heard directly before the judicial committee.

Article 127

The schedules of claims arising out of a contract of employment, certified by the bankruptcy judge, together with the decisions issued by the conciliation tribunal are recorded on the statement of claims filed with the court registry. Any interested party with the exception of those referred to in articles 123–125 may appeal or be joined as third party under the conditions referred to respectively in articles 103 and 104.

Section II: Priority of employees' claims

Article 128

Claims arising out of a contract of employment are protected in the event of commencement of proceedings for judicial reconstruction:

1. By the priority conferred under articles L.143-10, L.143-11, L.742-6 and L.751-15 of the employment code on the basis and in the amounts set out in these articles;
2. By the priority conferred under the 4th paragraph of article 2101 and the second paragraph of 2104 of the civil code.

Article 129

Notwithstanding the existence of any other claims, the claims protected by the priority conferred under articles L.143-10, L.143-11, L.742-6 and L.751-15 of the employment code must be paid by the administrator on the direction of the bankruptcy judge within ten days of issue of the order commencing proceedings for judicial reconstruction provided the administrator has the necessary funds at his disposal.

However, before any final drawing up of the amount of these claims, the administrator must, on the authority of the bankruptcy judge and in proportion to the available funds, immediately pay to the employees on a provisional basis a sum equal to one month's unpaid wages calculated by reference to the most recent payslip and without exceeding the limit set out in article L.143-10 of the employment code.

In the absence of available funds, the amount due under the two preceding paragraphs must be paid out upon the first receipt of funds on behalf of the business.

Section III: Protection for the payment of contract of employment claims

Article 130

Articles L.143-11-2, L.143-11-3, L.143-11-4 and L.143-11-6 of the employment code are renumbered respectively articles L.143-11-4, L.143-11-5, L.143-11-6 and L.143-11-8.

In article L.143-11-5 as renumbered, the words: 'of articles L.143-11-1 to L.143-11-7', are replaced by the words: 'of articles L.143-11-1 to L.143-11-9', and the words: 'to article L.143-11-2', by the words: 'to article L.143-11-4'.

Article 131

Article L.143-9 of the employment code is redrawn as follows:

> 'Art. L.143-9 – Without prejudice to the rule set out in articles 128 and 129 of law no. 85-98 of 25th January 1985 relating to the judicial reconstruction and liquidation of businesses, claims arising from the contract of employment or from the contract of apprenticeship are protected upon the terms set out in articles L.143-10 to L.143-11-9.'

Article 132

I In article L.143-11-6, as renumbered, of the employment code, the reference: 'section II of chapter I of part V of book III of the employment code' is replaced by the reference: 'section I of chapter I of part V of book III of this code'.

II In article L.143-11-8, as renumbered, of the employment code, the reference: 'article L.143-11-2' is replaced by the reference: 'article L.143-11-4'.

III In articles L.143-10 and L.143-11 of the employment code, the words: 'in the event of judicial regulation or of liquidation of assets' are replaced by the words: 'when proceedings for judicial reconstruction are commenced'.

Article 133

Article L.143-11-1 of the employment code is replaced by the following provisions:

'Art. L.143-11-1 – Every employer in the capacity of trader or artisan or body incorporated under private law who employs one or more employee must insure his employees, including salaried employees seconded abroad as well as the salaried expatriate employees referred to in article L.351-4, against the risk of non-payment of sums owing to them under the contract of employment in the event of proceedings for judicial reconstruction.

The insurance will cover:

1. Sums owing to employees on the date of the order commencing any proceedings for judicial reconstruction;
2. Claims arising from the breach of contracts of employment occurring during the period of observation, in the month following the order approving the reconstruction plan, in the fifteen days following the order for liquidation, and during the provisional continuation of the activity of the business authorised under the order for compulsory liquidation;
3. When the court orders compulsory liquidation, up to a maximum amount equal to one and a half month's work, the sums owing for the period of observation, the fifteen days following the order for liquidation, and during the provisional continuation of the activity of the business authorised under the order for liquidation.

'Art. L.143-11-2 – Claims resulting from the redundancy of employees entitled to special protection relating to redundancy will be covered by the insurance from the moment when the administrator, the employer or the liquidator, as the case may be, has shown during the periods referred to in the 2nd paragraph of article L.143-11-1 an intention to breach the contract of employment.

Art. L.143-11-3 – When such sums constitute claims against the business they will be covered by the insurance provided for in article L.143-11-1 if owed under a profit sharing scheme conforming with the provisions of articles L.441-1 and the following articles, or under an expansion participation scheme for employees conforming with the provisions of articles L.442-1 and the following articles, or under an agreement setting up an earnings fund under the conditions provided in articles L.471-1 and the following articles.

Those arrears of early retirement payments will also be covered by the insurance which are owed to an employee or a former employee under a professional or inter-professional agreement, under a collective convention or under an agreement concluded within the business itself. These provisions apply when the agreement provides for commencement of early retirement at the age of fifty five at the earliest. The protection provided under this paragraph will be limited under conditions fixed by decree.

The claims set out in the first and second paragraphs are protected:

– when they are due on the date of the order commencing proceedings;
– when, if a plan providing for survival of the business occurs as a result of the proceedings, they fall due as a consequence of the breach of the employment contract within the time limits provided for in the 2nd paragraph of article L.143-11-1;
– when an order pronouncing compulsory liquidation or approving the sale of the business as a whole is issued.'

Article 134

Article L.143-11-7 of the employment code is redrawn as follows:

'Art. L.143-11-7 – The creditors' representative will draw up the schedules of claims on the following conditions:

1. Claims referred to in articles L.143-10, L.143-11, L.742-6 and L.751-15 will be listed within ten days of issue of the order commencing proceedings;
2. Other claims also falling due on the date of the order commencing proceedings will be listed within three months of issue of the order;
3. Wages and paid holidays within the 3rd paragraph of article L.143-11-1 will be listed within ten days of expiry of the protected periods provided for under this 3rd paragraph up to the limit set out in articles L.143-10, L.143-11, L.742-6 and L.751-15;
4. Other claims will be listed within three months following expiry of the period of protection.

If the claims cannot be paid in whole or in part out of the funds available before expiry of the periods provided for above, the creditors' representative will request the institutions referred to in article L.143-11-4 to advance the necessary funds against presentation of the schedules of claims.

These institutions will pay to the creditors' representative the amounts stated in the schedules and remaining unpaid:

1. Within five days following receipt of the schedules of claims referred to in paragraphs 1 and 3 above;
2. Within eight days following receipt of the schedules of claims referred to in paragraphs 2 and 4 above.

The creditors' representative will immediately remit the sums received to the employee creditors to the exclusion of the subrogated creditors and will inform the employees' representative accordingly.

The institutions referred to above must remit the sums included in the lists even if disputed by a third party.

These institutions must also remit the sums corresponding to those claims which have been conclusively affirmed by judicial decision even though the protective periods have expired. In the event of termination of the appointment of the creditors' representative, the clerk of the court or the commissioner, as the case may be, will send a supplementary schedule to the institutions referred to above and will take on responsibility for remitting the sums to the employee creditors.'

Article 135

After article L.143-11-8 of the employment code, an article L.143-11-9 is inserted redrawn as follows:

'Art. L.143-11-9 – The institutions referred to in article L.143-11-4 are subrogated as regards the rights of the employees for whom advances have been made in respect of claims protected by the priority provided for in articles L.143-10, L.143-11, L.742-6 and L.751-15, and claims made under paragraph 3 of article L.143-11-1.'

'The other sums advanced will be reimbursed to the above-mentioned institutions under the conditions provided in law no. 85-98 of 25th January 1985 relating to the settlement of claims which arise before the order commencing proceedings and benefit from the preferential rights attached to such claims.'

Article 136

At the end of section II of chapter III of part IV of book I of the employment code, an article L.143-13-1 is inserted redrawn as follows:

'Art. L.143-13-1 – Foreigners referred to in article L.341-6-1 are entitled to the benefit of the provisions of this section is respect of the sums due to them under this article.'

PART II
SIMPLIFIED PROCEDURE APPLICABLE TO CERTAIN BUSINESSES

Article 137

Subject to the provisions of article 138 below, the individuals and bodies corporate referred to in the third paragraph of article 2 are entitled to the simplified procedure provided under this part II. The other provisions of this law apply to them insofar as those provisions are not inconsistent with the provisions of this part II.

Article 138

Until the order approving the plan has been issued, the court may, of its own motion or on the request of the debtor or the public prosecutor, decide to apply in full the procedure provided in part I if it considers that this is likely to benefit the reconstruction of the business.

In that event, the period of observation already passed is added to the period provided in the second paragraph of article 8.

CHAPTER I. THE ORDER COMMENCING PROCEEDINGS AND THE INQUIRY PROCEDURE

Article 139

In the order commencing proceedings for judicial reconstruction, the court will appoint the bankruptcy judge and one officer of the court responsible for representing the creditors. The court will invite the delegates of the work force or, failing which, the employees, to appoint an employees' representative from within the business.

In businesses which do not comply with the conditions provided in article L.421-1 of the employment code, the employees' representative will exercise, in addition, the functions allocated under the provisions of part I to the works council or, failing which, to the delegates of the work force.

Article 140

The observation period commences with a period of inquiry limited to thirty days, renewable once only on the direction of the president of the court upon the application of the debtor, the public prosecutor or the bankruptcy judge.

The bankruptcy judge, with the assistance of the debtor and the assistance, if required by the bankruptcy judge, of an expert of his choice, is responsible for initiating an enquiry with a view to drawing up a report on the economic and social position of the business and its prospects for reconstruction. The expert's opinion will be included in the bankruptcy judge's report.

The bankruptcy judge has the powers provided in article 19.

Article 141

During this period, the debtor will carry on the business unless it appears necessary to the court to appoint an administrator who may either be the expert referred to in article 140, or an official administrator, or any other qualified person. In that case, the debtor is either removed and thereafter replaced by the administrator, or he is assisted by the administrator.

In the absence of an administrator:

- the debtor will perform the functions allocated to the administrator under article 45; he will exercise the power conferred under article 121 and under article 37 if so authorised by the bankruptcy judge;
- the creditors' representative will perform the functions allocated to the administrator under article 28;
- for the purposes of article 22 an extraordinary general meeting, or a meeting of the partners of the business, will be called at the request of the bankruptcy judge who will determine the amount of the capital increase which is to be proposed in the meeting, in order to reconstitute the capital of the business.

Article 142

In the light of the report of the enquiry, the court will decide whether to continue the activity of the business with a view to preparing a draft business reconstruction plan, or to put the business into compulsory liquidation under the provisions of part III.

CHAPTER II. PREPARATION OF THE BUSINESS RECONSTRUCTION PLAN

Article 143

The business continues under the conditions provided in article 141 for a period of four months which may, by way of exception, be extended for two months by order of the court setting out its reasons, either of its own motion or on the application of the debtor, or, as the case may be, of the administrator and of the public prosecutor.

During this period, the debtor, or the administrator, if such has been nominated, will prepare a draft business reconstruction plan with the assistance, if so desired, of the expert who assisted the bankruptcy judge in his enquiry.

The debtor or the administrator will distribute the proposals for the discharge of the debts of the business as provided in article 24 to the creditors' representative and the bankruptcy judge, and will proceed with the information gathering and consultative measures provided in the third paragraph of article 20 and in article 25.

Article 144

If no administrator is appointed, the purchase offers referred to in articles 21 and 83 are addressed to the court registry which will distribute them to the bankruptcy judge, the debtor and the creditors' representative.

In this case, the debtor will set out in his draft plan all offers which the bankruptcy judge has verified.

Article 145

If no administrator is appointed, the debtor will file the draft business reconstruction plan at the court registry.

In this case, the bankruptcy judge will report to the court and submit the draft plan before it together with his opinion of the plan setting out his reasons.

Article 146

At any time during the proceedings, the court may, at the request of one of the persons referred to in article 36, or of its own motion, order one of the measures provided in that article.

CHAPTER III. IMPLEMENTATION OF THE BUSINESS RECONSTRUCTION PLAN

Article 147

In the absence of an administrator, the scheme commissioner will assist the debtor to perform the acts necessary to implement the plan.

PART III
COMPULSORY LIQUIDATION

CHAPTER I. THE LIQUIDATOR

Article 148

The court ordering compulsory liquidation will appoint the creditors' representative as liquidator. However, at the request of the administrator, a creditor, the debtor or the public prosecutor, the court may, in an order setting out its reasons, appoint the liquidator from among other official liquidators.

The court may either on its own motion or on the recommendation of the bankruptcy judge or at the request of the public prosecutor, replace the liquidator. The debtor or creditor may request the bankruptcy judge to apply to the court for this purpose.

The liquidator will proceed with the liquidation at the same time as completing, in the course of these procedures, the verification of claims and establishment of order of priority among the creditors. He will continue actions commenced by the administrator or by the creditors' representative before the liquidation order and he may initiate actions relating to the competence of the creditors' representative.

Redundancies caused by the liquidator in applying the decision of the court ordering liquidation are subject to the provisions of articles L.321-7, second paragraph, and L.321-10 of the employment code.

Article 149

No relative up to and including the fourth degree of the head of the business or its officers in the case of bodies corporate may be appointed as liquidator.

Article 150

The liquidator will keep the bankruptcy judge and the public prosecutor informed at least every three months of the progress of the liquidation.

Article 151

All sums received by the liquidator in the exercise of his functions will be paid immediately into a deposit account at the Central Deposit and Savings Bank. Any delay on the part of the liquidator in transferring such funds will attract interest for his own account at a rate equal to the legal rate of interest plus 5 points.

Article 152

The compulsory liquidation order is effective at law from the date of its issue to relieve the debtor of the administration and control of his property, including property acquired in whatever capacity as long as the compulsory liquidation has not terminated. The debtor's rights and any transactions relating to his property will be exercised by the liquidator during the entire period of compulsory liquidation.

However the debtor may be party to criminal proceedings with a view to establishing liability for a crime of which he is the victim provided his action is limited to the public prosecution of the crime and no civil remedy is sought.

Article 153

If required in the interests of the public and the creditors, the court may authorise the continuation of the business for a period not exceeding three months and only as is necessary for the compulsory liquidation. When the business is a farming business, this period is determined by the court by reference to the agricultural season then current and to the particular practices appropriate to the crop in question. The provisions of article 40 apply to claims originating during this period.

The administration of the business is handled by the administrator whose appointment continues by way of exception from the provisions of article 36, or, failing which, by the liquidator. The administrator, or, failing which, the liquidator will proceed with the redundancies subject to the conditions provided in the second paragraph of article L.321-7 and article L.321-10 of the employment code.

If the administrator does not have available the sums required for the continuance of the business, he may, on the authority of the bankruptcy judge, arrange to have these remitted by the liquidator.

CHAPTER II. REALISATION OF THE BUSINESS ASSETS

Article 154

Sales of real estate will take place in accordance with the formalities prescribed for the forced sale of real estate. However, following consultation with the inspectors and having heard or duly summoned before him the debtor and the liquidator, the bankruptcy judge will determine the lowest bid price and the main sale conditions and the means of publicising the sale.

Under the same conditions, the bankruptcy judge may, if the nature of the assets of the business, their arrangement, or offers received for them, are such as to permit an agreed transfer on the most favourable terms, authorise their sale either by agreed tender on the basis of the reserve price as determined by him, or by private contract for such price and other conditions as he may determine. An agreed tender may nevertheless be outbidded by a higher bid.

Sales by auction executed in accordance with the preceding paragraphs are effective to discharge any mortgages.

The liquidator will distribute the proceeds of sales and will regulate priority as between creditors subject to the hearing of any dispute before the civil court of first instance.

In the event of the compulsory liquidation of a farmer, and having regard to the debtor's personal and family situation, the court may grant the debtor extensions of time of such duration as the court may determine in order to leave his principal residence.

This article will be applied as prescribed by statutory instrument.

Article 155

Production units comprising all or part of the fixed or moveable assets may be transferred as a whole.

The liquidator will solicit offers to purchase and will determine the period during which these may be submitted. Any interested person may submit an offer to the liquidator.

However neither the officers of a body corporate in liquidation, nor any relative of these officers, or of the head of the business, up to and including the second degree, may act as purchasers.

Each offer must be in writing and must include the information provided in paragraphs 1 to 5 of article 83. Offers will be filed with the court registry where they are open to inspection by any interested party. Offers will be distributed to the bankruptcy judge.

Following consultation with the works council or, failing which, the delegates of the work force and after inviting comments from the debtor and the inspectors, the liquidator will select the offer which appears to him to be the most substantial and which, under the optimum circumstances, seems to him to ensure the most permanent employment prospects and the payment of creditors. The transfer is ordered by the bankruptcy judge.

A proportion of the transfer price is allocated to each of the assets sold for the purpose of distribution and in accordance with preferential rights.

Article 156

After hearing or duly summoning before him the debtor, and following consultation with the inspectors, the bankruptcy judge will order the sale of the other assets of the business by public auction or by private contract.

The bankruptcy judge may require the draft agreement for sale to be submitted to him to enable him to verify that the conditions fixed by him have been complied with.

Article 157

The liquidator will inform the administrative authority responsible for the keeping of records before any sale or destruction of the debtors records takes place. This authority is entitled to a pre-emptive right in respect of a sale or destruction of the records.

Article 158

With the authority of the bankruptcy judge, and after hearing or duly summoning the debtor before him, the liquidator may compromise and settle all disputes involving the creditors as a whole, including disputes relating to rights and actions in real estate.

If the object of the compromise or settlement is of uncertain value, or its value exceeds the limit of the court's competence in matters of final judgment, the compromise or settlement is submitted to the court for ratification.

Article 159

With the authority of the bankruptcy judge, the liquidator may, by payment of the debt or retaining an equivalent amount, discharge the security interest in any assets charged by the debtor as security for the debt.

Failing discharge, and within six months of the order for compulsory liquidation, the liquidator must apply to the bankruptcy judge for authority to commence the realisation of the relevant asset. The liquidator will notify the creditor of the grant of authority fifteen days before the realisation takes place.

The creditor entitled to the charge, even if he has not yet proved his claim, may request judicial allocation before realisation takes place. If the claim is rejected in whole or in part, he will restore the asset, or its value, to the liquidator without prejudice to the proven amount of his claim.

In the event of sale by the liquidator, the right of retention is transferred to the sale proceeds by operation of law. Any registration which may have been effected in order to preserve the charge is deleted at the instance of the liquidator.

CHAPTER III. DISCHARGE OF LIABILITIES

Section I: Satisfaction of creditors

Article 160

The order for compulsory liquidation accelerates claims which were not due on the date of the commencement of proceedings for judicial reconstruction.

If these claims are expressed in a currency other than the currency of the place where compulsory liquidation has been ordered, they will be converted into the currency of that place in accordance with the rate of exchange ruling at the date of the order.

Sub-section 1 – Right of individual action

Article 161

Creditors entitled to a preferential right, a charge over intangibles or moveable assets, or a mortgage, including the Treasury in respect of its preferential claims, may, as soon as their claims have been declared, and even though not yet admitted, exercise their right of individual action if the liquidator has not proceeded with the liquidation of the secured assets within a period of three months from the order for compulsory liquidation.

In the case of the sale of real estate, the provisions of the first and fourth paragraphs of article 154 will apply.

Sub-section 2 – Apportionment of the proceeds of compulsory liquidation

Article 162

If one or more distributions of funds takes place before distribution of the proceeds of sale of the real estate, the preferred creditors and mortgagees with admitted claims participate in the distribution of the proceeds in proportion to the total amount of their claims.

After sale of the real estate and final settlement of the order of priority among the preferred creditors and mortgagees, those of them who rank in priority for the whole of their claims in the proceeds of sale of the real estate will only collect the amount of their secured claim after deduction of sums already received by them.

Sums deducted in this way are available for the benefit of unsecured creditors.

Article 163

The rights of mortgagee creditors who are only entitled to prior rank in part of the distribution of the proceeds of sale of real estate are paid out in accordance with the amount remaining due to them after the distribution of the real estate proceeds. The excess of any dividend received by them in previous distributions over and above the dividend calculated after the settlement of their priority in respect of the real estate proceeds is deducted from the distribution to which they are entitled as mortgagees and included in the sums available to unsecured creditors.

Article 164

Preferred creditors or mortgagees whose claims are not met from the proceeds of sale of the real estate will compete with the unsecured creditors for whatever remains owing to them.

Article 165

Subject to the third paragraph of article 159, the provisions of articles 162–164 apply to creditors entitled to specific chattel security.

Article 166

The aggregate amount of the assets will be divided among the creditors in proportion to their admitted claims after deduction of the costs and expenses of the compulsory liquidation, the subsidies awarded to the head of the business or to the officers or managers of the business or their families, and the funds paid to the preferred creditors.

An amount equal to the claims awaiting definitive admission and, in particular, the officers' or managers' claims for remuneration insofar as no decision may have been taken regarding their position, will be held in reserve.

Section II: Termination of compulsory liquidation

Article 167

The court may order the termination of compulsory liquidation of its own motion, after the debtor has been heard or duly summoned, and on the report of the bankruptcy judge at any time when:

- there are no more debts due or the liquidator has raised sufficient sums to pay off the creditors; or
- continuation of the compulsory liquidation has become impossible due to insufficiency of assets.

Article 168

The liquidator will prepare the accounts for presentation. He is responsible for the documents entrusted to him in the course of the proceedings for five years after the accounts have been presented.

Article 169

The order terminating the compulsory liquidation on the grounds of insufficiency of assets does not restore to the creditors their right to take individual action against the debtor unless the claim arises either from a criminal conviction on facts which have no bearing on the debtor's professional activity or from rights of a personal nature.

The creditors' right of individual action is restored in the case of fraud on the creditors, personal bankruptcy, prohibition from the management or control of a commercial business or a body corporate, criminal bankruptcy, or when the debtor or the body corporate of which he was the manager has suspended payments and the proceedings have been terminated due to insufficiency of assets.

Creditors whose claims have been admitted and who have recovered their right of individual action are entitled to executory title on the direction of the president of the court.

Article 170

If termination of the compulsory liquidation is ordered on the grounds of insufficiency of assets, and if it appears that any assets have been concealed or, more generally, in the event of fraud on the part of the head of the business or the officers of the company, proceedings for compulsory liquidation may be re-opened at the request of any interested party by order of the court specifying the particular reasons for the decision and on proof that the funds necessary to pay for the costs of re-opening the proceedings have been remitted to the Central Deposit and Savings Bank.

PART IV
APPEALS

Article 171

The following decisions of the court are capable of being appealed to the Court of Appeal or to the Supreme Court:

1. Decisions relating to the commencement of proceedings on the part of the debtor, the plaintiff creditor, and also the director of public prosecutions even though he was not a principal party to the action;
2. Decisions relating to compulsory liquidation determining or rejecting the plan for survival of the business on the part of the debtor, the administrator, the creditors' representative, the works council or, failing which, the representatives of the works force and also the director of public prosecutions even though he was not a principal party to the action;
3. Decisions modifying the plan for survival of the business may be appealed on the part of the debtor, the commissioner, the works council, failing which, the representatives of the works force and also the director of public prosecutions even though he was not a principal party to the action.

Article 172

Decisions approving the plan for survival are not capable of being challenged by third parties.

Article 173

The following are not capable of being challenged whether by third parties or otherwise, or of appeal whether to the Court of Appeal or to the Supreme Court:

1. Judgments relating to the appointment or replacement of the bankruptcy judge;

2. Judgments of the court ruling on appeal against orders made by the bankruptcy judge acting within the limits of his powers, with the exception of judgments relating to the recovery of assets.

Article 174

The following are only capable of being appealed on the part of the public prosecutor even though he was not a principal party to the action:

1. Judgments relating to the appointment or replacement of the administrator, the creditors' representative, the liquidator, the inspectors or the experts;
2. Judgments ruling on the duration of the observation period, the survival or sale of the business or on the authorisation of a lease management contract under article 42.

Judgments approving or rejecting the business sale plan are only appealable on the part of the public prosecutor, even though he was not a principal party to the action, or the purchaser or the contracting party referred to in article 86; the purchaser may only file an appeal against the judgment approving the sale plan if, in breach of article 62, the plan imposes liabilities on him other than the undertakings entered into by him in the course of preparation of the plan; the contracting party referred to in article 86 may only file an appeal regarding that part of the judgment dealing with transfer of the relevant contract.

Judgments modifying the sale plan are only appealable on the part of the public prosecutor even though he was not a principal party to the action, or by the purchaser acting within the limits referred to in the preceding paragraph.

Article 175

However, judgments at first instance or on appeal in application of article 174 may not be challenged by third parties or appealed to the Supreme Court.

Article 176

As the director of public prosecutions is entitled to disclosure of proceedings for judicial reconstruction and actions relating to the responsibility of the officers of a company, it is only open to the director of public prosecutions to appeal to the Supreme Court on the grounds of failure to disclose.

Article 177

If the quashing of a judgment necessitates referral of the matter for reconsideration by the court, the Court of Appeal may commence a new observation period. The maximum duration of this period is three months reduced to one month when the simplified procedure provided in part II of this law applies.

In the event of appeal against the judgment ruling on compulsory liquidation or determining or rejecting the plan for survival or sale, and when provisional enforcement has been ordered, the observation period is extended pending judgment of the Court of Appeal.

PART V
SPECIAL PROVISIONS FOR BODIES CORPORATE AND THEIR OFFICERS

Article 178

The order commencing judicial reconstruction of a body corporate will operate in respect of every person being a member or associate of the body corporate and jointly and severally and without limit liable for the body corporate's liabilities. The court will commence proceedings for judicial reconstruction in respect of each of them.

Article 179

When proceedings for judicial reconstruction are commenced with respect to a body incorporated under private law and engaged in economic activity, the following provisions of this part apply to its officers, whether natural persons or incorporated bodies, as well as to the natural persons who act as permanent representatives of any of its incorporated officers.

Article 180

When the judicial reconstruction or compulsory liquidation of a body corporate discloses an insufficiency of assets, the court may, in the case of bad management having contributed to this insufficiency of assets, decide that the debts of the body corporate will be borne, wholly or in part, with or without joint liability, by all the officers or managers of the business who hold office in law or in fact, paid or unpaid, or by some of them.

Suit must be brought within three years of the judgment determining the reconstruction scheme, or, if there is none, within three years of the judgment ordering compulsory liquidation.

Sums paid by its officers by way of application of paragraph 1 are credited to the debtor's assets and are distributed in the event of the survival of the business in accordance with the methods provided under the plan for the discharge of liabilities. In the case of liquidation, these sums are distributed proportionally among all the creditors.

Article 181

The court may commence proceedings for judicial reconstruction with respect to the officers who have been made responsible for all or part of the liabilities of a body corporate, and who have not discharged this debt.

Article 182

In the event of judicial reconstruction of a body corporate, the court may start proceedings for judicial reconstruction in respect of any officer in law or in fact, paid or unpaid, against whom it is possible to establish one of the following facts:

1. He has disposed of the assets of the body corporate as if they were his own;
2. He has engaged in business for his own account under the guise of the body corporate and transacted business dealings in his personal interest;

3. He has used the assets or credit of the body corporate contrary to the interests of the body corporate for his own purposes or in favour of another body corporate or business in which he was directly or indirectly interested;
4. He has wrongfully carried on, for his own interests, a loss-making operation which could only lead to the cessation of payments by the body corporate;
5. He has kept false accounts or caused the accounting documents of the body corporate to disappear or has failed to keep all its accounts in accordance with the rules prescribed by law;
6. He has misappropriated or concealed all or part of the assets of the body corporate or has fraudulently increased its liabilities.

In the event of judicial reconstruction ordered by way of application of this article, the liabilities include the liabilities of the body corporate as well as the personal liabilities of any of its officers.

The date of cessation of payments is the date determined in the order commencing proceedings for judicial reconstruction with respect to the body corporate.

Proceedings will be instituted within three years of the order terminating the reconstruction plan or failing which, the order pronouncing compulsory liquidation.

Article 183

In the cases provided in articles 180 to 182, the court has jurisdiction of its own motion or on the application of the administrator, the creditors' representative, the commissioner, the liquidator, or the public prosecutor.

Article 184

For the purposes of applying the provisions of article 180 to 182, the court may of its own motion or on the application of one of the persons referred to in article 183 require the bankruptcy judge or, failing which, a designated member of the court, to obtain disclosure from public and administrative bodies, national insurance and social security organisations, and credit institutions, of every document or other piece of information, notwithstanding any provision of law to the contrary, relating to the personal wealth of the officers of a body corporate, whether they be natural persons or incorporated bodies, and also of the natural persons who act as permanent representatives of any of the incorporated officers of a body corporate referred to in article 179.

PART VI
PERSONAL BANKRUPTCY AND OTHER OFFENCES

Article 185

The provisions of this part apply to the following persons, once proceedings for judicial reconstruction have been commenced;

1. To natural persons carrying on the profession of trader, artisan or farmer; to natural persons who are traders or artisans;
2. To natural persons who are officers, in law or in fact, of incorporated bodies engaged in economic activities;

3. To natural persons who are permanent representatives of incorporated bodies, themselves being officers of the incorporated bodies defined in paragraph 2 above.

Article 186

A bankrupt is prohibited from the direction, management, administration or control, direct or indirect, of any commercial or artisan trading business, of any farming business and of any incorporated body engaged in economic activity.

Equally, the prohibitions and disqualifications applicable to persons declared bankrupt within the meaning given to that term before 1st January 1968 also apply.

Article 187

At any stage in the proceedings the court may order the bankruptcy of any natural person who is a trader, or of any farmer, or of any artisan against whom one of the following facts has been established:

1. He has wrongfully carried on a loss-making operation which could only lead to the cessation of payments;
2. He has omitted to keep accounts in accordance with the rules prescribed by law or caused all or some of the accounting documents to disappear;
3. He has misappropriated or concealed all or part of his assets or has fraudulently increased his liabilities.

Article 188

At any stage in the proceedings the court may order the bankruptcy of any officer, in law or in fact, paid or unpaid, of an incorporated body who has done one of the acts referred to in article 182.

Article 189

At any stage in the proceedings, the court may order the bankruptcy of any person referred to in article 185 against whom one of the following facts has been established:

1. He has engaged in any commercial, artisan or farming activity or the management or administration of an incorporated body contrary to a prohibition provided by law;
2. He has bought in order to re-sell below market price, or has used ruinous methods in order to obtain funds, in each case with the intention of avoiding or delaying the commencement of proceedings for judicial reconstruction;
3. He has undertaken contractual obligations on behalf of a third party and without consideration, which are held to have been excessive at the time of entering into them, having regard to the situation of the business or the incorporated body;
4. He has paid or caused to be paid one creditor in preference to others after the cessation of payments and with knowledge of the cessation of payments;
5. He has omitted to declare the date of cessation of payments for a period of fifteen days.

Article 190

The court may order the bankruptcy of the officer of an incorporated body who has not discharged those debts of the incorporated body for which he has been made responsible.

Article 191

The court, the administrator, the creditors' representative, the liquidator or the public prosecutor have jurisdiction in respect of the matters provided under articles 187–190.

Article 192

In the matters provided under articles 189 and 190, the court may, in place of bankruptcy, order prohibition from the direction, management, administration or control, direct or indirect, either of any commercial trading or artisan or farming business and any incorporated body, or of any one or more of these.

Article 193

Voting rights of officers of incorporated bodies who are subject to personal bankruptcy or to the prohibition provided under article 192 are exercised in meetings of incorporated bodies, which are themselves the subject of proceedings for judicial reconstruction, by an officer designated for that purpose by the court, on the request of the administrator, the liquidator or the commissioner.

The court may direct these officers of incorporated bodies, or some of them, to dispose of stocks or shares owned by them in the incorporated body or may order the forced sale of these at the hands of an officer of the court, if necessary after expert appraisal; the proceeds of sale are appropriated towards payment of part of the business debts in the event that these have been made the responsibility of the officers.

Article 194

The order of personal bankruptcy or the prohibition provided under article 192 entails removal of the capacity to perform any elected public office. This incapacity applies equally to every natural person in respect of whom compulsory liquidation has been ordered. It takes effect at law from the date when the relevant person receives notice from the competent authority.

Article 195

When the court orders personal bankruptcy or the prohibition provided under article 192, it will determine the duration of the prohibition, which may not be less than five years. The court may declare its decision to have provisional executory effect. The disqualifications, prohibitions and incapacity to perform elected public office automatically cease to have effect at law at the end of the fixed period without the necessity of a further order.

The duration of a period of incapacity to perform elected public office resulting from an order for compulsory liquidation is five years.

The termination order extinguishing the liabilities of the business restores the head of the business, or the officers of the incorporated body, to all of their rights. It removes, or relieves them from, all disqualifications, prohibitions and incapacity to perform elected public office.

In every instance, the relevant person may ask the court to remove in whole or in part the disqualifications, prohibitions and incapacity to perform elected public office if he has made sufficient contribution towards payment of the liabilities of the business.

When all disqualifications, prohibitions and incapacities have been lifted, the order of the court carries with it the recovery of all civil rights.

PART VII
CRIMINAL BANKRUPTCY AND OTHER OFFENCES

CHAPTER I. CRIMINAL BANKRUPTCY

Article 196

The provisions of this chapter apply:

1. To any trader, artisan or farmer;
2. To any person who has directly or indirectly, in law or in fact, controlled or put into liquidation a body incorporated under private law and engaged in an economic activity;
3. To natural persons who are permanent representatives of incorporated bodies, themselves being officers of the incorporated bodies defined in paragraph 2 above.

Article 197

In the event of commencement of proceedings for judicial reconstruction those persons referred to in article 196 are guilty of criminal bankruptcy if one of the following facts has been established against them:

1. He has bought in order to resell below market price, or has used ruinous methods in order to obtain funds, in each case with the intention of avoiding or delaying commencement of proceedings for judicial reconstruction;
2. He has misappropriated or concealed all or part of the debtor's assets;
3. He has fraudulently increased the debtor's liabilities;
4. He has kept false accounts or caused accounting documents of the business or the incorporated body to disappear or has failed to keep any accounts at all when so required by law.

Article 198

Article 402 of the penal code is amended as follows:

> 'Art. 402. – Those convicted of criminal bankruptcy are liable to imprisonment from three months to five years and a fine of 10,000 Ffrs to 200,000 Ffrs, or to one only of these penalties.
>
> In addition the deprivation of rights referred to in article 42 may be ordered against them.'

Article 199

Article 403 of the penal code is amended as follows:

> 'Art. 403. – Accessories in criminal bankruptcy are liable to the penalties provided in the preceding article even if they do not qualify as a trader or artisan or do not manage, directly or indirectly, in law or in fact, an incorporated body engaged in an economic activity.'

Article 200

Article 404 of the penal code is amended as follows:

> 'Art. 404. – Stockbrokers convicted of criminal bankruptcy or as accessories in criminal bankruptcy are liable to imprisonment from two to seven years and a fine of 20,000 Ffrs to 300,000 Ffrs or to only one of these penalties.
>
> In addition the deprivation of rights referred to in article 42 may be ordered against them.'

Article 201

The criminal court responsible for the conviction for criminal bankruptcy of one of the persons referred to in article 196 may in addition order the personal bankruptcy of that person or the prohibition provided under article 192.

When both a criminal court and a civil or commercial court have ordered by way of final decision the personal bankruptcy or the prohibition provided under article 192 with respect to the same person on the same facts, the criminal court judgment alone is executed.

Article 202

Article 55-1 of the penal code is amended by adding at the end the following paragraph:

> 'When the request relates to a disqualification, prohibition or incapacity ordered by way of application of article 201 of law no. 85-98 of 25th January 1985 relating to the judicial reconstruction and liquidation of businesses, the court may not award relief unless the relevant party has made a sufficient contribution towards payment of the debtor's liabilities.'

CHAPTER II. OTHER CRIMINAL OFFENCES

Article 203

The following are liable to imprisonment from three months to two years and a fine of 10,000 Ffrs to 200,000 Ffrs or to one or other of these penalties:

1. Any trader, artisan, farmer or any officer, in law or in fact, paid or unpaid, of an incorporated body who, during the observation period has granted a mortgage or preferential right or made any unauthorised sale as provided

under article 33, or paid in whole or in part a debt which arose before the decision to commence proceedings;

2. Any trader, artisan, farmer or any officer, in law or in fact, paid or unpaid, of an incorporated body who has made a payment contrary to the methods for the settlement of liabilities provided in the reconstruction plan, or who has made a sale without the authorisation provided under article 70;
3. Any person who has agreed with the debtor to perform one of the acts referred to in paragraphs 1 and 2 above or who has received an irregular payment from the debtor, in each case either during the observation period or in the course of implementation of the reconstruction plan, and in any event in full knowledge of the situation of the debtor.

Article 204

The following are liable to the penalties provided in article 402 to 404 of the penal code:

1. Those who, for the benefit of the persons referred to in article 196, have withdrawn, knowingly received or concealed all or part of the moveable or fixed assets belonging to the persons referred to in article 196, this all to be without prejudice to the application of article 60 of the penal code;
2. Those who have fraudulently declared false claims in the proceedings for judicial reconstruction either in their own name or in that of a third party;
3. Those who, while carrying on a trading, artisan or farming activity in the name of others or in a false name, are guilty of one of the offences provided under article 209.

Article 205

The spouses, issue, parents, grandparents or remoter ancestors, collateral relatives or relatives by marriage of the persons referred to in article 196 who have misappropriated, diverted or knowingly received chattels included in the assets of a debtor subject to proceedings for judicial reconstruction are liable to the penalties provided in the first paragraph of article 406 of the penal code.

Article 206

In the matters provided in the preceding articles including those relating to discharge the court with the relevant jurisdiction will adjudicate;

1. Upon the restoration to the debtor's estate of all assets, rights or claims which have been fraudulently removed;
2. Upon claims in damages.

Article 207

(Law no. 85-1407 of 30th December 1985, art. 85).

Any administrator, creditors' representative, liquidator or commissioner is liable to incur the penalties provided under the second paragraph of article 408 of the penal code who:

1. Has intentionally prejudiced the interests of the creditors or the debtor either in applying money for his own benefit or in obtaining pecuniary advantages to which he knew he was not entitled;
2. Has made use of his powers in his own interest in a way which he knew was contrary to the interests of the creditors or of the debtor.

Any administrator, creditors' representative, liquidator, commissioner and any other person, except the inspectors and employees' representatives, being a participant in any capacity in the proceedings, who has purchased for his own account, directly or indirectly, some of the assets of the debtor, or has used them for his own profit, is liable to incur the same penalties . The court will declare any such purchase null and void and will decide any resulting claim in damages.

Article 208

Any creditor who, after the commencement of proceedings for judicial reconstruction, has concluded a contract in terms particularly favourable to him to the disadvantage of the debtor is liable to incur the penalties provided under the first paragraph of article 406 of the penal code.

The court will declare any such contract null and void.

Article 209

The persons referred to in paragraphs 2 and 3 of article 196 are liable to incur the penalties provided under article 402–404 of the penal code who, with a view to removing all or part of their estate beyond the reach of an incorporated body in respect of which judicial reconstruction proceedings have been commenced, or of the associates or creditors of such incorporated body, have in bad faith misappropriated or concealed or attempted to misappropriate or conceal all or part of their own assets, or have fraudulently admitted debts which they did not owe.

CHAPTER III. RULES OF PROCEDURE

Article 210

As regards the provisions of chapters I and II of this part, the limitation period for a criminal action in open court only runs from the day of the order commencing proceedings for judicial reconstruction when the requisite facts have appeared before that date.

Article 211

The criminal court has jurisdiction either upon the application of the director of public prosecutions or on a petition for prosecution by the administrator, the creditors' representative, the employees' representative, the commissioner or the liquidator.

Article 212

The director of public prosecutions may require the administrator or the liquidator to hand over any contracts and documents retained by them.

Article 213

In the event of dismissal of the proceedings, the costs of the proceedings where instigated by the administrator, the creditors' representative, the employees' representative, the commissioner or the liquidator are borne by the Treasury.

In the case of conviction, the Treasury may only exercise its right of recourse for costs against the debtor after completion of the compulsory liquidation.

Article 214

Publication of judgments and appeals resulting in convictions issued by way of application of this part VII is at the expense of the convicted person.

PART VIII
MISCELLANEOUS PROVISIONS

Article 215

When the immediately available funds of the debtor are insufficient for that purpose, the Treasury will, on the order of the bankruptcy judge or the president of the court advance the costs and expenses, including notice and publicity expenses, relating to:

- decisions given in the course of the proceedings for judicial reconstruction in the joint interest of all the creditors and the debtor;
- maintenance of actions which have as their objective the conservation or restoration of the property of the debtor or carried on in the interests of the creditors jointly;
- maintenance of the actions set out in articles 187 to 190.

The Treasury will also, on the order of the president of the court, advance the costs and expenses, including notice and publicity expenses, relating to maintenance of the action terminating or modifying the plan.

These provisions apply to appeal procedures relating to all the decisions set out above both in the Court of Appeal and in the Supreme Court.

Reimbursement of the advances made by the Treasury is secured by the preferential right for legal costs.

Article 215A

The bankruptcy judge is entitled to reimbursement of his travelling expenses from the debtor's assets.

Article 216

Any person who carries on a professional activity or performs functions in breach of the prohibitions, disqualification or incapacity provided in articles 186, 192 and 194 of this law will be liable to imprisonment for six months to two years and a fine of 10,000 Ffrs to 2,500,000 Ffrs, or to only one of these two penalties.

Article 217

Article 1188 of the civil code is amended as follows:

'Art. 1188. – The debtor loses the benefit of the contractual term when he has diminished by his own action the value of the securities given to his creditor under the contract.'

Article 218

Paragraph 7 of article 1844-7 of the civil code is deleted and paragraph 8 becomes paragraph 7.

Article 219

Articles 768, 775 and 776 of the code of criminal procedure are modified in the following manner:

I The 5th paragraph of article 768 is amended as follows:

'5. In matters of judicial reconstruction, judgments ordering compulsory liquidation with regard to a natural person, bankruptcy or the prohibition provided under article 192 of law no. 85-98 of 25th January, 1985 relating to the judicial reconstruction and liquidation of businesses.'

II The 7th paragraph of article 775 is replaced by the following provisions:

'7. In matters of judicial reconstruction, judgments ordering bankruptcy or the prohibition provided under article 192 of law no. 85-98 of 25th January, 1985 aforesaid, when these measures are cancelled by a termination order issued on the grounds of discharge of the liabilities, by rehabilitation or by the expiry of a period of five years running from the day when these convictions became final, as well as the judgment ordering compulsory liquidation with respect to a natural person on the expiry of a period of five years from the day when this judgment became final, or after issue of a termination order on the grounds of discharge of the liabilities.

However, if the duration of the bankruptcy or the prohibition exceeds five years, the conviction relating to these measures will remain recorded in the 2nd official schedule during the whole of such period.'

III The 2nd paragraph of article 776 is amended as follows:

'2. To the military authorities in respect of persons on the army or navy lists and in respect of young persons applying for military service, and to the competent public authorities in the event of disputes regarding electoral rights or regarding the existence of any lack of capacity to perform an elected public office provided under article 194 of law no. 85-98 of 25th January 1985.'

Article 220

The 5th paragraph of article L.5 and article L.202 of the electoral code are amended as follows:

I 'Art. L.5. – 5. Persons declared bankrupt or whose bankruptcy has been declared in a judgment issued abroad but capable of execution in France.'

II 'Art. L.202. – In conformity with article 194 of law no. 85-98 of 25th January, 1985 relating to the judicial reconstruction and liquidation of businesses, those natural persons are not capable of being elected who are the subject of an order for compulsory liquidation, bankruptcy or the prohibition against management provided under article 192 of that law.'

Article 221

Articles L.113-6, L.132-14, L.132-17, L.326-1, L.326-6, L.326-11, L.328-5 and L.328-13 of the insurance code are modified in the following manner:

I Article L.113-6 is replaced by the following provisions:

'Art.L.113-6. – The insurance will remain in force in the event of the judicial reconstruction of the insured. The administrator or the debtor as authorised by the bankruptcy judge or the liquidator, as the case may be, and the insurer retain nevertheless the right to rescind the contract during a period of three months from this date. That part of the premium relating to the time when the risk is no longer covered by the insurer will be returned to the debtor.

In the event of judicial reconstruction of the insurer, the contract terminates one month after the commencement of proceedings subject to the provisions of article L.327-4. The insured may claim reimbursement of the premium paid for the period when cover has ceased.'

II In article L.132-14, the words: 'or by articles 29 and 31 of law no. 67-563 of 13th July 1967' are replaced by the words: 'or by articles 107 and 108 of law no. 85-98 of 25th January 1985 relating to the judicial reconstruction and liquidation of businesses'.

III In articles 132-17, the words: 'articles 56 and 58 of law no. 67-563 of 13th July 1967' are replaced by the words: 'articles 112 and 114 of law no. 85-98 of 25th January 1985'.

IV Article L.326-1 is amended as follows: 'Art.L.326-1. – The judicial reconstruction procedures enacted by law no. 85-98 of 25th January 1985, may only be commenced with regard to a business subject to the provisions of this book on the request of the minister for economy and finance; the court also has jurisdiction to commence these proceedings of its own motion or on the application of the public prosecutor, following the recommendation of the minister for economics and finance.

'The president of the court will only have jurisdiction to hear an application to commence the procedure for out-of-court settlement instituted under law no. 84-148 of 1st March 1984 relating to the prevention and out-of-court settlement of difficulties experienced by businesses with regard to one of the businesses mentioned above, following the recommendation of the minister for economics and finance.'

V In article L.326-6, the words: 'in articles 106 to 109 of law no. 67-563 of 13th July 1967' are replaced by the words: 'in articles 188 and 189 of law no. 85-98 of 25th January 1985'.

VI The second paragraph of article L.326-11 is amended as follows:

'After termination of this liquidation, compulsory liquidation may be carried out upon the conditions provided under law no. 85-98 of 25th January 1985.'

VII Article L.328-5 is amended as follows:

'Art. L.328-5. – The right of action available to the administrator or to the liquidator under article 211 of law no. 85-98 of 25th January 1985 is exercisable by the liquidator who must comply with the provisions of article 212 of that law.'

VIII Article L.328-13 is amended as follows:

'Art. L.328-13. – In the event of liquidation in accordance with the conditions provided under article L.326-2, the following provisions apply:

1. If the financial position of a business deteriorated as a result of final withdrawal of the administrative agreement giving rise to an insufficiency of assets in relation to liabilities which must be settled in the course of the liquidation, the court may decide, in the event of defective management contributing to that insufficiency of assets, and on the request of the liquidator or even of its own motion, that the debts of the business will be borne wholly or partially, with or without security, by all the officers or managers of the business in law or in fact, paid or unpaid, or by some of them.

   The action will be brought within three years from the filing of the liquidator's fourth half yearly report at the court registry.
2. Officers or managers of a business guilty of the dealings referred to in articles 188 and 189 of law no. 85-98 of 25th January 1985 may be subject to the sanctions provided under part VI of the said law and may be discharged from disqualifications and prohibitions under the conditions provided in article 195 of that law.'

Article 222

The second paragraph of article L.321-7 of the employment code is amended as follows:

'In the event of judicial reconstruction, the administrator or, in default, the employer or the liquidator, as the case may be, must inform and consult the competent administrative authority before proceeding with dismissals on the grounds of redundancy under the conditions provided in articles 45, 63, 148 and 153 of law no. 85-98 of 25th January 1985. The administrative authority may take ten days from the date of despatch of the redundancy proposal in order to make known its opinion. In default of a reply within this period, the opinion is deemed to have been given.'

Article 223

Article L.321-10 of the employment code is amended as follows:

'Art. L.321-10. – In the event of judicial reconstruction, the administrator or, failing which, the employer or the liquidator, as the case may be, who anticipates dismissals on the grounds of redundancy must call a meeting of, and consult, the works council, or in default, delegates of the work force under the conditions provided in articles L.321-3, L.321-4, L.422-1, fifth and sixth paragraphs, and articles L.432-1, third paragraph.'

Article 224

The fifth paragraph of article L.321-11 of the employment code is replaced by the following provisions:

'The employer, the administrator, or the liquidator is liable to the same penalties if he fails to observe the provisions provided in articles L.321-7, second paragraph, and L.321-10.'

Article 225

A paragraph in the following terms is added after the fourth paragraph of article L.432-1 of the employment code:

'He must also be informed and consulted before any declaration of cessation of payments and when the business is subject to judicial reconstruction, both before any decision relating to the survival of the business as well as at the time of preparation of the plan for the reconstruction of the business under the conditions provided in articles 20, 25 and 89 of law no. 85-98 of the 25th January 1985. The person or persons appointed by him in accordance with the provisions of article 226 of that law will be heard by the competent court under the conditions provided in articles 6, 23, 36, 61 and 68 of that law.'

Article 226

For the purpose of applying this law, the members of the works council or the delegates of the work force will appoint from among themselves the person designated to exercise any right of appeal in their name.

Article 227

A paragraph in the following terms is added to the end of articles L.412-18, L.425-1 and L.436-1 of the employment code:

'In the event of judicial reconstruction, every dismissal of an employee referred to in the preceding paragraph is subject to the procedure set out in this article.'

Article 228

Any dismissal of the employees' representative referred to in articles 10 and 139 which is anticipated by the administrator, the employer or the liquidator, as the case may be, must be submitted to the works council which will give its opinion on the planned dismissal.

The dismissal may not take place without authorisation by the labour inspector responsible for the establishment. When there is no works council in the establishment, the labour inspector has this responsibility.

However, in the event of serious misconduct, the administrator, the employer, or the liquidator, as the case may be, is competent to order the immediate temporary suspension of the employee concerned pending a final decision. In the event of rejection of the dismissal, the temporary suspension is cancelled and all its consequences are rectified.

The protection granted in favour of the employees' representative to enable him to carry out his task under article 44 ceases when all sums paid to the creditors' representative by the institutions referred to in article L.143-11-4 of the employment code in accordance with the tenth paragraph of article L.143-11-7 of the said code have been paid over by the latter to the employees.

When the employees' representative performs the functions of the works council, or, failing which, of the delegates of the work force, in accordance with article 139, the protection ceases at the end of the last hearing or consultation provided under the proceedings for judicial reconstruction.

Article 229

The following paragraph is added to the end of article 1 of decree no. 53-960 of 30th September 1953 regulating the relationship between lessors and lessees in connection with the renewal of leases of commercial, industrial or works premises:

'If the business is operated under lease management in accordance with law no. 56-277 of 20th March 1956 relating to the lease management of commercial and artisan trading businesses, the owner of the business will nevertheless enjoy the benefit of the provisions of this decree without having to prove registration with the commercial and company registry, or on the trade index.'

Article 230

Articles 22 (first paragraph), 33, 54, 67(2) (first paragraph), 68 (fifth paragraph), 114, 150, 199, 241 (fifth paragraph), 248, 249 (second paragraph), 331 to 337 and 473 (fourth paragraph) of law no. 66-537 of 24th July 1966 relating to commercial firms are modified as follows:

I The first paragraph of article 22 is amended as follows:

'When an order for compulsory liquidation or determining a plan for sale of the whole business, or a prohibition order against carrying on a commercial profession, or a disqualifying order is pronounced in respect of one of its jointly liable associates, the firm will be wound up unless its continuation is required by its articles of association or unless the other jointly liable associates unanimously decide upon its continuation.'

II Article 33 is amended as follows:

'Art. 33. – In the event of judicial reconstruction of a jointly liable partner, or of prohibition from carrying on a commercial profession or of disqualification affecting one of the jointly liable partners, the firm will be dissolved unless, if there is one or more other jointly liable partners, the continuation of the firm is required by its articles of association or the partners unanimously decide upon its continuation, in which case the provisions of the second paragraph of article 22 will apply'.

III Articles 54, 114, 150, 248 and the second paragraph of article 249 are amended as follows:

'In the event of commencement of proceedings for judicial reconstruction in accordance with law no. 85-98 of 25th January, 1985 relating to the judicial reconstruction and compulsory liquidation of businesses, the persons subject to that law may be held responsible for the liabilities of the business and are subject to prohibitions and disqualifications under the conditions provided in the said legislation.'

IV The first paragraph of article 67(2) is replaced by the following provisions:

'A private company with limited liability is not wound up when an order for compulsory liquidation, bankruptcy, prohibition from management provided under article 192 of law no. 85-98 of 25th January 1985 aforesaid, or disqualification, is issued with respect to one of its associates.'

V The fifth paragraphs of articles 68 and 241 are amended as follows:

'The provisions of this article do not apply to firms subject to judicial reconstruction.'

VI Article 199 is amended as follows:

'Art. 199. – When proceedings for judicial reconstruction are commenced with respect to a firm which has issued convertible bonds, the delay period provided for conversion of these bonds into shares starts to run from the order terminating the reconstruction plan and the conversion may take place at the request of each bondholder under the conditions provided in the scheme.'

VII Article 331 is amended as follows:

'Art. 331. – In the event of judicial reconstruction of the firm, the representatives of the general body of bondholders are enabled to act on behalf of the firm.'

VIII Article 332 is amended as follows:

'Art. 332. – The representatives of the general body of bondholders will declare in the liabilities of a firm subject to judicial reconstruction on behalf of all members of this body for the principal amount of the bonds remaining in circulation increased in accordance with a statement of the interest coupons due and unpaid contained in an account established by the creditors' representative. The bondholders representatives are not required to supply proof of their principals' title in support of this declaration.'

IX Article 333 is amended as follows:

'Art. 333. – In default of a declaration by the representatives of the general body of bondholders, an officer of the court will be appointed upon an order of the court at the request of the creditors' representative to be responsible for undertaking representation of the bondholders in the operations of judicial reconstruction and for declaring their claim.'

X Article 334 is repealed.

XI Article 335 is amended as follows:

'Art. 335. – The representatives of the general body of bondholders will be consulted by the creditors' representative regarding the methods for regulating bonds proposed in accordance with law no. 85-98 of 25th January 1985. They will give their agreement in the way indicated by the bondholders in ordinary general meeting called for this purpose.'

XII Article 336 is amended as follows:

'Art. 336. – The costs involved in the representation of the bondholders during the proceedings for judicial reconstruction of the firm are for the account of the company and are treated as costs of judicial administration.'

XIII Article 337 is amended as follows:

'Art. 337. – The judicial reconstruction of the company does not put an end to the functions and purpose of the general meeting of bondholders.'

XIV The fourth paragraph of article 473 is repealed.

Article 231

I In the first paragraph of article 30 of law no. 83-1 of 3rd January 1983 relating to the development of investments and the protection of savings, the words:

'of judicial regulation or liquidation of assets' are replaced by the words: 'of judicial reconstruction'.

II The second paragraph of article 30 of the aforesaid law is amended as follows: 'In the event of insufficient registrations, they will make a declaration to the creditors' representative up to the amount representing their combined rights.'

Article 232

Article 61 of law no. 57-298 of 11th March 1957 relating to literary and artistic property is amended as follows:

'Art. 61. – The judicial reconstruction of the editor does not involve termination of the contract.

When the activity is carried on in accordance with articles 31 and the following articles of law no. 85-98 of 25th January 1985 relating to the judicial reconstruction and liquidation of businesses, all the obligations of the publisher with regard to the author must be respected.

In the event of sale of the publishing business in accordance with articles 81 and the following articles of law no. 85-98 of 25th January 1985, the purchaser is responsible for the obligations of the vendor.

When the activity of the business has ceased for more than three months or when compulsory liquidation has been ordered, the author can request termination of the contract.

The liquidator may not proceed with the sale at a discount of finished copies or with their sale under the conditions provided in articles 155 and 156 of law no. 85-98 of 25th January 1985 aforesaid, until two weeks after notifying the author of his intention by registered letter requiring acknowledgement of receipt.

The author possesses a right of pre-emption in respect of all or some of the copies. In the absence of agreement, the sale price will be determined by an expert.'

Article 233

In all statutory provisions where the words: 'liquidation of assets', or the words: 'compulsory judicial settlement or liquidation of assets', appear, these words are replaced by the words: 'judicial reconstruction'.

A decree of the Council of State will deal with the adaptation in conformity with this law of references in other texts to former provisions applicable to matters pertaining to general proceedings for the discharge of liabilities and will delete such of these references which no longer serve any purpose.

Article 234

Articles 22, 23 and 24 of the law of 1st June 1924 relating to the introduction of French commercial law into the departments of Upper Rhine, Lower Rhine and Moselle are amended as follows:

'Art. 22. – Law no. 85-98 of 25th January 1985 relating to the judicial reconstruction and liquidation of businesses applies to natural persons domiciled in the departments of Upper Rhine, Lower Rhine and Moselle, and to their successors when such persons are publicly recognised as insolvent provided they are neither traders nor artisans nor farmers.

Disqualifications and prohibitions resulting from bankruptcy do not apply to these persons.

Art. 23. – In matters of judicial reconstruction and bankruptcy, the civil court at first instance or, if necessary, the commercial chamber of that court fulfils the functions attributed by law to the commercial court. However the functions of bankruptcy judge may also be exercised by a judge sitting in the civil court at first instance or by a judge serving the local court where the debtor is domiciled.

Art. 24. – The basis for the assessment and settlement of the taxation of legal costs relating to judicial reconstruction will be regulated temporarily in accordance with the provisions of local law.'

Article 234 – I

The provisions of article 1 of law no. 75-1256 of 27th December, 1975 relating to certain sales of real estate in the departments of Lower Rhine, Upper Rhine and Moselle are no longer applicable to the forced sale of real estate comprising part of the assets of a debtor subject to proceedings for judicial reconstruction commenced after 1st January 1986.

Article 235

I Article 58 of law no. 84-148 of 1st March 1984 is amended as follows:

'Art. 58. – Those provisions are repealed which derogate from the regulations set out in article 30 governing the appointment of auditors to state owned public institutions, the state shipping company (CGM), and the state corporation for research into, and construction of, aircraft engines (SNECMA).'

II In the first paragraph of article L.434-6 of the employment code, as amended by article 44 of law no. 84-148 of 1st March 1984, the words: 'in the tenth paragraph' are replaced by the words: 'in the fourteenth paragraph'.

Article 236

I In the first paragraph of article 17-3 of law no. 66-537 of 24th July 1966, as amended by law no. 84-148 of 1st March 1984, the words: 'the liabilities and remuneration of auditors of limited liability companies and the power to challenge their decisions or revoke their appointment' are replaced by the words: 'the liabilities and remuneration of auditors of limited liability companies and the power to challenge their decisions or revoke their appointment or appoint a substitute in their place'.

II In the first paragraph of article 66 of law no. 66-537 of 24th July 1966, the words: 'the responsibility for, and remuneration of, auditors of limited liability companies and the power to revoke their appointment' are replaced by the words: 'the responsibility for, and remuneration of, auditors of limited liability companies and the power to challenge their decisions, revoke their appointment or appoint a substitute in their place'.

III The second paragraph of article 27 of law no. 84-148 of 1st March 1984 is amended as follows:

'These bodies corporate are bound to appoint at least one auditor and one substitute from the list referred to in article 219 of law no. 66-537 of 24th July 1966 who will perform their functions in the manner provided under that law and subject to the regulations pertaining to them. The provisions of article 457 of law no. 66-537 of 24th July 1966 will apply.'

IV The following paragraphs are added to the end of article 28 of law no. 84-148 of 1st March 1984:

'These documents will be analysed in the written reports on the development of the body corporate drawn up by the organisation responsible for its administration. These documents and reports will be distributed simultaneously to the auditor, the works council and the supervisory organisation, if such exists.

In the event of failure to comply with the provisions of the preceding paragraphs, or if the information provided in the reports referred to in the preceding paragraphs calls for observations on his part, the auditor will make an appropriate reference to these matters in a written report which he will distribute to the organisation responsible for its administration or management. This report will be distributed to the works council. It will be disclosed at the next meeting of the consultative organisation.'

V At the end of the first sentence of the first paragraph of article 30 of law no. 84-148 of 1st March 1984, the words: 'at least one auditor' are replaced by the words: 'at least one auditor and a substitute'.

VI The following sentence is added to the end of the first paragraph of article 31 of law no. 84-148 of 1st March 1984: 'the provisions of article 457 of law no. 66-537 of 24th July 1966 aforesaid will apply'.

VII In the second paragraph of article 430 of law no. 66-537 of 24th July 1966, as modified by article 50 of the law of 1st March 1984, the words: 'when inspection or checking by the auditors has been wilfully hindered' are replaced by the words: 'when inspection or checking by the auditors or by experts nominated under article 64-2 has been wilfully hindered'.

Article 237

By way of exception to the provisions of article 33 of law no. 81-1162 of 30th December 1981 relating to the harmonisation of company law in accordance with the second directive adopted in 13th December, 1976 by the Council of the European Communities, limited liability companies which are protected by temporary suspension from suit or from compulsory judicial settlement as of 1st January 1985 will not be dissolved by operation of law due to the sole fact that their nominal capital on that date is less than 250,000 F.frs, or 1,500,000 F.frs, as the case may be. The same applies to companies in respect of which a decision accepting a plan for financial and economic reconstruction combined with a plan for discharge of liabilities, or confirming a creditors' composition agreement, has been taken between 1st July 1984 and 1st January 1985.

These companies have a period of a year from the decision accepting a plan for financial and economic reconstruction combined with a plan for discharge of liabilities, or confirming a creditors' composition agreement, in which to increase their nominal capital to the minimum required by law. In default, they will be dissolved by operation of law on expiry of this period.

The provisions of this article will come into force on 1st January 1985.

Article 238

The following are repealed:

1. Articles 10–19 of the decree of 8th August 1935 applying insolvency and bankruptcy laws to the officers and administrators of companies and instituting prohibition and disqualification from the right to manage and administer a company;
2. Articles 1–149 and 160–164 of law no. 67-563 of 13th July 1967 relating to compulsory judicial settlement, liquidation of assets, and criminal bankruptcy;
3. Order no. 67-820 of 23rd September 1967 made with a view to facilitating the economic and financial reconstruction of certain businesses.

Article 239

For a period of two years from the entry into force of this law, the insurance referred to in articles L.143-11-1 of the employment code will only cover the indemnities for paid holidays provided under the second paragraph of that article up to the amount of the employees' rights accrued at the end of the initial observation period.

During the same period, the maximum amount provided under the third paragraph of article L.143-11-1 of the employment code is limited to an amount equal to one working month's wages.

Article 240

The provisions of this law only apply to proceedings started after the provisions themselves have come into effect.

However, when proceedings for compulsory judicial settlement governed by law no. 67-563 of 13th July 1967 are converted into proceedings for the liquidation of assets after the entry into force of this law, the court may, in one and the same judgment, at the request of the public prosecutor, and if sales at an agreed price are envisaged, decide that the provisions of this law relating to sale of the business will apply, with the exception of the third paragraph of article 92. To this effect, the court will appoint an administrative officer responsible for submitting the draft sale plan to the court and for managing the business for the time being. This administrative officer will perform the functions of the creditors' representative. If the sale plan is rejected, the provisions of part III of this law will apply to these proceedings, with the exception of articles 169 and 170.

In proceedings for compulsory judicial settlement or liquidation of current assets, after the entry into force of this law, all monies received by the administrative officer in performance of his functions on behalf of the creditors or of the debtor whom he is assisting or representing, will be paid immediately into a deposit account at the Central Deposit and Savings Bank, or into the bank or post account of the business subject to compulsory judicial settlement or asset liquidation. Any delay on the part of the administrative officer in transferring such sums will attract interest for his own account at a rate equal to the legal rate of interest plus five points.

As from the entry into force of this law, the provisions of the fourth paragraph of article 195 will apply to bankruptcies and to the other sanctions ordered by way of application of articles 105–109 of law no. 67-563 of 13th July 1967.

Article 241

Presidents of, and judges appointed to, the commercial courts who have fulfilled three successive judicial sessions in their previous capacity, and who are due to retire from service in 1984, will continue in that capacity for a period of one year from 1st January 1985.

Presidents of, and judges appointed to, the commercial courts who are entitled to the benefit of the provisions of the previous paragraph will be placed on the supernumerary list of the complement of the judiciary to which they belong.

Article 242

With the exception of articles 130 to 136, this law applies to the overseas territories and to the community of Mayotte.

In the overseas territories, the measures required to put into effect the provisions of articles 2, 22, 24, 70, 73, 103 and 123 are determined by meetings of the competent council in the relevant territory.

Article 243

With the exception of articles 233, second paragraph, 235, 236, 237 and 241, the provisions of this law will enter into force on a date fixed by decree, and at the latest, on 1st January, 1986.

This law will take effect as a law of the State.

Made in Paris, 25th January 1985.

By the President of the Republic: FRANÇOIS MITTERRAND

The Prime Minister,
LAURENT FABIUS

Minister for Economy, Finance and Budgets,
PIERRE BÉRÉGOVOY

Keeper of the Seals, Minister of Justice
ROBERT BADINTER

Minister for the Interior
PIERRE JOXE

Minister for Social Security, Government Spokesman,
GEORGINA DUFOIX

Minister for Town Planning, Housing and Transport
PAUL QUILÈS

Minister for Commerce, Trade and Tourism
MICHEL CRÉPEAU

Minister for Employment
MICHEL DELEBARRE

Secretary of State at the Ministry for the Interior,
responsible for Overseas Departments and Territories
GEORGES LEMOINE

TABLE OF CHANGES IN LEGISLATION ARISING FROM THE LAW OF 25TH JANUARY 1985

AMENDED TEXTS	**ARTICLES – LAW NO. 85-98**
CIVIL CODE:	
Article 1188	217
Article 1844-7	218
ELECTORAL CODE:	
Article L. 5	220-I
Article L. 202	220-II
INSURANCE CODE:	
Article L. 113-6	221-I
Article L. 132-14	221-II
Article L. 132-17	221-III
Article L. 326-1	221-IV
Article L. 326-6	221-V
Article L. 326-11	221-VI
Article L. 328-5	221-VII
Article L. 328-13	221-VIII
CRIMINAL CODE:	
Article 55-1	202
Article 402	198
Article 403	199
Article 404	200
CRIMINAL PROCEDURE CODE:	
Article 768	219-I
Article 775	219-II
Article 776	219-III
EMPLOYMENT CODE:	
Article L. 143-9	131
Article L. 143-10	132-III
Article L. 143-11	132-III

AMENDED TEXTS	ARTICLES – LAW NO. 85-98
Article L. 143-11-1	133
Article L. 143-11-2	130-133
Article L. 143-11-3	130-133
Article L. 143-11-4	130
Article L. 143-11-5	130
Article L. 143-11-6	130-132-I
Article L. 143-11-7	134
Article L. 143-11-8	132-II
Article L. 143-11-9	135
Article L. 143-13-1	136
Article L. 321-7	222
Article L. 321-10.	223
Article L. 321-11.	224
Article L. 412-18.	227
Article L. 425-1	227
Article L. 432-1	225
Article L. 434-6	235-II
Article L. 436-1	227
Law of 1st June 1924:	
Articles 22, 23, 24	234
Decree of 8th August 1935:	
Articles 10 to 19	238-1
Decree No. 53-960 of 30th September 1953:	
Article 1	229
Law no. 57-298 of 11th March 1957:	
Article 61	232
Law no. 66-537 of 24th July 1966:	
Articles 22, 33, 54, 67(2), 114, 150, 199,	241, 248, 249,
331 to 337, 473	230
Article 17-3	236-I
Article 66	236-II
Article 430	236-VII
Law no. 67-563 of 13th July 1967:	
Articles 1 to 149 and 160 to 164	238-2
Orders No. 67-820 of 23rd September 1967	238-3
Law no. 84-148 of 1st March 1984:	
Article 27	236-III
Article 28	236-IV
Article 30	236-V
Article 31	236-VI
Article 58	Art. 235-I

DECREE NO. 85-1387 OF 27TH DECEMBER 1985 ISSUED BY WAY OF APPLICATION OF ARTICLES 2 AND 7 OF LAW NO. 85-98 OF 25TH JANUARY 1985 (OFFICIAL GAZETTE OF 29TH DECEMBER 1985)

Following the report of the Keeper of the Seals (Minister of Justice), and having regard to law no. 85-98 of 25th January 1985 concerning the judicial reconstruction and liquidation of businesses, and in particular articles 2 and 7, and having regard to decree no. 83-1020 of 29th November 1983 issued pursuant to law no. 83-353 of 30th April 1983 concerning the accounting obligations of businessmen and certain companies, and after hearing the views of the Council of State (Interior branch), the Prime Minister decrees as follows:

Article 1

In application of the third paragraph of article 2 of law no. 85-98 of 25th January 1985 concerning the judicial reconstruction and liquidation of businesses, the turn-over figure will be calculated in accordance with the provisions of the third paragraph of article 17 of decree no. 83-1020 of 29th November 1983. The figure taken is that relating to the last day of the most recent accounting period.

The turn-over threshold is fixed in the sum of twenty million francs.

The number of employees to be included in order to apply the third paragraph of article 2 of that law is the number of employees employed by the business either on the date of cessation of payments, or on the date of service of the creditor's summons, or on the date of the public prosecutor's petition, or, in the case of the court's own motion, on the date when the debtor is summoned by the president of the court.

Article 2

In application of article 7 of the law of 25th January 1985, the seat and jurisdictional district of the competent metropolitan courts will be determined in accordance with tables A and B attached hereto.

Article 3

The Keeper of the Seals, Minister of Justice, is charged with the execution of this decree, which will be published in the official gazette of the Republic of France.

Made in Paris, 27th December, 1985.

By the Prime Minister: LAURENT FABIUS

Keeper of the Seals, Minister of Justice
ROBERT BADINTER

ANNEXURE

TABLE A

Schedule of competent courts in metropolitan France to hear proceedings for judicial reconstruction and liquidation relating to traders and artisans under article 7 of law no. 85-98 of 25th January 1985 (As amended by Decree No 86-859 17th July 1986)

Department	*Competent court within the department*	*Jurisdictional district within which the court may exercise its powers*
Ain	Bourg-en-Bresse Commercial Court (CC)	Department
Aisne	Soissons CC	Department (exc. St. Quentin CFI)
	St. Quentin CC	
Allier	Moulins CC	Department
Alpes-de-Haute-Provence	Digne Civil Court of first instance (CFI)	Department
Alpes (Hautes-)	Gap CC	Department
Alpes-Maritimes	Nice CC	Nice Civil Court of first instance (CFI)
	Grasse CC	Grasse
Ardèche	Aubenas CC	Department
Ardennes	Charleville-Mézières CC	Department
Ariège	Foix CFI	Department
Aube	Troyes CC	Department
Aude	Carcassonne CC	Department
Aveyron	Rodez CC	Department
Bouches-du-Rhône	Aix-en-Provence CC	Tarascon C
	Marseille CC	Marseille CFI
Calvados	Caen CC	Department
Cantal	Aurillac CC	Department
	within the department	within which the court may exercise its powers
Charente	Angoulême CC	Department
Charente-Maritime	La Rochelle CC	Department
Cher	Bourges CC	Department
Corréze	Brive CC	Department (exc. Brive CFI)
	Tulle CC	
Corse-du-Sud	Ajaccio CC	Department
Corse (Haute-)	Bastia CC	Department
Côte-d'Or	Dijon CC	Department
Côtes-du-Nord	Saint-Brieuc CC	Department
Creuse	Guéret CFI	Department
Dordogne	Périgueux CC	Department
Doubs	Besançon CC	Department
Drôme	Romans CCT	Department
Essonne	Corbeil CC	Department
Eure	Évreux CC	Department
Eure-et-Loir	Chartres CC	Department
Finistére	Brest CC	Morlaix CFI
	Quimper CC	Quimper CFI
Gard	Nîmes CC	Department
Garonne (Haute-)	Toulouse CC	Department

Department	*Competent court within the department*	*Jurisdictional district within which the court may exercise its powers*
Gers	Auch CC	Department
Gironde	Bordeaux CC	Department
Hérault	Béziers CC	Béziers CF
	Montpellier CC	Montpellier CFI
Ille-et-Vilaine	Rennes CC	Department
Indre	Châteauroux CC	Department
Indre-et-Loire	Tours CC	Department
Isére	Grenoble CC	Department (exc. Bourgoin - Jallien CFI)
	Bourgoin – Jallien CFI	
Jura	Lons-le-Saunier CC	Department
Landes	Mont-de-Marsan CC	Department
Loir-et-Cher	Blois CC	Department
Loire	Saint-Étienne CC	Department
Loire (Haute-)	Le Puy CC	Department
Loire-Atlantique	Nantes CC	Nantes CFI
	Saint-Nazaire CC	Saint-Nazaire CFI
Loiret	Orléans CC	Department
Lot	Cahors CC	Department
Lot-et-Garonne	Agen CC	Department
Lozére	Mende CC	Department
Maine-et-Loire	Angers CC	Department (exc. Saumur CFI)
	Saumur CC	
Manche	Cherbourg CC	Department (exc. Avranches CFI)
	Granville CC	
Marne	Reims CC	Department
Marne (Haute-)	Chaumont CC	Department
Mayenne	Laval CC	Department
Meurthe-et-Moselle	Nancy CC	Department (exc. Briey CFI)
	Briey CC	
Meuse	Bar-le-Duc CC	Department
Morbihan	Lorient CC	Department (exc. Vannes CFI)
	Vannes CC	
Moselle	Metz CFI	CFI
	Sarreguemines CFI	CFI
	Thionville CFI	CFI
Nièvre	Nevers CC	Department
Nord	Cambrai CC	Cambrai/Douai
	Dunkerque CC	Dunkerque CFIs
	Lille CC	Lille CFIs (except for Roubaix-Tourcoing, and Hazebrouck CCs)
	Roubaix-Tourcoing CC	Roubaix-Tourcoing CC
	Valenciennes CC	Valenciennes/Avesnes CFIs
Oise	Beauvais CC	Department
Orne	Aleçon CC	Department
Paris	Paris CC	Department
Pas-de-Calais	Béthune CFI	Béthune/Arras CFI
	Boulogne CC	Boulogne/Saint-Omer CFIs
Puy-de-Dôme	Clermont-Ferrant CC	Department
Pyrénées-Atlantiques	Pau CC	Pau CFI
	Bayonne CC	Bayonne CFI
Pyrénées (Hautes-)	Tarbes CC	Department

Department	*Competent court within the department*	*Jurisdictional district within which the court may exercise its powers*
Pyrénées-Orientales	Perpignan CC	Department
Rhin (Bas-)	Strasbourg CC	Strasbourg/Saverne CFIs
Rhin (Haut-)	Mulhouse CC	CFI
	Colmar CC	CFI
Rhône	Lyon CC	Department
Saône (Haute-)	Vesoul CC	Department
Saône-et-Loire	Mâcon CC	Department
Sarthe	Le Mans CC	Department
Savoie	Chambéry CC	Department
Savoie (Haute-)	Annecy CFI	Department (exc. Thonon-les-Bains CFI)
	Thonon-les-Bains CFI	
Seine (Hauts-de-)	Nanterre CC	Department
Seine-Maritime	Havre CC	Le Havre CFI
	Rouen CC	Rouen/Dieppe CFIs
Seine-et-Marne	Melum CC	Department
Seine-Saint-Denis	Paris CC	Department
Sèvres (Deux-)	Niort CC	Department
Somme	Amiens CC	Department
Tarn	Castres CC	Department
Tarn-et-Garonne	Montauban CC	Department
Territoire de Belfort	Belfort CC	Department
Val-de-Marne	Créteil CC	Department
Val-d'Oise	Pontoise CC	Department
Var	Draguignan CC	Draguignan CFI
	Toulon CC	Toulon CFI
Vaucluse	Avignon CC	Department
Vendée	La Roche-sur-Yon CC	Department
Vienne	Poitiers CC	Department
Vienne (Haute-)	Limoges CC	Department
Vosges	Épinal CC	Department
Yonne	Auxerre CC	Department
Yvelines	Versailles CC	Department

TABLE B

Schedule of competent courts in metropolitan France to hear proceedings for judicial reconstruction and liquidation under article 7 of law n. 85-98 of 25th January 1985 relating to persons who are neither traders nor artisans

Department	*Competent court within the department (in each case the Civil Court of first instance)*	*Jurisdictional district within which the court may exercise its powers*
Ain	Bourg-en-Bresse	Department
Aisne	Laon	Department
Allier	Moulins	Department
Alpes-de-Haute-Provence	Digne	Department
Alpes (Hautes-)	Gap	Department

Department	*Competent court within the department (in each case the Civil Court of first instance)*	*Jurisdictional district within which the court may exercise its powers*
Alpes-Maritimes	Nice	Department
Ardèche	Privas	Department
Ardennes	Charleville-Mézières	Department
Ariège	Foix	Department
Aube	Troyes	Department
Aude	Carcassonne	Department
Aveyron	Rodez	Department
Bouches-du-Rhône	Marseille	Department
Calvados	Caen	Department
Cantal	Aurillac	Department
Charente	Angoulême	Department
Charente-Maritime	La Rochelle	Department
Cher	Bourges	Department
Corrèze	Tulle	Department
Corse-du-Sud	Ajaccio	Department
Corse (Haute-)	Bastia	Department
Côte-d'Or	Dijon	Department
Côtes-du-Nord	Saint-Brieuc	Department
Creuse	Guéret	Department
Dordogne	Périgueux	Department
Doubs	Besançon	Department
Drôme	Valence	Department
Essonne	Corbeil	Department
Eure	Évreux	Department
Eure-et-Loir	Chartres	Department
Finistére	Quimper	Department
Gard	Nîmes	Department
Garonne (Haute-)	Toulouse	Department
Gers	Auch	Department
Gironde	Bordeaux	Department
Hérault	Montpellier	Department
Ille-et-Vilaine	Rennes	Department
Indre	Châteauroux	Department
Indre-et-Loire	Tours	Department
Isére	Grenoble	Department
Jura	Lons-le-Saunier	Department
Landes	Mont-de-Marsan	Department
Loir-et-Cher	Blois	Department
Loire	Saint-Étienne	Department
Loire (Haute-)	Le Puy	Department
Loire-Atlantique	Nantes	Department
Loiret	Orléans	Department
Lot	Cahors	Department
Lot-et-Garonne	Agen	Department
Lozère	Mende	Department
Maine-et-Loire	Angers	Department
Manche	Coutances	Department
Marne	Châlons-sur-Marne	Department
Marne (Haute-)	Chaumont	Department
Mayenne	Laval	Department
Meurthe-et-Moselle	Nancy	Department

Department	*Competent court within the department (in each case the Civil Court of first instance)*	*Jurisdictional district within which the court may exercise its powers*
Meuse	Bar-le-Duc	Department
Morbihan	Vannes	Department
Moselle	Metz	Department
Nièvre	Nevers	Department
Nord	Lille	Department
Oise	Bèauvais	Department
Orne	Alençon	Department
Paris	Paris	Department
Pas-de-Calais	Arras	Department
Puy-de-Dôme	Clermont-Ferrant	Department
Pyrénées-Atlantiques	Pau	Department
Pyrénées (Hautes-)	Tarbes	Department
Pyrénées-Orientales	Perpignan	Department
Rhin (Bas-)	Strasbourg	Strasbourg/Saverne Civil Courts of first instance (CFIs)
Rhin (Haut-)	Colmar	Colmar/Mulhouse CFIs
Rhône	Lyon	Department
Saône (Haute-)	Vesoul	Department
Saône-et-Loire	Mâcon	Department
Sarthe	Le Mans	Department
Savoie	Chambéry	Department
Savoie (Haute-)	Annecy	Department
Seine (Hauts-de-)	Nanterre	Department
Seine-Maritime	Rouen	Department
Seine-et-Marne	Melum	Department
Seine-Saint-Denis	Bobigny	Department
Sèvres (Deux-)	Niort	Department
Somme	Amiens	Department
Tarn	Albi	Department
Tarn-et-Garonne	Montauban	Department
Territoire de Belfort	Belfort	Department
Val-de-Marne	Créteil	Department
Val-d'Oise	Pontoise	Department
Var	Toulon	Department
Vaucluse	Avignon	Department
Vendée	La Roche-sur-Yon	Department
Vienne	Poitiers	Department
Vienne (Haute-)	Limoges	Department
Vosges	Épinal	Department
Yonne	Auxerre	Department

DECREE NO. 85-1388 OF 27TH DECEMBER 1985 RELATING TO THE JUDICIAL RECONSTRUCTION AND LIQUIDATION OF BUSINESSES (OFFICIAL GAZETTE OF 29TH DECEMBER 1985)

Following the report of the Keeper of the Seals (Minister of Justice), the Minister for Economy, Finance and Budgets, and the Minister for Employment, and having regard to:

The civil code, the commercial code, the civil procedure code, the new civil procedure code, the employment code, the general taxation code, the social security code; and to:

The law of 1st June 1924 bringing into force French civil legislation in the departments of Upper Rhine, Lower Rhine and Moselle;

The law of 1st June 1924 introducing French commercial laws in the departments of Upper Rhine, Lower Rhine and Moselle;

Law no. 66-537 of 24th July 1966 relating to commercial companies, amended most recently by law no. 85-705 of 12th July 1985, together with decree no. 67-236 of 23rd March 1967 issued in order to apply that law, and as amended most recently by decree no. 85-295 of 1st March 1985;

Law no. 85-98 of 25th January 1985 relating to the judicial reconstruction and liquidation of businesses;

The decree of 17th February 1951 in connection with the formalities of the registration of preferential rights and regulating public administration, issued by way of application of the law of 18th January 1951 relating to the mortgaging of works equipment and materials;

Decree no. 55-22 of 4th January 1955 relating to the reform of publication of notices of interests in real estate.

Decree no. 63-608 of 24th June 1963 relating to the recovery of claims owed to the State, other than tax and property claims;

Decree no. 78-486 of 31st March 1978 establishing in each department a permanent commission consisting of the heads of the financial services divisions and representatives of the social security organisations in order to enquire into the situation of defaulting debtors;

Decree no. 83-359 of 2nd May 1983 relating to the regulation of transferable securities;

Decree no. 83-487 of 10th June 1983 relating to the trades register, amended by decree no. 84-170 of 5th March 1984;

Decree no. 84-406 of 30th May 1986 relating to the commercial and companies register, as amended by decree no. 84-1113 of 13th December 1984;

Decree no. 85-1387 of 27th December 1985 issued by way of application of articles 2 and 7 of law no. 85-98 of 25th January 1985;

and after hearing the views of the Council of State (Interior branch), the Prime Minister issues the following decree:-

Article 1

The court which is territorially competent to hear cases within the general regime of judicial reconstruction, or the simplified procedure applicable to certain businesses, is that which is located in the jurisdictional district where the debtor has his registered office, or, in the absence of a registered office in French territory, the debtor's principal place of business. However in the event of the change of registered office of a body corporate within the six months preceding the date of assumption of jurisiction the court in the jurisdictional district of the original registered office alone remains competent. This period runs from the date of amendment of the register of commerce and companies.

Article 2

Courts which, by way of exception, are not competent, are governed by articles 75–99 of the new civil procedure code subject to the provisions of articles 3, 4 and 5 below.

Article 3

When, in applying the second paragraph of article 7 of law no. 85-98 of 25th January 1985 relating to the judicial reconstruction and liquidation of businesses, a court hears an action which, either of its own motion or by way of exception, it believes not to be within its competence, the president of the court will send the court file setting out the grounds for the court's decision to the senior presiding judge at the Court of Appeal who will determine the competent jurisdiction after hearing the parties, or upon their being summoned by the clerk of the court.

The decisions of the president of the court and of the senior presiding judge at the Court of Appeal, will be immediately notified to the parties by the clerk of the court or of the Court of Appeal, and are not open to review.

The decision of the senior presiding judge is binding on the parties and on the judge to whom the case is remitted.

Pending the decision of the senior presiding judge, the court may appoint an agent who has been given ad hoc power on the authority of a judge empowered temporarily to that effect, to instigate, in particular, the proceedings provided in article 26 of the law of 25th January 1985. By way of provisional measures the court may also order an inventory of assets to be drawn up and seals to be affixed.

Article 4

In cases other than any resulting from the application of the second paragraph of article 7 of the law of 25th January 1985, the court may, if it declines jurisdiction, order the conservatory or provisional measures referred to in the last paragraph of the preceding article to be set in motion.

Article 5

When its competence is challenged, the court must, if it decides to accept jurisdiction, give its decision on the merits of the case in the same judgment.

PART I
GENERAL REGIME OF JUDICIAL RECONSTRUCTION

CHAPTER I. PROCEEDINGS FOR JUDICIAL OBSERVATION

Section I: Jurisdiction and decision of the court

Sub-section 1 – Debtor's application

Article 6

The declaration of cessation of payments, or of non-execution of financial obligations in out-of-court proceedings, is filed by the debtor at the registry of the competent court.

Besides the annual accounts for the last accounting period, the following documents drawn up on the date of the declaration are filed with it:

1. A transcript of the entry on the registries and directories referred to in article 21 below;

2. A financial statement dated within the last three months;
3. The number of employees and the turnover figure as defined in article 1 of decree no. 85-1387 of 27th December 1985 issued by way of application of articles 2 and 7 of law no. 85-98 of 25th January 1985;
4. The amount of claims and debts in figures, setting out the names and domicile of the creditors and, in the case of the employees, the total amount of sums unpaid;
5. The statement of guarantees taken and given, and of off-balance sheet transactions;
6. The summarised inventory of the debtor's assets;
7. If the case relates to a body corporate whose members are jointly liable for the company's debts, a list of the members setting out their names and domicile;
8. If already appointed, the names and addresses of the representatives of the works council or the delegates of the work force authorised to be heard by the court.

These documents must be dated, signed and certified as true and correct by the person making the declaration.

In the event that one or other of these documents cannot be supplied, or can only be supplied incomplete, the declaration must set out the reasons preventing proper production.

Sub-section 2 – Jurisdiction on a creditor's summons

Article 7

A creditor's summons must set out the nature and amount of the claim and indicate the proceedings or means of implementation to be undertaken in due course in order to recover the claim.

In the case of a farming business, the creditor will attach to his application a certificate issued by the clerk of the court to the effect that the president of the civil court of first instance has been seized for the purpose of arranging the appointment of a mediator.

Except in the case of failure to perform an out of court settlement, the application for commencement of proceedings for judicial reconstruction is liable to be declared inadmissible on the court's own motion. Such a declaration excludes all other action.

Sub-section 3 – Assumption of jurisdiction by the court or on the petition of the public prosecutor

Article 8

When the court assumes jurisdiction, the president of the court will summon the debtor at the instance of the clerk of the court through service of process by the court bailiff to appear before the court sitting in chambers within such time as the president may determine.

A memorandum is attached to the summons in which the president sets out the grounds for the court to assume jurisdiction.

The clerk of the court will send a copy of this memorandum to the public prosecutor notifying him of the date when the debtor will be heard by the court.

Judgment is pronounced in open court.

Article 9

If commencement of proceedings for judicial reconstruction is requested by the public prosecutor, he will file a petition with the court setting out the grounds for this application. The president of the court will summon the debtor at the instigation of the clerk of the court through service of process by the court bailiff to appear before the court sitting in chambers within such period of time as the president may determine.

The public prosecutor's petition is attached to this summons.

The public prosecutor will be notified of the date when the debtor will be heard by the court.

Judgment is pronounced in open court.

Article 10

The same procedures apply to the known heirs of the debtor when, in the circumstances provided in article 16 of the law of 25th January 1985, the court decides to assume jurisdiction or on the petition of the public prosecutor.

Article 11

If the Court of Appeal cancels or reverses a judgment in favour of judicial reconstruction or pronouncing compulsory liquidation, it may of its own motion either commence proceedings for judicial reconstruction or pronounce compulsory liquidation.

Sub-section 4 – Information before the court

Article 12

Before the decision is taken to commence proceedings, the clerk of the court, on the application of the president of the court, will notify the head of the business that he must hold a meeting of the works council, or, failing which, the delegates of the work force, in order to appoint the persons authorised to be heard by the court and to exercise the powers of appeal in accordance with article 226 of the law of 25th January 1985. A copy of this notice is sent by the clerk of the court to the secretary of the works council or, failing which, to the delegates of the work force. The names of the persons appointed are notified to the clerk of the court.

Article 13

Before the decision is made to commence proceedings, the president of the court, or the court itself, will, if such notice is considered useful, appoint an officer to collect all available information on the financial, economic and social condition of the business, and also on the number of employees and the turnover figure as defined in article 1 of decree no. 85-1387 of 27th December 1985. The appointed officer may be assisted by anyone he chooses. The statements of the assistant will be contained in the officer's report.

This report is filed at the the court registry and distributed by the clerk of the court to the public prosecutor.

The clerk of the court will notify the debtor and the plaintiff creditor that they may inspect the report within the time limits and in accordance with the methods laid down by the president of the court. He will inform the works council or, failing which, the delegates of the work force, that their representatives may inspect the report at the court registry and will notify them of the hearing date at the same time.

The president of the court will ensure that there is sufficient time between the clerk's notices and the hearing date.

Sub-section 5 – Commencement of proceedings

Article 14

The court will make its decision, upon the report of the appointed officer if relevant, in accordance with the conditions provided in article 6 of the law of 25th January 1985. If it is not possible to give judgment immediately, pronouncement is postponed for a future hearing, the date of which will be given to the debtor at the time of the hearing, and, if appropriate, to the plaintiff creditor.

The order commencing proceedings takes effect from its date.

Article 15

The administrator appointed in accordance with article 10 or article 141 of the law of 25th January 1985, or the head of the business, will hold a meeting of the works council and the delegates of the work force, or, failing which, the employees, to enable the employees' representative to be appointed within two days following the making of the order commencing proceedings.

Article 16

Upon notice filed at the registry, the district court has jurisdiction in respect of all disputes relating to the appointment of the employees' representative.

This notice is only valid if it is given within two days following the appointment of the employees' representative.

Within five days of the assumption of jurisdiction, the district court will issue its final decision without any award as to costs, and without formal proceedings, and upon simple notice given two days in advance to the interested parties.

The district court's decision is notified by the clerk of the court within two days by registered letter requiring acknowledgement of receipt.

The time limit for appeal is five days. The petition is lodged, commenced and heard under the conditions set down in articles 999–1008 of the new code of civil procedure.

Article 17

The dismissal of the employees' representative appointed under article 10 or 139 of the law of 25th January 1985 is governed by the provisions of articles R.436-1 to R.436-8, and article R.436-10 of the employment code.

Article 18

Notice to the debtor of the order commencing proceedings is given at the instance of the clerk of the court within eight days of the date of the order.

Article 19

The clerk of the court will immediately send a copy of the order commencing proceedings for judicial reconstruction:

(i) to the appointed officers of the court;
(ii) to the public prosecutor;
(iii) to the paymaster general of the department in which the debtor's registered office is located, and to the same officer of the department in which the debtor's principal place of business is located.

Article 20

The court will determine any extension of the observation period with due regard to the official receiver's report, and on the advice of the public prosecutor. It will assemble in advance any observations from the creditors' representative, the administrator and the debtor, provided that these persons are not plaintiffs in the action.

The decision extending the observation period will be distributed to the authorities referred to in article 19. It will also be noted in the registers and directories provided under article 21.

If the observation period is extended, the time limits provided in parts I and II of this decree, with the exception of those relating to jurisdiction and appeals, may be extended by order of the bankruptcy judge issued on his own motion, or at the instance of the administrator, the debtor or the creditors' representative.

Sub-section 6 – Publication of the order

Article 21

The order commencing proceedings for the judicial reconstruction of a debtor is noted, together with an indication of the powers conferred on the administrator, in the register of commerce and companies if the case concerns a trader or a body corporate listed on this register.

At the instance of the clerk of the court in which proceedings are commenced, the same entries are filed in the trades and business directories in the departments of Lower Rhine, Upper Rhine and Moselle if the case concerns an artisan.

Where a person is not listed on the register of commerce and companies and or the trades and business directories, entries are made on a register opened to that effect at the court registry of the civil court of first instance. In that event, the clerk of the court will note on the register the registered office of the business, and the name, forenames and address of the head of the business or of the company's officers.

Notice of the order will be publicised in the B.O.D.A.C.C. This notice will indicate the name of the debtor, the registered office of the business, its registration number in the registers and directories referred to above, the nature of the business and the date of the order commencing proceedings for judicial reconstruction. It will also set out the name and address of the creditors' representative and the administrator, if one has been appointed. Finally, it will direct the creditors to declare their claims to the creditors' representative.

The same notice will be published in the newspaper carrying legal notices for the place where the debtor's business has its registered office or any subsidiary establishments.

Publication of the order as set out above is effected by the clerk of the court without further instruction within eight days of the date of the order.

Article 22

Any decision amending the date of cessation of payments is noted on the registers and directories provided under article 21 above.

Section II: Organs of the court

Article 23

In the order commencing proceedings, or at any stage in the proceedings thereafter, the court may appoint a substitute bankruptcy judge who will perform the duties of a bankruptcy judge who has been temporarily incapacitated.

Article 24

Except as provided in article 26, following the report of the bankruptcy judge, the court will hear all disputes arising out of the judicial reconstruction or liquidation and brought before it.

Article 25

The bankruptcy judge will determine by way of order all actions, disputes and claims within his competence and also any objections raised against the actions of the administrator, the creditors' representative, the commissioner, the liquidator or the employees' representative.

If the bankruptcy judge has not given his decision within a reasonable time, the court will assume jurisdiction either of its own motion or at the request of a party to the action.

Orders issued by the bankruptcy judge will be filed immediately at the court registry and distributed to the officers of the court. They may be appealed by ordinary declaration made at the court registry within eight days either of this filing or of a notice in a form determined by the court and issued by the clerk of the court addressed to the plaintiff provided that he is not also an officer of the court and to the persons designated as such in the order.

The court may assume jurisdiction within the same time in order to cancel or amend the order.

Article 26

On penalty of being set aside, the bankruptcy judge may not sit in a judicial capacity when the court has jurisdiction by virtue of the provisions of the preceding article or is hearing an appeal lodged against one of its orders.

Article 27

The creditors' representative will do everything possible to inform and consult the creditors.

Article 28

The bankruptcy judge will authorise the administrator or the debtor to remit to the creditors' representative the monies necessary to enable the latter to perform his functions.

Article 29

One month after the order commencing proceedings, the administrator and the creditors' representative will report to the bankruptcy judge and the public prosecutor on the progress of the proceedings and the general situation of the business.

Article 30

When the bankruptcy judge hears an application for replacement in accordance with the second paragraph of article 12 or the second paragraph of article 148 of the law of 25th January 1985 and has not given judgment within three days, the application may be brought directly before the court by summons.

When the replacement of the persons referred to in the first two paragraphs of article 12 and in the second paragraph of article 148 of that law is requested by the public prosecutor, or when the court requests the same on its own motion, the summons is prepared in the manner and in accordance with the procedure provided in article 8 or 9 as the case may be.

In every case, the court will have regard to the report of the bankruptcy judge and will take advice from the public prosecutor.

The preceding provisions apply to the addition of one or more administrators.

Article 31

An officer of the court who retires from his office must account to the officer appointed in his place in the presence of the bankruptcy judge, the debtor being heard or summoned at the instance of the retiring officer.

Section III: The administrator's report and proposal

Article 32

Any offer received by the administrator as provided in article 21 of the law of 25th January 1985 will be filed at the court registry. When required, the offeror will attach the annual accounts relating to his last three trading years together with his draft accounts.

All offers and attached documents are distributed to the bankruptcy judge and, if requested, to the public prosecutor. They may be distributed to the debtor if the administrator considers this to be useful.

Article 33

When an extraordinary general meeting or a partners' meeting is to be held as provided under article 22 of the law of 25th January 1985, the administrator will call the meeting by registered letter requiring acknowledgement of receipt addressed to the board of directors or managers or to the managing director, as the case may be.

The letter calling the meeting will set out the agenda and will have attached to it a draft resolution and a report setting out the grounds for the proposed capital reorganisation.

Within three days of receipt of the administrator's letter calling the meeting, the board of directors or managers, or the managing director, must advise the administrator of the date fixed for the meeting, which must be within thirty days of receipt of the administrator's letter. In the absence of a reply the administrator will call the meeting himself.

Whoever calls the meeting, the meeting will be held in accordance with the formalities and time limits provided in decree no. 67-236 of 23rd March 1967 relating to commercial companies, with the exception of meetings of limited liability companies and partnerships limited to shares, in respect of which the provisions of articles 34–40 below will apply.

Article 34

Registered shareholders entitled to vote will be summoned by registered letter at the expense of the company. When the company's shares are registered with a stock exchange, or on the secondary market, or if they fulfil the conditions provided in article 163, eighth paragraph, of the general tax code, the meeting is called by a notice inserted in the Bulletin of obligatory legal announcements.

All joint shareholders or joint holders of an undivided share are summoned by registered letter if their rights are confirmed by entry of their names on the register. The same applies if the shares are charged with a usufructuary right in favour of the holder of the voting rights as provided in the first paragraph of article 163 of law no. 66-537 of 24th July 1966 relating to commercial companies.

Article 35

The notice convening the meeting will contain the information referred to in article 123 of decree no. 67-236 of 23rd March 1961.

It must also contain:

(i) the date on which the second meeting will be held should this prove necessary by reason of the first failing to achieve the required quorum;
(ii) the reminder of the time limit provided under the first paragraph of article 37 below.

The period of time between the first and second meetings must be at least six days.

Article 36

The period of time between the date of either insertion of the notice calling the meeting, or despatch of the letters calling the meeting, and the date for the first meeting, must be at least fifteen days.

Article 37

A shareholder's request to have a draft resolution included in the agenda for the meeting will be subject to the conditions for admissibility set out in article 128 of decree no. 67-236 of 23rd March 1967 and must be sent to the registered office of the company by registered letter requiring acknowledgement of receipt at least eight days before the date fixed for the first meeting.

Receipt of draft resolutions must be acknowledged within three days.

Article 38

Representation by proxy at a meeting is allowed under the conditions referred to in articles 132 and 134 of the decree of 23rd March 1967.

Proxy forms will be addressed to shareholders or bearers of voting certificates. They will contain:

(i) the agenda for the meeting;
(ii) the text of draft resolutions prepared by the board of directors or managers, the managing director, the administrator or the shareholders;
(iii) the auditors' report whenever this is required by the law of 24th July 1966 and the decree of 23rd March 1967.

Article 39

Within eight days before the date of the meeting, every shareholder or owner of a certificate of voting rights has the right to go to the registered office of the company and inform himself of the contents of, or take a copy of, the reports of the administrator, the auditors and also the draft resolutions.

Article 40

With effect from the date of notice of the calling of the meeting and up to and including the fifth day before the meeting, any shareholder owning registered shares may request the company or the administrator to send to him at a given address the reports of the administrator, the auditors, and also the draft resolutions.

The same right is open to any shareholder whose shares are bearer shares and who provides an intermediary's certificate as provided in the first article of decree no. 83-359 of 2nd May 1983 issued pursuant to article 94-II of the finance law for 1982 relating to the control of transferable securities. The certificate will confirm the non-transferability of shares registered on the share account up to the date of the meeting.

Article 41

The replacement of one or more of the officers of a body corporate may be requested as provided in article 23 of the law of 25th January 1985 at the latest at the time when the court issues its decision on the reconstruction plan. The officer or officers will be summoned at least eight days before the hearing by notice served by a court bailiff or in the manner provided under articles 8 and 9, as the case may be.

The clerk of the court will hear or summon the administrator, if he is not the plaintiff, the creditors' representative and the representatives of the works council or, failing which, the delegates of the work force, and also, if the second paragraph of article 139 of that law applies, the representative of the employees.

The hearings will take place in chambers: the bankruptcy judge is heard on the subject of his report, and the public prosecutor gives his opinion. Judgment is given in open court.

The clerk of the court is responsible for notifying the order to each manager who has been summoned, and to the legal representative of the body corporate. Notice of the order will be given to the authorities referred to in article 19 and also to the persons mentioned in paragraph 2 above. A note of the order will be entered in the registries or directories referred to in article 21.

The officer of the court referred to in the second paragraph of article 23 of the law of 25th January 1985 may also be the administrator.

Article 42

The proposals of the administrator or the debtor, as the case may be, relating to the deferred payment and remission of debts with a view to a plan for the survival of the business are communicated by registered letter requiring acknowledgement of receipt to the creditors' representative and to each creditor who is known or has declared his claim, and also to the institutions referred to in article L.143-11-4 of the employment code.

The letter will contain:

(i) a statement to the effect that an action has been started under article 23 of the law of 25th January 1985, or, if appropriate, a transcript of the decision given by the court;
(ii) an indication of the manner in which the reply should be given, whether by individuals or collectively;
(iii) a copy of the provisions of the second sentence of the second paragraph of article 24 of the law of 25th January 1985.

The following documents will be attached to this letter:

(i) a statement of the assets and liabilities setting out an estimate of the secured and unsecured debt;
(ii) the proposals of the administrator or the debtor and an indication of any guarantees which have been offered;
(iii) the opinion of the creditors' representative, and also of the auditors, if any have been appointed.

The creditors' representative will keep the administrator informed as and when replies are received.

Article 43

If the creditors' representative decides to consult the creditors as a whole, they will meet under his chairmanship at the place and time stated in the letter referred to in the preceding article. In addition, a notice of the meeting may be inserted in a local newspaper carrying legal notices based at or near the debtor's registered address.

The meeting must take place between the fifteenth and twenty-first day following despatch of the letter.

The creditors may be represented by a person authorised by a special power of attorney.

The creditors' representative will report to the creditors on the judicial reconstruction, and also on the survival of the business since the commencement of proceedings.

The agreement of each creditor present in person or by a representative on the proposals for the discharge of liabilities will be obtained in writing.

Failure to reply in writing within thirty days from receipt of the registered letter mentioned in the previous article will be deemed to constitute acceptance.

Article 44

At the latest within fifteen days before expiry of the observation period, the administrator will distribute the report drawn up in accordance with the provisions of article 18 and the last paragraph of article 21 of the law of 25th January 1985 to the authorities and persons referred to in article 25 of that law by registered mail requiring acknowledgement of receipt. The administrator or the debtor, as the case may be, will call a meeting of the works council or, failing which, the delegates of the works force in order to obtain their views on the report.

The debtor and the creditors' representative will make known their views to the administrator within eight days from the date of receipt of the letter referred to in the previous paragraph.

The report, and also the replies to the consultations and the official record referred to in article 25 of the same law, will be filed with the court registry. Each creditor may inform himself of the contents of these documents.

Article 45

If the report has not been filed by the administrator or the debtor, as the case may be, at least eight days before expiry of the observation period, or if it appears that it cannot be so filed, the bankruptcy judge will refer the matter to the court which will decide on the measures to be taken.

Section IV: Conduct of the business during the observation period

Sub-section 1 – Conservatory measures

Article 46

With effect from the order commencing proceedings, the debtor or any third party in possession is bound to return to the administrator on demand the documents and accounts of the business for examination by the administrator.

Article 47

In the event that the annual accounts have not been drawn up or are not placed at his disposal, the administrator will prepare a statement on the position of the business with the help of every available document or piece of information.

Article 48

If the bankruptcy judge has directed seals to be affixed to all or part of the debtor's assets, the procedure will follow the regulations for affixing seals upon death.

Notice of the affixing of seals is given to the bankruptcy judge who has ordered this to be done.

Article 49

An inventory of assets, documents and effects exempted from sealing or remaining unsealed on the decision of the bankruptcy judge will be taken immediately together with the administrator's estimate of their worth, or, if he has not been appointed, the creditors' representative's estimate. A brief description of the condition in which they were found will be noted on the official record of the affixing of seals.

The administrator or the creditors' representative may obtain assistance from any competent valuer.

Article 50

The administrator or the debtor will request the seals to be removed in order to enable the inventory to be taken.

Article 51

The administrator, or if none has been appointed, the creditors' representative, will proceed by taking an inventory of the debtor's assets in the presence of the debtor or of his known heirs, or upon their being summoned.

Two copies of the inventory are prepared. One is filed with the court registry, the other remaining in possession of the administrator or the creditors' representative.

If justified by the nature or value of the assets, the administrator or the creditors' representative may obtain assistance from any person competent in the drawing up of inventories just as in the case of the assets valuation.

Goods detained by customs or sold with reservation of title will be listed separately.

Article 52

The administrator will deliver a certificate permitting participation at the meetings of the company to those officers of the company whose shares representing their rights in the company have been transferred to the special account provided under article 28 of the law of 25th January 1985.

Unless the court determines otherwise, this special account will be closed at the request of the first interested party desiring to do so after the adoption of the reconstruction plan or upon termination of the procedure.

In the event of non-transferability of stocks, shares or certificates of investment or voting rights, or of the transfer of such instruments ordered under articles 23 and 193 of the law of 25th January 1985, the special account will be closed after the decision ordering the transfer or cancelling the non-transferability has been given the force of law.

Article 53

Remuneration and advances under article 30 of the law of 25th January 1985 will be fixed by the bankruptcy judge upon the advice of the administrator and the creditors' representative.

Sub-section 2 – Management of the business

Article 54

Any request to modify the administrator's terms of reference will be made by petition to the court which will give its decision on the basis of the official receiver's report and after obtaining the debtor's views, and also those of the persons referred to in the fourth paragraph of article 31 of the law of 25th January 1985, when these persons are not plaintiffs in the action.

Any decision modifying the administrator's terms of reference will be communicated to the authorities referred to in article 19, and will be noted on the registers or directories provided under article 21.

Article 55

If the bankruptcy judge gives a decision on a request for authorisation submitted by the administrator under the second paragraph of article 33 of the law of 25th January 1985, the clerk of the court will summon the debtor and, if appropriate, the creditors who hold specific security interests in the assets which are being considered for sale.

Article 56

The bankruptcy judge will give his decision on a request for substitution formulated in accordance with the second paragraph of article 34 of the law of 25th January 1985 after hearing the debtor or the administrator, the relevant creditor and the creditors' representative, or after those persons have been summoned by the clerk of the court.

Deletions and registrations of security will be petitioned by the plaintiff, or by the relevant beneficiary, upon demand made by the bankruptcy judge in his directions. The bankruptcy judge will also specify the person responsible for costs. A deletion cannot take effect until the substitute security is in place.

Sub-section 3 – Maintenance of the activity of the business

Article 57

When the court extends the observation period, the administrator must, at the end of each period fixed by the court, inform the bankruptcy judge, the public prosecutor and the creditors' representative of the trading results of the business.

Article 58

Decisions authorising conclusion of a lease management contract during the observation period, or which put into effect the sale of the activity of the business in whole or in part, will be communicated to the authorities referred to in article 19 and will noted on the registers or directories provided under article 21.

Article 59

If the business continues following the conclusion of a lease management contract, the administrator must take account, as provided in article 57, of the lease manager's performance of his undertakings and of the trading results of the business in his statement of the monies received from the lease manager.

The administrator may require the lease manager to hand over to him all documents and information, and may make any investigations necessary in order to accomplish his task.

Article 60

The decision by the bankruptcy judge authorising loans and granting extensions of time to pay in accordance with the paragraph numbered 3 of the second paragraph of article 40 of the law of 25th January 1985 will be noted on the registers or directories provided under article 21.

Article 61

Three months after expiry of the observation period the administrator or the debtor, as the case may be, will file at the court registry the list of unpaid claims referred to in article 40 of the law of 25th January 1985.

The clerk of the court will send a copy of this list to the commissioner, the liquidator and also, at his request, to the agent appointed to distribute the sale proceeds in accordance with the third paragraph of article 102. He will place a notice of this filing in the B.O.D.A.C.C.

The information on the list of these claims is available to all creditors. Disputes regarding the preparation of the list will be declared at the court registry where the proceedings for judicial reconstruction are being held and the administrator and the debtor will be summoned to the hearing. The time limit for disputes is two months from the public announcement provided under the second paragraph above; reference to this will be made in the notice

Article 62

The administrator and the creditors' representative will show the bankruptcy judge and the public prosecutor, if they so request, the balances on the bank and post office accounts of the business, and also the balances on the account at the Central Deposit and Savings Bank.

If the continued activity of the business so requires, the bankruptcy judge may modify the distribution of monies between, on the one hand the accounts of the business, and on the other hand, the accounts opened at the Central Deposit and Savings Bank.

Sub-section 4 – Employees' position

Article 63

The order issued by the bankruptcy judge under article 45 of the law of 25th January 1985 will show the number of employees whose dismissal has been authorised and also the occupations and professional categories involved.

The order will be notified to the works council, or, in default, to the delegates of the work force, and, if the second paragraph of article 139 applies, to the employees' representative.

Article 64

If, under article 63 of the law of 25th January 1985, the administrator or the debtor anticipates redundancies in his proposal, he will annex to the report filed at the court registry, or produce at the hearing, the following documents:

(i) the official record of the meetings of the works council or the delegates of the works force who have been consulted in accordance with article L.321-9 of the employment code;

(ii) the copy of the letter informing the administrative authority of the proposed dismissals in accordance with L.321-8 of the employment code.

The order approving the plan will show the number of employees whose dismissal has been authorised as well as the activities and professional categories involved.

CHAPTER II. DECLARATION AND VERIFICATION OF CLAIMS

Section I: Declaration of claims

Article 65

Proceedings suspended under article 48 of the law of 25th January 1985 will be reinstated at the instance of the plaintiff creditor as soon as he has produced to the court having jurisdiction over the proceedings a copy of the declaration of his claim, and has joined in the action the creditors' representative and also, if appropriate, the administrator.

At the request of the interested party, decisions having the force of law and given after reinstatement of proceedings are entered in the statement of claims by the clerk of the court where the proceedings for judicial reconstruction are being heard.

Article 66

Within eight days from the order commencing proceedings, the creditors' representative will notify the known creditors that they are required to have declared their claims to him within two months from the date of publication in B.O.D.A.C.C. of the order commencing proceedings. This period is increased by two months for creditors domiciled outside metropolitan France.

The notice issued by the creditors' representative will contain the legal and regulatory provisions relating to the time limits and formalities to be observed in the declarations of claims and in any action for disbarring relief.

The institutions referred to in article L.143-11-4 of the employment code will declare the claims set out in the lists provided under article 123 of the law of 25th January 1985 including those which, for whatever reason, they decline to settle. The period for declaration ends fifteen days after expiry of the periods for settlement provided under the third paragraph of article L.143-11-7 of the employment code.

As regards the contracting party referred to in article 37 of the law of 25th January 1985, the period for declarations expires fifteen days after the date on which disclaimer of continued performance is made if this date occurs after the date for publication provided in the first paragraph above.

Article 67

Besides the matters provided in article 51 of the law of 25th January 1985, a declaration of claim will contain:

(i) matters likely to establish the existence and the amount of the claim if the claim is not under a bond; or, in the absence of such evidence, an estimate of the claim if its amount has not yet been determined;
(ii) methods used in the calculation of interest which is still running. This will be noted in the declaration of the amount finally determined;
(iii) a note of the court hearing the claim, if the claim is being litigated.

The supporting documents are annexed by way of a memorandum to the declaration; these may be filed in the form of copies. At any time, the creditors' representative may require production of documents which should have been annexed.

Article 68

The threshold above which a claim must be certified under the third paragraph of article 51 of the law of 25th January 1985 is fixed in the principal sum of ten thousand francs.

An auditor's certificate or, in default, an accountant's certificate and, in the case of social security organisations, an accounts officer's certificate may be required by the bankruptcy judge.

Article 69

The list of creditors drawn up by the debtor under article 52 of the law of 25th January 1985 will indicate the name or firm name, registered office or domicile of each creditor, and will show the amount owing as at the date of commencement of proceedings, any sums falling due in the future, together with their due date, the nature of the claim and of any security or preferential right attaching to such claim.

The list is filed at the court registry and is sent to the creditors' representative within three days of the commencement of proceedings.

Article 70

If the bankruptcy judge is no longer in office, the court will give its decision on disbarring and will determine the amount of the proven claims. A note to this effect is entered by the clerk of the court on the statement of claims.

The costs of the action for disbarring relief are borne by the defaulting creditors.

Section II: Verification of claims

Article 71

In the event of sale of the business as a whole or of liquidation, the commissioner or the liquidator will, within one month of his appointment, submit to the bankruptcy judge a statement referring to the sale price or estimating the assets and the secured and unsecured debt.

After having regard to this statement, and after considering the views of the commissioner, the creditors' representative or the liquidator, as the case may be, the bankruptcy judge will decide whether or not it is appropriate under article 99 of the law of 25th January 1985 to undertake or proceed with the verification of claims.

Article 72

The verification of claims is made by the creditors' representative in the presence of the debtor, or upon his being called, and the administrator, if his terms of reference include undertaking administration of the verification with the assistance of auditors if any such are appointed.

If a claim is disputed other than those referred to in articles 106 and 123 of the law of 25th January 1985, the creditors' representative will notify the creditor by registered letter requiring acknowledgement of receipt. The period of thirty days provided under article 54 of that law runs with effect from receipt of this letter. The letter will specify the subject matter of the dispute; it will indicate the final amount of the claim for which registration is proposed, and will set out by way of reminder the provisions of the aforesaid article 54.

Article 73

The list or lists of claims containing the information to be provided under article 51 of the law of 25th January 1985, and also the proposals of the creditors' representative and the observations of the debtor will be submitted to the bankruptcy judge.

The bankruptcy judge will decide, if appropriate, on the admission of any claims which have not yet fallen due.

If the bankruptcy judge decides on the competence of the court to which he belongs, or on a claim disputed by the debtor or a creditor, the clerk of the court will summon the debtor and creditor by registered letter requiring acknowledgement of receipt. He will notify the creditors' representative or the administrator if appropriate.

Decisions regarding competence or determining a disputed claim are notified to the parties by the clerk of the court within eight days by registered letter requiring acknowledgement of receipt. In every case, the creditors' representative and the administrator are kept informed of the decisions given.

Undisputed decisions to admit claims are notified to the creditors by ordinary letter. The notice will specify on the one hand the amount in which the claim is admitted, and on the other hand any security and preferential rights attached to it.

Article 74

At the request of the Treasury, the bankruptcy judge will, after considering the opinion of the creditors' representative, order final admission to proof of claims admitted provisionally under the second paragraph of article 50 and in accordance with article 106 of the law of 25th January 1985, and which are executory in nature or are not disputed. When the bankruptcy judge is no longer in office, and on the summons of the representative of the Treasury, the President of the Court with jurisdiction will order final admission to proof. The decisions are entered on the statement of claims.

Any decisions given without regard to the provisions of the second paragraph of article 50 and the provisions of article 106 of the law of 25th January 1985 are open to appeal within the time limit provided in the third paragraph of article 157 below.

Article 75

Any person may obtain details at the court registry of the contents of the list of claims on which the decisions of the bankruptcy judge are entered and which specify, in the event of a claim admitted to proof, the amount of the claim and also any security and preferential right attaching to it.

Section III: Verification of claims arising under a contract of employment

Article 76

After having regard to the documents or information provided by the employees, the debtor, the administrator, and also by the employees' representative, the creditors' representative will verify claims arising under any contract of employment. This verification will take place even if there is no verification of unsecured claims.

If the employees' representative has not been involved in the verification procedure, the schedules of claims provided under article 123 of the law of 25th January 1985 will be sent to him as and when drawn up and, at the latest, three days or more before expiry of the period determined under article L.143-11-7 of the employment code in the case of the claims referred to in the paragraphs numbered 1 and 3 of this article, and ten days or more before expiry of the period determined under the paragraphs numbered 2 and 4 of the same article in the case of the claims referred to in those paragraphs. The creditors' representative will make available to the employees' representative the items from which the lists were drawn up and in particular the pay book and the personnel register. The employees' representative will sign the schedules, if necessary adding his reservations or other remarks. In the absence of signature the bankruptcy judge will confirm that the employees' representative has nevertheless completed his task.

At the instance of the creditors' representative the schedules will be certified by the bankruptcy judge. They will then be submitted by the creditors' representative to the institutions referred to in article L.143-11-4 of the employment code before expiry of the time limits provided for each class of claims in the aforesaid article L.143-11-7.

Article 77

The schedules of claims arising out of contracts of employment will identify each employee, the nature of his contract of employment, the date of commencement of his employment with the business, the position occupied and its description, whether or not he holds any representative status within the business, the date of breach of the contract of employment, and amounts already paid and still outstanding. The total amount will be calculated after the usual deductions and any deductions required by law.

Article 78

The creditors' representative will inform each employee by every available means of the nature and amount of admitted or rejected claims and will inform each employee of the date of filing of the claims at the court registry. He will remind the employees that the time limit provided under article 123 of the law of 25th January 1985 beyond which claims will be barred runs from and including the date of posting of public notice provided under the third paragraph below. Employees whose claims are admitted to proof will be informed of this at the time of payment.

An employee whose claim has been admitted to proof may be relieved from the time bar by the conciliation board within the period provided in the second paragraph of article 53 of that law. Relief from time bar may also accrue for the benefit of the institutions referred to in article L.143-11-4 of the employment code.

The public notification referred to in article 123 of that law is made at the instigation of the creditors' representative by the posting of a notice to the effect that all the lists of claims have been filed at the court registry. This posting will take place at the premises of the business and at its registered office, and on the gates of its premises, and also at the other works premises of the business and on their gates. It is effected at the latest three months from expiry of the final guarantee period provided under article L.143-11-1 of the employment code.

The notice, which is signed by the creditors' representative, is dated with the date of posting at the business premises. Time runs from this date for the purposes of the time bar provided under the aforesaid article 123.

If it is not possible to post the notices at the registered office of the business or at its business premises, the posting is effected at the town hall in the judicial district where the registered office or the business premises are located.

Article 79

The institutions referred to in article L.143-11-4 of the employment code will make known to the creditors' representative their refusal to settle a claim set out in a schedule within the same periods of time as those provided under article L.143-11-7 of the code in the case of payment in of outstanding amounts. These institutions will indicate the nature and the amount of the rejected claim and will also set out their grounds for rejection.

The creditors' representative will notify the employee of the refusal by the institution referred to above to settle the claim and will advise the employees' representative of the matter.

Article 80

The creditors' representative, the commissioner or the liquidator will restore to the institutions referred to in article L.143-11-4 of the employment code any sums advanced by the institutions which have not been collected by the employees before expiry of the validity of their claim for payment. These institutions will pay over to those employees who demand payment the amounts due to them.

Article 81

The administrator or the debtor, as the case may be, will give to the creditors' representative all useful information on any actions being heard before the conciliation board at the time of commencement of proceedings.

Section IV: Statement of claims

Article 82

The lists of claims and the schedules of claims arising from the employment contract will together constitute the statement of claims within the meaning of article 103 of the law of 25th January 1985.

Article 83

The clerk of the court will arrange for a notice to be published in the B.O.D.A.C.C. to the effect that the statement of claims has been finally constituted and filed at the court registry. The period within which the statement may be challenged is fifteen days from the date of publication; reference to this will be made in the notice.

Article 84

Claims by way of challenge from third parties are made by notice filed at the court registry and will be noted on the statement of claims by the clerk of the court. The clerk of the court will summon the interested parties by registered letter acquiring acknowledgement of receipt and will notify the creditors' representative and the administrator.

Within eight days the clerk of the court will notify them of the decisions of the bankruptcy judge by registered letter acquiring acknowledgement of receipt. The decisions are also notified to the creditors' representative and the administrator, if appropriate.

Article 85

Any creditor whose rights have been recognised in the form of a decision having the force of law will send a certified copy of the decision to the clerk of the court where the proceedings for judicial reconstruction are being heard. The clerk of the court will record the decision on the statement of claims.

CHAPTER III. PLAN FOR SURVIVAL OR SALE OF THE BUSINESS

Section I: Provisions common to all decisions of the court regarding the plan

Article 86

As soon as the administration report or the proposed plan has been filed at the court registry, the clerk of the court will, by registered letter requiring acknowledgement of receipt, summon before the court in chambers the debtor and representatives of the works council or, failing which, the delegates of the works force or, in the circumstances provided in the second paragraph of article 139 of the law of 25th January 1985, the employees' representative.

The date of the hearing will be notified to the public prosecutor, the administrator and the creditors' representative.

Every creditor or group of creditors representing at least 15% of the total amount of declared claims will be heard by the court if a reasoned submission to that effect has been lodged with the court registry.

Article 87

The order approving or rejecting the plan for survival or sale of the business is given in open court.

A copy of the order will be sent immediately by the clerk of the court to the authorities referred to in article 19 and also to the State Commissioner under the conditions provided in the paragraph numbered 3 of this article.

The order approving the plan is notified officially as provided in article 21.

Article 88

The administrator is accountable to the bankruptcy judge, if he still holds office, or to the president of the court, for the performance of those matters necessary to set the plan in motion in accordance with article 66 of the law of 25th January 1985.

The creditors' representative is accountable for his responsibilities to the bankruptcy judge who will supervise the termination of these once he is satisfied that the verification of claims has been completed and the amounts due to the employees have been paid as provided under article L.143-11-7 of the employment code.

The administrator and the creditors' representative will send to the debtor by way of notice, and will file at the court registry, within the two months following completion of their responsibilities, a copy of their accounts relating to receipts and expenses made through the Central Deposit and Savings Bank. These are open to inspection by every creditor at the court registry.

The debtor has a period of eight days from and including the date of notification within which to challenge the accounts in court by declaration filed at the court registry.

Article 89

The bankruptcy judge's functions will terminate as from presentation of the final accounts of the administrator and the creditors' representative.

Article 90

Any actions in which the administrator or the creditors' representative are parties and which have not finished by the time when these officers have completed their responsibilities, will be pursued by the scheme commissioner, or if he no longer holds office, by an ad hoc officer appointed by the court where the proceedings for judicial reconstruction were heard.

Article 91

The bankruptcy judge, or if he no longer holds office, the president of the court, will authorise the debtor or the purchaser to pay the commissioner the amounts necessary to enable the latter to accomplish his task.

Article 92

If replacement of the commissioner has been requested by the public prosecutor, or of the court's own motion, the interested party will be summoned in accordance with the formalities and procedure provided under articles 8 or 9 as the case may be.

Article 93

In the event of survival of the business following partial sales, the court may appoint one commissioner to be responsible for the implementation of all the operations.

Article 94

Any failure on the part of the debtor, the purchaser or any other person to carry out the plan will be noted by the commissioner in a report addressed to the president of the court and the public prosecutor.

The report will set out the views of the head of the business and will conclude by proposing action to be taken with the objective of enabling the plan to be carried out.

The commissioner will account to the president of the court for performance of his responsibilities. He will submit his accounts to the court registry within two months following completion of his task. The debtor or the purchaser, as the case may be, may challenge these accounts in accordance with the formalities and time limits provided under the fourth paragraph of article 88.

Article 95

Applications made under article 68 of the law of 25th January 1985 are made by way of statement by the debtor or purchaser filed at the court registry.

The clerk of the court will summon the representatives of the works council or, in default, the delegates of the works force appointed in accordance with article 12 to a hearing in chambers by registered letter requiring acknowledgement of receipt. He will notify the date of the hearing to the public prosecutor as well as to the commissioner.

When the modification affects the conditions for settling the liabilities of the business, the debtor will inform those creditors who are interested. In this event, every creditor, or group of interested creditors representing at least 15% of the total amount of claims admitted to proof, will be heard on application and to this end should file a reasoned statement at the court registry.

The court will give its decision in open court. The order is served and formally notified in accordance with the provisions of article 97 below.

Article 96

A copy of the order modifying the plan will be sent to the authorities referred to in articles 19 and 87. The order is officially publicised as provided in article 21.

Section II: Survival of the business

Article 97

The order approving or rejecting the plan for survival of the business is served at the instance of the clerk of the court within eight days of the date of the order on those persons other than the public prosecutor who are entitled to appeal. In addition the order is notified by the clerk of the court to every person responsible for execution of the order of accordance with article 62 of the law of 25th January 1985.

Article 98

The authorisation provided under article 70 of the law of 25th January 1985 is given by the court after having regard to the report submitted by the commissioner.

Article 99

A meeting of the partners, or an extraordinary general meeting, will be called in accordance with the formalities and within the time limits provided in articles 33 to 40 for the purpose of altering the articles of association in order to conform with the provisions of the plan.

Article 100

Any substitution of security as provided under article 78 of the law of 25th January 1985 will be ordered by the court where the proceedings for judicial reconstruction are being heard. The debtor, the creditor, and the commissioner are heard by the court, or are summoned to appear by the clerk of the court.

Deletion or registration of securities will be requested by the plaintiff or the beneficiary by way of application contained in the order. This will also identify the person responsible for costs. Deletion may not occur before the substitute security is in place.

Article 101

The maximum amount for claims which must be paid without deduction or delay in accordance with article 76 of the law of 25th January 1985 is 250 FFrs.

Article 102

The sale proceeds or a proportion of the sale proceeds of an asset referred to in articles 34 and 78 of the law of 25th January 1985 is paid into the Central Deposit and Savings Bank. The commissioner or the liquidator, as the case may be, will allocate the proceeds among the creditors, effect payment and proceed with deletion of the registrations.

In the event of a sale of real estate, the proceeds are paid after completion of the formalities for release of hypothecations prescribed by article 2181 and the following articles of the civil code, and in accordance with the priority proceedings described in articles 140 to 151 below.

If, when an asset referred to in article 78 of the aforesaid law is sold, the commissioner no longer holds office, distribution of the proceeds is made by an ad hoc officer of the court appointed by the president of the court where the proceedings are being heard.

Article 103

The debtor will make an annual report on the performance of his financial commitments within the time limits provided in the plan. He will submit this to the scheme commissioner and, if the latter is no longer in office, to the president of the court. This report is filed with the court registry where it is open to inspection by every creditor.

Section III: Sale of the business

Article 104

The sale of assets referred to in the last paragraph of article 81 of the law of 25th January 1985 is effected by the commissioner.

In this event, the bankruptcy judge will remain in office in order to perform the duties conferred on him by articles 154–156 of the aforesaid law.

The proceeds arising from the transfer of real estate will be allocated in accordance with the rules for priority proceedings provided in articles 140–151 below.

Article 105

When the court is required to rule on the transfer of the contracts referred to in article 86 of the law of 25th January 1985 or on the transfer of a prior charge referred to in article 93, the contracting party or parties, or the person entitled to the prior charge, will be summoned before the court at the instance of the clerk of the court by registered letter requiring acknowledgement of receipt.

Article 106

After completion of the transfer and the verification of claims, the bankruptcy judge will report to the court with a view to terminating the proceedings.

The order terminating the proceedings will be officially publicised as provided in article 21.

Article 107

For the purposes of article 90 of the law of 25th January 1985, the purchaser will be summoned by the clerk of the court to appear before the court in chambers.

Article 108

In the case provided under the last paragraph of article 93 of the law of 25th January 1985, the purchaser will inform the commissioner in advance of every sale of a transferred asset. The commissioner will notify those creditors entitled to institute proceedings.

Article 109

In a report addressed to the president of the court and the public prosecutor the commissioner will refer to any damage to the items under lease management contract, and also to any failure by the contract manager in the performance of his obligations. The report will set out the observations of the contract manager and will conclude with proposals for action to be taken with a view to assisting performance of the plan.

PART II
SIMPLIFIED PROCEDURE

Article 110

The provisions of part I above and of part III and the following parts apply to the simplified procedure to the extent that they do not conflict with the provisions of this part.

Article 111

After the parties and the persons referred to in article 6 of the law of 25th January 1985 have been heard in chambers, the court will commence proceedings by ordering the inquiry provided in article 140 of that law. The court may inform the parties present of the date of the hearing when the decision will be given regarding the enquiry report in accordance with article 142 of that law. The announcement of this date will replace the requirement to summons the parties. Persons not present or represented will be advised through the clerk of the court of the date of the hearing. The bankruptcy judge's enquiry report may be given orally.

Article 112

In the order determining survival of the business with a view to preparation of a proposal for a reconstruction plan the court will appoint the expert referred to in the second paragraph of article 143 of that law and whose assistance is considered necessary.

This appointment may be made at a later stage; it may be made of the court's own motion, or at the request of the debtor or the administrator, in each case following the report of the bankruptcy judge.

The order determining survival of the business is distributed to the authorities mentioned in article 19. It is noted on the registers and directories provided under article 21.

Article 113

One month after the order referred to in the previous paragraph, the creditors' representative and the administrator, if such has been appointed, will report to the bankruptcy judge and the public prosecutor on the progress of the proceedings and the situation of the business.

Article 114

In the absence of the administrator, the creditors' representative will perform the duties for which the administrator is responsible under article 52.

Article 115

Through the clerk of the court the bankruptcy judge will notify the legal representative of the company of the amount by which the capital should be increased for proposal before the extraordinary general meeting or before the partners in meeting in order to reconstitute the capital of the business.

Article 116

No later than fifteen days before expiry of the period provided under the first paragraph of article 143 of the law of 25th January 1985, the administrator or the debtor will distribute to the persons and authorities referred to in article 25 and in the second paragraph of article 139 of that law his proposal for a reconstruction plan to be prepared in accordance with paragraphs 3–5 of article 18 and the last paragraph of article 21 of that law. He will call a meeting of the delegates of the works force in order to obtain their views on the report.

The debtor, if the proposal has been distributed by the administrator, and also the creditors' representative and the employees' representative in the case referred to in the second paragraph of article 139 (paragraph 2) of the law of 25th January 1985, will make known their views to the administrator or the debtor as the case may be, and also to the bankruptcy judge within eight days following the date of receipt of the letter.

The proposed plan, the replies to the consultations and also the official record of the meetings of the delegates of the works force or the opinion of the employees' representative, are filed at the court registry.

Article 117

If the proposed plan has not been filed at the court registry at least five days before expiry of the observation period, or it if appears that this is not possible, the bankruptcy judge will refer the matter to the court. The court will determine the measures to be taken.

Article 118

When the proposed plan anticipates dismissals on economic grounds, the bankruptcy judge will annex the following documents to his report:

1. The official record of the meetings of the delegates of the works force consulted in accordance with article L.321-9 of the employment code or, in the circumstances provided under the second paragraph of article 139 of the law of 25th January 1985, the opinion of the employees' representative.
2. The copy of the letter informing the administrative authority of the proposed dismissals in accordance with L.321-8 of the employment code.

PART III
COMPULSORY LIQUIDATION

CHAPTER I. THE LIQUIDATOR

Article 119

The order for compulsory liquidation is given in open court. It is served at the instance of the clerk of the court on those persons other than the public prosecutor who are entitled to appeal. The order will be notified officially as provided in article 21. One copy of the order will be sent immediately by the clerk of the court to the authorities referred to in article 19.

Within time limits which are compatible with the time-barring provisions of article 53 of the law of 25th January 1985, the court may order extension of the period for declaration of claims which runs from publication of the order in B.O.D.A.C.C. In this event the official notice will refer to the extension of the period for declaration of claims.

Article 120

The liquidator, or the administrator responsible for the administration of the business after issue of the order for compulsory liquidation, will keep the bankruptcy judge and the public prosecutor informed of the trading results of the business up to expiry of the period during which it was carried on.

Article 121

The liquidator may operate under his signature the bank or post office accounts of the debtor for a period of six months from the date of the liquidation order. Beyond this period, use of these accounts is dependent on the authorisation of the bankruptcy judge and the opinion of the public prosecutor.

Article 122

The liquidator will complete the list of claims referred to in article 61. He will file the list at the court registry. The clerk of the court will publish a notice to this effect in B.O.D.A.C.C.

Creditors information, and disputes relating to the drawing up of the list, are governed by the provisions of the third paragraph of article 61 above. The liquidator will be summoned before the court at such time and place as the administrator may determine.

Article 123

Every three months the liquidator will submit a report to the bankruptcy judge and the public prosecutor setting out:

1. The various transactions dealing with realisation of assets;
2. The total amount paid into the Central Savings and Deposit Bank;
3. A statement of distributions to creditors.

Article 124

If, in accordance with article 158 of the law of 25th January 1985, it is appropriate for the bankruptcy judge to authorise the liquidator to settle or compromise a claim, the clerk of the court will, three days before issue of the bankruptcy judge's decision, summon the debtor to be heard before the bankruptcy judge, and will attach a copy of the liquidator's petition.

If the settlement or compromise must be submitted to the court for approval, the debtor will be summoned upon the same conditions.

Article 124-I

The decision granting the extensions of time referred to in the penultimate paragraph of article 154 of the law of 25th January 1985 will, even if issued subsequently, determine the rental compensation payable by the debtor.

CHAPTER II. REALISATION OF ASSETS

Section I: Sale of real property

Sub-section I – Forced sale by public auction or by agreed public tender

I. PROVISIONS COMMON TO BOTH METHODS

Article 125

The bankruptcy judge who authorises the sale of real estate by public auction or by agreed public tender as provided in article 154 of the law of 25th January 1985 will determine:

1. The reserve price for each of the assets for sale and the main conditions of sale;
2. The means for advertising the sale, having regard to the value, nature and location of the assets.

If the sale is at the instigation of a creditor as provided in article 161 of that law, the reserve price will be determined by agreement with the plaintiff creditor.

The bankruptcy judge may stipulate that, in the absence of bids reaching this reserve, the sale can proceed on the basis of a lower reserve price determined by him. He may, if the value and status of the assets justify such a measure, arrange for them to be appraised for sale either as a whole or in parts.

Article 126

The directions for sale will be officially notified through the clerk of the court in such manner as the bankruptcy judge may determine to both the debtor and those registered creditors whose names appear in the order at their chosen domicile.

The directions for sale replace the official order provided under articles 2217 of the civil code and 673 of the civil procedure code; at the instance of the liquidator or the plaintiff creditor, the directions will be officially notified at the hypothecation registry where the assets are located under the conditions provided for the official order in article 674 of the civil procedure code.

The hypothecation registrar will carry out the notification formalities for the directions even though official orders regarding the sale have already been published. Such official orders will cease to take effect as from publication of the directions for sale.

Article 127

The plaintiff, or the notary's clerk, will draw up a register.

The directions authorising the sale will appear in the register, as will the assets for sale, the reserve price, the conditions for sale and the methods for payment of the price in accordance with the regulations provided in article 140.

Article 128

The liquidator may not be declared highest bidder in the auction of the debtor's real estate, either in his own name or in the capacity of creditors' representative.

2. PARTICULAR PROVISIONS RELATING TO THE FORCED SALE OF REAL ESTATE

Article 129

The forced sale of real estate is subject to the provisions of part XII of book V of the code of civil procedure to the extent that these do not derogate from the provisions of this decree.

Article 130

The order authorising the forced sale of real estate issued on the application of the liquidator or a plaintiff creditor will contain, besides the matters referred to in article 125 above, the statements required by sub-paragraphs 4, 5, 6 and 7 of the second paragraph of article 673 of the civil procedure code.

Article 131

The bankruptcy judge may authorise the liquidator or the creditor to proceed simultaneously with the sale of more than one item of real estate, even if these are located in judicial districts which are far apart from each other.

He will decide whether the sale of these properties will take place before the court of first instance in the judicial district where each is located, or before the court in the judicial district where the debtor is domiciled or where the registered office of the business is located.

3. PARTICULAR PROVISIONS RELATING TO SALE BY AGREED PUBLIC TENDER

Article 132

The directions authorising sale by agreed public tender will contain, besides the matters referred to in article 125, the statements required by sub-paragraphs 4 and 5 of the second paragraph of article 673 of the civil procedure code. The directions will appoint the notary who will carry out the sale.

Article 133

At least two months before the date fixed for the sale, the notary will inform the registered creditors whose names appear on the statement delivered after publication of the directions by registered letter requiring acknowledgement of receipt that they should take note of the register filed in his office. He will record in the register their remarks and observations one month before the sale date. In the same letter, the notary will summon the creditors to the sale.

The liquidator and the debtor will be summoned by the notary to the sale at least one month in advance.

Article 134

Bids may be made without using the services of a lawyer. If no bid reaches the reserved price, the notary will determine the highest offer and may confer provisional title on the basis of the amount of this offer. The bankruptcy judge who fixed the reserve price, upon the request of the notary or any other interested party, may either declare the tender effective and the sale completed, or order a new sale to take place in accordance with one of the methods prescribed in article 154 of the law of 25th January 1985. If the new sale is an auction, he will fix the period within which it will take place, such period not to be less than fifteen days, and also the reserve price and the means by which the sale will be advertised.

Article 135

In the ten days following the sale by public tender, any person may tender a higher bid in a minimum amount of at least ten per cent above the sale price by declaration to the court registry at the court of first instance where the notary resides who carried out the sale.

The over-bidder will make this declaration by serving it personally on the highest bidder or at his address within the time limit fixed under article 709 of the code of civil procedure, and will inform the notary accordingly. The court, in any order validating the over-bid, will return the new highest public tender to the same notary who will proceed in accordance with the register already established.

If a second public tender takes place after an over-bid, no other over-bid may take place in respect of the same properties.

Article 136

If the bidder fails to pay the price bid, proceedings will be instituted before the civil court of first instance in the judicial district where the notary resides who carried out the sale. The certificate to the effect that the highest bidder has not performed the terms and conditions of the public tender will be filed by the liquidator. The official record of the sale by public tender will be filed at the registry of the civil court of first instance.

Article 137

Sale by agreed public tender is subject to the provisions of articles 701, 705–707, 711–713, 733–714(b) and 742 of the code of civil procedure.

Sub-section 2 – Sale by private contract

Article 138

The authority for the sale of one or more items of real estate by private contract under article 154 of the law of 25th January 1985 will set out the price of each property and the main conditions of sale.

The directions are notified officially in accordance with the first paragraph of article 126.

The liquidator will draw up the contracts necessary to effect the sale. He may not acquire for himself real estate belonging to the debtor either in his own name or in the capacity of creditors' representative.

Section II: Sale of production units

Article 139

The liquidator will assemble the opinions of the persons referred to in the fifth paragraph of article 155 of the law of 25th January 1985 on the offers received in accordance with that article. These opinions are attached to the sale application together with the observations of the debtor, the auditors if such have been appointed, and also the official minutes of the meetings of the works council, or, failing which, the delegates of the works force, and, under the conditions provided in the second paragraph of article 139 of that law, the opinion of the creditors' representative.

At his request, the public prosecutor will receive a copy of the purchase offer.

The liquidator will draw up the contracts necessary for completion of the sale. He may not acquire for himself any assets belonging to the debtor either in his own name or in the capacity of creditors' representative.

Section III: Priority of payment

Article 140

On penalty of resale on default terms at the instance of the liquidator, the winning bidder will arrange for the tender award or order to be recorded at the hypothecation registry within two months of its date of issue, and, in the event of appeal, within two months of the order confirming the decision.

Within three months of the auction, the winning bidder will pay into the deposit account opened by the liquidator at the Central Deposit and Savings Bank the total amount of the tender price including interest at the official court rate from the date when the sale became final up to the date of payment. If this time limit is exceeded, the liquidator will invite him by registered letter requiring acknowledgement of receipt to effect payment on penalty of resale on default terms.

Sub-section 1 – Priority ranking

Article 141

As soon as the sale has been recorded, the liquidator will request the hypothecations registrar to produce the statement of recorded entries in accordance with article 2196 of the civil code with a view to the regulation of priority among the creditors and the distribution of the sale proceeds.

In the case of private sale, after completion of the hypothecation redemption formalities provided in article 2181 and the following articles of the civil code and payment of the proceeds of sale into the Central Deposit and Savings Bank, the liquidator will, either on his own motion, or at the request of the purchaser or of any interested party, proceed with the commencement of priority proceedings.

Article 142

After payment in of the sale proceeds in the case of public tender, or completion of redemption formalities in the case of private sale, the liquidator will draw up the statement of priorities based on the registered entries, the claims admitted to proof, and the list of creditors referred to in article 40 of the law of 25th January 1985. He may, if he considers it would be useful to do so, call a meeting of the registered creditors and the winning bidder or the purchaser. The statement is filed at his instance at the registry of the court where the proceedings for judicial reconstruction were heard. This statement is open to inspection by any person.

The clerk of the court will advise the creditors and the winning bidder or the purchaser of the filing of the statement of priorities by notice in one or more official legal gazette and in a notice in B.O.D.A.C.C. naming the official legal gazette which carried the first announcement and referring to the time limit for appeals provided in article 148.

Unless the bankruptcy judge waives the requirement, the clerk of the court will distribute to each prior ranking creditor and to each creditor secured by entry registered against the real estate of the business, a copy of the statement of priorities, and will refer them to the methods of appeal and time limits provided in article 148.

Article 143

In the case of a registered preservation order, the creditor will only obtain payment against presentation of evidence of final registration as provided under article 54 of the civil procedure code. In the case of cancellation of the preservation order any interested party may require re-opening of the priority proceedings.

Article 144

If the priority is not contested, the liquidator is bound within the fifteen days which follow expiry of the time limit provided in the first paragraph of article 148 to proceed with bringing the priority proceedings to an end. He will file the official record of the termination of priority proceedings at the registry of the court where the proceedings for judicial reconstruction were heard.

Interest and arrears due to prior ranking creditors will cease to run against the debtor from the date of filing of the official record of termination of the priority ranking proceedings.

Sub-section 2 – Deletion of registered entries

Article 145

When the sale proceeds have been paid in accordance with the methods provided under article 140 and the creditors have not cancelled the registered entries relating to their security, the liquidator will cause deletion of the registered entries to be announced. The registrar of the civil court of first instance where the proceedings for judicial reconstruction were heard or in the jurisdictional district where these proceedings took place will have jurisdiction for this purpose. The liquidator will attach to his summons the statement of registered entries, the statement of priorities and documents supporting advance payment of the costs of sale referred to in article 713 of the civil procedure code. He will forward to the court the official record of the termination of priority ranking proceedings when these have been drawn up.

After completion of the redemption formalities and payment of the sale proceeds, the purchaser may request the court registrar referred to in the previous paragraph to order the deletion of registered entries. He will attach to his summons a statement of the registered entries and the documents supporting advance payment of the costs of sale referred to above.

The clerk at this court will notify those creditors who have not cancelled the registered entries relating to their security by registered letter requiring acknowledgement of receipt to their chosen address that they have thirty days from the date of despatch of the registered letter within which to raise objections.

The court registrar will issue his decision regarding any objections and will order deletion of the registered entries.

Article 146

The liquidator will submit to the hypothecations registrar a copy of the official record of the termination of priority proceedings and of either the order of the court registrar giving effect to the deletion of the registered entries or the deed by which the creditors cancelled the registered entries relating to their security.

The registrar will proceed with the deletion of the registered entries but remains bound to effect the final registration provided under article 54 of the civil procedure code.

Article 147

The liquidator will calculate the expenses incurred in the deletion of the registered entries and in pursuing the priority proceedings. These expenses will rank in priority in accordance with the regulations provided in article 40 of the law of 25th January 1985. In addition he will settle the expenses of every creditor whose claim has been satisfied, determine the amounts due to them and effect payment.

Sub-section 3 – Objections

Article 148

Objections will be formulated within thirty days of notice in B.O.D.A.C.C. of the filing of the statement of priorities. They are made by way of motion filed at the court of first instance where the proceedings for judicial reconstruction were heard or in the judicial district where the proceedings took place.

On penalty of being struck out on grounds of inadmissibility, the objection is notified within ten days of filing at the court registry by deed duly served by an agent of the court on the creditors who are parties to the suit, and on the liquidator. This deed will provide that the creditors or the liquidator should brief their lawyers to appear within fifteen days from the date of notification of the objection.

The objections are subject to the provisions of articles 761–764, and 766 and 788 of the civil procedure code.

Article 149

In the event of objections, the liquidator may nevertheless determine the priority ranking of, and deliver payment orders for, claims ranking ahead of the disputed claims. He may even determine the priority ranking for claims ranking after, if a sufficient sum is reserved for the disputed claims.

Article 150

In the course of the eight days following expiry of the time limit for appeal and in the case of an appeal within eight days of service of the decree, the liquidator will give his final ruling on the ranking of disputed claims and on the claims ranking after them in accordance with articles 144–147.

Article 151

In the event of a sale on default terms arising in the course of the priority proceedings, and even after the liquidator's final ruling, the liquidator will amend the statement of priorities and the amount due to the creditors registered on the official record of the proceedings following the result of the sale by public tender, and will effect payment accordingly.

CHAPTER III. TERMINATION OF OPERATIONS

Article 152

The order pronouncing termination of proceedings for extinction of liabilities or for insufficiency of assets will be officially published as provided in article 21.

Article 153

The liquidator will submit his accounts to the debtor and will file these at the court registry within three months of the termination of compulsory liquidation operations.

These accounts will give full details of the realisation of the assets of the business and of the distribution of the proceeds of sale. They are open to inspection by any creditor at the court registry.

The debtor may dispute these accounts in the manner provided in the fourth paragraph of article 88.

Article 154

On the directions of the president of the court issued on petition, a creditor whose claim has been admitted to proof and whose right of individual action has been restored in accordance with article 169 of the law of 25th January 1985, is entitled to claim title as provided under the third paragraph of that article.

In the case provided in the first paragraph of article 169 of that law, the directions are issued upon the debtor being heard by or summoned before the court.

The directions will confirm this creditor's final admission to proof and also the order terminating compulsory liquidation on the grounds of insufficiency of assets; the directions will contain the demand to pay and are drawn up as an enforceable order by the clerk of the court.

PART IV
APPEALS

Article 155

Orders and directions issued in judicial reconstruction and liquidation matters are provisionally enforceable as a matter of right except for those referred to in articles 34, 78, and in the second paragraph of article 159 of the law of 25th January 1985, and also except for those pronouncing personal bankruptcy or the prohibition provided under article 192 of that law.

Provisional execution of the judgments referred to in the second paragraph of article 177 of that law may only be stayed in the event of appeal by the senior presiding judge of the Court of Appeal, sitting in chambers, if the grounds supporting the appeal appear to have substance. The clerk of the Court of Appeal will inform the clerk of the court accordingly as soon as the decision of the senior presiding judge approving provisional execution has been issued.

Article 156

Appeals against decisions in judicial reconstruction and liquidation matters, in bankruptcy or other measures, may be filed by the parties themselves, or by third parties if admissible, by motion at the court registry within ten days of the date of issue of the decision.

However, in the case of decisions requiring the formality of publication in a gazette containing legal announcements or in B.O.D.A.C.C., the time limit will only run from the date of publication in B.O.D.A.C.C.

Article 157

The time limit for appeal by the public prosecutor and the transferee of the business against the orders referred to in article 174 of the law of 25th January 1985 is ten days from the date of issue of the order.

The clerk of the court will inform the contracting party in writing at the latest within forty-eight hours of the issue of the order in the circumstances provided under article 86 of the law of 25th January 1985, and the lessor in the circumstances provided under the third paragraph of article 82 of that law. The time limit for appeal by the contracting party and the lessor is ten days from the date of issue of the order.

The time limit for appeal against other decisions is ten days from the date of notification of the parties, or from receipt of the opinion given to the public prosecutor in the manner set out in article 19.

Article 158

Appeal by the public prosecutor is filed by a motion for appeal submitted or addressed to the registry of the Court of Appeal.

When this motion is effected by post, the date of the making of the appeal is the date of despatch.

Article 159

The person who appeals in the name of a works council or the delegates of the works force, or the employees' representative in the case provided under article 139 of the law of 25th January 1985, must prove his authority or is liable to be declared inadmissible.

Article 160

Appeal against the orders referred to in articles 171 and 174 of the law of 25th January 1985 will be drawn up, investigated and heard in accordance with the rules of procedure for cases requiring legal representation set out in articles 901–925 of the new code of civil procedure, subject as follows:

I Officers of the court who are not appellants must be summoned. In every case the public prosecutor will be notified of the date of the hearing.

II Appeal against orders approving or rejecting the plan for the sale of the business is subject to fixed day procedure.

III By way of exception to article 905 of the new code of civil procedure and save for cases subject to fixed day procedure, the filing of the motion for appeal constitutes application for entry on the cause list in cases other than those referred to in paragraph II above.

The case will then proceed in accordance with the provisions of the second paragraph of article 910 of the new code of civil procedure. The presiding judge may however decide that the proceedings will be investigated in accordance with the conditions set out in the first paragraph of the same article.

IV If they are not parties to the appeal, the following persons will be summoned to be heard by the court: the creditors' representative, the representatives of the works council, or the delegates of the works force and, in the circumstances provided under the second paragraph of article 139 of that law, the employees' representative and also, as the case may be, the purchaser, the contracting party referred to in article 86 of that law, the person entitled to the prior charge referred to in article 93 of that law, or the person entitled to the management contract. The summons is by ordinary letter from the clerk of the court.

V No interim application will be admitted within the ten days preceding the hearing date.

VI The Court of Appeal decision on the merits of the case will be given within four months following issue of the orders referred to in article 174 of the law of 25th January 1985.

Article 161

Within eight days of issue of the award of the court, the registrar of the Court of Appeal will send a copy of the award to the clerk of the civil court of first instance in order to enable the official notice formalities to be completed in accordance with article 21 if the award reverses a decision which has been officially notified.

He will notify the award to the parties by registered letter requiring acknowledgement of receipt and to the public prosecutor by recorded delivery. He will inform the persons referred to in article 160 of the issue of the award.

Article 162

Appeal to the Supreme Court on behalf of the director of public prosecutions is made by motion filed at the Supreme Court registry in accordance with the regulations provided in article 158.

PART V
SPECIAL PROVISIONS FOR BODIES CORPORATE AND THEIR OFFICERS

Article 163

The court competent to give judgment in the cases provided in articles 180, 181 and 182 of the law of 25th January 1985 is the same court which has ordered the judicial reconstruction of the incorporated body.

Article 164

In accordance with articles 180 to 182 of that law, the officer or officers of an incorporated body who are parties to the proceedings are summoned by due service of process at least eight days before they are due to be heard before the court in chambers, or as provided in articles 8 or 9.

The officers of the court referred to in article 183 of the law of 25th January 1985 are summoned by the clerk of the court if they are not plaintiffs in the proceedings.

The court will give its decision in open court and the bankruptcy judge will be heard on the subject of his report.

Article 165

When the officer of an incorporated body is already subject to proceedings for judicial reconstruction or liquidation, the total amount of the liabilities for which this officer is held to be responsible is determined by the court which has ordered the judicial reconstruction of the incorporated body after the creditors' representative or the liquidator appointed in the proceedings in respect of the officer have been made parties. At the request of the officer of the court who has instituted the proceedings, the decision of the court is entered in the statement of claims in the proceedings for judicial reconstruction in respect of the officer of the incorporated body.

Article 166

If judicial reconstruction is ordered in accordance with article 182 of the law of 25th January 1985 in respect of an officer who is already subject to proceedings for judicial reconstruction, the proceedings will be heard before the court which has already ordered judicial reconstruction in respect of that officer.

Creditors in the judicial reconstruction of an incorporated body are admitted as of right in the judicial reconstruction of its officer.

The date of cessation of payments in respect of the officer may not be after the date provided in the penultimate paragraph of article 182 of the law of 25th January 1985.

Article 167

Orders of the court given in accordance with articles 180–182 of the law of 25th January 1985 are sent by the clerk of the court to the authorities referred to in article 19. They will be noted in the registries and directories provided in article 21.

Only orders of the court given in accordance with articles 181 and 182 of that law will be officially notified in the form of an extract published in a gazette carrying legal announcements and in B.O.D.A.C.C. under the conditions provided in article 21. Publication in B.O.D.A.C.C. is made in respect of the partners in or officers of an incorporated body recorded in the register of commerce and companies under the same number as that incorporated body, and, if they are also traders, publication is additionally made in respect of their personal registration number at that registry.

Article 168

If the officers of the court referred to in article 191 of the law of 25th January 1985 have knowledge of the facts described in articles 187–190 of that law, they must inform the public prosecutor and the bankruptcy judge accordingly.

Article 169

In the circumstances provided under articles 187–190 of the law of 25th January 1985, the court may assume jurisdiction itself or under the conditions provided in article 164. The court will give its decision in the manner set out in that article.

Article 170

Independently of the references made in the register of previous convictions under article 768 (5th paragraph) of the criminal procedure code, orders of personal bankruptcy or the other sanctions provided under part VI of the law of 25th January 1985 will be officially notified as provided in article 21 and will be sent by the clerk of the court to the authorities referred to in article 19.

Article 171

Every request for relief from disqualification, prohibition and removal of capacity will be addressed by petition to the court which ordered judicial reconstruction. All documents evidencing contribution towards the discharge of liabilities will be annexed to the petition.

The court will give its decision in open court after hearing the plaintiff and the public prosecutor in chambers.

PART VI
MISCELLANEOUS PROVISIONS

Article 172

If funds owing to the debtor have been paid by third parties into the Central Deposit and Savings Bank, the bank will transfer these funds together with the rights, charges and notices attaching to the funds into the deposit account opened by the officer of the court acting as administrator, commissioner or liquidator. The officer of the court is responsible to the purchaser and the creditors for the performance of the obligations arising from these security interests.

Article 173

The payment of monies into the Central Deposit and Savings Bank is not open to challenge.

Article 174

The court with jurisdiction for proceedings for judicial reconstruction is competent in all matters relating to judicial reconstruction and liquidation, personal bankruptcy or the other sanctions provided under the law of 25th January 1985 with the exception of civil liability actions against the administrator, the creditors' representative, the commissioner or the liquidator which fall within the jurisdiction of the civil court of first instance.

Article 175

Proceedings before the civil court of first instance in matters regulated by the law of 25th January 1985 will be determined in accordance with article 853 and the following articles of the new civil procedure code for any matter which is not regulated by that law and this decree.

A party to the proceedings who does not act in person may only be represented by a lawyer.

Article 176

Proceedings before the civil courts of first instance in the departments of Lower Rhine, Upper Rhine and Moselle in matters regulated by the law of 25th January 1985 will be determined in accordance with article 31 of the law of 1st June 1924 governing the introduction of French commercial law into these departments and by articles 37–39 of the annex to the new civil procedure code as regards the application of that code in these departments.

Article 177

In the departments of Lower Rhine, Upper Rhine and Moselle, the administrative court is competent to decide:

1. Difficulties encountered in the enforcement of decisions taken by the bankruptcy judge in applying article 154 of the law of 25th January 1985;
2. Disputes relating to the regulation of priority as determined by the liquidator.

The administrative court will exercise the functions conferred by this decree on the executive judge of the civil court of first instance.

The liquidator may not, on his own behalf or as creditors' representative, be declared the successful tenderer for any real estate owned by the debtor.

Article 177 – 1

In the departments of Lower Rhine, Upper Rhine and Moselle:

1. The order provided in article 130 includes, besides the measures referred to in article 125, the statements set out in article 144 of the law of 1st June 1924 putting into effect French civil legislation in the departments of Lower Rhine, Upper Rhine and Moselle;
2. The order provided in article 132 includes, besides the measures referred to in article 125, the statements set out in the second paragraph of article 261 of the law of 1st June, 1924;
3. Sale by agreed public tender is subject to the provisions of articles 249–254 of the law of 1st June 1924.

Article 177 – 2

In the departments of Lower Rhine, Upper Rhine and Moselle, the distribution of the proceeds of sale and the regulation of priority among creditors by the liquidator referred to in the fourth paragraph of article 154 of the law of 25th January 1985 are exclusively governed by the provisions of this decree.

Article 178

In applying the provisions of this decree in the departments of Lower Rhine, Upper Rhine and Moselle, the words 'hypothecations bureau' or 'registrar of hypothecations' shall be deemed to mean 'land registry'.

Article 179

Remission or reduction in tax claims may be granted to businesses subject to proceedings for judicial reconstruction or liquidation within the limits and conditions set out in article L.247 of the tax procedure book.

Within the general regime of judicial reconstruction, the administrative authorities will rule on written demands submitted by creditors' representatives within six weeks of presentation. This time limit is extended to eight weeks when the authorities need to consult the contentious tax committee or the customs or exchange control committees. In the case of the simplified procedure, the authorities will give their decision within four weeks, extended to six weeks if committee consultation is necessary.

The time limits of thirty days and fifteen days provided under articles R.247-12 and R.247-13 of the tax procedures statute book do not apply.

In the absence of a response from the authorities within the prescribed time limits, the demands will be deemed to be rejected.

Article 180

The transfer of prior rank or hypothecation or the surrender of these securities provided under the third paragraph of article 24 of the law of 25th January 1985 may be granted without prior extinction of the claim after consultation with the commission of heads of finance divisions as provided in decree no. 78-486 of 31st March 1978. Expenses attributable to these procedures are for the account of the debtor.

Article 181

The head of legal services at the Treasury has power to grant remissions, as do also the paymasters-general in respect of claims of the State referred to in article 80 of decree no. 62-1587 of 29th December 1962 providing for the general regulation of public accountability.

Insofar as the need arises they may exercise these powers under the conditions provided in decree no. 86-620 of 14th March 1986.

However, the opinions assembled by the head of legal services at the Treasury acting either in the capacity of legal agent of the Treasury in accordance with article 17 of the decree of 14th March 1986 or as the delegate of the government minister in accordance with article 91 of the decree of 29th December 1962 are substituted by an opinion submitted by the working party of the litigation committee comprising the following members:

1. An examiner chief at the public audits tribunal, as president,
2. A principal at the appeals office of, or commissioner at, the state council;
3. The director of the public accounts department, or his representative.

Within the general regime of judicial reconstruction, the administrative authorities will rule on written demands submitted by creditors' representatives within six weeks of presentation. This time limit is extended to eight weeks when the authorities need to consult the contentious tax committee or the customs or exchange control committees. In the case of the simplified procedure, the authorities will give their decision within four weeks, extended to six weeks if committee consultation is necessary.

In the absence of a response from the authorities within the prescribed time limits, the demands will be deemed to be rejected.

Article 182

In the paragraph numbered 2 in article 425 of the new civil procedure code, the words: 'and in the case of incorporated bodies, proceedings for judicial regulation or liquidation of assets' are replaced by the words: 'and in the case of incorporated bodies, proceedings for judicial regulation or liquidation of assets, and also proceedings for judicial reconstruction and liquidation.'

Article 183

Article R.321-10 of the employment code is replaced by the following provisions:

'Art. R.321-10 – The request for an opinion on a proposal for dismissals by reason of redundancy submitted by the administrator or, failing which, by the employer or liquidator, by virtue of the second paragraph of article L.321-7, will include the following information:

1. Name and address of employer;
2. Nature of the business;
3. Date of the order commencing proceedings for judicial reconstruction;
4. The economic, financial or technical reasons for the dismissal plan;
5. The number of employees whose dismissal is contemplated;
6. The professional capacity of those concerned;
7. The number of employees, permanent or otherwise, employed in the establishment;
8. The measures taken to avoid the dismissal or limit the number concerned, and to facilitate the re-employment of those employees whose dismissal cannot be avoided;
9. Provisional timetable for the dismissals.

The official record of the meetings of the employees' representatives provided in article L.321-10, or the opinion of the employees' representative in the circumstances provided in the second paragraph of article 139 of law no. 85-98 of 25th January 1985 relating to the judicial reconstruction and liquidation of businesses will be sent to the administrative authority after expiry of the time limit referred to in article L.321-7.'

Article 184

The heading of chapter III of the decree of 17th February 1951 passed in order to apply the law of 18th June 1951 relating to the grant of security interests in works premises and equipment, is replaced by the following heading:

'Chapter III. – Registration formalities relating to the temporary inalienability of works equipment belonging to a business under judicial reconstruction subject to a survival plan.'

Article 185

Chapter III of the aforesaid decree of 17th February 1951 includes the following articles 8–11:

'Art. 8. – If, in applying article 70 of law no. 85-98 of 25th January 1985 relating to the judicial reconstruction and liquidation of businesses, the decision setting up or modifying the plan for survival of the business includes an order for the temporary inalienability of works equipment belonging to the debtor and has become final, the debtor, or, failing which, the commissioner, will request registration of the inalienability on the register provided under the first article of the decree of 28th August 1909 passed in order to apply the laws of 1st March and 1st April 1909 relating to the sale of, and prior charges in, businesses.'

'Art. 9. – The debtor or, failing which, the commissioner will present to the clerk of the commercial court in the judicial district where the business has its registered office, or will arrange for a third party to present to him, a copy of the decision as issued and to which are attached memoranda of the registered entry containing:

1. The name and forenames of the debtor, if a natural person, or the business name and description, if an incorporated body, the address of the registered office, the registered number in the commercial and company register or in the trades directory;
2. The date of issue of the decision;
3. The summary description of the works equipment subject to temporary inalienability, the place where this equipment has been placed in bonded storage, and an indication whether the equipment may be moved if the need arises;
4. Duration of the period of inalienability;

The clerk of the court will record on the memoranda the date when the registration was effected and the number of its entry on the register referred to in the preceding article.

The memoranda are drawn up and retained and one copy is given to the debtor under the conditions set out in articles 2 and 4 of this decree.

The clerk of the court will keep an alphabetical list of the debtors containing the numbers of the registered entries which concern them.'

'Art. 10. – The memoranda are given an entry number at the time they are produced.

These items are entered on the register referred to in article 8 of this decree; and a certified extract of the register is prepared containing:

1. The entry number affixed to the item as described in the preceding paragraph;
2. The date of deposit of the items;
3. The number and description of the items, showing the reason for their deposit;
4. The name or description of the debtor;
5. The nature and location of the transferable items of equipment and, finally, a note of the fact that they may be removed.'

'Art. 11. – The clerk of the court will refer, in the margin of the memorandum of registration, to the total or partial deletion of the inalienability relating to the items of equipment whose sale has been authorised by the court in accordance with the first paragraph of article 70 of the law of 25th January 1985.

When the time limit appointed for the temporary inalienability determined by the court has expired, the clerk of the court will, at his own instigation, make a note of the deletion in the margin of the memorandum. He will deliver a certificate of deletion to any debtor who requests it.

He is bound to deliver to all those who require it, a statement of the subsisting registrations with a note, if necessary, of any partial deletion.

Deletion expenses are included in the registration costs.'

Article 186

I Add the following paragraph to the end of paragraph 2 of article 28 of decree no. 55-22 of 4th January 1955 relating to the reform of publication of notices of interests in real estate:

'Judicial decisions establishing or modifying the plan for survival of the business issued in accordance with chapter II of law no. 85-98 of 25th January 1985 relating to the judicial reconstruction and liquidation of businesses, and which order the temporary inalienability of real estate belonging to the debtor upon the conditions set out in article 70 of that law;'

II In article 32 of decree no. 55-22 of 4th January 1955, the words: 'The notaries public, lawyers, service process agents and administrative authorities' are replaced by the words 'The notaries public, lawyers, service process agents, clerks of the court and administrative authorities'.

Article 187

The first paragraph of article 7 of decree no. 84-406 of 30th May 1984 relating to the commercial and companies register is replaced by the following provisions:

'Every natural person who is a businessman must request registration at the latest within fifteen days from the date of commencement of his business at the court registry in the judicial district where one of the following is located:

1. The registered office of his business, if this is different from his principal place of business; or
2. His principal place of business; or
3. In the absence of a place of business, his domicile, or if the need arises .....' (no change in the remainder of the paragraph).

Article 188

In paragraph A of article 8 of the aforesaid decree of 30th May 1984, the following sub-paragraph 1(b) is inserted between sub-paragraph 1. and sub-paragraph 2.:

'1(b) – The address of the registered office of the business if this is different from his principal place of business.'

Article 189

The following article 36-1 is added to the aforesaid decree of 30th May 1984:

'Art. 36-1. – The following are noted as a matter of course in the register: Declarations of cessation of payment, of non-performance of financial obligations under an out of court settlement, and also decisions issued in the course of proceedings for the judicial reconstruction or liquidation of businesses in accordance with law no. 85-98 of 25th January 1985:

1. Commencing proceedings for judicial reconstruction noting the powers conferred on the administrator;
2. Extending the observation period;
3. Amending the date of cessation of payments;
4. Amending the administrator's powers;
5. Deciding to continue the business in view of the drawing up of a reconstruction plan in accordance with article 142 of the law of 25th January 1985;
6. Authorising conclusion of a lease management contract in the course of the observation period;
7. Authorising loans or granting time for payment in accordance with article 40-3 of the law of 25th January 1985;
8. Making adoption of a reconstruction plan dependent on the replacement of one or more of the managers of the business;
9. Ordering the total or partial shut-down of the business;
10. Drawing up the plan for survival or sale of the business;
11. Amending the order drawing up the plan for survival or sale of the business;
12. Ordering compulsory liquidation;
13. Ordering termination of proceedings on the grounds of satisfaction of liabilities or insufficiency of assets;
14. Ordering termination of proceedings in the case of sale of the whole of the business in accordance with article 92 of the aforesaid law of 25th January 1985;
15. Ordering the discharge of the debts of the incorporated body in whole or in part by its officers or by some of them;
16. Ordering bankruptcy or the prohibition provided under article 192 of the law of 25th January 1985.'

Article 190

In the first sentence of article 37 of the decree of 30th May 1984, the words: 'In articles 35 and 36' are replaced by the words: 'In articles 35, 36 and 36-1'.

Article 191

Paragraph 1 of article 42 of the decree of 30th May 1984 is replaced by the following provisions:

'1. With effect from the termination of proceedings, whether for bankruptcy, or for liquidation of assets or on the grounds of insufficiency of assets or upon termination of the creditors' agreement, or for compulsory liquidation on the grounds of insufficiency of assets, or for judicial regulation under compulsory composition involving sale of all the interested party's assets;'

Article 192

Article 71 of the decree of 30th May 1984 is replaced by the following provisions:

'Art. 71. – The following may not be published:

1. In the case of proceedings commenced before 1st January 1986:
   (a) orders issued in matters concerning judicial reconstruction and liquidation in the case of termination on the grounds of satisfaction of liabilities;
   (b) orders issued in matters of judicial reconstruction in the case of performance of a survival plan and the agreed discharge of liabilities, and in the case of termination of proceedings in accordance with article 92 of the law of 25th January 1985;
   (c) orders to the effect that the debts of the incorporated body shall be borne wholly or partially by its officers, or by some of them, and following payment by the latter of the liabilities for which they have been held responsible;
   (d) orders for personal bankruptcy or the prohibition referred to in article 192 of the law of 25th January 1985 in the event of termination on the grounds of satisfaction of liabilities, total recovery of due debts, or forgiveness of debt.

2. In the case of proceedings commenced between 1st January 1968 and 1st January 1986:
   (a) orders issued in matters of judicial regulation, assets liquidation, personal bankruptcy or the other sanctions provided in the first chapter of title III of law no. 67-563 of 13th July 1967 in the case of termination upon satisfaction of liabilities, performance of a compulsory composition agreement, discharge from bankruptcy, or forgiveness of debt;
   (b) orders to the effect that all or part of the corporate debt shall be borne by the officers of the company following payment by the latter of the liabilities for which they have been held responsible;
   (c) orders issued in matters of provisional suspension from suit in the event of performance of a plan for reconstruction and the agreed discharge of liabilities.

3. In the case of proceedings before 1st January 1968: Orders issued in matters of personal bankruptcy, compulsory liquidation, judicial regulation following termination on the grounds of default in the payment of interest on the principal debt, performance of a compulsory composition agreement, discharge from bankruptcy, or forgiveness of debt;
4. Orders other than those provided under paragraphs 1, 2 and 3 above and involving removal of capacity to perform or prohibit from either performing a commercial or professional business activity, or managing, administering or directing an

incorporated body when the relevant party has been relieved of this incapacity or has benefited from bankruptcy discharge or forgiveness of debt;

5. Order of prohibition, or of nomination of judicial counsel, when these measures have been officially reported;
6. Demands for the separation of assets or for the anticipated liquidation of property acquired in common, and also demands formulated on the basis of article 1426 of 1429 of the civil code when these have been rejected by the court, and also the orders rejecting these demands.'

Article 193

Article 76 of the decree of 30th May 1984 is replaced by the following provisions:

'Art 76 – The notices provided under the previous articles are drawn up and gazetted by the clerk of the court within eight days of the relevant registration, or, in the case of a principal registration, upon notification of the identity number by the National Institute for Statistics and Economic Research.'

Article 194

The following article 10-1 is added to decree no. 88-487 of 10th June 1983 relating to the trades directory:

'Art 10-1. – The president of the trades chamber will proceed in due course to note in the trades directory decisions issued in judicial reconstruction and liquidation matters with regard to businesses registered in this directory each time provision for such notification is made under decree no. 85-1388 of 27th December 1985 relating to the judicial reconstruction and liquidation of businesses.

An extract of the decision is sent by the clerk of the court where the proceedings where commenced to the competent president of the trades chamber.

The order referred to in article 10 of this decree will determine the list of decisions to be referred to in the trades directory and also the means whereby these decisions will be communicated.'

PART VII
TRANSITIONAL PROVISIONS

Article 195

When, in proceedings for judicial regulation or liquidation of assets, the trustee in bankruptcy makes a payment after 1st January 1986 into the deposit account at the Central Savings and Deposit Bank, any funds previously remitted under the same proceedings will be transferred to the deposit account upon authorisation by the bankruptcy judge.

Nevertheless, if funds due to the debtor have been paid in by third parties before commencement of proceedings for judicial regulation or liquidation of assets, they will remain in the retention account opened in the debtor's name.

Articles 25 and 86 of decree no. 67-1120 of 22nd December 1967 do not apply to funds paid into the deposit account or remitted as provided in this article.

PART VIII
FINAL PROVISIONS

Article 196

The following are cancelled:

1. Decree no. 67-1120 of 22nd December 1967 relating to judicial regulation, liquidation of assets and personal bankruptcy;
2. Decree no. 67-1254 of 31st December 1967 providing for jurisdictions to hear proceedings for provisional suspension of suit and the agreed discharge of liability as instituted by order no. 67-820 of 23rd September 1967 passed in order to facilitate the economic and financial reconstruction of certain business, as modified by decree no. 73-12 of 2nd January 1973;
3. Decree no. 67-1255 of 31st December 1967 passed in order to facilitate the economic and financial reconstruction of certain business.

Article 197

With the exception of the provisions relating to the institutions referred to in article L.143-11-4 of the employment code, this decree applies to the territorial community of Mayotte.

Article 198

Subject to paragraphs 2, 3 and 4 of article 240 of the law of 25th January 1985 and with the exception of article 195 above, the provisions of this decree are only applicable to proceedings commenced after their entry into force.

Article 199

The provisions of law no. 85-98 of 25th January 1985 and of this decree enter into force on 1st January 1986.

Article 200

The following persons are responsible, insofar as it concerns each of them, for performance of this decree which will be published in the Official Journal of the French Republic: the Minister for Economy, Finance and Budgets, the Keeper of the Seals, Minister of Justice, Minister for the Interior, the Minister for Social Security, Government Spokesman, the Minister for Commerce, Trade and Tourism, the Minister for Employment, the Secretary of State at the Ministry for the Interior, responsible for Overseas Departments and Territories.

Made in Paris, 27th December 1985.

By the Prime Minister: LAURENT FABIUS

Keeper of the Seals, Minister of Justice
ROBERT BADINTER

Minister for Economy, Finance and Budgets
PIERRE BÉRÉGOVOY

Minister for Commerce, Trade and Tourism
MICHEL CRÉPEAU

Minister for Employment
MICHEL DELEBARRE

Secretary of State at the Ministry for the Interior, responsible for Overseas Departments and Territories
GEORGES LEMOINE

JUDICIAL RECONSTRUCTION AND COMPULSORY LIQUIDATION OF BUSINESSES

Extract from:

NO: 1034 – OFFICIAL GAZETTE OF THE FRENCH REPUBLIC

GERMANY

The translated texts are of the Bankruptcy Code of 10th February 1877, the Scheme of Arrangement Code of 26th February 1935, the Avoidance Law of 21st July 1879 and, finally, certain articles from the Joint Stock Companies' Law, the Limited Liability Companies' Law and the Commercial Code. The translation is of the law as it was on 1st July 1991.

The Bankruptcy Code consists of two Books, each of eight chapters, the first dealing with the substantive law and the second containing the procedure.

While the Scheme of Arrangement Code is largely either procedural or administrative, there are important substantive provisions concerning the revival of liability (section 9), excluded claims (section 29), the effect of the Scheme (chapter V), legal capacity of a debtor subject to the Scheme (chapter VI), the effect of a ratified Scheme of Arrangement (chapter IX) and the effect of termination and discontinuance proceedings (chapters X and XI). There are special Schemes of Arrangement provisions for joint stock companies, unlimited commercial partnerships and registered co-operative societies.

The Avoidance Law deals with the avoidance of transactions where the debtor is not a bankrupt, and the special insolvency provisions for joint stock companies, limited liability companies and unlimited partnerships are set out in the articles from the relevant laws at the end of the translated texts.

Germany has enacted a new bankruptcy law, but it is not scheduled to come into effect until later in the 1990s.

CHAPTER THREE

German Insolvency Laws

TABLE OF CONTENTS

BANKRUPTCY CODE OF 10TH FEBRUARY 1877

(RGB1.p. 351) as published on 20 May 1898 (RGB1 p. 612) (BGBl.III 311-4)

PART I. LAW OF BANKRUPTCY

Chapter I: General provisions

1. Bankrupt's estate

(1) Bankruptcy proceedings apply to all the property of the bankrupt which is open to judicial execution and which is owned by him at the date of commencement of the proceedings.

(2) The limitations provided under section 811 paragraphs 4 and 9 of the Code of Civil Procedure and section 20 of the Law on the Postal System of the German Reich of 28th October 1871 are not applicable in bankruptcy proceedings.

(3) The bankrupt's books of account form part of the bankrupt's estate.

(4) Assets which are not open to seizure or attachment do not form part of the bankrupt's estate.

2. Joint property of spouses

(1) If the joint property of spouses is administered by one of the spouses alone under the marital property regime and bankruptcy proceedings are commenced against the assets of that spouse, the joint property will form part of the bankrupt's estate; no formal division of the joint property between the spouses may be made. The joint property will not be affected by bankruptcy proceedings against the property of the other spouse.

(2) If the spouses jointly administer the joint property, the joint property will not be affected by bankruptcy proceedings against the property of one spouse; separate bankruptcy proceedings in respect of the joint property can be brought under sections 236a-236c.

(3) In the case of continuation of joint ownership of property, the provisions of subsection (1) above apply on the basis that where the spouse who administers the joint property dies, the surviving spouse is substituted for that spouse and the descendants are substituted for the non-administering spouse.

3. Creditors in bankruptcy

(1) The bankrupt's estate is to be applied in joint settlement of the claims of all creditors who have a claim for money or money's worth against the assets of the bankrupt which was established at the date of commencement of the proceedings.

(2) Maintenance claims which are established against the bankrupt under sections 1351*, 1360, 1361, 1578 to 1583, 1586**, 1601 to 1615 and 1708 to 1714 of the Civil Code and claims arising under sections 1715 and 1716 of the Civil Code and which will fall due in the future may only be asserted in so far as the bankrupt is liable as heir to the original debtor.

* Now section 39 subsection 2 of the matrimonial law.

** Now section 1569 et seq. of the Civil Code.

4. Satisfaction of preferred claims

(1) A claim for preferential payment out of the chattels which form part of the bankrupt's estate may only be asserted subject to the provisions of this law.

(2) Payment of secured claims is made independently of the bankruptcy proceedings.

5. Foreign creditors

(1) Foreign creditors are treated in the same way as German creditors.

(2) With the consent of the Federal Council the relevant Government Minister can order that a right of retaliation be applied against a foreign state, its subjects and their legal successors.

6. Rights of administration and disposal

(1) At the commencement of the proceedings the bankrupt loses his powers of management and disposal over the assets that form part of the bankrupt's estate.

(2) The rights of management and disposal will be exercised by a judicial receiver.

7. Transactions performed by the bankrupt after the commencement of bankruptcy proceedings

(1) Transactions performed by the bankrupt after the commencement of proceedings are not valid as against the bankrupt's creditors; the provisions of sections 892 and 893 of the Civil Code and sections 16 and 17 of the Rights in Registered Ships and Ships under Construction Law of 15 November 1940 (RGBl. I p. 1499) remain unaffected.

(2) The other party is to be reimbursed for its consideration from the bankrupt's estate in so far as the latter was enlarged by that consideration.

(3) Transactions performed by the bankrupt on the day that proceedings were commenced are deemed to have been effected after such commencement.

8. Benefits obtained by the bankrupt after the commencement of the bankruptcy proceedings

(1) Performance of an obligation which is to be discharged in favour of the bankrupt's estate and which is effected in favour of the bankrupt after the commencement of the proceedings will only discharge the performing party as against the creditors of the bankrupt to the extent that it benefits the bankrupt's estate.

(2) Performance effected prior to public announcement of the commencement of the proceedings discharges the performing party unless it is proved that he was aware of the commencement of proceedings at the time of performance.

(3) Performance effected after such public announcement discharges the performing party if he proves that he was unaware of the commencement of the proceedings at the time of performance.

9. Inheritance

An inheritance or other testamentary gift which accrues to the bankrupt prior to the commencement of the proceedings can only be accepted or renounced by the bankrupt. The same applies to rejection of a continuation of joint ownership of property.

10. Conduct of litigation

(1) Litigation to which the bankrupt is a party concerning assets which form part of the bankrupt's estate and which is pending at the commencement of the bankruptcy proceedings may be adopted by the judicial receiver in the procedural state in which it is at such time. If there is any delay in the adoption of the litigation the provisions of section 239 of the Code of Civil Procedure will apply accordingly.

(2) If the judicial receiver disclaims his right to take up the litigation, both the bankrupt and the other party may do so in his place.

11. Particular types of litigation

(1) Litigation which is pending against the bankrupt concerning the segregation of a chattel out of the bankrupt's estate or preferential payment, or claims which are to be regarded as preferential debts, may be adopted both by the judicial receiver and by the other party.

(2) If the judicial receiver recognises the claim immediately he will not bear the costs of those proceedings.

12. Disputes over debts in bankrupt's estate

Creditors of the bankrupt may only pursue their claims to security or satisfaction out of the bankrupt's estate subject to the provisions of the bankruptcy procedure.

13. Restraint on alienation

Restraint on alienation of the type described by sections 135 and 136 of the Civil Code which is in force against the bankrupt is void as against the creditors of the bankrupt; however, a seizure resulting from judicial execution against immoveable property remains valid.

14. No individual enforcement

(1) No attachments or executions in favour of individual creditors of the bankrupt, whether against assets within the bankrupt's estate or other assets of the bankrupt, will be carried out during the bankruptcy proceedings.

(2) No priority notice obtained by injunction in favour of individual creditors of the bankrupt may be entered during the bankruptcy proceedings in respect of real property, registered ships and ships under construction belonging to the bankrupt's estate, nor may such a notice be entered against the rights of the bankrupt registered against such real property, registered ships, ships under construction or registered rights.

15. Partially ineffective acquisitions of title

After commencement of the bankruptcy proceedings, title to assets within the bankrupt's estate as well as preferential rights to and liens on such assets may not be validly acquired as against the creditors of the bankrupt even if such acquisition did not result from the act of the bankrupt. The provisions of sections 878, 892 and 893 of the Civil Code, section 3 sub-section 3, and sections 16 and 17 of the Rights to Registered Ships and Ships under Construction Act of 15 November 1940 (RGBl. I. p. 1499) and section 20 sub-section 3 of the Maritime Allotment Code of 25 July 1986 (BGBl. I p.1130) remain unaffected.

16. Joint rights

(1) Where the bankrupt is co-owner or in an association or other joint undertaking with a third party, any formal division or other distribution of property will take place outside the bankruptcy proceedings.

(2) An agreement in respect of a tenancy in common which stipulates that the right to demand termination of the co-ownership is excluded forever or temporarily or is subject to a period of notice, has no legal effect as regards the bankrupt's estate. The same applies to a direction to that effect made by a testator in respect of the joint ownership of the estate by co-heirs.

Chapter II: Performance of transactions

17. Judicial receiver's right to choose in bilateral contracts

(1) Where at the time of the commencement of the bankruptcy proceedings a bilateral contract has not, or has not fully, been performed by the bankrupt and the other party, the judicial receiver may perform the contract in the place of the bankrupt and may demand performance from the other side.

(2) Upon demand by the other party the judicial receiver will inform him without delay, even if performance is not yet due, whether he wishes to insist on performance. If he fails to do so he will not be able to insist on performance.

18. Transactions to be performed within a given period of time

(1) Where goods with a price quoted on a market or stock exchange are to be delivered on a particular date or within a certain period of time and that date or time period occurs after the commencement of the proceedings, it is not possible to demand performance. Only a claim for non-performance may be brought.

(2) The amount of such a claim will be determined by the difference between the purchase price and the price quoted on the market or stock exchange which applies at the place of performance or the relevant place of trade for such transactions with a fixed time for performance on the second working day after commencement of the proceedings.

(3) Sub-section 1 above does not apply where the relevant market or stock exchange quoted price cannot be ascertained.

19. Leases and tenancies

Where a chattel rented by, or leased to, the bankrupt is handed over to him before the commencement of the proceedings, both the judicial receiver and the other party may terminate the lease or tenancy. The statutory period of notice applies unless a shorter one was agreed. Where the judicial receiver terminates the lease or tenancy the other party is entitled to claim compensation for damages incurred by reason of the termination of the contract.

20. Landlord's cancellation rights in leases or tenancies

(1) Where a chattel rented by, or leased to, the bankrupt is not handed over to the bankrupt before commencement of the proceedings the other party is entitled to cancel the contract.

(2) Upon demand by the judicial receiver the other party must inform him without delay whether he wishes to cancel the contract. If he fails to do so the provisions of section 17 above apply.

21. Validity in relation to the bankrupt's estate

(1) Where the bankrupt handed over a chattel which he rented or leased out to prior to commencement of the proceedings, the tenancy or lease agreement is valid in relation to the bankrupt's estate.

(2) Where a piece of real property or residential or other property is rented or leased out, any disposition by the bankrupt made prior to the commencement of the proceedings in relation to rent due in the future and especially the collection of rent, is valid in relation to the bankrupt's estate only in so far as the disposition relates to the calendar quarter* in which the proceedings were commenced; if the bankruptcy proceedings are commenced in the second half of the last month of a calendar quarter**, the disposition is also valid in so far as it relates to the rent for the following calendar quarter*.

(3) In so far as the payment of the rent is valid in relation to the bankrupt's estate the tenant or lessee may set off any claim he has against the bankrupt against any rent demand by the bankrupt's estate.

(4) Any voluntary sale by the judicial receiver of real property or a registered ship rented or leased out by the bankrupt takes effect as a judicial sale in relation to the tenancy or lease in so far as the property or ship was handed over to the tenant or lessee before commencement of the proceedings. The provisions of sections 576 and 169, subsection 2, of the law on judicial rules and receivers will, nevertheless not be applied.

22. Service contracts

(1) A service contract entered into in the household, undertaking or business of the bankrupt may be terminated by either party. The statutory notice period applies unless a shorter one was agreed.

(2) Where the judicial receiver gives notice of termination, the other party is entitled to claim compensation for damages incurred by reason of termination of the service contract.

23. Mandate; Agency agreements

(1) A mandate given by the bankrupt is cancelled by the commencement of the proceedings unless it relates to property outside the bankrupt's estate. Where the mandate is cancelled, the provisions of section 672 second sentence and section 674 of the Civil Code apply accordingly.

* Now: calendar month, section 12 of the law containing regulations for the enforcement of judgments, 26th March 1933, refers.

** Now: after the 15th day of that month, see previous footnote. (2) The same applies where responsibility has been assumed through a service or work contract for performing on behalf of the bankrupt a transaction which the bankrupt has delegated to him by way of agency.

24. Priority notices

Where a priority notice has been entered in the land register, the register of ships or the register of ships under construction as security for a claim for the granting or setting aside of rights to a real property or a registered ship or a ship under construction belonging to the bankrupt or to a right registered in the name of the bankrupt or as security for a claim for alteration of the scope or ranking of such a right, the creditor may demand satisfaction of his claim from the judicial receiver. This also applies where the bankrupt assumed further obligations towards the creditor and these have not or have not fully been fulfilled.

25. Other effects of the commencement of bankruptcy proceedings

In so far as the civil law contains certain provisions concerning the effect of the commencement of bankruptcy proceedings on legal relationships which do not fall within sections 18 to 24 above, those provisions apply.

26. No rights of restitution

Where an obligation of the bankrupt is not fulfilled or a legal relationship to which the bankrupt is a party is avoided by reason of the commencement of the bankruptcy proceedings, the other party is not entitled to require the bankrupt's estate to fulfil the obligation or restore the legal relationship, which remain matters within the bankrupt's control. Unless he has a right to preferential payment of a secured claim he may only make a claim for the non-performance or avoidance as a creditor in bankruptcy.

27. Claims for compensation

Where a mandate given by the bankrupt or a service or works contract of the type described in section 23 sub-section 2 above is cancelled by reason of the commencement of proceedings, the other party is, in respect of claims for compensation arising after the commencement of proceedings, a preferred creditor where section 672 second sentence of the Civil Code applies and a creditor in bankruptcy where section 674 of the Civil Code applies.

28. Rights of managing partners

Where a partnership established pursuant to section 705 of the Civil Code is dissolved by reason of the commencement of bankruptcy proceedings over the property of one of its partners, the managing partner is a preferred creditor in respect of those claims which are due to him for the temporary continuation of the business under section 728 second sentence of the Civil Code, and creditor in the bankruptcy for claims due to him under section 729 of the Civil Code, without prejudice to the provisions of section 51.

Chapter III: Avoidance

29. General principle

Transactions performed prior to the commencement of the bankruptcy proceedings may be challenged as void against the creditors in bankruptcy in accordance with the following provisions.

30. Avoidance of transactions of the bankrupt

The following are voidable:

(1) transactions entered into by the bankrupt after the cessation of payments or the petition for the commencement of bankruptcy proceedings which prejudice creditors in bankruptcy where the other party knew of the cessation of payments or the application at the time he entered into the transaction; and transactions performed after the cessation of payments or the application which provide security or satisfaction for a creditor in bankruptcy where the creditor knew of the cessation of payments or the petition at the date of performance;
(2) transactions performed after or within the last ten days before the cessation of payments or petition for commencement of bankruptcy proceedings which provide security or satisfaction for a creditor in bankruptcy to which he was not entitled or not of that type or not at that time unless he proves that at the time of the transaction he had no knowledge of both the cessation of payments and the petition, or of the intention of the bankrupt to prefer him over the other creditors.

31. Avoidance of intentional acts

The following are voidable:

(1) transactions which the bankrupt carried out with the intention, known to the other party, of prejudicing his creditors;
(2) non-gratuitous contracts made by the bankrupt during the last year preceding the commencement of the proceedings
   - with his spouse either before or during their marriage
   - with his or his spouse's relations, whether ancestors or descendants; with his or his spouse's brothers and sisters or half-brothers and sisters or the spouse of any such person, in so far as conclusion of the contract prejudices the creditors of the bankrupt and the other party does not prove that at the time of the conclusion of the contract he was unaware of an intention of the bankrupt to prejudice his creditors.

32. Avoidance of gratuitous dispositions

The following are voidable:

(1) gratuitous dispositions made by the bankrupt during the last year preceding the commencement of the proceedings in so far as they were not usual or occasional gifts.
(2) gratuitous dispositions made by the bankrupt in favour of his spouse during the last two years preceding the commencement of bankruptcy proceedings.

32a. Repayment of Loans

Transactions which provide security for a creditor in respect of a demand covered by section 32a sub-sections 1 and 3 of the law on limited liability companies are voidable.

The same applies to transactions which provide satisfaction for a creditor in respect of such demands where the transaction was carried out during the last year preceding commencement of the bankruptcy proceedings.

33. Previous transactions

Transactions which took place more than six months before the commencement of the proceedings may not be avoided by reason of knowledge of the cessation of payments.

34. Payments by bills of exchange or cheques

(1) Payments by bill of exchange by the bankrupt may not be reclaimed from the recipient under section 30 paragraph 1 if, under the law of bills of exchange, the recipient was obliged to accept payment in the case of loss of his claim on the bill against other parties liable on the bill.

(2) The amount paid on the bill must be reimbursed by the last debtor against whom recourse on the bill may be made, or if he negotiated the bill for the account of a third party, by that third party, if the former or the latter was aware of the circumstances set out in section 30 paragraph 1 at the time he issued the bill of exchange or caused it to be issued.

(3) Sub-sections 1 and 2 above apply accordingly to payments by cheque.

35. Executory awards and judicial execution

Avoidance is not excluded by the fact that an executory award has been obtained in respect of the voidable transaction or the fact that it was effected by way of judicial execution or enforcement of an attachment.

36. Exercise of the right of avoidance

The right of avoidance will be exercised by the judicial receiver.

37. Restitution

(1) Any part of the bankrupt's property which is sold, given away or relinquished through a voidable act must be restored to the bankrupt's estate.

(2) A bona fide recipient of a gratuitous performance need only restore what he received to the extent that he was enriched by it.

38. Consideration/Counter-performance

Consideration is to be repaid from the bankrupt's estate, in so far as it is within it, or in so far as the estate is enriched by its value. Any other claim may only be brought as a claim in bankruptcy.

39. Reinstatement of a demand

If the recipient of a voidable performance restores what he received, his claim is reinstated.

40. Avoidance as against successors in title

(1) Avoidance established against the testator is good against the successor in title.
(2) Avoidance which has been established against a person in respect of which the voidable act was performed is good against another successor in title of that person:

1. If the circumstances which gave rise to the avoidability of the acquisition by his predecessor in title were known to him at the time of his acquisition;
2. If he belongs to the persons named in section 31 paragraph 2 unless, at the time of his acquisition, he did not know of the circumstances which gave rise to the avoidability of the acquisition of his predecessor in title;
3. If he received it for no consideration.

(3) In the case of sub-section 2 paragraph 3 the provisions of section 37 sub-section 2 apply to the liability of the successor in title.

41. Time-limit for avoidance

(1) Avoidance may only be effected within one year of the commencement of proceedings. The provisions of section 203 sub-section 2 and section 207 of the Civil Code apply by analogy for the duration of this period. Avoidance pursuant to section 31 paragraph 1 and the first sentence of section 32a is prohibited if more than thirty years have passed since the act was done.
(2) The judicial receiver may refuse to perform an obligation of the bankrupt where the obligation results from the voidable act even if avoidance is excluded under sub-section 1.

42. Transactions after the commencement of bankruptcy proceedings

The regulations which apply to avoidance of transactions performed prior to the commencement of proceedings apply equally to transactions which were performed after the commencement of proceedings in so far as the latter are effective as against the creditors in bankruptcy under section 892 and 893 of the Civil Code and section 16 and 17 of the Rights in Registered Ships and Ships under Construction Law of 15 November 1940 (RGBl. I p. 1499). The period for exercising the right of avoidance begins with the performance of the transaction.

Chapter IV: Separation of property

43. Claims for separation of property

Claims for separation from the bankrupt's estate of an asset which does not belong to the bankrupt on the basis of a personal right or a right in rem are determined according to the general law and not to the laws relating to bankruptcy proceedings.

44. Right of pursuit

(1) A vendor or buying agent may reclaim goods which were sent to the bankrupt from another place and which have not yet been fully paid for by the bankrupt in so far

as they had not arrived at the place of delivery prior to commencement of the proceedings and had not come into the custody of the bankrupt or another person on his behalf.

(2) The provisions of section 17 apply.

45. (Cancelled)

46. Substitution of consideration for separated property

Where assets, in respect of which a claim could have been made for separation from the bankrupt's estate, have been disposed of by the bankrupt prior to the commencement of proceedings, or thereafter by the judicial receiver, the person entitled to separation is entitled to demand transfer to himself of the right to consideration in so far as consideration has yet to be made. He may demand consideration from the estate in so far as the consideration was brought into the estate after the commencement of the proceedings.

Chapter V: Preferential rights

47. Immoveable Assets

Assets subject to execution as real property (immoveable assets) are available for preferential payment to those entitled to a right to satisfaction from them.

48. Contractual liens

Creditors who have a contractual lien on an asset which forms part of the bankrupt's estate may demand preferential payment out of the asset pledged to them as security for their claim first for costs, secondly for interest and lastly for the capital sum.

49. Other parties entitled to preferential rights

(1) The following enjoy the same rights as creditors entitled to the rights of lien described in section 48:

1. The state treasury, regional treasury offices and local authorities, and also the municipal, county and provincial councils, for rates and taxes on items retained or confiscated subject to customs or excise duties;
2. Those who have a lien on certain assets arising by operation of law or by virtue of an attachment; the lien to which the landlord or lessor is entitled under sections 559, 581 and 592 of the civil code may not be enforced in respect of rent for any period of time earlier than the year preceding the commencement of proceedings nor in respect of a compensation claim of the landlord or lessor arising from termination of the contract by the judicial receiver; the lien of a landlord of agricultural property is not subject to this limitation in respect of rent;
3. Those who have caused some benefit to attach to an item, for monies spent up to the value of the benefit still remaining in respect of the item retained.

4. Those who have a right of retention in respect of certain items under the commercial code.

(2) The rights in sub-section 1 paragraph 1 have priority over those in sub-section 1 paragraph 2-4 and section 48; this does not apply to maritime liens (section 754 of the Commercial Code).

50. Liability for compensation

Anyone who assigns a claim against the bankrupt's estate to the overseas resident owner of an asset which forms part of the bankrupt's estate or to a third party with the intention that the former should appropriate the claim after the commencement of bankruptcy proceedings or knowing that an application has been made for their commencement or that payments have ceased, is under a duty to repay to the bankrupt's estate the amount by which it was diminished by reason of the owner exercising a right of security against the asset under the foreign law in contravention of this law. The provisions of section 33 apply accordingly.

51. Co-ownership

Anyone who owns property jointly with the bankrupt in partnership or some other form of association, may demand preferential payment in respect of claims arising out of such a relationship out of the bankrupt's share established upon division or other form of apportionment.

52. (Obsolete)

Chapter VI: Set-off

53. Declaration unnecessary

To the extent that he is entitled to set-off, a creditor does not need to assert his claim in the bankruptcy.

54. Non-monetary claims and claims not accrued due

(1) Set-off is not precluded by reason of the claims or one of them not yet having accrued due or still being contingent at the date when proceedings were commenced, or because the creditor's claim was not for a monetary sum.

(2) A creditor's claim which has not yet accrued due will be calculated in accordance with the provisions of section 65 for purposes of the set-off.

(3) For the purpose of calculating a claim subject to a condition precedent, the creditor may demand security when the condition comes into effect to the extent that the claim equals the debt payable by him.

(4) A non-monetary claim of a creditor will be calculated according to section 69 and 70 for the purposes of set-off.

55. Set-off not allowed

Set-off is not allowed in bankruptcy proceedings:

1. If the claim against the bankrupt arose before or after the commencement of proceedings but the indebtedness to the estate only arose after the commencement of proceedings;
2. If the indebtedness to the bankrupt arose before the commencement of proceedings but the claim against the bankrupt arose thereafter even if the same claim arose in respect of another creditor before the commencement of proceedings;
3. If the indebtedness to the bankrupt arose before the commencement of proceedings and the claim against the bankrupt was acquired through a transaction with him or through assignment of a right from, or payment to, a creditor, provided that the person acquiring the claim knew at the time he acquired the claim that the bankrupt had ceased to make payments or that a petition had been made to commence bankruptcy proceedings. The provisions of section 33 apply accordingly.

   Set-off is allowed if the person acquiring the claim was under an obligation to do so or to pay the creditor and he did not know of the cessation of payments or of the petition at the time he assumed the obligation.

56. Liability for compensation

The provisions of section 50 apply accordingly if a debtor resident overseas enforces under foreign law a set-off against a bankruptcy claim assigned to him which is not allowed under section 55.

Chapter VII: Preferred creditors

57. Prior payment

Preferential debts of the estate and the costs of the bankruptcy proceedings are to be paid first out of the estate.

58. Costs of the bankruptcy estate

These are:

1. Court fees for the joint proceedings;
2. Expenses incurred in the administration, realisation and distribution of the estate;
3. Maintenance costs allowed to the bankrupt and his family.

59. Preferential debts of the estate

(1) These are:

1. Claims arising from the transactions or acts of the judicial receiver;
2. Claims under bilateral contracts where performance is demanded from the estate or must be made after commencement of proceedings;
3. Claims, arising in respect of arrears for the six months prior to commencement of proceedings or the death of the bankrupt:
   (a) of employees for earnings for employment by the bankrupt, of those employed as trainees for earnings during their training with the bank-

rupt, and also of those employed in domestic work and those engaged on like terms in respect of their employment by the bankrupt,

(b) of employees for reimbursement under an agreement with the bankrupt restricting competition,

(c) of commercial agents for remuneration including commission against the bankrupt in so far as they are within the class of persons for whom the lower limit of contractual performance by their principals may be stipulated under section 92a of the Commercial Code and they are still not, and were not, owed more than on average one thousand Deutschmarks per month during the last six months of the contractual relationship (or all of it where the contract is for a shorter time) in respect of remuneration including commission and compensation for expenses incurred in the ordinary course of business,

(d) of persons entitled to benefits from a company pension scheme as against the bankrupt,

(e) of the social security agencies and the federal employment agency for contributions including surcharges for overdue contributions and other charges;

4. Claims in respect of an unjust enrichment of the estate.

(2) If the claims under sub-section 1 paragraph 3 (a) are transferred to the federal employment agency under section 141m sub-section 3 first sentence of the Law to Promote Employment or section 9 sub-section 3 first sentence of the Law on Optional Early Retirement, they will be discharged as claims in the bankruptcy with the same order of priority as those in section 61 sub-section 1 paragraph 1. The same applies to claims for contributions under sub-section 1 paragraph 3 (e) which remain in force as against the bankrupt under section 141m sub-section 2, first sentence, of the Law to Promote Employment.

60. Priority of costs of the bankruptcy proceedings and preferential debts of the estate

(1) As soon as it has been ascertained that the estate will not be sufficient to pay off all preferential creditors, the costs of the bankruptcy proceedings and the preferential debts of the estate will, to the extent that these claims are monetary, be discharged in accordance with the following order of priority, and, where they rank equally, in proportion to their amounts:

1. Preferential debts of the estate as described in section 59 sub-section 1 paragraphs 1 and 2.
2. Costs of the bankruptcy estate as described in section 58 paragraphs 1 and 2, and of those, first, the cash expenses.
3. Preferential debts of the estate as described in section 59 sub-section 1 paragraphs 3 and 4.
4. Costs of the bankruptcy proceedings as described in section 58 paragraph 3.

(2) Section 13 sub-section 1, second sentence, of the law relating to the avoidance of transactions of a debtor not subject to bankruptcy proceedings, as published on 20 May 1898 (RGBl.p.709) and as amended by the Judicial Scheme of Arrangement Code of 5 July 1927 (RGBl.Ip 139) remains unaffected.

Chapter VIII: Creditors in bankruptcy

61. Priority of claims in bankruptcy

(1) Claims in bankruptcy will be discharged according to the following priority:

1. In respect of arrears for the year preceding the commencement of proceedings or the death of the bankrupt, the claims:
   (a) of employees for earnings for employment by the bankrupt, of those employed as trainees for earnings during their training with the bankrupt and also of those employed in domestic work and those engaged on like terms in respect of their employment by the bankrupt,
   (b) of employees for reimbursement under an agreement with the bankrupt restricting competition,
   (c) of commercial agents for remuneration including commission against the bankrupt in so far as they are within the class of persons for whom the lower limit of contractual performance by their principals may be stipulated under section 92a of the Commercial Code and they are still not, and were not, owed more than on average one thousand Deutschmarks per month during the last six months of the contractual relationship (or all of it where the contract is for a shorter time) in respect of remuneration including commission and compensation for expenses incurred in the ordinary course of business,
   (d) of persons entitled to benefits from a company pension scheme as against the bankrupt,
   (e) of the social security agencies and the federal employment agency for contributions including surcharges for overdue contributions and other charges,

   in so far as the claims are not preferential debts of the estate.
2. The claims of the state treasury, the regional treasury offices and local authorities and also the municipal, county and provincial councils for rates and taxes which fell due in the year preceding the commencement of proceedings or which are deemed due under section 65; it makes no difference if the organisation responsible for collecting the relevant tax has already paid the tax in advance to the treasury office.
3. The claims of churches and schools, of public associations and compulsory public fire insurance companies for rates payable and benefits granted by law or under the constitution for the year preceding the commencement of proceedings.
4. The claims of doctors, surgeons, veterinary surgeons, chemists, midwives and nurses for medical and nursing costs for the year preceding the commencement of proceedings, in so far as the amount of the claims does not exceed the amount fixed by tariff.
5. The claims of children, wards and those in care and of those whom the bankrupt has been ordered to maintain as regards any of their property placed under the bankrupt's administration by order of law; this privilege is lost if the claim is not asserted in court within two years following the end of the administration of the said property and pursued up to commencement of proceedings.
6. All remaining claims in bankruptcy.

(2) Claims within the same paragraph of sub-section 1 rank equally. Equally ranking claims in the bankruptcy will be discharged in proportion to their amounts.

62. Ancillary claims

The following claims rank equally with the principal claim:

1. Costs incurred by the creditor before the commencement of proceedings;
2. Contractual penalties;
3. Interest accrued up to the commencement of proceedings.

63. Excluded claims

The following claims may not be asserted in bankruptcy proceedings:

1. Interest accrued since the commencement of proceedings;
2. Costs incurred by individual creditors for their participation in the proceedings;
3. Monetary penalties or fines, fines for contempt of court and administrative fines as well as any incidental legal consequences of a criminal or administrative offence which entail a monetary payment;
4. claims resulting from a gratuitous disposition made by the bankrupt inter vivos or on death.

64. Claims made for shortfalls where there is a secured asset

A creditor who demands payment of a secured claim, may assert the claim against the estate if the bankrupt is also personally liable, but he may only demand satisfaction for the amount claimed to the extent to which he waives his right to preferential payment or to the extent that he was not fully paid in a preferential payment.

65. Claims not accrued due

(1) Claims not accrued due are deemed due and payable.

(2) A non-interest bearing contingent claim which has not accrued due will be reduced to the amount which is equal to the total amount of the claim including interest at the rate stipulated by law for the period from commencement of proceedings to maturity.

66. Claims subject to conditions subsequent

Claims subject to conditions subsequent may be asserted in the same way as unconditional claims.

67. Claims subject to conditions precedent

Claims subject to conditions precedent only confer entitlement to security.

68. Joint and several debtors

Where bankruptcy proceedings are commenced in respect of the property of several or one of several persons who are jointly and severally liable for the whole amount in respect of the same obligation, a creditor may claim that amount in each set of proceedings in which he could claim at the commencement of such proceedings until his claim is fully satisfied.

69. Indeterminate claims

Claims which are not for a monetary sum or whose monetary value is indeterminate or uncertain or not established in the currency of the state, will be asserted for their estimated value in the currency of the state.

70. Instalments

Instalments due in a certain amount and over a fixed period of time will be capitalised by adding together the individual instalments and discounting the interim interest (section 65). The total amount may not exceed the amount of the capitalised instalments discounted at the rate of interest stipulated by law.

PART II. BANKRUPTCY PROCEDURE

Chapter I: General provisions

71. Competent district court

(1) The district court has exclusive competence for bankruptcy procedure for the district in which the bankrupt has his principle place of business or, in the absence of the latter, where it has general jurisdiction.

(2) Where several courts have competence, the court in which the proceedings were first commenced overrides the others.

(3) Provincial governments are empowered by means of decree to refer bankruptcy matters in respect of districts served by several district courts to a single district court, provided that consolidation is necessary in order to expedite the proceedings. The provincial governments may delegate their power to the provincial Department of Justice.

72. Application of the Civil Procedure Code

The rules of the Civil Procedure Code apply to bankruptcy procedure unless inconsistent with the provisions of this law.

73. Principles of procedure; accelerated appeals

(1) Decisions in insolvency proceedings may be taken without a prior hearing.

(2) Service of notices will be effected by the court of its own motion.

(3) Accelerated appeals may be made against the decisions made during the bankruptcy proceedings unless this law provides to the contrary.

74. The effectiveness of the court's decision on appeal

The decision of the court hearing determining the appeal is only effective when it becomes final. The court may however order that its decision shall take effect immediately.

75. Enquiry by the court

The bankruptcy court may order any necessary enquires, in particular the examination of witness and experts, in order to clarify all the circumstances relevant to the proceedings.

76. Public announcements

(1) Public announcements are effected by at least one entry in a newspaper designated for the publication of official court announcements. The entry may appear in the form of an extract. The announcement is deemed effective two days after the publication of the newspaper containing the entry or the first entry.

(2) The court may order further announcements.

(3) Public announcement is deemed made to all interested parties, even if this law requires in addition special notice to be served.

77. Service; notices without prescribed form

(1) If a special notice is required in addition to the public announcement it can be effected by post. Certification of the document to be served is not required.

(2) The notices which the judicial receiver is obliged to serve can be effected directly with no prescribed form required.

78. Appointment of the judicial receiver

(1) The judicial receiver is appointed by the court.

(2) The court may require the judicial receiver to provide security.

79. Several judicial receivers

If the judicial receivership includes different branches of the business, several judicial receivers may be appointed. Each of them manages his part of the business in an independent capacity.

80. Election of another judicial receiver

In the creditor's meeting following the appointment of a judicial receiver, the creditors may elect another person instead of the appointed judicial receiver. The court may reject the appointment of the elected person.

81. Publication of the appointment of the judicial receiver

(1) The name of the judicial receiver will be announced in public.

(2) The judicial receiver shall be given written confirmation of his appointment. He shall hand this written confirmation back to the court upon termination of his office.

82. Liabilities of the judicial receiver

The judicial receiver is liable to all interested parties for the performance of his duties.

83. Supervision by the bankruptcy court

The judicial receiver is under the supervision of the bankruptcy court.

84. Fines

(1) The court may fine the judicial receiver. It may dismiss the judicial receiver on its own motion prior to the creditors meeting following the appointment of the receiver.

Afterwards, it may only dismiss the judicial receiver at the request of the creditors' meeting or the creditors' committee.

(2) A warning must be given before the judicial receiver is fined. The judicial receiver has a right to be heard before issue of the decision under the second sentence of subsection 1.

85. Expenses; remuneration

(1) The judicial receiver is entitled to reimbursement for reasonable cash expenses and to remuneration for his business management. The bankruptcy court will determine the expenses and the remuneration.

(2) The provincial Department of Justice can make general regulations for the remuneration to be granted to the judicial receiver.

86. Final accounts

The judicial receiver must present the final accounts to a creditors' meeting upon termination of his office. The accounts must be submitted with supporting invoices at least three days before the meeting for inspection by the interested parties at the court's administrative offices, and, if a creditors' committee is called, with the committee's comments. The bankrupt, each creditor and any subsequent judicial receiver are entitled to object to the accounts. The accounts are deemed to be agreed so long as no objections are raised during the meeting.

87. Creditors' committee

(1) Before the first creditors' meeting the court may appoint a creditors' committee from among the creditors or representatives of the creditors.

(2) The creditors' meeting must decide on the appointment of a creditors' committee. The members of the creditors' committee must be elected by the creditors' meeting. Creditors or other persons may be elected as members.

88. Functions

(1) The members of the creditors' committee must supervise and support the judicial receiver during his management of the business. The members may inform themselves about the running of the business, may inspect the books and documents of the judicial receiver and examine the state of his accounts.

(2) The creditors' committee is entitled to demand a report from the judicial receiver as regards the progress of the case and the management of the business. It is obliged to arrange for the judicial receiver's accounts to be checked at least once a month by one of its members.

89. Members' liabilities

The members of the creditors' committee are liable to all interested parties for the performance of their duties.

90. The passing of resolutions

A resolution passed by the creditors' committee is valid if the majority of the members has voted and the resolution was passed by an absolute majority of those who voted.

91. Expenses; remuneration

(1) The members of the creditors' committee are entitled to reimbursement for reasonable cash expenses and to remuneration for their business management. The bankruptcy court will determine the expenses and the remuneration following discussion at a creditors meeting.

(2) The provincial Department of Justice may make general regulations for the remuneration to be granted to the members of the creditors' committee.

92. Revocation of the appointment

The appointment of a member of the creditors' committee effected by the court may be revoked by the court; the appointment of a member of the creditors' committee effected by a creditors' meeting may be revoked by a resolution of the creditors' meeting.

93. Calling a creditors' meeting

(1) The court decides whether to call a creditors' meeting. A meeting must be called if it is requested by the judicial receiver, the creditors' committee or by at least five creditors in bankruptcy whose claims, as estimated by the court, amount to one-fifth of the total debts.

(2) The calling of the meeting will be announced in public. Public announcement is not necessary if an adjournment of the proceedings is ordered in a creditors' meeting.

94. Supervision of meetings and passing of resolutions

(1) The creditors' meeting will be held under the supervision of the court.

(2) Resolutions passed by the creditors' meeting will require an absolute majority. A simple majority suffices in order to elect the members of the creditors' committee.

(3) The majority of the votes is calculated according to the value of the claims. Where the value of the claims is equal, the number of creditors is decisive.

95. The right to vote

(1) Admitted bankruptcy claims confer a right to participate in the voting process. As regards a disputed claim, the question will be discussed at the hearing for the investigation of claims whether, and to what extent, a permanent right to vote should be granted. In the absence of agreement, the bankruptcy court will decide the issue. The court may revise its decision upon the further application of a party.

(2) The question whether, and to what extent, bankruptcy claims not investigated confer the right to vote in a creditors' meeting is decided by the court upon the objection of a creditor or of the judicial receiver.

(3) The decision may not be challenged.

96. The right to vote in special cases

(1) The question whether, and to what extent, claims relating to any estimated shortfall suffered in connection with the satisfaction of preferred claims, and also bankruptcy claims subject to conditions precedent, confer the right to vote in a creditors' meeting is decided by the court upon the objection of a creditor or of the judicial receiver.

(2) The decision may not be challenged.

97. Counting of votes

Only the votes of those creditors present at the creditors' meeting are counted. Creditors not present are bound by the resolutions of the meeting.

98. Publication of the resolutions

The subject matter of a resolution passed in a creditors' meeting will be made public at the time when the meeting is called.

99. Prohibited implementation of a resolution

Upon application by the judicial receiver or an outvoted creditor during a creditors' meeting, the court will prohibit implementation of a resolution passed by the creditors meeting, if the resolution conflicts with the common interests of the creditors in bankruptcy.

100. Bankrupt's duty to provide information

The bankrupt is obliged to provide information to the judicial receiver, the creditors' committee and, upon order of the court, to the creditors meeting, regarding all the circumstances relating to the bankruptcy proceedings.

101. Bankrupt's duty to attend

(1) The bankrupt will only leave his place of residence with the court's consent.

(2) If the bankrupt does not fulfil the duties imposed on him by law, or if it appears necessary to protect the assets of the bankrupt, the court may compel the bankrupt to appear and, after hearing the bankrupt, may order his detention.

Chapter II: Commencement of bankruptcy proceedings

102. Inability to pay debts as they fall due

(1) The bankrupt's inability to pay debts as they fall due is a precondition to the commencement of bankruptcy proceedings.

(2) In particular, inability to pay will be presumed if the bankrupt has ceased to pay his debts.

103. General principles applying to a petition in bankruptcy

(1) The proceedings may only be commenced upon petition.

(2) The bankrupt, each preferential creditor according to section 59, sub-section 1, paragraph 3 and each creditor in bankruptcy is entitled to make a petition.

104. Petition documents

If the bankrupt petitions for commencement of proceedings he will provide a schedule of creditors and debtors together with a summary of the assets of the bankruptcy estate upon filing the petition, or, if this is not possible, he will supply these documents without delay.

105. Grant of the petition

(1) A creditor's petition for the commencement of proceedings will be admitted if evidence is produced supporting the creditor's claim and the bankrupt's inability to pay.

(2) If the petition is admitted, the court will hear the debtor and, if the latter does not admit inability to pay or cessation of payments, the court will order whatever investigation it considers necessary.

(3) The hearing of the debtor may not take place if it would require service of a notice by public announcement, or service of a notice abroad. In this event, if possible, a representative or relative of the debtor will be heard in his place.

106. Protective measures

(1) The court may compel the appearance and detention of the debtor. It may order interim injunctions for the protection of the estate. In particular the court may issue the debtor with a general prohibition order against disposal of assets.

(2) Upon rejection of a petition to commence proceedings, any protective measures ordered will be suspended.

107. Rejection of the petition to commence proceedings on the grounds of insufficiency of assets

(1) A petition to commence proceedings will be rejected, if, in the opinion of the court, the value of the bankrupt's estate is insufficient to meet the costs of the proceedings. Rejection will not arise if a sum of money sufficient to cover the costs set out in section 58, paragraph 1 and 2 is advanced.

(2) The court will maintain a register of those debtors in respect of whom a petition to commence proceedings was rejected on the grounds set out in the first sentence of sub-section (1). Inspection of the register is open to all. After five years following rejection of the petition to commence proceedings, the entry in the register will be deleted so that the debtors name is rendered illegible.

108. The time of commencement of bankruptcy proceedings

(1) Any resolution for the commencement of bankruptcy proceedings will state the time of commencement of proceedings.

(2) If this is omitted, time of the commencement of proceedings is deemed to be midday of the day when the resolution was passed.

109. Accelerated appeals

The bankrupt alone is entitled to file an accelerated appeal against a resolution for the commencement of bankruptcy proceedings; only the petitioner for commencement of bankruptcy proceedings may file an accelerated appeal against a decision rejecting the petition.

110. Court orders upon the commencement of bankruptcy proceedings

(1) Upon the commencement of bankruptcy proceedings, the court will nominate the judicial receiver, and appoint a date not more than one month later for the election of any other judicial receiver and a creditors' committee. The court will also order the

general attachment of assets, determine the deadline for the declaration of claims and appoint the date for the hearing for the investigation of claims.

(2) The court may combine the meetings if the bankrupt's estate is small or the number of creditors is limited, or if the debtor has proposed a compulsory judicial composition.

111. Public announcement

(1) The administrative office of the court will announce in public any resolution passed in order to commence bankruptcy proceedings, any general attachment of assets, any deadline for the declaration of claims, and any other dates required.

(2) Notwithstanding the provisions of section 76 sub-section 1, the announcement will be inserted in the Official Gazette.

(3) Special notice will be served on those creditors and debtors of the bankrupt whose place of residence is known.

112. Notice to registries

The administrative office of the court will submit a certified form of the resolution to commence bankruptcy proceedings indorsed with the name of the judicial receiver to the authority responsible for the trade, cooperative, or suchlike registers and also to any other authority entitled to accept proceedings on behalf of the bankrupt.

113. Registry entries

(1) Any general prohibition against the disposal of assets issued by the bankruptcy court under section 106, and also the commencement of the bankruptcy proceedings, will be entered in the Land Register, the Ships Register and the Register of Ships under Construction:

1. With regard to land, registered ships and ships under construction, when the bankrupt's name has been entered as the owner in the land registry, ships register and the register of ships under construction;
2. With regard to rights in land, registered ships, ships under constructions and other rights, registered in favour of the bankrupt, if, depending on the nature of the right and the circumstances at the time, omission of entry could adversely affect the rights of the creditors.

(2) The bankruptcy court will, of its own motion, request the Land Registry, or the court administering the appropriate register, to make the relevant entry in so far as it is aware of any such right, on any land, registered ships or ships under construction.

(3) The judicial receiver may also apply for entry to the Land Registry, or to the court administering the appropriate register.

114. Cancellation of the entry in the register

If land, registered ships, ships under construction or rights in respect of which an entry has been made under section 113, sub-sections 1 and 2, is released or disposed of for consideration by the judicial receiver, the bankruptcy court may, upon application, request the Land Registry or the court administering the appropriate register to strike out the entry.

115. No fees payable

No fees are payable on the making or cancellation of any entries under sections 113 or 114.

116. Public announcement of the cancelling resolution

As soon as a decision cancelling a resolution for commencement of bankruptcy proceedings becomes absolute, the cancellation of proceedings will be publicly announced. The provisions of sections 111, sub-section 2, 112, 113 and 191 apply accordingly.

Chapter III: The bankruptcy assets.

117. Duties of the judicial receiver

(1) After the commencement of proceedings the judicial receiver will immediately take possession and be responsible for the administration of all the assets which constitute the bankrupt's estate and will apply the latter accordingly.

(2) The business records of the bankrupt may only be disposed of with the business as a whole, and only insofar as they are necessary for the continuation of the business.

118. General attachment

All persons who have in their possession an asset belonging to the bankrupt's estate, or who are indebted to the bankrupt's estate are ordered by way of public announcement of the general attachment of assets not to hand over anything to, or to perform any obligation for, the bankrupt and are all obliged to notify the judicial receiver within a specified time limit regarding their possession of any asset and regarding any claim they may have for a security interest in the asset entitling them to preference upon disposal.

119. Breach of the duty to notify

Any person who fails to notify his possession of assets of the bankrupt within the specified time limit is liable for all resulting damages arising from such failure or delay in notification.

120. Duty to present assets for inspection

Creditors who claim a security interest in an asset in their possession will present the asset for inspection by the judicial receiver on demand and will permit the asset to be valued.

121. Interception of mail

(1) The post and telecommunication organisations are obliged, upon the order of the bankruptcy court, to hand over to the judicial receiver all parcels, letters and telegrams intended for the bankrupt. The judicial receiver is entitled to open such mail. The bankrupt may demand inspection of the mail and, if its contents do not relate to the bankrupt's estate, may require any such mail to be handed over to him.

(2) After consulting the judicial receiver, the court may withdraw or limit this order upon application by the bankrupt.

122. Sealing

(1) In order to protect the assets forming part of the bankrupt's estate, the judicial receiver may have such assets sealed by a person legally empowered to perform such acts.

(2) The trading accounts of the bankrupt will be closed by the clerk of the bankruptcy court.

123. Listing of the assets forming part of the bankrupt's estate

(1) The judicial receiver will list and value the individual items forming part of the bankrupt's estate. If required, the value will be assessed by an expert. An authorised person or official will be present during the listing. The bankrupt will be present if he is available without delay.

(2) At the request of the judicial receiver and the creditors' committee, if any has been appointed, the court may permit the listing of the items to be omitted or carried out in the absence of an authorised person or official.

124. Inventory, balance sheet

The judicial receiver will prepare an inventory and a balance sheet. He must file a signed copy of the inventory and balance sheet at the administrative office of the court for inspection by all concerned, together with a statement in writing of any sealing or unsealing of assets which may have taken place.

125. Sworn affidavit

Following preparation of the inventory, either the judicial receiver or a creditor may invite the bankrupt to a hearing of the district court before which the bankruptcy proceedings are pending for the swearing of an affidavit of the debtor's statement of affairs.

126. Compulsory administration and forced sale by auction

The compulsory administration and forced sale by auction of any real estate forming part of the bankrupt's estate may be conducted by the judicial receiver before the competent authority.

127. Realisation of property charged by way of security

(1) The judicial receiver is entitled to dispose of any item forming part of the bankruptcy estate which a creditor claims is charged to him by way of security or over which an equivalent right or lien is claimed. Disposal will take place in accordance with the provisions for compulsory execution against property or for the sale of pledged property. The disposal is not open to challenge by the creditor; he may however exercise his rights over the proceeds of sale.

(2) If the creditor is entitled to realise his security without court proceedings, the bankruptcy court may, at the request of the judicial receiver and after hearing the creditor, set a time limit within which the creditor must dispose of the item. After the time limit has expired, the provisions of sub-section 1 will apply.

128. Reversionary succession

If the bankrupt is a life tenant, the receiver may not dispose of the items comprising the inheritance if the disposal is ineffective under section 2115 of the Civil Code as against the reversionary owner upon maturity of the reversionary interest.

129. Maintenance for the bankrupt

(1) Until the passing of an appropriate resolution by the creditors, the receiver may provide the bankrupt and his family with any necessary maintenance out of the bankrupt's estate either with the court's approval or, if a creditors' committee has been appointed by the court, with such committee's approval.

(2) Until the passing of an appropriate resolution by the creditors, the receiver will, at his discretion, either close down or continue to run the bankrupt's business. He will deposit any monies, securities and valuable objects as ordered by the court. If a creditors' committee has been appointed by the court, it will determine the closing down or continuation of the business and the deposit arrangements for any monies, securities or valuable objects.

130. Closing down of the business

(1) If the business of the bankrupt is to be closed down as provided in section 129, the judicial receiver will inform the bankrupt of the intended action if it is possible to communicate with him without delay, before the creditors' committee has passed the relevant resolution or, if a creditors' committee has not been appointed, before the closing down of the business.

(2) On application of the bankrupt, the court may prohibit the closing down of the business if the bankrupt has submitted a proposal for compulsory judicial composition.

131. The report of the judicial receiver

At the first creditors' meeting, the judicial receiver will report on the original causes of the bankrupt's inability to pay, on the current state of affairs, and on the measures taken so far.

132. Resolutions to be taken at the creditors' meeting

(1) The creditors' meeting will take decisions on the maintenance to be granted to the bankrupt and his family, on the closing down or continuation of the business, and the place of deposit and the terms of any deposit or investment arrangements for any monies, securities and objects of value.

(2) The creditors' meeting will decide how and how often the judicial receiver should report and account to the creditors' meeting or committee on the administration and disposal of the bankrupt's estate.

133. Approval of the creditors' committee

If a creditors' committee has been appointed, its consent must be sought by the judicial receiver:

1. If, before the preliminary hearing to admit claims has been held, or before a proposal for a compulsory judicial composition submitted before the end of

that meeting has been settled, objects are to be sold, the sale of which may be postponed without obvious disadvantage to the bankrupt's estate and the sale of which is not caused by the continuation of the business;

2. If performance of the bankrupt's contracts is required, or if legal proceedings are to be instigated or their admission rejected, or if settlements or arbitration contracts are to be agreed, or if claims are to be acknowledged relating to assets not belonging to, and separated out of, the bankrupt's estate or for which a preferential right is asserted, or if claims of preferred creditors under sections 57 to 60 are to be acknowledged, or if security over pledged assets should be discharged, or if claims should be assigned, provided always that in these cases the relevant asset is worth more than three hundred deutschmarks.

134. Consent in special cases

The judicial receiver must obtain the consent of the creditors' committee or, if a committee has not been appointed, the consent of a creditors' meeting:

1. If real property is to be sold by private contract, or the business or stock of the bankrupt is to be sold as a whole, or the right to receive regular income is to be sold;
2. If loans are to be obtained or third party liabilities adopted or assets forming part of the estate are to be pledged, or if land is to be purchased.

135. Duty to provide information to the bankrupt; provisional prohibition of certain transactions

(1) The judicial receiver will inform the bankrupt if he is readily available of any proposed action under sections 133 or 134 before the passing of the relevant resolution of the creditors' committee or the creditors' meeting and before the performance of the relevant transaction in the case of section 133, if no creditors' committee has been appointed.

(2) The court may, upon application by the bankrupt and provided always that the creditors' meeting has not consented to the transaction, provisionally prohibit performance of a particular transaction and call a creditors' meeting in order to pass a resolution on the matter.

136. Validity of transactions as against third parties

The validity of a transaction by the judicial receiver as against third parties is unaffected by the provisions of sections 133 to 135.

137. Joint signature of a member of the creditors' committee

If a creditors' committee has been appointed, and the creditors' meeting does not resolve otherwise, receipts given by the judicial receiver for monies, securities or valuable objects removed from deposit and instructions given by the judicial receiver regarding the place of deposit require the joint signature of a member of the creditors' committee.

Chapter IV: The bankruptcy debts

138. Time-limit for the declaration of claims

The period within which bankruptcy claims will be declared is from two weeks to three months. The period between expiry of the time-limit for the declaration and the preliminary hearing to admit claims will be at least one week and at most two months.

139. Contents of the declaration of claim

A declaration of claim must specify the amount and the ground for the claim as well as any priority right relied on by the claimant. The declaration may be filed at the court in writing or recorded at the administrative offices of the court. The original documents supporting the claim or a copy are to be included.

140. Claims register

(1) Declarations of claim will be filed at the administrative office of the court for inspection by the participating parties.

(2) The registrar of the administrative office of the court will enter each declaration immediately after it has been filed, in the order of priority relied upon by the claimant, in a register which must be lodged in the administrative office of the court for inspection by participating parties, and give a copy to the judicial receiver during the first third of the period between expiry of the time-limit for the declaration of claims and the hearing for the investigation of claims.

141. Procedure for the investigation of claims

(1) The amount and priority rights of each of the claims which have been declared will be discussed at the hearing for the investigation of claims.

(2) The bankrupt must provide explanations for the claims.

142. Claims declared out of time

(1) Claims declared after expiry of the period for declaration of claims will also be examined at the hearing for the investigation of claims if neither the judicial receiver nor a creditor has objected to this; otherwise a special hearing for the investigation of such claims will be arranged at the expense of the defaulting creditor.

(2) The previous provision applies likewise to priority rights claimed out of time and to miscellaneous amendments to the declaration of claims.

(3) Creditors who file declarations of claims after the hearing for the investigation of claims will bear the costs of any special hearing for the investigation of such claims.

143. Absence of a creditor

Examination of a declared claim will take place even if the claiming creditor is absent from the hearing for the investigation of claims.

144. Admission of claims

(1) A claim will be deemed admitted if neither the judicial receiver nor a creditor in

bankruptcy objects during the hearing for the investigation of claims, or if any objection raised has been settled.

(2) If the claim is disputed by the bankrupt in the hearing for the investigation of claims, any action pending at the time of commencement of bankruptcy proceedings concerning the disputed claim may be adopted.

145. Entry in the claims register

(1) After discussion of each claim, the court will enter the result in the register. The registrar of the administrative office of the court will note admission of the claim on any bills of exchange and similar debt instruments.

(2) As regards the amount of, and priority rights attaching to, admitted claims, entry in the register constitutes executory judgment as against all creditors in bankruptcy.

146. Actions on the admission of a claim

(1) It is for the creditors whose claims are disputed to start proceedings for the admission of their claims as against those opposing the claims. To this effect the court will make available for the creditors certified extracts from the register.

(2) The admission of claims will be determined in ordinary civil proceedings. The district court before which the bankruptcy proceedings are pending or, if the matter in dispute is not within the competence of a district court, the regional court having jurisdiction over the area in which the bankruptcy court is located, has exclusive competence to hear the action.

(3) If an action was pending with regard to the claim at the time of commencement of the bankruptcy proceedings, the action will be pursued in order to determine whether the claim should be admitted.

(4) Admission of a claim may only be based on the ground and for the amount for which the claim was declared or in respect of which it was presented at the hearing for the investigation of claims.

(5) The provisions of sub-sections 1, 3 and 4 apply likewise to claims admitted in hearings within the jurisdiction of a special court, an administrative body or an administrative court.

(6) Objection to a claim for which an executory title, a final judgment or an enforcement order exists will be at the instance of the opposing party.

(7) The successful party is responsible for rectification of the register.

147. Extent of legal validity

To the extent that a claim has been finally admitted or an objection declared valid by an executory judgment, that judgment is effective as against all creditors. If the action was only conducted against some creditors, those creditors may request reimbursement of their legal costs out of the bankrupt's estate to the extent that the estate has benefited from the judgment.

148. Value of disputed matters

The value to be given to an action relating to the verification or priority of a claim will be determined by the court at its own discretion on the basis of the ratio of the assets of the estate to the debts of the estate.

Chapter V: Distribution

149. Interim distribution

Following the hearing for the investigation of claims, a distribution to the creditors in bankruptcy should follow whenever sufficient funds are available.

150. Approval of the creditors' committee

Before making any distribution the judicial receiver must obtain the approval of the creditors' committee, if such has been appointed.

151. Schedule of creditors

Before making any distribution the judicial receiver must file at the court registry for the inspection of the participants a schedule of all the claims which have to be taken into account at the distribution. He must also announce in public the amount of the claims and the amount of funds available for distribution.

152. Limitation period

There is a limitation period of two weeks from the date of the public announcement by the judicial receiver for those creditors whose claims have not been admitted and for which no final judgment, enforcement order or executory judgment has been produced. Such creditors must prove to the judicial receiver within those two weeks that they have commenced proceedings for the admission of their claims, and for what amount, or that they have recommenced proceedings which were previously pending. If they fail to produce evidence within this time limit their claims will not be considered in the forthcoming distribution.

153. Payment of secured claims

(1) Creditors demanding payment of their secured claims have until the end of the limitation period to prove to the judicial receiver either that there has been a shortfall in a preferential payment as provided under section 64, or that they have waived their claims. Unless evidence is produced within that time limit, their claims will not be taken into account in the forthcoming distribution.

(2) In order to share in an interim distribution it is sufficient to prove to the judicial receiver before the end of the limitation period that the assets to be used in satisfaction of the secured claim have been disposed of and to prove the amount of the presumed shortfall.

154. Claims subject to a condition precedent

(1) At an interim distribution, claims subject to a condition precedent will participate in the amount that the claim would have if it was unconditional.

(2) If the possibility of fulfilment of the condition is so remote that the conditional claim has no current value, it cannot be taken into account at the final distribution.

155. Subsequent satisfaction

Creditors not included in an interim distribution may subsequently claim the dividend which has been determined so far from whatever funds remain available as soon as they have complied with the provisions of sections 152 and 153 and insofar as these funds are not required for a new distribution following the end of the limitation period.

156. Increasing the funds available for final distribution

The creditors' percentage dividends in previous distributions in which they participated according to sections 153 sub-section 2 or 154 sub-section 1 will apply at the final distribution, provided that either at this distribution the provisions of section 153 sub-section 1 have not been complied with, or recognition of the claims subject to a condition precedent has been excluded under section 154 sub-section 2.

157. Amending the schedule of creditors

The judicial receiver has three days from expiry of the limitation period in order to effect the necessary amendments to the schedule on the grounds set out in the preceding provisions.

158. Objections to the schedule of creditors

(1) In the event of an interim distribution, objections to the schedule must be made at the bankruptcy court within one week following expiry of the limitation period.

(2) The court will determine any objections. Any decision ordering rectification of the schedule must be filed at the court registry. The period for filing an accelerated appeal against the court's decision runs from the day on which the decision is filed.

159. Percentage dividend in interim distributions

(1) At an interim distribution the judicial receiver or the creditors' committee, if such has been appointed, will determine the percentage dividend to be paid.

(2) The judicial receiver must notify the percentage share to the relevant creditors.

160. Deferral in the case of a proposal for judicial composition

At the request of the bankrupt the court may order that the interim distribution be deferred if the bankrupt has proposed a compulsory judicial composition, and so long as the limitation period has not expired.

161. Final distribution

(1) The final distribution will follow as soon as the assets have been realised.

(2) The final distribution must be approved by the court.

162. Final hearing

(1) Upon not less than three weeks and not more than one month's notice in advance the court will fix a final hearing date for delivery and approval of the final accounts, for objections to be made against the closing schedule, and for the creditors to pass a resolution regarding disposal of any unrealisable assets.

(2) The provisions of section 158 sub-section 2 apply to the final distribution.

163. Termination of bankruptcy proceedings

(1) After the final hearing the court will order the termination of bankruptcy proceedings. No appeal lies against this order.

(2) The order must be made public together with the reason for the termination.

(3) The provisions of sections 111 sub-section 2, 112, and 113 apply accordingly.

164. Unsatisfied creditors; extracts from the claims register as evidence of executory title

(1) After termination of bankruptcy proceedings, the unsatisfied bankruptcy creditors may enforce their claims against the debtor without restriction.

(2) For those creditors whose claims have been admitted and were not expressly disputed by the bankrupt at the hearing for the investigation of claims, execution will be levied against the debtor based on the entry in the claims register. Sections 724–793 of the Civil Procedure Code apply accordingly.

(3) The court designated under section 146 sub-section 2 has jurisdiction to hear actions for endorsing executory judgments, and also actions in which the claim itself is disputed, or actions challenging the occurrence of a fact which was presumed at the endorsing of the executory judgment where execution is based on the entry in the register, or actions challenging a legal succession which is presumed to have occurred.

165. Reinstatement

If the debtor was not present at the hearing for the investigation of claims, he may request reinstatement. The provisions of section 51 sub-section 2, section 85 sub-section 2, and sections 233 to 236 of the Civil Procedure Code apply accordingly. The written submissions requesting reinstatement must be served on any creditor whose claim is to be disputed subsequently. If reinstatement is granted, objections in the written submission have the same effect as objections made at the hearing for the investigation of claims and should be entered in the schedule.

166. Supplementary distribution

(1) If, after completion of the final distribution, funds which were withheld for the estate become available, or sums which were paid out of the estate are repaid, these amounts will be used by the judicial receiver for a supplementary distribution in accordance with the final schedule of creditors following an order of the bankruptcy court. The accounts concerning the administration and distribution of such amounts are subject to the examination of the bankruptcy court.

(2) This will also apply to any property found to belong to the bankrupt's estate following the final distribution or following termination of proceedings.

167. Carrying out the distribution

Each distribution will be effected by the judicial receiver.

168. Retention of distributions

Any participations in claims which:

1. are being challenged in court following an objection raised at the hearing for the investigation of claims;
2. rely on conditions precedent;
3. entitle the claimant to preferential payment and in respect of which the provisions of section 153 sub-section 2 have been satisfied; and
4. are subject to performance of a condition subsequent, provided that the creditor is obliged to provide security and fails to do so;

will be withheld.

169. Remaining funds to be deposited

Any funds withheld after the final distribution or which have not been claimed by that date will be deposited under a court order for the benefit of the participating creditors.

170. Advance payment of preferential claims

With the authorisation of the court, the judicial receiver may make payments in respect of admitted preferential claims independently of the distributions.

171. Funds reverting to the bankrupt's estate

Any funds which have been deposited for the satisfaction of a creditor entitled to conditional set-off under section 54 sub-section 3 will revert to the bankrupt's estate for the final distribution if the possibility of the condition being fulfilled is so remote that the conditional claim has no current value.

172. Postponed announcement of claims

Claims of preferred creditors under sections 57 to 60 which have not been made known to the judicial receiver at the date when the dividend was fixed, or by the end of the final hearing, or at the date of the announcement of a supplementary distribution, may not be enforced against the funds to be used in payment of the determined dividend or against the funds to be used in the final or supplementary distribution.

Chapter VI: Compulsory judicial composition

173. Admissibility

As soon as the hearing for the investigation of claims has been held, and as long as the final distribution has not been approved, a compulsory judicial composition between the bankrupt and the non-preferential creditors may be drawn up at the request of the bankrupt.

174. Contents of the proposal for composition

The composition proposal must state how the creditors will be satisfied as well as whether and how their claims may be secured.

175. Inadmissibility

A compulsory judicial composition will be inadmissible if:

(1) the bankrupt has absconded or if he refuses to comply with the sworn affidavit referred to in section 125; or

(2) a criminal investigation or reinstated proceedings are pending against the debtor on the grounds of bankruptcy pursuant to section 283 sub-sections 1–3 and section 283(a) of the Criminal Code; or

(3) the bankrupt has been convicted for criminal bankruptcy pursuant to section 283 sub-sections 1–3 and section 283(a) of the Criminal Code.

176. Rejection of the composition proposal by the court

On application by the judicial receiver and by the creditors' committee, if such has been appointed, the court may reject the composition proposal, either if the creditors or the court have already rejected a proposal in the bankruptcy proceedings or if it has been withdrawn by the bankrupt after the announcement of the composition hearing.

177. Statement of creditors' committee

(1) Unless the composition proposal is rejected by the court, the creditors' committee will state whether it is acceptable or not.

(2) If the creditors' committee states that the proposal is not acceptable, the bankrupt will not be permitted to challenge the realisation of the estate.

178. Filing the composition proposal

The proposal and the statement of the creditors' committee will be filed and made available to the participants at the court registry.

179. Announcement of the hearing

(1) The composition hearing should not be fixed more than a month in advance. The hearing date will be publicly announced. The bankrupt and the judicial receiver will be summoned to the hearing as well as those non-preferential creditors who have declared their claims. At the same time they will be informed of the composition proposal and of the issue of the statement of the creditors' committee.

(2) The announcement of the hearing will state that the composition proposal and the statement of the creditors' committee have been filed and are available for the participants to inspect at the registry of the bankruptcy court.

180. Combination with the hearing for the investigation of claims

On the application by the bankrupt and by the creditors' committee, if such has been appointed, the court may combine the composition hearing with the hearing for the investigation of claims.

181. Equal rights for creditors

The composition must grant all non-preferential creditors equal rights. Unequal allocation of rights is only permissible with the express consent of the creditors who have been ranked lower. Any other agreement by the bankrupt or by any other person which prefers individual creditors is void.

182. Required majorities

(1) Acceptance of the composition is conditional on:

1. The majority of creditors entitled to vote, who are present at the hearing, expressly agreeing to the composition; and
2. The total claims of those creditors in agreement amounting to at least three-quarters of the total of all the claims of those entitled to vote.

(2) If only one of the required majorities is achieved, the bankrupt may request before the end of the hearing that the vote be repeated once at a new hearing. The court must appoint a date for the new hearing and announce it at the hearing.

183. Bankrupt's spouse

(1) The calculation of the required majorities pursuant to section 182 sub-section 1, paragraphs 1 and 2 does not include a bankrupt's spouse who has voted in favour of the composition.

(2) The same applies to anyone to whom the bankrupt's spouse has transferred a claim against the bankrupt during the bankruptcy proceedings or in the year prior to the commencement of proceedings, provided that a voting right attaches to the claim which has been transferred. This provision does not apply if the spouse was obliged to make the transfer by law or by a contract which was concluded more than a year before the commencement of bankruptcy proceedings.

184. Approval of compulsory judicial composition

(1) Once the compulsory judicial composition has been accepted by the creditors the approval of the bankruptcy court is required.

(2) The court will reach its decision after hearing the creditors, the judicial receiver and the creditors' committee either at the composition hearing or at a future hearing.

185. Announcement of the court's decision

The decision approving or rejecting the compulsory judicial composition will be announced in public.

186. Rejection of the compulsory judicial composition by the court of its own motion

The composition will be rejected if:

1. The procedural and voting provisions for the composition have not been complied with and the omissions are not capable of rectification;
2. The compulsory judicial composition subsequently becomes inadmissible.

187. Grounds for rejection

The composition must be rejected if it does not satisfy the creditors to the extent of at least one-fifth of their claims and if this is a result of improper acts on the part of the bankrupt and particularly if the bankrupt causes the commencement of bankruptcy proceedings to be delayed by such an act. The composition may be rejected if the same result was achieved by the careless act of the bankrupt.

188. Application for rejection of the compulsory judicial composition

(1) The composition must be rejected on an application by a non-preferential creditor who had a voting right or who substantiates his claim if:

1. The composition results from preferring a creditor or from any other improper act;
2. The composition conflicts with the common interests of the non-preferential creditors in bankruptcy.

(2) The application is only admissible if the facts on which it is based are substantiated.

189. Accelerated appeal

(1) An accelerated appeal against the decision confirming or rejecting the composition may be filed by the bankrupt and any non-preferential creditor entitled to vote or who substantiates his claim.

(2) The time limit for filing an accelerated appeal runs from the announcement of the decision.

(3) There is no further appeal from the decision of the court hearing the appeal.

190. Termination of bankruptcy proceedings

(1) As soon as the composition has become finally binding, the court will order the termination of bankruptcy proceedings. No appeal lies against this order.

(2) The order and the ground for termination must be announced in public.

(3) The provisions of section 111 sub-section 2, sections 112 and 113 apply accordingly.

191. Claims of preferred creditors under sections 57 to 60; preferential claims

(1) The judicial receiver will satisfy claims of preferred creditors under sections 57 to 60 out of the bankruptcy estate. If contested these claims will be protected.

(2) Preferential claims in bankruptcy will be satisfied to the extent that they are admitted, and secured to the extent that they are shown to be valid.

192. Bankrupt's right of disposal

The bankrupt's right to make disposals from the bankrupt's estate will be restored to him as long as the compulsory judicial composition makes no provision to the contrary.

193. Effect of compulsory judicial composition

Once the compulsory judicial composition has been ratified it will take effect for and against all ordinary creditors even if they have not taken part in the bankruptcy proceedings or in the voting on the composition or voted against the composition. The rights of the creditors against joint debtors and guarantors of the bankrupt are not affected by the compulsory judicial composition. This applies also to liens relating to a claim, and also to mortgages, other charges, annuities or ship mortgages relating to a claim or to any registered priority notices.

194. Execution following compulsory judicial composition

After ratification of the compulsory judicial composition, execution will be levied in accordance with sections 724-793 of the Civil Procedure Code and section 164 sub-section 3 of this law on behalf of all those creditors whose claims have been admitted and which were not expressly disputed by the bankrupt at the hearing for the investigation of claims. Execution will be levied against the bankrupt and anyone who has assumed liability jointly with the bankrupt for the performance of the judicial composition and without reserving a right to demand prior enforcement against the bankrupt.

195. No action for annulment on non-performance

No proceedings may be filed for annulment of a compulsory judicial composition on the grounds of non-performance.

196. Appeal on grounds of fraud

(1) If a compulsory judicial composition has been arranged fraudulently, every creditor may contest the partial waiver of his claim without prejudicing his rights under the composition.

(2) An appeal is only admissible if the creditor's inability to prove the grounds for appeal in the hearing to approve the composition was not due to his own negligence.

197. Criminal conviction for bankruptcy

(1) Final criminal conviction for bankruptcy pursuant to sections 283 sub-sections 1–3 and 283(a) of the Criminal Code will revoke for all creditors any waiver based on a compulsory judicial composition without prejudicing the rights conferred on them by the composition.

(2) On the application of a creditor the bankruptcy court may order protective measures to be made against the bankrupt, even before his final criminal conviction.

198. Reinstatement of bankruptcy proceedings

(1) In the event of a final criminal conviction, bankruptcy proceedings will be reinstated on the application of a bankruptcy creditor provided that either there are sufficient assets or that a satisfactory sum for discharging the costs of the bankrupt's estate under sections 58 sub-sections 1 and 2 is advanced.

(2) Reinstatement is by court order. The provisions of sections 108, 111–113 will apply at the time of the reinstatement and the public announcement of the reinstatement of proceedings.

199. Challenge and set-off on reinstatement

For the purposes of contesting transactions undertaken in the period between the termination and reinstatement of bankruptcy proceedings the date of the first judgment convicting the bankrupt is deemed to be the date when payments cease, provided there has been no actual cessation of payments in the meantime. This also applies to rights of set-off arising during the same period.

200. Participating creditors

(1) Creditors for and against whom the compulsory judicial composition took effect may participate in the reinstated proceedings to the extent of the unredeemed amounts of their original claims.

(2) New creditors of the bankrupt are entitled to participate in the proceedings. They have no claim for satisfaction from any security created for the execution of the compulsory judicial composition.

201. Re-hearing bankruptcy proceedings

(1) The proceedings must be re-heard so far as is necessary.

(2) Claims which had been examined already will only be examined again with regard to any interim satisfaction.

Chapter VII: Termination of proceedings

202. Bankrupt's petition for termination

(1) Bankruptcy proceedings will terminate on petition by the bankrupt, if, after the expiry of the time limit for the declaration of claims, he obtains the consent of all bankruptcy creditors who have declared a claim. The bankruptcy court will decide in its discretion the extent to which approval of, or security for, the creditors who have declared claims which have not been admitted, is necessary.

(2) Proceedings may be terminated before the expiry of the time limit for the declaration of claims, on petition by the bankrupt, provided that no other creditors are known except those whose approval the bankrupt obtains.

203. Procedure for petitions for termination

(1) The petition will be publicly announced and filed at the court registry for the inspection of the creditors together with the statements of approval. The creditors may object to the petition within one week of the date of the public announcement. In the case of section 202 sub-section 1 objections may be made by any creditor who has declared his claim before the expiry of the time limit.

(2) The court will rule on the termination after hearing the bankrupt and the judicial receiver. If there are any objections, the creditor raising the objection will also be heard.

204. Termination on the grounds of lack of assets

(1) The court may terminate the bankruptcy proceedings as soon as it appears that the bankrupt's estate is not sufficient to cover the costs of the proceedings. There will be no termination if an adequate amount is advanced to cover the estate costs referred to in section 58 paragraphs 1 and 2.

(2) The creditors will be heard before proceedings are terminated.

205. Announcement of termination

(1) The decision to terminate proceedings and the grounds for termination will be publicly announced.

(2) The provisions of sections 111 sub-section 2, 112, 113 and 191 apply accordingly.

206. Bankrupt's right of disposal

(1) The bankrupt's right of disposal over the bankrupt's estate is restored to him.

(2) The provisions of section 164 apply accordingly.

Chapter VIII: Miscellaneous provisions

207. Joint stock company

(1) Bankruptcy proceedings will apply to the assets of a joint stock company in the event of inability to pay debts as they fall due as well as where the liabilities exceed the assets.

(2) Proceedings may be commenced after the winding-up of a joint stock company as long as the distribution of assets has not been completed.

208. Persons entitled to petition for the winding-up of a joint stock company on the grounds of insolvency

(1) Members of the board of management and liquidators as well as creditors are entitled to petition for the commencement of proceedings.

(2) If the petition is not made by all members of the board of management or all liquidators it will be allowed if it is proved either that the corporation is unable to pay its debts as they fall due or that its liabilities exceed its assets. The court must hear the other creditors or liquidators pursuant to the provisions of section 105 sub-sections 2 and 3.

209. Partnerships with limited and unlimited liability

(1) If an unlimited partnership, a limited partnership or a partnership limited by shares is unable to pay its debts as they fall due, separate bankruptcy proceedings will be instituted against the partnership assets. Separate bankruptcy proceedings will also be instituted against the assets of a partnership limited by shares if its liabilities exceed its assets. The same applies to bankruptcy proceedings concerning the assets of unlimited partnerships or limited partnerships where none of the personally liable partners is a natural person, unless one of them is either another unlimited partnership or a limited partnership in which one of the personally liable partners is a natural person.

(2) The provisions of section 207 sub-section 2 will apply accordingly.

210. Persons entitled to petition for the bankruptcy of partnerships

(1) Apart from the creditors, every personally liable partner and every liquidator is entitled to petition for the commencement of bankruptcy proceedings.

(2) If the petition is not made by all personally liable partners or all liquidators it will be allowed if, in the case of a partnership limited by shares, or an unlimited partnership or a limited partnership in each case of the type described in the third sentence of

section 209 sub-section 1, there is a good arguable case that the bankrupt is unable to pay his debts as they fall due or that his liabilities exceed his assets, or, in the case of an unlimited partnership or limited partnership of any other type, that the bankrupt is unable to pay his debts as they fall due. The court will hear the other personally liable partners or liquidators as provided under section 105 sub-sections 2 and 3.

(3) In the case of an unlimited partnership or limited partnership as described in the third sentence of section 209 sub-section 1, sections 208 sub-section 2 and 210 sub-section 2 will apply accordingly to the officers of the partnership and the liquidators of those partners who are empowered to represent the partnership. The same applies if the officers of the partnership are partnerships themselves of the type described in the third sentence of section 209 sub-section 1 or if the structural relationships between the partnerships continue in this way.

211. Compulsory judicial composition in the case of partnerships

(1) A compulsory judicial composition may only be concluded if the proposal is made by all the partners who are personally liable.

(2) The compulsory judicial composition will, when it takes effect, limit the extent of the partners' personal liability subject to any provision to the contrary.

212. Bankruptcy of a partner

(1) In bankruptcy proceedings concerning the private property of a personally liable partner the partnership creditors may ask for satisfaction only in respect of those amounts for which they received no satisfaction in the partnership proceedings, if bankruptcy proceedings against partnership assets have commenced.

(2) In any distribution, the percentage dividend of any claim on the partnership estate will be withheld until the shortfall in the partnership assets has been ascertained.

(3) Furthermore the provisions of sections 64 and 96 apply to such claims.

213. Bodies corporate, associations

The provisions of sections 207 and 208 apply accordingly to bankruptcy proceedings concerning the assets of a body corporate or association which is capable of being sued in its own name.

214. Bankruptcy of the estate of a deceased person

The district court which had general jurisdiction over the testator at the time of his death has sole jurisdiction over the deceased's estate for bankruptcy proceedings.

215. Estate liabilities to exceed estate assets

Bankruptcy proceedings may not be commenced unless the liabilities of the deceased's estate exceed the estate assets.

216. Commencement of bankruptcy proceedings over the deceased's estate

(1) The commencement of proceedings will not be affected by the fact that the heir has not yet accepted his inheritance or because of his unlimited liability for estate obligations.

(2) If there are several heirs it is also permissible to commence proceedings after the division of the estate.

217. Persons entitled to petition for bankruptcy proceedings over the deceased's estate

(1) All heirs and executors as well as other administrators of the estate or executors who are entrusted with the administration of the estate and all estate creditors are entitled to petition for the commencement of proceedings.

(2) If the petition is not made by all the heirs it will be allowed if there is a good arguable case that the liabilities exceed the assets. The court will hear the remaining heirs if necessary.

(3) If the administration of the estate is entrusted to an executor, he will be heard if an heir petitions for the commencement of proceedings, and, if the executor is the petitioner, the heir will be heard.

218. Deceased's estate forming part of joint property

(1) If an estate of a deceased person forms part of the jointly owned property of both spouses, both the spouse who is an heir and the spouse who is not an heir, but is administering the general property alone or together with his spouse, may petition for the commencement of proceedings without the consent of the other spouse. Spouses retain these powers after the joint ownership of property terminates.

(2) If the petition is not made by both spouses it must be allowed if there is a good arguable case that the liabilities of the estate exceed the assets. If necessary, the court will hear the other spouse.

219. Excluded estate creditors

(1) An estate creditor who is excluded in officially notified proceedings for the declaration of claims or is an excluded creditor pursuant to section 1974 of the Civil Code, may only petition for the commencement of proceedings if bankruptcy proceedings have been commenced over the assets of the heir. The same applies to a legatee or anybody else entitled to demand satisfaction of a testamentary disposition imposed by the deceased over the estate.

(2) If the heir is a spouse and the deceased's estate forms part of the joint property administered by the other spouse alone, the creditors referred to in sub-section 1 above may only make an application if bankruptcy proceedings have been commenced over the assets of the other spouse. If the joint property is administered by both spouses, the creditors may only make an application if bankruptcy proceedings have been commenced over the joint property.

220. Time-limit for petitions

An estate creditor may not petition for the commencement of proceedings after two years from the date the inheritance was accepted.

221. Post-succession judicial execution

(1) Preferential payment may not be demanded following an order for judicial execution or for seizure of goods against the estate issued after succession has occurred.

(2) A priority notice obtained by interlocutory injunction issued after succession has occurred is void.

222. Voidable transactions of the heir

If the heir has satisfied the minimum statutory entitlements, or has paid legacies or discharged testamentary dispositions out of the estate before the commencement of bankruptcy proceedings, such transactions are voidable in the same way as any gratuitous disposal by the heir.

223. Expenses of the heir

The heir has no right to withhold payment of expenses for which he is entitled to reimbursement out of the estate by virtue of sections 1978 and 1979 of the Civil Code.

224. Priority for debts upon bankruptcy of the deceased's estate

(1) Apart from the obligations described in section 59 sub-section 1 estate debts also include:

1. Expenses for which the heir is entitled to reimbursement out of the estate by virtue of sections 1978 and 1979 of the civil code;
2. The cost of a suitable funeral for the testator;
3. In the event of an official declaration of the testator's death, the costs of the proceedings which have to be borne by the estate;
4. The costs of obtaining probate, of an order securing the estate, of the administration of the estate, of officially notified proceedings for the declaration of claims and of the production of an inventory;
5. Any liabilities arising as a result of transactions performed by an administrator of the estate or an executor;
6. Liabilities incurred in the course of business on behalf of the heir by an administrator of the estate, an executor or an heir who has rejected his inheritance, provided that the estate creditors would have been liable if the business has been carried out on their behalf by these persons.

(2) The liabilities set out in sub-section 1 will have the priority provided under section 60 sub-section 1, paragraph 3.

225. Cessation of merger of claims and debts

(1) An heir may assert any claims he had against the deceased.

(2) If the heir satisfies a liability of the estate and, unless his liability for estate debts is unlimited, he will be subrogated to the creditor unless satisfaction pursuant to section 1979 of the Civil Code is not deemed to have been made for the estate's account.

(3) If the heir's liability to an individual creditor is unlimited, he may assert the claim of such creditor if the creditor does not do so himself.

226. Liabilities of the deceased's estate

(1) Every liability of the deceased's estate may be asserted in the proceedings.

(2) The following liabilities will be satisfied only after all other liabilities and in the following order and, if they are within the same rank, pro rata:

1. Interest on claims set out in section 61 accruing since the commencement of proceedings;

2. Penalties imposed on the testator following a crime or infringement of the law punishable by a fine;
3. Liabilities arising from the testator's gratuitous dispositions other than testamentary dispositions;
4. Liabilities owed to persons with minimum statutory entitlements to the estate;
5. Liabilities arising from legacies and other testamentary dispositions imposed by the deceased;
6. Liabilities owed to those entitled to statutory rights of inheritance other than as heirs.

(3) A legacy which excludes a beneficiary's rights to a minimum statutory share in accordance with section 2307 of the Civil Code will rank equally with a right to a minimum statutory share to the extent it does not exceed it. If the testator has provided in his will that a legacy or other testamentary disposition should be satisfied before another legacy or disposition, that legacy or disposition will have priority.

(4) Liabilities, in respect of which a creditor is either excluded by virtue of officially notified proceedings for the declaration of claims or is treated as an excluded creditor pursuant to section 1974 of the Civil Code, will only be satisfied after the liabilities set out in sub-section 2 paragraphs 1–3 and, if they are among the liabilities set out in sub-section 2 paragraphs 4–6, they will only be satisfied after the liabilities with which they would have ranked without this restriction. Otherwise priority is not changed by this restriction.

227. Interest on debts of the deceased's estate

Interest accrued up to the date of commencement of proceedings and interest accrued since the commencement will rank equally with claims set out in sections 226 sub-section 2 paragraphs 2–6 and 226 sub-section 4.

228. Returned items

(1) Whatever is returned to the deceased's estate, as a consequence of a transaction of the testator being avoided, may not be used to satisfy obligations set out in section 226 sub-section 2 paragraphs 4 to 6.

(2) In respect of items which the heir has returned to the deceased estate pursuant to sections 1978 to 1980 of the Civil Code, creditors who are excluded in officially notified proceedings for the declaration of claims or who are treated as excluded creditors under section 1974 of the Civil Code, may only claim to the extent to which the heir would be liable to pay compensation under the provisions for unjust enrichment.

229. Declaration by way of officially notified proceedings

Claims declared and not excluded in officially notified proceedings for the declaration of claims undertaken in order to exclude estate creditors are deemed to have been declared in an estate bankruptcy provided that the public notice is issued by the court which has jurisdiction over the bankruptcy and the procedure is not completed before the commencement of bankruptcy proceedings without issue of an exclusion order.

230. Compulsory judicial composition in estate bankruptcy

(1) A compulsory judicial composition may only be concluded if proposed by all the heirs.

(2) Creditors with claims under section 226 sub-section 2 paragraphs 2–6 and sub-section 4 will not take part in the compulsory judicial composition; such creditors will nevertheless be heard before the composition is approved. If one of them shows that it is arguably correct that the compulsory judicial composition is detrimental to his interests, the composition will be rejected on his application; if the composition is approved he has an immediate right of appeal under section 189.

231. Reversionary succession

The provisions of sections 223, 224 sub-section 1, paragraph 1, and 225 sub-sections 2 and 3, apply to life tenants also after reversionary succession.

232. Purchase of an inheritance

(1) If the heir sells his inheritance, the purchaser will take his place in the proceedings.

(2) The heir is entitled to apply for the commencement of proceedings in the same way as any estate creditor in respect of any estate liability for which the purchaser is liable as against the heir. He will have the same right with regard to any other estate liability, unless he is liable for it without limit or an estate administration has been ordered. The provisions of sections 223, 224 sub-section 1, paragraph 1, and 225 apply to the heir even after the sale of the inheritance.

233. Sale of the inheritance

The provisions of section 232 will apply accordingly to the sale of an inheritance acquired by contract or to any other binding obligation for the disposal of an inheritance which has been received or otherwise acquired.

234. Simultaneous bankruptcy of the heir

(1) The provisions of sections 64, 96, 153, 155, 156, 168, paragraph 3, and 169 apply accordingly to estate creditors to whom the heir is liable without limit in bankruptcy proceedings relating to the property of the heir, if, simultaneously, bankruptcy proceedings are commenced over the estate or if an estate administration is ordered.

(2) If the heir is a spouse and the estate forms part of the joint property which is administered by the other spouse alone, the same applies to bankruptcy proceedings relating to the property of the other spouse and if the joint property is administered jointly, the same will apply to bankruptcy proceedings relating to the joint property and in bankruptcy proceedings relating to the other property of the spouse who is not an heir.

235. No bankruptcy proceedings against part of a deceased's estate

Bankruptcy proceedings may not be commenced against part of a deceased's estate.

236. Bankruptcy proceedings in connection with joint property where joint ownership is continued

The provisions of sections 214–234 will apply accordingly to bankruptcy proceedings over joint property if the joint ownership of the property is continued. The creditors in bankruptcy consist only of those creditors of the joint property whose claims already existed at the time of the joint ownership. A creditor is not entitled to apply for the commencement of bankruptcy proceedings if the surviving spouse was already personally liable to him at that time. Issue entitled to shares in the joint property are not entitled to apply; the court will hear them if it thinks necessary.

236a. Independent bankruptcy proceedings against joint property which is jointly administered

(1) If the spouses have joint ownership and administer the joint property jointly, independent bankruptcy proceedings against the joint property will be allowed if the spouses are unable to pay their debts as they fall due.

(2) If one of the preferred creditors referred to in section 59, sub-section 1, paragraph 3, or an ordinary bankruptcy creditor, is entitled to demand satisfaction of a debt out of the joint property, he may petition for the commencement of bankruptcy proceedings against the joint property.

(3) The same applies to each spouse. If the petition is not filed jointly by both spouses it is only allowed if the inability to pay debts is arguably correct. The court will hear the other spouse if necessary.

236b. Compulsory judicial composition

(1) A compulsory judicial composition may only be concluded if proposed by both spouses.

(2) The compulsory judicial composition will limit the extent of the personal liability of the spouses subject to any provisions to the contrary.

236c. Simultaneous bankruptcy proceedings against the joint property and other property of a spouse

(1) If bankruptcy proceedings are commenced against joint property which is administered jointly by the spouses as well as over the other property of one of the spouses, the creditors in bankruptcy may only seek satisfaction against the other property of one of the spouses in respect of the amounts for which they have received no satisfaction in the bankruptcy proceedings over the joint property.

(2) In any distribution, the percentage dividends will be withheld until any shortfall in the bankruptcy over the joint property has been ascertained.

(3) Furthermore the provisions of sections 64 and 96 apply accordingly to such claims.

237. Foreign bankruptcy proceedings

(1) If bankruptcy proceedings have been commenced abroad against assets of a debtor who has assets in the Federal Republic of Germany, execution may be granted against the domestic assets.

(2) Exceptions to this provision may be made by order of the relevant Government Minister with the approval of the Federal Council.

238. Restrictions on the scope of bankruptcy proceedings

(1) Bankruptcy proceedings will only affect property situated in the Federal Republic of Germany, if the debtor has his principle place of business in the Federal Republic of Germany but has no other place where he may be sued in the Federal Republic of Germany.

(2) If the debtor has no principle place of business in the Federal Republic of Germany and has no other place where he may be sued in the Federal Republic of Germany, bankruptcy proceedings will be commenced against the debtor's property situated in the Federal Republic of Germany if he acts as owner, beneficiary or lessee in respect of land in the Federal Republic of Germany which includes residential and commercial buildings. The district court in the area where such land is situated will have exclusive jurisdiction in the proceedings.

(3) If bankruptcy proceedings are commenced abroad no proof of inability to pay debts is necessary in order to commence domestic proceedings.

SCHEME OF ARRANGEMENT CODE OF 26TH FEBRUARY 1935

(RGB1.I p.321-356)(BGB1.III 311-1)

1. General principle

The avoidance of bankruptcy by way of scheme of arrangement according to the provisions of this law.

Chapter I: Petition for the commencement of proceedings; Proposal for scheme of arrangement

2. Petition for the commencement of proceedings

(1) The petition for the commencement of scheme of arrangement proceedings is filed with the court which has jurisdiction to commence bankruptcy proceedings. The petition may only be filed by the debtor. The petition is admissible under the same requirements as those governing petitions for bankruptcy.

(2) Once bankruptcy proceedings have been commenced, the petition may no longer be filed.

3. Contents of the petition

(1) The petition must contain the proposed scheme of arrangement and must indicate whether and how performance of the scheme of arrangement should be ensured.

(2) The debtor will list in the petition:

1. Whether and when he has made any out-of-court settlements with his creditors within the last five years prior to the date of filing the petition;
2. Whether and when within the same period of time either domestic bankruptcy proceedings or a domestic scheme of arrangement in relation to his property has been effectively commenced at law or whether commencement of either of these proceedings was finally refused due to lack of sufficient assets;

3. Whether, when and with what result he has within the same period of time been required to give an affidavit of his statement of affairs in domestic execution proceedings as a result of a demand for money;
4. When and where he was born.

(3) In the case of sub-section 2 paragraphs 2 and 3, the court in which proceedings are or have been pending must be stated.

(4) The debtor will swear by way of affidavit as to the truth of his statements (in sections 2 and 3) or establish this by public deed.

4. Enclosures to the petition

(1) The petition will include the following:

1. A review of the debtor's financial position (section 5);
2. A schedule of creditors and debtors giving details of all claims and debts (section 6);
3. A declaration by the debtor as follows:
   (a) whether within the year prior to the date of the petition there has been a financial settlement between him and either his spouse before or during the marriage or some other close relative (sub-section 2), as well as
   (b) whether and what dispositions he has made during the two years prior to the date of the petition for the benefit of either his spouse before or during the marriage or for any other close relative; normal everyday gifts are not included;
4. If security is to be offered for the performance of the scheme of arrangement, the exact nature of the security and, if the security is in the form of a guarantee, the surety bond;
5. A declaration by the debtor that he is ready to swear the affidavit mentioned in section 69 sub-section 2.

(2) The following are deemed to be close relatives:

1. The debtor's spouse;
2. The debtor's or his spouse's direct ancestors or descendants;
3. Full or half-brothers and sisters of the debtor and his spouse;
4. The spouses of those persons named in paragraphs (2) and (3) above.

(3) The application and its enclosures will be made in duplicate.

5. Financial statements

(1) In the financial review, all assets and liabilities must be stated and recorded against each other according to their amount or value (section 4 sub-section 1 paragraph 1). Doubtful assets or those which cannot be brought into account should be indicated. Where land, registered ships and ships under construction are among the assets, their title or registered entries will also be stated.

(2) Where the debtor is required by commercial law to keep statutory books, he must submit the opening balance sheet and profit and loss accounts as well as the financial statements; where he has traded for over three years, it is sufficient to present the balance sheets and profit and loss accounts for the preceding three years.

6. Schedule of creditors and debtors

(1) The schedule of creditors and debtors (section 4 sub-section 1 paragraph 2) will include all creditors and debtors. The amount and cause of the indebtedness are to be stated in respect of each claim and liability. Ancillary rights must be shown, particularly in the case of the transfer of title as security, retention of title, mortgages, land charges, ship mortgages, liens and guarantees as well as claims on bills of exchange issued or received; in the case of a claim, all available proof of that claim is to be adduced; for mortgages and land charges the land registry references for the land subject to a charge will be stated and for ship mortgages the ship-registry references will be stated for a ship or ship under construction which is subject to a charge. Where a claim or a debt is disputed, this will be indicated. Creditors who are not creditors in the scheme of arrangement are to be listed separately. In the case of a creditor who may demand preferential payment of a secured claim in the event of a bankruptcy, the presumed shortfall of his claim must be stated.

(2) Where a creditor or debtor is a near relative (section 4 sub-section 2) of the scheme of arrangement debtor or his legal representatives, this will be indicated. Where a creditor or debtor is an employee of the scheme of arrangement debtor or his legal representatives or is in partnership or has some other form of joint undertaking with the debtor or his legal representative, this will also be stated together with details of the partnership or other joint undertaking.

(3) The addresses of all creditors and debtors will be stated. If a creditor lives abroad or his place of residence is unknown but has a designated domestic representative who is known to the scheme of arrangement debtor and who can receive service on behalf of the creditor, the address of that representative will also be stated.

7. Contents of the proposed scheme of arrangement (minimum dividend)

(1) The proposal for the scheme of arrangement must be clearly defined. The scheme of arrangement creditors must be paid a minimum of 35% of their claims (the minimum dividend provision).

(2) The minimum dividend rises to 40% if the debtor requires a repayment period of more than one year from the court's ratification of the scheme of arrangement. The debtor may only seek a repayment period of more than eighteen months to the extent that his offer exceeds 40% of the claims.

(3) The minimum repayments must be made in cash.

(4) A scheme of arrangement in which the debtor agrees with his creditors that they may realise all or part of his property on the condition that, in so doing, that part of the claims not satisfied by the sale will be waived, is only acceptable if it is anticipated that the realisation of the assets will satisfy at least 35% of the creditors' claims and, should the realisation make less, the waiver will not apply to that part of the claim below the 35% level.

8. Equal treatment of creditors

(1) The scheme of arrangement must afford equal rights to all the creditors concerned.

(2) Unequal treatment of creditors is only admissible if:

1. The majority of the scheme of arrangement creditors who will be thus prejudiced and who are present at the scheme of arrangement hearing and entitled

to vote agree to the above; creditors agreeing in writing will be treated in the same way as those present at the scheme of arrangement hearing; and

2. The total amount of the claims of these consenting creditors make up at least three-quarters of the claims of those deferred creditors entitled to vote. The provisions of section 75 are to be applied accordingly.

(3) Every other agreement by the debtor or other persons with individual creditors which creates a preference is void.

9. Revival of liability

(1) Should claims be deferred or partially waived by way of scheme of arrangement, that deferment or waiver will be invalid as against a creditor against whom the debtor defaults in the performance of the scheme of arrangement; default is only deemed to have occurred in the performance of a scheme of arrangement if the debtor has not satisfied a due debt despite a written demand from the creditor served on the debtor which extends the date for repayment by at least one week.

(2) If bankruptcy proceedings are initiated over the debtor's property before performance of the scheme of arrangement, any deferment or waiver of claims is invalid against all creditors.

(3) In the case of section 7 sub-section 4, if the debtor defaults in the repayment of the sum outstanding after his property has been realised for the benefit of his creditors, and for which he is still liable because the minimum repayment level or a pre-arranged higher amount has not been reached, the provisions of the preceding sub-section 1 do not apply. In the case of section 7 sub-section 4, where bankruptcy proceedings are initiated after realisation of the debtor's property for the benefit of the creditors but before repayment of the amount for which the debtor is liable because the minimum repayment level or a pre-arranged higher amount has not been reached, the provisions of the preceding sub-section 2 do not apply.

(4) The provisions of the preceding sub-sections 1 to 3 are only applicable insofar as the scheme of arrangement does not provide otherwise, with the proviso however that the second half of the second sentence of sub-section 1 and sub-section 3 cannot be excluded or restricted so as to prejudice the debtor.

10. Extension of time

Where the debtor fails to produce the enclosures to the petition listed in section 4 sub-section 1, or where the petition and the enclosures do not satisfy the provisions of sections 3 to 7, the court may allow the debtor more time for the production of the documents unless the deficiency is inexcusable. The extension of time should not exceed two weeks. Where the scheme of arrangement concerns a large business or if there are any other special circumstances, the extension may be granted for a longer period not exceeding four weeks.

Chapter II: Commencement of proceedings

11. Appointment of a provisional judicial administrator

(1) The court will appoint a provisional administrator immediately after the petition is filed, and will announce in public the filing of the petition and the name of the provisional judicial administrator.

(2) The same provisions apply accordingly to the provisional administrator as apply to the administrator appointed in the scheme of arrangement (sections 38–43).

12. Protective measures

The court will take all measures which appear necessary in order to prevent any change in the debtor's financial position which might be prejudicial to his creditors until a ruling is made on the petition. In particular, the court may impose restrictions on the debtor's authority to dispose of his assets and can order that the debtor be subject to the restrictions laid out in section 57 and that the provisional administrator shall have those powers granted in section 57 to the scheme of arrangement administrator. The restrictions on the debtor's authority to dispose of his assets are subject to the provisions of sections 59–65.

13. Temporary suspension of enforcement proceedings

(1) On application by the provisional administrator, the court dealing with the scheme of arrangement may order that an execution action pending against the debtor at the time of the filing of the petition, or which becomes pending thereafter, is to be temporarily suspended until a ruling is made on the petition; such suspension is to last no longer than six weeks. The order will only be made if either it is advantageous to the outcome of the disposal of assets or it is imperative to avoid the impending detriment of the creditors. The order will only be granted if the execution creditor would be a scheme of arrangement creditor or would be one of the creditors referred to in section 29 paragraphs 3 and 4, if, in either case, scheme of arrangement proceedings were commenced.

(2) The petition will be refused if it is filed too late to enable the court to assess its requirements.

14. The views of business representatives

If the debtor is involved in commerce or trade or is a farmer, the court will hear official professional representatives from industry, commerce, trade or agriculture as appropriate before it decides on the petition and regardless of its duty under section 116. The representatives will comment on the petition immediately or within one week at the latest. The court may extend this period for a further week on application by the representatives.

15. Procedure should the scheme of arrangement petition have no purpose or be withdrawn

(1) The measures provided under sections 11 to 14 will not be implemented if one of the grounds set out in section 17 and 18 applies so as to prevent the commencement of scheme of arrangement proceedings and where the elimination of this ground is either impossible or may not be predicted with certainty.

(2) Should the debtor withdraw the scheme of arrangement petition before proceedings commence, the court will cancel the measures taken under sections 11–13. The withdrawal of the petition and the termination of office of the provisional administrator will be made public unless the court has declined to make the public announcement provided for in section 11 sub-section 1 on the grounds of sub-section 1 above.

16. Ruling on the commencement of proceedings

Once the requisite enquiries have been made and in particular after the official business representatives have been heard or after the time limits set out in section 14 have expired, the court will decide whether scheme arrangement proceedings should commence.

17. Grounds for refusal

The commencement of proceedings will be refused:

1. If the requirements of sections 3–7 are not satisfied and such deficiency cannot be remedied within the time limit imposed under section 10;
2. If the debtor absconds or goes into hiding or fails to obey a court direction to appear before the court (section 116) without adequate excuse;
3. If a judicial investigation or a recommencement of proceedings is pending against the debtor on the grounds of bankruptcy under section 283 subsection 1–3 and 283a of the criminal code or if the debtor has been finally convicted for one of these crimes;
4. If within the five years preceding the date of the petition, domestic bankruptcy or scheme of arrangement proceedings over the debtor's assets have either been initiated or finally refused due to lack of funds;
5. If, within the same period of time, the debtor has given an affidavit of his statement of affairs in domestic execution proceedings on a demand for money or has refused to give such an affidavit without giving reasons;
6. If the debtor's assets are insufficient to cover the projected costs of the proceedings, including the administrator's remuneration (sections 11 and 20); there will be no such refusal if sufficient funds to cover these costs are advanced or guaranteed in some other satisfactory manner when the petition is made;
7. If the debtor refuses to allow the provisional administrator to inspect his books and business papers or refuses without good reason to give him any information or explanation;
8. If the business records of the debtor are so deficient that they do not enable a satisfactory review of his financial position to be made;
9. If a debtor contravenes an order of the court made under section 12 and his conduct in so doing is inexcusable.

18. Additional grounds for refusal

Commencement of proceedings will also be refused if it appears from the debtor's petition or from the documents produced and statements made by him or from the court's investigations or from the official business representatives' report:

1. That the debtor has caused his financial ruin by dishonesty, under-pricing or his own recklessness; or
2. That, in the opinion of the ordinary businessman, the debtor has wrongfully delayed the petition to commence proceedings for a scheme of arrangement; or
3. That the proposal for the scheme of arrangement does not correspond with the debtor's financial position, whether the debtor offers too much or too little; or

4. That, in the event of the continuation of the business, it is evident that its survival will not depend on the scheme of arrangement.

19. Court ruling on the commencement of bankruptcy proceedings

(1) If the commencement of scheme of arrangement proceedings is refused, the court will rule of its own motion on the commencement of bankruptcy proceedings.

(2) Within one week, the debtor may file an accelerated appeal against the decision either to commence bankruptcy proceedings or to refuse to commence bankruptcy proceedings (section 121). The debtor may assert in his appeal that the commencement of scheme of arrangement proceedings has been unjustly refused.

(3) If bankruptcy proceedings are not commenced an order under section 12 lapses when the order refusing the commencement of scheme of arrangement or bankruptcy proceedings becomes final.

(4) The office of the provisional administrator terminates when the order commencing scheme of arrangement or bankruptcy proceedings is made, or when the order refusing the commencement of scheme of arrangement or bankruptcy proceedings becomes final.

(5) The order commencing scheme of arrangement or bankruptcy proceedings or refusing commencement of scheme of arrangement and bankruptcy proceedings, as well as any orders made on any appeals, will also be served on the provisional administrator. Once the order refusing the commencement of scheme of arrangement or bankruptcy proceedings becomes final, it will be published in the same way as the announcement under section 11 sub-section 1 is made.

20. Contents of the order to commence proceedings

(1) If scheme of arrangement proceedings are commenced, the court will name an administrator for the scheme of arrangement and appoint a date for the hearing of the scheme of arrangement proposal (the scheme of arrangement hearing).

(2) The scheme of arrangement hearing will be set down within one month.

(3) The commencement order will contain:

(i) name (business name), forenames, occupation or area of business, residence or principal place of business of the debtor;
(ii) name and address of the administrator in the scheme of arrangement;
(iii) time and place for the hearing of the scheme of arrangement;
(iv) a request for creditors to declare their claims immediately.

21. Time for commencement of scheme of arrangement proceedings

(1) The order commencing scheme of arrangement proceedings will state the time when proceedings commence.

(2) If this is omitted, time for the commencement of proceedings is deemed to be midday of the day when the order as made.

22. Notice of the order to commence proceedings

(1) The court registry will publish the order to commence proceedings immediately.

(2) The debtor, the scheme of arrangement creditors listed in the schedule of creditors, and also the administrator of the scheme of arrangement will be summoned to

attend the scheme of arrangement hearing by way of a specially served notice of both the order to commence proceedings and the scheme of arrangement proposal.

(3) The public notice and the summons will indicate to the creditor that the petition to commence proceedings, its attachments and the findings of any enquiries may be inspected at the court.

23. Entry in the companies' register

(1) If the debtor is entered in the companies' register, the court registry will send a copy of the resolution to commence proceedings to the authorities responsible for keeping the register.

(2) The registration authorities will officially enter the commencement of scheme of arrangement proceedings in the companies' register. There will be no public notification of this entry. The provisions of section 15 of the Commercial Code will not apply.

24. Continuation of restrictions on the disposal of assets

Where restrictions on the debtor's authority to dispose of assets are ordered in accordance with section 12, these will be deemed to be restrictions under sections 58–65 after the commencement of proceedings.

Chapter III: Scheme of arrangement creditors

25. General principle

(1) Insofar as this law does not provide otherwise, all personal creditors of the debtor will participate in the scheme of arrangement proceedings (scheme of arrangement creditors) if, at the time when the proceedings commence, they have a claim against the debtor.

(2) Those entitled to maintenance are only scheme of arrangement creditors insofar as they would be able to assert their claim in bankruptcy proceedings.

26. Creditors not involved in scheme of arrangement proceedings

(1) Creditors entitled to demand separation of assets or substitution of consideration for separated property or who have a right to recovery from third parties, and also creditors who have priority rights in a bankruptcy and creditors whose claims are secured by a priority notice, are not scheme of arrangement creditors.

(2) Court fees and expenses and also the claims of the provisional administrator are not included as scheme of arrangement claims even if they were incurred before proceedings were commenced. Furthermore, claims which in bankruptcy proceedings are preferential debts of the estate in accordance with section 59 sub-section 1 paragraph 3 of the Bankruptcy Code, are not included as scheme of arrangement claims.

27. Creditors with preferential claims

(1) Creditors who have preferential claims in bankruptcy proceedings are scheme of arrangement creditors in spite of the provisions of section 71 sub-section 3 insofar as the debtor is personally liable to them and they have waived their preferential right or remain unpaid. As long as the shortfall has not been determined, they will be included

in the scheme of arrangement settlement up to the limit of the presumed shortfall, provided that an arrangement more favourable for the debtor is not agreed in the scheme of arrangement proceedings.

(2) The regulations governing creditors with preferential claims also apply to creditors to whom an asset or a right has been transferred in order to secure a claim, as well as to those creditors entitled to satisfaction in bankruptcy and for whom the provisions for creditors with preferential claims are applied correspondingly.

28. Exclusion period

(1) Creditors who have obtained security by way of execution remain creditors in the scheme of arrangement if they obtained the security within thirty days before the presentation of the petition to commence proceedings. This provision also applies to creditors who have achieved full satisfaction of their claims by way of execution.

(2) The day when the petition was presented is not included in calculating the above period.

29. Excluded claims

The following claims may not be asserted in scheme of arrangement proceedings:

1. Interest running from the commencement of proceedings;
2. Costs which individual creditors incur by reason of their participation in proceedings;
3. Fines, payment orders and compulsory payments as well as penalty payments incurred as a result of criminal acts or any infringements;
4. Claims caused by the debtor's gratuitous acts.

30. Claims not accrued due

Claims not accrued due are deemed due and payable. If they are interest free, they will only be included in the proceedings in an amount equal to the total amount of the claim including statutory interest for the period from commencement of proceedings to maturity.

31. Contingent claims

Claims subject to a condition subsequent are included in proceedings in the same way as unconditional claims.

32. Liability of jointly and severally liable debtors

A creditor to whom several people are liable for the whole debt may take part in the scheme of arrangement proceedings against every debtor for the whole amount to which that creditor was entitled when scheme of arrangement proceedings commenced up until the point when he obtains complete satisfaction of his claim.

33. Rights of jointly and severally liable debtors and guarantors

Co-debtors and guarantors are scheme of arrangement creditors to the extent of any future claim which they could raise against the debtor as a result of their satisfaction of the creditor's claim only if this creditor does not assert this claim in the scheme of arrangement proceedings.

34. Conversion of claims

Non-monetary claims or claims for an unliquidated amount or claims which are denominated in a non-domestic currency are included at their estimated value in domestic currency at the time of commencement of scheme of arrangement proceedings.

35. Recurring obligations

Claims requiring performance at repeated intervals, where the amount and the duration of the obligation are fixed, are included in the proceedings for the amount of the total liabilities still outstanding after deduction of the interim interest described in section 30. Where the duration of the obligation is not fixed, section 34 applies accordingly.

36. Claims arising out of reciprocal contracts

(1) A creditor whose claim is based on a reciprocal contract is not a scheme of arrangement creditor if, at the time scheme of arrangement proceedings are commenced, no party to the agreement has yet performed the contract in full.

(2) If the obligations owed by the parties to the agreement are severable and if, at the time scheme of arrangement proceedings are commenced, the creditor has partially performed his obligation under the agreement, he is a scheme of arrangement creditor for an amount corresponding to his partial performance. Because of this partial performance, once proceedings are commenced, the creditor may no longer seek to exercise an express or implied right to disclaim the contract.

(3) If the creditor's performance is not regarded as fully completed because performance of his obligations is defective, the creditor is still, despite his own defective performance, a scheme of arrangement creditor with a claim to such reciprocal performance as he is entitled; the rights to which the debtor is entitled because of the defective performance are unaffected.

37. Foreign creditors

Foreign creditors are treated in the same way as domestic creditors.

Chapter IV: Scheme of arrangement administrator; Creditors' steering committee

38. Appointment of the scheme of arrangement administrator

The scheme of arrangement administrator must be a person competent in business affairs and independent of the creditors and the debtors.

39. Duties of the scheme of arrangement administrator

The scheme of arrangement administrator will examine the financial position of the debtor and supervise the management of the business as well as the living expenses of the debtor and his family.

40. Further powers and duties of the scheme of arrangement administrator

(1) The scheme of arrangement administrator is authorised to enter the debtor's business premises and institute investigations there. The debtor will allow the scheme of arrangement administrator to inspect his books and business papers; he and his employees will supply the administrator with all the information he requests.

(2) The scheme of arrangement administrator must immediately report to the court if matters become known to him which would justify court intervention, and in particular the imposition of restrictions on the disposal of assets, the termination of scheme of arrangement proceedings or the refusal to ratify the scheme of arrangement proposals. He will provide the court with information on demand at any time.

(3) At the scheme of arrangement hearing, the scheme of arrangement administrator will report on the debtor's position, and in particular on the causes of the debtor's financial collapse, the adequacy of the scheme of arrangement proposal and on the prospects of the scheme of arrangement being successful. On the basis of the results of his investigations (section 39), the court may order the scheme of arrangement administrator to produce a written report on the matters mentioned at the scheme of arrangement hearing and also to distribute copies of the report to the scheme of arrangement creditors.

41. Court supervision

(1) The scheme of arrangement administrator is supervised by the court.

(2) The court may impose fines on the scheme of arrangement administrator. It may remove him from office if it has good cause.

(3) The court will first threaten to impose a fine. The scheme of arrangement administrator will be heard before a decision is made under the second sentence of subsection 2 above.

(4) The scheme of arrangement administrator may file an accelerated appeal against a decision to impose a fine (section 121). The court may grant relief.

42. Liability of the scheme of arrangement administrator

The scheme of arrangement administrator is responsible to all participants in the proceedings for the satisfactory performance of his duties.

43. The scheme of arrangement administrator's fees and expenses

(1) The scheme of arrangement administrator may demand from the debtor a refund of his reasonable cash expenses and a reasonable fee for his management of the debtor's business. The scheme of arrangement administrator may only claim reimbursement of expenses which he has incurred by appointing an expert to examine the debtor's books and estimate his stocks if the court has agreed to the appointment of an expert in advance; such agreement should only be given if the examination or the estimation pose particular difficulties.

(2) The court will fix the amount of the administrator's fees and expenses. If scheme of arrangement proceedings continue after ratification of the scheme of arrangement, the court will only determine the administrator's remuneration for his involvement up to the date of ratification. His fees for any involvement after this point will be decided separately after completion of his duties. In this connection, particular regard is to be taken of whether or not the scheme of arrangement has been performed successfully.

(3) Notice of the court's decision will be served on the scheme of arrangement administrator, the debtor and every member of the creditors' steering committee and may be challenged by any of these persons (section 121). The court hearing the scheme of arrangement proceedings may grant relief.

(4) Agreements between the scheme of arrangement administrator and the debtor or a scheme of arrangement creditor regarding the amount of the administrator's fees and expenses are invalid.

(5) The Minister of Justice may issue regulations regarding the administrator's remuneration.

44. Creditors' steering committee

(1) Where the size of the debtor's business appears to require such a step, the court may appoint a creditors' steering committee to support and supervise the work of the scheme of arrangement administrator. Bodies corporate may also be appointed to the creditors' steering committee.

(2) At any time the court may revoke an appointment of a member of the steering committee.

(3) The members of the steering committee are responsible to all participants for the performance of their duties.

(4) A resolution of the steering committee is valid if the majority of the members have participated in the voting and the resolution has been passed by a simple majority.

45. Rights and duties of the members of the creditors' steering committee

(1) The members of the creditors' steering committee are entitled to inspect the books of account and business documents of the debtor and the administrator and to require an explanation in response to any questions which may arise. They shall notify the court immediately upon becoming aware of facts capable of justifying an intervention by the court, in particular the issue of restrictions on the disposal of assets, the termination of the scheme of arrangement proceedings or the refusal to ratify the scheme of arrangement.

(2) The members of the creditors' steering committee may require the debtor to reimburse their reasonable cash expenses and also to pay them compensation for time spent as committee members. The provisions of section 43 sub-sections 2–5 apply accordingly.

Chapter V: Effects of the commencement of scheme of arrangement proceedings

46. Prohibition of bankruptcy proceedings

From the time when the petition for the commencement of the scheme of arrangement proceedings has been filed until the time when the decision terminating the proceedings becomes finally binding, any decision on a petition for the commencement of bankruptcy proceedings will be stayed.

47. Prohibition of execution proceedings

After the scheme of arrangement proceedings have commenced, the scheme of arrangement creditors and also the creditors described in section 29 will not carry out execution proceedings against the debtor until the decision terminating the proceedings has become finally binding.

48. Execution proceedings pending

(1) Execution proceedings against the debtor and in favour of a scheme of arrangement creditor or one of the creditors described in section 29 paragraphs 3 and 4, which are pending at the time of commencement of the scheme of arrangement proceedings, are temporarily stayed by operation of law until the decision terminating the proceedings comes into force.

(2) Upon application by the scheme of arrangement administrator, the court may order the final termination and the cancellation of an executory measure (sub-section 1), if disposal of the asset affected by the executory measure is necessary in the interests of the scheme of arrangement creditors.

49. Court actions after the commencement of the proceedings

Where a scheme of arrangement creditor brings an action for specific performance after the proceedings have commenced, he will bear the court and legal costs pertaining to that action if the debtor admits the claim immediately. This will not apply if, at the time of bringing the action, the creditor either did not know the scheme of arrangement proceedings had commenced or had a legitimate interest in obtaining an immediate judgement.

50. Termination of contracts by disclaimer

(1) The debtor may disclaim performance or the continued performance of a contract if, at the time when the scheme of arrangement proceedings commenced, no party has completed performance of the contract. In the case described in section 36 sub-section 2, disclaimer is only admissible if the other party to the contract claiming reciprocal performance is not a scheme of arrangement creditor.

(2) In order to be able to disclaim, the debtor must obtain prior authorisation from the court. The request for authorisation may be presented to the court at the same time as the filing of the petition for the commencement of proceedings and at the latest within two weeks after public notification of the resolution to commence proceedings (section 22). Before making a decision the court will hear the administrator (sections 11 and 20) and the other party to the contract. A hearing need not take place if it is unnecessary. The authorisation should only be granted if the performance or continued performance of the contract would jeopardise the realisation or performance of the scheme of arrangement and the disclaimer of performance will not result in the other party to the contract suffering disproportionate damage. The decision on the request for authorisation will be served on the debtor, the administrator and the other party to the contract.

(3) The debtor may only disclaim performance within two weeks after he has been served with a court order giving authorisation. After voting on the proposed scheme of arrangement has commenced, the disclaimer may no longer be declared.

(4) If a priority notice has been lodged in order to secure a creditor's claim, the debtor is not entitled to exercise the right of disclaimer as against the creditor as provided under sub-section 1 above. This will also apply if the debtor has assumed further obligations as against the creditor and these have not, or have only partially, been fulfilled.

51. Tenancies, leases and service contracts

(1) The provisions in section 50 do not apply to tenancies or leases where the debtor is the lessor or to service contracts where the debtor is the party obliged to perform the service.

(2) In respect of tenancies and leases, where the debtor is lessee and the leasehold property has already been transferred to him before the proceedings have commenced, and in respect of service contracts, where the debtor is the party entitled to receive the service, the provisions in section 50 will apply with the modification that the power to disclaim performance is substituted by the right to terminate the contractual arrangement within the statutory termination notice period irrespective of the contractual duration.

52. Damages for the termination of reciprocal contracts

(1) The party with whom the debtor has contracted may claim damages for non-performance of the contract if the performance or continued performance of a contract is disclaimed on the grounds stated in section 50 or if a tenancy, lease or service contract is prematurely terminated on the basis of section 51 sub-section 2. He will participate in the scheme of arrangement proceedings to the extent of his claim for damages, and is subject to the scheme of arrangement.

(2) The lessor's right of lien under sections 559, 581 and 592 of the Civil Code may not be asserted over a claim for damages made in accordance with sub-section 1 as a result of a premature termination of the agreement.

53. Mandatory application of sections 50–52

The contracting parties are not entitled to rely on any prior mutual agreement between themselves that the provisions of sections 50–52 are to be excluded or restricted in their application.

54. Set-off

The scheme of arrangement creditors and the creditors described in section 29 remain entitled to set-off after commencement of the proceedings; the provisions of sections 54 and 55 of the Bankruptcy Code concerning the facilitation and the limitation of set-off apply accordingly. In so far as set-off is admissible under these provisions the entitlement to set-off is not affected by the scheme of arrangement.

55. Suspension of the limitation period

Subject to section 96 sub-section 3, the limitation period for the claims of scheme of arrangement creditors is suspended from the commencement of the scheme of arrangement proceedings until the time when the decision terminating the proceedings becomes final.

Chapter VI: Legal capacity of the debtor to assume obligations and to dispose of his assets after the commencement of scheme of arrangement proceedings

56. Duty to maintain a modest lifestyle

During the scheme of arrangement proceedings the debtor may only make use of the means available for him and his family to lead a modest lifestyle.

57. Position of the debtor as against the scheme of arrangement administrator

(1) The debtor should only enter into obligations which do not normally arise during the ordinary course of business operations with the consent of the scheme of arrangement administrator. He should also refrain from entering into obligations which normally arise during the course of business operations if the administrator objects.

(2) If required to do so by the administrator, the debtor will consent to all incoming monies being received exclusively by the administrator and all payments being made by the administrator.

58. Restrictions on the power of disposal

(1) At any time the court may of its own motion or upon application from the scheme of arrangement administrator, a member on the creditors' steering committee or a scheme of arrangement creditor, impose restrictions on the power of the debtor to dispose of his assets.

(2) At the commencement of proceedings the court will examine whether such restrictions are to be imposed on the debtor.

59. General and specific prohibition against disposals of assets

The restrictions on the power to dispose of assets may take the form of the debtor being prohibited generally from disposing of any assets or of him being prohibited from exercising his right to dispose of specific assets. The general prohibition against disposing of any assets includes property which the debtor has acquired after the prohibition has been issued. The effects of these measures will otherwise be determined exclusively in accordance with the provisions of sections 62 to 64.

60. Commencement of the general prohibition to dispose of assets

(1) The order prohibiting the general disposition of assets will record the time when the prohibition is issued. If this is omitted then the effective time of the general prohibition of disposing assets is midday of the day on which the resolution was issued.

(2) The general prohibition against disposing assets will be publicly announced and served on the scheme of arrangement debtor as well as his debtors and the scheme of arrangement administrator. At the same time the court will prohibit third party debtors from paying the debtor.

61. Entering the prohibition on the Land Register and Register of Ships

(1) The general prohibition against disposing assets will be entered on the Land Register, the Register of Ships and the Register of Ships under Construction:

1. In respect of real freehold property, registered ships and ships under construction where the debtor is registered as owner;
2. In cases where the debtor has registered rights in real freehold property, registered ships or ships under construction, if, due to the type of the debtor's right and the circumstances of the particular case, omitting to register the general prohibition against disposing assets would adversely affect the scheme of arrangement creditors.

(2) In so far as it has notice of such real freehold property, registered ships and ships under construction or rights therein, the scheme of arrangement court will either of its own motion or upon application from the scheme of arrangement administrator require the Land Registry or Court of Registration to make the entry on the appropriate register.

(3) The provisions of sub-sections 1 and 2 above will apply accordingly if, at any time when the general prohibition against disposing assets is in force, the debtor acquires real property, a registered ship or ship under construction, a right in such an asset or a right over such a right.

(4) The entry is free of charge.

62. Effects of the general prohibition against disposing assets

(1) The effect of the general prohibition against disposing assets is that any disposal made after the prohibition has been issued is void as against the scheme of arrangement creditors.

(2) If the debtor has made a disposal on the day on which the general prohibition against disposing assets was issued, it is presumed that he made it after the prohibition had been issued.

(3) The provisions of sections 892 and 893 of the Civil Code and sections 16 and 17 of the Rights in Registered Ships and Ships under Construction of 15th November 1940 (Reich Law Gazette I p. 1499) remain unaffected.

(4) Unless section 893 of the Civil Code and section 17 of the Law on Registered Ships and Ships under Construction provide otherwise, the restriction of the right to dispose of assets will only come into effect as against a debtor of the scheme of arrangement debtor when the restriction is made known to the former. Such knowledge is presumed to exist if the judicial decree of the general prohibition against disposing assets is publicly announced or served on the third party debtor (section 60 sub-section 2).

63. Prohibition against disposing specific assets

(1) The prohibition against disposing specific assets will be served on the debtor and scheme of arrangement administrator. If the debtor has been prohibited from exercising his right of disposal in relation to a claim, in particular the collection of a debt, the prohibition will also be served on the third party debtor; the court will in this case prohibit the third party debtor from performing his contractual obligations in favour of the debtor.

(2) The provisions of sections 61 sub-sections 1, 2 and 4 will apply accordingly if the debtor has been prohibited from exercising his rights of disposal in relation to real property, a registered ship or ship under construction, a right over such an asset or a right over such a right.

(3) The prohibition against exercising the right of disposal in relation to specific assets has the effect of making a disposal of such an asset void as against the scheme of arrangement creditors. The provisions in favour of those persons who derive rights from an unauthorised person or a person who does not have title to such rights will apply accordingly. The provisions in section 62 sub-section 4 apply accordingly as against a third party debtor.

64. The scheme of arrangement administrator's power of approval

A restriction on the right of disposal will not affect the validity of a disposal if the scheme of arrangement administrator approves of the disposal. The court may exclude or limit the scheme of arrangement administrator's power of approval.

65. Removal of restrictions on the power of disposal

(1) A restriction on the power of disposal will be removed when it becomes unnecessary.

(2) The removal of a restriction will be served, publicly announced and entered on the Land Register, the Register of Ships or the Register of Ships under Construction in the same way as the order imposing the restriction (sections 60 sub-section 2, 61, 63 sub-sections 1 and 2).

Chapter VII: Declaration of claims; Scheme of arrangement hearing

66. Settlement of the scheme of arrangement

(1) During the scheme of arrangement hearing the proposed scheme of arrangement will be negotiated and voted upon, and the voting rights of the claims, if in dispute, will be determined. The proposed scheme of arrangement will be read out; the contents of a statement of the official professional representatives obtained in accordance with section 14 will be announced.

(2) The creditors not participating in the scheme of arrangement proceedings may attend the scheme of arrangement hearing and will be heard at their request.

67. Declaration of claims

(1) A scheme of arrangement creditor whose claim has not been entered on the schedule of creditors (section 4 sub-section 1 paragraph 2 and section 6) will be taken into consideration at the voting if he declares his claim in writing or records it at the administrative office of the court before voting commences on the proposed scheme of arrangement. Written declarations of claims will be submitted in duplicate.

(2) The declaration of claim will contain the amount and the grounds for the claim; originals or copies of pieces of documentary evidence will be annexed to the declaration. If the original is not annexed to the claim, its production may be required at the scheme of arrangement hearing.

(3) The register of the administrative office of the court will rectify the schedule of creditors in accordance with the declaration of claims.

68. Debtor's and scheme of arrangement administrator's duty to attend

(1) The debtor and the scheme of arrangement administrator will appear in person at the scheme of arrangement hearing.

(2) The debtor may only be represented by proxy if he is able to prove that important reasons prevent him from being able to attend in person.

69. Debtor's obligation to provide information and to swear an affidavit of his statement of affairs

(1) Upon demand by the scheme of arrangement administrator or a scheme of arrangement creditor, the debtor is obliged to disclose all relevant information needed in order to enable an assessment to be made of his financial position as well as the suitability and feasability of the proposed scheme of arrangement; in particular he will

explain the declaration given in accordance with section 4 sub-section 1 paragraph 3 and give detailed particulars about the assets listed in the schedule of assets and also explain where the assets are located and in whose control they are.

(2) Whenever the court considers such measures necessary for the production of truthful particulars, the court will either of its own motion or upon application from the administrator or a scheme of arrangement creditor, order the debtor to place on record a sworn affidavit that he has provided details of his property and liabilities and disclosed the requested information fully to the best of his knowledge and ability. The provisions of sections 478 to 480 and 483 of the Civil Procedure Code apply in accordance with their terms. If the debtor is not requested to give any information the court will restrict the extent of the sworn affidavit accordingly.

70. Discussion of claims

The scheme of arrangement creditors' claims will be discussed on the basis of the rectified schedule of creditors; the debtor will give an explanation for each claim.

71. Determination of the right to vote

(1) If a claim is not contested by either the debtor, the administrator or a scheme of arrangement creditor, it will confer a right to vote. The scheme of arrangement administrator will contest a claim where there are grounds to doubt the legitimacy of the claim arising from the debtor's books of account and records or otherwise, and the debtor is unable to dispel such doubts.

(2) If a claim is contested and the debtor, the administrator and the scheme of arrangement creditors who attended the hearing are unable to agree on the voting right being granted, the court will decide the matter. Upon application from the debtor, one of the scheme of arrangement creditors who attended the hearing, or the administrator, the court may alter its decision at any time before the commencement of voting on the proposed scheme of arrangement. The effect of the decision is limited to determining the right to vote and the legal consequences described in section 97.

(3) The provisions of sub-section 2 above apply accordingly to claims subject to a condition precedent and to preferential claims.

(4) After a claim has been discussed, the register of the administrative office of the court will record in the schedule of creditors whether and by whom the claim was contested. If the participants have agreed amongst themselves or the court has decided on the right to vote, this agreement or decision will be recorded as well.

72. Right to vote in exceptional cases

(1) Scheme of arrangement creditors whose claims for a principal sum are not prejudiced under the proposed scheme of arrangement are not entitled to vote.

(2) One vote will be given to those creditors who have a joint claim or whose claims formed a single claim until the commencement of the debtor's inability to pay his debts. This provision applies likewise where a pledge or usufruct attaches to the claim.

73. Written consent

(1) A creditor may also consent to the proposed scheme of arrangement in writing; the declaration will only be taken into consideration if it has been filed at the court before the voting has terminated.

(2) Consent is also deemed to have been given if the claim of the consenting creditor is contested, unless consent was excluded upon such an event.

74. Voting on the proposed scheme of arrangement

(1) In order for the proposed scheme of arrangement to be accepted it is necessary that

1. The majority of those creditors entitled to vote and present at the hearing, including those creditors who have consented in writing, give their approval to the proposed scheme of arrangement; and
2. The total sum of the claims of the consenting creditors aggregates to at least three quarters of the claims of the creditors entitled to vote.

(2) The majorities will be calculated according to the rectified schedule of creditors.

(3) If the proposed scheme of arrangement does not grant the creditors at least half of their claims, the requisite total sum of the consenting creditors referred to in sub-section 1 paragraph 2 above must equal at least four-fifths of the creditors entitled to vote.

75. Right to vote for spouses and their successors in title

(1) For the purposes of calculating the majorities the debtor's spouse will be disregarded if he or she has consented to the proposed scheme of arrangement.

(2) The same applies to a person to whom the spouse either after the commencement of the scheme of arrangement proceedings or during the previous year has assigned a claim against the debtor if the right to vote derives from the assigned claim. This provision does not apply if the spouse was obliged to assign the claim at law or by virtue of an agreement entered into within one year prior to the commencement of the scheme of arrangement proceedings.

76. Amending the proposed scheme of arrangement to the disadvantage of the creditors

If the proposed scheme of arrangement is amended to the disadvantage of the creditors after the commencement of the scheme of arrangement proceedings and not all of the scheme of arrangement creditors are present at the scheme of arrangement hearing, the court may only permit the amended proposal to be voted on if the proposal has been sent to the scheme of arrangement creditors by the court prior to the hearing; creditors, who have declared their claims at such a late stage that they could not be informed of the amended proposal in time, will not be taken into consideration. The court will decide whether the proposal has been amended to the disadvantage of the creditors.

77. Adjournment of the scheme of arrangement hearing

(1) Upon application from the debtor the scheme of arrangement hearing will be adjourned if only one of the majorities required under section 74 for acceptance of the proposed scheme of arrangement has been achieved; a further adjournment is not permissible.

(2) The scheme of arrangement hearing may be adjourned if three-quarters of the scheme of arrangement creditors present apply for it and it is expected that the new hearing will lead to a scheme of arrangement. The provisions of section 75 apply accordingly.

(3) The scheme of arrangement hearing may be adjourned if the debtor has been represented at the hearing as permitted (section 68 sub-section 2) and the court deems it necessary for the affidavit referred to in section 69 sub-section 2 to be given.

(4) The new date for the hearing will be fixed as soon as possible and should not as a rule take place more than two weeks later.

Chapter VIII. Ratification of the scheme of arrangement by the court

78. Ratification proceedings

(1) The accepted scheme of arrangement requires ratification by the court.

(2) Prior to reaching a decision on the ratification the court will hear representations from the debtor, the administrator and the creditors' steering committee.

(3) The court's decision on the ratification will be announced at the scheme of arrangement hearing, or at a later date to be fixed immediately and which will not be more than one week in advance of the hearing.

(4) If the scheme of arrangement is ratified by the court, the main contents will be communicated to the scheme of arrangement creditors who appear on the schedule of creditors as amended together with a reference to the ratification.

79. Grounds for rejection by the court

Ratification will be rejected by the court if:

1. The regulations for the contents and the making of the scheme of arrangement, or the regulations regarding the procedure after the commencement of scheme of arrangement proceedings have not been observed in a material respect, and the failure cannot be rectified;
2. The debtor has absconded or has gone into hiding or if a criminal investigation or a recommencement of proceedings is pending against the debtor on the grounds of bankruptcy under section 283 subsection 1 to 3 and 283(a) of the criminal code, or if he has been finally convicted of one of these crimes;
3. The scheme of arrangement has arisen dishonestly, in particular through the preference of a creditor;
4. The scheme of arrangement is inconsistent with the common interests of the creditors.

80. The court's ruling on the commencement of bankruptcy proceedings upon refusal to ratify a scheme of arrangement

(1) If the court refuses to ratify the scheme of arrangement it will decide on the commencement of bankruptcy proceedings on its own motion.

(2) Within one week the debtor may file an accelerated appeal against the decision either to commence bankruptcy proceedings or to refuse to commence bankruptcy proceedings (section 121). The debtor may assert in his appeal that the ratification has been unjustly refused.

(3) The court's decision refusing ratification, and its decision concerning the commencement of bankruptcy proceedings, are effective only when they become final.

81. Procedure when bankruptcy proceedings are not commenced

(1) The order refusing ratification where bankruptcy proceedings are not commenced, will be announced in public, notified, and recorded in the public register after it comes into force in the same way as the commencement of proceedings (sections 22 and 23); the order will also be served on the members of the creditors' steering committee; and a certified copy of the order will be filed with the registration authority.

(2) Any restriction on the right to dispose of property will cease to have effect. Section 65 sub-section 2 applies accordingly.

(3) The administrator and the members of the creditors' steering committee will cease to hold office.

Chapter IX: Effects of a ratified scheme of arrangement

82. General principles

(1) A scheme of arrangement is effective for and against all creditors, even if they did not take part in the proceedings or voted against the arrangement.

(2) The creditors' rights against jointly liable debtors and guarantors of the debtor, and also their rights under a pledge, lien or under a mortgage, land charge or annuity charge, or under a priority notice existing in order to secure the claim, will, without prejudice to the provision in section 87, be unaffected by a scheme of arrangement. The debtor will however be released by the scheme of arrangement as against the jointly liable debtor, guarantor or other party entitled to recourse in the same way as the debtor is released as against the creditor.

83. Effect on particular claims

(1) A scheme of arrangement will also have the effect set out in section 82 in favour of and against claims arising from the debtor's gratuitous dispositions.

(2) Interest running from the date of commencement of the scheme of arrangement and arising from the claims affected by the arrangement, and also costs incurred for the account of the creditors as a result of their participation in the proceedings, or in any action for enforcement which has become ineffective under section 87, are deemed to be waived, unless the scheme of arrangement provides otherwise.

84. Effect on a petition for commencement of bankruptcy proceedings

If a scheme of arrangement is ratified, any petition for commencement of bankruptcy proceedings subject to a decision suspended pursuant to section 46, shall be deemed never to have been made.

85. Execution of the scheme of arrangement

(1) Execution against the debtor will take place under a ratified scheme of arrangement in connection with an extract from the creditors' schedule as amended, for the claims under the arrangement which are recorded in the schedule. Execution will take place in the same way as an enforceable court judgment, provided that no note is made in the creditors' schedule that the claim has been disputed by the debtor or by the arrangement administrator.

(2) The same applies to execution against a third party who has assumed liability for the performance of the scheme of arrangement jointly with the debtor, without reserving a right to proceed first against the debtor, by way of a written declaration lodged at the court where the arrangement proceedings are pending or an oral declaration recorded on the official record at the arrangement hearing. It makes no difference whether the declaration regarding the liability to be assumed has been appended to the arrangement proposal under section 4 sub-section 1 paragraph 4 or if it was only later lodged with the court.

(3) If the creditor asserts those rights open to him upon the debtor's default, then no proof that the debtor is in default is required for the issue of the execution order relating to these rights and for performance of the order except for proof of the issue of the formal notice of demand and of the expiry of the additional period of time (section 9).

86. Jurisdiction over execution of a scheme of arrangement

Where execution takes place under a ratified scheme of arrangement (section 85), the district court at which the arrangement proceedings are or were pending and, if the amount in dispute exceeds the jurisdiction of the district court, the provincial court of the area in which the court where the arrangement proceedings are pending is situated, will have exclusive jurisdiction for hearing actions on the issue of the execution order, as well as actions contesting the claim itself or, in relation to the issue of the execution order, contesting the admissibility of conditions accepted as proven in connection with its issue.

87. Consequences of the exclusion period

(1) If a scheme of arrangement creditor or one of the creditors described in section 29 paragraphs 3 and 4 has obtained a security for, or satisfaction of, his claim by way of execution within thirty days of the filing of a petition to commence proceedings for an arrangement, the security is rendered ineffective by the ratification of the arrangement and anything obtained by way of satisfaction of his claim will be returned in accordance with the provisions for restitution in the event of unjust enrichment.

(2) Section 28 sub-section 2 applies accordingly.

88. Termination of the effects of the scheme of arrangement

(1) A scheme of arrangement will cease to have effect for all participating creditors without prejudice to their rights under the arrangement if the debtor is finally convicted for criminal bankruptcy under section 283 sub-sections 1–3 and 283(a) of the Criminal Code in connection with the arrangement proceedings or if he is finally convicted because he deliberately submitted a false affidavit under section 3 sub-section 4 or under section 69 sub-section 2.

(2) The court at which the scheme of arrangement proceedings are or were pending may, on the application of a participating creditor, make orders for the preservation of assets even before the final conviction of the debtor, and in particular the court may restrict the debtor's right to dispose of property in accordance with sections 59–65.

89. Opposition to the scheme of arrangement

(1) Each of the creditors affected by a scheme of arrangement may, without prejudice to the rights protected by the arrangement, dispute the arrangement, if it has arisen through deceit and the creditor was unable, through no fault of his own, to make his submission in opposition during the arrangement proceedings.

(2) An action may not be brought for annulment of a scheme of arrangement on the ground that the arrangement has not been performed.

Chapter X: Termination of proceedings; Supervision of performance of the scheme of arrangement

90. Termination of the proceedings

(1) Scheme of arrangement proceedings will be terminated upon ratification of the arrangement:

1. If the creditors participating in the arrangement apply for termination at the creditors' meeting prior to ratification by the court in the same majority as was required to accept the arrangement.

2. If the total amount of the claims capable of execution does not exceed twenty thousand deutschmarks without taking into account the waiver agreed under the arrangement.

(2) If termination of the proceedings is inconsistent with the common interest of the creditors under the scheme of arrangement, the court will reject, on the application of one of the participating creditors, or of its own motion, an application under sub-section 1, paragraph 1 above and will refuse to grant termination under sub-section 1, paragraph 2 above.

91. Supervision of the debtor under the scheme of arrangement

(1) Scheme of arrangement proceedings will also be terminated upon ratification of the arrangement, if the debtor has subjected himself in the arrangement to supervision by one or more persons named in the arrangement as administrative agent of the creditors. Supervision continues until the arrangement has been performed in full or until fulfilment of one of the conditions set out in the arrangement.

(2) The provisions of sections 92–95 apply to supervision of the debtor under sub-section 1. Regulations other than those set out in sections 92, 93 sub-sections 1 and 3 may be agreed under the arrangement.

92. The supervision regulations

(1) The administrative agent will have the same rights and duties as the arrangement administrator provided in sections 39, 40 sub-section 1, 42 and 57. Where there are several administrative agents, they will manage the business jointly.

(2) The court may remove an administrative agent from his office on any grounds of substance; The court will hear the agent before it reaches its decision.

(3) If an administrative agent refuses to take up office or is removed from office or otherwise ceases to hold office the court may appoint another administrative agent in his place.

(4) If the debtor has granted a power of attorney to the administrative agent under the arrangement, the power of attorney may not be revoked until the administrative agent has completed his duties.

(5) If assets belonging to the debtor have been transferred to the administrative agent for the purposes of performing the arrangement, the provisions of civil law concerning the liability of the transferee will not apply.

93. Mortgage security under a supervised scheme of arrangement

(1) If the scheme of arrangement contains a provision to create a mortgage to secure performance of the arrangement, the mortgage may be registered in such a manner that the creditors under the arrangement are designated as beneficiaries of the security and without any requirement to provide further details.

(2) The security granted by this mortgage is only fully effective in the hands of the creditors. To this extent it will be valid as security even if it not designated as such in the Land Register.

(3) The administrative agent for the time being has the right to deal with the mortgage in favour of and against the mortgagees. He will be recorded in the Land Register as representative of the mortgagees. If the mortgagor is entitled to require the mortgagees to deal with the mortgage in a manner in which the administrative agent is authorised,

he may require the administrative agent to execute any such dealing on their behalf.

(4) These provisions apply likewise if performance of the scheme of arrangement is secured by a mortgage over a ship.

94. Continuation of the restrictions on the power of disposal of assets by the debtor under a supervised scheme of arrangement

(1) Restrictions on the power of disposal will continue, and further restrictions may be ordered, on application by the administrative agent. The restrictions on disposal will be lifted when the supervision ends.

(2) In other cases the provisions in sections 59 to 65 will apply in accordance with their terms; the administrative agent being substituted therein for the arrangement administrator.

95. Termination of supervision of a scheme of arrangement

Termination of the supervision is announced in public at the expense of the debtor and on petition by the debtor or the administrative agent by means of the court where the scheme of arrangement proceedings are pending. The debtor's petition will only be granted if the debtor establishes to the satisfaction of the court that the arrangement has been performed or that the condition specified in the arrangement has been fulfilled. The fact that the debtor has not yet paid the amount for which he will continue to be liable upon realisation of the property under section 7 sub-section 4 does not prejudice termination of the supervision.

96. Continuation of scheme of arrangement proceedings

(1) If the scheme of arrangement proceedings do not terminate upon ratification of the arrangement (sections 90 and 91), they will continue in accordance with the following provisions.

(2) The arrangement administrator will supervise performance of the scheme of arrangement.

(3) The protections against bankruptcy proceedings and stay of execution granted to the debtor under sections 46 and 47, and also the suspension of the limitation period provided under section 55 will terminate upon ratification of the scheme of arrangement.

(4) The proceedings will terminate if the arrangement administrator reports that the debtor has performed the scheme of arrangement, or if the debtor petitions for termination upon establishing to the satisfaction of the court that the arrangement has been performed. The fact that the debtor has not yet paid the amount for which he will continue to be liable under section 7 sub-section 4 upon realisation of the property does not prejudice termination of the proceedings.

(5) The court will decide on its own motion in respect of the commencement of bankruptcy proceedings if the arrangement administrator reports to the court that the scheme of arrangement cannot be performed, or if, within two weeks after the expiry of the latest payment date under the arrangement, the arrangement administrator has not submitted a report concerning the performance of the arrangement or the debtor has not petitioned for termination of the proceedings, or if this application has been rejected after expiry of the latest payment date under the arrangement. Before reaching its decision the court will hear both the debtor and the arrangement administrator.

(6) If, during proceedings continued in accordance with sub-section 1, bankruptcy proceedings are commenced over the debtor's property either on petition or by the

court of its own motion, or if commencement of bankruptcy proceedings is rejected on the grounds of insufficient assets, termination of the arrangement proceedings will be declared at the same time. The provisions of sections 80 sub-sections 2 and 3, and 81 will apply with the modification that the debtor may also assert in his appeal that termination of the arrangement proceedings has been unjustly refused.

(7) In the cases set out in sub-section 5, the court may refrain from making a decision on its own motion in respect of commencement of bankruptcy proceedings if the remaining part of the scheme of arrangement to be performed is relatively insignificant. In such a case the court may terminate the arrangement proceedings.

97. Treatment of disputed and partly secured claims

(1) If a claim is disputed by the debtor or the arrangement administrator, or if the amount of the shortfall is not yet clear in the case of a partly secured claim (section 27) and no decision as to this has been made under section 71 sub-sections 2 or 3, the court before which the arrangement proceedings are pending will, upon application by the debtor or the creditor, irrespective of whether the proceedings were terminated after the ratification, ascertain the presumed amount of the disputed claim or the shortfall. The court's decision has the effect set out in the following subsection.

(2) The legal consequences of default in the performance of the scheme of arrangement (section 9 sub-section 1) may not affect the debtor if, in performing the arrangement, he takes into account the contested or partly secured claim up to final determination of the contested claim or of the shortfall to an extent which complies with a decision reached by the court under sub-section 1 or in accordance with section 71 sub-sections 2 or 3.

(3) After final determination of the amount of the contested claim or shortfall, a debtor who has taken these claims into account in the course of performance of the scheme of arrangement to the lesser extent determined by the court will pay the amount outstanding. Default in performance of the arrangement will however only be deemed to arise when the debtor has not paid the amount outstanding despite a formal notice served on him by the creditor granting him an additional period of time of at least two weeks.

(4) If the final assessment reveals that the debtor has paid too much, he may only reclaim back the excess to the extent that the creditor has received more from the payments than the total amount due to him under the arrangement, even if the claim has not yet accrued due.

98. Effect of the termination of proceedings

(1) The appointments of arrangement administrator and the members of the creditors' steering committee lapse upon the termination of proceedings.

(2) Any restriction on the debtor's right to dispose of his assets will cease to have effect so long as nothing else arises from the operation of section 94. Section 65 sub-section 2 applies by analogy.

(3) Termination of the proceedings will be announced in public, notified, and recorded in the public register in the same way as the commencement of proceedings (sections 22 and 23); the order will also be served on the members of the creditors' steering committee; a certified copy of the order will be delivered to the registrar. If the debtor has submitted to supervision by an administrative agent of the creditors, this fact will be indicated in the notice. Termination of proceedings is only recorded in the public register after termination of the supervision.

Chapter XI: Discontinuance of proceedings

99. Discontinuance due to withdrawal of the proposal for a scheme of arrangement

Arrangement proceedings are discontinued if the debtor withdraws the petition for a scheme of arrangement (section 2). Withdrawal of the petition is admissible until voting on the proposal for an arrangement has been completed.

100. Further grounds for discontinuance

(1) Scheme of arrangement proceedings are also discontinued:

1. If it is shown that commencement of the proceedings should have been refused; discontinuance will not take place if the defect can be corrected or the proposal for a scheme of arrangement has already been accepted (section 74);
2. If the debtor absconds, goes into hiding or fails to comply without good excuse with a summons of the court (section 116);
3. If the debtor fails to comply without good excuse with the restrictions on his capacity to enter into obligations or to dispose of assets (sections 57–65);
4. If the debtor refuses to permit the arrangement administrator or a member of the creditors' steering committee to examine his books and business papers or refuses without sufficient reason to give information or explanations;
5. If the debtor is in breach of his duty to live modestly (section 56);
6. If the debtor fails to appear at the scheme of arrangement meeting or to arrange for representation if such is permitted;
7. If the debtor refuses to give the affidavit provided under section 69 subsection 2;
8. If the necessary majority for acceptance of the proposal for an arrangement is not reached at the scheme of arrangement meeting and a request for adjournment of the meeting is not made or is refused.

(2) In the case of paragraph 6 above, the order to discontinue will not be issued before the third working day after the day of the meeting. Discontinuance will not take place if, before issue of the order, the debtor establishes to the satisfaction of the court that he or his representative, if such was permitted, was prevented from appearing at the meeting by an event which could not be avoided even with the utmost care, and also that he was not able to indicate this to the court before the meeting. Discontinuance may not take place if three-quarters of the arrangement creditors present at the meeting agree that the proceedings will continue; the provisions of section 75 apply accordingly. If the proceedings are not discontinued, a further arrangement meeting will be fixed as soon as possible and which should not be more than two weeks later.

(3) The provisions of sub-sections 1 and 2 do not apply to proceedings which have been continued under section 96.

101. The court's decision on the commencement of bankruptcy proceedings

If the scheme of arrangement proceedings are discontinued, the court will, of its own motion, at the same time make a decision on the commencement of bankruptcy proceedings. The provisions of section 80 sub-sections 2 and 3 and section 81 will apply save that the debtor may also assert in appeal that the proceedings were wrongfully discontinued.

Chapter XII: Subsequent bankruptcy proceedings

102. Basic principle

(1) If bankruptcy proceedings are commenced following rejection of commencement of scheme of arrangement proceedings, refusal of ratification, discontinuance of the arrangement proceedings or in proceedings continued under section 96, they will be designated in the order commencing proceedings as subsequent bankruptcy consequent upon previous proceedings.

(2) The provisions of sections 103–107 apply to subsequent bankruptcy proceedings.

103. Effect of the restrictions on disposal of assets under the scheme of arrangement proceedings

An order restricting on the debtor's rights to dispose of his assets order under the arrangement proceedings is deemed to be made for the benefit of the bankruptcy creditors.

104. Consequences of the exclusion period

(1) If a scheme of arrangement creditor, or one of the creditors described in section 29 paragraphs 3 and 4 has obtained a security for, or satisfaction of, his claim by way of execution, within thirty days of the filing of a petition to commence proceedings for an arrangement, the security is rendered ineffective by the commencement of bankruptcy proceedings and anything obtained by way of satisfaction of this claim will be returned in accordance with the provisions for restitution in the event of unjust enrichment.

(2) Section 28 sub-section 2 applies accordingly.

105. Costs of the arrangement proceedings allowed as costs of bankruptcy proceedings

The court costs of the arrangement proceedings as well as the amounts prescribed by the court under sections 11, 43 and 45 for the provisional administrator, the arrangement administrator or the members of the creditors' steering committee, are included in the costs of the bankruptcy proceedings within the meaning of section 58 paragraphs 1 and 2 of the Bankruptcy Code.

106. Claims arising from loans to the debtor allowed as preferential debts of the estate

Claims arising from loans made to the debtor during the arrangement proceedings with the consent of the arrangement administrator (in the case of section 96 up to ratification of the scheme of arrangement) in order to continue his business and in particular to pay wages or similar claims, or in the interest of the commencement or the performance of the arrangement, and in particular in order to pay off small creditors, constitute preferential debts of the estate within the meaning of section 59 sub-section 1 paragraph 1 of the Bankruptcy Code.

107. Avoidance of transactions. Extension of time limits

(1) For the purposes of avoidance of transactions, a petition to commence bankruptcy proceedings has the same effect as a petition to commence arrangement proceedings.

(2) Time-limits calculated from the day of commencement of bankruptcy proceedings under section 31 paragraph 2, sections 32, the second sentence of section 32a, 33, 55 paragraph 3, and section 183 sub-section 2 of the Bankruptcy Code and section 237 of the Commercial Code and the first sentence of section 32b of the Limited Liability

Companies Law are calculated from the day of the commencement of the arrangement proceedings.

Chapter XIII: Special types of scheme of arrangement proceedings

108. Joint stock companies etc

(1) In the case of joint stock companies, companies with limited liability and other legal entities and also associations which may be sued as such, scheme of arrangement proceedings are, subject to section 112, only permitted to the extent that their assets are open to bankruptcy proceedings. In the case of registered associations, the commencement of scheme of arrangement proceedings will be entered in the register of associations under section 23.

(2) In the case of scheme of arrangement proceedings in respect of a company with limited liability, the shareholders and former shareholders who have withdrawn from the company in the year preceding the application for commencement of scheme of arrangement proceedings are deemed to be affiliates of the company (section 4 subsection 2). This also applies to the close relatives of the shareholders referred to in the first sentence. For the purpose of sections 13, 47, 48, 87 and 104 the creditors referred to in section 32 a subsection 1 and 3 of the Limited Liability Companies Law are treated in the same way as the creditors referred to in section 29 paragraphs 3 and 4.

109. Unlimited commercial partnerships etc

(1) The following special provisions apply to unlimited commercial partnerships, limited partnerships, and partnerships limited by shares:

1. The proposal for the scheme of arrangement will be made by all partners who are personally liable. In any other case proceedings may be commenced when it is possible to show that the partner who has not consented to the proposal was prevented by important reasons from so doing; in such a case, his consent must be declared at the latest at the scheme of arrangement hearing before voting on the proposal for the scheme of arrangement.
2. Insofar as the conduct of the debtor is relevant to the commencement or continuation of proceedings, it is sufficient to refuse commencement of proceedings or ratification of scheme of arrangement proceedings or to terminate proceedings if a ground for such action exists in respect of any one personally liable partner, or, in the case of section 100 sub-section 1 paragraphs 3, 4, 6 and 7 in respect of a person entitled to represent the partnership.
3. Unless it provides otherwise, the scheme of arrangement will limit the extent of the personal liability of the partners.

(2) In scheme of arrangement proceedings over the assets of a partnership under sections 129a or 172 of the Commercial Code, section 108, sub-section 2, third sentence applies to the creditors referred to in those sections.

110. Judicial scheme of arrangement proceedings and bankruptcy proceedings over a partner's property

(1) If scheme of arrangement or bankruptcy proceedings have been commenced over the partnership property, the partnership creditors will participate in scheme of

arrangement proceedings over the personal property of a personally liable partner in an unlimited commercial partnership, a limited partnership or a partnership limited by shares to the extent that they remain unsatisfied in the partnership proceedings. Sections 7, subsection 2 and section 97 apply accordingly.

(2) Scheme of arrangement proceedings in respect of the property of an unlimited commercial partnership, a limited partnership or a partnership limited by shares are equivalent to bankruptcy proceedings as far as concerns the satisfaction of the partnership creditors in bankruptcy proceedings over the personal property of a personally liable partner of such a partnership.

111. Registered co-operative societies.

The following special provisions apply to scheme of arrangement proceedings in respect of registered co-operative societies subject to the law relating to producers' and consumers' co-operative societies:

1. Each member of the managing board is entitled to file the petition. If the petition is not filed by all the members of the managing board, the court will hear those members of the managing board who have not filed the petition before making its decision.
2. The schedule of creditors (section 4, sub-section 2[1], paragraph 2) will state whether a creditor is a member of the co-operative society; this also applies to a declaration under section 67. The petition will also name the auditing association to which the co-operative society belongs or has belonged in the past three years before the filing of the petition. If the co-operative society did not belong to any auditing association during that period, the petition will name the relevant professionally competent auditing association of the district where the co-operative is located. The petition and supporting documents will be submitted in triplicate.
3. The auditing association to which the co-operative belongs will be heard in accordance with section 14 before the court rules on a petition to commence scheme of arrangement proceedings. If the co-operative does not belong to an auditing association, a hearing will be granted to the auditing association to which the co-operative belonged in the last three years before the filing of the petition, or, if, during this period, the co-operative did not belong to any auditing association, the auditing association of the district where the co-operative is located which is professionally competent in the matter. If more than one auditing association is involved, the court will decide which will be heard.
4. The commencement of scheme of arrangement proceedings will be entered in the co-operative's register in accordance with section 23.
5. It is a requirement of a scheme of arrangement that the creditors who are members of the co-operative and the creditors who are not members of the co-operative agree separately to the scheme of arrangement in the majorities required under section 74.
6. If a member of the co-operative has declared his resignation from the co-operative or if the creditor of a member of the co-operative has exercised his right to give notice of termination of membership, the member of the co-operative will not retire before the end of the financial year in which the scheme of arrangement proceedings end or, if a moratorium has been granted in a scheme of arrangement, until expiry of the moratorium. The

declaration of the member of the co-operative, or the creditors, concerning the resignation or the notice of termination of membership will be recorded in the list of the members of the co-operative at the latest six weeks before the end of the financial year in which the member of the co-operative retires, or, immediately, if the scheme of arrangement proceedings end within the last six weeks of that year. The year-end when the member of the co-operative retires will be recorded in the list of members of the co-operative only after termination of the scheme of arrangement proceedings; if recorded previously, a note will be made afterwards to the effect that scheme of arrangement proceedings have been commenced. The provision contained in the first sentence will not apply if the member of the co-operative had already validly retired from the co-operative at the time of presentation of the petition for the scheme of arrangement.

112. Insurance institutions and building societies

(1) Scheme of arrangement proceedings may not be commenced with the intention of avoiding bankruptcy proceedings in respect of the assets of insurance institutions or building societies subject to supervision under the Law Regulating Private Insurance Institutions or the Law Regulating Building Societies.

(2) A petition for the commencement of scheme of arrangement proceedings over the assets of a credit institution which is subject to supervision under the Law of Credit Institutions but is not a building society may only be filed with the consent of the Federal Supervision Authority of Credit Institutions.

113. Judicial scheme of arrangement proceedings over a deceased's estate

(1) The following special provisions apply to scheme of arrangement proceedings commenced with the intention of avoiding bankruptcy of the estate of a deceased person:

1. The petition may be filed by those entitled to petition for the commencement of bankruptcy proceedings with the exception of the creditors of the deceased's estate. The provisions of section 217 sub-section 3 and section 218 sub-section 2 of the bankruptcy code apply accordingly. Where there is more than one heir, all the heirs will file the petition jointly.
2. The petition may be filed before acceptance of the deceased's estate.
3. The petition may not be filed if the heir or one of the heirs is liable without limit for the obligations of the estate in favour of some or all of the creditors of the estate or if the estate has already been distributed.
4. As regards the liability of an heir for the obligations of the estate, the scheme of arrangement proceedings and any scheme of arrangement concluded in the proceedings will take effect as a bankruptcy of the estate and a compulsory scheme of arrangement concluded in bankruptcy proceedings.
5. As far as the conduct of the debtor is relevant to the commencement or the continuation of proceedings it is sufficient to refuse commencement of proceedings or ratification of scheme of arrangement proceedings or to terminate proceedings if a ground for such action exists in respect of any one of several co-heirs.
6. The obligations set out in section 224 of the bankrutpcy code will not form part of the scheme of arrangement proceedings and are not affected by a

scheme of arrangement if those obligations had already accrued at the time of the commencement of the proceedings.

7. The creditors named in section 226 sub-sections 2 and 4 of the bankruptcy code will not take part in the scheme of arrangement proceedings and are not affected by a scheme of arrangement; however, during the period when scheme of arrangement proceedings are pending, they may not carry out any execution against the estate and in particular they may not execute attachments or interlocutory injunctions against the estate.

(2) If bankruptcy proceedings are commenced over an estate of a deceased person or if an administration of the estate is ordered, the provisions of section 234 of the Bankruptcy Code will apply in accordance with their terms to a creditor of the estate who also takes part in the scheme of arrangement proceedings over the property of the heir, or if there is joint ownership of property in the scheme of arrangement proceedings over the property of his spouse or over the jointly owned property.

114. Judicial scheme of arrangement proceedings over jointly owned property under a continuing joint ownership of property

The provisions of section 113 apply likewise to scheme of arrangement proceedings for the avoidance of bankruptcy in respect of the jointly owned property under a continuing joint ownership of property. Before the court rules on the petition to commence proceedings it will, as far as practicable, hear the descendants entitled to a share of the property.

114a. The following special provisions apply to scheme of arrangement proceedings over jointly owned property in continuing joint ownership:

1. The petition must be presented by both spouses.
2. As far as the conduct of the debtor is relevant to the commencement or continuation of proceedings, it is sufficient to refuse commencement of proceedings, or ratification of the scheme of arrangement, or to terminate proceedings, if a ground for such action exists in respect of either of the spouses.
3. Unless it provides otherwise the scheme of arrangement will limit the extent of the personal liability of the spouses.

114b.

(1) If scheme of arrangement proceedings or bankruptcy proceedings are commenced in respect of the jointly owned property of spouses managed jointly by them, and scheme of arrangement proceedings are commenced over the other property of a spouse, creditors of the jointly owned property may only participate in the scheme of arrangement proceedings over the other property of the spouse to the extent that they are not satisfied in the proceedings over the jointly owned property. Section 71 sub-section 2 and section 97 apply in accordance with their terms.

(2) Scheme of arrangement proceedings over the jointly owned property are equivalent to bankruptcy proceedings as regards satisfaction of the creditors of the jointly owned property in bankruptcy proceedings over the other property of a spouse.

Chapter XIV: General procedural rules

115. Basic principle

So long as this law does not provide otherwise, the provisions of the Code of Civil Procedure will apply to these proceedings in accordance with their terms.

116. Court functions

The court will carry out all investigations concerning the proceedings. To this end the court may, in particular, hear the debtor, interrogate witnesses and experts, and call a meeting of creditors; in order to call this meeting it is sufficient to make a public announcement of the appointed date.

117. Oral hearing

Decisions of the court may be made without an oral hearing.

118. Service

(1) Service will be effected ex officio by post. It is not necessary to certify the documents to be served.

(2) Where the person to be served is abroad service will be effected by registered letter.

(3) Documents will not be served on persons whose address is not known. If they have a representative entitled to accept service residing in the jurisdiction and known to the court, service will be effected on the representative.

119. Public announcements

(1) The debtor will be named accurately in public announcements, in particular, his address and business will be stated.

(2) Public announcement is effected by at least one entry in a newspaper designated for the publication of official court announcements; the entry may appear in the form of an extract. The announcement is deemed to take effect from the end of the second day after the appearance of the newspaper containing the entry or the first insertion.

(3) The announcement will be entered by way of extract in the Federal Gazette; the court may also order further public announcements.

(4) Public announcement is deemed to constitute good service on all interested parties even if this law requires additional service to be effected in a particular way.

120. Inspection of the files

(1) The debtor, the provisional scheme of arrangement administrator for the time being, the scheme of arrangement administrator and every creditor may inspect the files; the debtor, the provisional administrator and the scheme of arrangement administrator are also entitled to transcripts of the files.

(2) The creditors will be denied inspection of those parts of the files which do not concern them or the confidentiality of which is claimed by the debtor to be necessary for the carrying on of his business.

(3) The presiding judge may allow inspection of the files by persons other than those named in sub-section 1 without the consent of the debtor only upon proof of a legitimate interest.

121. Appeals

(1) The decision of the court may only be contested as provided under this law.

(2) A decision may be contested by way of accelerated appeal. The time limit for appeal (final date) is one week. Time runs from the announcement of the decision or, if not announced, from service of the decision.

(3) There is no further appeal.

122-123.

Chapter XV: Final and transitional provisions

124. Attachment and interlocutory injunctions

Execution within the meaning of this law also includes the seizure of goods or the execution of an injunction.

125-129. Changes to other laws

130. Coming into force

(1) This law will come into force on 1st April, 1935.

(2) At the same time the law on the Judicial Scheme of Arrangement to prevent Bankruptcy (Judicial Scheme of Arrangement Code)* of 5th July, 1927 (RGBl I p. 139), with the exception of sections 97 to 100, will be repealed. Where reference is made in other laws to the repealed law, the corresponding provisions of this law will take their place.

131. Obsolete

132. Implementing provisions

The Minister of Justice will issue the necessary legal and administrative provisions for the performance (and supplementing) of this law.

THE LAW RELATING TO THE AVOIDANCE OF TRANSACTIONS OF A DEBTOR NOT SUBJECT TO BANKRUPTCY PROCEEDINGS OF 21ST JULY 1879 (RGBL. P. 277), AS PUBLISHED ON 20TH MAY 1898 (RGBL. P. 709), AND AMENDED BY THE LAW OF 5TH JULY 1927 (RGBL. I P. 139)

1. Admissibility of proceedings for avoidance

Transactions by a debtor not subject to bankruptcy proceedings may be avoided as ineffective in favour of a creditor and if made with the objective of the satisfaction of that creditor's claim in accordance with the following provisions.

2. Persons entitled to avoid

Each creditor, who has obtained an executory title and whose claim has accrued due, is entitled to avoidance provided that either judicial execution against the assets

* These provisions confirm changes to other laws.

of the debtor has not resulted in the complete satisfaction of the creditor, or it can be assumed that judicial execution will not result in his complete satisfaction.

3. Avoidable transactions

(1) The following transactions are avoidable:

1. Transactions which the debtor has performed with the intention of prejudicing his creditors, and where the other party was aware of this intention;
2. Contracts for which the debtor has given consideration and entered into by him in the year prior to the proceedings for avoidance: with his spouse prior to or during the marriage, with his or his spouse's relatives in ascending or descending line, with his or his spouse's brothers and sisters and half-brothers and half-sisters, or with the spouse of one of these persons, provided that the debtor's creditors are prejudiced by the making of the contract and the other party does not prove that at the time of the making of the contract he was not aware of an intention of the debtor to prejudice the creditors.
3. Gratuitous disposals made by the debtor in the year prior to the proceedings for avoidance, unless the subjects of these disposals were usual everyday gifts;
4. Gratuitous disposals made by the debtor for the benefit of his spouse in the last two years prior to the proceedings for avoidance.

(2) In the calculation of these periods time shall not be taken into account during which proceedings for a scheme of arrangement were pending with the object of avoiding bankruptcy proceedings.

3a. Transactions performed by the heir

If an heir has performed duties arising from claims for compulsory portions, legacies or testamentary burdens arising out of the estate, a creditor of the estate whose claim in bankruptcy proceedings relating to the estate would rank in priority to, or pari passu with, the beneficiary, may avoid these transactions in the same manner as a gratuitous disposal by the heir.

4. Notification of the party opposing avoidance

If a creditor has notified the party in whose favour a transaction as described in section 3 paragraphs 2 to 4 has been performed of his intention to avoid the transaction by serving a notice in writing before obtaining an executory title or before his claim has accrued due, the period will be calculated from the time of service provided the debtor was already unable to meet his obligations at that time and provided the avoidance occurred within two years of such time.

5. Avoidance as a ground for defence

A claim for avoidance may be asserted by way of defence before an executory title to the claim has been obtained; the creditor has, however, to procure executory title before the decision within a period to be determined by the court.

6. Judicial execution

The right to avoid is not excluded if executory title has been obtained under the transaction which is disputed or if the transaction has been completed through judicial execution or by enforcing an attachment.

7. Claim for restitution

(1) Insofar as is necessary for satisfaction of his claim, the creditor may demand that those assets which have been disposed of, given away or withdrawn from the debtor's property be returned by the donee so as to restore title to the debtor.

(2) The bona fide donee of a gratuitous disposal will return the gift but only to the extent that he would otherwise be enriched thereby.

8. Claim of the party opposing avoidance

The donee only has recourse against the debtor for reimbursement of the consideration he has given, or in the event of avoidance of his claim against the debtor.

9. Specific demand for relief

If avoidance is claimed by way of legal action, the demand for relief shall designate specifically to what extent and in what manner the restitution will be effected by the donee.

10. Preliminary executory title

If a creditor has only a preliminary executory title to his claim or the judgment in his favour is provisional (Civil Procedure Code Sections 540 and 599), his executory title under a judgment awarding avoidance is conditional upon the preliminary executory title or provisional judgment becoming final or unqualified.

11. Avoidance against a successor in law

(1) A well-founded claim for avoidance against the deceased may be asserted against the heir.

(2) A well-founded claim for avoidance may be asserted against another successor in law of the party in favour of whom the avoidable act has been performed:

1. If at the time of acquisition he was aware of the circumstances which formed the basis for the avoidability of acquisition by his predecessor at law;
2. If he is one of the persons listed in section 3 paragraph 2 unless, at the time of his acquisition, he was not aware of the circumstances which formed the basis for the avoidability of acquisition by his predecessor at law;
3. If the disposal to him was gratuitous.

(3) In the case of sub-section 2, paragraph 3, the liability of the successor at law will be subject to section 7 sub-section 2.

(4) It is sufficient for the purposes of the running of time under the limitation periods in accordance with section 4 if the writ is served on the successor in law against whom the avoidance proceedings will be instituted.

12. Time limit for avoidance proceedings

(1) Proceedings for avoidance of a transaction which is avoidable under section 3 paragraph 1 may only be commenced within ten years. The provisions of section 203 sub-section 2 and sections 206 and 207 of the Civil Code relating to the limitation of actions apply accordingly.

(2) The period starts to run from the time when the creditor obtained an executory

title and his claim accrued due; if, however, the transaction was performed after this period of time, time starts to run from the time when the act was performed.

(3) No action for avoidance will lie if 30 years have elapsed since the transaction was performed.

13. Commencement of bankruptcy proceedings

(1) If bankruptcy proceedings are commenced in respect of the property of the debtor, the judicial receiver is entitled to pursue claims for avoidance asserted by creditors in bankruptcy. The costs of their original proceedings shall be repaid to the creditors out of the proceeds of the action.

(2) The court proceedings relating to the claim for avoidance shall be stayed if they are still pending. In case of delay in pursuing the action, the provisions of section 239 of the Code of Civil Procedure apply accordingly. The judicial receiver may extend the scope of the claim under sections 37–39 and 41 of the Bankruptcy Code in accordance with sections 268 and 529 of the Code of Civil Procedure. If the judicial receiver refuses to adopt the action, the action may be pursued by each party in respect of the costs of the proceedings. The power of the judicial receiver to exercise the right of avoidance under the provisions of the Bankruptcy Code is not excluded by the refusal to adopt the action.

(3) If the creditor has obtained security or payment out of the item which has to be returned, the provisions of section 30, paragraph 1 apply accordingly.

(4) After the termination of bankruptcy proceedings the rights of avoidance which enured for the benefit of the judicial receiver may be pursued by the individual creditors in accordance with this law, provided that objections to the claim for avoidance have not been sustained by the judicial receiver. If avoidance had not been undertaken at the time of the commencement of bankruptcy proceedings, the period specified in section 3, paragraphs 2–4 will be calculated from this point of time provided the avoidance takes place within one year after the termination of bankruptcy proceedings.

(5) Transactions which the bankrupt has performed in relation to any part of his property which does not form part of the bankrupt's estate may also be avoided during bankruptcy proceedings as provided in this law.

EXTRACTS FROM THE JOINT STOCK COMPANIES LAW, THE LIMITED LIABILITY COMPANIES LAW, AND THE COMMERCIAL CODE RELATING TO INSOLVENCY

Joint Stock Companies Law

92. Duties of the executive board of directors in the event of loss, excess of liabilities over assets, or inability to pay debts as they fall due

(1) If during preparation of the annual balance sheet or an interim balance sheet it becomes apparent that a loss exists of one half or more of the capital of the company, or if that assumption follows upon due exercise of proper discretion, the executive board will call a shareholders' meeting without delay and will notify the shareholders accordingly.

(2) If the company is unable to pay its debts, the executive board will petition for commencement of bankruptcy or scheme of arrangement proceedings without undue delay and at the latest within three weeks after the inability to pay first arose. The same

shall apply, unless the context requires otherwise, if the assets of the company are insufficient to meet its liabilities. The filing of the petition will not be unduly delayed if the executive board arranges for the commencement of proceedings for a scheme of arrangement with the diligence of a prudent and conscientious business manager.

(3) After the company has become unable to pay its debts as they fall due or when its liabilities exceed its assets, the executive board will stop making payments. This provision does not apply to payments made after this time in accordance with the diligence of a prudent and conscientious business manager.

262. Grounds for winding up

(1) A joint stock company will be wound up

1. ...
2. ...
3. Upon commencement of bankruptcy proceedings over the assets of the company;
4. When the order refusing the commencement of bankruptcy proceedings on the grounds of lack of assets to meet the costs of the proceedings becomes final.
5. ...

Limited Liability Companies Law

60. Grounds for winding up

(1) A limited liability company will be wound up

1. ...
2. ...
3. ...
4. Upon commencement of bankruptcy proceedings; the shareholders may resolve that the company will continue if bankruptcy proceedings are terminated after a compulsory judicial composition has been fulfilled or upon application of the bankrupt.

63. Bankruptcy proceedings

(1) Bankruptcy proceedings take place over the assets of the company in the event of its inability to pay its debts as they fall due or when its liabilities exceed its assets.

(2) The provisions of section 207 sub-section 2 and section 208 of the Bankruptcy Code relating to bankruptcy proceedings over the assets of a joint stock company apply to a limited liability company in accordance with their terms.

64. The obligation to petition for bankruptcy proceedings

(1) If the company is unable to pay its debts as they fall due, the directors will without undue delay and at the latest within three weeks after the inability to pay first arose, file a petition for commencement of bankruptcy or for scheme of arrangement proceedings. The same shall apply, unless the context requires otherwise,

if during preparation of the annual balance sheet or of an interim balance sheet, it appears that the assets of the company no longer suffice to meet its obligations. The directors' petition will not be unduly delayed if the commencement of proceedings for a scheme of arrangement is arranged with the diligence of a prudent business man.

(2) The directors are liable to compensate the company for any payments made after the company has ceased to be able to pay its debts as they fall due or after the excess of its liabilities over its assets has been discovered. This provision does not apply to payments made after this time in accordance with the diligence of a prudent businessman. The provisions of section 43 sub-sections 3 and 4 apply to the compensation claim in accordance with their terms.

Commercial Code (insolvency provisions relating to unlimited partnerships)

130a. Insolvency of the partnership

(1) If a partnership in which no partner is a natural person becomes unable to pay its debts or if the assets of the partnership are insufficient to meet its liabilities a petition will be made for the commencement of bankruptcy proceedings or for a scheme of arrangement. This does not apply if one of the partners of the unlimited partnership and the partners with unlimited liability is a natural person. The obligation to make the petition lies with the statutory representatives of the partners who are authorised to represent the partnership and with the liquidators. The petition will be filed without undue delay and at the latest within three weeks after the inability to pay or the insufficiency of assets to meet liabilities arose. The petition will not be unduly delayed if those obliged to make the application conduct the commencement of proceedings for a scheme of arrangement with the diligence of a prudent and conscientious business manager.

(2) After the partnership has become unable to pay its debts as they fall due or it appears that its liabilities exceed its assets, the statutory representatives of the partners authorised to represent the partnership and the liquidators will stop making payments for the partnership. This does not apply to payments effected even after this time in accordance with the diligence of a prudent and conscientious business manager.

(3) If, in violation of sub-section (1), the petition for the commencement of bankruptcy proceedings or of the scheme of arrangement is not filed at all or in due time or if, in violation of sub-section (2), payments are made after the partnership has become unable to pay its debts as they fall due or after it appears that its liabilities exceed its assets, the statutory representatives of the partners who are authorised to represent the partnership and the liquidators are jointly liable to the partnership to make good the damages arising therefrom. If it is disputed whether they displayed the diligence of a prudent and conscientious business manager they bear the burden of proof. The liability may not be limited or excluded by agreement with the partners. So far as is necessary for the satisfaction of the partnership's creditors the liability may not be revoked by either a waiver or a settlement of the partnership or by the fact that the act was based on a decision taken by the partners. A compulsory judicial composition or a settlement reached in the process of a scheme of arrangement is effective both for and against the partnership's claim. Claims under these provisions expire in five years.

(4) These provisions apply accordingly if the statutory representatives mentioned in sub-sections (1)–(3) are themselves partnerships none of whose partners are natural persons or if the connection between partnerships goes further in the same way.

130b. Penal provisions

(1) Imprisonment up to three years or a fine will be inflicted on any person who contrary to section 130 sub-sections (1)–(4) being a statutory representative or liquidator fails to petition for the commencement of bankruptcy proceedings or for judicial scheme of arrangement proceedings when the partnership becomes unable to pay its debts as they fall due or when the assets of such partnership are insufficient to meets its liabilities.

(2) If the act was committed negligently, the punishment shall be imprisonment up to one year or a fine.

131. Grounds for dissolution

An unlimited partnership will be dissolved:

1. On expiry of the period for which it was formed;
2. By a resolution of the partners;
3. By the commencement of bankruptcy proceedings over the property of the partnership;
4. By the death of one of the partners unless the partnership agreement provides otherwise;
5. By the commencement of bankruptcy proceedings over the property of one of the partners; and
6. By notice of termination and by judicial decision.

137. Death and insolvency of a partner

(1) If a partnership is dissolved due to the death of a partner, the heir of the deceased partner will notify the other partners of the death immediately and in the case of imminent risk he will carry on any business which needed to be looked after by the deceased until the other partners are able to make arrangements with him in some other manner. The other partners are obliged in the same way to carry on for the time being the business which requires their attention. To this extent the partnership is deemed to continue to exist.

(2) The provisions of sub-section (1) second and third sentences also apply in the event of a dissolution of the partnership due to the commencement of bankruptcy proceedings over the property of one of the partners.

138. Withdrawal of a partner

If the partnership agreement provides that when a partner gives notice or dies or when bankruptcy proceedings are commenced over his property the partnership will continue to exist between the other partners, the partner who is affected by such occurrence will leave the partnership with effect from the time at which the partnership would have been dissolved in the absence of such a provision.

141. Continuation by resolution

(1) If a personal creditor of a partner makes use of the rights he is entitled to under section 135, the other partners may on the basis of a resolution passed by them declare to the creditor that the partnership will continue to exist between them. In this case the affected partner will leave the partnership at the end of the business year.

(2) When bankruptcy proceedings are commenced over the property of a partner these provisions will apply provided that declaration is made to the judicial receiver and that the bankrupt is deemed to have left the partnership on the date of the commencement of bankruptcy proceedings.

142. Take-over of the business by one partner

(1) If there are only two partners and with regard to one of them the requirements are fulfilled under which in case of a larger number of partners his expulsion from the partnership would be permissible, the other partner may upon his petition be declared by the court to be entitled to take over the business with its assets and liabilities without liquidation.

(2) If, in the case of a partnership consisting of two partners, a personal creditor of a partner makes use of the right he is entitled to under section 135 or if bankruptcy proceedings are commenced as to the property of one of the partners the other partner is entitled to take over the business as set out above.

(3) Regarding the settlement of accounts the provisions which are applicable in the case of a withdrawal will apply accordingly.

144. Continuation after bankruptcy

(1) If the partnership is dissolved due to the commencement of bankruptcy proceedings over its property, but the bankruptcy proceedings are terminated after conclusion of a compulsory judicial composition or are stayed upon a petition by the bankrupt, the partners may pass a resolution for the continuation of the partnership.

(2) The continuation will be notified for registration in the Commercial Register by all the partners.

NOTE: By section 161 sub-section 2, and section 177a of the Commercial Code these provisions relating to unlimited partnerships also apply to limited partnerships.

ITALY

The translated text is of the Bankruptcy Law of 16th March 1942 as amended up to 1st January 1993, together with the Decree of Extraordinary Administration of 30th January 1979.

It is arranged in six titles. Title I, which is very short, governs the application of the insolvency procedures available under Italian law to particular types of business activity. Title II contains the entire procedural and substantive scheme of bankruptcy, as such. Save for the first article of the title (article 5) which defines bankruptcy and article 11, which voids Civil Code preferences on death in the event of bankruptcy, chapters I and II of Title II are largely procedural. Chapter III effectively contains all the substantive provisions. Chapters IV, V, VI and VII deal with the administration, realisation and distribution of assets. Chapters VIII and IX contain the termination and discharge provisions (but chapter VIII also includes a section on settlement agreements). Chapter X contains special provisions for company officers and the members of co-operatives and limited liability companies, and chapter XI sets out the summary procedure in cases where liabilities are less than 1.5 million lire.

Titles III, IV and V deal, respectively, with the procedures of preventive creditors' settlement, supervised administration and compulsory administrative liquidation. Title VI contains the criminal bankruptcy provisions, and the Decree governs the special procedure of Extraordinary Administration.

CHAPTER FOUR

Italian Insolvency Laws

Note: Articles indicated by an asterisk* are those which have been in part declared invalid by the Constitutional Court. The parts deleted are omitted from the translation. The text is correct as of 1st January 1993. The text does not include the exception to Article 67 in favour of factors (Law no. 52 of 21st February 1991), or the right of first refusal granted to a lessee of a business subject to one of the bankruptcy procedures (Law no. 223 of 23rd July 1991 – art. 3, paras. 1 & 4).

TABLE OF CONTENTS

BANKRUPTCY LAW, 16TH MARCH 1942, AS AMENDED UP TO DATE OF PUBLICATION IN 1987

TITLE I. GENERAL PROVISIONS

1. (Undertakings subject to bankruptcy, preventive creditors' settlement and supervised administration.) All traders who carry on a commercial enterprise are subject to the provisions of the law on bankruptcy, preventive creditors' settlement and supervised administration – with the exception of traders who carry on small businesses and of public entities controlled by public authorities.

*Traders carrying on small businesses are those traders who carry on an activity which is assessed as having an income below the minimum level for the purposes of taxes on personal property. In the absence of such assessment, small businesses are those carrying on a commercial activity funded with capital not exceeding 900.000 lira. Commercial companies are never considered to be small businesses.

2. (Compulsory administrative liquidation and bankruptcy.) Undertakings subject to compulsory administrative liquidation, the circumstances in which compulsory administrative liquidation may be ordered, and the competent authority to order it, are determined by law.

Unless otherwise provided by law, undertakings subject to compulsory administrative liquidation are not subject to bankruptcy.

Where the law provides for application of the procedures of both compulsory administrative liquidation and bankruptcy, the provisions of art. 196 will apply.

3. (Compulsory administrative liquidation, preventive creditors' settlements and supervised administration.) Unless otherwise provided by law, those undertakings which are subject to compulsory administrative liquidation may be subject to the procedures for preventive creditors' settlements and supervised administration subject always to the provisions of paragraph (7) of art. 195 for companies which are excluded from bankruptcy. Undertakings which are lending institutions are not subject to supervised administration as provided under this law.

4. (Specific laws.) Stockbrokers may become bankrupt in circumstances determined by specific laws, subject always to the provisions of specific laws concerning the declaration of bankruptcy of tax-payers on account of any tax liability.

TITLE II. BANKRUPTCY

Chapter I: Declaration of bankruptcy

5. (State of bankruptcy.) A trader is declared bankrupt when he is in a state of insolvency. A state of insolvency is shown by non-payment of a debt or other external factors which indicate that the debtor is unable to meet his obligations on a regular basis.

6. (Application for a declaration of bankruptcy.) Bankruptcy is declared on the petition of the debtor or one or more creditors or on application by the public prosecutor or by the court of its own motion.

7. (State of bankruptcy resulting in criminal proceedings.) If the insolvency is manifested as a result of the trader absconding or going into hiding, or by the closure of the premises of his firm, by his or her theft, or by the fraudulent substitution of, or reduction in the company's assets, the public prosecutor proceeding against the trader must petition the competent court for a declaration of bankruptcy.

8. (State of bankruptcy resulting in civil proceedings.) If, in the course of civil proceedings, a party to the proceedings appears to be insolvent, the judge must refer the matter to the competent court for a declaration of bankruptcy.

9. (Jurisdiction.) Bankruptcy is declared by the court in the jurisdiction where the principal office of the business is located.

A trader who has his principal office abroad may be declared bankrupt in the Republic of Italy even if a declaration of bankruptcy has been pronounced abroad and subject always to international conventions.

10. (Bankruptcy of a trader who has ceased to carry on business.) A trader who, for whatever reason, has ceased to carry on business may be declared bankrupt within one year from the date of cessation of business, provided the insolvency has occurred before the date of cessation or within the following year.

11. (Bankruptcy of a deceased trader.) Deceased traders may be declared bankrupt if the conditions set out in the previous article apply.

The heir may request that the deceased be declared bankrupt provided that the inheritance and the estate of the heir have not already been merged.

Preferential treatment by way of separation of assets obtained by the creditors of the deceased in accordance with the civil code ceases to have legal effect after the declaration of bankruptcy of the deceased has been pronounced.

12. (Death of the bankrupt trader.) If a trader dies after he has been declared bankrupt, the legal procedure continues with regard to his heirs even if they have accepted the inheritance to the extent that debts are not in excess of assets.

If there is more than one heir, the legal procedure is directed at the heir who has been designated a personal representative. If there is no agreement in designating the personal representative within fifteen days of the death of the bankrupt person, nomination will be made by the judge.

In the case referred to in art. 528 of the civil code, the legal procedure is directed at the administrator of the relevant unclaimed inheritance and in the case referred to in art. 641 of the civil code it is directed at the administrator appointed pursuant to art. 642 of the civil code.

13. (Duty to transmit list of protests.) Public officials authorised to collect protests of bills are under a duty to transmit every fifteen days, a list of protests for non-payments collected during the previous fifteen days to the president of the court in the jurisdiction where they act. The list must contain the date of each protest, surname and address of the person to whom the protest is addressed and that of the person requesting it, date of expiry of the bill protested, the amount owed and the reasons for the refusal of payment.

Procurators of the registry are under the same obligation as regards refusals of payment made in accordance with the law governing promissory notes.

14. (Duties of traders who petition for their own bankruptcy.) A trader who petitions for his own bankruptcy is under a duty to file, at the court registry, his books of account and the balance sheet with the profit and loss account for the previous two years or from the commencement of the business if it has been in existence for less than two years. He must also file a detailed statement and estimate of his assets, a list of his creditors by name and the amount of the respective debts, and another list containing the names of those who claim rights *in rem* against chattels in his possession and indicating the grounds of such claims.

15. *(Power of the court to hear the debtor.) The court may summon a trader to appear in chambers, and hear him alone or in the presence of his creditors, before it declares him bankrupt.

16. (Judgment in which bankruptcy is declared.) The judgment declaring bankruptcy is pronounced in chambers.

In the judgment the court:

(1) appoints the bankruptcy judge in charge of the procedure;
(2) appoints the administrator;
(3) orders the bankrupt to file, within twenty four hours, his balance sheet and books of account if he has not already done so in accordance with art. 14.
(4) grants a period to creditors and third parties who claim rights *in rem* against chattels in the possession of the bankrupt of up to thirty days from the date on which the judgement has been published for the submission of their claims to the court registry;
(5) appoints the place, date and time (to be within twenty days of the date indicated at paragraph (4) above) of the meeting of creditors at which the indebtedness position will be examined.

The judgment is provisionally enforceable.

In the same judgment or in a subsequent decree the court will order the arrest of the bankrupt or of any others responsible for committing offences contemplated in this law if the circumstances described in art. 7 exist, or if there are other facts evidencing their guilt. The sentence or the decree will be communicated to the public prosecutor who will be responsible for its execution.

17. (Notification and publication of the judgment in which bankruptcy is declared.) An abstract of the judgment in which bankruptcy is declared is communicated in accordance with art. 136 of the code of civil procedure, to the debtor, to the administrator and to the petitioning creditor no later than one day following the date in which the judgment is given. The abstract will contain the names of the parties, the verdict and the date of the judgment.

Within the same period of time the registry will ensure that the abstract is attached to the external door of the court and is communicated to the public prosecutor, to the office of the registrar of the companies for registration (this to be done within twenty four hours of its receipt), and to the court registry in the jurisdiction where the debtor was born or the company was incorporated. Moreover, the provisions of the code of criminal procedure relating to criminal records must be observed.

In addition the court registry will ensure that the abstract of the judgment is gazetted in the provincial journal for legal notices.

18. ★(Objections to the declaration of bankruptcy.) The debtor and any other interested parties may file an objection to the declaration of bankruptcy within fifteen days from the publication of judgment. The objection may not be made by the same persons who petitioned for the declaration of bankruptcy.

Objection is made by means of a writ of summons to be notified to the administrator and to the creditor who has petitioned for the declaration of bankruptcy.

★The lodging of an objection does not suspend execution of the judgment.

19. (Judgment on the proceedings for objection and appeal.) A judgment revoking the bankruptcy will be notified to the administrator, to the creditor who petitioned for the declaration of bankruptcy and to the debtor, if he is not the appellant. It must be published, communicated, attached and registered in accordance with art. 17.

A judgment rejecting the objection will be notified to the party who appealed.

In both cases the judgment may be appealed within a period of 15 days from notification.

The provisions of the first and second paragraphs apply to the appeal judgment.

20. (Death of the bankrupt during the objection proceedings.) If the bankrupt dies during the objection proceedings, the hearing will continue with regard to the persons referred to in art. 12 and follows the provisions of art. 299 et seq. of the code of civil procedure.

21. (Revocation of the declaration of bankruptcy.) If a judgment declaring bankruptcy is revoked, the consequences of acts legally carried out by the administrative organs of the court appointed in bankruptcy cases remain effective at law.

Legal costs and remuneration for the administrator are settled by the court on the basis of the report of the bankruptcy judge in a decree which is not subject to appeal.

★Legal costs and the administrator's remuneration are paid by the creditor who has lodged the petition, where he has been ordered to pay damages for having wrongfully requested the declaration of bankruptcy. If that is not the case the administrator may obtain payment, in whole or in part, in accordance with the procedures set out in the regulation in force for the allocation of remuneration to administrators who are unable to obtain adequate remuneration.

22. (Appeal from an order disallowing bankruptcy.) A court which disallows a petition for the declaration of bankruptcy must give reasons for its order in the decree.

The petitioning creditor may lodge an appeal against the decree within fifteen days at a court of appeal which, after hearing the petitioning creditor and the debtor, will pronounce judgment in chambers.

★If the court of appeal allows the appeal it will return the file to the court of its own motion for the declaration of bankruptcy to be pronounced.

Chapter II: Administrative organs of the court appointed in cases of bankruptcy

Section I: The bankruptcy court

23. (Powers of the bankruptcy court.) The court which issues a declaration of bankruptcy is responsible for the entire procedure; it will rule on disputes arising from the procedure itself, which are not within the jurisdiction of the bankruptcy judge, and it will make decisions on appeals against the acts of the bankruptcy judge. The court has

the power, at any time, to hear in chambers the administrator, the bankrupt and the committee of creditors, and to replace the bankruptcy judge. The measures taken by the court in relation to the matters provided for by this article are not subject to appeal.

24. *(Jurisdiction of the bankruptcy court.) The court which has issued a declaration of bankruptcy is competent to ascertain all legal actions which derive from the case whatever their value and even if they relate to labour matters, except in the case of actions ***in rem*** with respect to property where the ordinary rules of jurisdiction will remain applicable.

Section II: The bankruptcy judge

25. (Powers of the bankruptcy judge appointed to the case.) The bankruptcy judge is in charge of the operation of the bankruptcy, supervises the actions of the administrator and in addition to this:

(1) refers to the court any new matter for which a tribunal ruling is necessary;
(2) issues, or calls on the competent authority to issue, measures necessary for the conservation of the assets;
(3) calls a meeting of the creditors' committee in the cases provided for by the law and whenever he thinks it appropriate;
(4) authorises the administrator to nominate the persons whose acts are required in the interests of the bankruptcy unless the nomination is reserved to the bankruptcy judge by law;
(5) within the shortest possible time, rules on any objections raised against the actions of the administrator;
(6) authorises the administrator in writing to represent the bankrupt in court, either as plaintiff or defendant; appoints lawyers and attorneys; authorises the administrator to carry out acts of special administration, with the exception of those provided under art. 35. The authorisation must always be given for specified transactions and must be given for proceedings at each level of jurisdiction;
(7) supervises the actions of anyone connected with the case in the interests of the bankruptcy and, if appropriate, discharges him from his duty and pays any remuneration due to him after hearing the administrator;
(8) proceeds, with the cooperation of the administrator, with the preliminary examination of claims, of rights in rem claimed by third parties, and of the documentation relating thereto.

Actions taken by the bankruptcy judge are ordered by decree.

26. *(Appeal against the decree of the bankruptcy judge.) Within three days of the issuing date of the decree, appeals may be raised by the administrator, the bankrupt person, by the creditors' committee or by any other interested party.

The court will issue its decision by way of decree in chambers.

The appeal does not suspend execution of the decree.

Section III: The administrator

27. (Role of receivers.) Repealed.

28. (Requirements for the nomination of administrator.) A person may not be appointed administrator and, if appointed, loses his position, if he has been disqualified from holding office, has been declared unable to transact business, has been declared bankrupt, or has been punished under a sentence involving being barred, even temporarily, from holding public office. Moreover, the spouse, any relative of up to the fourth degree, creditors and whoever has been employed in a professional capacity by the bankrupt, or has, during the two years previous to the declaration of bankruptcy, been in any way connected with the business of the bankrupt, may not be appointed administrator.

29. (Acceptance of the appointment of administrator.) The administrator will communicate his acceptance of the appointment to the bankruptcy judge within two days of his nomination. If the administrator does not comply with this duty, the court sitting in chambers will urgently attend to the appointment of another administrator.

30. (Capacity of public official.) In the exercise of his functions the administrator acts in the capacity of a public official.

31. (Powers of the administrator.) Under the direction of the bankruptcy judge, the administrator is responsible for the administration of the bankrupt's assets.

He may not take part in legal proceedings without the written approval of the bankruptcy judge except in matters relating to disputes and in late notifications of claims and of rights *in rem* against chattels in the possession of the bankrupt.

The administrator may not act as lawyer or attorney in legal proceedings relating to the bankrupt.

32. (Non-transferable powers of the administrator.) The administrator will exercise the functions of his office personally and may not delegate his powers to others, with the exception of a specific operation, and then only provided he has obtained authorisation from the bankruptcy judge.

Following the prior opinion of the creditors' committee he may be authorised by the bankruptcy judge to be assisted in his task on his own responsibility by experts or other paid persons, including the bankrupt himself.

33. (Report to the bankruptcy judge.) Within one month following the declaration of bankruptcy the administrator will submit to the bankruptcy judge a detailed report on the causes and circumstances of the bankruptcy, on whether the bankrupt was negligent in carrying out his business, on his standard of living and that of his family, on the responsibility of the bankrupt and of others for his bankruptcy, and on anything else that may be of interest for the purpose of the criminal inquiry.

The administrator will also refer in his report to any transactions of the bankrupt already challenged by the creditors, as well as those which he himself intends to challenge. The bankruptcy judge may even request a summary report from the administrator before the prescribed time.

In the case of a company, the report will set out any facts certified and information collected relating to the directors, statutory auditors, partners and, if necessary, other third parties. In the first five days of each month the administrator will submit to the bankruptcy judge a report on his administration with, if requested, any supporting documents.

34. (Deposit of collected sums.) Sums collected by the administrator on any grounds whatsoever (after deduction of the amount which the bankruptcy judge by decree

declares to be necessary for administrative and legal costs) will be deposited at the post office within five days according to the procedure stipulated by the bankruptcy judge, or in a credit institution indicated by the bankruptcy judge. The amount deposited is the sum which remains after deduction of legal and administrative costs in such amount as the bankruptcy judge may by decree determine.

The deposit will be made in the name of the bankruptcy registry and may not be withdrawn except on the basis of a payment order made by the bankruptcy judge.

In the event of failure to effect the deposit within the prescribed time the court will order the discharge of the administrator.

35. (Integration of the powers of the administrator.) After consulting the creditors' committee the bankruptcy judge may, by way of a reasoned decree, authorise the administrator to consent to the reduction of credits, to make settlements and compromises, to withdraw from litigation, to acknowledge the rights of third parties, to cancel mortgages, to give back pledged property, to discharge bonds and to accept inheritances and donations.

If these transactions have an undefined value, or a value of more than 200,000 lira, the appropriate organ to give such authorisation is the court upon the recommendation of the bankruptcy judge, after he has consulted the creditors' committee. The authorisation is given by reasoned decree, and is not subject to appeal.

As far as possible, the bankrupt must also be consulted.

36. (Appeal against the acts of the administrator.) The bankrupt and any other interested party, may protest against the acts of the administrator to the bankruptcy judge who will issue his decision by way of reasoned decree.

The decree of the bankruptcy judge may be appealed to the court within three days of the decree. The court will issue its decision by way of a reasoned decree after consulting both the administrator and the appellant.

37. (Discharge of the administrator.) The court may discharge the administrator at any time, at the instance of the bankruptcy judge, or on request of the creditors' committee, or of its own motion. After consulting the administrator and the public prosecutor, the court will issue its decision by way of decree.

38. (Liability of the administrator.) The administrator will carry out his activities with customary diligence. He will keep a register, certified by the bankruptcy judge, free of charge, and make daily entries of the actions relating to his office. A new administrator, with prior authorisation from the bankruptcy judge, may sue the discharged administrator for any liability he has incurred. An administrator who leaves his office, even during bankruptcy, will give account of his administration in accordance with art. 116.

39. (Remuneration of the administrator.) Even if the bankruptcy terminates in a preventive creditors' settlement, the remuneration and costs owing to the administrator must be paid at the request of the administrator upon the final decree of the court, following the report of the bankruptcy judge and pursuant to the provisions set out in the decree of the Minister of Justice.

Remuneration is effected after approval of the accounts and, as the case may be, after performance of the creditors' settlement. The court has the power to grant the administrator advances on account of his remuneration when justified on reasonable grounds.

No other remuneration beyond that already given by the court may be made to the administrator, not even for reimbursement of his expenses. Promises and payments made contrary to this prohibition are considered void. It is always possible to claim back whatever has been paid independently of criminal proceedings.

Section IV: The creditors' committee

40. (Appointment of the committee.) The creditors' committee will be appointed within ten days of the decree referred to in art. 97: it may be appointed on a provisional basis even before this time if the bankruptcy judge considers this to be appropriate.

The committee is appointed by decision of the bankruptcy judge and will be composed of three or five members chosen from among the creditors. The president of the committee will be chosen from among these members by the bankruptcy judge.

The bankruptcy judge may replace members of the committee.

41. (Functions of the committee.) In addition to the cases expressly provided by law, the committee may also be consulted when the court or the bankruptcy judge considers this to be appropriate. The president will summon the committee whenever it is asked to give its opinion or whenever he considers this to be appropriate. Decisions of the committee are taken by a majority vote of its members. At any time the committee and any of its members may inspect the books of account and the documents of the bankrupt and has the right to ask for information and clarification from the administrator and the bankrupt. The committee members are only entitled to reimbursement of costs.

Chapter III: Consequences of bankruptcy

Section I: Consequences of bankruptcy for the bankrupt

42. (The bankrupt's property.) With effect from its date, a declaration of bankruptcy deprives the bankrupt of the ability to administer and dispose of any of his property existing at the time of the declaration of bankruptcy. Property obtained by the bankrupt during the bankruptcy is also included in the bankruptcy subject to any indebtedness incurred upon its acquisition or by way of maintenance.

43. (Procedural statements.) The administrator will represent the bankrupt in any legal proceedings, even if already pending, relating to rights of the bankrupt included in the bankruptcy.

The bankrupt may join in the proceedings only in matters which may raise an imputation of criminal bankruptcy against him or if the law provides expressly for him to join in the proceedings.

44. (Transactions entered into by the bankrupt after the declaration of bankruptcy.) All transactions and payments made by the bankrupt after the declaration of bankruptcy are void as regards creditors.

Payments received by the bankrupt after the declaration of bankruptcy are also void.

45. (Formalities carried out after the declaration of bankruptcy.) If formalities required to make transactions effective as against third parties are completed after a bankruptcy has been declared they have no effect on creditors.

46. (Property not included in the bankruptcy.) Property not included in the bankruptcy includes:

(1) Property and rights of a wholly personal nature;
(2) Alimonies, salaries, pensions, wages and the bankrupt's earnings up to the amount necessary to provide for his own and his family's living needs;
(3) Income derived from any legal usufruct over the property of his children and the income from property which constitutes the family estate, save as otherwise provided for by arts. 170 and 326 of the civil code;
(4) Income from dowry property and dotal credits, save as otherwise provided for by art. 188 of the civil code;
(5) Items which are not available for attachment at law.

The amount referred to in paragraph (2) of this article is fixed by order of the bankruptcy judge.

47. (Food allowances for the bankrupt and his family.) If the bankrupt ceases to have any livelihood, and after consultation with the administrator and the committee of creditors, if it has been nominated, the bankruptcy judge may grant him a subsidy in the form of a food allowance for himself and his family.

In so far as this is necessary to accommodate the bankrupt and his family, the house owned by the bankrupt may not be put to other use until the end of the liquidation.

48. (Correspondence addressed to the bankrupt.) Correspondence addressed to the bankrupt must be handed over to the administrator who is entitled to withhold correspondence concerning financial or commercial matters. The bankrupt has the right to see such correspondence.

The administrator is obliged to keep confidential the contents of any correspondence which does not concern financial or commercial matters.

49. (Residence obligations of the bankrupt.) The bankrupt may not leave his residence without the permission of the bankruptcy judge, and whenever he is summoned either by the judge, the administrator or the creditors' committee he must present himself in person. If he has a legitimate excuse the judge may authorise him to appear before the court by proxy.

The judge may order the bankrupt to be accompanied by the police if he refuses to appear as provided above.

50. (Public register of bankrupt persons.) A public register is kept in each court registry of the names of those who have been declared bankrupt by that court as well as the names of those who have been declared bankrupt elsewhere if their place of birth falls within the jurisdiction of that court.

The names of bankrupt persons may be removed from the register following judgment by the court.

While his name appears on this register, the bankrupt is subject to the legal incapacity imposed by law on bankrupt persons.

The procedural rules for the maintenance of the register will be issued by the Ministry of Justice. Pending institution of the register the names of the bankrupt persons will be entered on the schedule of bankrupt persons already in existence.

Section II: Consequences of bankruptcy for the creditors

51. (Prohibition of executory action by individuals.) Unless otherwise provided for by law, no individual executory proceeding may be initiated or brought against property within the bankruptcy estate.

52. (Creditors' participation.) The declaration of bankruptcy enables creditors to concur in claiming against the property of the bankrupt person.

*Save as otherwise provided by law, every creditor, even those with preferential rights, will be assessed in accordance with the provisions of chapter V.

53. (Creditors possessing pledges or other prior rights over chattels.) Claims secured by pledges or protected by other prior rights in accordance with the terms of art. 2756 and 2761 of the civil code may be paid during the bankruptcy after they have been admitted as preferential debts.

In order to obtain authority for a sale the creditor will apply to the bankruptcy judge who, after consulting the administrator and the creditors' committee, will appoint by decree the time of the sale and specify whether it is to be carried out by a private offer or by auction; he will also determine the relevant procedure.

After consulting the creditors' committee, if appointed, the bankruptcy judge may also authorise the administrator to take back property subject to pledges or other preferential rights by paying off the relevant creditor or to carry out a sale in accordance with the procedure referred to in the preceding paragraph.

54. (Rights of preferred creditors in the distribution of the assets.) The preferential claims of creditors with mortgages, pledges and other preferential rights are satisfied as regards capital, interest, and expenses, from the sale proceeds of the secured property; if their claims are not fully satisfied they will participate together with the unsecured creditors in the distribution of the remaining assets.

They also have the right to participate in any distribution carried out before distribution of the sale proceeds of the secured property. In that event, and if their claim (calculated first to include interest and thereafter capital) is paid in full, the amount they receive is reduced by the sum which they have already received, and an amount equal to that sum is divided among the creditors with unsecured debts. If only part of the secured debt is paid the secured creditors are only entitled to participate in respect of the unsatisfied part of their claim as to principal only in the percentage dividend allocated to unsecured creditors.

*The extension of preferential rights to interest is regulated by art. 2788 and the second and third paragraphs of art. 2855 of the civil code, a declaration of bankruptcy being considered the same as an attachment of property.

55. *(Consequences of the declaration of bankruptcy on monetary debts.) A declaration of bankruptcy suspends the running of ordinary or legal interest as regards the participation of creditors until the close of bankruptcy proceedings save for debts secured by mortgage, pledge or other preferential right and except as provided under the third paragraph of the previous article.

As regards the participation of creditors, monetary debts are deemed to fall due on the date of the declaration of bankruptcy.

Creditors with contingent debts take part in the distribution of assets in accordance with the terms of articles 95 and 133. Included in contingent debts are all debts which may not be claimed against the bankrupt unless all remedies against the principal debtor have been exhausted.

56. (Set off during bankruptcy.) Creditors are entitled to set off debts owed to the bankrupt against debts owed to them by the bankrupt even if the debts owed by the bankrupt had not accrued due before the declaration of bankruptcy.

As regards the claims of creditors which have not yet accrued due, set-off may however not take place if the creditor's claim was acquired after the declaration of bankruptcy or in the previous year.

57. (Claims bearing no interest.) Claims bearing no interest which have not yet fallen due on the date of the declaration of bankruptcy are included as liabilities for the entire sum that is due. However for each single distribution they will be discounted by compound interest, calculated at the rate of 5% per year, from the date of the order for payment to the maturity date of the claim.

58. (Debentures.) Debentures issued by joint stock companies are valued at their face value reduced by the amount of any repayments.

Debentures which are repayable by lots, at more than the face value, are valued at an amount equal to their principal amount by reducing the aggregate amount of all debentures which have not yet been allocated by lots, to the current value on the basis of compound interest of 5%. The value of each debenture is equal to the sum calculated by dividing this principal amount by the number of debentures not yet paid off. In any event debentures will not be given a value lower than the face value after deduction of any amount which has been paid as a repayment of principal.

59. ★(Non-monetary debts.) Claims which must be discharged by a payment in cash determined by reference to other values or by performance other than payment in cash, and which have not yet fallen due, participate according to their value on the date of the declaration of bankruptcy.

60. (Perpetual annuities and life annuities.) If debts in the form of perpetual annuity form part of the bankruptcy, they are redeemed in accordance with art. 1866 of the civil code.

The claim of a beneficiary of a life annuity is admitted among the debts of the bankruptcy for a sum equal to the capital value of the annuity on the day of the declaration of bankruptcy.

61. (Creditors of jointly liable debtors.) Creditors of jointly liable debtors will participate in the bankruptcy of those debtors who are bankrupt for the whole amount of the claim as to capital and other sums until payment is made in full.

Actions for recovery as between bankrupt joint debtors may be commenced only after the claim of the creditor of those joint debtors has been entirely satisfied.

62. (Creditors of joint debtors, whose claims have been partially satisfied.) Creditors who, before the declaration of bankruptcy, have received payment for part of the claim owed to them from a debtor liable jointly with the bankrupt, or from a guarantor, may join in the bankruptcy proceedings to claim for that part of the debt which has not yet been recovered.

A joint debtor who has a right of recovery against the bankrupt is entitled to claim the amount of his payment in the bankruptcy proceedings.

However the creditor is entitled to an assignment of the share of the distribution due to the joint debtor until payment in full of the amount still owed to him. The creditors' claim against the joint debtor will survive to the extent that the creditor is not fully satisfied.

63. (Joint debtor or guarantor of the bankrupt with security.) A joint debtor or guarantor of the bankrupt who has a security interest or a mortgage over the bankrupt's property as a guarantee for his obligations will take part in the bankruptcy proceedings for the sum in respect of which he has been given a mortgage or a security interest.

The proceeds of sale of the mortgaged property or of chattels pledged by way of security are given to the creditor to be deducted from the amount due to him.

Section III: Consequences of the declaration of bankruptcy on transactions prejudicial to creditors

64. Transactions for no consideration entered into by the bankrupt during the two years prior to the declaration of bankruptcy are void as against the creditors, with the exception of customary gifts and acts performed by way of fulfilment of a moral duty or acts for the public good where the generosity of the donor is in proportion to his property.

65. (Payments.) Payments of debts which fall due on the day of or after the declaration of bankruptcy are void as against the creditors if these payments were made by the bankrupt in the two years before the declaration of bankruptcy.

66. (Ordinary avoidance actions.) The administrator may apply for transactions carried out by the debtor to the prejudice of creditors to be set aside in accordance with procedure set out in the civil code.

67. (Transactions for valuable consideration, payments, guarantees.) Unless the other party can prove that he was not aware of the insolvency of the debtor, the following transactions are set aside:

(1) transactions for valuable consideration carried out in the two years prior to the declaration of bankruptcy in which the values of the financial or other obligations undertaken by the bankrupt party are considerably greater than what was given or promised to him;
(2) extinction by the bankrupt of monetary debts which were due and payable and which have not been paid in money or in any other normal form of payment, if carried out in the two years prior to the declaration of bankruptcy;
(3) pledges, antichrisis and mortgages for no consideration granted in the two years prior to the declaration of bankruptcy for pre-existing debts which had not yet fallen due;
(4) pledges, antichrisis and mortgages for no consideration or judicial mortgages granted within one year prior to the declaration of insolvency for debts which were due and payable.

If the administrator can prove that the other party was aware of the insolvency of the debtor, payment of due debts in cash, transactions for valuable consideration and those which constitute a right of priority for debts formed in the same context are also set aside if carried out within one year prior to the declaration of bankruptcy.

Subject always to the provisions of special laws, this article does not apply to the Bank of Italy, to other institutions authorised to grant credit facilities secured by pledge (but with limitation to those transactions), or to building societies.

68. (Payment of expired bills of exchange.) Notwithstanding the second paragraph of art. 67, payment of a bill of exchange may not be set aside if the holder had to accept it in order not to lose his rights of recovery against joint obligors under the bill of exchange. In such cases, if the administrator can prove that the last joint obligor under the bill was aware of the insolvency of the principal debtor when he issued or endorsed the bill of exchange, he will return the payment to the administrator.

69. (Transactions between spouses.) Transactions between spouses of the type described in art. 67 performed during the time when the bankrupt spouse was managing a commercial enterprise are set aside if the other spouse is not able to prove that he or she was not aware of that spouse's state of bankruptcy.

If the husband was managing a commercial enterprise at the time of their marriage, or if he started a commercial enterprise in the following year, the legal mortgage to secure the dowry property does not extend to the property acquired by the husband during the marriage by means other than inheritance or gift.

In such cases the wife may not exercise against the creditors in the bankruptcy proceedings advantages in her favour deriving from the contract of marriage and equally the creditors have no claim to the advantages in favour of the husband deriving from the contract of marriage.

70. (Property acquired by the bankrupt's spouse.) Property acquired by the spouse of the bankrupt for valuable consideration in the five years prior to the declaration of bankruptcy, is presumed as far as the creditors are concerned, and unless proved otherwise, to be acquired with money belonging to the bankrupt. Such property is considered to be the bankrupt's property and the administrator is legally entitled to take possession of it. If the same property has in the meantime been transferred or mortgaged, the transaction may not be set aside to the detriment of a third party if the latter can prove he acted in good faith.

71. (Consequences of setting aside.) Those who, in order to comply with the above provisions for setting aside transactions, have given back what they received, may participate in the bankruptcy for the amount of the debt owed to them, if any.

Section IV: Consequences of bankruptcy on pre-existing legal relationships

72. (Sale not yet completed by both the contracting parties.) If a contract of sale has not been performed either in whole or in part by both parties when the buyer is declared bankrupt, the seller is entitled to complete the performance of the contract and claim in the bankruptcy for the amount of the price.

If he does not wish to exercise this right, performance of the contract is suspended until the administrator, with the authorisation of the bankruptcy judge, declares either that he will take the place of the bankrupt party in the contract and in so doing adopt all the relevant obligations under the contract or, alternatively, that he elects to terminate the contract.

The seller may place the administrator on notice by causing the bankruptcy judge to give the administrator up to eight days in which to complete the contract failing which the contract is terminated.

In the event of bankruptcy of the seller, if the article traded has already become the property of the buyer, the contract may not be terminated. If the item traded has not already become the property of the buyer, the administrator may elect to perform or to terminate the contract. In the event of termination of the contract the buyer has the right to claim for the amount owed to him in the bankruptcy but without an indemnity for damages.

73. (Sales with deferred payment or with payment in instalments.) In the event of the bankruptcy of the buyer, if the price is payable by a certain date or in instalments, the administrator may adopt the contract, with the authorisation of the bankruptcy judge; the seller may however demand a payment guarantee unless the administrator pays the balance due after deduction of interest at the legal rate.

In sales with payment in instalments and under reservation of title, the declaration of bankruptcy of the seller does not give rise to a right to terminate the contract.

74. (Supply contracts.) In the case of sales where delivery is by instalments and in supply contracts the provisions of the second, third and fourth paragraphs of art. 72 will apply.

If the administrator adopts the contract he must pay the full price for deliveries already made.

75. (Restitution of items not paid for.) If the object of the sale is a chattel and has been sent to the buyer before he is declared bankrupt but is not yet in his possession or at the final destination and no one else has claimed rights over the item, the seller may repossess the chattel by assuming liability for the costs and by returning any advance payment received, unless he prefers to enforce the contract by claiming in the bankruptcy for the balance of the price, or unless the administrator indicates his intention to take delivery of the item by paying the price in full.

76. (Forward stock exchange transactions.) If the performance of a stock exchange transaction falls due after the declaration of bankruptcy of one of the contracting parties, the contract is deemed to be terminated on the date of the declaration of bankruptcy. The difference between the contract price and the value of the items or of the securities on the date of the declaration of bankruptcy is paid to the bankrupt party if it is a credit otherwise it is added to the liabilities of the bankrupt party.

77. (Capital ventures.) Capital ventures are terminated by the bankruptcy of the partner who, by agreement, received the capital contributions of the venture. The other partner has the right to claim in the bankruptcy for that part of his contribution which is not absorbed by the losses of the venture to be borne by him.

He must pay to the bankruptcy creditors the balance due of his contribution to the extent of the losses to be borne by him.

The procedure provided under art. 150 is applied to him.

78. (Current accounts, mandates, commission agencies.) Current accounts, agreements, mandates, and commission agency contracts are terminated by the bankruptcy of one of the parties.

79. (Temporary possessions of the bankrupt.) If items which a bankrupt must return are no longer in his possession on the day of the declaration of bankruptcy and the administrator is unable to recover them, the person who has title may claim in the bankruptcy for the value of the items on the date of the declaration of bankruptcy.

If the bankrupt's possession ceased after the seals had been affixed, the person who has title may claim payment in full for the value of the item.

This article is subject to the provisions of art. 1706 of the civil code.

80. (Leases.) The declaration of bankruptcy of the lessor, unless otherwise agreed, does not terminate a lease, and the administrator will adopt the contract.

In the event of bankruptcy of the tenant, the administrator may withdraw from the contract at any time on payment of proper compensation to the lessor. If the amount due cannot be agreed between the parties, it will be determined by the bankruptcy judge after he has consulted the interested parties. The claim payable as compensation is a preferred claim in accordance with the terms of art. 2764 of the civil code.

81. (Contracts for work and materials.) A contract for work and materials is terminated if one of the two parties is declared bankrupt unless the administrator, on hearing the creditors' committee, if nominated, and after he has obtained the authorisation of the bankruptcy judge, declares his intention to adopt the contract and notifies the other party of his intention within twenty days from the declaration of bankruptcy and offers appropriate guarantees.

In the event of the bankruptcy of the contractor, continued performance of the contract is not permitted where the personal skills of the bankrupt are crucial to the contract.

This article is subject to the provisions of the law governing contracts for public works.

82. (Insurance contracts.) The declaration of bankruptcy of the insured, unless otherwise agreed, does not terminate a contract of insurance against damage and save as otherwise provided for by art. 1898 of the civil code if the bankruptcy aggravates the insured risk.

If the contract continues, the debt owed to the insurer for the unpaid premiums must be paid in full, even if the premiums fall due before the declaration of bankruptcy.

83. (Publishing contracts.) The consequences of bankruptcy of the publisher under a publishing contract are regulated by special laws.

Chapter IV: The control and administration of assets within the bankruptcy estate

84. (Affixing the seals.) After the declaration of bankruptcy has been issued, the bankruptcy judge or, if this is not possible, the judge of the lower court, will proceed immediately in accordance with the procedures set out in the code of civil procedure with the affixing of seals on all assets located at the debtor's principal place of business and on any other possessions of the insolvent debtor. The affixing of seals at the principal place of business will be witnessed by the administrator unless there is a legitimate reason which prevents him from so doing.

As regards possessions located elsewhere, the bankruptcy judge will apply through the clerk of the court to the competent judge of the lower court to proceed with the affixing of seals. The written report of the judge of the lower court will be submitted immediately to the bankruptcy judge.

The judge who effects the affixing of seals may take such provisional and conservatory measures as he thinks fit, including authorising the sale of perishable goods.

85. (The affixing of seals by the judge of the lower court.) A judge of the lower court who has knowledge of a declaration of bankruptcy may effect the affixing of seals

within his jurisdiction even before he has received the application referred to in the second paragraph of the preceding article.

86. (Items not subject to seals.) In addition to the items listed in the code of civil procedure the following items are excluded from the affixing of of seals:

(1) items which are instrumental to the exercise of the debtor's business if in the opinion of the judge this should not be interrupted immediately;
(2) the books of account;
(3) bills of exchange and other securities which have fallen due or are about to fall due and which must be given to the administrator for collection;
(4) all sums in cash which must also be given to the administrator who will deposit these sums in accordance with the provisions of art. 34.

A description of all these items is entered in the report.

After they have been stamped by the presiding judge the books of account will be deposited at the court registry. The bankruptcy judge may however authorise the administrator to retain the books temporarily subject to the obligation to produce them upon lawful request.

87. (Removing of the seals; and establishment of the inventory.) Within the shortest possible time the administrator will ask the judge to remove the seals and draw up the inventory. He will proceed with this in accordance with the rules laid down in the code of civil procedure and in the presence of, or after notice to, the bankrupt and the committee of creditors, if nominated, and with the assistance of the clerk of the court or, as the case may be, of the clerk of the lower court, who writes the report. The creditors may attend.

The bankruptcy judge may order special procedures to be followed and precautionary measures to be taken in the drawing up of the inventory and if necessary he may nominate a valuer.

Before completion of the inventory the administrator will ask the bankrupt or, in the case of a company, its directors to declare whether they have knowledge of other activities which should be included in the inventory, and will warn them of the criminal penalties provided under art. 220 for a false declaration or omission.

Two copies of the inventory are produced and signed by all present. One of the originals is deposited in the court's offices.

88. (Transfer of the assets of the bankrupt to the administrator.) The assets of the bankrupt will be transferred to the administrator together with the books of account and the documents of the bankrupt as and when entered in the inventory.

If the bankrupt owns property or any other assets which require registration, the administrator will serve notice by way of an abstract of the declaration of bankruptcy on the competent registrars in order to ensure that these are duly entered in the public registries.

89. (Lists of the creditors and of the holders of rights *in rem* in chattels; and the balance sheet.) The administrator will compile a list of creditors on the basis of the books of account and any other information he is able to collect. The list will set out creditors' claims and preferential rights and will specify those creditors holding rights *in rem* over chattels which are in the possession of the bankrupt and their respective rights.

The lists are kept in the court offices.

Moreover, the administrator must draw up the balance sheet for the last financial year, if this has not already been done by the bankrupt within the prescribed time limit, and make the necessary corrections and any additions to the balance sheet and to the lists submitted by the bankrupt in accordance with the terms of art. 14.

90. (Temporary operation.) After the declaration of bankruptcy has been issued the court may order the temporary continuation of the business of the bankrupt if sudden interruption could cause serious and irreparable damage to the business.

After the decree provided under art. 97 has been issued, the creditors' committee will declare whether it is in favour of allowing the operation of the business of the bankrupt to continue, or to be taken in hand, in whole or in part, and will set out the appropriate terms and conditions. The continuation or the taking in hand of the business may be granted by the court only if supported by the creditors' committee.

If, in accordance with the preceding paragraph, temporary continuation of the business is ordered, the committee of creditors is required by the bankruptcy judge to be kept informed at least every two months by the administrator regarding the state of the management of the business and to declare whether it is in favour of allowing the business to continue its operations. The court may order interruption of the temporary continuation of the business if the creditors' committee so requests, or at any other time if he considers such action to be appropriate.

In each of the above instances the court, having heard the administrator, will meet in chambers to issue its decree, which is final.

91. (Advances for legal costs by the Treasury.) If, from the time of the declaration of bankruptcy to the completion of the bankruptcy procedure, the bankrupt does not have sufficient funds to pay legal costs in respect of matters required by the law, the Treasury will advance the necessary sums for the payment.

As far as stamp duty and registration fees are concerned, the advance of costs will be made in respect of each matter required by the procedure by means of registering the debt in accordance with the decree of the bankruptcy judge. Other costs are paid directly by the registrars to the claimants as indicated by the decree of the bankruptcy judge. The costs of the bankruptcy procedure paid for by the Treasury are listed in a register kept by the clerk of the court. The clerk of the court will arrange for the recovery of the costs by drawing from the proceeds of the liquidation of the assets as soon as funds are available, even before completion of the bankruptcy procedure.

Chapter V: Assessment of the liabilities of the bankruptcy estate and of rights *in rem* in chattels belonging to third parties

92. (Notice of inspection to creditors.) The administrator will send notices by registered post to the creditors and the other interested parties included in the lists referred to in art. 89, specifying the length of time available to them to submit their applications to the court registry as well as the provisions of the order for the declaration of bankruptcy relating to the statement of liabilities.

Notice is sent to the representatives of the creditors and the other interested parties who are not resident in Italy. If there is no representative in the Republic of Italy, the judge may grant an extension and give notice of the extension to all other creditors and interested parties.

93. (Application to be admitted to the statement of liabilities.) The application to be admitted to the statement of liabilities will indicate the full name of the creditor, specify the sum and the grounds for the claim, any preferential rights and include the documents evidencing the claim.

If the creditor is not resident in the municipality within the jurisdiction of the court, the application will also appoint an agent for service in that municipality otherwise all subsequent notices to the creditor will be served at the court registry.

Any documents not included in the application must be submitted before the verification meeting.

At the request of the holder of bearer securities, the judge may arrange for the clerk of the court to take a copy of these in order to include them in the statement of the liabilities and thereafter return them to the holder endorsed with a note to the effect that they have been presented for admission to the statement of liabilities.

94. (Consequences of the application.) The application to be admitted to the statement of the liabilities has the same effect as a judicial application and prevents the expiry of time limits for transactions which cannot be completed during the bankruptcy proceedings.

95. (Preparation of the statement of liabilities.) The clerk of the court will compile a chronological list of the applications to be included in the statement of the liabilities and submit it to the bankruptcy judge. With the assistance of the administrator and having heard the bankrupt and having gathered the appropriate information, the bankruptcy judge will examine the applications, and on the basis of these he will prepare the statement of liabilities of the bankrupt. The judge will indicate clearly the claims which he considers should be included, specifying in each case if they are protected by priority rights, pledges or mortgages, and indicating those which he considers should not be included in their entirety or only in part, giving a brief account of the reasons for the total or partial exclusion of these claims or of any guarantees relating to those claims.

The claims referred to in the last paragraph of art. 55 and those for which the supporting documents have not yet been submitted, will be conditionally admitted to the statement of liabilities. If the claim is the result of a judgment which has not become final, an appeal is necessary in order to exclude the claim.

The statement of liabilities prepared by the bankruptcy judge will be filed at the court registry at least three days before expiry of the time limit fixed by art. 16 paragraph (5). This document is open to inspection by the creditors.

96. (Verification of the statement of liabilities.) At the meeting of creditors provided for in paragraph (5) of art. 16, the statement of liabilities prepared by the judge is examined in the presence the administrator and of the bankrupt. Subsequent applications for admission to the statement of the liabilities together with applications submitted at the meeting are also examined.

After hearing the objections and observations of interested parties and inspecting any new documents which have been submitted, the judge will incorporate any comments and make such amendments to the statement of liabilities as he considers appropriate.

If these matters cannot be completed in one meeting, the judge will adjourn the meeting to a date within eight days, without further notice to either those present or the absentees.

In any event the judge has the right to postpone preparation of the statement of liabilities until fifteen days after the meeting of creditors has concluded this business.

97. (Executory effect of the statement of liabilities.) The statement of liabilities is signed by the judge and the clerk of the court and concludes with the decree of the judge which declares it to be executory as from the date on which the meeting of creditors concluded its business or as from any subsequent date appointed as provided under the fourth paragraph of the preceding article.

The statement of liabilities together with the judge's decree is deposited in the court registry where it is open to inspection by the creditors.

In any case where applications of admission to the statement of liabilities are rejected or partially accepted or conditionally accepted, the administrator will immediately inform those creditors who have been excluded, or admitted conditionally, by registered post with acknowledgement of receipt.

98. *(Objection on the part of excluded or conditionally admitted creditors.) Creditors who have been excluded or conditionally admitted may dispute the statement within fifteen days of submission of the statement of liabilities to the court registry by submitting an objection to the bankruptcy judge.

The judge will appoint the date of the hearing by decree at which all the petitioning creditors and the administrator will appear in court to be heard. The decree will also provide for the period of time allowed to give the administrator notice of the objection and the order.

The creditors will file their submissions at least five days before the hearing. If no submissions are filed, the objection will be considered to be withdrawn. Other creditors may intervene in the objection proceedings.

99. (Directions for the objection and the order relating to the objection.) The bankruptcy judge deals with the proceedings in respect of the various objections and will duly appoint a date for the hearing before the tribunal in accordance with the procedure set out in art. 189 of the code of civil procedure.

If some of the objections require a longer period of time for all the information provided to be heard, the judge may make an order to separate out these objections and submit to the tribunal those where decisions may be taken.

The court will make a single judgment on all the objections submitted before it. Under the circumstances referred to in the first paragraph of art. 279 of the code of civil procedure, the court may temporarily include in the statement of liabilities those debts which are being disputed.

The judgment will be affixed to the external door of the court within eight days of its publication and is provisionally executory. The clerk of the court will give immediate notice of its publication to the representatives of the parties in accordance with the provisions of art. 136 of the code of civil procedure.

*There is a fixed period of fifteen days for appeal from the publication of the judgment. The same provisions of the preceding paragraphs apply to the hearing of the appeal where appropriate. The time limit for appeal to the Supreme Court is calculated from the day of publication of the judgment and is one half of the fixed period referred to above.

*Appeal is not allowed in respect of objections relating to amounts which do not exceed those within the competence of the lower court.

100. *(Objections to claims admitted to the statement of liabilities.) Within fifteen days of the filing of the statement at the court registry, any creditor may, by way of appeal to the bankruptcy judge, challenge claims admitted to the statement of liabilities.

*The judge will appoint by decree the final date for the hearing, at which all petitioning creditors and the administrator will appear before him, together with the period of time allowed to communicate the objections and the decree to the administrator and the creditor whose claims have been challenged. The parties will make their appearance in accordance with the provisions of the third paragraph of art. 98.

If the parties do not reach agreement at this hearing the judge will make a final order to the effect that, in the event of a distribution of the proceeds of the bankruptcy, the shares of the contested creditors be set aside.

The provisions of the preceding article apply to the procedure and the decision on the disputed claims, and the judgment and the relevant proceedings must all be dealt with together with those in respect of the disputed claims.

101. (Late filing of claims.) Creditors may ask to be admitted to the statement of liabilities by making an application to the bankruptcy judge, even after the decree issued under art. 97 and up until all the proceeds of the bankruptcy have been distributed.

The judge will appoint by decree the date of the hearing in which the petitioner and the administrator will appear before him, and will determine the period of time allowed to notify the administrator of the appeal and the decree. The parties will make their appearance in accordance with the provisions of the third paragraph of art. 98. The other creditors may intervene.

If the administrator does not contest the inclusion of the new claim at the hearing, and the judge regards it as well-founded, the claim is included by way of decree; otherwise the judge will commence proceedings in accordance with the provisions of art. 175 of the code of civil procedure.

The creditor will bear the costs incurred as a consequence of the late petition unless the delay was caused by circumstances not attributable to him.

102. (Petition to revoke claims admitted to the statement of liabilities.) If, before the close of the bankruptcy proceedings, it is discovered that the inclusion of a claim or of a guarantee has resulted from fraud, mistake or substantial error as to the merits or that significant documents are found which were previously unknown, the administrator or any creditor may present a petition to revoke the decree of the bankruptcy judge or the judgment of the court in respect of the relevant claim or guarantee.

The petition will take the form of an appeal to the bankruptcy judge. The judge will appoint by decree the date of the hearing for the parties and the period of time allowed to notify the administrator and the other parties of the appeal and the decree. He will then issue directions for the proceedings.

The administrator may intervene in the proceedings.

Pending resolution of the dispute the judge may make an order to the effect that, in the event of a distribution of the proceeds of the bankruptcy, the shares of the contested creditors be set aside pending a final decision.

If the bankruptcy proceedings are closed before the dispute is resolved, the hearing will continue at the same court.

103. (Applications to claim ownership, recovery and separation of chattels.) The provisions of arts. 93 and 102 also apply to applications for claiming ownership, recovery and separation of chattels in the possession of the bankrupt.

On the basis of the list of all the applications the judge will prepare a statement of those which have been accepted or refused in accordance with the provisions of arts. 95, 96 and 97.

If the applications have been submitted late in accordance with art. 101 the bankruptcy judge may suspend the sale of the items claimed, or in respect of which recovery or separation is requested, with or without requiring security.

In all cases the judge must consult the bankrupt as far as possible before he proceeds with the claim.

Applications for claiming ownership, recovery and separation made with respect to the price received under a sale which has already taken place will not prejudice distributions already made and may be made in respect of any monies still available for distribution.

Chapter VI: Realisation of the assets

Section I: General provisions

104. (Commencement.) Under the direction of the bankruptcy judge and having heard the creditors' committee (if the committee has been appointed) the administrator will proceed with the sale of the assets after issue of the decree of the court in accordance with art. 97, insofar as this does not impede any permitted temporary continuation of the business.

The administrator may be authorised by reasoned decree of the bankruptcy judge to proceed with the sale of the assets before expiry of the term referred to in the first paragraph above.

105. (Applicable provisions.) The provisions of the civil procedure code relating to execution proceedings apply to the sale of the bankrupt's assets, whether in the form of chattels or real estate, save as otherwise provided in the following sections.

Section II: Sale of chattels

106. (Procedure for the sale of chattels.) After hearing the administrator and the creditors' committee, the bankruptcy judge will appoint a date for the sale of chattels (including the income of real estate), direct whether this should be by means of sale or auction, describe the procedure to be followed and, if necessary, will consult a valuer.

If the bankruptcy judge considers it necessary or desirable, he may authorise the block sale of the whole or part of the chattels and order special measures to advertise such block sale.

Section III: Sale of real estate

107. (Forced sale.) If proceedings for the forced sale of one or more of the items of the bankrupt's real estate have been commenced by a creditor prior to the declaration of bankruptcy, the administrator will be substituted for that creditor in the proceedings.

The creditor, the debtor or any other interested party may appeal to the bankruptcy judge in accordance with art. 36 in the event of unjustified delays on the part of the administrator.

If the procedure for the distribution of the proceeds of the sale has commenced, this must be carried out with the participation of the administrator.

The administrator will keep a special account in relation to the sale proceeds of each item of real estate and of its income from the date of declaration of bankruptcy. The income derived from any item of real estate is added to the proceeds of its sale.

108. (Procedure for the sale of real estate.) The sale of real estate is by means of public auction unless the bankruptcy judge decides to dispense with a sale by public auction, should he consider this more advantageous. This may only arise following the request of the administrator and after having heard the creditors' committee and having obtained the consent of the creditors whose claims have been accepted and who have a preferred right in the real estate in question.

The bankruptcy judge will order the sale at the request of the administrator and the sale is carried out in the presence of the judge, save as otherwise provided by art. 578 of the civil procedure code.

The judge may suspend the sale if he considers that the price offered is inappropriately low.

The administrator must give notice of the order for sale to each creditor whose claim has been accepted and who has preferred rights in the real estate in question and to the creditors registered as mortgagees.

109. (Distribution of the proceeds of sale.) The bankruptcy judge will distribute the proceeds of sale in accordance with the provisions of the following chapter.

The bankruptcy judge will issue a decree determining, if appropriate, the amount to be paid to the administrator on account of his final compensation payable in accordance with art. 39. This amount is deducted from the proceeds of sale, together with procedural and administrative expenses.

Chapter VII: Distribution of the assets

110. (Distribution.) Unless the judge orders otherwise, every two months from the date of the decree referred to in art. 97 the administrator must submit to the bankruptcy judge a statement of available funds, together with a distribution plan, inclusive of a reserve against the cost of the bankruptcy proceedings.

The judge, after hearing the creditors' committee, may vary the plan if he considers it appropriate; he will order the plan to be deposited in the court's offices and that all the creditors be notified.

The creditors may file written comments within ten days of notice. After expiry of this ten-day period and after having considered the creditors' written comments, the judge will issue a decree to the effect that the distribution plan be deemed final and shall have executory effect.

111. (Order of entitlement.) The proceeds of sale of the assets will be applied as follows:

(1) towards payment of the costs of the bankruptcy proceedings, including costs advanced by the Treasury, and expenses incurred in the administration of the bankruptcy and in the continuation of the business if such continuation has been authorised;
(2) towards satisfaction of any claims admitted with preferred rights on the asset sold, in accordance with the order of priority provided by law (arts. 2754 et seq. of the civil code);
(3) towards satisfaction of the unsecured debts and the balance of the indebtedness owing to the creditors referred to in (2) above if such indebtedness has not been fully discharged out of the amount received, in equal proportions between themselves.

The expenses referred to in (1) above are determined by decree of the bankruptcy judge.

112. (Participation of creditors with late petitions.) Creditors admitted in accordance with art. 101 are only considered for distributions taking place after their admission and in proportion to their respective claims unless they are creditors with preferred rights. If, however, from the decree granted under art. 101 it appears that the delay in submitting their claims was due to reasons out of their control, these creditors are also allowed to participate in the amount which, in a previous distribution, would have been theirs from the proceeds of sale of any assets not yet distributed.

113. (Partial distributions.) When partial distributions (which cannot exceed 90 per cent. of the total amount to be distributed) are made, the bankruptcy judge will order the withholding and deposit of the sums allocated:

(1) to creditors resident abroad whose claims await confirmation under an extended time limit;
(2) to creditors whose claims have been ordered to be set aside and to creditors whose claims have been admitted subject to presentation of the relevant documentation of their rights;
(3) to creditors whose claims are subject to conditions not yet satisfied, including debts which cannot be enforced against the bankrupt before enforcement of a principal obligation;
(4) to meet future costs in an amount considered appropriate by the judge and to pay for the remuneration and expenses of the administrator.

114. (Restitution of sums received.) If any of the situations contemplated by art. 102 arises, creditors who have participated in any distribution must refund the sum received together with statutory interest.

115. (Payment.) The administrator will pay the creditors in accordance with the distribution plan and the procedures as ordered by the bankruptcy judge.

116. (Final account of the administrator.) The administrator will submit the final account of his administration to the bankruptcy judge after realisation of the assets has taken place and before final distribution.

The judge will order the final account to be deposited in the court office and will appoint the date and time of a hearing at which all interested parties may raise objections. The date appointed for the hearing must be after expiry of a fifteen-day period from the deposit of the final account in the court office.

Notice of deposit of the final account and of the date appointed for the hearing will be given immediately to the bankrupt and the creditors.

If no objections are raised or if agreement is reached at the hearing, the judge will approve the final account of the administrator; if the judge is not able to give his approval and no agreement is reached at the hearing, the judge will arrange a second hearing before the tribunal within twenty days in accordance with art. 189 of the civil procedure code.

117. (Final distribution.) After approval of the final account and payment of the compensation due to the administrator, and after considering any proposals submitted

by the administrator, the bankruptcy judge will order the final distribution in accordance with the preceding articles.

The funds set aside under art. 113 above are included within the final distribution unless, in relation to paragraph (3) of art. 113, the condition has not been satisfied. In this event the sum will be deposited according to the instructions of the bankruptcy judge and will be paid to the relevant creditors if found to be entitled to it or, if not found to be entitled to it, will be included in a further distribution among the other creditors.

Sums due to creditors who do not report to the court or who are not traceable will be deposited with a credit institution. The certificate of deposit constitutes a good receipt.

Chapter VIII: Termination of bankruptcy proceedings

Section I: Termination of proceedings

118. (Grounds for termination.) Save in the case of a creditors' settlement as provided in the following section, the bankruptcy proceedings are terminated:

(1) if no application for admission of a claim in the statement of liabilities is made within the time limit specified in the declaration of bankruptcy;
(2) when all the claims are settled in full by means of the distribution of the assets, even before the final distribution, including the costs of the bankruptcy proceedings and the expenses of the administration;
(3) after completion of the final distribution;
(4) when insufficiency of assets prevents continuation of the proceedings.

119. (Termination decree.) Bankruptcy proceedings are terminated by decree of the court issued of its own motion, or on the petition of either the administrator or the debtor, and are published in accordance with art. 17.

The order is subject to appeal to the Court of Appeal within fifteen days of the date of display. The court will decide in chambers and issue its judgment after having heard the appellant, the administrator and the bankrupt.

120. (Consequences of the termination.) Upon termination of the proceedings, the assets of the bankrupt are released from the bankruptcy proceedings and the bankruptcy organisation is dismantled.

Unpaid creditors may commence separate enforcement proceedings for capital and interest in respect of the unsatisfied share of their claim.

121. (Re-opening of the bankruptcy proceedings.) In the events provided under paragraphs (3) and (4) of art. 118 the bankruptcy proceedings may be reopened within five years of termination upon a petition presented by a creditor or by the debtor himself if he provides a guarantee for payment of at least ten per cent of old and new claims, and provided it appears that there are sufficient assets owned by the bankrupt to make re-opening worthwhile.

If the court allows the petition, it will issue a final judgment in chambers which:

(1) reinstates the bankruptcy judge and the administrator to their offices or reappoints them;

(2) fixes time limits shorter by not more than one half of those provided in paragraphs (4) and (5) of art. 16.

The judgment is published in accordance with art. 17.

The bankruptcy judge appoints the creditors' committee, taking into account any new creditors.

The provisions of the preceding chapters apply to the reopened proceedings.

122. (Participation of old and new creditors.) The creditors' claims in the new distribution are for the amounts owed to them by the debtor at the time of the reopening of the proceedings, less any amount received in the previous distribution subject always to the rights of preferred claimants.

The judgment made previously remains valid in accordance with arts. 93–105.

123. (Consequences of the reopening on transactions prejudicial to the creditors.) In the event of a reopening of the bankruptcy proceedings, the time limits applicable to an avoidance action under arts. 65, 67 and 70 for transactions of the debtor performed after the termination of the proceedings, are calculated from the date of the judgment of court declaring the reopening of the proceedings.

Transactions for no consideration entered into by the bankrupt after the termination and before the reopening of the bankruptcy proceedings are void as against the creditors.

Section II: Creditors' settlement

124. (Settlement proposal.) Upon issue of a decree of the court in accordance with art. 97, the bankrupt may propose a settlement to the creditors by lodging a petition with the bankruptcy judge. The petition must contain the time requested for payment of debts, the percentage of the original amount of the unsecured debts which is proposed to be paid, and details of the guarantees offered for the payment of the debts, of the costs of the proceedings and of the administrator's compensation.

The assignment of avoidance actions as a condition of the settlement is allowed only for the benefit of a third party who undertakes the obligations under the settlement and is limited to those actions already commenced by the administrator.

Assignment of avoidance actions is not allowed in favour of the bankrupt or his guarantors.

125. (Examination of the proposal.) The bankruptcy judge will seek the opinion of the administrator and of the creditors' committee on the settlement and, if he considers the settlement to be appropriate, he will arrange for it, together with these preliminary approvals, to be notified immediately by registered post to the creditors. Dissenting creditors must lodge a formal objection within twenty to thirty days, as determined by the judge. The objection may be written at the foot of the notification.

Voting intentions are noted in a special report, signed by the judge and the clerk of the court.

After a settlement has been proposed, the bankruptcy judge may stay the sale of assets.

If there are bond holders the settlement proposal will be communicated to their representative and the period of time granted to the creditors to make their formal objections is doubled.

126. (Numerous creditors.) If there are so many creditors that the individual notifications referred to in article 125 are impracticable, the court, having heard the public prosecutor and the administrator, may authorise the bankruptcy judge to order that the settlement proposal and the opinions of the administrator and the creditors' committee be instead published in the Official Gazette and if necessary in other journals.

127. (Voting rights with respect to a settlement proposal.) All the creditors whose claims have been admitted in the statement of liabilities, with or without reservation, are entitled to vote.

Creditors who have a preferential right, a lien or a mortgage (even if contested) over an asset are not entitled to vote unless they renounce their priority rights. The renunciation may be partial, as long as it relates to more than one third of the entire claim including interest. The affirmative vote of these creditors must be express and entails the waiving of the priority rights in relation to their entire claim if the vote is given without a declaration of partial renunciation. If the settlement proposal is not approved, or if it is annulled, the effect of the renunciation ends.

The debtor's spouse, his relatives and in-laws up to the fourth degree and any transferee or assignee of their claims if the transfer or assignment took place within less than a year are not entitled to vote or to be considered in determination of the majority required.

Assignment of claims after the commencement of the bankruptcy proceedings does not entail the right to vote.

128. (Approval of the settlement proposal.) The settlement proposal is passed by a simple majority of the creditors entitled to vote, provided they also represent two thirds of the aggregate amount of all their claims.

Approval is considered to be impliedly given by creditors who do not raise formal objection within the time limit specified in accordance with art. 125, subject to the provisions of the second paragraph of the preceding article.

A change in the number of creditors or the amount of the individual claims taking place subsequently to the time limit specified in art. 125 does not affect the computation of the majority.

129. (Ratification.) If after expiry of the time limit specified for the vote the requisite majority is not reached, the bankruptcy judge will declare by way of notice attached to the proposal as provided in art. 125 that the scheme of arrangement is rejected. If the required majority has approved the scheme, a further and final ratification is required, and the bankruptcy judge will appoint the date and time of a hearing to take place not earlier than fifteen days nor later than thirty days. The order is published by way of official display.

Dissenting creditors and other interested parties may challenge the ratification by submitting their objection to the administrator and the bankrupt not later than five days before the date fixed for hearing. The grounds of objection must be stated.

At the hearing the administrator will make an oral report and the judge will hear the parties, the chairman of the committee of creditors and the bankrupt. He will then proceed, in accordance with art. 183 and the civil procedure code, to appoint the date and time for the hearing before the tribunal within the next ten days.

Five days before the final hearing before the tribunal the administrator will submit a written report to the court stating his final opinion. The creditors' committee may submit a similar report.

130. (Ratification order.) The court will verify that all the formalities for the presentation and approval of the settlement have been complied with, consider the

merits of the proposal and the reliability of the guarantees given, and determine all objections in a single judgment. The court will then ratify or reject the creditors' settlement.

The ratification judgment may set out the procedure for payment of the sums owing to the creditors by way of performance of the settlement or may delegate this responsibility to the bankruptcy judge whose decision is final.

If mortgages are given to secure the settlement, the ratification order may provide for a period of time during which the administrator will register such mortgages.

The ratification judgment will be published in accordance with art. 17.

The judgment is temporarily executory. If it has not become final before the expiry of the time period fixed for payment under the settlement, the sums required to fulfil the debtor's obligations under the settlement must be deposited with a credit institution designated by the bankruptcy judge.

131. (Appeal against the judgment.) The bankrupt and the dissenting parties may appeal against the judgment ratifying or rejecting the settlement within fifteen days of publication.

Notice of appeal must be given to the administrator, the bankrupt and any parties who filed an objection.

The judgment given on appeal is published in accordance with art. 17 and the time limit for appeal to the Supreme Court is reduced by half from the day of publication.

When the ratification judgment becomes final the insolvency procedure is terminated.

132. (Intervention of the public prosecutor.) The public prosecutor may intervene either at first instance or on appeal.

133. (Costs of the ratification on proceedings.) The bankruptcy judge will authorise withdrawal of the funds necessary to pay the costs of the ratification proceedings. If there is insufficient liquidity, the judge will order the costs to be paid by means of borrowing from the Treasury. Costs paid in advance by the Treasury will be reimbursed in accordance with art. 91.

134. (Final account of the administrator.) When the ratification judgment becomes final the administrator will submit the final accounts of his administration in accordance with art. 116.

135. (Consequences of the scheme of arrangement.) Once ratified, the settlement binds all the creditors whose debts were incurred before the commencement of the bankruptcy proceedings including creditors who did not submit a petition to have their claim considered. Those creditors, however, do not benefit from guarantees given by third parties under the settlement.

The creditors retain their right of action for the whole amount of their claims against co-obligors, guarantors and prior obligors.

136. (Performance of the settlement.) After ratification of the settlement the bankruptcy judge, the administrator and the committee of creditors will supervise performance of the settlement in accordance with the procedure set out in the ratification judgment.

Any sums due to creditors whose claims are contested or subject to a condition and to creditors who cannot be found are deposited in accordance with the procedure set out by the bankruptcy judge.

Once the bankruptcy judge is satisfied that performance of the settlement is completed, he will order the release of the guarantees and the annulment of the charges registered as security.

The order is published in accordance with art. 17. The debtor is liable to pay the costs.

137. (Cancellation of the settlement.) The administrator must notify the court if the promised guarantees are not given in accordance with the settlement or if the bankrupt is in breach of its obligations under the settlement and the ratification judgment. The court will summon the bankrupt and the guarantors, if any, and will order the cancellation of the settlement by way of final judgment in chambers. The court may proceed also on the petition of one or more creditors or on its own motion.

The order cancelling the settlement reopens the bankruptcy proceedings.

The settlement cannot be cancelled after expiry of a period of one year from the date fixed for the last payment to be made under the settlement.

The provisions of this article do not apply when the obligations under the settlement have been undertaken by a third party with immediate discharge of the debtor.

138. (Annulment of the settlement.) The ratified settlement may be annulled by the court on the petition of the administrator or of a creditor if it is discovered that the liabilities have been fraudulently exaggerated or that the existence of certain assets has not been disclosed.

The judgment annulling the settlement reopens the bankruptcy proceedings and is temporarily executory.

The action for annulment must be commenced within six months of the discovery of the fraud and, in any event, within two years from the date fixed for the last payment under the settlement.

139. (Provisions applicable to the reopening.) The judgment referred to in arts. 137 or 138 on the reopening of the bankruptcy proceedings will make provisions in accordance with the second and following paragraphs of art. 121.

140. (Consequences of the reopening.) The consequences of the reopening are set out in arts. 122 and 123.

Any avoidance action interrupted by ratification of the settlement may be reinstated.

Creditors retain the benefit of the guarantees given to them under the cancelled or annulled settlement and may keep any amount received under the scheme.

Those creditors will continue to participate for the original amount of their claim less any amount received by virtue of the partial execution of the settlement.

141. (New settlement proposal.) As soon as a new statement of liabilities has been finalised, the bankrupt may propose a new settlement. This settlement proposal may only be ratified if, prior to the hearing, the entire amount needed for its fulfilment is deposited in accordance with the instructions of the bankruptcy judge.

Chapter IX: Discharge of the bankrupt

142. (Discharge.) Discharge puts an end to the restrictions affecting the bankrupt under the bankruptcy judgment.

Discharge is ordered by the court by way of judgment in chambers after hearing the public prosecutor in the cases provided under the following articles on application by the debtor or his heirs.

The discharge order provides for the name of the bankrupt to be removed from the register referred to in art. 50 and is communicated to the Companies Registry for registration.

143. (Conditions.) Discharge is given to a bankrupt who is capable of satisfying the following requirements:

(1) payment in full of all claims submitted in the bankruptcy, including interest and costs;
(2) proper performance of the obligations arising from any creditors' settlement ratified by the court, after taking into account the causes and the circumstances of the bankruptcy, the conditions of the settlement and the percentage of claims satisfied. Discharge cannot be granted if the percentage payable to unsecured creditors is less than 25 per cent. in addition to interest and is payable over more than six months;
(3) good conduct for five years after conclusion of bankruptcy proceedings.

144. (Procedure.) The application for discharge is published by way of display on the outer door of the court. The court may order other means of publication.

Anyone wishing to oppose the discharge may lodge his formal objection in court within thirty days from publication.

After the expiry of this thirty day period the court will either approve or reject the application for discharge.

The judgment may be appealed to the Court of Appeal by the debtor-applicant, his heirs, dissenting creditors or the public prosecutor within fifteen days from publication of the discharge order. The Court of Appeal will decide the appeal in chambers.

145. (Criminal convictions preventing discharge.) Discharge cannot be granted to a bankrupt who has been convicted of fraudulent bankruptcy or of a crime against property, against public policy, national economy, industry and commerce, and who has not been discharged in accordance with the criminal code.

The court will not consider making a discharge order until the proceedings referred to in the above paragraph, if any, have been terminated.

Chapter X: Corporate bankruptcy

146. (Directors, general managers, auditors and liquidators.) The directors and the liquidators of an incorporated body are subject to the duties imposed on a bankrupt natural person under art. 49. They must be heard in all cases in which the law requires that a bankrupt natural person be heard.

Proceedings against the directors, the auditors, the general managers and the liquidators referred to in arts. 2393 and 2394 of the civil code are instituted by the administrator with prior authorisation of the bankruptcy judge and after having heard the committee of creditors.

The bankruptcy judge may, in authorising the administrator, order certain conservatory measures.

147. *(Unlimited companies.) When a declaration of bankruptcy is made in relation to an unlimited company, a declaration of bankruptcy is also made in relation to each member of the company.

If, after the company has been declared bankrupt, the existence of new members with unlimited responsibility is discovered, the court may declare the bankruptcy of these members after having heard them in chambers. The court may do so on its own initiative or on petition of the administrator.

The decision of the court is open to objection in accordance with art. 18.

The provisions of this article do not apply to cooperative companies.

148. (Bankruptcy of the company and its members.) In the situation contemplated by art. 147 the court will appoint one administrator only for both the bankruptcy of the company and the bankruptcy of the members, but the court may appoint more than one committee of creditors.

The assets of the company and the assets of its members are kept separate.

The claims submitted by the creditors of the company in the company's bankruptcy proceedings are treated as also submitted in the bankruptcy proceedings relating to the members. The creditors of the company are entitled to participate in every distribution until complete satisfaction of their claims, subject to the right of each member's bankruptcy estate to recover from the others any amount paid in excess of its proportionate participation in the company.

The creditors of a member only participate in the bankruptcy proceedings relating to that member.

Each creditor is entitled to contest the claims of the creditors with whom he is competing.

149. (Member's bankruptcy.) The bankruptcy of one or more members with unlimited responsibility does not cause the bankruptcy of the company.

150. (Payments by members with limited responsibility.) In the event of the bankruptcy of a limited company, the bankruptcy judge may, on the proposal of the administrator, order the members and any previous owners of stocks and shares to pay any outstanding contributions in respect of their shares even if the period fixed for payment has not expired.

151. (Cooperative companies.) In the event of the bankruptcy of a cooperative company with subordinated limited responsibility or with unlimited responsibility, the bankruptcy judge may, after making the order referred to in art. 97, authorise the administrator to request the members to pay the amount necessary to discharge the liabilities of the company in accordance with art. 2263 of the civil code. Contributions due from members who are insolvent are transferred to the other members.

For the above purpose, the administrator will prepare a distribution plan and will file it at the court registry. Notice will be given to the company members by recorded delivery post with proof of receipt to be returned to the sender. Members intending to submit written comments as regards their status or the extent of their liabilities must file these within forty days from submission of the distribution plan. After hearing the administrator and considering the members' written comments, the bankruptcy judge will make appropriate modifications to the distribution plan. The distribution plan will become final upon the decree of the judge and will be deposited at the court registry where it may be inspected by any interested party.

Those who have contested their status in the proceedings or the extent of their liabilities are entitled to file an objection to the court within fifteen days from filing of the distribution plan at the court registry. The objection does not suspend execution of the distribution plan, even as regards the opposing party. In any other case an appeal is allowed in accordance with art. 26.

If it appears at a later stage that the collection of a share of contribution included in the distribution plan is not practicable, a supplementary distribution plan may be prepared in accordance with the above paragraphs.

Recourse action is available as between members in accordance with art. 1299 of the civil code, as is action for reimbursement of a sum remaining after discharge of the liabilities.

In order to secure payment of the members' contributions, the administrator may apply to the bankruptcy judge who may order the seizure of the assets of the members.

152. (Settlement proposal.) Any proposed creditors' settlement relating to a bankrupt company must be signed by the company's statutory representatives.

Creditors' settlements relating to partnerships and limited partnerships must be approved by members representing an absolute majority of capital. As regards joint stock companies, partnerships limited by shares and cooperative companies, creditors' settlements must be approved by an extraordinary general meeting unless the relevant powers have been delegated to the directors.

153. (Consequences of a creditors' settlement.) Unless otherwise agreed, a creditors' settlement made by an unlimited company is also valid with regard to the members and terminates their bankruptcy. The creditors of a member may file an objection in accordance with the second paragraph of art. 129 against the termination of the bankruptcy proceedings of that member.

The judgment given on the objection is final.

154. (Creditors' settlements relating to the bankruptcy of the member.) In the event of the bankruptcy of an unlimited company, each of the members declared bankrupt may submit a creditors' settlement to the creditors of the company and to his own creditors in relation to his own bankruptcy.

Chapter XI: Summary proceedings

155. (Applicable provisions.) If, at the time of the declaration of bankruptcy or preparation of the statement of liabilities, it appears that the debts of the debtor do not exceed one million five hundred thousand lire, the court may, in the judgment declaring the bankruptcy or in a subsequent order to be published in accordance with art. 17, declare that the bankruptcy proceedings be carried out by means of summary proceedings. If it subsequently appears that the total amount of the debts exceeds one million five hundred thousand lire, the judge must inform the court which will order the continuation of bankruptcy proceedings in the normal way. Any actions already completed will remain valid.

The preceding provisions relating to bankruptcy proceedings apply to summary proceedings in so far as they are consistent with the following provisions.

156. (Organs of the court and conservatory measures.) The functions of the bankruptcy judge may be entrusted to the judge at first instance of the principal place of business of the company. The nomination of the creditors' committee is optional.

The procedure of affixing seals may be omitted.

157. (Verification of claims.) The administrator will prepare the list of creditors on the basis of the company's books, the debtor's declarations and any other information received by the administrator.

The list and supporting documents is submitted to the judge who will proceed with the preparation of the statement of liabilities, which is made executory by him. The statement of liabilities together with the bankruptcy order are filed at the court registry for inspection.

The administrator will notify each creditor of the measures concerning them within three days from the date of deposit by means of recorded delivery.

Within fifteen days from the date of deposit of the statement of liabilities at the court registry the creditors not included in the statement of liabilities are entitled to file an objection to the judge.

In the same period of time objections to the admitted claims may be put forward by the other creditors.

The judge will appoint the day and the time of the hearing to discuss objections and appeals.

He will try to resolve disputes amicably, but, should he not succeed, he will pronounce judgment.

158. (Applications to claim ownership, restitution and separation of chattels.) The provisions of the preceding article also apply to the petitions to claim ownership, restitution and separation of chattels in the possession of the bankrupt.

159. (Settlement.) A creditors' settlement proposal will be approved if it has the consent of the majority of the creditors in number who are entitled to vote and who hold the majority in value of the debts.

The judge, having ascertained that the majority requirement has been satisfied, will indicate his approval of the settlement proposal by decree and will proceed by granting its execution.

No appeal lies against the decree approving or rejecting the settlement proposal.

TITLE III. PREVENTIVE CREDITORS' SETTLEMENT

Chapter I: Admission to the procedure of preventive creditors' settlement

160. (Conditions of admission to the procedure.) A trader who becomes insolvent may, prior to a declaration of bankruptcy being made, propose a preventive creditors' settlement in accordance with the provisions of this title, provided that:

(1) he has been registered in the trades register for at least two years or since the start of his business if it has had a shorter life, and he has kept regular accounts for that period;
(2) he has not been declared bankrupt or admitted to the procedure of preventive creditors' settlement during the preceding five years;
(3) he has not been convicted of fraudulent bankruptcy or of a crime against property, public policy, national economy, industry or commerce.

The proposed creditors' settlement must fulfil one of the following conditions:

(1) the debtor provides appropriate security or personal guarantees for the payment, within six months of the date of approval of the proposal, of at least 40 per cent. of the amount of unsecured debts. If a longer delay is proposed, he must provide similar guarantees for the payment of interest owing at law on all sums accruing due after the first six months;
(2) the debtor transfers to his creditors, in payment of his debts, all his assets as at the date of the proposal of the creditors' settlement, apart from those referred to in art. 46, and the valuation of these assets allows the creditors to be satisfied at least to the extent mentioned in (1) above.

161. (Application for creditors' settlement.) The request for admission to the procedure of preventive creditors' settlement is made by means of an application signed by the debtor to the court of the place where the head office of his business is situated.

The applicant must explain in his application how his insolvency was caused and his reasons for proposing a creditors' settlement.

The debtor must submit with his application the books of accounts, a detailed statement and estimate of the assets and a list of creditors.

In the case of companies, the application must be approved and signed in accordance with art. 152.

162. *(Inadmissibility of the application.) After hearing the public prosecutor and, if necessary, the debtor, the court will, by way of a final decree, declare the proposal inadmissible if the conditions set out in the first paragraph of art. 160 are not satisfied, or if it considers that the proposed scheme of arrangement does not satisfy the conditions of the second paragraph of the same article.

In this event, the court will declare the bankruptcy of the debtor of its own motion.

163. (Admission to the procedure.) If the court considers the proposal to be admissible, the court will order the commencement of the procedure of preventive creditors' settlement by way of a final decree. In the same order the court will:

(1) appoint a judge to the creditors' settlement proceedings;
(2) order a meeting of the creditors to be held within thirty days from the date of the order and fix the deadline for sending notice of it to the creditors;
(3) appoint the judicial commissioner, chosen from the register of legal administrators in accordance with arts. 27, 28 and 29;
(4) fix a period of not more than eight days before the expiry of which the applicant must deposit at the court registry the sum considered necessary for the whole procedure.

If the required deposit is not made, the court will proceed according to the second paragraph of the previous article.

164. (Decrees of the bankruptcy judge.) The decrees of the bankruptcy judge are open to objection in accordance with art. 26.

The decree of the court which determines the objection is not subject to appeal.

165. (Judicial commissioner.) In the exercise of his functions the judicial commissioner acts in the capacity of public official.

Arts. 36, 37, 38 and 39 apply to the judicial commissioner.

166. (Publication of the order.) The order is published by way of display on the outer door of the court and is notified for registration to the registrar of the trades register. It is also published in the local legal announcements journal and, in other journals as ordered by the court.

If the debtor owns immoveables or other assets subject to public registration, the provisions of the second paragraph of art. 88 will apply.

Chapter II: Consequences of admission to preventive creditors' settlement

167. (Administration of the assets during the procedure.) During the procedure of preventive creditors' settlement the debtor continues to administer his assets and to run his business under the supervision of the judicial commissioner and at the direction of the bankruptcy judge.

Loans, even by way of promissory notes, settlements, compromises, transfers of immoveables, the grant of mortgages and pledges, guarantees, renunciation of lawsuits, acknowledgments of the rights of third parties, cancellations of mortgages, and redemptions of pledges and acceptances of inheritances and donations and, in general, all acts of extraordinary administration made, in each case, without the written authorisation of the bankruptcy judge, are void as against creditors whose claims arose prior to the creditors' settlement.

168. (Consequences of the application.) From the date of submission of the application and until issue of the judgment approving the creditors' settlement, creditors whose claims are antecedent to the order may not, at the risk of having their actions invalidated, begin or continue proceedings against the debtor's assets.

Time barring provisions will remain suspended and forfeitures may not take place.

Creditors may not acquire rights ranking in priority over the rights of competing creditors unless authorised by the judge as provided in the preceding article.

169. (Applicable provisions.) Arts. 55, 56, 57, 58, 59, 60, 61, 62 and 63 apply in relation to the date of application for creditors' settlement.

Chapter III: Immediate measures

170. (Books of accounts.) The bankruptcy judge will, immediately after the order of admission to the creditors' settlement has been made, make a note to that effect below the last entry in the books submitted.

The books are then returned to the debtor who must keep them at the disposal of the bankruptcy judge and the judicial commissioner.

171. (Meeting of the creditors.) The judicial commissioner will proceed with the verification of the list of creditors and debtors as disclosed by the books of accounts submitted in accordance with art. 161 and will make the necessary rectifications.

The judicial commissioner will notify the creditors, by registered post or by telegram, of the date of the meeting and of the debtor's proposals.

If the giving of notice as mentioned in the preceding paragraph is impracticable due to the number of creditors or due to the difficulty of identifying them all, the court may, after consultation with the judicial commissioner, give the authorisation referred to in art. 126.

If there are bondholders, the time limit mentioned in item (2) of the first paragraph of art. 163 must be doubled.

In any event, notice of the meeting is given to the bondholders' representative.

The provisions of royal decree no. 136 of 8th February 1924 with respect to credit institutions will prevail.

172. (Acts and reports of the commissioner.) The judicial commissioner will prepare an inventory of the debtor's assets and a detailed report on the causes of the insolvency, the debtor's conduct, the proposed creditors' settlement and the guarantees offered to the creditors. He will file these at the court registry not less than three days before the creditors' meeting.

At the request of the judicial commissioner, the judge may appoint a valuer to assist him in the valuation of the assets.

173. (Declaration of bankruptcy in the course of the procedure.) If the judicial commissioner discovers that the debtor has concealed part of the assets or has fraudulently omitted to report one or more credits or has declared non-existent losses or committed other acts of fraud, the commissioner will immediately notify the bankruptcy judge who, after appropriate investigation, will arrange for a declaration of bankruptcy to be made by the court.

A declaration of bankruptcy will also be made if the debtor participates in unauthorised transactions within the meaning of art. 167 or acts constituting a fraud on the creditors during the procedure of a creditors' settlement or if, at any time, the conditions for the admissibility of creditors' settlement may no longer be satisfied.

Chapter IV: Examination of the preventive creditors' settlement

174. (Meeting of the creditors.) The bankruptcy judge will preside over the creditors' meeting.

Every creditor is entitled to be represented by an agent whose power of attorney may be informally written on the notice of meeting.

The debtor or his statutory representative will attend in person. He may only be represented by an agent in the event of unavoidable impediment, verified by the bankruptcy judge.

Co-obligors, the debtor's guarantors and subordinated obligors may also attend.

175. (Discussion of the proposed creditors' settlement.) The judicial commissioner will present his report and the debtor's final proposal at the creditors' meeting.

Each creditor may give his reasons for not considering the proposed creditors' settlement admissible or acceptable and he may raise objections as regards competing creditors.

The debtor may then answer and object to the claims. He is under a duty to supply the judge with satisfactory explanations.

176. (Provisional admission of disputed claims.) The bankruptcy judge may admit disputed claims on a provisional basis, in their entirety or in part, for the purpose of voting and the calculation of majorities, without compromising the final decision on the admissibility of these claims.

Creditors whose claims have been excluded may, at the ratification stage in the creditors' settlement procedure, object to their exclusion if admission of their claims would have affected the formation of the majorities.

177. (Majority required for approval of the scheme of arrangement.) The scheme of arrangement must be approved by a majority of the creditors entitled to vote who also represent two thirds of all claims. Creditors with preferential rights over the debtor's assets are not entitled to vote unless they renounce their preferred claim. This renunciation may be partial, as long as it relates to more than one third of the entire claim, including interest.

The consequences of renunciation terminate if the creditors' settlement is not approved or if it is subsequently cancelled or annulled. The vote of these creditors entails the waiving of preferred status in relation to their entire claim if the vote is given without a declaration of partial renunciation.

The debtor's spouse, his relatives and in-laws up to the fourth degree and any transferee or assignee of their claims within less than a year prior to the proposal of the creditors' settlement are likewise excluded from voting and from the calculation of the majorities.

178. (Acceptance of the proposed creditors' settlement.) The votes of the creditors, whether in favour or against the proposal, will be recorded in the minutes of the creditors' meeting together with details of the voters' names and the amount of their respective claims.

The minutes are signed by the bankruptcy judge, the judicial commissioner and the clerk of the court.

If all the business of the meeting cannot be concluded on the appointed day, it will be continued at a subsequent meeting fixed by the judge and held within eight days. Absentees need not be notified.

Communications of approval by letter or telegram made within twenty days of the closure of the minutes will be noted by the clerk of the court at the end of the minutes. If the majority of the creditors entitled to vote at the meeting approved the creditors' settlement but the two thirds majority of the claims was not reached, those approvals are taken into account for the purpose of calculating the majority of the claims.

Chapter V: Ratification of the preventive creditors' settlement

179. (Rejection of the creditors' settlement.) If the majorities required by arts. 177 and 178 are not reached within the prescribed time limit, the bankruptcy judge will immediately notify the court which will proceed in accordance with the second paragraph of art. 162.

180. (Approval of the creditors' settlement and ratification hearing.) If the required majorities are reached, the bankruptcy judge will, by means of an order published by way of official display, appoint a date for a hearing to be held within thirty days from the date of the order.

Dissenting creditors and other interested parties may oppose the ratification by notifying their objection to the debtor and the judicial commissioner and by registering their appearance in court not later than five days before the date fixed for the hearing. The objection must set out the grounds on which it is based.

Within the same time limit the judicial commissioner will file his reasoned opinion at the court registry.

The debtor may attend the hearing and be heard by the judge even if he did not register his appearance.

The judge will then proceed, in accordance with art. 183 and the following articles of the civil procedure code, and will appoint a date for a further hearing to be held within the following ten days.

181. (Ratification judgment.) Once the court has verified that the conditions of admission of the creditors' settlement are still satisfied and that all the formalities have been complied with, it will consider:

(1) the economic benefit of the creditors' settlement for the creditors having regard to the existing assets and the efficiency of the business;
(2) whether the majorities required by law have been reached, taking also into account the provisionally excluded creditors who have objected to their exclusion;
(3) whether the guarantees offered will secure performance of the creditors' settlement and, in the case specified in paragraph (2) of art. 160, whether the assets offered are sufficient for the payment of the creditors;
(4) whether the debtor deserves the benefit of the creditors' settlement having regard to the causes of the insolvency and his conduct.

If these conditions are satisfied, the court will ratify the settlement; otherwise, it will declare the debtor's bankruptcy.

In the ratification order the court will determine the amount to be deposited by the debtor in respect of disputed claims in accordance with the creditors' settlement. The court will also give instructions concerning payment of the sums owing to the creditors in performance of the creditors' settlement or will delegate this responsibility to the bankruptcy judge who will do so in a separate order.

The last two paragraphs of art. 130 apply.

182. (Measures to be taken in the event of transfer of assets.) Unless otherwise stated, if the creditors' settlement provides for the transfer of assets the court will, in the ratification judgment, appoint one or more liquidators and a committee of three to five creditors in order to assist the liquidation. It will also determine the liquidation procedure (art. 1977 of the civil code).

183. *(Appeal against the ratification order.) The dissenting parties and the debtor may appeal against the judgment ratifying or rejecting the creditors' settlement within fifteen days of publication.

Notice of appeal must be given to the debtor, the judicial commissioner and the other parties who appeared before the court.

Judgment will be published in accordance with art. 17, and the time period for appeal to the Supreme Court runs from the date of publication (art. 339 of the civil procedure code).

184. (Consequences of the creditors' settlement on the creditors.) The ratified creditors' settlement is binding on all the creditors whose claims are antecedent to the decree

commencing the procedure. However, these creditors retain their rights of action against co-obligors, the debtor's guarantors and any other obligors.

Unless otherwise agreed, a creditors' settlement in respect of a company takes effect as regards members with unlimited liability (arts. 2291 and 2313 of the civil code).

Chapter VI: Performance, cancellation and annulment of the preventive creditors' settlement

185. (Performance of the creditors' settlement.) After ratification of the creditors' settlement, the judicial commissioner will supervise its performance in accordance with the guidelines given in the ratification judgment. He must notify the judge of anything which might be prejudicial to the creditors.

The second paragraph of art. 136 applies.

186. (Cancellation and annulment of the creditors' settlement.) The provisions of arts. 137 and 138 apply to the creditors' settlement where references to the administrator are construed as references to the judicial commissioner.

If the creditors' settlement provides for transfer of assets in accordance with item (2) of the second paragraph of art. 160, the creditors' settlement will not be cancelled if, after realisation of the assets, the sum obtained represents a dividend less than 40 per cent.

The judgment cancelling or annulling the creditors' settlement will also constitute a declaration of bankruptcy.

TITLE IV. SUPERVISED ADMINISTRATION

187. (Request for admission to the procedure.) A trader who has temporary difficulties in fulfilling his obligations may apply to the court for supervision of the management of his business and the administration of his assets in the interests of his creditors for a period not exceeding two years, provided the conditions numbered 1, 2 and 3 of the first paragraph of art. 160 are satisfied and the business has real recovery prospects.

The request is made in the form prescribed by art. 161.

188. (Admission to the procedure.) If the legal conditions are satisfied, and the court considers that the debtor deserves the benefit, the court will admit the applicant to the procedure of supervised administration by way of decree which is not subject to review. In the same order the court will:

(1) appoint a judge to the proceedings;
(2) order a meeting of the creditors to be held within thirty days from the date of the order and fix the deadline for sending notice of it to the creditors;
(3) appoint a judicial commissioner in accordance with arts. 27, 28 and 29;
(4) fix a period of not more than eight days before the expiry of which the applicant must deposit at the court registry the sum considered necessary for the whole procedure.

The decree is published in accordance with art. 166 and, during the procedure, has the consequences provided under arts. 167 and 168.

The provisions contained in arts. 164, 165 and 170–173 also apply.

189. (Creditors' meeting.) The provisions of arts. 174, 175, 176 (first paragraph), 177 (fourth paragraph) and 178 (first, second and third paragraphs) apply to the creditors' deliberations.

Votes made by letter or by telegram are taken into consideration provided they were received prior to the close of proceedings.

The debtor's proposal must be approved by the vote of the majority of the creditors who also represent the majority of the claims with the exception of those creditors with preferential rights over the debtor's assets.

If the required majorities are not reached, the admission decree ceases to be effective.

190. (Power of the bankruptcy judge.) If the required majorities are reached and after taking into account the opinion of the creditors expressed at the meeting, the bankruptcy judge will appoint by decree a committee of three or five creditors to assist the judicial commissioner.

Any interested party may appeal against the order of the judge within ten days of the date of the order. The court will decide the appeal in chambers by way of a decree which is not subject to review.

191. (Administrative powers of the judicial commissioner.) At the request of any interested party or on its own motion, and after having heard the creditors' committee, the court may at any time during the procedure, by means of a final decree, entrust part or the whole of the management of the business and the administration of the debtor's assets to the judicial commissioner and determine his powers.

The decree will be published in accordance with art. 166.

In such a case the commissioner will submit the accounts of his administration in accordance with art. 116.

192. (Commissioner's report and revocation of supervised administration.) The judicial commissioner will report every two months to the bankruptcy judge on the progress of the business.

*The judicial commissioner and the creditors' committee must also report to the bankruptcy judge any fact which may justify revocation of the supervised administration as soon as they became aware of it.

If it appears at any time that the supervised administration may not be carried on profitably, the bankruptcy judge will propose that the court issues a declaration of bankruptcy. However, the trader's option to propose a preventive creditors' settlement in accordance with the provisions of the preceding title is preserved.

193. (Termination of the supervised administration.) A debtor who proves that he can regularly meet his obligations may ask the court to close the procedure even before expiry of the period fixed for its duration. In this event the court will issue a decree for publication in accordance with art. 17.

If, after the termination of the supervised administration, the business is not in a position to fulfil its obligations on a regular basis, the third paragraph of the preceding article will apply.

TITLE V. COMPULSORY ADMINISTRATIVE LIQUIDATION

194. (Applicable provisions.) Compulsory administrative liquidation is regulated by the provisions of this title, save as otherwise provided by special laws.

Provisions of special laws which are incompatible with arts. 195, 196, 200, 201, 202, 203, 209, 211 and 213 are repealed.

195. (Judicial assessment of the state of insolvency prior to the compulsory administrative liquidation.) If a business subject to compulsory administrative liquidation to the exclusion of bankruptcy is in an insolvent position, the court of the place where the head office of the business is situated will, on the application of one or more creditors, declare the business insolvent by way of a judgment in chambers. In the same judgment, or in a subsequent order, the court will provide for appropriate conservation measures in the interest of the creditors prior to the commencement of the liquidation procedure.

*Before taking any action, the court must hear the governmental authority responsible for supervising the business.

The judgment will be notified to the competent authority within three days in accordance with art. 136 of the civil procedure code in order to enable it to proceed to the liquidation. It is also notified and published in the manner and within the period provided for declarations of bankruptcy.

Within thirty days following publication and after taking into account the observations of the commissioner, any interested party may oppose the judgment in the court which pronounced it.

The time limit for the appeal is fifteen days from notification of the judgment.

The judgment rejecting the petition for the declaration of insolvency is given by way of a reasoned decree. Appeal against the decree may be made in accordance with art. 22.

The court will proceed of its own motion to the declaration of insolvency in accordance with this article when, during the procedure of preventive creditors' settlement or of supervised administration of a business which is also subject to compulsory administrative liquidation to the exclusion of bankruptcy, the conditions set out in titles III and IV for a declaration of bankruptcy occur.

The provisions of this article do not apply to public entities.

196. (Concurrence of bankruptcy and compulsory administrative liquidation.) As regards those businesses subject to compulsory administrative liquidation, and for which the law does not exclude the procedure of bankruptcy, a declaration of bankruptcy will preclude compulsory administrative liquidation, and a declaration of administrative liquidation will preclude a declaration of bankruptcy.

197. (Liquidation provisions.) The order for liquidation will be published in its complete form within ten days by the issuing authority in the Official Gazette of the Republic of Italy and will be notified to the registry of businesses for registration, in addition to the other forms of publicity prescribed by the order (art. 2188 of the civil code).

198. (Persons appointed in administrative liquidation.) A liquidator is appointed in the order for liquidation, or in a subsequent order. A supervising committee is also appointed which consists of between three and five members chosen from experts in the same type of activity as the business, possibly from among the creditors.

Whenever the importance of the business so requires, three liquidators may be appointed. In this case decisions are taken by a majority and representation is exercised jointly by any two of them. The appointment of a supervising committee is optional in the case of liquidation of cooperatives.

199. (The liabilities of the liquidator.) In the exercise of his functions the liquidator acts in the capacity of a public official.

During the liquidation, any proceedings for liability against a liquidator who has been removed from his office will be taken by the new liquidator with the consent of the authority supervising the liquidation.

The provisions of arts. 32, 37 and 38, first paragraph, apply to the liquidator and the powers of the authority supervising the liquidation are considered to replace those of the court and the bankruptcy judge.

200. (Consequences of the order for liquidation on the business.) Arts. 42, 44, 45 and 47 apply as from the date of the order for liquidation, If the business is a company or a legal person, any powers exercised in meetings and the function of the administrative and supervising bodies will cease save as provided in art. 214.

The liquidator will represent the business in any legal proceedings, even if already pending, relating to the rights of the business itself.

201. (Consequences of the liquidation on the creditors and on the pre-existing legal relationships.) The provisions of title II, chapter III, section II (art. 51 and the following articles) and section IV (art. 72 and the following articles) and the provisions of art. 66 apply as from the date of the order for liquidation.

*The administrative authority supervising the liquidation is considered to be substituted for the court and the bankruptcy judge. The liquidator is considered to be substituted for the administrator and the supervising committee is considered to be substituted for the committee of creditors.

202. (Judicial assessment of the insolvency.) If, at the time of the liquidation order, the business was in an insolvent position not previously declared in accordance with the provisions of art. 195, the court of the place where the head office of the business is situated will, on application made by the liquidator or at the request of the public prosecutor, assess the insolvency in chambers even if the liquidation has been ordered on the grounds of insufficient assets.

The provisions of the first, second, third, fourth, fifth and sixth paragraphs of art. 195 will apply.

203. (Consequences of judicial assessment of the insolvency.) Once the insolvency has been judicially assessed in accordance with art. 195 or 202, the provisions of title II, chapter III, section III apply from the date of the order for liquidation also to shareholders or partners with unlimited liability. The provisions of arts. 216 to 219 and 223 to 225 apply to such shareholders or partners, the directors, the general managers, the liquidators and the supervising bodies.

The liquidator is responsible for pursuing avoidance actions relating to transactions made to the detriment of creditors.

The liquidator will submit a report to the public prosecutor in accordance with the first paragraph of art. 33.

204. (Liquidator.) The liquidator is responsible for all matters concerning the liquidation in accordance with the directives of the authority supervising the liquidation and under the control of the supervising committee.

He will take over all the assets included in the liquidation, the books of account and other documents belonging to the business and may request, where necessary, the assistance of a notary.

The liquidator will then prepare an inventory and, if necessary, appoint one or more valuers for the valuation of the assets.

205. (Liquidator's report.) The trader, or, if the business is a company or a legal person, the directors, must submit the administration accounts to the liquidator for the period following the latest balance sheet.

The liquidator is not required to prepare the annual balance sheet but at the end of every six months he must submit a report to the authority supervising the liquidation on the financial state of the business and on the status of its management, accompanied by a report of the supervising committee.

206. (Liquidator's powers.) In accordance with arts. 2393 and 2394 of the civil code, any liability action against the directors and the members of the supervising bodies of the business being liquidated will be brought by the liquidator with the consent of the authority supervising the liquidation.

Performance of the transactions referred to in art. 35 as either of no specified value or of a value exceeding two million lire, and the continuation of the business' activity by the liquidator, must be authorised by this authority, following consultation with the supervising committee.

207. (Notice to creditors and third parties.) Within one month following his appointment the liquidator will notify each creditor by means of registered letter with acknowledgement of receipt the amounts owing by the business according to the books of account and the business' documents. The notice is considered to be given subject to any objections.

The same notice is given to those entitled to bring actions for avoidance or restitution or for separation of the business chattels.

Creditors, and the other parties referred to in this paragraph, may submit their objections or petitions to the liquidator within fifteen days from receipt of the registered letter.

208. (Requests of the creditors and third parties.) Within sixty days of publication of the orders in the Official Gazette, creditors and the other parties referred to in the preceding article who have not received this notice may submit a request by registered letter for their claims to be acknowledged and their assets restored.

209. (Preparation of the statement of liabilities.) Unless special laws provide for a longer term, the liquidator must draw up the list of admitted and rejected claims, and of the claims referred to in the second paragraph of art. 207, whether accepted or rejected, within ninety days from the date of the liquidation order. He must then file it at the court registry of the place where the head office of the business is situated, and notify it by registered post to those whose claims have been rejected or partly admitted. The list becomes executory upon filing at the court registry.

*Objections (in accordance with art. 98) and appeals (in accordance with art. 100), are submitted within fifteen days from the filing of the statement, by way of summary application to the president of the court, having due regard to the provisions of the second paragraph of art. 93.

The president of the court will appoint an investigating judge who will also deal with any further decisions. Arts. 98 to 103 will be observed where applicable when the bankruptcy judge is replaced by the investigating judge, and the administrator is replaced by the liquidator.

The provisions of special laws regulating the assessment of unsecured claims in the liquidation of credit institutions will prevail.

210. (Liquidation of the assets.) The liquidator has all the powers necessary for the liquidation of the assets insofar as not restricted by the authority supervising the liquidation.

In any event, the consent of the authority supervising the liquidation and the opinion of the supervising committee will be requested for the sale of real estate and the block sale of chattels.

In the event of a company whose members have limited liability the court may, on the proposal of the liquidator, order to be paid up outstanding portions of subscribed capital due from the limited liability members and from those transferors by way of the relevant proportions and shares although the time for payment has not yet expired.

211. (Company with members having secondary limited, or unlimited, liability.) In the event of liquidation of a company whose members have secondary limited, or unlimited, liability the liquidator may ask the members to pay the sums he considers necessary for the payment of debts after obtaining authorisation of the authority supervising the liquidation and after filing the list referred to in art. 209 at the court registry. Art. 151 applies in respect of the remainder of the procedure, when the powers of the president of the court are substituted for the bankruptcy judge's powers, the liquidator replaces the administrator, and the appeal referred to in art. 26 is excluded.

212. (Distribution of the assets.) The sums received from liquidation of the assets are distributed in the order referred to in art. 111.

After obtaining the opinion of the supervising committee and authorisation from the authority supervising the liquidation, the liquidator may make partial distributions, either to all creditors or to particular categories, even before all the assets have been realised and all the liabilities have been ascertained.

Late submissions for the admission of claims or for the acknowledgment of property rights do not prejudice the distributions already made and may be satisfied out of the sums not already distributed in accordance with the provisions of art. 112.

The provisions of art. 113 apply to partial distributions.

213. (Termination of the liquidation.) The final liquidation account, together with the management account and the distribution plan and a report of the supervising committee must be submitted to the authority supervising the liquidation before the final distribution to the creditors. The supervisory authority will authorise the filing of these at the court registry and will pay the liquidator's compensation. The filing will be notified by means of publication in the Official Gazette of the Republic of Italy and in newspapers as indicated by the authority supervising the liquidation.

Within twenty days from publication in the Official Gazette, the parties concerned may submit their objections to the court. These are notified by the registrar to the authority supervising the liquidation, the liquidator and the supervising committee. The observations of these bodies may be filed at the court registry within twenty days. The president of the court will appoint an investigating judge who will also deal with any further decisions under art. 189 of the civil procedure code.

If no observations are submitted during this period, the final account, the administration account and the distribution plan are approved, and the liquidator will proceed with the final distribution to creditors. The provisions of art. 117 and, if necessary, of arts. 2456 and 2457 of the civil code will apply.

214. (Creditors' settlement.) After filing of the list under art. 209 the authority supervising the liquidation may, after hearing the liquidator and the supervising committee, authorise the business in liquidation to propose a creditors' settlement. If the business is a limited liability company, the provisions of article 152 shall apply.

The proposed creditors' settlement must set out the conditions and any relevant guarantees. It will be filed at the court registry together with the opinions of the liquidator and the supervising committee and published in accordance with the instructions of the authority supervising the liquidation. Within thirty days of filing, interested parties may submit objections to the registrar. These will be communicated to the liquidator.

After hearing the opinion of the authority supervising the liquidation the court will decide on the creditors' settlement by way of a judgment issued in chambers and after taking into consideration any objections. The judgment approving the scheme will be published as provided in art. 17 and in accordance with the instructions of the court.

The business in liquidation, the liquidator and any objectors may each appeal against the judgment, whether accepting or rejecting the scheme, within fifteen days of attachment of the order to the external door of the court. The appeal judgment will be published in accordance with the preceding paragraph and the period of time for appeal to the Supreme Court will run from the date of publication of the judgment.

The liquidator, with the assistance of the supervising committee, will supervise execution of the creditors' settlement.

215. (Cancellation and revocation of the creditors' settlement.) If the creditors' settlement is not implemented, the court will, at the request of the liquidator or of one or more creditors, pronounce the cancellation of the creditors' settlement by way of a judgment in chambers not subject to appeal. The provisions of art. 137 paragraphs 3 and 4 will apply.

At the request of the liquidator or the creditors the creditors' settlement may be annulled in accordance with art. 138.

Once the creditors' settlement has been cancelled or annulled, the administrative liquidation will reopen and the authority supervising the liquidation will take such measures as it considers necessary.

TITLE VI. CRIMINAL PROVISIONS

Chapter I: Crimes committed by the bankrupt party

216. (Fraudulent bankruptcy.) A trader who has been declared bankrupt may be sentenced to imprisonment for three to ten years if he has:

(1) misappropriated, concealed, dissembled, destroyed or dissipated, in whole or in part, his property, or disclosed or recognised non-existent debts with the aim of prejudicing his creditors;
(2) stolen, destroyed or falsified, in whole or in part, books of account or other documents relating to accounts, with the aim of obtaining for himself or for others illicit profits or of prejudicing creditors, or kept these books or documents in such a way as to render impossible the reconstruction of the assets or commercial activities of the business.

The same penalties apply to a trader who, having been declared bankrupt, during the bankruptcy procedure commits any of the offences described in paragraph 1 above or if he steals, destroys or falsifies books of account or other documents relating to accounts.

The bankrupt may be sentenced to imprisonment for one to five years if, before or during the bankruptcy procedure, he makes payments or fraudulently creates preferred rights with the aim of obtaining preferences for any one of the creditors.

In addition to the further penalties set out in title III, sub-title II, book I of the penal code, conviction for one of the offences provided under this article carries disqualification from commercial business practice and from the occupation of management positions for ten years.

217. *(Simple bankruptcy.) A trader who has been declared bankrupt may be sentenced to imprisonment for six months to two years if he has, apart from the offences described in the preceding article:

(1) incurred disproportionate expenditure on himself or his family having regard to his financial position;
(2) squandered a sizeable part of his assets in transactions which depend on pure luck or through manifest imprudence;
(3) demonstrated grave imprudence while attempting to delay bankruptcy;
(4) aggravated his own difficulties by not requesting a declaration of bankruptcy or through any other serious fault;
(5) not satisfied the obligations accepted by him under a prior preventive creditors' settlement or a bankruptcy settlement.

The same penalty will apply to a bankrupt who, during the three years prior to the declaration of bankruptcy or from the commencement of trading, if it had a shorter duration, has not kept the accounts or other documents relating to accounts required by the law, or if he has kept them in an irregular or incomplete manner.

In addition to the penalties set out in title III, sub-title II, book I of the penal code, a conviction for this offence carries disqualification from commercial business practice and from the occupation of management positions for up to two years.

218. (Unlawful recourse to credit.) Unless the offence constitutes a more serious offence than provided for herein, a person who, while conducting commercial transactions, incurs or continues to incur debts while concealing his bankruptcy, may be sentenced to up to two years imprisonment.

In addition to the further penalties set out in title III, sub-title II, book I of the penal code, the conviction carries disqualification from commercial business practice and from the occupation of management positions for up to three years.

219. (Aggravating and extenuating circumstances.) Where the offences provided under articles 216, 217 and 218 have caused loss or damage of a serious nature to the assets of the bankrupt, the sentences specified in those articles may be lengthened by up to a half.

The sentences specified in these articles will be lengthened:

(1) if the guilty party has committed more than one of the offences provided for in the above articles;
(2) if the guilty party could not carry on business due to legal disqualification.

Where the offences described in paragraph 1 have caused loss or damage to the assets and the loss or damage is of a particularly minor nature, the sentences may be reduced by up to one-third.

220. (Naming of fictitious creditors and other offences by the bankrupt.) A bankrupt who, apart from the offences provided under article 216, names fictitious creditors in the list of creditors or omits to mention the existence of assets which should be included in the inventory, or fails to observe the requirements imposed in articles 16 (para 3) and 49, may be sentenced to imprisonment for six to eighteen months.

If the bankruptcy has occurred due to the fault of the bankrupt, he may be sentenced to imprisonment for up to one year.

221. (Bankruptcy with summary proceedings.) If summary proceedings are brought against the bankrupt, the penalties provided for under this chapter will be reduced to one-third.

222. (Bankruptcy of a company in common ownership or in limited partnership.) Where bankruptcy affects companies in common ownership or a limited partnership, the provisions of this chapter will apply to the offences committed by partners with unlimited liability.

Chapter II: Offences committed by persons other than the bankrupt

223. (Fraudulent offences committed in bankruptcy.) The penalties specified in article 216 will apply to directors, general managers, auditors and liquidators of businesses declared bankrupt, when they have committed any of the offences provided under that article.

The penalties specified in article 216 paragraph 1 will apply to the above persons when:

(1) they have committed any of the offences provided under articles 2621, 2622, 2623, 2628 and 2630 (first paragraph), of the civil code;
(2) they have caused the bankruptcy of the company by fraud or by fraudulent means.

The provisions of the last paragraph of article 216 will apply in each case.

224. (Simple bankruptcy offences.) The penalties specified in article 217 will apply to directors, general managers, auditors and liquidators of businesses declared bankrupt, when they have:

(1) committed any of the offences provided under that article;
(2) contributed in causing or aggravating the failure of the business by failing to meet the requirements imposed by the law.

225. (Unlawful recourse to credit.) The penalties specified in article 217 will apply to directors and to general managers of businesses declared bankrupt, when they have committed the offence created by that article.

226. (Declaration of non-existent debts.) The penalties specified in article 220 will apply to directors, general managers and liquidators of businesses declared bankrupt, when they have committed the offences created in that article.

227. (Offences committed by agents.) The penalties specified in articles 216, 217, 218 and 220 will apply to the agent of a bankrupt, declared insolvent, when he has committed the offences provided under those articles in the course of the management entrusted to him.

228. (Private interests of the administrator in the bankruptcy actions.) Except when articles 315, 317, 318, 319, 321, 322 and 323 of the penal code apply, an administrator who acquires a private interest in any bankruptcy action either directly or through a third party or through concealed transactions will be punishable by imprisonment for from two to six years and a fine of no less than 400 000 lire.

The conviction carries disqualification from public office.

229. (Acceptance of remuneration not due.) An insolvency administrator who receives or arranges for remuneration, in money or another form, above the amount provided to be paid to him during the liquidation by the court or the bankruptcy judge, will be punished by imprisonment for from three months to two years and a fine of between 200 000 and one million lire.

In the most serious cases temporary disqualification from the office of director for no less than two years may be added to the above penalties.

230. (Failure to deliver or deposit property related to the bankruptcy.) An administrator who does not comply with the judge's order to deliver or deposit money or other property relating to the bankruptcy which he holds on account of his office, will be punished by imprisonment for up to two years and a fine of up to two million lire.

If the offence is due to negligence, imprisonment for up to six months or a fine of up to 600 000 lire are applicable.

231. (Official delegates of the administrator.) The provisions of articles 228, 229 and 230 will also apply to persons who act as official delegates of the administrator during the management of the bankruptcy.

232. (Applications for the admission of fictitious debts or misappropriations without collusion with the bankrupt.) A person who, in circumstances other than collusion with the bankrupt, presents a fraudulent application to admit a fictitious debt in the bankruptcy, even through a third party, will be punished by imprisonment for from one to five years and by a fine of from 100 000 lire to one million lire.

If the application is withdrawn before verification of the state of liabilities, the penalty is reduced by a half.

Imprisonment for from one to five years will apply to any person who:

(1) after the declaration of bankruptcy, in circumstances other than collusion with bankrupt, or of aiding and abetting, takes, misappropriates, purchases knowingly, or, either in the case of private or public declarations, conceals goods of the bankrupt;
(2) with full knowledge of the financial distress of the bankrupt, misappropriates or purchases knowingly goods or assets of the bankrupt, or acquires

them at a price markedly less than the current value, if the bankruptcy takes place thereafter.

In the cases provided under paragraphs 1 and 2, the penalty is increased if the party taking the goods or assets is engaged in commercial activity.

233. (Trafficking in votes.) A person who, being a creditor of the bankrupt, agrees terms in his own favour with the bankrupt or with others acting in the interests of the bankrupt, in exchange for giving his vote in the creditors' settlement or in the deliberations of the committee of creditors, will be punished by imprisonment for from six months to three years and by a fine of not less than 200 000 lire.

The moneys and the goods received will be confiscated. The same penalty applies to the bankrupt and to a person who makes such arrangements with a creditor in the interests of the bankrupt.

234. (Unlawful practice of a commercial activity.) A person who undertakes a commercial activity while disqualified from such activity by criminal conviction will be punished by imprisonment for up to two years and by a fine of no less than 200 000 lire.

235. (Failure to transmit the list of bills under protest.) A person acting in the capacity of a public official whose responsibility it is to protest bills who, without good cause, fails to send the lists of bills under protest for non-payment to the president of the court within the prescribed period, or sends incomplete lists, will be punished by a fine of up to 500 000 lire.

The same penalty will apply to a person who, acting in the capacity of attorney for the registrar, fails to transmit the list of declarations of refusal of payment in accordance with article 13 within the prescribed period, or who sends an incomplete list.

Chapter III: Provisions applicable in the case of preventive creditors' settlement, supervised administration and compulsory administrative liquidation

236. (Preventive creditors' settlement and controlled administration.) A trader may be sentenced to imprisonment for one to five years, if, with the sole aim of securing admission to a preventive creditors' settlement or supervised administration, he attributes to himself fictitious activities, or, in order to influence the formation of a voting majority, makes a claim which is fictitious wholly or in part.

In the event of preventive creditors' settlement or supervised administration:

(1) the provisions of articles 223 and 224 will apply to the directors, general managers, auditors and liquidators;
(2) article 227 will apply to the agents of the bankrupt;
(3) the provisions of articles 228 and 229 will apply to the judicial commissioner under the preventive creditors' settlement or under the supervised administration;
(4) the provisions of articles 232 and 233 will apply to the creditors.

237. (Compulsory administrative liquidation.) In the event of compulsory administrative liquidation, the provisions of articles 228 and 229 will apply to the liquidator,

the provisions of articles 232 and 233 to creditors, and the provisions of articles 220 and 226 to the trader.

Chapter IV: Procedural provisions

238. (Criminal proceedings in respect of offences related to bankruptcy.) In respect of the offences created by articles 216, 217, 223 and 224, criminal proceedings may be commenced following the publication of the declaration of bankruptcy provided under article 17.

Criminal proceedings may be commenced still earlier in the circumstances provided under article 7 and in all other circumstances where there are serious and consistent motives and where a request for the declaration of bankruptcy has already been made or is made at the same time.

239. Repealed.

240. (Civil proceedings.) In the case of the offences provided under this section, the administrator, the receiver and the liquidator may decide to commence civil proceedings in the criminal proceedings set out in this title, even against the bankrupt.

The creditors may join in the criminal proceedings in the case of a fraudulent bankruptcy when the administrator, the receiver and the liquidator do not do so, or when they intend to bring a personal claim.

241. (Rehabilitation.) Civil rehabilitation of the bankrupt extinguishes the offence of simple bankruptcy. In the event of a conviction, rehabilitation cancels execution of the conviction and its consequences.

DECREE, 30TH JANUARY 1979
EXTRAORDINARY ADMINISTRATION

Legislative decree no. 26 of 30th January 1979. Urgent provisions for the extraordinary administration of large businesses in difficulty (Official Gazette no. 36, dated 6th February 1979), enacted, with amendments by Law no. 95 of 3rd April 1979 (Official Gazette no. 94, dated 4th April 1979).

1. (Businesses subject to extraordinary administration and applicable regulations.) Businesses referred to in article 1 paragraph 1 of Royal Decree no. 267 dated 16th March 1942 on the regulation of bankruptcy, creditors' settlements, supervised administration and compulsory administrative liquidation, are subject to the extraordinary administration procedure instead of bankruptcy, provided that they have, and have had for a period of at least one year, no less than three hundred employees, including those qualifying for government subsidy provided for in legislative decree no. 788 dated 9th November 1945, as amended, and provided that they have a total of indebtedness to credit companies, special credit institutions, and social security and welfare institutions, amounting to not less than 544.113 billion lire, and more than five times the paid up capital on the basis of the most recent approved set of accounts. This amount of indebtedness will be reviewed each year on the 30th April by means of a

decree issued by the Minister of Commerce and Industry who will apply the gross national product index published in the general reports on the economic condition of the country.

This last requirement also applies to companies which have controlled other companies for a period of at least one year by way of subsidised financing granted to those other companies.

The above provision will also apply to bankruptcy proceedings, creditors' settlements, supervised administration and compulsory administration in respect of which revocation or appeals proceedings are in progress.

When calculating the amount of the indebtedness for the purpose of the first paragraph, debts owed to publicly owned companies are taken into account if they derive from financings granted pursuant to the provision of business plans approved by CIPI (Interministerial Committee for the Coordination of Industrial Policy) under laws for the restructuring of specific sections of industry.

When the state of insolvency of a business has been judicially determined in accordance with articles 5 and 195 of the bankruptcy law on the court's own motion, or on the initiative of those persons listed in article 6 of the that law, or where there has been a default in payment of at least three months wages to employees, the Minister of Commerce and Industry together with the Treasury Minister will institute by decree proceedings for extraordinary administration.

The procedure is implemented by one or three liquidators working under the supervision of the Minister of Commerce and Industry and in accordance with the conditions laid down in articles 195 ff. and 237 of the bankruptcy law, except as otherwise provided in this decree. Revocation of the appointment of a liquidator will be implemented on the basis of the favourable opinion of CIPI. The supervisory committee must include one or two unsecured creditors (depending on whether it is composed of three or five members) with experience in the activities with which the business is concerned. For the purposes of the bankruptcy law, the decree specified in the preceding paragraph is deemed to constitute the decree ordering compulsory administrative liquidation.

2. (Powers and remuneration of commissioners.) Subject to consideration of the interests of creditors, the decree ordering the extraordinary administration procedure may provide that the business continues trading under the supervision of the judicial commission for a period of time with the approval of CIPI, which may be extended no more than twice for up to two years. Subject to any requests which might be made by the supervisory committee and subject to the approval of the CIPI, subsequent decrees may revoke completely or in part the decree authorising the continued trading.

Where businesses connected in the manner laid down in article 3 of this decree are subject to extraordinary administration, subject to the approval of the CIPI, and in accordance with the following provisions, the Ministry of Commerce and Industry may fix a single period of time, running from the date of the last decree, for the continued trading of all of these businesses, however, the period of continued trading may amount to a total of no more than five years from the date of the first decree in respect of such businesses.

If business and management solutions are being prepared and provided these safeguard adequately the assets and employment level of the business, the period of time specified in the paragraph above may be further extended for up to a maximum of eight months for those businesses where extraordinary administration is due to end before 31st December 1984, in order to permit substantive reform of law no. 95 dated 3rd April 1979, as amended.

In order to implement the extension referred to in the paragraph above, the extraordinary administration commissioner will present a special plan for approval by the Minister of Commerce and Industry and which also requires to be approved by the CIPI. In the decree approving the plan the Minister will determine the duration of the extension of the period of time referred to in the paragraph above.

The commissioner will prepare a programme to be approved by the CIPI in advance. Implementation of the programme must be authorised by the supervising authority. Insofar as is possible and after taking into consideration the interests of the creditors, the programme will provide for a recovery plan in conformity with the principles of industrial policy, and will include specific details of which facilities should be restored to operation and which projects should be completed, as well as which facilities or units should be disposed of and details of any new participant in the business; as far as possible the integrity of the operative units must be maintained, including those which should be disposed of.

Until the programme is put into effect, administrative actions which go beyond ordinary management must be specifically authorised by CIPI or in default will be null and void. Authorisation is not necessary for the actions provided under article 35 of the bankruptcy code, provided their value does not exceed 200 million lire.

Employees, and industrial and artisan businesses with no more than one hundred employees, are given preferential treatment in the distribution of advance payments provided under paragraph 2 of article 212 of the bankruptcy law.

The remuneration of the commissioner will be settled by the supervising authority based on the level of fees received by heads of public businesses and after taking into consideration the size of the businesses being managed.

2. (part 2) (State guarantees.) The State Treasury may guarantee in whole or in part any debts incurred by businesses under extraordinary administration with credit institutions for the purpose of financing current management and facilities, and the reactivation or completion of facilities and projects, real estate and industrial equipment.

The sum total of the guarantees given in respect of guaranteed businesses pursuant to the above paragraph may not exceed 700 billion lire.

The conditions and methods of guarantees are regulated by decree of the Treasury Minister and approved by the CIPI.

Expenses arising under these guarantees are met from capital budgeted by the Treasury Minister, and classified as obligatory expenses.

3. (Subsidiary or guaranteed businesses, and businesses under one management.) From the date of publication in the Official Gazette of the decree providing for the extraordinary administration of a business as described in paragraph 1 of article 1, the following businesses will also be subject to the same procedure in accordance with this decree, even where they do not fall within the provisions of that paragraph:

(a) a company which controls, directly or indirectly, the business under extraordinary administration;
(b) companies controlled, directly or indirectly, by the business under extraordinary administration;
(c) companies which, on the basis of the composition of their respective administrative bodies, are under the same management as the business under extraordinary administration;
(d) companies which have extended credit facilities or guarantees to the business under extraordinary administration and to the businesses referred to in

(a), (b) and (c) the total amount of which exceeds one third of the aggregate value of their activities according to the most recent set of accounts.

Judicial verification of the insolvency of these businesses will be made by the court in accordance with paragraph 2 of article 1 at the instance of the commissioner or commissioners. The same administrative organs appointed in the decree referred to in paragraph 1 must be appointed for the extraordinary administration procedure to be instituted by separate decree for each company, except for the membership of the supervisory committee which may be increased even by exceeding the maximum number provided in article 198 of the bankruptcy law.

With regard to the companies referred to in paragraph 1, even where a state of insolvency has not been determined, the commissioner or commissioners responsible for the businesses under extraordinary administration may commence actions for avoidance under article 67 of the bankruptcy law, in respect of the transactions referred to in sub-paragraphs 1, 2 and 3 of the first paragraph of that article which took place up to five years before the declaration of insolvency of the company under extraordinary administration, and in respect of transactions referred to in sub-paragraph 4 of the first paragraph and in the second paragraph of the same article which took place three years before the relevant declaration of insolvency.

If the commissioner or commissioners take such action, they may request information from the National Commission for Business and the Stock Exchange (CONSOB), and from any other public office. These offices are required to furnish the necessary information within thirty days. In addition, the liquidators may request CONSOB to institute the investigations permitted by law no. 216 dated 7th June 1974 with the aim of verifying all legal transactions relating to assets belonging to businesses under extraordinary administration. Verification must be completed within 120 days of the date of the request.

The commissioner is entitled to start legal proceedings under article 2409 of the civil code against the directors and statutory auditors of the businesses referred to in sub-paragraphs (a), (b) and (c) of paragraph 1 of this article. Where the court ascertains the existence of serious irregularities under article 2409 of the civil code, the commissioner may be appointed judicial manager of the company whose managers have been party to these irregularities.

The judicial applications referred to in the preceding paragraph, and the liability proceedings which the commissioner is entitled to institute under paragraph 1 of article 206 of the bankruptcy law, must be made before the court which determined the initial state of insolvency under paragraph 2 of article 1 in accordance with the procedure provided under law no. 533 dated 11th August 1973. The judgments of the court are provisionally enforceable.

The provisions of the preceding paragraphs also apply to transactions and matters which existed prior to the entry into force of this decree.

In order to verify whether there are companies which fall within the conditions set out in paragraph 1, the Ministry of Commerce and Industry and the commissioner may request information from CONSOB and from any other public office. These are required to furnish the required information within fifteen days.

For the same purpose they may also request that the nominee companies referred to in law no. 1966 dated 23rd November 1939 provide particulars of the beneficial owners of shares registered in their names. These companies are also required to respond within fifteen days.

In the case of businesses connected in the manner set out in the first paragraph of this article, where there is a single body of management, the directors responsible will respond severally with the directors of the businesses under extraordinary administration for the losses caused to the company.

4. (Substitution of proceedings in insolvency.) Wherever, following the entry into force of this decree and after hearing the statutory representative of the business, the bankruptcy administrator and, if named, the commissioner, a company is declared insolvent under article 3, the court will declare in chambers that the company is subject to the extraordinary administration procedure. The court may make this declaration on the petition of any interested party or of its own motion.

The judgment is provisionally enforceable. The provisions of paragraphs 3, 4, 5 and 6 of article 195 of the bankruptcy law will also apply.

From the date of the order for extraordinary administration, the organs appointed in the bankruptcy procedure will cease to function. Completed legal transactions, however, remain in force.

5. (Intervention by consortia.) With the aim of acquiring business, business facilities or plants belonging to businesses under extraordinary administration in accordance with this decree, the consortia referred to in law no.787 dated 5th December 1978, may form new joint-stock companies.

The provisions of this decree do not apply from the date of constitution of the relevant consortium and for the duration of its existence to businesses for the recovery of which consortia have been authorised to be formed under law no. 787 dated 5th December, 1978, which control them in accordance with paragraph 2 of article 2 of that law. However the relevant consortium may at any time apply for a judicial declaration of insolvency of such businesses in the manner provided in this decree and for the purposes of this decree.

5. (part 2) (Tax relief on transfer.) Transfer of businesses or of going concerns belonging to businesses under extraordinary administration under this decree, including single branches of the activities of a business, are subject to a fixed stamp duty of one million lire.

6. (Rules of procedure.) The court which initially determined the insolvency of a business as provided in paragraph 2 of article 1 of this decree is competent to hear petitions against declarations of insolvency and to make the judgments provided in article 4 of this decree and will apply those provisions of the bankruptcy law which apply to businesses in extraordinary administration.

An appeal does not suspend enforcement of the judgment of the court.

A decree of the Minister of Commerce and Industry is required to redeem mortgages registered over properties of businesses under extraordinary administration sold by commissioners.

The suspension of time limits in judicial proceedings as provided in law no. 742 dated 7th October 1969, does not apply to procedures to determine the insolvency, or to those provided in article 4, or to appeals related to those procedures.

Provision will be made for termination of the extraordinary administration procedure in the circumstances provided in paragraphs 2 and 4 of article 118 of Royal Decree no. 267 dated 16th March 1942.

Termination of an administration is declared by decree of the supervising authority on petition of the liquidator or of the court's own motion. The decree is published in the Official Gazette of the Republic of Italy by the authority which issued it and is transmitted for registration at the registered office of the business in addition to any other forms of publicity set out in the order.

6. (part 2) (Methods of disposal of going concerns.) In the event of disposal of businesses, facilities or going concerns, or of real estate or chattels en bloc, sale without auction and sale by private offer are permissible, subject to the authorisation of the supervising authority and after the opinion of the supervisory committee has been heard.

In these cases, the value of the items to be disposed of will be determined by one or more experts nominated by the commissioner who will take account of the criteria for valuation appropriate for each of the items to be disposed of including profitability at the time of the estimate of the value of the item and two years later.

6. (part 3) (Applicability.) The provisions of this decree will apply until the entry into force of a new law for the reform of business regulations.

7. (Entry into force.) This decree will enter into force upon publication in the Official Gazette of the Republic of Italy, and will be presented to Parliament to be made law.

LUXEMBOURG

The basic provisions of Luxembourg's insolvency law are contained in Book III of the Commercial Code. The translation is of the law as it was on 1st January 1992. This follows, paragraph number by paragraph number and, almost, word for word, the equivalent Belgian text. As with the Belgian text, Book III is set out in four parts or titles. Part I deals with the whole of the bankruptcy laws, as described in the chapter headings. All the chapters are procedural except for chapter II (the effect of bankruptcy) and chapter VII (creditors' rights). Part II deals with bankruptcy offences, Part III with discharge, and Part IV with the suspension of payments provisions.

There are important supplementary laws, notably the law of 14th April 1886 relating to judicial schemes of arrangement; the law of 30th June 1930 regarding creditors' committees; the decree of 24th May 1935 supplementing the laws relating to suspension of payments, judicial schemes of arrangement and bankruptcy; and finally articles 38 to 46 of the law of 27th November 1984, as amended, relating to access to, and supervisory control of, the financial sector.

CHAPTER FIVE

Luxembourg Insolvency Laws

TABLE OF CONTENTS

COMMERCIAL CODE
BOOK III. BANKRUPTCY, FRAUDULENT BANKRUPTCY AND SUSPENSION OF PAYMENTS

General provisions

437. Any trader who ceases making payments and whose credit is unsound is in a state of bankruptcy.

Any person who has ceased trading may be declared bankrupt if he had ceased making payments at a time when he was still trading.

A trader may be declared bankrupt after his death if he had ceased making payments by the time of his death.

438. Bankruptcy is designated as non-fraudulent bankruptcy and will be punished by a fine if the bankrupt trader's act or omission is within one of the categories of serious misdemeanour contained in chapter I of part II.

Bankruptcy is designated as fraudulent bankruptcy and will be punished as a crime if the bankrupt trader's act or omission is within one of the categories of fraud contained in chapter II of part II.

439. Applications for suspension of payments will be presented and determined in accordance with the provisions of part IV.

PART I. BANKRUPTCY

Chapter I: Admission and declaration of bankruptcy, and cessation of payments

440. Any person who is bankrupt must make an admission at the registry of the district commercial court for the area in which he resides within three days of cessation of payments. The three day period includes the day on which he ceased making payments.

In the case of a bankrupt partnership, the admission will contain the name and address of each of the partners who is jointly liable; it will be made at the registry of the district commercial court for the area in which the principal office of the partnership is situated.

Where a limited company has been declared bankrupt, the proceedings will be brought against the directors, who, whenever so requested will appear before, and provide all required information to, the bankruptcy judge and the trustees.

441. The following documents will be attached to the admission:

(1) a balance sheet of the bankrupt's business or a memorandum explaining the reasons why this cannot be filed;
(2) the registers required to be kept by articles 8 and 9 of the Commercial Code; these registers will be closed by the clerk of the court who will make a record of the state in which he finds them.

The balance sheet will contain a list and valuation of all the real and personal property of the debtor, a list of assets and liabilities, the profit and loss account, and a schedule of expenses; the balance sheet will be certified as correct, dated and signed by the debtor.

At the foot of the bankrupt's admission and any attached documents the clerk of the court will certify the date on which they were received at the registry and, if required, provide a receipt.

Delivery to the registry of all other documents relating to the bankruptcy will be recorded in the same manner, but it will not be necessary to file any other document at the court.

442. Bankruptcy is declared by judgment of the district commercial court upon either the bankrupt's admission or on the petition of one or more creditors, or on its own motion.

By the same judgment or by a later judgment made on the report of the bankruptcy judge, the district commercial court will determine the time at which the bankrupt ceased making payments either on its own motion or on request by any interested party.

Except as provided by article 613, the time at which payments ceased to be made may not be fixed at a date which precedes the declaratory judgment of bankruptcy by more than six months.

Unless specifically determined otherwise, the cessation of payments will be presumed to have occurred with effect from the time when the judgment of bankruptcy is declared or, where the bankruptcy is declared after the death of the bankrupt, with effect from the date of death.

Without prejudice to the appeal procedure available to interested parties under article 473, no application for the date of cessation of payments to be fixed at a time other than that which would have been established by the declaration of bankruptcy or by a later judgment, will be admissible after the day appointed for the close of proceedings for the verification of claims.

443. Repealed.

Chapter II: The effect of bankruptcy

444. From the date of declaration of the judgment of bankruptcy, the bankrupt ceases at law to have control over his entire estate, including any property which becomes his during his bankruptcy.

All payments, transactions and legal documents made by the bankrupt and all payments made to the bankrupt after the judgment has been declared are void at law.

445. The following transactions are void and without legal effect in so far as they relate to the bankruptcy estate if performed by the debtor after the time fixed by the court as the time of cessation of payments or within the previous ten days.

All gratuitous transfers of personal or real property, as well as legal documents, transactions, barter agreements or contracts for valuable consideration, if the value of that which was given by the bankrupt is substantially greater than the value received by him in return.

All payments, whether in cash, by assignment, sale, set-off or otherwise for any debt whether due or not and all payments made otherwise than in cash or by bill of exchange.

All contractual or judicial mortgages, and all rights under assignments by way of security of income from real property, or security taken over the assets of the debtor for previously contracted debts.

446. All other payments made by the debtor on debts accrued due and all other transactions entered into by him for value by him after cessation of payments and before the declaration of bankruptcy may be avoided if those who received value from the debtor or who contracted with him, were aware that the debtor had ceased to pay his debts.

447. Rights validly acquired under a mortgage or charge may be registered up to the date of declaration of bankruptcy.

Nevertheless, registrations made within ten days before the cessation of payments, or after, may be declared void if registration of the mortgage or preferential right takes place more than fifteen days after its creation.

448. All transactions or payments made with intent to defraud creditors are void, irrespective of the date or when they were made.

449. Where payment under a bill of exchange has been made after the date fixed as the time of cessation of payments and before the declaration of bankruptcy, proceedings to recover the payment may only be brought against the person for whose benefit the bill was issued; in the case of a promissory note the proceedings may only be brought against the first endorser.

In each case, it is necessary to prove that the person from whom recovery is sought was aware of cessation of payments at the time of issue of the bill or note.

450. A judgment by way of declaration of bankruptcy accelerates any debts of the bankrupt which are not yet due and payable. If the bankrupt is the issuer of a promissory note, the acceptor of a bill of exchange or the drawer in the case of dishonour, the other obligors will be obliged to provide a guarantee for payment on maturity unless they prefer to pay immediately.

However debts not accrued due which do not carry interest and which are due to expire in more than one year will not be admitted as a liability without deduction of the legal interest calculated from the declaration of bankruptcy up to maturity.

If one co-obligor makes immediate payment under a promissory note or a non-interest bearing bill of exchange which has not yet accrued due, the payment will be subject to deduction of the legal interest for the period remaining until expiry.

451. Interest is suspended as regards the bankruptcy estate only, from the time of the declaration of bankruptcy, on all claims which are not secured by pledge, mortgage or other preferential right or lien.

Interest on secured claims may only be claimed on the proceeds of sale of assets which are pledged or mortgaged or charged with some other preferential right.

452. From the time of declaration of bankruptcy, actions and enforcement proceedings against the bankrupt's personal and real property may only be continued, instituted or exercised against the trustees of the bankruptcy estate.

The court may nevertheless admit the bankrupt as an intervening party.

453. A judgment by way of declaration of bankruptcy terminates execution of any arrest warrant on the bankrupt and any distraint proceedings brought by unsecured and unpreferred creditors over the bankrupt's personal and real property.

If, before this judgment, the date for the compulsory sale of any distrained real or personal property has already been fixed and officially published, the sale will take place on behalf of the bankruptcy estate.

Nevertheless, if the interests of the bankruptcy estate so require, the court may, at the request of the trustees, authorise rescheduling of the sale to another time.

454. All enforcement proceedings against personal property forming part of the bankruptcy estate to obtain payment of preferred claims are suspended until close of proceedings for the verification of claims without prejudice to any protective and legal measures available to a landlord for the repossession of rented properties.

In the latter case, suspension of enforcement procedures under the present article ceases as a matter of law in favour of the landlord.

Chapter III: Administration and liquidation of the bankruptcy estate

Section I: General provisions

455. Upon the recommendation of the High Court of Justice, sworn liquidators may be appointed by order of the State to particular areas served by the district commercial courts if the number and importance of bankruptcies renders this necessary.

456. The trustees of the bankruptcy estate will be appointed from among the sworn liquidators who are established in the district unless a different choice is required for reasons of distance, kinship, conflict of interest, or on other legitimate grounds, or for the proper administration of the bankruptcy estate.

If there are no sworn liquidators, and in such cases where, in accordance with the previous paragraph, the court believes it ought to make another choice, the trustees of the bankruptcy estate will be appointed from those having the highest reputation for intelligence and honesty as administrators.

These trustees will have the same rights and powers and will be subject to the same control and duties as if they have been appointed from amongst the sworn liquidators.

457. The number of sworn liquidators will be determined by Royal Decree on the advice of the Court of Appeal and the district commercial court according to the requirements of the service.

They are appointed by Royal Decree from two lists in duplicate put forward by these same bodies.

458. The sworn liquidators are appointed for five years and retain this function, in all cases, until their successors are sworn in. They may be reappointed.

A sworn liquidator, who is not reappointed, will nevertheless conclude all the operations entrusted to him and the liquidation of the bankruptcy estate for which he had been appointed trustee.

459. The sworn liquidators are under the supervisory control of the district commercial court. They may be removed from the office by Royal Decree.

460. Within fifteen days of their appointment, the liquidators will make oath, at an open session of the district commercial court, to properly and faithfully fulfil their duties as trustees in bankruptcy.

461. The district commercial court will determine the fees of the trustees, depending on the nature and size of the bankruptcy, and in accordance with the scales established by Royal Decree.

462. The district commercial court may, at any time, replace the bankruptcy judge for a particular bankruptcy by another of its members, and may also remove one or more of the trustees from the office, replace them or increase their number.

Any trustee who has been removed from office will first be given a hearing before the court in chambers. The decision will be announced in public.

463. The bankruptcy judge is specifically empowered to expedite and control the operations, management and liquidation of the bankruptcy estate; he will make a report in public on all disputes arising from it; he will order any urgent measures necessary for the security and preservation of the assets of the bankruptcy estate and will preside at creditors' meetings.

Orders of the bankruptcy judge are provisionally enforceable. Any appeal against these orders will be brought before the district commercial court.

464. The public prosecutor may intervene in any of the operations of the bankruptcy, inspect the books and papers of the bankrupt, assess his financial position and obtain from the trustees any information he considers useful.

465. All orders made in relation to the bankruptcy are provisionally enforceable; the normal time limit for appeals is fifteen days from notification of the order.

The following decisions may not be contested, and are not open to appeal, or to review by the Supreme Court on a question of law:

(1) Decisions relating to the appointment or replacement of the bankruptcy judge or to the appointment or dismissal of trustees;
(2) Decisions concerning applications for safe conduct permits, for provisional release from arrest, or for assistance for the bankrupt and his family;
(3) Decisions authorising the sale of personal effects or goods forming part of the bankruptcy estate, or, in accordance with article 453, paragraph 3, postponement of the sale of any distrained items;
(4) Decisions which suspend any judicial scheme of arrangement;
(5) Decisions on appeal from orders issued by the bankruptcy judge and made within his competence.

Section II: Formalities relating to the declaration of bankruptcy and initial provisions concerning the bankrupt and his property

466. In the same judgment as the declaration of bankruptcy, the district commercial court will appoint the bankruptcy judge and order the affixing of seals. The court will appoint one or more trustees, depending on the size of the bankruptcy. The court will order the bankrupt's creditors to declare their claims at the registry within a period not exceeding twenty days from the date of the judgment declaring the bankruptcy and will indicate, in accordance with article 472, the journals in which this order and the order determining the date of cessation of payments will be published.

The same order will also designate the times and dates for the close of the official record of proceedings for the verification of claims with the court and for the hearing in court of any disputes arising from the verification. These dates will be arranged so that there will be not less than five or more than twenty days between expiry of the time limit fixed for the declaration of claims and the time limit for the filing of the official record of the verification of claims, and a similar interval between then and the date fixed for the hearing of any disputes.

467. Repealed.

468. If the court considers that an inventory of the assets of the estate may be drawn up in one day, it will order the inventory to be made immediately in the presence of the bankruptcy judge or a clerk of the court delegated by him and without first affixing the seals.

469. The clerk of the district commercial court will immediately give the public prosecutor and the trustees notice of the provisions of the order for the fixing of the seals, for the committal or detention of the bankrupt, and for the appointment of the trustees.

The seals will be affixed by a clerk of the court delegated by the bankruptcy judge.

Only in cases where the debtor has either absconded or dissipated all or part of his assets, may the local court judge or a clerk of the court delegated by him order the seals to be affixed before issue of the order, either of his own motion or on the application of one or more creditors.

470. The appointed trustees will begin their duties immediately after the declaration of bankruptcy; if they have not been chosen from amongst the sworn liquidators, they will first swear before the bankruptcy judge properly and faithfully to fulfil the functions entrusted to them; they will manage the bankruptcy estate with due diligence and in good faith under the supervision of the bankruptcy judge, and they will, if necessary, order the seals to be affixed immediately.

The seals will be affixed to the shops, counters, tills, portfolios, books, documents, furniture and personal effects of the bankrupt.

In the case of a bankrupt partnership or limited partnership, the seals will be affixed in the residence of each of the jointly liable partners as well as in the principal office of the partnership.

In every case, the clerk of the court will immediately inform the president of the district commercial court and the trustee appointed over the bankruptcy estate, that the seals have been affixed by him.

471. The following items will not be sealed, or, if a seal is affixed, the items will be removed and handed over to the trustees:

(1) The bankrupt's books, once they have been closed by the clerk of the court, who will record in his report the state in which he finds them;
(2) Short-term bills or bills capable of immediate acceptance, or requiring protective measures: a schedule of these will be provided to the bankruptcy judge;
(3) Items which may perish or depreciate in the immediate future;
(4) Items used in the running of a business in the circumstances provided in article 475;
(5) Items included in the list referred to in article 476.

An inventory of the items referred to in this article will be drawn up by the trustees in the presence of the clerk of the court delegated by the bankruptcy judge, who will sign the memorandum.

472. At the instigation of the trustees and within three days of the date on which they were issued, the declaration of bankruptcy and the order which finally deter-

mined the date of cessation of payments will be posted on the noticeboard at the commercial court where they will remain for three months. Within the same three days, summaries will be published in the journals printed in the areas or towns closest to where the bankrupt has his residence or business premises and designated by the district commercial court.

Pages of the journals containing the summaries signed by the printer and attested by the mayor are proof of their publication.

473. The declaration of bankruptcy and order determining the date of cessation of payments may be contested by interested persons who were not parties to the relevant orders.

Opposition is only permissible if made by the bankrupt within eight days, and, by all other interested persons, within fifteen days, of publication of the orders in the journals mentioned in article 472 printed in the place nearest to their residence.

474. If a debtor, who has admitted his bankruptcy, has declared that his assets are more than sufficient to pay all his debts, and has requested a stay of execution, the district commercial court may, without halting the progress of bankruptcy, order an immediate appraisal of the state of his affairs by one or more experts; and if, after the result of this appraisal, the court agrees that the assets of the debtor exceed his liabilities, it will order an immediate meeting of creditors and the matter will proceed as provided in part IV.

475. In the case provided in the preceding article, and in every case where the bankrupt has requested a judicial scheme of arrangement, and if required in the interests of the creditors, the court may, following the report of the bankruptcy judge, and having heard the trustees, order that the commercial operations of the bankrupt be continued provisionally by them or by a third party under their supervision. The court may also, following the report of the bankruptcy judge and having heard the trustees, modify or revoke this order.

476. On the authorisation of the bankruptcy judge, the trustees may deliver to the bankrupt and his family, suits, clothes, linen, furniture and personal effects necessary for their personal use. The trustees will draw up a list of these items.

Furthermore, the bankrupt may obtain maintenance for himself and his family at a level determined by the court on the recommendation of the trustees and following the report of the bankruptcy judge.

477. On the authority of the bankruptcy judge, the trustees may sell immediately any items liable to perish or depreciate in the immediate future.

Before rejection of a judicial scheme of arrangement, other items may only be sold with the authority of the court; the court will determine the manner and conditions of sale following the report of the bankruptcy judge and after having duly summoned or heard the bankrupt.

478. Letters addressed to the bankrupt will be handed over to the trustees who will open them; if the bankrupt is available, he will be present when the letters are opened.

479. The trustees will pursue and recover all claims or sums due to the bankrupt and issue a receipt. The proceeds of sale and recoveries by the trustees will be deposited at the office of the public trustee within eight days of receipt after deduction of any

amounts required by the bankruptcy judge. If deposit is delayed, and without prejudice to the application of articles 459 and 462, the trustees will owe commercial interest on any amounts not deposited.

480. The sums deposited in the Public Trustee Office on account for the estate of the bankrupt may only be withdrawn with the authority of the trustees endorsed by the bankruptcy judge. The withdrawal can be made without any other formalities, for the account or to the order of the creditors in bankruptcy.

481. In the case where the court has ordered the committal or detention of the bankrupt, the bankruptcy judge may, after reviewing the state of his affairs, propose to give him bail. The court, in giving bail, may oblige the bankrupt to provide a guarantee to reappear against the payment of a sum determined by the court and, if necessary, this will be debited to the estate.

The bankrupt may request his release from the court, and the court will pronounce judgment in open court after hearing evidence from the bankruptcy judge.

482. The bankrupt may only absent himself on the authority of the bankruptcy judge. He is obliged to attend all meetings called either by the bankruptcy judge or by the trustees.

In all cases where the presence of the incarcerated or detained debtor is necessary in the bankruptcy proceedings, he will, by order of the bankruptcy judge, be removed from prison or from where he is being detained and escorted to the place where his presence is required.

483. The trustees will summon the bankrupt in order to close and draw up the books and accounts in his presence.

484. The trustees will proceed immediately to verify and correct the balance sheet. If it has not already been filed, they will draw up the balance sheet with the aid of the bankrupt's books and documents and any other information which they may obtain, and will file it at the registry of the district commercial court.

485. The bankruptcy judge is authorised to summon the bankrupt, his book-keepers and employees and any other person to be heard before him, either in relation to the verification or the drawing up of the balance sheet, or in connection with the causes or circumstances of the bankruptcy.

486. Where a trader has been declared bankrupt after his death or, where the bankrupt has died after filing an admission of bankruptcy, his widow, children or heirs may present themselves or send a representative to fulfil the role which the bankrupt would have had in the production of the balance sheet or in any other stage of the bankruptcy.

487. From the moment when the trustees assume office, they are personally liable to ensure that everything necessary is done to preserve the rights of the bankrupt as against his debtors.

They are also obliged to require registration of any mortgages over the properties of the bankrupt's debtors if the bankrupt has not himself required this to be done; registration by the trustees will be in the name of the bankruptcy estate, the trustees will attach to their memorandum a certificate of the clerk of the court in support of their appointment.

Further, they are obliged to ensure that any real property of the bankrupt of which they are aware is registered in the name of the creditors as a group. Registration is made on a short memorandum recording that a bankruptcy has occurred and showing the date of the order appointing the trustees.

488. Within three days of assuming office, the trustees will if necessary demand removal of the seals and proceed to draw-up an inventory of the bankrupt's assets in the bankrupt's presence or after he has been duly summoned.

On the authority of the bankruptcy judge, the trustees may request the assistance of any person they think suitable to draw up the inventory and value the relevant items.

489. Whenever seals are removed from an item, it will be included in the inventory drawn up by the trustees; the clerk of the court delegated by the bankruptcy judge will attend and attest each removal; a record will be deposited at the registry within twenty four hours of final completion of the inventory. The trustees may take copies free of charge and against reimbursement of their travelling expenses.

In accordance with article 471, items which have not been placed under seal or from which the seal has been removed and which have been entered in the inventory will be placed in the custody of the trustees.

490. Where bankruptcy is declared after death, and where an inventory has not been drawn up before this declaration or where the bankrupt dies before an inventory has been commenced, an inventory will be drawn up immediately in the manner prescribed in the preceding article, in the presence of the heirs or after they have been duly summoned.

491. Once the inventory has been completed, the goods, money, current title deeds and bills of exchange, assets, furniture and personal effects of the debtor will be returned to the trustees who will make a note to that effect at the foot of the inventory.

492. On the authority of the bankruptcy judge, and after the bankrupt has been duly summoned, the trustees may settle all disputes relating to the estate, including disputes concerning shares and real property rights.

If the settlement relates to real property rights or if the subject matter of the settlement is of undetermined value or exceeds 300 Francs, it will only be enforceable after its approval has been confirmed in the report of the bankruptcy judge. If the settled dispute was within the competence of court of first instance, the settlement must be ratified by that court.

The bankrupt will be summoned to attend the approval of any such settlement; in every case he will have the opportunity to dispute the settlement. If the object of the settlement is real property, opposition by the bankrupt will suffice to block the settlement.

On the authority of the district commercial court and after the bankrupt has been duly summoned, the trustees may also give their sworn support to the opposing parties in the determination of any disputes arising from the bankruptcy.

493. The trustees may employ the bankrupt to facilitate and clarify any matter arising from their administration. The bankruptcy judge will decide the conditions of his employment.

494. In every bankruptcy, and within fifteen days of assuming office, the trustees must provide the bankruptcy judge with a memorandum or summary of the apparent state of the bankruptcy, giving its main causes, apparent features and circumstances.

The bankruptcy judge will immediately send the memorandum with his observations to the public prosecutor. If it has not been sent within the prescribed time limit, he will inform the public prosecutor and provide reasons for the delay.

495. If proceedings against the bankrupt are brought for simple or fraudulent bankruptcy and if an order to appear or warrant for arrest has been issued against him, the public prosecutor will notify the bankruptcy judge without delay, and in that event the bankruptcy judge may not recommend, and the court may not grant, either the release of the bankrupt or his safe-conduct.

Chapter IV: Declaration and verification of claims

496. The bankrupt's creditors are required to file a declaration of claims at the registry of the district commercial court together with proof of title within the time limit fixed in the declaration of bankruptcy. The clerk will retain the declaration of claims and issue a receipt.

The creditors will receive notice to this effect in the publications prescribed in article 472. They will also be advised by a circular letter which the trustees will send to them by registered post as and when their existence becomes known to the trustees. This circular will set out the time and dates fixed for the close of proceedings for the verification of claims and for hearing any disputes arising from the verification.

Certificates of posting will be annexed to, and will remain annexed to, a memorandum of the circular which will be endorsed by the bankruptcy judge.

497. If there are any creditors residing or domiciled outside the Grand Duchy for whom the time limit fixed by the declaration of bankruptcy is too short, the bankruptcy judge may extend it for their benefit according to the circumstances; any such extension will be referred to in the circulars addressed to the creditors in accordance with article 496.

498. The declaration of claims of each creditor will contain his surname, first names, occupation and address, the amount and grounds for his claim, any preferential rights, mortgages or pledges relevant to it and the documents evidencing the claim.

The declaration will end with an affirmation in the following terms:

'I swear that this my claim is sincere and true.'

The declaration will be signed by the creditor or by his attorney in his name; in that event, the power of attorney will be annexed to the declaration, and will state the amount of the claim and contain the affirmation prescribed by this article.

499. The declaration of claims of any creditor not domiciled in the district where the commercial court is situated will contain an election of domicile in that district.

In the absence of an election of domicile, all notices and information may be left at the court registry.

500. The trustees will verify the claims as and when the declarations of claim are filed at the registry; verification will take place in the presence of the bankruptcy

judge and also the bankrupt who is entitled to intervene, or after the bankrupt has been duly summoned. The documents evidencing the claim will be checked against the accounts and records of the bankrupt.

The trustees' claims will be verified by the bankruptcy judge.

A report on the progress of the bankruptcy will be drawn up by the trustees and signed at each meeting by them and the bankruptcy judge. It will contain the addresses of the creditors and their attorneys. It will contain a summary description of the documents provided, refer to any additions, deletions and omissions, and state whether the claim is admitted or denied.

If the claim is denied or if it does not appear fully justified, the trustees will adjourn their decision until the close of proceedings for the verification of claims and if the creditor is not present in person or represented by his attorney at the time of this adjournment, they will notify him immediately by registered letter.

501. On his own motion or otherwise, after each claim has been declared and up until the date fixed for the hearing of any disputes which may have arisen regarding it, the bankruptcy judge may order the creditor or his attorney or any person who could provide information to appear in person. He will draw up a report of their statements. He may also order production of the creditor's books or demand by order for discovery that a transcript be made of them by the local judge.

502. At the meeting fixed in order to close the proceedings for the verification of claims, submissions from both sides will be heard in respect of all declared claims which are disputed or which have not yet been admitted. The trustees will endorse the document evidencing each of the admitted and uncontested claims with a declaration in the following terms:

> 'Admitted as a liability in the bankruptcy of .... in the amount of .... dated ....'

The bankruptcy judge will sign the declaration; he will refer all disputes relating to disputed claims to the court. If there are any matters in dispute which are not within the jurisdiction of the commercial court, they will be referred to the competent judge for decision upon the merits, and to the court for judgment, in accordance with article 504, on their value. This will determine the extent to which a disputing creditor may participate in any meetings relating to a scheme of arrangement.

503. The bankrupt and any creditors whose claims have been verified or entered on the balance sheet may attend the verification of claims meeting and object to any verifications which have been made or remain outstanding. After close of the proceedings for the verification of claims, any objections to verifications made and contained in the official record must, at the risk of being declared void, be formally served in writing on the creditors who have declared their claims and must be filed at the registry together with the relevant evidence of title two days before the date fixed for the hearing of the disputed claims.

Objections to verifications made after close of the proceedings for the verification of claims will, also at the risk of being declared void, be served within ten days after admission of the disputed claim. However, as regards creditors admitted after this period, the time limit will only run from the date of verification of their claims.

504. The bankruptcy judge will submit his report on the day fixed for the hearing of disputed claims in the declaration of bankruptcy. Once the court has received the re-

port, it will, as a matter of urgency, suspend all other business, and, if possible in a single judgment, proceed to settle all the disputes relating to the verification of claims without prior summons and without awaiting expiry of any time limits which have been extended under article 497. This judgment will be made after having heard all the submissions of the trustees, the bankrupt and any admitted or objecting creditors who have attended the hearing.

The hearing of any disputes which cannot be settled immediately will be adjourned. The court may however in either case make an interim order that the disputed creditors will be admitted up to a sum specified in the same order for the purpose of participating in the discussions on the preparation of any judicial scheme of arrangement. If the court does not make a decision to this effect, the disputing creditors may not take any part in the administration of the bankruptcy until the dispute has been decided.

No appeal or application to set aside lies against the order made under this article, or against any judgment at a later stage on any disputes which have been postponed. Furthermore, no appeal or appeal on a point of law lies against an interim order provisionally admitting disputed creditors.

505. All disputes concerning the liquidation of bankruptcy estates which are within the jurisdiction of the civil courts will be brought before them as quickly as possible and heard as a matter of urgency. The same applies to all disputes of this nature which are brought before the High Court of Justice.

506. Until judgment is pronounced on the disputes, all declarations of claims, documents produced in support and all deeds, reports, objections and applications relating to them will remain on file at the registry and will be made available to interested parties on request.

507. For every bankruptcy, the clerk of the court will keep a schedule divided into columns and containing the following information for each declared claim:

(1) The reference number;
(2) The surname, first names, occupation and address of the creditor filing his declaration of claim, together with evidence of his title to the claim;
(3) The date of filing;
(4) The amount of the declared claim;
(5) A summary of the assets or items over which a mortgage or other preferential charge is claimed;
(6) Whether the claim is included in the liabilities of the bankruptcy or if it has been rejected by the trustees;
(7) The date of the admission or rejection;
(8) The objections to the claim;
(9) The names of those objecting;
(10) The dates of the objections;
(11) The date of close of proceedings for the verification of claims;
(12) The date of commencement of the hearing of submissions on disputed claims;
(13) A summary of the final decision;
(14) The date of this decision;
(15) Other information which could be useful to interested parties.

This schedule will be drawn up by the clerk of the court; the prescribed information will be entered on a day-to-day basis as and when the facts and circumstances to which the information relates come to light; it will be made available to any interested party on request.

508. Any person, known or unknown, who fails to declare or affirm his claim within the time limit fixed by the declaration of bankruptcy as extended under article 497, will not be included in the distributions. However, such persons may declare and affirm their claims up to and including the last distribution of proceeds. Their declarations will not suspend distributions which have already been ordered; however, if new distributions are ordered after such declarations, they shall be included up to an amount which will be fixed provisionally by the bankruptcy judge and will be held in reserve until their claims have been admitted. In each case, any expenses incurred in the verification and admission of such claims will the creditor's responsibility and may not be reclaimed from the distributions ordered before their declarations; if they can prove that it was impossible for them to make their declaration and affirmation within the prescribed time limit, they will have the right to draw on any undistributed assets for the dividends attributable to their claims in the first distributions.

Chapter V: Judicial scheme of arrangement

Section I: Creditors' meeting

509. The parties will proceed with the formation of the scheme of arrangement immediately after issue of the judgment in accordance with article 504 and without waiting for expiry of the time limits allowed under article 497.

To this end, the bankruptcy judge will summon a meeting of creditors and fix the place, date and time of the meeting.

The date of the meeting will be arranged so that it takes place within fifteen days of the judgment issued under article 504 and so that, between receiving notice of the meeting and the date of the meeting, a period of two days increased by one day for each five myriameters between his actual residence and the place of meeting is allowed for each creditor.

510. Notice of the meeting will be given to creditors within five days of the summons of the bankruptcy judge; it will be given under the direction of the trustees by notices, by publication and by circular letter individually addressed to the creditors whose claims have been definitively or provisionally admitted, all in accordance with the manner and form prescribed by articles 472 and 496.

511. The meeting will take place under the chairmanship of the bankruptcy judge at the place, date and time fixed by him. Only creditors admitted definitively or provisionally or their attorneys will be permitted to attend.

The bankrupt will be summoned to the meeting; he may send a representative only if he has valid reasons which have been approved by the bankruptcy judge.

The bankruptcy judge will verify the powers of those attending the meeting under power of attorney. The trustees will report on the progress of the bankruptcy, on the formalities carried out and any steps already taken, and on the probable outcome of the liquidation. The bankrupt will be accorded a hearing. The trustee's report will be signed and given to the bankruptcy judge who will draw up a report on what has been discussed and decided at the meeting.

Section II: Formation of the scheme of arrangement

512. Except as provided under article 520, no agreement may be made between the creditors determining the matter and the bankrupt debtor until the formalities prescribed above have been fulfilled.

An agreement by way of scheme of arrangement may only be made by a majority in number of those creditors who represent three quarters of the total claims which have been definitively or provisionally admitted in accordance with chapter IV: if these conditions are not fulfilled the agreement is void.

513. Creditors with registered mortgages or mortgages not requiring registration or other preferential rights or who are secured under pledges may not vote in respect of these secured claims on any business relating to a scheme of arrangement, and their votes will not be counted unless they surrender their mortgages, preferential rights or pledges.

This surrender will arise by operation of law if a secured creditor votes on the scheme of arrangement; if the scheme of arrangement is not accepted the surrender will be of no effect.

A secured creditor may only vote on the scheme of arrangement by surrendering his preferential right, mortgage or pledge to the extent of the equivalent of at least half of the amount of his claim. In this event, the claim will only be counted to that extent in any matters relating to the scheme of arrangement.

514. There will be no scheme of arrangement if the bankrupt is within article 495 or if he has been convicted of fraudulent bankruptcy.

When article 495 applies, creditors called to the meeting to discuss the scheme of arrangement may vote in the same majorities prescribed by article 512 to postpone their decision until after proceedings have been issued. Rejection of any motion to postpone will result in rejection of the scheme of arrangement.

515. The scheme of arrangement will be signed while the meeting is in session or may otherwise be declared void. The meeting will be postponed for eight days if only a majority in number or a majority of three-quarters of the total claims agree the scheme of arrangement. In this instance, any resolutions made or agreement concluded at the time of the first meeting will be of no effect.

516. Any creditor entitled to take part in agreeing the scheme of arrangement, or who would have been so entitled after it has been agreed, may object to it.

Reasons for the objection will be given and should be notified to the trustees and the bankrupt within five days following the scheme of arrangement, failing which the objection may be declared void. Within five days of this notification, the trustees and the bankrupt may give notice of their application in reply to the objection and file it at the registry together with any documents on which they rely.

Immediately after this period of time and without any other formalities or proceedings, the bankruptcy judge will report on the bankruptcy, and on the acceptability of the scheme of arrangement, and the court will issue in a single judgment a decision ratifying the scheme of arrangement and any objections to it. Nevertheless, the parties may appear or be represented at the meeting to present a summary of any evidence in support of their submissions.

If only one trustee has been appointed and he opposes the scheme of arrangement, he must arrange for another trustee to be appointed in order to fulfil the requirements of this article.

If the judgment on the objections involves decisions on issues outside the competence of the district commercial court because of the subject matter concerned, the court will defer judgment until after these issues have been resolved.

517. If the above provisions are not observed, or if the scheme of arrangement is not in the public interest or in the interests of the creditors, the court will refuse to ratify it. In such cases the scheme of arrangement is deemed to be set aside as regards all interested parties.

518. Ratification of the scheme of arrangement renders it binding on all creditors, proven or unproven, whether or not they are listed on the balance sheet, including those creditors referred to in article 497, together with all those who would have been admitted to the discussions by virtue of article 504 whatever amount is ultimately awarded to them in the final judgment.

It will preserve for the benefit of each of the creditors the mortgage registered in accordance with the last paragraph of article 487 over the bankrupt's real property. To this end, and unless the scheme of arrangement provides otherwise, the trustees will register the ratifying judgment on the mortgages.

519. The trustees' duties terminate as soon as the judgment ratifying the scheme of arrangement has become final.

The trustees will present their final account to the bankrupt in the presence of the bankruptcy judge; the account will be completed following discussion. The trustees will return the whole of his assets to the bankrupt, including books, documents and personal effects; the bankrupt will provide a receipt for these items, and the bankruptcy judge will draw up a comprehensive report.

Any objection will be settled by the district commercial court following the report of the bankruptcy judge.

520. Repealed.

Section III: Cancellation and dissolution of the scheme of arrangement

521. The scheme of arrangement will be void at law if the bankrupt is convicted of fraudulent bankruptcy after ratification of the scheme.

If, after ratification of the scheme of arrangement, proceedings for fraudulent bankruptcy are brought against the bankrupt, or a warrant of committal or arrest, or an order to prevent him absconding, is issued against him, the district commercial court may make any appropriate protective orders following the report of the bankruptcy judge. These orders will cease to take effect at law from the date of a declaration that there are no grounds to proceed or when the case is dismissed or the bankrupt is acquitted.

522. After the scheme has been ratified, no action may be brought to have it declared void except for reasons of fraud discovered after the ratification and taking the form of either concealment of assets or the exaggeration of liabilities.

The setting aside of the scheme of arrangement either for fraud or following conviction for fraudulent bankruptcy operates at law as of right even as regards the guarantors.

523. If the conditions of the scheme of arrangement are not fulfilled by the bankrupt, an action to rescind the scheme may be brought against him before the district commercial court in the presence of the guarantors, if any, or after the guarantors have been duly summoned.

Rescission of the scheme of arrangement does not release any guarantors who intervened to guarantee its total or partial implementation.

524. In the judgment ordering either the setting aside or rescission of the scheme of arrangement, or in the cases provided under article 521, the district commercial court may, by a judgment made on the application of one or more creditors, or even of its own motion following the report of the bankruptcy judge, instruct the previously nominated trustees to take up their duties or instruct new trustees and order the persons who have becomes creditors of the bankrupt since notification of the scheme of arrangement to declare their claims within the time limit fixed under article 466.

The provisions of articles 469 and 472 will be followed with respect to this judgment.

The trustees may have seals affixed. Without delay and with the help of the magistrate or the bankruptcy judge, if responsible for the affixing of seals, the trustees will proceed on the basis of the original inventory, taking any securities, shares and bills into safe custody and if necessary drawing up a supplementary inventory. They will prepare a supplementary balance sheet and send the circular letter referred to in article 496 to the new creditors.

525. Any new claims must be declared, affirmed and proved in accordance with the provisions of chapter IV.

No new proof of the claims already admitted as liabilities is necessary, but this will nevertheless not affect the rejection or reduction of those which have since been extinguished in whole or part.

526. Those transactions referred to in article 445 and made by the bankrupt after the judgment ratifying the scheme of arrangement and before it has been set aside or rescinded are void and of no effect. Other transactions of the bankrupt during this period will only be set aside if they were made with the intention of prejudicing performance of the scheme of arrangement or of defrauding the creditors.

527. Those who were already creditors before the scheme of arrangement will retain all their rights as against the bankrupt himself; but their participation rights in the bankruptcy estate are only as follows:

If they have not received any dividend, the whole of their claim; if they have received part of their dividend, that part of their initial claim which corresponds to the proportion of the promised dividend which has not been received.

The provisions of this article apply in cases where a second bankruptcy has begun without prior setting aside or rescission of the scheme of arrangement.

Chapter VI: Liquidation of the bankruptcy estate

528. If no scheme of arrangement is agreed, the trustees will continue to represent the creditors as a whole and will proceed with the liquidation of the bankruptcy estate: they will arrange for the sale of any real property, goods and personal effects and the payment of debts owed to and by the bankrupt; the whole procedure will be

under the supervision of the bankruptcy judge in accordance with the provisions of articles 479 and 480 and without any need for the bankrupt to appear in person before the court.

They may compromise any of the rights of the bankrupt in the manner prescribed by article 492 notwithstanding any objections by him.

529. Nevertheless, the creditors may authorise either the trustees or a third party under the trustees' supervision to continue using the available assets for the benefit of the estate.

The decision conferring this authority will also determine its scope and duration and fix the amount which the trustees may retain to cover their costs and expenses; the decision must be taken in the presence of the bankruptcy judge immediately after rejection of the scheme of arrangement and by the majority in number and amount provided under article 512.

The bankrupt and any objecting creditors may challenge this decision, but this will not suspend execution.

If the transactions of the trustees, or of those duly authorised, result in liabilities which exceed the available assets, only those creditors who authorised these liabilities will be personally liable over and above their share in the assets, but only up to the limits of the authority granted by them. Their contributions will be pro rata to their proven claims.

530. Where a partnership is in bankruptcy, the creditors may only enter into a scheme of arrangement with one or more of the partners; in such cases the whole of the partnership's assets remain subject to the bankruptcy; the personal assets of those with whom the scheme of arrangement has been agreed will be excluded, and the particular agreement concluded with them may only include an obligation to make a payment relating to those assets which are outside the partnership assets.

A partner who has agreed a special scheme of arrangement will be discharged from joint liability.

531. Immediately following the rejection of a scheme of arrangement, the creditors will be consulted in meeting as regards the continuation of maintenance provided in accordance with article 476 or of whatever maintenance may ultimately be available to the bankrupt and his family from the assets of the bankruptcy. With the agreement of the majority of creditors present, maintenance will be granted or allowed to continue. The trustees will propose an amount which will be agreed by the bankruptcy judge and may only be appealed by the trustees to the district commercial court.

532. After the scheme of arrangement has been set aside or rejected, the bankruptcy judge may summon the creditors if he considers this is necessary.

By simple majority vote and with the authorisation of the court after the bankrupt has been duly summoned, the creditors in meeting may instruct the trustees to forfeit and dispose of all or part of any unrealised rights or causes of action.

533. When the liquidation has been completed the creditors will be summoned by the bankruptcy judge. He may order the trustees' report of the liquidation to be annexed to the summons.

The report will be discussed at this meeting, with the bankrupt in attendance or after he has been duly summoned. The final distribution will be made from the balance shown in the report.

If any objection is made, the procedure set out in article 519 paragraph 3 will be followed.

At the same meeting, the creditors will give their opinion on whether the bankrupt should be released from further liability. A minute of the meeting will be drawn up in which each creditor may record his statements and observations.

534. The bankruptcy judge will present the court in chambers with the decision of the creditors as regards the release of the bankrupt and will report to the court in chambers on the characteristics and circumstances of the bankruptcy. The court will decide whether or not the bankrupt should be released.

No release will be granted to the following persons:

Fraudulent bankrupts of whatever kind; persons convicted for theft, forgery, extortion, deceit or breach of trust; and bailees; guardians; administrators or other persons liable to account who have not submitted and balanced their accounts.

535. No trader who is a debtor will be allowed to petition for his release on the grounds of assignment of his assets.

If the bankrupt is declared released, he will also be released from the warrant of arrest as regards the creditors of his bankruptcy, and except as provided in particular statutes, proceedings may be brought by them only against his assets.

If he is not declared released, the creditors retain the right to take individual action either against the bankrupt personally or against his assets.

536. If at any time before the creditors are summoned to discuss the scheme of arrangement, it becomes clear that there will be insufficient assets to pay for the estimated administration and liquidation costs, the district commercial court may, even of its own motion, and following the report of the bankruptcy judge pronounce termination of the bankruptcy proceedings. In such cases the creditors retain the right to take individual action against the bankrupt personally and against his assets.

In the same judgment the court may issue its decision on the release of the bankrupt.

Implementation of a judgment pronouncing termination of the bankruptcy proceedings is suspended for one month.

At any time the bankrupt or any other interested person may restore the proceedings before the district commercial court by proving that sufficient funds exist to cover the bankruptcy proceedings or by depositing a sufficient sum with the Public Trustee. The costs of proceedings brought under this article must in any event be paid in advance.

536-1. If the liquidation is closed due to lack of assets, the costs incurred by the trustees will be taxed by the commercial court. The court will also approve fees after taking into account the nature and importance of the trustees' services, although the fees must be within limits laid down by regulation of the Grand Duchy.

Fees and expenses are paid by the administrative registry in accordance with the conditions established by the law of 29th March 1893 concerning legal aid and the procedure for settling debts.

Chapter VII: Different categories of creditors and their rights

Section I: Co-obligors and guarantors

537. A creditor entitled to performance of any obligation underwritten, endorsed or guaranteed jointly by the bankrupt and other bankrupt co-obligors, will participate in

distributions from each bankruptcy estate and will participate for the full nominal value of his claim until full and final payment.

538. Recourse by one co-obligor against another for dividends which have been paid is only available where the total dividends from these bankruptcies exceed the amount of the principal claim plus interest in which case the excess will be distributed to those obligors who are guaranteed by the other obligors according to the priority of their obligations.

539. If a creditor entitled to performance of obligations owed jointly by the bankrupt and other co-obligors or obligations secured by guarantee, has received a partial payment for his debt before the bankruptcy, he will only be included in the estate after deduction of this payment and only retain his rights against the co-obligors or the guarantor for what remains due to him.

540. Any amount which a co-obligor or guarantor making a part payment has paid to discharge the bankrupt will be taken into account.

541. Notwithstanding any scheme of arrangement, creditors will retain their rights to the whole of their claim against the co-obligors of the bankrupt.

Section II: Creditors secured by pledges, and creditors secured by charges or other preferential rights and charges over personal property

542. Account of the bankrupt's creditors who are validly secured by pledges will only be taken for the record.

543. At any time, and on the authority of the bankruptcy judge, the trustees may release pledges in favour of the bankruptcy estate by repaying the debt owed by it.

544. If a pledge is not released by the trustees and if the pledged item is sold by the creditor for a price which exceeds the claim, any surplus will be recovered by the trustees. If the price is less than the claim, the secured creditor will be entitled to claim for the shortfall against the estate as an ordinary creditor.

545. Employees' claims for remuneration and benefits arising from the last six months of a contract of employment, together with indemnity claims for breach of contract of employment, will be admitted as preferred claims with the same priority and conditions as the prior right created under paragraphs (1) and (2) of article 2101 of the Civil Code.

546. The preferential right and right of claim established by article 2102, paragraph 4, of the Civil Code in favour of a vendor of chattels and also the right of rescission, are not available in cases of bankruptcy.

This preferential right will nevertheless continue to exist for two years from delivery in favour of suppliers of machines and equipment used in industrial businesses.

It will only be effective if, within fifteen days of delivery, the document evidencing the sale is transcribed into a special register kept for this purpose at the registry of the commercial court for the district in which the debtor is domiciled or, failing which, is resident.

The clerk of the court is bound to inform anyone who asks that this transcription has been effected.

The preferential right is available even where the machines and equipment have become real property by virtue of their intended use or by incorporation.

Subject to proof to the contrary, delivery is evidenced by the vendors' accounts.

Where the bankruptcy of a debtor is declared before expiry of the two years preference period, the preferential right will continue to exist until after liquidation of the bankruptcy estate.

547. The trustees will present the bankruptcy judge with a list of those creditors claiming preferential rights or other charges over the personal property within the bankruptcy estate and the bankruptcy judge will, if necessary, authorise payment of such creditors from the first proceeds recovered.

If a preferential right is disputed, the court will settle the dispute.

Section III: The rights of creditors with mortgages or preferential rights or other charges over real property

548. Where the proceeds of sale of real property are distributed before the proceeds of sale of personal property, or at the same time, creditors with charges or mortgages which have not been satisfied by the proceeds of sale of real property will compete with the unsecured creditors for the amount which remains due to them, and will be paid from the proceeds allocated to the unsecured creditors, provided however that their claims have been affirmed and approved according to the procedure described above.

549. If other distributions are made before the proceeds of sale of real property are distributed, the creditors with charges or mortgages over real property will compete in these distributions in proportion to their total claims and without, in that event, allowing for deductions calculated in accordance with the following provisions.

550. After sale of the real property and final arrangement of the order of priority between creditors with mortgages and other preferential rights and charges, those who have priority in the proceeds of sale of real property up to the total amount of their claim, will not receive the amount to which they are entitled under their mortgage ranking until after deduction of any amounts received by them from the unsecured estate.

Such deducted amounts do not continue to form part of the mortgaged estate, but go to the unsecured estate for the benefit of which the deduction was effected.

551. As regards those mortgaged creditors who rank only partially in the distribution of the proceeds from real property, the procedure will be as follows: Their rights over the unsecured estate will be finally determined according to the sums for which they remain creditors after the prior ranking secured creditors have been satisfied, and the proceeds of sale received by them from the preceding distribution in excess of the amount of their unsecured claim will be retained from the amount received by them as secured creditors and held for the creditors.

552. Mortgage creditors without effective priority will be considered as unsecured creditors and subject as such to the terms of the scheme of arrangement and to all dealings in the unsecured estate.

Section IV: The effects of bankruptcy of a married person with regard to his or her spouse

553. The spouse of the bankrupt is entitled to retake possession of his or her own property and any which forms part of their joint estate.

554. Repealed.

555. Whatever matrimonial regime applies, the legal presumption is that all moveable or real property belongs to the bankrupt and has been paid for out of his or her money, and must be included in the total of his or her assets, save where the spouse can provide evidence to the contrary in accordance with the rules provided under article 1402 of the Civil Code.

556. A solvent spouse's action for repossession will only be brought for debts and mortgages secured on property which is legally encumbered, whether voluntarily or compulsorily.

557. If the bankrupt was a trader at the time of the marriage or became a trader within two years of his marriage, his spouse may bring no action in the bankruptcy by reason of benefits conferred under the marriage contract; and, in this case, the creditors may not avail themselves of the benefits given by the spouse to the bankrupt in the same contract.

558. If the spouse has discharged any debts on account of the bankrupt, the legal presumption is that he or she has done so out of the bankrupt's own funds and the spouse may not, therefore, bring any action in the bankruptcy, except on the production of evidence to the contrary, as provided under article 555.

559. Repealed.

560. Repealed.

Chapter VIII: Distribution among creditors

561. After the costs and expenses of the administration of the bankruptcy, the maintenance granted to the bankrupt or his family and the sums paid to preferred creditors have been set aside, the amount of the bankrupt's liquid assets will be distributed among all the creditors in proportion to their declared and verified claims.

To this end, the trustees will provide the bankruptcy judge every month with a report on the position of the bankruptcy and a statement of the proceeds deposited with the Public Trustee; the bankruptcy judge will, if necessary, order a distribution to be made to the creditors in an amount determined by him.

The creditors will be advised of the decisions of the bankruptcy judge and of the commencement of the distribution by circular letter sent by post in the manner provided in article 496.

562. If there are any creditors with claims not admitted to proof and for whom the time limit as extended under article 497 has not yet expired, or creditors whose claims, which were declared and affirmed within the prescribed time limit, have given rise to objections which have not yet been determined, no distribution will be made until

after an amount equal to the dividend to which they would be entitled has been put in reserve. In the former case the amount will be the amount entered on the balance sheet; in the latter case the amount will be the amount declared and affirmed.

Where claims of creditors domiciled or resident outside the Grand Duchy, for which the time limit has been extended in accordance with article 498, have not been entered on the balance sheet in an exact manner, the bankruptcy judge may decide that the reserve be increased. The trustees may dispute this decision before the district commercial court.

563. No payment may be made by the trustees without production of the document evidencing the claim.

The trustees will enter on the document the sum paid or authorised in accordance with article 480. Where it is not possible to produce the document, the bankruptcy judge may authorise payment after having regard to the official record of the verification of claims. In every case, the creditor must acknowledge receipt in the margin of the distribution statement.

Chapter IX: The sale of real property belonging to the bankrupt

564. If proceedings for the compulsory purchase of real property have not been commenced before the rejection or setting aside of a scheme of arrangement, the trustees alone may proceed with a sale of real property. They must do so within eight days, on the authority of the bankruptcy judge and in accordance with the particular applicable laws.

On the authority of the district commercial court, and after summoning the bankrupt, the trustees may stay any proceedings which have been commenced at any time, by proceeding in accordance with the same method with the sale of any real property which has been attached.

In this case the trustees must notify the creditor who has brought proceedings and the debtor at least eight days prior to the sale, of the place, date and time at which the sale will take place.

A similar notification will be made within the same period of time to all creditors who are registered at their chosen place of domicile in the document registering their debt.

565. During the fifteen days following the sale by auction, all persons are entitled to make an overbid. The overbid must exceed by one tenth the principal sum reached in the auction. It will be made by writ of summons, served by a court process server, and notified to the notary public who instituted the auction, to the trustees and to the successful bidder. Award to the successful bidder following the overbid will be made on the petition of the trustees without further authorisation, by the same public official and in the same manner as the first award.

All persons are entitled to compete in this auction, which constitutes the definitive sale, and will not be followed by any subsequent overbid.

Chapter X: Action for repossession

566. An action for repossession in the event of bankruptcy may be brought with respect to negotiable instruments and other unpaid instruments of title which were

still in that form in the bankrupt's possession at the date of the judgment declaring the debtor's bankruptcy. Such an action may be brought where delivery of the instrument has been made by an owner duly authorised to recover sums due under the instrument and to retain the amount at the disposal of the creditor, or where the instrument has been specially appropriated to particular payments.

567. An action for repossession may also be brought in respect of any goods consigned to the debtor by way of bailment or for him to sell on behalf of the shipper so long as they remain in their original state, either as a whole or in part.

An action may also be brought for the price or for any part of the price of these goods which has not been paid or settled in some other way, or for which monies have been paid into a current account between the bankrupt and the purchaser.

568. An action for repossession may also be brought in respect of goods sent to the bankrupt, so long as passing of property in the goods did not occur in the bankrupt's shops or to those of an agent responsible for selling the goods on behalf of the bankrupt.

Nevertheless this action for repossession will not be allowed if, prior to their arrival, the goods have been lawfully sold against invoices with bills of lading or waybills signed by the shipper of the goods.

569. A person bringing an action for repossession is obliged to reimburse the creditors with any amount which he has received, together with the balance of any advances of freight or consignment costs, commission, insurance or other expenses, and to pay any such sums which may be due for these items.

570. The vendor may retain any goods sold but not yet delivered to the bankrupt or which have not yet been sent, either to the bankrupt or to any third party on the account of the bankrupt.

571. In the cases referred to in articles 568 and 570, and on the authority of the bankruptcy judge, the trustees have the power to require delivery of the goods by paying to the vendor the price agreed between the vendor and the bankrupt.

572. The trustees may, with the approval of the bankruptcy judge, admit applications for repossession, and if these are disputed, the court will decide the issue on its merits on the basis of a report prepared by the bankruptcy judge.

PART II. NON-FRAUDULENT AND FRAUDULENT BANKRUPTCY

Chapter I: Non-fraudulent bankruptcy

573. A bankrupt trader will be declared a non-fraudulent bankrupt in the following cases:

(1) If his personal or household expenses are judged excessive;
(2) If he has spent large sums on gambling, or on deals of pure chance, or on fictitious trading on the stock exchange or in the commodity markets;

(3) If, with intent to delay his bankruptcy, he has bought goods with a view to resale below the market price, or if, with the same intention, he has taken out loans, endorsed negotiable instruments or used other onerous methods of procuring funds;
(4) If he fabricated fictitious expenses or losses, or if he cannot prove the existence or use of any assets appearing in his latest stock inventory or of any cash, securities, furniture and personal effects of any nature whatsoever received after the date of the latest stock inventory;
(5) If, after he ceased to make payments, he has made a payment to or has preferred any creditor to the prejudice of his general creditors.

574. A trader may be declared a non-fraudulent bankrupt in the following situations:

(1) If, without receiving value in exchange, he has undertaken on behalf of any third party, obligations which are too great considering his situation at the time he undertook these obligations;
(2) If he is declared bankrupt for a second time, without having satisfied his obligations under a previous scheme of arrangement;
(3) If, having contracted out of the statutory matrimonial regime, he has not complied with article 69;
(4) If he has not admitted his inability to make payments within the time limits prescribed by article 440; if this admission does not contain the names of all his jointly liable partners; if in making this admission he has not supplied the information and explanations required by article 441 or if such information and explanations are inaccurate;
(5) If he absconds without the authority of the bankruptcy judge or if, without a legitimate excuse, he has not attended hearings in person on the summons of the bankruptcy judge or the trustees;
(6) If he has not kept the statutory books required by article 8, if he has not drawn up the inventory prescribed by article 9, if his statutory books and inventories are incomplete or irregularly kept, or if they do not show the true position of his assets and liabilities, but without there being any fraud.

575. The following persons will be ordered to pay fines for non-fraudulent bankruptcy without prejudice, if appropriate, to the application of article 578:

(1) Those who, in the interests of the debtor, have taken possession of, hidden or knowingly received all or part of the assets (whether fixed or moveable) of the debtor;
(2) Those who have fraudulently claimed in the debtor's bankruptcy and have claimed, either in their own name or by third parties, fictitious or exaggerated debts;
(3) A creditor who has obtained for himself, either with the debtor or with other persons, any particular advantages by reason of his vote at any meetings concerning the bankruptcy or who has entered into a particular agreement by which he has obtained an advantage over the assets of the bankrupt;
(4) A trustee who is found guilty of a misappropriation of funds.

Any person found so liable, will in addition, be ordered to pay a fine equal to the value of the illegal advantages which he has obtained or to make restitution and pay damages with interest to the general body of creditors in a sum of not less than one hundred francs.

576. The directors of limited liability companies who have not supplied the information requested of them, either by the bankruptcy judge or by the trustees, or who have given inaccurate information, may also be liable to be ordered to pay fines for non-fraudulent bankruptcy.

This also applies to those persons who, without a legitimate excuse, have not appeared before the bankruptcy judge or the trustee when so requested.

Chapter II: Fraudulent bankruptcy

577. A bankrupt trader will be guilty of fraudulent bankruptcy in any of the following situations:

(1) If he has removed the accounts books, or if he has fraudulently removed, erased or altered the contents;
(2) If he has diverted or concealed any part of his assets;
(3) If, in any written document, whether public or private, or in the balance sheet of his business he has fraudulently purported to be a debtor for sums which he does not owe.

578. Those persons who, by one of the means indicated in article 60 of the Penal Code, have instigated any of the situations referred to in the preceding article or have given instructions to do so, and those who have knowingly helped the fraudulent bankrupt in his plans or have facilitated his bankruptcy, or have assisted in the circumstances which give rise to it, will be held to be accomplices in fraudulent bankruptcy.

Chapter III: General provisions

579. In the cases referred to in articles 575, 577 and 578 and even if a party is acquitted the court hearing the case will:

(1) of its own motion order any assets, rights or actions which have been fraudulently removed to be restored to the general creditors;
(2) decide on any award sought for damages and interest and granted in any order or decree.

Contractual agreements will, in addition, be declared void with regard to all persons including the bankrupt.

A creditor will be obliged to account to the person entitled for money or securities received from any agreement declare void.

580. Where the avoidance of the fraudulent deeds or agreements referred to in articles 575 and 577 is sought under civil law, proceedings will be brought before the commercial court in the judicial district in which the bankruptcy proceedings were commenced.

581. Costs arising in fraudulent or non-fraudulent bankruptcy proceedings will only be borne by the general creditors when the accused is acquitted and the trustees

authorised by a majority of the creditors present have also brought proceedings for civil compensation in the criminal proceedings.

582. In the event of a scheme of arrangement, the Treasury may only recover costs from the bankrupt after completion of the conditions agreed in the scheme.

583. Any judgments or convictions under articles 573 to 578 will be notified and published in the manner and following the procedures set out in article 472 at the expense of the guilty party.

Chapter IV: The administration of assets in fraudulent and non-fraudulent bankruptcy

584. In all proceedings and convictions for fraudulent or non-fraudulent bankruptcy, civil actions, other than those referred to in article 579, remain separate, and all provisions relating to assets forming part of the bankruptcy will be implemented without being applied to, or invoked in, the criminal courts or the assize court.

585. However, trustees in bankruptcy are obliged to deliver to the public prosecutor all documents, documents of title, papers and information requested of them. During the proceedings these documents, deeds and papers will be held, and made available if required, by the clerk of the court. They will be delivered at the request of the trustees who will be able to take extracts for use in the civil courts or require copies to be delivered to them free of expense by the clerk of the court. Any documents, documents of title and papers which have not been officially filed on the instructions of the court will, after the order or judgment has been issued, be returned to the trustees who will give a receipt for them.

PART III. DISCHARGE

586. A bankrupt who has paid all of the principal amount, interest and expenses which he owes in full, may obtain his discharge.

He will not obtain a discharge if he is jointly liable as a partner in a trading company which is bankrupt until he can prove that all the debts of the company have been paid in full as to principal, interest and expenses, even though a special scheme of arrangement has been agreed with him and the company.

A bankrupt may be discharged after his death.

587. All applications for discharge will be sent to the High Court of Justice. The person making the application will attach to his application all receipts and other supporting documents.

The Director of Public Prosecutions at the High Court of Justice, acting on the application submitted to him, will send certified copies to the public prosecutor and to the president of the commercial court in which the person making the application is resident and if there has been a change of residence since the bankruptcy, the papers will be sent to the public prosecutor at the court and to the president of the commercial court for the area where the bankruptcy took place, requesting them to obtain all available information on the truth of the facts as now disclosed.

To this effect, on the request of the public prosecutor, a copy of the application will be displayed for a period of two months both in the civil and commercial courts, and in the town hall, and will be inserted by way of extract in the official journals.

588. Any creditor whose debt has not been fully paid as to the principal amount, interest and expenses, and any other interested party, may, during the period while the application is on display, oppose the discharge by filing a notice at the court registry accompanied by supporting documents. A creditor opposing the petition for discharge will never become a party to the proceedings relating to the discharge.

589. After the expiry of two months the public prosecutor and the president of the commercial court will send, separately, to the Director of Public Prosecutions at the High Court of Justice, the information which they have collected and any opposing statements which have been made. They will also add their recommendation on the petition for discharge.

The Director of Public Prosecutions at the High Court of Justice will pronounce judgment by way of acceptance or rejection of the petition for discharge. If the petition is rejected, a further petition may not be made until the expiry of one year.

590. The judgment granting a discharge will be sent both to the Public Prosecutor and to the president of each of the courts to which the application has been submitted. The judgment will be read aloud in the courts and a transcript will be recorded in their registers.

591. The following will not be discharged from bankruptcy: fraudulent bankrupts of whatever kind, persons convicted of theft, forgery, extortion, deceit or breach of trust, bailees, guardians, administrators or other persons liable to account who have not submitted and balanced their accounts.

A non-fraudulent bankrupt who has suffered the penalty to which he was sentenced may be discharged from bankruptcy.

592. No bankrupt trader may act as adviser or represent parties at the commercial court unless he has obtained his discharge.

PART IV. SUSPENSION OF PAYMENTS

593. Suspension of payments is only granted to a trader who, as a consequence of extraordinary and unforeseen events, is obliged temporarily to cease payments but who also, after due verification of his balance sheet, has assets or means sufficient to satisfy all his creditors both as to principal and interest.

Suspension of payments may also be granted if there is a serious possibility that the trader's assets will eventually balance his liabilities, although at the time of the suspension he may be insolvent.

In the event of death of a trader, suspension of payment of his debts may be granted to his successors for the reasons and on the conditions mentioned in the previous paragraph.

594. The debtor will apply simultaneously to the commercial court in the area in which he is resident and to the High Court of Justice. He will annex to his application:

(1) A summary of the events on which he bases his application;
(2) A detailed list of his assets and liabilities together with an estimate;
(3) A list of the names and addresses of his creditors indicating the amount of his debts to them.

The application addressed to the High Court of Justice will be notified by the president of the court to the Director of Public Prosecutions. It must be signed by a lawyer attached to that court.

595. The application addressed to the commercial court will be delivered to the clerk of the court who will give a good receipt without drawing up a formal deed of deposit for it.

Following this application, the president of court will appoint the place, date and time on which, within fifteen days, the creditors will be summoned to appear, and he will indicate the journals which will carry the notice of the meeting.

The court, if necessary in extraordinary session, will appoint one or more experts who will proceed with the verification of the debtor's state of affairs and will appoint one of its judges to supervise the case.

The court may either immediately or during the course of the proceedings grant the debtor a provisional suspension of payments.

In this event, the court will appoint one or more administrators who will be responsible for supervising and controlling the debtor's business transactions throughout the whole of the suspension period.

596. The creditors will be summoned individually by the bankruptcy judge by registered letter posted at least eight days before the date of the meeting. This notice will, in addition, be inserted on three different occasions in the journals selected by the bankruptcy judge.

The notice will reproduce the text of articles 579 and 599 of the Commercial Code as completed and modified by the present legislation.

One copy of the journals carrying the notice of the meeting will be filed at the court registry before the creditor's meeting.

The debtor will deposit the sum considered necessary to cover the expenses of the summons and insertions with the clerk of the court responsible for these arrangements.

597. On the appointed day, the bankruptcy judge will report to the court in the presence of the creditors or their authorised representatives.

The creditors or their authorised representatives will be heard in argument against the debtor. They will declare individually the amount of their claims, and whether or not they agree with the debtor's application. Each creditor may also make a valid written declaration stating the amount owed and recording his vote; this must arrive at the court registry before the date appointed for the creditors' meeting.

A detailed minute of the meeting will be made to which will be attached any documents produced by the creditors and by the debtors.

The court will attach its reasoned opinion to this minute.

598. The court's opinion, together with all the documents relating to the application, will be sent within three days to the Director of Public Prosecutions at the High Court of Justice who will submit them, with his conclusions, to the president. The latter will

nominate an adviser, and the court will issue its decision on the basis of his report within eight months of receipt of the documents.

599. The court may not grant a suspension of payments, even though the trader has performed the conditions set out in article 593, unless the majority of creditors whose claims represent three-quarters of all sums due, have expressed their agreement with the application.

The majority by number of creditors and amount of claims will be established by counting the claims of creditors who have made no written or verbal declarations as agreeing with the application for the full value of their claims.

Those claims which are declared as preferred claims under article 605 and the persons to whom such claims are owed, will not count at all in the calculation.

600. The court will determine the duration of any suspension of payments.

The court will appoint one or more administrators who will be responsible for supervising and controlling the debtor's business transactions throughout the whole of the suspension period.

The suspension of payments may be extended on application by the debtor, with any submissions by the public prosecutor being given in writing. The application will be addressed to the High Court of Justice and will be signed by a lawyer attached to that court. The court will hear the debtor and the administrator(s).

At law, rejection of the application entails revocation of the provisional suspension of payments.

Successors of the debtor do not benefit from a suspension of payments granted to a debtor unless they accept the succession on terms that liability does not exceed the value of the assets inherited.

601. An order granting a provisional suspension or the decree granting a final suspension of payments will, within three days of its date, be published at the instigation of the supervising administrators by way of notice in the chamber of the commercial court and in journals selected by the judge in accordance with article 595.

602. Experts and commissioners will be chosen from persons resident in the debtor's area.

Before taking up their appointments, the experts will swear on oath before the judge faithfully and properly to carry out their duties.

The commissioners will also swear the same oath before the president of the commercial court.

Their fees will be taxed by the commercial court in accordance with the nature and importance of the debtor's business. Their fees and disbursements will be paid in priority to other debts.

Any creditor of the debtor appointed as a commissioner will not be paid a fee.

603. Payment of claims existing at the time of the application may not be made by instalments throughout the period of the suspension of payments, unless all the creditors are finally paid pro rata according to the amount of their claims.

When claims are contested, article 562 of this Code will apply.

Without the authority of the supervising commissioners, the debtor may not transfer, charge, or mortgage his property, whether real or personal, settle or attempt to settle, or, borrow or receive any sum or make any payment or make himself available for any act of administration.

The commercial court will determine any dispute.

604. During the period of the suspension of payments, no execution may be made against the debtor's person or property. Distraints and attachments made before the suspension of payments will remain in force but the court may, depending on the circumstances, lift such measures after hearing submissions from the debtor, the creditor and the supervising administrators.

Suspension of payments does not suspend proceedings which have been commenced nor the bringing of new actions against the debtor unless these actions are solely aimed at obtaining payment of a debt which is not in dispute.

However, it is not possible during a provisional or final suspension of payments, to register any mortgage on the debtor's real property arising as a result of any orders of the court issued during that time.

605. Suspension of payments only applies to obligations contracted prior to the grant of the suspension. It does not apply in favour of co-debtors, or any guarantors who have renounced the benefit of preliminary proceedings. It does not apply in relation to:

(1) Taxes or other public charges;
(2) Preferred claims or claims secured by mortgages or other charges;
(3) Claims for maintenance;
(4) Claims for the supply of necessaries to the debtor and his family during a period of six months preceding the suspension of payments.

606. During the suspension of payments, the secured or preferred creditors may not proceed to have any buildings or fixtures used in the course of the profession or business of the debtor, attached or sold, provided that any interest due on the secured claims is paid in full and promptly.

607. Revocation of the suspension of payments may be demanded by one or more creditors, or by the administrators, if the debtor has been found guilty of fraud or of acting in bad faith, if he is in breach of article 603, or if it appears that his assets no longer cover all his debts in full.

The application to revoke the suspension of payments will be made to the commercial court, which, after hearing the debtor's submissions, will give a decision, if the provisional suspension of payments is in issue, or will issue its opinion, if a final suspension of payments is in issue.

Any decree or judgment relating to the revocation of the suspension of payments will be published in the manner and in the places prescribed under article 601.

608. Any withdrawal of an application for suspension of payments will be sent both to the High Court of Justice and to the commercial court.

It will be put into effect on the production of proof that a notice announcing the application to withdraw has already been published in the form prescribed in article 595.

609. A judgment which grants, refuses or revokes a provisional suspension of payments will not be open to challenge or appeal.

A debtor may however oppose a judgment which revokes a provisional suspension of payments if he has been legitimately prevented from attending the hearing.

Any decree ordering suspension of payments may be referred to the High Court of Justice by way of an application in civil proceedings.

610. Any instruments, documents or other written material which might assist the court and the High Court of Justice to reach a view on the request for a suspension of payments may be produced and filed by the debtor, the creditors or the supervising administrators and without any need to have them formally stamped or registered.

Judgments relating to the grant, extension or revocation of provisional suspensions of payments will be registered against a fixed rate fee of three francs.

611. The debtor is subject to the same penalties as a non-fraudulent bankrupt:

(1) If, in order to determine or to facilitate the grant of a suspension of payments, he has in any manner whatsoever voluntarily concealed a part of his liabilities or exaggerated his assets;
(2) If the debtor has caused or allowed one or more fictitious creditors or creditors whose claims have been exaggerated to appear in any meetings relating to his application for a suspension of payments.

612. Any person who, without being a creditor, has taken part in meetings relating to the application for the suspension of payments or who, being a creditor, has fraudulently exaggerated the claims entitling him to take part in these meetings, will be liable to the same penalty.

613. In the event of bankruptcy of a debtor within six months following expiry of the period of suspension of payments, the date of cessation of payments, by way of derogation from article 422, will, as a matter of law, be deemed to be the date of the application for the suspension of payments.

In addition to the void transactions referred to in article 445, all transactions entered into by the debtor without the authority of the administrators, where authorisation was required, are void and of no legal effect.

614. Suspension of payments is available to owners of industrial properties who are not considered as traders at law.

All the provisions of this part IV apply to a suspension of payments of this type with the exception of article 613.

If, on expiry of the period of suspension of payments, there is a liquidation or sale of assets, mortgages effected pursuant to judgments rendered during this period, and also all transactions entered into by the debtor without the authority of the administrators, where authorisation was required, will be void and of no legal effect.

LAW OF 14TH APRIL 1886 – JUDICIAL SCHEMES OF ARRANGEMENT

1. A debtor who is a trader may avoid a declaration of bankruptcy, if he obtains a judicial scheme of arrangement from his creditors in the form and on the terms prescribed by this law.

This scheme of arrangement may also be granted after the debtor's death.

2. This type of scheme of arrangement will only arise if the majority of creditors, represented by uncontested claims or claims provisionally admitted in accordance with article 16, and representing three-quarters of all sums due, have accepted the debtor's application.

Majorities of the number of creditors and of claims are established by counting as assenters to the request in the sum of their claims, those creditors who have not made a verbal or written declaration.

When calculating the majority by number, if bearer obligations exist, the only creditors who will be counted in those matters which concern them are those whose entitlements have been proved in accordance with articles 9 and 14 of this law.

The scheme of arrangement will only take effect after it has been ratified by the commercial court.

Ratification will only be granted in favour of a debtor who has suffered misfortune and who has acted in good faith.

3. The debtor will address his application by petition to the district court where he resides. He will attach to his petition:

(1) a summary of the events on which he bases his application;
(2) a detailed list and estimated account of his assets;
(3) a list of the names of his creditors, acknowledged or presumed, with their addresses and the amount of their claims;
(4) the proposals for a scheme of arrangement.

The debtor will deposit at the court registry the amount considered necessary to cover the cost of the proceedings for the grant of a scheme of arrangement.

4. The petition will be delivered to the court registry and entered in a special list. The clerk of the court will give a receipt for the petition without charge or other formality.

If the request is presented by a limited partnership or a limited company, the petition must be signed either by its members or its officers.

The clerk will give notice of the petition to the public prosecutor's office at the district court within twenty-four hours.

The documents referred to in the preceding article will remain at the court registry for inspection by interested parties.

5. Before examining whether there are grounds to allow the petition, the court, meeting in chambers, will assign one of its judges to investigate the situation of the debtor and the report to the court within a short period so that a decision may be taken at the latest within eight days.

Before the court issues its decision, the petitioner or his legal representative may make representations if they so request. The court may, on its part, require the petitioner to attend in person.

The assignment of the case to the appointed judge will be endorsed and dated on the petition.

The court's decision that there is no ground to commence proceedings for the grant of a judicial scheme of arrangement will be argued in chambers; it will be issued in the form of a reasoned decision in open court. Bankruptcy will be declared by way of the same judgment. An appeal may be made within fifteen days of its date.

If the court considers that proceedings for the grant of a judicial scheme of arrangement may be commenced, it will immediately appoint the place, date and time of the creditors' meeting, and will nominate one or more journals which will carry a notice of the meeting for three days. The judge appointed in accordance with paragraph 1 will be chairman of the creditors' meeting and will oversee the implementation of the scheme of arrangement. The decision of the court assigning one of its judges to investigate the debtor's situation will include as of right a provisional stay, for the benefit of the debtor, on all subsequent levying of execution. The provisional stay will not benefit co-debtors or guarantors who have renounced the benefit of preliminary proceedings.

6. During proceedings for a scheme of arrangement, the debtor may not dispose of, mortgage or otherwise deal with his property, without the authority of the judge.

7. Either immediately, or before his report to the court, or during the examination of the debtor, the appointed judge may appoint one or more experts who, after having sworn on oath to carry out their duty in good faith, will proceed to verify the state of the debtor's affairs.

Their fees will be taxed by the court. These fees together with their disbursements will be paid in priority to other claims.

8. On the instructions of the appointed judge, the clerk of the court will summon a creditors' meeting by registered letter delivered by post at least eight days before the date appointed for the meeting.

This letter will contain the proposals for the scheme of arrangement.

Creditors living abroad may be summoned by registered telegram indicating the subject matter of the meeting but without the need to include the proposals.

One copy, duly attested, of the journals carrying the notice of meeting and a memorandum of the letter and telegram sent to creditors and a summary of the recommendations will be filed at the court registry before the creditors' meeting.

9. On the date appointed for the creditors' meeting, the judge will make his report on the debtor's state of affairs.

The debtor in person, or, if permitted by the judge, an authorised representative, will put forward his proposals. The creditors, either in person or through their authorised representatives, will declare in writing the amount of their claims and state whether or not they assent to the scheme of arrangement.

Any persons who claim to be creditors and who have not been summoned will be allowed to make their declarations of claim.

Any creditor may make a valid tender of his declaration and vote to the office of the clerk of the court, even before the creditors' meeting.

Any creditor's declaration may be contested either by the debtor or by the other creditors.

10. Creditors secured by a mortgage, lien or other charge or preferential right, will only be able to vote in respect of their claims in the scheme of arrangement if they surrender their security.

Any creditor voting in the scheme of arrangement renounces his security as a matter of law. This surrender will not take effect if the scheme of arrangement between creditors is not accepted.

These creditors may however vote in the scheme of arrangement without renouncing their liens, mortgages or other charges or preferential rights, but only for an amount equivalent to one half of their claims. In this event, these claims will only be counted for this pro rata amount in the scheme of arrangement.

Before the vote is taken, creditors secured by a mortgage, lien or other charge or preferential right will be advised by the judge of the consequences of their vote.

11. The appointed judge is entitled to adjourn the creditors' meeting. He may also adjourn the meeting to take place at the latest within fifteen days from the date of this decision. Any adjournment will be noted in the minutes. In the event of adjournment, the creditors will be summoned again to the meeting in accordance with articles 5 and 8.

12. The minutes of the creditors' meeting will include:

(1) A list of creditors attending the meeting, either upon summons or voluntarily, with details of the amount and the nature of their claims;
(2) Any objections raised, in particular regarding the existence and amount of the claims;
(3) The definitive proposals put forward by the debtor;
(4) The result of the ballot on these proposals;
(5) The date on which the appointed judge will report to the court, and when the court will be requested to rule on the objections and on the ratification of the arrangement, and will determine the time when cessation of payments occurred.

The minutes will be signed during the meeting.

Any documents produced by the debtor and the creditors will be annexed to the minutes.

13. The minutes of the creditors' meeting, drawn up in accordance with article 12 and the documents annexed thereto, will immediately be filed at the registry for inspection by interested parties.

14. During the week following this meeting, any claim may be filed at the court registry together with the supporting documents by any of the creditors referred to in the list delivered by the debtor to the court in accordance with article 3.

Creditors who do not appear on the above list and who do not appear voluntarily at the meeting may also produce proof of any claim at the court registry, as long as it is supported by the original deed or by good documentary evidence.

Any documents supporting the claim will be put on file.

Any new claim will be submitted with an indication of its acceptance or refusal under the scheme of arrangement.

15. On the date appointed in accordance with article 12, paragraph 5, the judge will read his report in open court. The creditors and the debtor, or their authorised representatives, may be heard and the court will then, in one single judgment and following

the submissions of the public prosecutor's office, issue its ruling on any objections and on the ratification of the scheme of arrangement; at the same time the court will determine the time when cessation of payments occurred.

16. The decision of the court with regard to disputed claims will not turn on the substance of the objection but will merely govern the admission of creditors, for the whole or part of their disputed claims, to meetings in connection with the formation of the scheme of arrangement.

17. If these provisions are not observed or if the scheme of arrangement is unable to proceed on grounds relating to public interest or to the interests of creditors, the court will refuse to ratify the scheme of arrangement.

18. If, in the course of considering the application for a scheme of arrangement, the court considers that the debtor is not acting in good faith, it may at any moment declare the debtor bankrupt.

19. The judgment ratifying the scheme of arrangement will be published on the instructions of the judge within three days of its issue in the form of an extract of the judgment in the journals referred to in article 5.

20. This judgment may not be contested except by creditors who were not summoned to the meeting, who did not present themselves voluntarily at the creditors' meeting, or who have not made use of the right provided under article 19.

This opposition, which does not suspend execution of the decision, must be supported by written submissions and notified to the debtor within a week, starting from the date of publication in the journals, and must be accompanied by a writ requesting the debtor's appearance before the court.

Only one day's delay in appearance will be permitted; the court will rule on all matters pending before it.

The judgment ratifying the scheme of arrangement may only be revoked if the court considers there has been bad faith on the part of the debtor.

21. The judgment is open to appeal by the debtor, or by any creditors who were not summoned to appear at the meeting, or who voted against adoption of the scheme of arrangement, or whose claims have been rejected in whole or in part, or who dispute the date fixed for cessation of payments.

An appeal does not suspend execution of the judgment.

As regards creditors it must be made within one week running from the date of the publications referred to in article 19, and as regards the debtor, the date of issue of the judgment.

The appeal will be formulated by way of declaration filed at the court registry and entered in a special register; a copy of this declaration certified by the clerk of the court, will be sent by him to the registry at the High Court of Justice, together with the whole court file on the case, within forty-eight hours.

Furthermore, an appeal made by the creditors will be notified to the debtor with a writ requesting the debtor to appear before the High Court of Justice within four clear days.

The case will come before the court at one of the earliest hearings. The court will rule on all matters pending before it. The public prosecutor will be heard by the court.

All creditors who have made their rights known before the commercial court may intervene in the appeal; intervention is made by a simple petition, notified to the appeal bailiff. It cannot delay the hearing.

The judgment of the High Court of Justice will be published in accordance with article 19.

22. The decrees determining ratification of the scheme may be referred to the Supreme Court of Appeal.

The appeal must be formally constituted within eight days following publication of the court's decree in court and in the journals.

23. Ratification of the scheme of arrangement by the court is binding on all creditors; it only applies to obligations contracted prior to ratification by the court. When these are contested claims, the procedure for application of the provisions of article 562 of the law of 2nd July 1870 should be followed.

24. Neither co-debtors nor joint guarantors who have renounced the opportunity for negotiation may benefit from a scheme of arrangement.

Without derogation from article 36, it is without effect as regards:

(1) Taxes and other public charges;
(2) Claims secured by liens, mortgages or other charges or preferential rights;
(3) Claims due by way of alimony.

25. A debtor who has been granted a scheme of arrangement must, where his circumstances have improved, pay his creditors in full.

26. Guarantors and other creditors bound by the scheme of arrangement may request its dissolution if a conviction for non-fraudulent or fraudulent bankruptcy is made after the ratification by the court of the arrangement between creditors, or if fraud arising either from dissipation of the debtor's assets or from exaggeration of his liabilities is discovered after the date of the scheme of arrangement.

In these two cases the court may also, following the report of the appointed judge and after hearing the debtor and the guarantors, or once these have been duly summoned, of its own motion rescind the arrangement and declare the debtor bankrupt.

A setting aside of a scheme of arrangement releases any guarantor as of right.

27. In the event of non-performance of the scheme of arrangement, an application to dissolve it may be heard in the presence of the guarantors, or after these have been duly summoned if they have guaranteed total or partial performance of the arrangement.

Dissolution of the arrangement will not release these guarantors.

28. At least every three months, the appointed judge must examine the state of the scheme of arrangement with the assistance of one or more experts appointed by him, if he considers this would be useful.

The judge will report to the court, which, after hearing the debtor and the guarantors, or having duly summoned them at the instigation of the judge by recorded delivery post, may order dissolution of the scheme of arrangement and declare the debtor bankrupt.

29. In the event of bankruptcy of the debtor within the six months which follow dissolution of the scheme of arrangement, the time when cessation of payments occurs may, by derogation from article 442 of the law of 2nd July 1820, be put back to the date when the application was made for the scheme of arrangement.

30. The provisions of the law of 8th July 1870 on stamping rights and registration of documents relating to bankruptcy and suspension of payments apply to documents produced in court or prepared in the carrying out of this law.

31. The debtor is subject to the same penalty as for non-fraudulent bankruptcy:

(1) If in order to terminate or facilitate the formation of a scheme of arrangement he has, in any manner whatsoever, voluntarily dissipated part of his assets or exaggerated his assets.
(2) If he has made or knowingly permitted one or more fictitious creditors or creditors whose claims have been exaggerated to intervene in the meetings.
(3) If he has knowingly omitted one or more creditors from the list of creditors.

32. All persons who, not being creditors, have fraudulently taken part in meetings concerning the scheme of arrangement, or, being creditors, have exaggerated their claims, and those persons who have either with the debtor or with other persons obtained a preferential position arising out of the use of their vote in scheme of arrangement meetings or who have concluded a special agreement resulting in a preferential position with regard to the debtor's assets will be subject to the fine set out in article 490 of the Penal Code.

33. Article 520 of the law of 2nd July 1870 is repealed.

34. Where the scheme of arrangement is by way of surrender of assets, the debtor and the creditors must appoint in the scheme one or more persons charged with realising the assets of the debtor under the supervision of the judge. In such a case, the liquidators will also be able, in the absence of an express provision to the contrary and with the authority of the judge, either in the name of the debtor or the creditors, to appear in court, settle, take the judicial oath, compromise and sell real property.

The judge will decide the terms and conditions of the sale of goods and moveables without having regard to the provisions of the law of lst December 1854 on the sale by auction of new goods.

The judge will also decide the conditions of sale of real property and will appoint the notary responsible for effecting the public sale of such property.

In a single instrument, the creditors will appoint one or more persons whose task will be to pursue any avoidance action which may arise for the benefit of the creditors by reason of acts of the debtor defrauding them of their rights which took place before the commencement of proceedings for the scheme of arrangement.

If the debtor and the creditors fail to comply with these provisions, liquidators will be appointed by the commercial court either in the judgment ratifying the scheme or in a later judgment given at the request of the most diligent party.

It is open to the debtor and the creditors to select the debtor himself; but in this event the creditors, or the court in the name of the creditors, must at the same time appoint a person other than the debtor to pursue, if the need arises, the avoidance actions envisaged in paragraph 4.

The liquidator's fees will be taxed by the tribunal; these, and any disbursements, constitute privileged debts.

35. A trader who has been granted a scheme of arrangement, even by way of surrender of assets, is not struck off the electoral register.

36. In the event of a scheme of arrangement by way of surrender of assets, liquidation will take place as for bankruptcy.

The judgment ratifying the scheme will determine the time of cessation of payments.

In any event this may not take place on a date more than six months before the decision of the court to the effect that proceedings may commence for the grant of a scheme of arangement.

Acts of the debtor in accordance with article 6 are valid.

LAW OF 30TH JUNE 1930 – CONCERNING THE CREATION OF A CREDITORS' COMMITTEE WHOSE FUNCTION IS TO SAFEGUARD THE INTERESTS OF CREDITORS IN BANKRUPTCIES AND SCHEMES OF ARRANGEMENT

Official Gazette, 1930, 637

1. Within fifteen days of the declaration of all bankruptcies, the bankruptcy judge will appoint a creditors' committee consisting of three members chosen from the principal unsecured creditors domiciled in the Grand Duchy or having a place of business there.

Nevertheless the commercial court may order a creditors' committee not to be appointed if it seems certain that the bankruptcy will be completed in a short time, whether because of a shortfall of assets, or by way of liquidation.

The decision of the court that a creditors' committee will not be appointed may be revoked at any time; if this happens, the bankruptcy judge must appoint the members of the committee within eight days of this decision.

The decisions of the commercial court referred to in this article are taken in chambers.

2. In all cases, the bankruptcy judge must appoint a creditors' committee within eight days of expiry of a period of six months from the declaration of bankruptcy if, at that time, no order terminating the bankruptcy or approving a scheme of arrangement has been issued.

3. The duties of a member of the creditors' committee are performed personally by the creditors; if a creditor is a body corporate, it may be represented by its duly appointed proxy.

4. The function of the creditors' committee is to assist the trustee in bankruptcy and to supervise the progress of the bankruptcy.

The creditors' committee is only a consultative body. It meets when summoned either by the bankruptcy judge or the trustee in bankruptcy every time that this seems necessary in order to consider what measures to take in the interests of the estate. It must however be summoned at least once every three months by the bankruptcy judge in order to hear the report of the trustee in bankruptcy on the state of the liquidation.

5. In the event of a scheme of arrangement by way of surrender of assets after bankruptcy, the creditors' committee previously appointed, if any, stays in office unless decided otherwise by a majority of the unsecured creditors present in person or by proxy at the creditors' meeting. If the existing creditors' committee is discontinued or one of its members ceases to serve, or if at this time a creditors' committee has still not been appointed, the unsecured creditors present either in person or by proxy will immediately make the necessary replacements or, as the case may be, appoint a creditors' committee, selecting the members by the same majority.

In the absence of agreement by the unsecured creditors, the appointed judge will select the members of the creditors' committee immediately after ratification of the scheme of arrangement.

6. The procedure for the appointment of the creditors' committee set out in article 5 above will also be followed in the case of either a scheme of arrangement by way of surrender of assets, or a scheme of arrangement before or after bankruptcy which does not result in the surrender of assets.

7. In the case of a scheme of arrangement other than by way of surrender of assets, the function of the committee is to supervise the commercial activities of the debtor until performance of the scheme is complete, and without prejudice to the provisions of article 28 of the law of 14th April 1886.

Any dispute shall be referred by the committee to the appointed judge who will decide how the supervision is to be carried out.

Any action by the debtor hindering the activities of the committee may lead to annulment of the scheme.

8. The members of the creditors' committee will be dismissed and replaced by the bankruptcy judge or the appointed judge, as the case may be, unless otherwise provided for in this law.

No appeal lies from the decision of the bankruptcy judge or the appointed judge, as the case may be.

9. The services of members of the creditors' committee are unpaid.

DECREE OF 24TH MAY 1935 SUPPLEMENTING THE LAWS RELATING TO SUSPENSION OF PAYMENTS, JUDICIAL SCHEMES OF ARRANGEMENT AND BANKRUPTCY: CONTROLLED MANAGEMENT

Official Gazette, 1935, 439

1. A trader whose credit is unsound or who is unable to perform his obligations in full may apply for relief by way of controlled management with a view to either the reorganisation of his business or the proper realisation of his assets.

To that effect, an application setting out the grounds and accompanied by supporting documents including in particular a list of creditors, will be submitted to the commercial court in the district where he has his principal place of business or, in the case of a company, where it has its registered office.

In the latter case the request will be submitted at the instigation of a majority of the directors or members of the board or at the instigation of a majority of the auditors.

The application ceases to be admissible when the applicant has been declared bankrupt by a judgment which has become *res judicata.*

2. The court will hear the applicant and consider the application in chambers.

The application will be rejected if the information produced does not show that the remedy sought would be capable of either ensuring the restoration and normal operation of the applicant's business over a period of time, or improving the conditions for the realisation of his assets.

If the application is not rejected, the court will appoint one of its judges to make a report to the courts within such period as it may determine.

In order to verify the state of the applicant's business the appointed judge may arrange to be assisted by an expert who will undertake, on oath, properly and faithfully to discharge his duties.

3. The decision of the court appointing the judge will take effect at law for the benefit of the applicant and, until the definitive decision is given on the application, suspends all further executory measures, including those instituted by mortgagees, pledgees or other secured creditors.

As from the date of this decision and without the written authorisation of the judge dealing with his case, the trader may not alienate, pledge, or mortgage any of his assets, or enter into any contracts, or receive any transferable capital, upon penalty of the transaction being declared void.

4. Once the report is submitted, the court will hear the applicant in chambers and, giving judgment in open court, will either reject the application or place the applicant's assets under the control of one or more supervisory agents. This decision will be published at the instigation of the commissioners in the Official Gazette in summarised form.

If, on placing the management of the applicant's assets under the control of one or more commissioners, the court ascertains that the applicant has suspended payment of his debts, the court may, in the same or a subsequent judgment, determine at what time the cessation of payments occurred; the time so determined may not however be a date more than six months earlier than the date of the application to the court. However, where a declaration of bankruptcy is appropriate, no such declaration may be made until after issue of the definitive decision rejecting the application in accordance with the foregoing paragraph and articles 2 and 9.

5. The commissioners will forthwith prepare an inventory of the property within the administration and also a statement of the assets and liabilities of the trader; if a company is involved they will also prepare the balance sheets in accordance with the law or any relevant statutory instrument.

The trader may not, without the authority of the auditors, alienate, charge or mortgage his moveable or immoveable property, engage in any legal proceedings, compromise his debts, borrow or receive any monies, make any payment or carry out any administrative act, upon penalty of the transaction being declared void. The commissioners may also prescribe any measures which they consider to be in the interests of the trader or his creditors.

The court will decide any objection which may arise; no appeal lies against the court's decision.

The commissioners are entitled to bring actions under article 448 of the Commercial Code and actions for avoidance of transactions in breach of this decree. They may also bring the following actions with leave of the court:

(a) Actions under articles 59, 62(3) and 103 of the law of 10 August 1915 on commercial companies and, in the case of co-operative companies, actions under arts. 1991, 1992, 1993 and 1995 of the Civil Code.
(b) In the case envisaged in the second paragraph of article 4 of this decree, actions for avoidance of the transactions listed in articles 445, 446 and 447 of the Commercial Code, in each case in accordance with the conditions prescribed in those articles.

In the case of a company limited by shares or a co-operative company, the commissioners may attend the meetings of the board of directors or management; they must be invited to such meetings; they are also themselves entitled to convene meetings of those boards.

At the request of the trader, and also on its own motion, the court may replace a commissioner after hearing his views. No appeal lies against the decision of the court.

6. The commissioners will prepare within the time limits prescribed by the court either a proposal for the reorganisation of the trader's business or a proposal for the realisation and distribution of his assets.

7. The proposal for reorganisation, or for realisation and distribution of the assets will deal fairly and equitably with all the interests involved. It will observe the order of priority of any charges and mortgages in accordance with the law and will ensure that no contractual clauses providing for forfeiture, rescission or penalties operate in a manner prejudicial to the reorganisation, or to the realisation and distribution of the assets.

8. The commissioners will deliver the proposal for controlled management to the creditors and to the co-obligors and any known guarantors; in the case of a company a summary of the proposal will also be published in the annexes to the Official Gazette. It will first be submitted to the court for approval.

Within fifteen days of the delivery or public announcement of the proposal referred to in the previous paragraph, the creditors will give notice to the court registry of their acceptance of, or opposition to, the proposal submitted by the commissioner. They, and also the trader, the shareholders, the co-obligors and the guarantors, may address written observations to the court registry.

The court will hear the trader in chambers; it may also invite any interested parties who submitted observations or objections to attend at the hearing.

The judgment will be delivered in open court.

The court may only approve the commissioners' proposal if it is accepted by more than one half of the creditors who have claims not contested by the commissioners and who represent more than one half of the liabilities. Creditors who abstain will be deemed to have accepted the proposal.

9. If the court considers it cannot approve the commissioners' proposal it will reject the application or prescribe a short period within which the commissioners must prepare a new proposal.

Any new proposal will be published in accordance with article 8 and the procedure provided under that article will be repeated.

10. The judgment approving the commissioners' proposal is binding on the trader, his creditors and, even if they have discharged the debt after the judgment, on any jointly liable co-debtors and guarantors. A summary of the judgment will be published at the instigation of the commissioners in the Official Gazette and in a journal designated by the court.

11. Judgments given in accordance with articles 2, 4, 9 and 10 are provisionally enforceable with the exception of any rejecting the application; all are subject to appeal by the trader and his creditors; there are no other rights of appeal.

The time limit for appeals is eight days from the date of publication of the judgment, where publication is prescribed, and from the date of the judgment in other cases.

Appeals are subject to the formalities provided under paragraphs 4 to 7 of article 21 of the law of 14 April 1886 as amended by the law of 1 February 1911 concerning judicial schemes of arrangement.

No further appeal lies from the judgment on appeal.

If the court reverses the decision of the lower court given under the second paragraph of article 2, or the decision refusing to place the management of the applicant's assets under the control of one or more commissioners, it will order the proceedings to take place before the commercial court.

12. The fees of the commissioners and the experts will be assessed by the court according to the difficulty of their tasks; these fees and any disbursements will be borne by the applicant and rank as preferred claims.

Any creditors of the applicant appointed as commissioners are not entitled to fees.

13. At the risk of imprisonment for a term of from eight days to five years, and a fine of between 2,501 and 150,000 francs, the commissioners may not participate in the supervision or administration of the companies whose management they have controlled for five years following completion of their tasks.

14. All deeds, instruments or documents which might assist the lower or appeal courts regarding applications for controlled management may be produced and filed without need for the prior formality of stamping or registration.

15. Any trader who, during the course of the proceedings governed by this order,

(a) in any way deliberately conceals part of his liabilities or exaggerates his assets, or
(b) arranges for or allows the intervention of one or more sham creditors or creditors whose claims have been exaggerated,

is liable to the penalty provided under article 13.

16. The same penalty will apply to any person who, not being a creditor, purports to be a creditor during the course of the proceedings governed by this decree or who, being a creditor, fraudulently exaggerates his claim.

17. In the event of the bankruptcy of the trader within the six months following either the judgment rejecting the application provided under the first paragraph of article 4 or article 9 or the judgment approving the auditors' proposal provided under article 10, the time of cessation of payments may, in derogation from article 442 of the Commercial Code, be put back to six months prior to the date of the application.

18. Relief by way of controlled management may be granted to persons operating industrial establishments who are not at law regarded as traders.

The provisions of this decree will apply to such a controlled receivership, except those contained in the second paragraph of article 4 and article 17.

The provisions of this decree and those of the decree of 4 October 1934 supplementing and amending certain provisions of the Commercial Code concerning suspension of payments and judicial schemes of arrangement will apply to public notaries.

EXTRACT FROM THE LAW OF 27TH NOVEMBER 1984 AS AMENDED RELATING TO ACCESS TO, AND SUPERVISION OF, THE FINANCIAL SECTOR: SUSPENSION OF PAYMENTS, CONTROLLED MANAGEMENTS AND THE LIQUIDATION OF CREDIT INSTITUTIONS

Section 1 – Suspension of payments and controlled managements

Article 38

(1) Total suspension of payments by a financial institution referred to in article 1(1) and 1(2) may take place in the following circumstances:

- (a) when the credit of the institution is unsound or when it encounters a liquidity crisis, whether cessation of payments occurs or not;
- (b) when full and proper performance of the obligations of the business is compromised;
- (c) when the authorisation under article 4 has been withdrawn but this decision is not yet final.

(2) The board of the Luxembourg Monetary Institute or the financial institution itself may ask the district commercial court to rule upon the suspension of payments referred to in paragraph (1).

(3) The application for suspension supported by reasons and documents, will be filed at the registry of the court in the district where the institution is based.

(4) When the application is from the institution itself it must first notify the board of the Luxembourg Monetary Institute and unless there is an emergency, annex the Institute's observations on the application, before laying the case before the judge.

(5) When the application is from the board of the Luxembourg Monetary Institute, the Institute must notify, or serve formal notice on, the institution by registered letter or by the bailiff.

(6) Filing of the application under paragraph (3) of the present law at the registry of the commercial court following performance of the conditions outlined in the preceding paragraph results, as a matter of law, in the suspension of all payments by the financial institution, and in the prohibition of all action save to preserve assets, without authorisation of the management of the Luxembourg Monetary Institute, until a final decision on the application has been made.

(7) The court will give its decision within a short time. If it considers it has sufficient information it will give a ruling without hearing the parties in open court.

If necessary, the clerk of the court will summon the parties within three days of the application. The court will hear the parties in chambers and give its ruling in open court.

(8) The judgment determines the conditions and terms of the suspension of payments. The period of the suspension may not exceed six months.

(9) The judgment, even if given without having heard the parties, may not be opposed. It is provisionally enforceable immediately, before registration and without any requirement for security, notwithstanding all appeals.

(10) The board of the Luxembourg Monetary Institute and the institution itself may appeal within 15 days of service of the judgment by the clerk of the court. The appeal is heard summarily and without any particular formalities by a commercial or civil division of the Court of Appeal. The parties are summoned by the clerk of the court within eight days. The parties are heard in chambers, and the decision is given in open court. There is no need to be legally represented.

(11) If one of the parties fails to appear, a judgment given in default may not be opposed.

Article 39

(1) A judgment granting suspension of payments in accordance with article 38 will contain the appointment of one or more commissioners.

(2) Written authorisation from the commissioners is obligatory for all acts and decisions of the institution subject to the judgment; the penalty for non-compliance is nullity. The court may in any event limit the scope of activities subject to authorisations.

The commissioners may submit any proposals they think appropriate for consideration by the relevant welfare authorities.

They may take part in the meetings of the administrative, management and supervisory committees of the institution.

(3) The court has the final decision in the event of any dispute between the institution and the commissioners; this is not subject to appeal.

(4) The board of the Luxembourg Monetary Institute exercises the full role of commissioner until a decision has been made on the application under article 38.

(5) The court will determine the costs and fees of the commissioners; it may grant them advances of costs and fees.

Article 40

On the request of any interested party, the court may amend the terms of the judgment given under articles 38 and 39.

Article 41

(1) Within eight days of the decision, the judgment granting a suspension of payments under article 38, and appointing one or more commissioners in accordance with article 39(1), together with any amending rulings under article 40, will be published either in whole or in summary form, at the expense of the financial institution, by the commissioners in the Official Gazette and in at least three

Luxembourg or foreign journals designated by the court and having an adequate circulation.

(2) Any decision amending the judgment set out in paragraph (1) will be published without delay, either in whole or in summary form at the expense of the losing party, by the board of the Luxembourg Monetary Institute in the Official Gazette and in the same journals as those in which the judgment was published.

Section 2 – Liquidation of credit institutions

Article 42

(1) At the request of the public prosecutor or the board of the Luxembourg Monetary Institute, the district commercial court may pass judgment on the dissolution and liquidation of an institution of the type referred to in article 1 when:

(a) it appears that the suspension of payments under article 38 which was granted earlier has not rectified the situation which originally justified the suspension;
(b) the financial situation of the institution is so unsound that it can no longer satisfy its obligations towards all its creditors and the holders of other rights of participation;
(c) authorisation under article 4 has been withdrawn and this decision is final.

(2) At the same time as ordering liquidation, the court will appoint a bankruptcy judge together with one or more liquidators. It may apply the rules governing bankruptcy, as far as it thinks fit.

In that event, it may fix the date when cessation of payments took place as any day not more than six months before the filing of the application under article 38.

The method of liquidation may be modified later, either on the application of the liquidators or as a matter of course.

(3) A judgment ordering dissolution and liquidation is provisionally enforceable.

(4) From the date of the judgment, all actions against the institution, and all enforcement measures, may only be commenced or continued by, or exercised against, the liquidators.

(5) The liquidators are responsible to third parties and to the credit institution for the proper performance of their functions and for any mistakes made under their management.

(6) Judicial decisions ordering dissolution or liquidation of a credit institution are published, either in whole or in extracts and at the expense of the institution, by the liquidators, in the Official Gazette and in at least three Luxembourg or foreign journals designated by the court and having an adequate circulation.

(7) The court will determine the costs and the fees of the liquidators; it may grant them advances of costs and fees. If the bankruptcy judge holds that there are insufficient assets, court documents will be exempted from all registration fees, and the

costs and fees of the liquidators are borne by the Treasury and written off as judicial costs.

(8) Monies due to any creditors who failed to appear at the termination of the liquidation are deposited at the public trustees' office for the benefit of whoever may be concerned.

(9) When the liquidation is at an end, the liquidators will report to the court regarding the employment of the institution's assets, and will submit their liquidation accounts together with supporting documents. The court will appoint commissioners to examine the documents.

Following the commissioners' report, the court will issue its decision regarding the management of the institution by the liquidators on the termination of the liquidation. This will be published in accordance with paragraph (6) above.

The public announcement will contain, among other things:

(a) The address of the place designated by the court where the institution's books and documents must be kept for at least five years.
(b) Any measures taken in accordance with paragraph (8) in order to deposit monies due to creditors and shareholders which could not have been returned to them earlier.

(10) All actions against the liquidators as such have a limitation period of five years from public announcement of the termination of liquidation contemplated by paragraph (8).

Actions against the liquidators based upon acts in the course of their duties have a limitation period of five years from the relevant act or, if the act was concealed by fraud, five years from the discovery of the relevant act.

Article 43

(1) A credit institution may only put itself into voluntary liquidation after having informed the Luxembourg Monetary Institute at least one month before the notice calling an extraordinary general meeting.

This notice must contain the agenda and is served by advertisements in the Official Gazette, and in a journal and published in the Grand Duchy twice at an interval of at least eight days and at least eight days before the meeting. The penalty for non-compliance is nullity.

(2) A decision to put the institution into voluntary liquidation does not give the board of the Luxembourg Monetary Institute or the public prosecutor the power to ask the court to dissolve or put the institution into liquidation under Article 42.

Article 44

Without prejudice to the provisions of article 42(2), the provisions of the law of 4th April 1886 as amended concerning judicial schemes of arrangement, and the provisions of the decree of 24th May 1935 supplementing the laws relating to suspension of payments, judicial schemes of arrangement and bankruptcy by way of controlled management, do not apply to the institutions referred to in article 1, Part III, of the Commercial Code.

Section 3 – General provisions

Article 45

All deeds, instruments and documents submitted for the information of the court under articles 38, 40 and 42 may be produced and filed without the need to have them first stamped or registered.

Article 46

The fees of the commissioners and liquidators, together with all other expenses incurred in procedures under this chapter are borne by the institution in question. The fees and expenses are considered as administration costs and are deducted from the assets before any distribution of monies.

NETHERLANDS

Netherlands' insolvency law is contained in the Bankruptcy and Suspension of Payments Law of 30th September 1893, as amended. The translation is of the law as it was on 1st January 1992 and includes the amendments introduced by the Implementation Act of that date. It is set out in two parts or titles. Title I contains the bankruptcy provisions, as such, and Title II contains the suspension of payments provisions. The headings of the eleven chapters of Title I are self-explanatory. Broadly, all are procedural except for chapter II (consequences of the declaration of bankruptcy) which contains the more important substantive provisions. Title II consists of two chapters only. The substantive provisions for suspension of payments are found towards the end of the first chapter in articles 230–241, inclusive. The second chapter sets out in detail the provisions of the suspension of payments scheme of arrangement.

CHAPTER SIX

Netherlands Insolvency Law

TABLE OF CONTENTS

LAW OF 30TH SEPTEMBER 1893
BANKRUPTCY AND SUSPENSION OF PAYMENTS

TITLE I. BANKRUPTCY

Chapter I: The declaration of bankruptcy

Article 1

1. A debtor who has ceased to pay will be declared bankrupt by a court order either on his own application or at the request of one or more of his creditors.

2. The bankruptcy order may also be issued for reasons of public interest or on the demand of the public prosecutor.

Article 2

1. The declaration of bankruptcy is pronounced by the district court of the residence of the debtor.

2. If the debtor has left European Holland, the district court of his last residence is the competent court.

3. With respect to partners under a general partnership, the district court of the district where the office of the partnership is established, is also competent.

4. If the debtor does not have an address within European Holland but does have his profession or company there, the district court of the district in which his office is situated is the competent court.

5. If, in the cases referred to under the third and fourth paragraph above, bankruptcy orders are issued by more than one competent court on different dates, only the first order will have legal effect. If the orders of the different courts are issued on the same date, only the order of the court listed first in the law of 10th August 1951, Statute-Book 347, will have legal effect.

6. Repealed by the law of 8th April 1976.

Article 3

Repealed by the law of 14th June 1956.

Article 4

1. The bankruptcy application is made and the bankruptcy petition filed at the office of the clerk of the court and will be heard in chambers without delay. The public prosecutor will be heard.

2. A married debtor may only apply for bankruptcy with the cooperation of his spouse, unless joint ownership has been excluded between the spouses.

3. In the event of a general partnership, the application must contain the names and residence of each of the partners, who are jointly and severally responsible for the whole partnership.

4. The bankruptcy order will be issued at a public hearing and is enforceable irrespective of appeal.

Article 5

The petitions referred to in the preceding article and in articles 8, 9, 10, 11, 67, 155, 166, 198 and 206, will be filed by an attorney-at-law.

Article 6

1. The court may order the debtor to be summoned to be heard either in person or by proxy. The clerk of the court will arrange for the summons to be processed in the manner provided by order in council.

2. If the debtor summoned to be heard is married, his spouse is also authorised to appear in person or by proxy.

3. The declaration of bankruptcy will be pronounced if facts or circumstances have been summarily proved which show that the debtor has ceased to pay; where the petition is made by a creditor, such creditor's right to claim must also be proved summarily.

Article 7

1. Pending investigation, the court may, if so required, grant the petitioner leave to have the assets and estate of the debtor put under seal. The court may grant such leave on the condition of security to be given in such amount as it may determine.

2. The seals will be affixed by a civil law notary appointed by the court when granting leave. The goods referred to in article 21 will not be sealed, but will be briefly described in the protocol.

Article 8

1. A debtor declared bankrupt after he has been heard by the court at the time of the petition for a bankruptcy order, has the right to appeal within eight days following the date of the order.

2. If he has not been heard, he has the right to oppose the order within fourteen days after the day of the order. If he is not within European Holland at the time the order is issued, this term will be extended to one month.

3. The debtor may appeal against a judgment given in opposition within eight days following the date of the judgment.

4. The opposition or appeal will take the form of a petition submitted to the office of the clerk of the court to be seized with the appeal. The president of the court will forthwith determine the date and time for the appeal to be heard. Ultimately on the fourth day following the day on which he has filed his petition, the debtor will arrange for a writ to be served on the attorney-at-law who issued the petition for his bankruptcy, informing him of the opposition or appeal and of the time appointed for the hearing of the matter.

5. This writ will serve as a summons for the creditor who instigated the declaration of bankruptcy.

6. The matter will be handled as provided under article 4.

Article 9

1. If an application or petition for a declaration of bankruptcy is rejected, an appeal may be filed within eight days following the date of rejection.

2. The same applies if a declaration of bankruptcy is nullified following opposition, in which case the clerk of the court of appeal before which the appeal proceedings were

initiated will forthwith notify the clerk of the court which ordered the nullification of the declaration of bankruptcy.

3. The appeal proceedings will be instituted and heard as provided under articles 4 and 6.

Article 10

1. Each creditor, except the creditor who has requested the declaration of bankruptcy, and each party interested has the right to oppose the declaration of bankruptcy within eight days following the date of the order.

2. Opposition will be by way of a petition submitted to the clerk of the court which has issued the bankruptcy order.

3. The president of the court will determine forthwith the date and time of the hearing of the matter. Ultimately on the fourth day following the day on which he has filed his request, the person making the request will arrange for a writ to be served on the debtor and, if the declaration of bankruptcy was requested by a creditor, on the attorney-at-law who applied for the bankruptcy, informing them of the opposition and of the time appointed for the hearing of the matter.

4. This writ will serve as a summons for the debtor and the creditor who instigated the declaration of bankruptcy.

5. The matter will proceed as provided under article 4.

Article 11

1. The creditor or the party interested, whose opposition (referred to in the previous article) has been rejected by the court, has the right to appeal within eight days following the date of rejection.

2. The debtor, the creditor who requested the bankruptcy and the public prosecutor have the same right of appeal if the bankruptcy is nullified by the court as a result of such opposition, in which case the second paragraph of article 9 will apply.

3. The appeal proceedings will be instituted and heard as provided under articles 4 and 6.

4. If the opposition was submitted to the court of appeal, there is no further possibility of appeal.

Article 12

1. The debtor, the creditor who requested the bankruptcy, the creditor or party interested referred to in article 10 and the public prosecutor have the right to request a review of the judgment rendered by the court of appeal during a period of eight days after the date of the judgment.

2. The request for review will be filed and heard as provided under articles 4, 6 and 8.

3. If the request for review is directed against a judgment nullifying the bankruptcy order, the clerk of the supreme court will forthwith notify the clerk of the court of appeal which rendered the judgment.

Article 13

1. If, as a result of opposition, appeal or review proceedings, the declaration of bankruptcy is nullified, the acts performed by the bankruptcy trustee prior to or on the day

on which the requirement of notification in accordance with article 15 has been fulfilled remain nevertheless valid and binding as regards the debtor.

2. Pending opposition, appeal or review proceedings, no bankruptcy scheme of arrangement may be discussed nor may the bankruptcy estate be liquidated without the consent of the debtor.

Article 14

1. The bankruptcy order will give directions for the appointment of one of the members of the court as bankruptcy judge and also for the appointment of one or more trustees. The judge who issues the bankruptcy order will also authorise the trustee by such order to open letters and telegrams addressed to the bankrupt.

2. The clerk of the court will forthwith notify the post office of the declaration of bankruptcy. The authorisation referred to in the previous paragraph will be referred to in the notice.

3. An extract from the bankruptcy order, setting out the name, residence or office and the profession of the bankrupt, the name of the bankruptcy judge, the name and address or office address of the trustee, the date of the order, together with the name, profession and address of each member of the provisional committee of creditors, if any, will forthwith be published by the trustee in the Netherlands State Gazette and in one or more journals indicated by the bankruptcy judge.

Article 15

1. As soon as a bankruptcy order has been nullified as the result of opposition, appeal or review proceedings, and when, in the first two cases, the time limit for lodging appeal or review proceedings has expired without appeal or review proceedings being lodged, the clerk of the court which ordered the nullification will notify the trustee and the post office of such nullification. The trustee will announce this nullification in the journals referred to in article 14.

2. A similar notification will be given to the clerk of the court which rendered the judgment in the event that a bankruptcy order is nullified in appeal or review proceedings.

3. The judge who ordered the nullification of a bankruptcy will also determine the amount of the costs of the bankruptcy and the fee of the trustee. He will charge this amount to the party who requested the bankruptcy, or to the debtor, or to both, in a proportion determined by him. No appeal lies against this decision. An enforcement order will be issued in this respect for the benefit of the trustee.

Article 15a

If the declaration of bankruptcy is ordered in appeal or review proceedings nullifying the judgment by which the application or petition for bankruptcy was rejected, the clerk of the court which ordered the bankruptcy will notify the clerk of the court to which the application or petition was submitted.

Article 16

1. If the condition of the estate so requires and upon the recommendation of the bankruptcy judge and after having heard the creditors' committee, if any, the court

may order either that the bankruptcy proceedings shall be free of charges or, after having heard or duly summoned the bankrupt, that the bankruptcy be terminated. In the latter case the order must be pronounced in public.

2. The judge who orders the termination of the bankruptcy, will also determine the amount of the bankruptcy costs and, if there is reason to do so, the fees of the trustee. He will charge these amounts to the debtor. They will have priority over all other debts.

3. No appeal lies against this decision. An enforcement order will be issued for the benefit of the trustee.

4. By way of exception from the provisions of the second paragraph, the costs of the announcements provided in Title I of this law, will be charged to the state in so far as they cannot be paid out of the bankruptcy estate. The clerk of the court ordering the termination of the bankruptcy will arrange for payment of the amount determined by the court to be paid by the state.

Article 17

An order to the effect that the bankruptcy proceedings are free of charges will result in an exemption from court fees.

Article 18

1. The order for termination of the bankruptcy will be made public in the same way as the bankruptcy order and the debtor and creditors may appeal against this order in the same manner and in the same terms as provided for appeal against the judgment by which a declaration of bankruptcy is rejected.

2. If another petition for bankruptcy is filed within three years after termination, the debtor or the petitioner will be obliged to demonstrate that there are sufficient assets to cover the costs of the bankruptcy.

Article 19

1. The clerk of each court will keep a public register setting out for each bankruptcy and referring to the date of each entry:

(1) an extract from the court decisions by which the bankruptcy order was declared or terminated;
(2) the brief contents and formal approval by the court of the bankruptcy scheme of arrangement;
(3) the dissolution of the bankruptcy scheme of arrangement;
(4) the payments made in case of liquidation;
(5) the termination of the bankruptcy pursuant to article 16;
(6) the rehabilitation.

2. Further provisions as to the form and contents of the register will be provided by order in council.

3. The clerk of the court is obliged to keep the register available for inspection by everyone at no cost and to provide an extract from the register against payment.

Chapter II: Consequences of the declaration of bankruptcy

Article 20

The bankruptcy estate will include the entire property of the debtor at the time of the declaration of bankruptcy as well as any property which he obtains in the course of the bankruptcy.

Article 21

Nevertheless, the following will remain outside the bankruptcy:

(1) the goods referred to in article 447, sub-paragraphs 1-3 of the Code of Civil Procedure, the equipment of members of the army in accordance with their service and rank and any copyright not subject to arrest; as well as the items described in the first paragraph of article 448 of that Code, unless there are creditors who have the claims referred to in the second paragraph of that article;

(2) everything which the bankrupt obtains in the course of the bankruptcy through personal activities, or as remuneration for an office or service or as pay, wages, or pension, if and to the extent determined by the bankruptcy judge;

(3) moneys given to the bankrupt to enable him to comply with his legal liability for maintenance;

(4) an amount determined by the bankruptcy judge from the proceeds of the usufruct referred to in article 251 of Book I of the Civil Code in order to cover the charges referred to in article 252 of Book 1 of that Code, and the costs for the care and education of a child;

(5) the amount deposited with the court pursuant to article 320c of the Code of Civil Procedure;

(6) the assets referred to in article 60a, third paragraph.

Article 22

The definition of 'bankrupt' in the previous article also includes the spouse of the bankrupt in the event that they are married with jointly owned property.

Article 23

As a result of the declaration of bankruptcy the debtor loses the right at law to dispose of and control property falling within the bankruptcy estate with effect from and including the day on which the bankruptcy order is issued.

Article 24

The bankruptcy estate will only be liable for undertakings of the debtor made after the declaration of bankruptcy to the extent that the bankruptcy estate may benefit therefrom.

Article 25

1. Legal proceedings concerning rights or obligations which belong to the bankruptcy estate will be instituted by as well as against the trustee.

2. If proceedings initiated or pursued by or against the bankrupt result in a judgment against the bankrupt, such judgment will have no force in law as against the bankruptcy estate.

Article 26

Legal proceedings during the bankruptcy relating to claims against the bankrupt for payment may only be instituted against the bankrupt by submitting the claim to the trustee for verification.

Article 27

1. If legal proceedings are pending at the time of the declaration of bankruptcy and were instituted by the bankrupt, the proceedings will be adjourned at the request of the defendant so that he may summon the trustee within a period fixed by the judge to take over the proceedings.

2. If the trustee does not answer this summons, the defendant has the right to request the proceedings to be dismissed; failing such request the proceedings between the bankrupt and the defendant may be pursued without cost to the estate.

3. Whether or not he has been summoned, the trustee has the power to take over the proceedings at any time in the place of the bankrupt.

Article 28

1. If legal proceedings are pending at the time of the declaration of bankruptcy and were instituted against the bankrupt, the claimant has the right to ask for an adjournment in order to summon the trustee within a period determined by the judge.

2. By appearing in court, the trustee takes over the proceedings and the bankrupt is discharged from the proceedings at law.

3. If the appearing trustee immediately consents to the claim, the costs of litigation of the opposing party will not form a debt of the bankruptcy estate.

4. If the trustee does not appear, the provision in the second paragraph of article 25 does not apply to the judgment against the bankrupt.

Article 29

To the extent that legal proceedings relating to claims against the bankrupt for payment are pending at the time of the declaration of bankruptcy, the action will be adjourned after the declaration of bankruptcy and will only be pursued if verification of the claim is disputed.

In such a case the person disputing the verification becomes a party to the action instead of the bankrupt.

Article 30

1. If prior to the declaration of bankruptcy the court was asked to render judgment, the second paragraph of article 25 and articles 27-29 are not applicable.

2. Articles 27-29 will nevertheless apply if this judgment results in the action being pursued before the judge dealing with the matter.

Article 31

If an action is pursued by or against the trustee, and also, if article 29 applies, against a creditor, the trustee or such creditor may avoid acts performed by the debtor in the action before he was declared bankrupt, if it is proved that the debtor deliberately caused all creditors to suffer loss through such acts and that this was known to the other party.

Article 32

Repealed by the law of 3rd December 1987, Statute Book 591.

Article 33

1. The bankruptcy order means that all judicial enforcement against any part of the property of the debtor commenced prior to the bankruptcy ends immediately and that with effect also from the same moment, no judgment may be enforced by arrest *in personam.*

2. Attachments made will lapse; the registration of a statement to that effect from the bankruptcy judge authorises the keeper of the public register to delete the attachments. As soon as a bankruptcy ends as a result of the nullification or termination of the bankruptcy, the attachment will revive provided the asset is still part of the estate. If the registration of the attachment in the public register has been deleted, the revival will lapse in the absence of registration within fourteen days following the revival of a writ informing the debtor of such revival.

3. If the debtor is imprisoned for debt, and save as provided in article 87, he will be released as soon as the bankruptcy order has become final.

4. The provisions of this article do not apply to arrest *in personam* in the cases referred to in article 598a of the Code of Civil Procedure.

Article 33a

Repealed by the law of 23rd March 1977, Statute Book 184.

Article 34

If prior to the declaration of bankruptcy of the debtor the realisation of his property is at the stage where the date of sale has already been determined, the trustee may pursue the sale for the account of the bankruptcy estate, after being authorised to that effect by the bankruptcy judge.

Article 35

1. If on or after the date of the declaration of bankruptcy some of the transactions necessary in order to complete a delivery of goods by the debtor have not been performed, the delivery can no longer be validly made.

2. If before the date of the declaration of bankruptcy the debtor has agreed to deliver future goods in advance, those goods will belong to the estate if they were obtained by

him after the beginning of the day of the declaration of bankruptcy, unless the goods are fruits or plants which have not yet been harvested and to which the debtor was entitled already before the declaration of bankruptcy by virtue of a right in rem or a rent or lease agreement.

3. For the purpose of articles 86 and 238 of Book 3 of the Civil Code, the party to whom the debtor has made the delivery is deemed to have been aware of the debtor's lack of capacity after the publication of the declaration of bankruptcy referred to in article 14, third paragraph.

Article 35a

If no notice of a covenant under article 252 of Book 6 of the Civil Code has been entered in the public registers on or before the date of the declaration of bankruptcy, the trustee may sell the property, in accordance with articles 101 or 176, in respect of which the covenant has been made without the covenant having effect.

Article 35b

No rights against the estate arise in favour of the donee of a gift made by the debtor under a condition subsequent or to occur at a time following the date of the declaration of bankruptcy.

Article 36

1. If a limitation period in respect of a court action as provided in article 26 would otherwise lapse during the bankruptcy or within six months following termination of the bankruptcy, the limitation period will continue until six months following the termination.

2. The first paragraph applies by analogy to time limits which begin by force of law.

Article 36a

If, prior to the declaration of bankruptcy, a time period applies to the debtor, by virtue of article 55, second paragraph, of Book 3, or article 88 of Book 6 of the Civil Code, and it had not yet expired at the time of the declaration of bankruptcy, the time period will continue to the extent necessary in order to enable the trustee to determine his standpoint. The opposing party may cause a new reasonable time period to apply to the bankruptcy trustee for that purpose.

Article 37

1. If, at the time of the declaration of bankruptcy a contract has not been performed, or has only partially been performed by both the debtor and the other party and if the trustee fails to declare himself bound by the contract within a reasonable time period fixed by the other party, the contract is dissolved and the other party may file a claim for damages as an unsecured creditor.

2. If the trustee declares himself bound by the contract, he is obliged to put up security for the proper performance of the contract at the time of his declaration.

3. The previous paragraphs do not apply to agreements which only require personal performance by the bankrupt.

Article 37a

The other party may file a claim as unsecured creditor in respect of claims which he has against the bankrupt by virtue of the dissolution or cancellation of an agreement concluded with the bankrupt before the declaration of his bankruptcy or in respect of claims under an indemnity for failure to pay a claim accruing against the bankrupt prior to his declaration of bankruptcy.

Article 38

If, in the circumstances referred to in article 37, delivery of goods traded on a commodity market is required at a fixed time or within a certain period, and if this is after the declaration of bankruptcy, the agreement is dissolved by the declaration of bankruptcy and the opposing party may file a claim for damages as an unsecured creditor. If the bankruptcy estate suffers loss because of this dissolution, the other party is obliged to pay such loss.

Article 38a

1. If the bankrupt is a party to a hire-purchase contract, the trustee as well as the seller may declare the contract, or any agreement for the hire-purchase of a ship, dissolved.

2. This dissolution has the same consequences as dissolution of a contract on the grounds of non-performance of a buyer's obligations.

3. The seller may file a claim for the amount due as an unsecured creditor.

Article 39

1. If the bankrupt is a tenant, the trustee as well as the landlord may terminate the lease before expiry provided the notice of termination is given within a period in accordance with local practice for such leases. Nevertheless, the agreed or usual notice period must be observed, provided however that three months' notice is in any case sufficient. If rent has been paid in advance, termination may not take place earlier than the end of the period which had been paid for. The rent will be a debt of the bankruptcy estate as from the date of the declaration of bankruptcy.

2. If the bankrupt is a lessee, the above applies by analogy.

Article 40

1. Employees in the service of the bankrupt may terminate their employment and their employment may be mutually terminated by the trustee with due observance of the agreed or legally prescribed terms.

2. The employee will nevertheless not have to observe the term referred to in article 1639j, first paragraph, of the Civil Code, and he may in any case terminate the employment by six weeks' notice.

3. The trustee may in any case terminate the employment by six weeks' notice which notice period is extended pursuant to article 1639j, second paragraph, of the Civil Code, with regard to employees between 45 and 65 years of age.

4. From the date of the declaration of bankruptcy the salary and premiums relating to the employment agreement are debts of the bankruptcy estate.

5. This article applies by analogy to agency agreements.

Article 41

1. Inheritances falling in and becoming due to the bankrupt during the bankruptcy will only be accepted by the trustee subject to his consideration of a detailed inventory of the inheritance.

2. The trustee requires the approval of the bankruptcy judge in order to disclaim an inheritance.

Article 42

1. The trustee may, for the benefit of the estate, avoid every transaction voluntarily performed by the debtor and prior to the declaration of bankruptcy which he knew or should have known at that time would prejudice the creditors. Article 50, second paragraph, of Book 3 of the Civil Code does not apply.

2. A transaction, other than for no consideration, which is either multilateral or unilateral and to which one or more persons are party, may only be avoided on the grounds of prejudice to the creditors if the parties with or in favour of whom the bankrupt performed the transaction, also knew or should have known that it would prejudice the creditors.

3. If a transaction for no consideration is avoided on the grounds of prejudice to the creditors, such nullification has no effect in respect of a beneficiary who neither knew or should have known that the transaction would prejudice the creditors, provided that he proves that he had not benefited from the transaction at the time of the declaration of bankruptcy.

Article 43

1. If the transaction prejudicing the creditors was performed within one year prior to the declaration of bankruptcy and if the debtor was not already legally committed to the transaction before the beginning of this period, the knowledge referred to at the end of article 42, first paragraph, first sentence, is presumed to exist on both sides in the absence of proof to the contrary:

(1) in the case of contracts in which the value of the debtor's obligation considerably exceeds the value of the other party's obligation;
(2) in the case of transactions constituting payment of, or security for, a debt which is not yet payable;
(3) in the case of transactions performed by a debtor who is an individual with or as against:
  (a) his spouse, foster child or a relative up to the third remove;
  (b) a body corporate in which he, his spouse, his foster child or a relative up to the third remove, is a director or officer or in which these persons, severally or jointly, participate directly or indirectly as shareholders up to at least half of the subscribed capital;
(4) in case of transactions performed by the debtor being a body corporate with or as against an individual:
  (a) who is the director or officer of the body corporate, or with or as against such person's spouse, foster child or relative up to the third remove;
  (b) who, together or not with his spouse, foster children and relatives up to the third remove, participates directly or indirectly as a shareholder up to at least half of the subscribed capital;

(c) whose spouse, foster children or relatives up to the third remove, severally or jointly, participate directly or indirectly as shareholders up to at least half of the subscribed capital;

(5) in the case of transactions performed by a debtor being a body corporate with or as against another body corporate, if:

(a) one of these bodies corporate is the director of the other;

(b) a director, an individual, of one of these bodies corporate, or his spouse, foster child or relative up to the third remove, is a director of the other body corporate;

(c) a director, an individual, or a member of the supervisory board of one of these bodies corporate, or his spouse, foster child or relative up to the third remove, severally or jointly, participates directly or indirectly in the other body corporate as a shareholder up to at least half of the subscribed capital;

(d) the same body corporate or the same individual, together or not with his spouse, foster children and relatives up to the third remove, participates directly or indirectly in both bodies corporate up to at least half of the subscribed capital;

(6) in case of transactions performed by the debtor who is a body corporate with or as against a group company.

2. A spouse includes any other life partner. A foster child means a child which is raised and educated as an own child.

A director, member of the supervisory board or shareholder includes any person who was a director, member of the supervisory board or shareholder less than one year prior to the performance of the legal act.

If the director of a body corporate director is a body corporate itself, this body corporate shall be treated as if it was the body corporate director itself.

3. Article 138, tenth paragraph, of Book 2 of the Civil Code applies if the debtor is a legal entity.

Article 44

Repealed. (Implementation Act 1st January 1992, Books 3, 5 and 6, first part.)

Article 45

In the event of prejudice to the creditors caused by a transaction for no consideration performed by the debtor within one year before the declaration of bankruptcy it is presumed that he performed the transaction with the knowledge that it would prejudice the creditors.

Article 46

Repealed. (Implementation Act 1st January 1992, Books 3, 5 and 6, first part.)

Article 47

Payment by the debtor of a claim which has accrued due may only be avoided if it is proved either that the person receiving the payment knew that the bankruptcy of the debtor had already been applied for or that the payment was the result of negotiations between the debtor and the creditor with the intention of preferring that creditor over other creditors.

Article 48

1. By virtue of the previous article no reimbursement may be claimed from a person who, as holder of a negotiable instrument made out to order or bearer, was obliged to accept the payment in view of his legal relationship with former holders.

2. In such event the party in whose favour the negotiable instrument was issued is obliged to reimburse the amount paid by the debtor to the bankruptcy estate if it is proved either that at the time the negotiable instrument was issued he had the knowledge referred to in the previous article or that the negotiable instrument was issued as a result of the negotiations referred to in that article.

Article 49

1. Legal proceedings based on the provisions of articles 42 to 48 are commenced by the trustee.

2. Nevertheless the creditors are able to dispute the admission of a claim on grounds derived from these provisions.

Article 50

Termination of the bankruptcy by means of the court's approval of a bankruptcy scheme of arrangement results in the lapse of the legal proceedings referred to in the previous article unless it is a liquidation scheme of arrangement in which case the legal proceedings may be pursued or commenced by the liquidators of the estate for the benefit of the creditors.

Article 51

1. Assets removed from the property of the debtor due to an unlawful act must be returned to the trustee by the persons who are parties to the transaction which has been avoided with due regard to section 2 of title 4 of Book 6 of the Civil Code.

2. Rights which have been acquired by third parties in good faith against payment will be honoured. Assets obtained by a third party in good faith for nothing will not be claimed back to the extent that as the third party proves that at the time of the declaration of bankruptcy he had not benefited as a result of the transaction.

3. Assets received by the debtor under a transaction which has been avoided or the value thereof, will be returned by the trustee to the extent that this benefits the bankruptcy estate. The person who is a party to the transaction which has been avoided may file a claim for the deficit as an unsecured creditor.

Article 52

1. Payment to the bankrupt after the declaration of bankruptcy, but before public announcement thereof, in performance of obligations towards him entered into before the declaration of bankruptcy will release the party paying as against the bankruptcy estate as long as it is not proved that he knew of the declaration of bankruptcy.

2. The payment referred to in the previous paragraph made to the bankrupt after public announcement of the declaration of bankruptcy will only release the party

paying as against the bankruptcy estate if he proves that the declaration of bankruptcy could not have been known at the time by legal publication in his place of residence subject to the right of the trustee to prove that it was nevertheless known to him.

3. Payment to the bankrupt will in any case release the debtor from liability to the bankruptcy estate to the extent that as the funds paid by him accrued to the benefit of the bankruptcy estate.

Article 53

1. A person who is both a debtor and a creditor of the bankrupt may claim set-off if both the claim and the debt occurred before the declaration of bankruptcy, or if they resulted from transactions entered into with the bankrupt before the declaration of bankruptcy.

2. The claim against the bankrupt will, if necessary, be calculated in accordance with the rules set out in articles 130 and 131. The bankruptcy trustee may not invoke article 135 of Book 6 of the Civil Code.

Article 54

1. Nevertheless, a person who has been assigned a debt owed to, or a claim against, the bankrupt before the declaration of bankruptcy may not apply for set-off if he has not acted in good faith with respect to such assignment.

2. Set-off is never permitted for claims or debts assigned after the declaration of bankruptcy.

Article 55

A debtor of the bankrupt who wishes to set off his debt against a claim to order or bearer, must prove that he was already the owner in good faith of the negotiable instrument made out to order or bearer at the time of the declaration of bankruptcy.

Article 56

A person who owns property jointly with the bankrupt, the joint ownership of which is separated during the bankruptcy, may invoke article 184, first paragraph, of Book 3 of the Civil Code; this also applies if the debt of the bankrupt to the joint ownership is a debt under a condition subsequent which has not yet been fulfilled. Articles 130 and 131 apply.

Article 57

1. Creditors holding a mortgage or a pledge may exercise their rights as if there were no bankruptcy.

2. At the time of the judicial distribution creditors with a limited preferential right, whose right had vested prior to the declaration of bankruptcy but had expired due to execution by a creditor holding a mortgage or a pledge, may file their claim for indemnification as provided in article 282 of Book 3 of the Civil Code.

3. At the time of the distribution the trustee will exercise for the benefit of the estate those rights which the law confers on those who attach an asset. He is bound also to represent any preferred creditors who rank ahead of pledge and mortgage holders and ahead of creditors with limited preferential rights.

4. Any determination of the order of priorities which may be necessary will be requested from the president of the court of which the bankruptcy judge is a member. The distribution will take place before the bankruptcy judge in the manner prescribed in the Code of Civil Procedure.

Article 58

1. The trustee may determine a reasonable period within which the mortgage creditor and the pledgee referred to in the previous article must exercise their rights in accordance with the previous article. If the mortgage creditor or pledgee has not sold the security within this period, the trustee may claim the assets and sell them in accordance with articles 101 or 176, but without prejudice to the right of the mortgage creditor or pledgee to the proceeds. The bankruptcy judge may extend the period one or more times at the request of the mortgage creditor or pledgee.

2. The trustee may, until the time of the sale, release mortgaged or pledged assets against payment of the amount of the mortgage or pledge and also of the execution costs already incurred.

Article 59

If the proceeds are insufficient to pay off the mortgage creditor or the pledgee or any person whose limited preferential right has expired because of the execution, he may file his claim for the deficit as unsecured creditor.

Article 60

1. A creditor having a right of retention does not lose this right because of the declaration of bankruptcy.

2. The asset may be claimed by the trustee and sold in accordance with article 101 or 176 without prejudice to the priority right conferred on the creditor in article 292 of Book 3 of the Civil Code. To the extent that the estate will benefit, the trustee may also return the asset to the estate by payment of the debt in respect of which the right of retention may be executed.

3. The creditor may allow the trustee a reasonable period in which to proceed with the application of the previous paragraph. If the trustee has not sold the asset within this period, the creditor may sell the asset with analogous application of the provisions concerning execution by a pledgee without recourse to the court or, in case of immovable property, the provisions concerning execution by a mortgage holder without recourse to the court. The bankruptcy judge may extend the period one or more times at the request of the trustee.

4. In the case of immoveable property the creditor must, within fourteen days after expiry of the period referred to in the previous paragraph – failing which he will lose his right of prompt execution – serve a writ on the trustee notifying the trustee that he will proceed with the execution and have this writ recorded in the public registers.

Article 60a

1. If the property of the bankrupt contains any goods under administration, and creditors have submitted claims for verification, who would otherwise be entitled to sell off these assets without mandate from the administration, the trustee will claim these assets from the administrator and take control and sell them to the extent that

this is necessary for the payment of these creditors from the proceeds. The administration of an asset terminates upon the trustee claiming it. The proceeds will be distributed among the creditors in accordance with this law to the extent that their claims have been verified. The trustee will transfer the amount which remains from the proceeds after the distribution to the administrator, unless the other creditors are entitled to sell off the assets under administration, in which case the remainder will be distributed among these creditors in accordance with this law.

2. If the only creditors who have submitted claims for verification are those entitled to sell off the assets while maintaining the administration, these assets will be sold by the trustee while maintaining the administration in accordance with articles 101 or 176.

3. Except as provided in the previous paragraphs the assets under administration will be kept outside the bankruptcy and the trustee will only be paid the net sale proceeds of the assets.

4. The administrator is at all times obliged to account to the trustee if the latter requires this.

Article 60b

1. If, by virtue of the previous articles, assets have been kept outside the bankruptcy, and the administrator has ceased to pay the creditors otherwise entitled to sell off these assets without mandate from the administration, the court which issued the bankruptcy order may instruct the trustee at the request of each of the creditors otherwise unable to file their claim in the bankruptcy, to assume the control of these assets and to arrange for them to be sold off for their benefit.

2. The provisions concerning a declaration of bankruptcy and bankruptcy apply by analogy.

Article 61

1. The spouse of the bankrupt will take back all goods belonging to him which are not jointly owned.

2. As regards third parties, ownership of instruments endorsed to bearer and assets not capable of registration which are excluded from joint ownership under the contract of marriage may only be proved as provided under article 130 of Book 1 of the Civil Code.

3. Ownership by the bankrupt's spouse of instruments endorsed to bearer and of assets not capable of registration and regarding which the last will of the testator or the intention of the donor is that they are not part of the joint ownership of the spouses, must, in the event of a dispute, be identified by description or in documents. The same applies to such instruments and assets in respect of which title has become vested in the spouse by inheritance, legacy or gift in the course of the marriage and which, by virtue of the contract of marriage, are not owned jointly by the spouses.

4. Assets resulting from investment or reinvestment of moneys which belong to a spouse and are not jointly owned, will likewise be taken back by such spouse, provided that, in the event of a dispute, the investment or reinvestment is proved by ample documentary evidence to the satisfaction of the judge.

5. If assets belonging to the spouse of the bankrupt have been disposed of by the bankrupt, but the purchase price has not yet been paid or the proceeds of sale have been kept separated from the bankruptcy estate, the spouse may exercise his right to receive the purchase price or the available proceeds of sale.

6. The spouse of the bankrupt is a creditor for his personal claims.

Article 62

The spouse of the bankrupt has no claim against the estate for any consideration due under the contract of marriage. By the same token, the creditors may not benefit from any consideration granted to the bankrupt by his spouse under the contract of marriage.

Article 63

1. The bankruptcy of a spouse married with joint ownership of property will be deemed to constitute the bankruptcy of such joint ownership. It will include all jointly owned assets save for assets excepted under article 21, and benefits all creditors entitled to recourse against jointly owned assets. Assets of the bankrupt which are not jointly owned are only available for the satisfaction of debts which could be settled from those assets if no joint ownership existed.

2. If the bankrupt is married with joint ownership of property the provisions of this law in respect of acts of the bankrupt will apply to transactions which legally bind the jointly owned property, regardless of which spouse performed these acts.

Article 63a

1. At the request of each party interested, or of his own motion, the bankruptcy judge may issue an order stipulating that for a period of one month at most each right of third parties for recourse against assets belonging to the estate or to claim assets which are in the control of the bankrupt or the trustee, may only be executed with his authorisation. The bankruptcy judge may extend this period once for at most one month.

2. The bankruptcy judge may limit this order to certain third parties, and may impose conditions both on the extent of the order and on the authorisation of a third party to execute a right to which he is entitled.

3. During the periods referred to in the first paragraph, any other periods of time imposed in respect of the entitlements of these third parties will continue in so far as may reasonably be required to enable the third party or the trustee to determine his standpoint after expiry of such periods. The party imposing the period of time is entitled to impose a further reasonable period of time.

4. At the request of the party who applied for the bankruptcy or of the debtor the decision referred to in the first sentence of the first paragraph may also be rendered by the judge issuing the bankruptcy order.

Chapter III: Administration of the bankruptcy estate

Section 1. The bankruptcy judge

Article 64

The bankruptcy judge is charged with supervision of the administration and liquidation of the bankruptcy estate.

Article 65

Before issuing a decision on any matter in respect of the administration or liquidation of the bankruptcy estate, the court is obliged to hear the bankruptcy judge.

Article 66

1. The bankruptcy judge is competent to hear witnesses or to order an expert's investigation in order to clarify all circumstances relating to the bankruptcy.

2. The witnesses will be summoned on behalf of the bankruptcy judge. Article 203 of the Code of Civil Procedure applies by analogy.

3. Articles 197-201 of the Code of Civil Procedure apply if the witnesses do not appear or refuse to take the oath or to give evidence.

4. The spouse or former spouse, the children and more remote descendants and the parents and grand-parents of the bankrupt may invoke their right to refuse to testify.

Article 67

1. Appeal may be lodged at the district court against any order of the bankruptcy judge within five days. The court will issue its decision after hearing the interested parties or after they have been duly summoned.

2. Nevertheless no appeal lies against the orders referred to in articles 21 (2) and (4), 34, 58, first paragraph, 60, third paragraph, 73a, second paragraph, 79, 94, 98, 100, 102, 125, 127, fourth paragraph, 174, 175, second paragraph, 176 first and second paragraph, 177, 179 and 180.

Section 2. The trustee

Article 68

1. The trustee is charged with the administration and liquidation of the bankruptcy estate.

2. Except for verification disputes and the matters referred to in articles 37, 39, 40 and 58, second paragraph, 60, second and third paragraphs and 60a, first paragraph, the trustee requires the approval of the bankruptcy judge before appearing as such in court.

Article 69

1. Each of the creditors, the appointed creditors' committee, and also the bankrupt, may file a petition with the bankruptcy judge by way of objection to any act of the trustee or to request the bankruptcy judge to order the trustee to perform or refrain from performing any act.

2. The bankruptcy judge will issue his decision within three days after hearing the trustee.

Article 70

1. If more than one trustee has been appointed, the consent of the majority of the trustees or, in the event of a split vote, a decision of the bankruptcy judge is required in order to make their acts legally binding.

2. A trustee assigned to a specific task under the bankruptcy order will have the power to act independently within the limits of his task.

Article 71

1. Without prejudice to the provisions of article 15, third paragraph, the fee of the trustee will be determined by the court in each bankruptcy.

2. In the case of a bankruptcy scheme of arrangement the fee is set down in the judgment by which the court has formally approved the scheme of arrangement in bankruptcy.

Article 72

Absence of authorisation by the bankruptcy judge where this is required, or non-observance of the provisions of articles 78 and 79, does not affect the validity as regards third parties of any act performed by the trustee. In such event, the trustee is only liable as regards the bankrupt and the creditors.

Article 73

1. The court is competent to dismiss the trustee at all times after he has been heard or duly summoned, and to replace him by someone else or to appoint one or more co-trustees, in each case either on the recommendation of the bankruptcy judge or upon the reasoned petition of one or more of the creditors, the creditors' committee or the bankrupt.

2. The dismissed trustee must account for his administration to the trustee who replaces him.

Article 73a

1. Every three months, the trustee will submit a report on the state of the bankruptcy estate. The trustee will submit his report to the clerk of the court where it is available for inspection by everyone free of charge. There is no charge for the submission of the trustee's report.

2. The period referred to in the previous paragraph may be extended by the bankruptcy judge.

Section 3. The creditors' committee

Article 74

1. If necessitated by the importance or the nature of the estate and as long as no decision has been taken in respect of the appointment of the committee referred to in the following article, the court may appoint in the declaration of bankruptcy, or at a later time, a provisional committee of between one and three creditors in order to advise the trustee.

2. If a member of this provisional committee does not accept his appointment, resigns or dies, the court will fill the vacancy by choosing one of the two candidates recommended by the bankruptcy judge.

Article 75

1. Whether or not a provisional creditors' committee has been appointed, the bankruptcy judge will consult the creditors on the appointment of a definitive creditors' committee at the verification meeting after the verification has been completed. If the meeting considers such committee desirable, the bankruptcy judge will forthwith proceed with the appointment of the committee. The definitive creditors' committee will also consist of one to three members.

2. A report of the discussions on this issue is included in the minutes of the verification meeting.

3. If a member of the definitive committee does not accept his appointment, resigns or dies, the bankruptcy judge will fill the vacancy.

Article 76

The committee may require to see the books and documents relating to the bankruptcy at any time. The trustee is obliged to provide the committee with all information required from him.

Article 77

In order to obtain the advice of the committee, the trustee will meet with the committee as often as he considers desirable. He will preside over, and prepare the minutes of, these meetings.

Article 78

1. The trustee is obliged to obtain the advice of the committee before commencing or pursuing any legal proceedings, or opposing any proceedings, whether already instituted or pending, except in the case of proceedings relating to verification disputes. He will also obtain the advice of the committee on whether or not to continue the business of the bankrupt and also in the cases referred to in articles 37, 39, 40, 58, second paragraph, 73, second paragraph, 100, 101, 175, last paragraph and 177, and generally in respect of the liquidation and realisation of the bankruptcy estate and the time and amount of the payments to be made to creditors.

2. This advice is not required if the trustee has called a meeting of the committee upon adequate notice in order to obtain such advice and no advice was rendered.

Article 79

The trustee is not bound to accept the advice of the committee. If he does not agree with their advice, he will forthwith notify the committee which may then request the bankruptcy judge to determine the matter. If the committee has declared that it wishes to obtain the decision of the bankruptcy judge, the trustee is obliged for three days to suspend performance of any intended transaction which is contrary to the advice of the committee.

Section 4. Creditors' meetings

Article 80

1. The bankruptcy judge will preside over the creditors' meetings.

2. The presence of the trustee or of a substitute approved by the bankruptcy judge is imperative.

Article 81

1. At the creditors' meetings the decisions are taken by an absolute majority of votes of the creditors present. Each creditor may cast one vote per hundred guilders.

One vote is also cast for claims or remaining parts of claims of less than one hundred guilders.

2. Division of a claim after the declaration of bankruptcy does not give title to a vote.

Article 82

Creditors whose claims have been admitted or provisionally admitted and bearers of verified claims endorsed 'to bearer' are entitled to vote.

Article 83

1. The creditors may appear at the meeting in person, by written proxy or by an attorney-at-law.

2. As regards creditors represented at the meeting, all notices convening later meetings will be addressed to the representatives, unless the creditors request the trustee in writing that notices of meetings and other notifications be forwarded to themselves or to another representative.

Article 84

1. Except for the meetings provided under this law, a meeting of creditors will be held as often as the bankruptcy judge considers necessary, or whenever he receives a reasoned request for such a meeting from the creditors' committee or from at least five creditors representing one fifth of the claims admitted and provisionally admitted.

2. The bankruptcy judge will determine the date, hour and place of the meeting to which the creditors with a right to vote will be invited at least ten days in advance by announcement in the journal or journals referred to in article 14, and by letter, both setting out the matter to be discussed at the meeting.

Section 5. Court orders

Article 85

All orders in matters relating to the administration or liquidation of the bankruptcy estate are issued by the court by way of final judgment, unless the court orders otherwise.

Article 86

All orders in matters relating to the administration or liquidation of the bankruptcy estate, including those not issued by the court, are enforceable irrespective of appeal and on production of the original of the instrument, unless ordered otherwise.

Chapter IV: Interim judicial provisions following the declaration of bankruptcy; administration of the estate by the trustee

Article 87

1. At the same time as the bankruptcy order or at any time thereafter, but in the latter case only on the recommendation of the bankruptcy judge or at the request of the

trustee or of one or more of the creditors after having heard the bankruptcy judge, the court may order the bankrupt to be taken into custody, either in prison or in his own house under the supervision of an officer of the state.

2. This order will be executed by the office of the public prosecutor.

3. The order will be valid for not more than thirty days calculated from the day on which it has been executed. At the end of this period the court may extend the order for at most another thirty days on the recommendation of the bankruptcy judge or upon request and after having heard the bankruptcy judge as referred to in the first paragraph. Thereafter further extensions may be granted in the same way each time and for thirty days at most.

Article 88

1. On the recommendation of the bankruptcy judge or at the request of the bankrupt the court has the power to release the bankrupt from custody, with or without requiring provision of security against his appearance upon first summons.

2. The amount of the security will be determined by the court and, in the event of non-appearance of the bankrupt, this amount will be credited to the bankruptcy estate.

Article 89

The application to take the bankrupt into custody must be granted if it is based on the bankrupt's deliberate failure without good reason to perform the obligations imposed on him under articles 91, 105 and 116.

Article 90

1. In any cases where the presence of the bankrupt is required in connection with a particular activity relating to the bankruptcy estate, he will, if he is in legal custody, be brought on the instructions of the bankruptcy judge from the place where he is being kept.

2. This instruction will be executed by the office of the public prosecutor.

Article 91

During the bankruptcy the bankrupt may not leave his residence without the consent of the bankruptcy judge.

Article 92

Immediately after the trustee has accepted his appointment he will safeguard the bankruptcy estate by all necessary and proper means. He will immediately take and give receipt for any documents, moneys, jewels, stock and other securities. He is entitled to deposit moneys with the court's clerk.

Article 93

1. If the trustee or the bankruptcy judge deems this desirable, the trustee may immediately have the estate sealed by a civil law notary.

2. The items referred to in articles 21, paragraph 1 and 92 and also the assets required

for the business of the bankrupt, if such business is to be continued, are not put under seal but these goods are briefly described in the protocol of sealing.

Article 94

1. As soon as possible the trustee will proceed with the inventory of the estate.

2. The inventory may be drawn up by a deed between the parties and the assessment may be done by the trustee, subject to the approval of the bankruptcy judge.

3. The members of the provisional committee of creditors are entitled to attend the drawing up of the inventory.

Article 95

A list setting out the items referred to in article 21, paragraph (1), no. 1, is attached to the inventory. The goods referred to in article 92 are included in the inventory.

Article 96

Immediately after the inventory has been drawn up, the trustee will prepare a statement listing the nature and amount of the assets and liabilities of the estate, the names and addresses of the creditors together with the amount of the claims of each of them.

Article 97

1. Copies of the inventory and the statement referred to in the previous article certified by the trustee are available for inspection to everybody, free of charge, at the office of the clerk of the district court and the cantonal court, in which jurisdiction the domicile or office or place of residence of the bankrupt is situated depending on which court issued the bankruptcy order. If the cantonal court is in the same municipality as the district court before which the bankruptcy proceedings are pending, the inventory will only be filed with the clerk of the district court.

2. The filing is free of charge.

Article 98

The trustee may continue the business of the bankrupt. If a creditors' committee has not been appointed, authorisation to continue the business is required from the bankruptcy judge.

Article 99

1. In accordance with the authority referred to in article 14, the trustee will open letters and telegrams addressed to the bankrupt. He will forthwith pass on to the bankrupt those letters and telegrams which do not relate to the bankruptcy estate. Upon receipt of a notification from the clerk of the court and until either released by the trustee or the bankruptcy judge from this obligation or receipt of the notification referred to in article 15, the post office must deliver to the trustee letters and telegrams addressed to the bankrupt. The authority of the court for the trustee to open letters and telegrams ceases to be valid at the time referred to in the previous sentence when the post office's obligation to deliver the letters and telegrams to the trustee has ceased.

2. Protests, writs, statements and notices of time periods relating to the bankruptcy estate must be addressed to the trustee.

Article 100

Depending on the circumstances the trustee may pay such amount as the bankruptcy judge may determine for the maintenance of the bankrupt and his family.

Article 101

1. The trustee has the power to dispose of assets belonging to the bankruptcy estate if and to the extent necessary to cover the costs of the bankruptcy or if and to the extent that retention of the assets results in loss for the bankruptcy estate.
2. The provisions of article 176 are applicable.

Article 102

1. The trustee will immediately take custody of all moneys, jewels, stock and other securities, unless some other means of custody has been determined by the bankruptcy judge.
2. Cash which is not necessary for the administration will be invested by the trustee on behalf of the estate in such manner as the bankruptcy judge may approve.

Article 103

The trustee may not dispose of moneys, jewels, stock and other securities retained by a third party on the instruction of the bankruptcy judge, or of invested moneys, other than on the authority of documents executed by the bankruptcy judge by way of approval.

Article 104

Following the advice of the creditors' committee, if any, and with the approval of the bankruptcy judge, the trustee has the power to enter into settlements, agreements or compromises.

Article 105

1. Whenever summoned, the bankrupt is obliged to appear before the bankruptcy judge, the trustee or the creditors' committee and to provide them with all information required.
2. In the event of the bankruptcy of a married person whose entire property is jointly owned with the other spouse, the obligation to provide information rests upon each spouse, in as far as each such spouse has undertaken transactions relating to the jointly owned property.

Article 106

In the event of the bankruptcy of a body corporate, the provisions of articles 87–91 apply to the directors and the provisions of article 105, first paragraph, apply to the directors and members of the supervisory board.

Article 107

1. The clerk of the court is obliged to hand to each creditor, at his request and for his account, a copy of the documents filed at the office of the clerk of the court under any provision of this law.

2. The clerk of the court is likewise obliged to provide anyone, at his request and for his account, with a copy of the documents available for inspection at the office of the clerk of the court under any provision of this law.

Chapter V: The verification of claims

Article 108

1. Within fourteen days at most after the bankruptcy judgment has become final the bankruptcy judge will determine:

(i) the latest possible date for the submission of claims;
(ii) the date, hour and place for the creditors' meeting.

2. There must be at least fourteen days between the dates referred to in paragraphs (i) and (ii) above.

Article 109

The trustee will forthwith notify these dates by letter to all known creditors and he will also announce these dates in the journals referred to in article 14.

Article 110

1. Claims must be submitted to the trustee in the form of an invoice or other written statement setting out the nature and amount of the claim accompanied by documentary evidence or copies thereof and also by a statement as to whether or not a priority right, pledge, mortgage or right of retention is claimed.

2. The creditors may require a receipt from the trustee.

Article 111

The trustee will compare the invoices submitted with the notes and records of the bankrupt; if he objects to the admission of a claim, he will contact the creditor involved, and may require the submission of any missing documentation as well as inspection of the creditor's notes and original documents.

Article 112

The trustee will prepare a list of provisionally admitted claims and a separate list of the disputed claims setting out the grounds of his opposition.

Article 113

In the lists referred to in the previous article each claim is described together with an indication whether or not the trustee considers the claim to be preferred or secured by a mortgage or pledge or whether or not a right of retention may be exercised in respect of this claim. If the trustee only disputes the priority right or right of retention, the claim is placed on the list of provisionally admitted claims together with a note of the trustee's opposition and the grounds therefor.

Article 114

1. The trustee will file copies of the lists referred to in article 112 at the offices of the clerks of the district court and of the cantonal court indicated in article 97, in order that these may be available for inspection without charge to anyone during the seven days which precede the creditors' meeting.

2. No charge will be made for this filing.

Article 115

The trustee will notify all known creditors in writing of the filing of the lists as provided in article 114. This notice will also contain an invitation to the creditors' meeting and will indicate whether or not a bankruptcy scheme of arrangement has been filed by the bankrupt at the office of the clerk of the court.

Article 116

The bankrupt will attend the creditors' meeting personally in order to give all information with regard to the causes of the bankruptcy and the condition of the estate required of him by the bankruptcy judge. The creditors may request the bankruptcy judge to ask information from the bankrupt in respect of specific issues indicated by them. The questions put to the bankrupt and the answers given by him are recorded in the minutes of the creditors' meeting.

Article 117

If the bankrupt is a body corporate, the obligation imposed on the bankrupt under the previous article is imposed on the directors of such body corporate.

Article 118

Repealed by the law of 6 May 1976.

Article 119

1. At the meeting the bankruptcy judge will read out the list of the provisionally admitted claims and the list of the disputed claims. Each creditor whose name is shown on a list is entitled either to ask information from the trustee with regard to each claim and its position on one of the lists or to dispute the correctness, the alleged preference or the alleged right of retention or to declare that he concurs with the objections raised by the trustee.

2. The trustee is entitled to withdraw a provisional admission or opposition, or to require a creditor to affirm on oath a claim which is not contested either by the trustee or by any of the other creditors; if the original creditor has died, the persons entitled

must state under oath that they believe in good faith that the claim exists and has not yet been settled.

3. If it is necessary to adjourn the meeting, the meeting will be continued within eight days at a time fixed by the bankruptcy judge without further notice.

Article 120

1. The affirmation on oath referred to in the second paragraph of the previous article is taken in person or through a special proxyholder before the bankruptcy judge either immediately at the meeting or at a later date determined by the bankruptcy judge. The proxy may be granted by deed between the parties.

2. If the creditor who must affirm his claim on oath is not present at the meeting, the clerk of the court will forthwith notify him of the required affirmation on oath and the date fixed therefor.

3. The bankruptcy judge will provide the creditor with a statement of his affirmation on oath, unless the affirmation on oath is made in the course of a creditors' meeting, in which event the affirmation on oath is recorded in the minutes of such meeting.

Article 121

1. The undisputed claims are set out on a list of creditors whose claims have been admitted and such list is included in the minutes of the meeting. The trustee makes a note of the admission on any negotiable instruments endorsed either to order or to bearer.

2. The claims for which the trustee has required affirmation on oath are provisionally admitted until, on the date referred to in the first paragraph of article 120, a final decision is made on their admission depending on whether or not the affirmation on oath took place.

3. The minutes of the meeting are signed by the bankruptcy judge and the clerk of the court.

4. The admission of a claim recorded in the minutes of the meeting is final in the bankruptcy. The trustee may only assert the nullity of such a claim in the event of fraud.

Article 122

1. If a claim is disputed and the bankruptcy judge is unable to reconcile the parties and the dispute is not already the subject of proceedings, the bankruptcy judge will refer the matter to the court and no writ of summons is required to be served.

2. The attorneys-at-law representing the parties will make a statement to that effect at the hearing.

3. If the creditor requesting verification of a claim does not appear at the hearing, his request is deemed to have been withdrawn; if the person who has disputed the claim does not appear, he is deemed to have withdrawn his opposition and in such case the judge will admit the claim.

4. Any creditor who failed to dispute a claim at the creditors' meeting may not join or intervene in the proceedings.

Article 122a

1. If a claim is disputed by the trustee, the proceedings will be adjourned if ratification by the court of a bankruptcy scheme of arrangement has become final, unless the court

has already been asked to render judgment, in which event the claim, if admitted, is considered as admitted in the bankruptcy and the bankrupt will be substituted for the trustee as regards the decision as to who shall bear the costs of the proceedings.

2. The bankrupt may file a notice containing the appointment of another attorney-at-law, in which the bankrupt states that he takes over the proceedings in place of the trustee with effect from the date of issue of the latest court documents.

3. As long as this has not happened, the other party is entitled to summon the bankrupt to take over the proceedings.

4. If the bankrupt does not appear, the first paragraph of article 261 of the Code of Civil Procedure applies.

5. If a claim is disputed by another creditor, the proceedings may be pursued by the parties after the ratification of a bankruptcy scheme of arrangement has become final only in order to obtain a decision as to who shall bear the costs of the proceedings.

Article 123

A creditor whose claim is disputed is not obliged to produce any further evidence in support of his claim than he would have to produce to the bankrupt.

Article 124

1. If a creditor whose claim is disputed is not present at the creditors' meeting, the clerk of the court will forthwith notify him of the opposition and of the matter being referred to the court.

2. In the proceedings the creditor may not plead absence of such notification.

Article 125

Claims which are disputed may be provisionally admitted by the bankruptcy judge up to an amount determined by him. If the priority ranking of a claim is disputed, the bankruptcy judge may provisionally allow the priority ranking claimed.

Article 126

1. The bankrupt may also dispute the admission of a claim, either in whole or in part, or the omission of any alleged priority ranking, briefly setting out his grounds for opposing the claim or the priority ranking. In such event the fact of the opposition and the grounds are recorded in the minutes without the parties being referred to the court and without preventing admission of the claim in the bankruptcy.

2. Any opposition which is not supported by a statement of grounds, or which does not include the whole claim and does not indicate which part of the claim is admitted and which part is not, will not be considered.

Article 127

1. Claims which are submitted to the trustee after the period referred to in article 108, first paragraph, but at least two days prior to the day of the creditors' meeting, are admitted at the meeting upon request, unless the trustee or any of the creditors present objects.

2. Claims submitted after this date, will not be verified.

3. The provisions of the first and second paragraph do not apply if the creditor lives outside European Holland and was therefore unable to submit his claim earlier.

4. If objection is raised under the first paragraph or if there is disagreement concerning the inability to submit a claim earlier as referred to in the third paragraph, the bankruptcy judge will determine the matter after consulting the meeting.

Article 128

Interest running after the declaration of bankruptcy may not be verified unless secured by a pledge or mortgage. In that event interest will be verified *pro memoria.* To the extent that the interest is not covered by the proceeds of the security the creditor may not derive any rights from the admission.

Article 129

A claim subject to a condition precedent is verified for the total amount, without altering the effect of the condition when it is fulfilled.

Article 130

1. A claim subject to a condition subsequent may be verified for its value at the date of the declaration of bankruptcy.

2. If the trustee and the creditors are unable to reach agreement on such verification, the claim is conditionally admitted for the full amount.

Article 131

1. A claim with an uncertain due date or which entitles the claimant to periodic payments is verified for its value at the date of the declaration of bankruptcy.

2. Claims which become payable within one year after the bankruptcy declaration are considered payable as of the date of the bankruptcy declaration. Claims which become payable after one year are admitted for their value one year from the date of the bankruptcy declaration.

3. Only the time and method of instalment payments, any profit opportunity and, if the claim bears interest, the agreed rate of the interest, are taken into account in order to determine these values.

Article 132

1. Creditors whose claims are secured by a mortgage or pledge or a right of retention or who have a priority interest in an item and who can prove that it is likely that a part of their claim will not be recovered from the proceeds of the item subject to the security interest, may require that the rights of an unsecured creditor are conferred on them for that part, while they retain priority to the extent of their security interest.

2. The amount which mortgage creditors or pledgees may be able to recover from the proceeds is determined pursuant to article 483e of the Code of Civil Procedure, provided that the time of drafting of the statement is substituted by the beginning of the day when the bankruptcy was declared.

Article 133

Claims having an indefinite or uncertain value, or where the value is not expressed in Netherlands currency or not expressed in a currency at all, are admitted for their estimated value in Netherlands currency.

Article 134

Claims endorsed to bearer may be admitted in the name 'bearer'. Each admitted claim endorsed to bearer is considered as a claim of a separate creditor.

Article 135

Repealed. (Implementation Act 1st January 1992, Books 3, 5 and 6, first part.)

Article 136

1. If one or more than one of many debtors jointly and severally liable under one claim has been declared bankrupt, the creditor may claim against each of the bankruptcy estates of the debtors for the total amount due to him at the time of the declaration of bankruptcy until his claim has been settled in full.

2. A jointly and severally liable debtor may be admitted, if necessary on a provisional basis, for the amounts for which he has, or will obtain, a recourse claim against the bankrupt pursuant to their mutual relationship. The admission may only take place:

(a) to the extent that the creditor is not able to submit a claim, or does not submit a claim even though he is entitled to submit it;
(b) in the event that the creditor is paid during the bankruptcy for the total amount of this alleged claim;
(c) to the extent that, for any other reason, the admission does not prejudice the unsecured creditors in respect of the percentages to be distributed to them.

Article 137

1. After verification of the claims the trustee will submit a report on the bankruptcy estate and will provide all information required by the creditors in connection with the estate. The report and the minutes of the creditors' meeting are filed at the office of the clerk of the court and are open to inspection by everyone free of charge. The filing is also free of charge.

2. After the report and the minutes have been filed the trustee, and also the creditors and the bankrupt, many request the court to amend the minutes if the documents show that the minutes contain a mistake.

Chapter VI: The bankruptcy scheme of arrangement

Article 138

The bankrupt is entitled to offer a scheme of arrangement to his creditors as a body.

Article 139

1. If the bankrupt has filed a draft scheme of arrangement for public inspection free of charge at the office of the clerk of the district court and of the cantonal court referred to in article 97 at least eight days prior to the creditors' meeting, this will be discussed and a decision will be reached on it in the creditors' meeting after the admission of claims, subject always to the provisions of article 141.

2. A copy of the draft bankruptcy scheme of arrangement must be sent to the trustee and the members of the provisional committee of creditors at the same time as it is filed at the office of the clerk of the court.

Article 140

The trustee and the creditors' committee are each obliged to submit a written opinion on the proposed bankruptcy scheme of arrangement.

Article 141

The discussion and the decision will be adjourned for a further meeting which must take place within three weeks on a date appointed by the bankruptcy judge:

(1) if, during the meeting, a definitive committee of creditors is appointed which does not consist of the same persons as the provisional committee and the majority of the creditors present at the meeting require from this committee a written opinion on the proposed bankruptcy scheme of arrangement;
(2) if the draft bankruptcy scheme of arrangement was not filed in time and the majority of the creditors present at the meeting express themselves in favour of an adjournment.

Article 142

If the discussion and vote in respect of the bankruptcy scheme of arrangement are adjourned under the provisions of the previous article, the trustee will forthwith inform any creditor whose claim has been verified or conditionally admitted and who was not present at the meeting by means of a letter containing a summary of the bankruptcy scheme of arrangement.

Article 143

1. Preferred creditors including those creditors whose priority ranking is disputed, are excluded from the voting in the bankruptcy scheme of arrangement unless they have waived their priority interest in favour of the bankruptcy estate prior to the vote.

2. By this waiver they become unsecured creditors even if the bankruptcy scheme of arrangement is not accepted.

Article 144

The bankrupt is entitled to be heard in support of the bankruptcy scheme of arrangement and with regard to amendment of the scheme of arrangement during the meeting.

Article 145

In order to be accepted, the bankruptcy scheme of arrangement must be approved by two thirds of the unsecured creditors with admitted and provisionally admitted claims representing three quarters of the total amount of the admitted or provisionally admitted unsecured claims.

Article 146

If two thirds of the creditors present at the meeting and representing more than half of the total amount of claims carrying voting rights consent to the bankruptcy scheme of arrangement, a second ballot will be taken within eight days without further notification being required. In the second ballot no one is bound by his first vote.

Article 147

Any later changes in the number of creditors or the amount of the claims will not influence the validity of the acceptance or refusal of the bankruptcy scheme of arrangement.

Article 148

1. The minutes of the meeting will set out the contents of the scheme of arrangement, the names of the voting creditors present at the meeting, their vote, the result of the ballot and any further proceedings of the meeting. The minutes are signed by the bankruptcy judge and the clerk of the court.

2. The minutes are available for inspection free of charge at the office of the clerk of the court for a period of eight days.

Article 149

If the documents show that the bankruptcy judge wrongly considered the bankruptcy scheme of arrangement rejected, the creditors who have voted in favour of the scheme of arrangement, and the bankrupt, may request the court to amend the minutes within eight days after the meeting.

Article 150

1. If the bankruptcy scheme of arrangement is accepted, the bankruptcy judge will, before the meeting is closed, appoint the date on which the court will determine the ratification of the scheme of arrangement.

2. If article 149 applies, the court will determine this date by order. The trustee will notify the order to the creditors.

3. The hearing will be held at least eight days and at most fourteen days after the ballot on the scheme of arrangement or, if article 149 applies, after the order of the court.

Article 151

During this period the creditors may advise the bankruptcy judge in writing why they consider the court should refuse to ratify the bankruptcy scheme of arrangement.

Article 152

1. At the hearing fixed for the ratification of the scheme of arrangement the bankruptcy judge will provide a written report and each creditor may explain either in person, by written proxy or through an attorney-at-law why he is either for or against the ratification.

2. The bankrupt is allowed to be heard in support of his interests.

Article 153

1. The court will issue its reasoned decision on that same date or as soon as possible thereafter.

2. The court will refuse to ratify the bankruptcy scheme of arrangement:

(1) if the assets of the estate considerably exceed the liabilities of the estate under the bankruptcy scheme of arrangement;
(2) if the performance of the bankruptcy scheme of arrangement is insufficiently secured;
(3) if the bankruptcy scheme of arrangement was concluded as a result of fraudulent transactions or the undue preference of one or more creditors or other unfair means and regardless of whether the bankrupt or any other party co-operated to this effect.

3. The court may also refuse to approve the scheme of arrangement on other grounds or of its own motion.

Article 154

If the court refuses to ratify the bankruptcy scheme of arrangement, the creditors who voted in favour of the scheme of arrangement, and also the bankrupt, may file an appeal within eight days after the order; the same applies to the creditors who voted against or who were not present at the ballot if the scheme of arrangement is approved. In the latter case the creditors who voted in favour of the scheme of arrangement, have the same right, but only if one or more of the grounds referred to under article 153, third paragraph, is discovered by them after the ratification of the bankruptcy scheme of arrangement.

Article 155

1. Appeal proceedings will be instituted by submitting a petition to the office of the clerk of the court of appeal which will hear the matter. The president of the court of appeal will forthwith appoint the date and time of the hearing which must take place within twenty days. The clerk of the court before which the appeal proceedings were instituted will forthwith notify the clerk of the court which issued the order relating to the ratification of the scheme of arrangement.

2. Article 152 and article 153, first paragraph, apply to the appeal proceedings with the exception of the provisions relating to the bankruptcy judge.

Article 156

Review proceedings must be initiated and heard within the same terms and in the same way and manner.

Article 157

A bankruptcy scheme of arrangement which has been ratified is binding on all unsecured creditors without exception, regardless of whether or not they have filed their claim with the trustee.

Article 158

After the court has refused to approve a bankruptcy scheme of arrangement or after the ratification has been rejected, the bankrupt may not offer another bankruptcy scheme of arrangement in the same bankruptcy.

Article 159

Once ratification of the bankruptcy scheme of arrangement has become final, this, together with the minutes of the creditors' meeting, will constitute a writ of execution against the bankrupt and any guarantors acceded to the bankruptcy scheme of arrangement, on behalf of those creditors whose claims have been admitted and have not been disputed by the bankrupt in accordance with article 126.

Article 160

Notwithstanding the scheme of arrangement the creditors will retain all their rights against any guarantors and other co-debtors of the bankrupt. Any rights which they may have over goods belonging to third parties are maintained as if no bankruptcy scheme of arrangement had been concluded.

Article 161

As soon as the ratification of the scheme of arrangement has become final, the bankruptcy will terminate. The trustee will arrange for this to be announced in the journals referred to in the third paragraph of article 14.

Article 162

1. After the ratification of the scheme of arrangement has become final, the trustee must account to the bankrupt before the bankruptcy judge.

2. Unless the scheme arrangement provides otherwise, the trustee will release to the bankrupt all goods, moneys, books and documents belonging to the bankrupt estate.

Article 163

1. Any amount which may be claimed by admitted creditors under an admitted priority interest, and the costs of the bankruptcy, will be paid to the trustee unless the bankrupt has issued security therefor. As long as this requirement has not been fulfilled, the trustee must retain all moneys and goods belonging to the bankrupt estate until this amount and the costs referred to have been paid to the appropriate parties.

2. If after one month following ratification of the bankruptcy scheme of arrangement no payment has been made by or on behalf of the bankrupt, the trustee will proceed with payment of these amounts from the assets of the estate.

3. If necessary, the amount referred to in the first paragraph and the parts of it attributable to each creditor under his priority interest will be estimated by the bankruptcy judge.

Article 164

In the case of claims where the priority interest has been provisionally admitted, the obligation of the bankrupt referred to in the previous article is limited to issuing security; in the absence of the issue of such security the trustee must only reserve from the assets of the bankrupt estate the amount to which the priority interest relates.

Article 165

1. Any creditor whom the bankrupt fails to satisfy under the bankruptcy scheme of arrangement may request dissolution of the scheme of arrangement as ratified.
2. The bankrupt must prove that he has performed his obligations under the bankruptcy scheme of arrangement.
3. The judge may on application or on his own motion grant an extension of one month to the bankrupt to perform his obligations.

Article 166

Any claim to dissolve the bankruptcy scheme of arrangement must be instituted and determined in the same way as provided in articles 4, 6–9 and 12 in respect of the bankruptcy petition.

Article 167

1. A judgment by which a bankruptcy scheme of arrangement is dissolved will also contain an order to reopen the bankruptcy and to appoint a bankruptcy judge and a trustee together with a creditors' committee, if such committee had already existed in the bankruptcy.
2. It is preferable for the same persons to be appointed who occupied these positions earlier in the bankruptcy.
3. The trustee will arrange for the judgment to be announced as provided under article 14, third paragraph.

Article 168

1. Articles 13, first paragraph, 15–18 and those contained in the second, third and fourth chapter of this title, will apply if the bankruptcy is reopened.
2. The provisions of the chapter on the verification of claims apply likewise save that the verification is limited to claims which had not been verified before.
3. Nevertheless the creditors whose claims have already been verified are also invited to attend the creditors' meeting and they have the right to dispute any claims for which admission is sought.

Article 169

Any transactions performed by the bankrupt in the period between the ratification by the court of the bankruptcy scheme by arrangement and the reopening of the bankruptcy are binding on the estate, subject to the application of article 42 and the following articles, if there are grounds for those articles to apply.

Article 170

1. When a bankruptcy has been reopened, no further bankruptcy scheme of arrangement may be offered to the creditors.

2. The trustee will forthwith proceed with the liquidation of the estate.

Article 171

1. If, at the time when the bankruptcy is reopened, the bankruptcy scheme of arrangement has been performed in whole or in part as against some creditors, at the distribution under the reopened bankruptcy the amounts promised under the bankruptcy scheme of arrangement will be paid in advance to the new creditors and to those among the old creditors who at that time had not yet received payment, and creditors who had received partial payment will receive, also in advance, the balance of the amount promised.

2. Any amount remaining in the estate will be equally divided among all the creditors, old and new.

Article 172

The previous article will also apply if the estate of the bankrupt is declared bankrupt again before the bankrupt has fully performed the bankruptcy scheme of arrangement.

Chapter VII: Liquidation of the estate

Article 173

1. If no bankruptcy scheme of arrangement has been offered at the creditors' meeting or if the proposed bankruptcy scheme of arrangement has been rejected or ratification of it has been finally refused by the court, the estate is insolvent at law.

2. Articles 98 and 100 will cease to apply when the decision has been taken in accordance with the following articles that the business of the bankrupt will not be continued or when the business ceases after having been continued.

Article 173a

1. If no bankruptcy scheme of arrangement has been offered at the creditors' meeting or if the proposed bankruptcy scheme of arrangement has been rejected, the trustee or a creditor present at the meeting may propose that the business of the bankrupt be continued.

2. The creditors' committee, if any, and the trustee in the event that the proposal has been made by a creditor, will advise on this proposal.

3. At the request of the trustee or of any of the creditors present the bankruptcy judge will adjourn the discussion and the decision on the proposal until a meeting which must take place within fourteen days.

4. The trustee will forthwith notify the creditors who were not present at the meeting of such later meeting by letter setting out the proposal and drawing their attention to article 114.

5. During this meeting the claims which were submitted after the time provided in article 108, paragraph 1, and which have not already been verified under article 127, will be verified. The trustee will act in respect of these claims in accordance with the provisions of articles 111–114.

Article 173b

1. The proposal will be accepted if creditors representing more than half of the admitted and provisionally admitted creditors whose claims are not secured by pledge or mortgage or right of retention declare themselves in favour of the proposal.

2. In such event, and if there is no creditors' committee, article 75 will likewise apply.

3. The minutes of the meeting will list the names of the creditors present at the meeting, their votes, the result of the ballot, and any further proceedings of the meeting.

4. The minutes will be available for inspection at the office of the clerk of the court for a period of eight days.

Article 173c

1. If, within eight days after ratification of the bankruptcy scheme of arrangement has been finally refused by the court, the trustee or a creditor submits a proposal to the bankruptcy judge to continue the business of the bankrupt, the bankruptcy judge will immediately order a creditors' meeting at a date, time and place determined by him in order to discuss and decide on the proposal.

2. The trustee will notify the creditors at least ten days prior to the meeting by letter, setting out the proposal and drawing their attention to article 114. He will also make an announcement in the journals referred to in article 14.

3. Article 173a, paragraphs 2 and 5, and article 173b will apply.

Article 173d

The trustee and the creditors may request the court within eight days after the meeting to declare that the proposal has been accepted or rejected if it appears from the documents that the bankruptcy judge wrongly considered the proposal rejected or accepted.

Article 174

1. At the request of a creditor or the trustee, the bankruptcy judge may order the continuation of the business to cease. The creditors' committee, if any, and the trustee, if the request was not made by him, will be heard.

2. The bankruptcy judge may also hear each creditor and the bankrupt.

Article 175

1. If a proposal to continue the business is not made or is not made in time or if the business ceases after having been continued, the trustee will forthwith proceed with the liquidation and sale of the estate without requiring the consent or cooperation of the bankrupt.

2. The bankrupt may keep some household effects as determined by the bankruptcy judge.

3. Even if the business is continued, assets of the estate which are not essential for the continuation of the business may be sold.

Article 176

1. The assets will be sold either in a public sale or, with the consent of the bankruptcy judge, in a private sale.

2. The trustee will dispose of items which are not capable of being sold quickly or at all in a manner approved by the bankruptcy judge.

Article 177

The trustee may make use of the services of the bankrupt in the liquidation at a level of remuneration to be determined by the bankruptcy judge.

Article 178

After the bankrupt has become insolvent, the bankruptcy judge may order a creditors' meeting at a date, hour and place determined by him in order to discuss, if necessary, the liquidation of the estate and to verify any claims submitted after the time referred to in article 108, paragraph 1 and which have not yet been admitted in accordance with article 127. In respect of these claims the trustee will act in accordance with articles 111–114. At least ten days prior to the meeting he will send a letter to the creditors summoning them to the meeting and setting out the issues of the meeting and drawing their attention to article 114. He will also make a similar announcement in the journals referred to in article 14.

Article 179

Whenever the bankruptcy judge considers that there are sufficient funds available he will order a payment to the admitted creditors.

Article 180

1. The trustee will prepare a plan of the distributions and submit this to the bankruptcy judge for his approval. The plan will contain an account of the revenue and expenditure (including the fee of the trustee), the names of the creditors and the verified amount of each claim together with the amount to be paid.

2. The percentage dividend as determined by the bankruptcy judge will be reserved for the unsecured creditors. For the preferred creditors, regardless of whether their priority interest is disputed, who have not been paid in accordance with the provisions of article 57 or 60, paragraph 3, the amount for which they are secured will be reserved from the proceeds of sale of the assets to which their priority interest related. If the proceeds are less than the total amount of their claims, the balance, or, if the assets to which the priority interest related have not yet been sold, the amount of their total claim will be reserved in the same percentage dividend as the unsecured creditors.

Article 181

In the distribution plan the percentage dividend to be reserved for provisionally admitted claims is calculated by reference to the total amount of the claims.

Article 182

1. The general bankruptcy costs are apportioned over each part of the estate with the exception of any part which, after execution in accordance with article 57 or 60, third paragraph, second sentence, vests in creditors secured by a pledge or mortgage or with a right of retention, or to creditors with limited preferential rights, tenants and lessees whose right has expired or been lost because of the execution, but including the amount paid to the trustee for the benefit of a creditor who ranked above one or more of the above-mentioned creditors.

2. The exception referred to in the previous paragraph also applies to aircraft sold by a creditor in accordance with article 38 of the law on registered aircraft.

Article 183

1. The distribution plan approved by the bankruptcy judge will be available for inspection by the creditors free of charge at the office of the clerk of the court for a period of ten days.

2. The trustee will also file a copy for the same purpose with the office of the clerk of the cantonal court referred to in article 97. No charge will be made for this filing.

3. The trustee will arrange for the filing of the distribution plan to be announced in the journals referred to in article 14. The filing will also be notified to each of the creditors whose claim has been admitted or provisionally admitted with a note of the amount reserved for him.

Article 184

1. During the period referred to in the previous article each creditor may oppose the distribution plan by submitting a petition to the clerk of the court against receipt.

2. The petition will be attached to the distribution plan.

Article 185

1. If a petition disputing the distribution plan has been filed, the bankruptcy judge will determine the date on which the petition will be heard at a public hearing immediately after the inspection period. The order to this effect will be available for inspection free of charge at the office of the clerk of the court. The clerk of the court will also give written notification to the petitioners and to the trustee. The day of the hearing may not be later than fourteen days after expiry of the period referred to in article 183.

2. At the hearing the bankruptcy judge will submit a written report and the trustee and each of the creditors, either in person or by proxy or represented by an attorney-at-law, may submit grounds in support of or against the distribution plan.

3. The court will issue its reasoned order on the same date or as soon as possible thereafter.

Article 186

1. A creditor whose claim has not been verified and a creditor whose claim has been verified for an insufficient amount, albeit in accordance with his own statement, may also file a petition disputing the distribution plan, provided always that he submitted his claim, or the unverified part of it, to the trustee at least two days prior to the day of

the hearing, has attached a copy of his claim, as submitted, to the petition and has also requested in the petition that this claim be admitted.

2. Verification as provided under article 119 and the following articles will then take place at the public hearing at which the petition disputing the distribution plan is heard and before this hearing has started.

3. If the only purpose of the petition disputing the distribution plan is the admission of a claim and if no one else has filed a petition disputing the distribution plan, the costs of the proceedings will be borne by the negligent creditor.

Article 187

1. Within eight days after the court has issued its order the trustee and each creditor may file a request to review such order.

2. The review must be requested by means of a petition filed with the office of the clerk of the supreme court. The president of the supreme court will forthwith determine the date and time of the hearing which must take place within twenty days. The clerk of the supreme court will immediately notify the clerk of the court which issued the order in opposition.

3. The review request will be heard at a public hearing. The trustee and all creditors may attend the hearing.

4. The distribution plan will become binding after expiry of the period provided under article 183 or, if it has been disputed, after the order relating to it has become final.

Article 188

1. Upon transfer following a sale by the trustee and payment of the purchase price, all mortgages on the item sold will lapse and any limited preferential rights which may not be invoked against the admitted creditors will expire.

2. Upon request, the bankruptcy judge will issue a statement to the buyer of the lapsed and expired rights. This statement may be registered in the registers at the time of or after the transfer. The statement will then authorise the keeper of the registers to delete the registrations involved.

3. Article 575 of the Code of Civil Procedure applies to sales by the trustee of any ships which belong to the estate.

Article 189

1. The amount reserved for a creditor whose claim has been provisionally admitted will not be paid as long as no decision has been made in respect of his claim. If the final result is that he has nothing to claim or that his claim is reduced, the moneys which have been reserved for him will be retained for the benefit of the other creditors either in whole or in part.

2. Payments reserved for claims where the prior ranking is disputed and where the payments may amount to more than the percentage dividend to be paid on unsecured claims are postponed until a decision on the priority has been made.

Article 190

If an asset charged with a priority interest is sold after a payment has been made to the secured creditor pursuant to article 179 in connection with the last part of article 180, he will only receive in any later distribution the amount to which his priority ranking in the proceeds of sale of the asset entitles him after deduction of the percentage dividend which he already received on his claim.

Article 191

1. Creditors whose claims are only verified after payments have taken place due to their negligence, will receive an amount in advance from the available funds which is proportional to the amounts already received by the other admitted creditors.

2. If they are secured creditors, they will forfeit their priority interest to the extent that the proceeds of sale of the asset to which the priority attached have already been allocated to other creditors with a priority right.

Article 192

After expiry of the inspection period referred to in article 183, or after an order in respect of the petition disputing the distribution plan is issued, the trustee is obliged to proceed immediately with payment. Any amounts not disposed of within one month or reserved pursuant to article 189 will be deposited by him with the court.

Article 193

1. As soon as the admitted creditors have received the full amount of their claims or as soon as the final distribution plan has become binding, the bankruptcy will terminate save as provided in article 194. This will be announced by the trustee in accordance with article 14.

2. After one month the trustee will account for his administration to the bankruptcy judge.

3. Any books and documents which the trustee found in the estate will be surrendered by him to the bankrupt against proper receipt.

Article 194

If, after the final distribution pursuant to article 189, amounts reserved flow back into the estate or if it appears that funds may still be available to the estate which were not known at the time of the liquidation, the court will order the trustee to proceed with the liquidation and distribution thereof on the basis of the previous plans of distribution.

Chapter VIII: The position of the bankrupt in law after the liquidation

Article 195

After the final plan of distribution has become binding, the creditors' execution rights on the goods of the bankrupt are restored to them to the extent that their claims have remained unpaid.

Article 196

Admission of a claim in accordance with the fourth paragraph of article 121 is binding on the bankrupt; the minutes of the creditors' meeting provide executory title regarding the admitted claims.

Article 197

The previous article does not apply if and to the extent that the claim has been disputed by the bankrupt in accordance with article 126.

Chapter IX: Bankruptcy of the estate of a deceased person

Article 198

The estate of a deceased person will be declared bankrupt, if one or more creditors has filed a petition for bankruptcy and has proved that the deceased had ceased to pay his debts or that the inheritance at the time of death was not sufficient to pay the debts of the deceased.

Article 199

1. The petition is submitted to the court which was competent to declare the bankruptcy at the time of the death of the debtor.

2. The heirs will be heard or summoned to be heard by a writ served at the domicile of the deceased without it being necessary to mention them by their specific names and, to the extent that they are known, also by means of a letter from the clerk of the court.

Article 200

The declaration of bankruptcy takes effect at law to separate the estate of the deceased from the estate of his heirs in accordance with article 1153 of the Civil Code.

Article 201

A petition for a declaration of bankruptcy may be filed up to three months after acceptance of the estate by the heirs and up to six months after the death of the debtor.

Article 202

The sixth chapter of this title does not apply to the bankruptcy of the estate of a deceased person; nor does the eighth chapter unless the inheritance has been accepted unconditionally.

Chapter X: Provisions of international law

Article 203

A creditor whose claim has been satisfied either in whole or in part after the declaration of bankruptcy from assets of the bankrupt which are abroad and not charged by way of security must pay the amount recovered into the bankruptcy estate.

Article 204

1. A creditor who assigns his claim against the bankrupt, either in whole or in part, to a third party in order to enable the third party to recover the claim, either in whole

or in part, from assets of the bankrupt which are abroad, must pay the amount recovered into the bankruptcy estate.

2. Unless proved to the contrary, the assignment is deemed to have been effected with this purpose if it was known to the parties that an application for bankruptcy had been made or would be made.

Article 205

1. A similar obligation to pay any amount recovered into the estate lies with any creditor who assigns his claim or his debt, either in whole or in part, to a third party who is then in a position to effect a payment abroad which is not allowed under the present law.

2. The second paragraph of the previous article applies.

Chapter XI: Rehabilitation

Article 206

After the bankruptcy has terminated in accordance with articles 161 or 193, the bankrupt, or his heirs, also if article 198 applies, may submit a petition for rehabilitation to the court which has ordered the bankruptcy.

Article 207

This petition is not admissible unless proof is submitted together with it that all admitted creditors have been paid to their satisfaction.

Article 208

The petition is announced in the Netherlands State Gazette and in one or more journals indicated by the court.

Article 209

1. Each admitted creditor may oppose the petition within two months after the announcement by means of a reasoned notice of objection submitted to the office of the clerk of the court; the clerk of the court will issue a receipt for the notice of objection.

2. The only possible ground for opposition is that article 207 has not been duly performed.

Article 210

After expiry of this period of two months the court will either allow or refuse the petition upon the advice of the public prosecutor and regardless of whether or not opposition has been filed.

Article 211

No further appeal lies against the decision of the court.

Article 212

The judgment allowing the rehabilitation is pronounced at a public hearing and is also recorded in the register referred to in article 19.

TITLE II. SUSPENSION OF PAYMENTS

Chapter I: Suspension of payments and its consequences

Article 213

A debtor who foresees that he will be unable to continue to pay his debts which have accrued due may apply for suspension of payments.

Article 214

1. To this end he must submit to the court referred to in articles 2 or 3 a petition which is accompanied by a statement in the form referred to in article 96 which in turn is supported by the necessary documents and is signed by himself and his attorney-at-law.

2. A draft suspension of payments scheme of arrangement may be added to the petition.

Article 215

1. The petition together with the relevant documents will be filed at the office of the clerk of the court for public inspection free of charge.

2. The court will immediately allow the provisional suspension of payments requested and will appoint one or more administrators who will administer the affairs of the debtor together with the debtor. The court will also order the known creditors and the debtor to be summoned by the clerk of the court by letter on a date appointed by the court in order to be heard on the petition before the court decides on the final grant of the suspension of payments. The summons will refer to the date and place of the hearing and will state whether or not a draft suspension of payments scheme of arrangement was added to the petition.

Article 216

The clerk of the court will forthwith make a public announcement in the Netherlands State Gazette, and in one or more journals indicated by the court, of the submission of the petition, the provisional suspension of payments, the name of the suspension of payments judge, if any, the names and addresses of the administrators appointed and the date determined in accordance with the second paragraph of the previous article. The announcement will also state whether or not a draft suspension of payments scheme of arrangement was added to the petition.

Article 217

The suspension of payments is considered effective as of the beginning of the day on which it was provisionally granted.

Article 218

1. On the appointed day the court in chambers will hear the debtor, the suspension of payments judge, if any, the administrators and the creditors present either in person or by proxy or represented by an attorney-at-law. A creditor is allowed to attend the hearing even if he has not been summoned to it.

2. The court may grant final suspension of payments unless objection is made either by creditors holding more than one fourth of the total amount of the claims represented at the hearing and referred to in article 233 or by more than one third in number of the creditors holding such claims.

3. In the event of a dispute the court will decide whether or not a creditor is eligible to vote.

4. Final suspension of payments will never be granted if there are good grounds for suspecting that the debtor will try to prejudice the creditors during the suspension of payments or if it is not anticipated that the debtor will be able to pay his creditors in due course.

5. If the court rejects the petition it may declare the debtor bankrupt by the same order. If bankruptcy is not ordered, the provisional suspension of payments is maintained until the court order has become final.

6. If the petition for a declaration of bankruptcy and the petition for suspension of payments are submitted simultaneously, the petition for suspension of payments will be heard first.

7. The order issued on the application will be fully reasoned and will be pronounced at a public hearing.

Article 219

1. If the application is rejected, the debtor may appeal within eight days following the date of the judgment; if the application is allowed, each creditor who has not declared himself in favour of the petition, may appeal within eight days following the date of the judgment.

2. The appeal is instituted by a petition to the clerk of the court of appeal to be seized with the matter. The president of the court will forthwith determine the date and hour of the hearing.

3. If the appeal is lodged by a creditor he will inform, by means of a writ, the attorney-at-law who has submitted the petition for suspension of payments within four days that an appeal has been commenced and the date and time of the hearing. This writ serves as summons on the debtor.

4. The clerk of the court of appeal will announce the appeal and the date and time of the hearing in the journals in which the application for suspension of payments was announced under article 216. He will also notify the appeal to the clerk of the court from whom he receives the documents referred to in article 214 which are then filed in his office for inspection free of charge.

Article 220

1. At the appeal hearing the application will not be re-submitted to vote but each creditor is entitled to participate either in person or by proxy or represented by an attorney-at-law, in opposing or supporting the judgment under appeal.

2. The hearing takes place in chambers. The judgment is pronounced at a public hearing.

Article 221

1. If the suspension of payments has been refused the debtor may apply for a review of the judgment issued by the court of appeal within eight days following the judgment; and, if suspension of payments has been granted, each creditor who has not declared himself in favour of the application may also request a review of the judgment issued by the court of appeal within eight days following the date of the judgment.

2. The review proceedings are instituted by a petition to the clerk of the supreme court. The president of the court will forthwith determine the date and time of the hearing.

3. The clerk of the supreme court will announce the application for review and the date and time of the hearing in the journals in which the application for suspension of payments was announced pursuant to article 216. He will also notify the clerk of the court of appeal from whom he receives the documents referred to in article 214 which are filed in his office for inspection free of charge.

4. The provisions of the third paragraph of article 219 and of the second paragraph of article 220 apply accordingly.

Article 222

1. The order by which suspension of payments is finally granted is enforceable irrespective of appeal.

2. It is announced in the manner provided in article 216.

Article 222a

1. The clerk of each court will keep a public register setting out for each suspension of payments the date and:

(1) an extract from the court order granting provisional or final suspension of payments or extending or terminating a suspension of payments;
(2) the appointment of a suspension of payments judge;
(3) a summary of the contents of the suspension of payments scheme of arrangement and the ratification of it by the court;
(4) the dissolution of the suspension of payments scheme of arrangement.

2. Further rules as to the form and contents of the register are provided by order in council.

3. The clerk of the court is obliged to keep the register available for inspection by the public free of charge and to provide transcripts and extracts from the register against payment.

Article 223

1. When suspension of payments is finally granted, the court will determine its duration at one and a half years at most. If the suspension of payments is terminated because this period has expired, the administrators will announce this in the journals referred to in article 216.

2. Prior to the termination of the suspension of payments the debtor may once or more often apply for an extension for at most one and a half years. The application is heard in the

same manner as an application for suspension of payments. If at the time of termination of a suspension of payments no decision is made on an application for extension, the suspension of payments will be maintained until such decision is made. The order issued by the court will be announced in the manner provided in the first paragraph.

Article 223a

At the time when the suspension of payments is provisionally granted or at any later date the court may appoint one of its members as suspension of payments judge in order to advise the administrators.

Article 223b

1. At the request of the administrators the suspension of payments judge may hear witnesses or order an experts' investigation to clarify the circumstances concerning the suspension of payments. The witnesses are summoned on behalf of the bankruptcy judge. Article 203 of the Code of Civil Procedure applies by analogy.

2. In the event of non-appearance or refusal to take the oath or to testify, articles 197-201 of the Code of Civil Procedure will apply by analogy.

3. The spouse or former spouse, the children and further descendants and the parents and grandparents of the debtor may be exempt from giving testimony.

Article 224

1. If more than one administrator has been appointed, the consent of the majority of the administrators or, in the event of a split vote, a decision of the suspension of payments judge, if appointed, or in the absence of a suspension of payments judge, a decision of the president of the court, is required in order to make their acts legally binding. The second paragraph of article 70 applies by analogy.

2. The court is competent to dismiss an administrator at all times after he has been heard or properly summoned and to replace him by someone else or to appoint one or more co-administrators, all this either at his own request or at the request of the other administrators or of one or more of the creditors or on the recommendation of the suspension of payments judge, if appointed, or on the court's own motion.

Article 225

1. In the order granting provisional suspension of payments the court will make such provisions as it considers necessary to safeguard the interests of the creditors.

2. The court may also act in this way during the suspension of payments on the recommendation of the suspension of payments judge, if appointed, or at the request of the administrators or of one or more creditors or on the court's own motion.

Article 226

1. When the suspension of payments has been provisionally granted, the court may appoint one or more experts in order to investigate the position of the estate and to submit a report of their findings within a period determined by the court which may be extended. The last paragraph of article 225 applies by analogy.

2. The experts' report will contain a fully reasoned opinion on the reliability of the statement and documents submitted by the debtor and on the likelihood that the debt-

or will be able to pay his creditors in due course. The report will indicate, if possible, the measures which must be taken to achieve the payment of creditors.

3. The experts will file their report at the office of the clerk of the court for public inspection free of charge. No charge will be made for the filing of the report.

4. The final paragraph of article 224 will apply by analogy with regard to the experts

Article 227

1. Every three months the administrators will report on the position of the estate. This report will be filed as provided in the third paragraph of article 226.

2. The period referred to in the previous paragraph may be extended by the bankruptcy judge, if appointed, or, if not, by the court.

Article 228

1. During the suspension of payments, the debtor may not perform any act in relation to the control or disposal of the estate without the cooperation, authorisation or assistance of the administrators. If the debtor is in breach of this provision, the administrators are entitled to do everything necessary to ensure that the estate is not prejudiced.

2. The estate is only liable for obligations entered into by the debtor after the beginning of the suspension of payments without the cooperation, authorisation or assistance of the administrators to the extent to which the estate has benefited therefrom.

Article 229

If the debtor shares the ownership of his property with his spouse, the revenue and costs of this property are included in the estate.

Articles 61 and 62 apply accordingly.

Article 230

1. During the suspension of payments the debtor may not be compelled to pay the debts referred to in article 233 and all foreclosure actions to recover these debts are suspended.

2. Unless so ordered by the court at an earlier date at the request of the administrators, any attachments made will expire and a debtor who is imprisoned will be released as soon as the order granting the suspension of payments or ratifying the suspension of payments scheme of arrangement has become final. The registration of a statement to this effect issued by the suspension of payments judge, if any, or otherwise by the president of the court at the request of the administrators, will authorise the keeper of the public registers to delete the attachments.

3. The provisions of the preceding paragraphs do not apply to executions and attachments commenced in connection with claims secured by a priority right over certain assets in so far as the assets to which the priority right relates are concerned.

4. Article 36 applies by analogy to the debts referred to in the first paragraph.

Article 231

1. Suspension of payments does not stop any pending proceedings or prevent the commencement of new proceedings.

2. If however the proceedings merely concern a claim for payment of a debt acknowledged by the debtor, and the plaintiff does not require a judgment in order to assert rights against third parties, the judge may, after noting the acknowledgement of the claim, adjourn judgment until the suspension of payments has terminated.

3. Without the cooperation of the administrators the debtor may not act in court either as plaintiff or as defendant in legal proceedings relating to rights and obligations of the estate.

Article 232

1. Suspension of payments does not take effect in respect of:

(1) preferred claims except in so far as these may not be recovered from the assets to which the priority right relates;
(2) claims for maintenance, care or education costs which constitute legal obligations and which have been determined by an agreement or by a judgment unless accrued prior to the suspension of payments and the court has determined the amount which is subject to the suspension of payments;
(3) instalments due under hire-purchase agreements (including those relating to ships).

Article 233

Payment of all other debts existing prior to the suspension of payments may only be made during the suspension of payments to all joint creditors in proportion to their claims.

Article 234

1. Set-off is available to a person who is both a debtor and a creditor of the estate if the claim and the debt both arose prior to the suspension of payments or resulted from transactions with the debtor performed prior to the suspension of payments.

2. If necessary the claims against the debtor will be calculated in accordance with the rules set out in articles 261 and 262.

3. An estate under suspension of payments may not invoke article 136 of Book 6 of the Civil Code.

Article 235

1. Nevertheless, a person who has been assigned a debt owed to, or a claim against, the estate before the suspension of payments may not apply for set-off if he has not acted in good faith with respect to such assignment.

2. Set-off is never permitted for claims or debts assigned after the suspension of payments.

3. Articles 55 and 56 apply by analogy.

Article 236

1. If at the beginning of the suspension of payments a contract either has not been performed or has only partially been performed by both the debtor and the other party, and the debtor and the administrators have not declared within a reasonable

term imposed by the other party whether they wish to continue the contract, they will lose their right to claim the performance of the contract. If the debtor and the administrators declare that they will continue to perform the contract, the other party may require security for the proper performance of the contract.

2. These provisions do not apply to contracts in which the debtor's obligations only consist of acts which must be performed by the debtor personally.

Article 236a

Claims which a contracting party has against the debtor pursuant to the dissolution or cancellation of a contract concluded with the debtor prior to the beginning of the suspension of payments, or claims constituting indemnification against failure in the performance of an obligation of the debtor prior to the beginning of the suspension of payments, may be submitted as provided under article 233.

Article 237

If, under the circumstances referred to in article 236, the delivery of goods traded on the commodities market has been fixed to occur at a particular date or within a particular period and either the date occurs or the period expires after the beginning of the suspension of payments, the contract will terminate because of the provisional suspension of payments and the party contracting with the debtor may submit a claim for damages in accordance with article 233. If the estate suffers loss because of the termination of the contract, the other party is obliged to pay this loss.

Article 237a

1. As soon as the suspension of payments has commenced, a debtor who is a hire-purchaser or the seller under a hire-purchase agreement, may declare the hire-purchase agreement terminated, including any hire-purchase agreement for a ship.

2. This termination has the same consequences as the termination of a contract due to non-performance of a buyer's obligations.

3. The seller may submit a claim for the amount due to him in accordance with article 233.

Article 238

1. As soon as the suspension of payments has commenced, a debtor who is a tenant may terminate the tenancy before expiry in accordance with article 228, provided the notice of termination is given for a period of time which is in accordance with local practice for such agreements. The agreed or usual notice period must be observed, provided however that in any event a term of three months is sufficient. If the rent has been paid in advance, the tenancy may only be terminated on the date on which the period covered by the advance payment terminates.

2. The rent is a debt of the estate as from the beginning of the suspension of payments.

3. If the debtor is a leaseholder, this provision will apply by analogy.

Article 239

1. As soon as the suspension of payments has commenced, the debtor may terminate employment contracts with his employees with due regard to the provisions of article 228 and to the contractual or legal notice period, provided however that the

employment may always be terminated at six weeks' notice or, if the notice period prescribed in article 1639j, first and second paragraphs, of the Civil Code is more than six weeks, in accordance with such notice period.

2. As soon as the suspension of payments has commenced, a debtor's employees are not obliged to apply the provisions of article 1639j, first paragraph, of the Civil Code, when terminating their employment contracts.

3. As from the beginning of the suspension of payments, salary and other costs relating to the employment contract are debts of the estate.

4. This article applies by analogy to agency agreements.

Article 240

1. Payment to the debtor after the suspension of payments has provisionally been granted, but before the public announcement thereof, in performance of obligations towards him entered into before the suspension of payments will release the party paying as against the bankruptcy estate as long as it is not proved that he knew of the provisional suspension of payments.

2. The payment referred to in the previous paragraph made to the debtor after the public announcement of the suspension of payments will only release the party paying as against the bankruptcy estate if he proves that the provisional suspension of payments could not have been known at the time through the channel of legally prescribed announcements subject to the right of the administrators to prove that it was nevertheless known to him.

3. Payment to the debtor will in any event release the party paying from liability to the bankruptcy estate to the extent that the payment accrued to the benefit of the estate.

Article 241

Suspension of payments does not take effect in favour of guarantors and other debtors.

Article 241a

1. At the request of the debtor or the administrator the court may issue an order stipulating that rights of recourse of third parties either against assets belonging to the estate or to claim assets which are in the control of the debtor or the administrators may be executed only with the authorisation of the court or, if appointed, of the suspension of payments judge, for a period of one month at most. The court may extend this period once for at most one month.

2. The court may limit its order to certain third parties and attach conditions thereto. The court and the suspension of payments judge may attach conditions to the authorisation of a third party to execute a right to which he is entitled.

3. During the periods referred to in the first paragraph, any other periods of time imposed in respect of the entitlements of third parties will continue, in as far as may reasonably be required to enable the third party or the debtor or the administrators to determine his standpoint after expiry of such periods. The party imposing the period of time is entitled to impose a further reasonable period of time.

Article 242

1. After suspension of payments has been granted it may be terminated either upon recommendation of the suspension of payments judge, if appointed, or on the applica-

tion of the administrators or of one or more of the creditors or on the court's own motion:

(1) if the debtor has acted in bad faith in administering the estate during the suspension of payments;
(2) if the debtor attempts to prejudice his creditors;
(3) if the debtor acts in breach of article 228, first paragraph;
(4) if the debtor fails to perform any transactions imposed upon him by the court at the time the suspension of payments was granted, or at a later date, or which the administrators require him to perform in the interests of the estate;
(5) if, pending the suspension of payments, the estate appears to be in a position where it is no longer desirable to maintain the suspension of payments or if it is unlikely that the debtor will be able to pay his creditors in due course.

2. In the circumstances referred to in sub-paragraphs (1) and (5) the administrators are obliged to apply for termination of the suspension of payments.

3. The petitioner, the debtor and the administrators will be heard or duly summoned. The summons will be issued by the clerk of the court for a date appointed by the court. The order must contain the reasons for the court's decision.

4. If suspension of payments is terminated under this article, the bankruptcy of the debtor may be declared in the same order. If bankruptcy is not declared, the suspension of payments is maintained until the order of the court has become final.

Article 243

1. Within eight days following the order, if the suspension of payments is terminated, the debtor may appeal against the order of the court, and, if the termination of the suspension has been refused, the party who made the application to terminate the suspension has the right to appeal against the order of the court.

2. The appeal is commenced by way of petition submitted to the clerk of the court of appeal seized with the matter. The clerk of the court of appeal will forthwith notify the clerk of the court which issued the order.

3. The president of the court of appeal will determine forthwith the date and time of the hearing of the matter. Without delay the clerk of the court of appeal will summon the parties which requested termination of the suspension of payments, the debtor and the administrators to appear at the hearing.

4. The clerk of the court of appeal will forthwith notify the clerk of the district court of the order issued by the court of appeal.

Article 244

1. During a period of eight days following the order of the court of appeal the unsuccessful party has the right to apply for a review.

2. Review proceedings are instituted by means of a petition submitted to the clerk of the supreme court. The clerk of the supreme court will forthwith notify the clerk of the district court.

3. The president of the supreme court will determine forthwith the date and time of the hearing of the matter. Without delay the clerk of the court of appeal will summon the parties involved to appear at the hearing. The clerk of the supreme court will forthwith notify the clerk of the district court of the order issued by the supreme court.

Article 245

As soon as an order terminating suspension of payments has become final, this will be announced in public as provided under article 216.

Article 246

1. If the court considers that the hearing of the application to terminate the suspension of payments will not have been completed before the date on which the creditors are heard as provided in article 215, second paragraph, the court will order the clerk of the court to inform the creditors in writing that their hearing will not be held on this date.

2. If necessary the court will later appoint another date for this hearing; the creditors will be summoned by the clerk of the court.

Article 247

1. The debtor may always request the court to terminate the suspension of payments on the grounds that the financial position of the estate allows him to commence paying his debts. The administrators and, if final suspension of payments has been granted, the creditors, are heard or duly summoned.

2. The summons will be issued in writing by the clerk of the court at a date fixed by the court.

Article 248

1. It is impossible to request the bankruptcy of the debtor during suspension of payments otherwise than pursuant to the provisions of this title.

2. If a bankruptcy is declared pursuant to the provisions of this title, article 14 will apply by analogy; if the bankruptcy is terminated pursuant to these provisions, articles 13 and 15 will apply by analogy.

Article 249

1. If bankruptcy is declared pursuant to the provisions of this title, or within one month after termination of a suspension of payments, the following provisions will apply:

(1) time counts from the commencement of the suspension of payments for the purposes of the periods referred to in articles 43 and 45 of the present law and in articles 138, sixth paragraph, and 248, sixth paragraph, of Book 2 of the Civil Code;

(2) the trustee has the powers attributed to the administrators in the first paragraph of article 228;

(3) transactions performed by the debtor with the cooperation, approval or assistance of the administrators are deemed to be transactions of the trustee, and debts of the estate incurred during the suspension of payments will be deemed to be debts of the estate in the bankruptcy;

(4) the estate is not liable for obligations of the debtor entered into during the suspension of payments without the cooperation, approval or assistance of the administrators save to the extent that the estate has benefited as a consequence thereof.

2. If an application is made for suspension of payments within one month after the termination of an earlier suspension, the provisions of the first paragraph will also apply in respect of the period of the next suspension.

Article 250

1. The administrators' fees and the fees of experts appointed pursuant to the provisions of article 226 are determined by the court and are paid as the highest ranking preferential claims.
2. This also applies to their expenses and to the expenses of the clerk incurred in accordance with the provisions of this title.

Article 250a

1. If the Central Bank of the Netherlands considers that a company or institution which is not registered in accordance with articles 13 or 30, third paragraph, of the law governing finance companies, and following enquiries under this law by the Central Bank, is unable to pay its immediate debts, the Central Bank may, with the consent of the president of the competent court, apply for a suspension of payments of such company or institution in the manner provided in article 214, first paragraph.
2. The president of the court will decide as soon as possible on an application for the consent referred to in the first paragraph but only after the company or institution has been given an opportunity to submit its views on the matter.
3. In the event referred to in the first paragraph the suspension will not become final if the company or institution opposes the application.
4. Articles 215–250 and 251 apply by analogy.
5. If the application is refused on a ground other than contained in the third paragraph, the Central Bank has the right to appeal and to apply for a review in accordance with the provisions of articles 215 and 221. The Central Bank is allowed to participate in the hearing of both the appeal and the review.

Article 251

The provisions relating to foreign jurisdictions in articles 203 and 205 apply by analogy in the event of suspension of payments.

Chapter II: The suspension of payments scheme of arrangement

Article 252

Upon submitting an application for suspension of payments, or at any later date, the debtor may offer a scheme of arrangement to those creditors who are affected by the suspension.

Article 253

1. If the draft scheme of arrangement has not already been filed at the office of the clerk of the court under article 215, it will be filed there for public inspection free of charge.

2. The administrators and experts must be sent a copy as soon as possible.

Article 254

The draft scheme of arrangement will terminate if a court decision relating to the termination of the suspension of payments becomes final before the judgment approving the scheme of arrangement has become final.

Article 255

1. If the draft scheme of arrangement was filed at the office of the clerk of the court at the same time as the petition for the suspension of payments, the court may, after hearing the suspension of payments judge, if appointed, and the administrators, order that the hearing referred to in article 218 will not take place, in which event the court will also determine:

(1) the latest date on which the claims affected by the suspension must be submitted to the administrators;
(2) the date and time when the proposed scheme of arrangement will be discussed and determined either before the suspension of payments judge or in chambers, if no such judge has been appointed.

2. There must be at least 14 days between the dates referred to under sub-paragraphs (1) and (2).

3. If these matters are not determined by the court, or if the draft scheme of arrangement was not filed at the same time as the petition, the court will, after hearing the suspension of payments judge, if appointed, and the administrators, determine the dates and times referred to in the first paragraph as soon as the order granting the definitive suspension of payments has become final or, if the draft scheme of arrangement was filed at a later date, immediately after it has been filed.

Article 256

1. The administrators will announce the order referred to in the previous article together with the filing of the draft scheme of arrangement – unless this has already been announced in accordance with article 216 – in the Netherlands State Gazette and in the journals nominated by the court under article 216.

2. The administrators will also notify all known creditors in writing. This notice will refer to the provisions of article 257, second paragraph.

3. The creditors may appear either in person or by written proxy or by an attorney-at-law.

4. The administrators may require the debtor to provide them in advance with an amount determined by them to cover the costs of these announcements and notices.

Article 257

1. The claims must be submitted to the administrators by means of presentation of an invoice or other written statement indicating the nature and the amount of the claim with supporting evidence or copies thereof.

2. Claims not affected by the suspension may not be submitted. If they are nevertheless submitted, the suspension of payments will then affect these claims, and any

priority right, right of retention, pledge or mortgage will be forfeited. This does not apply if the claim is withdrawn before the ballot is taken on it.

3. The creditors may require a receipt from the administrators.

Article 258

The administrators will compare the invoices submitted with the notes and records of the debtor; they will consult the creditor if they object to the admission of a claim; they may require any missing documents to be submitted by the creditor, and also to be given an opportunity to investigate the creditor's notes and original evidence.

Article 259

The administrators will prepare a list of the claims submitted, setting out to the names and addresses of the creditors, the amount and description of the claims together with a note as to whether or not the claims are acknowledged by the administrators.

Article 260

1. If the list contains an interest-bearing claim, interest will be included in the listed claim until the date of commencement of the suspension of payments.

2. Articles 129, 133–135 and 136, first and second paragraphs, apply by analogy.

Article 261

1. A claim subject to a condition subsequent may be included in the list for its value at the commencement of the suspension of payments.

2. If the administrators and the creditors do not agree on the determination of this value, the claim will be provisionally admitted for the full amount.

Article 262

1. A claim of uncertain due date or which entitles the claimant to periodical payments will be included in the list for its value at the commencement of the suspension of payments.

2. All claims which become due within one year following the commencement of the suspension of payments are considered as being due at that time. All claims which become due after one year will be included in the list for their value after expiry of one year.

3. In calculating their value only the time and method of payment, the probability of profit, if any, and, if the claim is interest-bearing, the agreed rate of interest, are taken into account.

Article 263

1. The administrators will file a copy of the list referred to in article 259 at the office of the clerk of the court for public inspection free of charge during the seven days preceding the meeting referred to in article 255.

2. No charge will be made in respect of this filing.

Article 264

1. The suspension of payments judge, if appointed, or if not, the court, may, on the application of the administrator, or of its own motion, postpone the discussion and ballot on the scheme of arrangement.

2. In such an event article 256 applies by analogy.

Article 265

1. At the meeting, the administrators and any experts will submit a report concerning the proposed suspension of payments scheme of arrangement. Article 144 applies by analogy.

2. Claims which are submitted to the administrators after expiry of the period referred to in article 255, sub-paragraph (1), but at the latest two days before the day of the meeting, will be included in the list if so requested at the meeting and if neither the administrators nor any of the creditors present object.

3. Any claims which are submitted after that time will not be included in the list.

4. The provisions of the two preceding paragraphs do not apply to creditors living outside European Holland and thus unable to submit their claim earlier.

5. If the objection referred to in the second paragraph is raised, or if there is disagreement concerning the inability to file claims referred to in the fourth paragraph the suspension of payments judge, if appointed, or otherwise the court, will determine the objection or dispute after consulting the meeting.

Article 266

1. At the meeting the administrators may withdraw any of their prior admissions or refusals of claims.

2. The debtor, and also each creditor present, may dispute a claim which is admitted by the administrators either in whole or in part.

3. Refusals or admissions made during the meeting will be included in the list.

Article 267

The suspension of payments judge, if appointed, or, if not, the court will decide whether, and if so, for what amount the creditors whose claims are disputed will be allowed to vote.

Article 268

1. In order to be accepted the suspension of payments scheme of agreement must be approved by two thirds of the admitted and provisionally admitted creditors representing three quarters of the amount of the admitted and provisionally admitted claims. The approval of an admitted or provisionally admitted creditor whose claim is based on a forfeited penalty is not required.

2. Articles 146 and 147 apply by analogy.

Article 269

1. The minutes of the meeting must contain the contents of the scheme of arrangement, the names of the creditors present entitled to vote, a record of their votes, the

result of the ballot and a record of all further proceedings. The list of creditors as drawn up by the administrators and as supplemented or amended during the meeting is certified by the suspension of payments judge, if appointed, or, if not, by the president and the clerk of the court and is attached to the minutes of the meeting.

2. A copy is available free of charge at the office of the clerk of the court during eight days.

Article 269a

If the discussion took place before a suspension of payments judge and the suspension of payments scheme of arrangement is rejected, the suspension of payments judge will immediately notify the court of the rejection by means of a copy of the draft suspension of payments scheme of arrangement and the minutes of the meeting referred to in article 269. The creditors who voted in favour, and also the debtor, may apply to the court to amend the minutes within eight days following the meeting if it appears from the documents that the suspension of payments judge erred in considering the scheme of arrangement rejected.

Article 269b

1. If the suspension of payments scheme of arrangement is accepted, the suspension of payments judge will, before closing the meeting, appoint the date when the court will consider ratification of the suspension of payments scheme of arrangement.

2. If article 269a applies, the court will appoint the date for the hearing in its order. The administrators will notify the creditors of the order.

3. The hearing will be held at least eight and at most fourteen days after the ballot relating to the suspension of payments scheme of arrangement, or, if article 269a applies, after the order issued by the court.

4. During this period the creditors may submit a statement to the bankruptcy judge setting out the reasons why they consider the scheme of arrangement should not be approved by the court.

Article 270

1. If the discussion of the scheme of arrangement took place in chambers, and if it appears from the documents that the court erred in considering the scheme of arrangement rejected, the creditors who voted in favour of the scheme of arrangement, and also the debtor, may within eight days following the ballot apply to the court of appeal to amend the minutes of the meeting.

2. If the court of appeal amends the minutes, it will in the same order appoint a date when the court will discuss the ratification of the scheme of arrangement. This date will be at least eight and at most fourteen days following the order. The administrators will notify the creditors of the order. This order has the effect that any bankruptcy pronounced under article 277 is null and void at law.

Article 271

1. If the scheme of arrangement is accepted, the suspension of payments judge, if appointed, will submit a written report on the date appointed for the hearing, and the administrators, and also each creditor, may submit grounds for or against the ratification of the agreement. Article 152, second paragraph, applies by analogy.

2. The court may determine that the ratification hearing will take place at a later date, and, if so, this date will be specified immediately.

Article 272

1. The court will issue its order as soon as possible.
2. The court will refuse ratification:

(1) if the assets of the estate exceed the amount agreed under the suspension of payments scheme of arrangement;
(2) if performance of the suspension of payments scheme of arrangement is not sufficiently guaranteed;
(3) if the suspension of payments scheme of arrangement was reached by means of fraudulent acts or the preference of one or more creditors or other unfair means and regardless whether or not the debtor or any other party co-operated to this effect;
(4) if the fees and expenses of the experts and the administrators have not been paid to the administrators or if no security for these has been issued.

3. The court may also refuse to ratify the suspension of payments scheme of distribution on other grounds or on its own motion.
4. In refusing to ratify the scheme of arrangement the court may, in the same order, declare the bankruptcy of the debtor. If bankruptcy is not declared, the suspension of payments will terminate as soon as the order refusing the ratification has become final. The administrators will announce the termination in the journals referred to in article 216.
5. Articles 154–156 and 160 are applicable by analogy.

Article 273

A suspension of payments scheme of arrangement which has been ratified is binding on all creditors for whom the suspension of payments was effective.

Article 274

Ratification of the suspension of payments scheme of arrangement in conjunction with the minutes referred to in article 269 constitutes a writ of execution against the debtor and any guarantors acceded to the suspension of payments scheme of arrangement on behalf of those creditors whose claims have not been disputed by the debtor.

Article 275

As long as no final decision has been made in respect of the proposed suspension of payments scheme of arrangement, suspension of payments may not terminate by the mere expiry of the period for which it was granted.

Article 276

Suspension of payments will terminate as soon as the ratification comes into force. The administrators will announce the termination in the journals referred to in article 216.

Article 277

If the scheme of arrangement is not accepted, the court may declare the debtor bankrupt. If bankruptcy is not declared, the suspension of payments will terminate upon expiry of the unused part of the period referred to either in article 269a or article 270, or if the court has refused to amend the minutes of the meeting. The administrators will announce the termination in the journals referred to in article 216.

Article 278

1. If the court has declared the debtor bankrupt, the debtor may lodge an appeal against the declaration of bankruptcy within eight days following expiry of the unused part of the period referred to either in article 269a or in article 270, or if the court has refused to amend the minutes of the meeting.

2. The appeal will take the form of a petition submitted to the clerk of the court of appeal seized with the matter. The president will forthwith determine the date and time of the hearing.

3. The clerk of the court of appeal will announce the appeal and the date and time of the hearing in the journals in which the application for suspension of payments was announced in accordance with article 216. Each creditor may take part in the hearing.

Article 279

1. If the court of appeal confirms the bankruptcy the debtor may apply for a review of the decision, and, if the court of appeal rejects the bankruptcy, each creditor taking part in the appeal proceedings may apply for a review of the decision.

2. The application for a review must be submitted and heard within the same period and in the same manner as the appeal, save that the announcement in the journals is substituted by a writ which must be served upon the other party within four days after the appeal has been lodged.

Article 280

1. As regards any termination of the scheme of arrangement, articles 165 and 166 apply by analogy.

2. The debtor will be declared bankrupt in the judgment ordering dissolution of the scheme of arrangement.

Article 281

If a bankruptcy is declared as provided in articles 272, 277 or 280, a bankruptcy scheme of arrangement may not be offered.

Chapter II(A): Special provisions

Article 281a

1. If there are over 10,000 creditors, the list to be submitted by the debtor with his application under article 214 need not contain the names and residences of the creditors

nor the amount of the individual claims; it will suffice for the list to refer to the different groups of creditors divided according to the nature of their claim, and the total number and total amount of the aggregate claims of each group.

2. If the number of creditors is between 5,000 and 10,000, the court may permit the debtor to submit a list in accordance with the previous paragraph.

Article 281b

1. If the number of creditors appears to be over 5,000, the court may, at the request of the administrators, make the arrangements described in articles 281c–281f.

2. The arrangements made under articles 281d and 281e may only be made in combination.

Article 281c

The court may determine that the notices referred to in articles 215, second paragraph, 256, second paragraph, and 264, second paragraph, will not be served individually but by announcements in the journals indicated by the court. In that event the court will also determine the latest date on which these announcements must be made and which matters must be included in the announcements.

Article 281d

The court may determine that certain types of claims or claims below a certain amount – which may however not exceed Dfl. 1,000 – need not be included in the list referred to in article 259.

Article 281e

1. The court may appoint a representative committee of creditors, consisting of at least nine members. This committee must consist of persons considered to represent the major groups of creditors.

2. Only the members of the committee are entitled to vote in the ballots referred to in articles 218 and 268.

3. A final suspension of payments may not be granted if more than one-quarter of the members of the committee present at the meeting held to determine the matter have voted against the suspension.

4. Acceptance of a suspension of payments scheme of arrangement is subject to the approval of three quarters of the members of the committee present at the meeting. If at least two thirds of the members have not appeared at the meeting, the ballot on the scheme of arrangement is postponed until a later date. A further creditors' meeting is not required but the members of the committee will be summoned by the administrators in writing to attend the next meeting. At this meeting a ballot will be taken irrespective of the number of committee members present.

5. By way of application of articles 269, first paragraph, first sentence, 270 and 272, and the analogous application of article 154 , the words 'members of the committee' are substituted for 'creditors' and in article 271 instead of 'each creditor' the words 'each creditor and each committee member' are substituted.

Article 281f

If it is anticipated that more than one distribution to creditors must be made, the court may, in ratifying the scheme of arrangement, determine that bills of exchange endorsed to bearer will be issued with the first distribution to creditors and that payment of the next distributions may only be claimed through presentation of these bills of exchange.

Chapter III: Final provisions

Article 282

No appeal lies against decisions of the court issued under the provisions of this Title, except where the contrary has been provided and save for the possibility of review in the interests of the law.

Article 283

1. Applications submitted under articles 219, 223, 225, 242, 243, 247, 270, 272, final paragraph, 278 and 280, first paragraph, must be signed by an attorney-at-law except when the application is made by the administrators.

2. In order to commence review proceedings the assistance is required of an attorney-at-law accredited at the supreme court.

General final provision

Article 284

The Statute of Limitations is not applicable to the time limits provided in articles 39, 40, 238 and 239.

SWITZERLAND

Swiss insolvency law is contained in the Federal Law of 11th April 1889, relating to proceedings in debt and bankruptcy, as amplified by the very brief Federal Law of 29th April 1920 relating to the public law consequences of unsatisfied distraint and bankruptcy. The text is as of 1st January 1991.

The 1889 law is divided into 13 chapters. Chapter I is administrative. Chapters II, III and IV deal with proceedings for debt enforcement, distraint and the realisation of security. Some important substantive provisions will be found in these chapters, for example: article 96(2) – any disposal of assets to the prejudice of creditors' rights by the debtor is void save in favour of a third party acting in good faith; and articles 135(1), 142, and 146(2) – preservation of creditors' rights and ranking in the event of a sale of mortgaged property. The bankruptcy laws as such are set out in chapter V and the following chapters. These are all mainly administrative or procedural except for chapter VI (the effect of bankruptcy on the debtor's estate and creditors' rights, generally) and chapter X (actions to set aside). The law does not apply to issuing banks or federal railways and shipping companies (article 30). The law dealing with the public law consequences of bankruptcy is confined merely to provisions regarding the holding of public office and the voting rights of bankrupts.

CHAPTER SEVEN

Swiss Insolvency Laws

TABLE OF CONTENTS

THE FEDERAL LAW RELATING TO PROCEEDINGS IN DEBT AND BANKRUPTCY, 11TH APRIL, 1889

THE FEDERAL ASSEMBLY OF THE SWISS CONFEDERATION PURSUANT TO ARTICLE 64 OF THE FEDERAL CONSTITUTION, DECREES:

CHAPTER I. GENERAL PROVISIONS

I: Organisation

Article 1

1. The area of each canton comprises one or several districts for the administration of bankruptcies and where debt enforcement actions may be brought.

2. The cantons will determine the number and area of these districts.

3. The bankruptcy districts may be further divided into several districts where debt enforcement actions may be brought.

Article 2

1. Each debt enforcement action district will have an administrative debt office managed by a superintending officer.

2. The superintendent will be replaced by a substitute if his competence is challenged or he is prevented from carrying out his duties.

3. The administration of the office is the responsibility of each canton.

Article 3

Each bankruptcy district will have an administrative bankruptcy office. The administration of this office is likewise the responsibility of each canton.

Article 4

The debt enforcement office and bankruptcy office may be combined.

Article 5

1. The superintendents and other officials of the bankruptcy office are responsible for any loss caused by their own errors or the errors of employees appointed by them. Actions for such losses will be heard before a judge.

2. Employees of bankruptcy and debt enforcement offices appointed by a public body have the same responsibility for loss caused by them.

Article 6

1. The canton is responsible for any loss which is not met by the officers or employees who were responsible, or their guarantors.

2. The canton has rights of recourse against the electoral districts responsible for the appointment of the official or the employee.

3. The cantons may demand security bonds from the officials and employees for whom they are responsible.

Article 7

1. Any action for damages with interest must be brought within a year of the date when the injured party realised that the loss had taken place and in all cases within ten years of the date when the loss occurred.

2. However, if the loss arises from a criminal act which is subject to a longer limitation period under criminal law, the same limitation period will apply to the civil action.

Article 8

1. The bankruptcy offices and debt enforcement offices will draw up a report on their operations and also on any claims and official notifications that they receive.

2. Anyone who can establish an interest may consult the registers and request extracts.

3. The minutes of the debt and bankruptcy offices are proof of their contents unless the contrary is proven.

Article 9

The debt and bankruptcy offices are required to deposit with the public trustee treasury office any monies, shares and valuable objects not applied by them within three days of receipt.

Article 10

1. No official or employee may carry out the functions of his office in the following cases:

- (i) If he himself has an interest;
- (ii) If his wife, his fiancée, his parents or relatives in a direct ascending or descending line or in a collateral line up to and including the third degree have an interest;
- (iii) If he is the legal representative, agent or employee of the interested party.

2. Any superintendent who finds himself in such a position will immediately transfer the matter to his substitute and notify the creditor of the position.

Article 11

It is forbidden, and any such transaction will be null and void, for officials and employees of debt and bankruptcy offices to deal on their own account with any matter connected with a debt enforcement action or with an item which is being sold.

Article 12

1. The debt enforcement office is bound to accept payments made for the account of the plaintiff creditor.

2. The debtor is freed from his obligations to the extent of such payments.

Article 13

1. Each canton will appoint a supervisory authority for the debt and bankruptcy offices.

2. The cantons may also set up subordinate supervisory authorities for one or more districts.

Article 14

1. The supervisory authority will inspect each office at least once a year.

2. The supervisory authority may subject the official or employee to the following penalties:

(i) A reprimand;
(ii) A fine of up to 200 francs;
(iii) Suspension for up to six months;
(iv) Dismissal.

Article 15

1. The federal court exercises the ultimate supervisory powers in matters of bankruptcy and debts and will apply this law in a consistent and uniform manner.

2. The federal court will issue by decree any necessary regulations and enforcement orders.

3. The federal court may give instructions to the cantonal supervisory authorities and ask them for their annual reports.

4. In particular the federal court will arrange for the debt offices to maintain a register of persons subject to bankruptcy proceedings living in their district.

Article 16

1. The federal council will set the level of charges to be applied by the debt and bankruptcy officers.

2. Documents relating to debt enforcement actions and bankruptcy are exempt from stamp duty.

Article 17

1. Except in cases where judicial process is required by law, the supervisory authority may be petitioned if the debt or bankruptcy office has behaved unlawfully or appears to have acted without justification.

2. The petition must be lodged within ten days of the petitioner having knowledge of the act in question.

3. The petitioner may also bring an action at any time for breach of natural justice or for non-justifiable delay.

Article 18

1. Any decision of the subordinate authority may be referred to the cantonal supervisory authority within ten days of its publication.

2. At any time the cantonal authority may be petitioned for breach of natural justice or for non-justifiable delay on the part of the subordinate authority.

Article 19

1. Any decision of the cantonal supervisory authority issued contrary to the present law may be referred to the federal court within ten days of its publication.

2. At any time the federal court may be petitioned for breach of natural justice or for non-justifiable delay on the part of the supervisory authority.

Article 20

In debt proceedings concerning bills of exchange the time limits within which a petition may be brought, or redress may be sought, is only five days in each case; the supervisory authority is obliged to issue its decision within the same period.

Article 21

If a petition is substantiated, the supervisory authority will annul or reverse the decision which was the object of the petition; the supervisory authority will order those matters to be done which the official has delayed or has unreasonably refused to perform.

Article 22

1. The cantons will appoint the judicial authorities responsible for issuing decisions dealing with matters which this law requires to be decided by a judge.

2. The cantons may appoint a single judge, a court or a division of a court.

Article 23

1. The cantons will also appoint authorities responsible for:

(i) Authorising sequestration (art. 271–281);
(ii) Evicting a tenant or farmer (art. 282);
(iii) Ruling on schemes of arrangement (art. 293–317); this service may be organised on one or two levels.

2. These matters may be referred either to judicial or to administrative bodies.

Article 24

The cantons will appoint the public trustee treasury offices and be responsible for them.

Article 25

The cantons will issue decrees required in order:

(i) To institute summary civil proceedings. In proceedings of this kind the parties must be summoned at short notice and the actions must be determined by the final cantonal authority within six months from commencement of proceedings.
(ii) To institute summary proceedings in bankruptcy applications, whether contested or not.
(iii) ... [repealed]

Article 26

[Repealed]

Article 27

1. The cantons may administer the professional body of commercial officers. In particular, they may regulate its conduct in matters of competence and integrity, regulate the remuneration of the commercial officers and impose on them the obligation to put up security.

2. Nobody may be compelled to use these officers. Their remuneration may not be charged to the debtor.

Article 28

1. The cantons will supply the federal court with details of the operational districts of their bankruptcy and debt enforcement offices, the administration of these offices, the authorities set up in order to enforce this law and the names of the superintendents, their substitutes and any officials of the bankruptcy office.

2. The federal court will give the necessary official publicity to these matters.

Article 29

The laws and regulations made by the cantons in performance of articles 13, 25, 27, 45 and 111 are subject to the approval of the Federal Council.

Article 30

This law does not apply to:

(i) The compulsory liquidation of railways and shipping firms operating under a federal concession;
(ii) The compulsory liquidation of issuing banks;
(iii) Enforcement action against cantons, districts and communes for any matters relating to federal or cantonal law.

II: Miscellaneous regulations

Article 31

1. Any time limit in days does not include the day from which is starts to run.

2. Any time limit in months or years expires on the day corresponding to the day on which it starts; if there is no corresponding day in the final month of the time limit, it expires on the last day of that month.

3. When the last day of the time limit falls on a Sunday or a day which is a legal holiday the time limit expires on the first working day afterwards.

4. ... [repealed]

Article 32

When notice is given by post, the time limit is deemed to be complied with if the letter is posted during the period.

Article 33

1. Any agreement modifying the limitation periods provided under this law is null and void.

2. When a limitation period has not been observed the debtor may waive his right to invoke this defence.

Article 34

Any communications made by the offices will be made in writing; they will be effected by registered post, or by direct delivery against receipt, unless the law provides otherwise.

Article 35

1. Public notices will be inserted in the official journal of the canton and in any event in the federal commercial journal if the debtor is subject to bankruptcy proceedings. In this event, insertion of a notice in the federal commercial journal is good notice for the purpose of the calculation of limitation periods and the consequences of publication.

2. If the circumstances so require, publication may also be made in other journals or by the town crier.

Article 36

A petition, appeal and further appeal only take effect to suspend the decision when so determined by the authority ruling on the matter or by its president. The parties are informed immediately of any such suspension.

Article 37

1. The expression 'mortgage' as used in this law includes mortgages, mortgage certificates and land charge notes, charges on real estate under laws no longer in force, land charges, special preferential rights pertaining to certain land and charges on the appurtenances of a building.

2. The expression 'charge over moveables' includes charges over intangibles and chattels, charges over livestock, retention rights, charges over debts and other rights.

3. The expression 'charge' used on its own includes charges over moveables and charges over real estate.

CHAPTER II. DEBT ENFORCEMENT ACTIONS

I: Various types of debt enforcement action

Article 38

1. Enforcement against a sum of money under a guarantee operates as a debt enforcement action.

2. The action is begun by notification of an order to pay. it is continued by proceedings for distraint, for realisation of security or for bankruptcy.

3. The superintendent will decide which method will be applied.

Article 39

1. Proceedings will be in bankruptcy, either as 'ordinary proceedings in bankruptcy' (art. 159–174); or as 'proceedings for recovery under bills of exchange' (art. 177–189) when the debtor is entered on the trade register in one of the following capacities:

(i) head of the business (art. 865, 2nd and 4th para. of the federal code of obligations);
(ii) a partner in a partnership (art. 553 of the federal code of obligations);
(iii) a partner with unlimited liability in a limited partnership (art. 591 of the federal code of obligations);
(iv) manager of a partnership limited by shares (art. 676 of the federal code of obligations);
(iv) managing partner in a company with limited liability (art. 811 of the federal code of obligations);
(v) as a partnership (art. 552 of the federal code of obligations);
(vi) as a limited partnership (art. 590 of the federal code of obligations);
(vii) as a limited company or partnership limited by shares (art. 623 and 676 of the federal code of obligations);
(vii) as a limited liability company (art. 772 of the federal code of obligations);
(viii) as a co-operative society (art. 678 of the federal code of obligations);
(ix) as any other business association (art. 716 of the federal code of obligations).

2. [Repealed]
3. The entry takes effect on the day after publication in the federal commercial journal.

Article 40

1. Those who have been entered in the trade register and who have been struck off remain subject to bankruptcy proceedings for the six months following publication of their striking off in the federal commercial journal.
2. Proceedings in which bankruptcy has been threatened or an order to pay under bills of exchange has been made before expiry of this period, are continued in bankruptcy.

Article 41

1. When the subject matter of the proceedings is a debt secured by a charge, the proceedings will take the form of realisation of the security (art. 151–158), even as against debtors subject to proceedings by way of bankruptcy. This does not apply to the provision in article 177 concerning the proceedings relating to bills of exchange.
2. At the choice of the creditor, where the proceedings concern interest payments or annuities guaranteed by a mortgage, these will operate either by realisation of the security or by distraint or by bankruptcy, depending upon the means of the debtor.

Article 42

1. In all other cases proceedings will be by way of distraint (art. 88–150).

2. When a debtor is entered on the trade register, distraints made previously against him will continue in force as long as he is not declared bankrupt.

Article 43

Actions for the recovery of taxes, rates, duty, fees, fines or other general dues owing to a public authority treasury or official are always made by way of distraint or realisation of security.

Article 44

The realisation of items confiscated under the fiscal or penal laws of the Confederation and the cantons will take place in accordance with the provisions of these laws.

Article 45

These laws do not apply to the provisions of the Swiss Civil Code concerning a pawnbroker's right of sale.

II: Jurisdiction

Article 46

1. The forum for debt proceedings is the debtor's domicile.

2. The bodies corporate and companies entered on the trade register are sued at their registered office. Bodies corporate not entered on the trade register are sued at their principal place of business.

3. Each co-owner of a debt in a co-ownership which has no representative may be sued in the place where the co-ownership operates.

Article 47

1. If the debtor has a legal representative the proceedings take place at the domicile of the legal representative and it is to him that all steps in the proceedings are notified.

2. If the legal representative has not yet been appointed the proceedings take place at the registered office of the authority responsible for the appointment or for taking care of the debtor's interest temporarily and that is where steps in the proceedings are notified.

3. However, in the case of claims concerning the carrying on of a profession or an activity authorised by virtue of article 412 of the Swiss Civil Code, proceedings will be directed against the debtor himself in the place where he carries on his profession or activity.

Article 48

A debtor who has no fixed abode may be sued in any place where he may be found.

Article 49

So long as division of property under a will has not yet taken place or a contractual co-ownership has not been constituted or an official declaration of bankruptcy has not been ordered, a deceased person's estate will be sued in the place where the deceased could himself be sued at the time of his death and according to the applicable method.

Article 50

1. A debtor living abroad who has a business in Switzerland may be sued there for the debts of the business.

2. A debtor domiciled abroad whose chosen domicile for the purposes of performance of a legal obligation is Switzerland may be sued there for that particular debt.

Article 51

1. Where the debt is secured by a charge over moveables, proceedings take place either at the debtor's domicile, or at the place where the security, or that part of the security which is of the greatest value, is located.

2. When the debt is guaranteed by a mortgage, the proceedings take place where the property is located, or if the mortgage is over several properties in different districts, in the place where the property having the highest value is located.

Article 52

Proceedings following sequestration take place where the sequestrated item is located; however, the threat and the application for bankruptcy itself may only be notified officially in the usual forum.

Article 53

If the debtor changes domicile after notice of distraint, after threat of bankruptcy or after notice of an order to pay bills of exchange, proceedings will continue in the original domicile.

Article 54

The bankruptcy of an absconding debtor is declared in the area of his last domicile.

Article 55

Bankruptcy proceedings may not be commenced at the same time in several areas of Switzerland. Proceedings are deemed to be commenced where the bankruptcy was pronounced for the first time.

III: Public holidays and the staying of proceedings

Article 56

Except in case of sequestration or urgent protective measures, no proceedings may be instituted:

(i) Before 8 am. or after 7 pm;
(ii) On Sundays and public holidays;
(iii) During non-working days: seven days before and after Easter, Whitsunday, federal fasting day and Christmas; except for proceedings under bills of exchange;
(iv) When the debtor is entitled to a stay of proceedings (art. 57–62) or to a stay under a scheme of arrangement (art. 295).

Article 57

1. Proceedings against a debtor on military service are suspended during such period of service.

2. When the debtor has completed without major interruption at least thirty days service before discharge or going on leave, proceedings remain postponed for the two weeks following discharge or going on leave.

3. Military service means all military or supplementary service completed in Switzerland qualifying for pay including anti-aircraft service.

4. As regards periodic payments of alimony, proceedings by way of distraint or realisation of security may take place even during the stay of proceedings provided that the stay has lasted for three months.

Article 57(a)

1. When a particular step in the proceedings cannot be carried out because a debtor is engaged in military service, adult persons in the debtor's household and, when notice of the step in the proceedings is published in an industrial or commercial firm, the employees, and, if applicable, the employer, must inform the official of the date of call up and the military address of the debtor, as well as his date of birth.

2. If requested, the competent officer will notify the debt enforcement office when the debtor will be discharged or will go on leave.

3. The penalty provided for non-compliance with a decision of the authorities (art. 292 CP) or for failing to observe the military regulations (art. 72 CPM) applies to those who refuse to supply the necessary information.

Article 57(b)

1. Security for mortgage interest payments (art. 818, Ch3, CC) is extended for the duration of the stay of proceedings as against any debtor benefiting from the stay by reason of military service.

2. In proceedings for realisation of security, the order to pay must also be given during the stay of proceedings provided the stay has lasted three months.

Article 57(c)

1. If the debtor benefits from a stay of legal proceedings on the grounds of military service, the creditor may ask the debt enforcement office to draw up an inventory which takes effect as provided under article 164 for the duration of the stay. The creditor must, however, be able to show that he has a genuine claim and that it is open to compromise by actions of the debtor or any third party tending to favour

certain creditors to the detriment of others or to the disadvantage of all the creditors.

2. The inventory will not be drawn up if the debtor supplies security for the claim of the petitioning creditor.

Article 57(d)

A stay of legal proceedings on the grounds of military service may be revoked with immediate effect by the judge either for all debts generally or for certain specific debts, on the petition of a creditor who shows it is probable:

(i) That the debtor has withdrawn assets beyond the reach of his creditors or that he is taking measures to favour certain creditors to the detriment of others or that he is prejudicing the rights of all the creditors; or
(ii) That the debtor, if he has made a voluntary disposition, does not need a stay of legal proceedings to safeguard his financial situation; or
(iii) That the debtor is making a voluntary disposition in order to avoid his responsibilities.

Article 57(e)

1. The provisions relating to the stay of legal proceedings apply equally to persons and companies whose legal representative is performing military service as long as they are unable to appoint another representative.

2. Debtors who are doing their service as civil servants, employees or workers of the Confederation or of a canton are not entitled to a stay.

Article 58

Proceedings instituted against a debtor whose spouse, parent or child, by blood or marriage, has just died, are suspended for two weeks from the date of death.

Article 59

1. Proceedings for debts which encumber an inheritance are suspended for two weeks from the date of the death as well as during the period granted for accepting or repudiating the inheritance.

2. Proceedings begun before the death may be continued against the deceased's estate under article 49.

3. The proceedings continue against the heir only if they concern the realisation of security or if, in proceedings for distraint, the agreed period of settlement under articles 110 and 111 has elapsed.

Article 60

When proceedings are instituted against a prisoner who has no representative, the superintendent will grant a period of time to appoint a representative, unless such is appointed by the guardian authority. Proceedings are suspended during this period.

Article 61

In the case of serious illness of the debtor, the superintendent may suspend proceedings for a fixed period of time.

Article 62

In cases of epidemics, public disaster or war, proceedings may be suspended in a particular part of the territory or as regards certain categories of people. This will be announced by way of decree by the cantonal authority with the assent of the Federal Council.

Article 63

Time limits continue to run during public holidays and stays of proceedings; but if the end of the period coincides with a public holiday or a day during a stay, the period is extended to the third working day.

IV: Notice of proceedings

Article 64

1. The debtor is given notice of proceedings at his home or at the place where he normally carries on his business. If he is absent, notice can be given to an adult person of his household or in his employ.

2. If so required, the notice is given to a local official or to the police who are then responsible for delivering it to the debtor.

Article 65

1. When proceedings are instituted against a body corporate or a company, notice of the proceedings is sent to the representative as follows:

(i) To the president of the executive authority, in the case of a commune, a canton or the Confederation;
(ii) To a board member or an attorney in the case of a limited company or a cooperative or a company listed on the commercial register;
(iii) To the president of the board or the manager, in the case of any other body corporate;
(iv) To one of the managing partners or the attorney in the case of a partnership or a limited partnership.

2. When the persons mentioned above are absent from their offices, notice can be left with another official or employee.

3. Notice of proceedings instituted against the undivided estate of a deceased person is given to the appointed representative of the estate or, if there is no known representative, to one of the heirs.

Article 66

1. When the debtor does not live near the place where proceedings have been instituted, notice is sent to the person or left at the place designated by him.

2. If no such designation is made, notice is served by the debt enforcement office at his domicile or through the post.

3. When the debtor lives abroad, notice is given through the local authorities at his residence or through the post.

4. If the debtor has no known address, notice is given by public announcement.

5. In the cases provided in paragraphs 2, 3 and 4 of this article the superintendent may extend the time limits depending on the circumstances.

V: Application for proceedings

Article 67

1. Application for proceedings is addressed to the debt enforcement office in writing or is orally communicated. It will state:

- (i) The name and address of the creditor and, if applicable, of his representative; his chosen address in Switzerland, if he lives abroad. Failing election, the address of the debt enforcement office is deemed to be his chosen address.
- (ii) The name and address of the debtor and, if appropriate, of his legal representative; in the case of application for proceedings against a deceased person's estate, the heirs to whom notice is to be given must be named;
- (iii) The amount in Swiss currency of the amount owing or security demanded; if the debt carries interest, the rate and the day from which it runs;
- (iv) Proof of title to the claim and the date when it arose; if there is no title, the reason for the debt.

2. An application made in respect of secured debt must contain in addition the information required under article 151.

3. On request the creditor is entitled to receive free of charge a receipt for the application for proceedings.

Article 68

1. The costs of the proceedings are borne by the debtor. The creditor pays them in the first instance. The debt enforcement office may postpone any action where costs have not been advanced by the creditor; but it must inform the creditor of this.

2. The creditor may recover his costs from the first payments made by the debtor.

V(2): Proceedings against spouses whose property is owned jointly

Article 68(a)

1. When proceedings are instituted against a spouse whose property is owned jointly, the debtor's spouse will also be given notice of the order to pay and of all the other proceedings; if it becomes apparent during the course of the proceedings that the debtor's spouse holds the property jointly, the debt enforcement office will notify the spouse immediately.

2. Either spouse may oppose the order to pay.

3. A debtor or his spouse who claims that the debt attaches only to the debtor's personal property or to his share of the joint estate must state the reasons for this claim.

Article 68(b)

1. Each spouse may claim by way of proceedings for the recovery of property (arts. 106 to 109) that the property distrained is part of the personal property of the debtor's spouse.

2. When the proceedings concern only the personal property of the debtor and his share in the joint estate, each spouse may also oppose the distraint of property in the joint estate by way of the proceedings for the recovery of property (art. 106–109).

3. If the proceedings continue against the personal property of the debtor and against his share in the joint estate, the distraint and subsequent sale of this share are governed by article 132.

4. A spouse's share in the joint estate may not be sold at auction.

5. The supervising authority may apply to the judge to order a division of the estate.

VI: The order to pay and opposition to the order

Article 69

1. Upon application for proceedings, the debt enforcement office will draw up the order to pay.

2. This contains:

(i) The arrangements prescribed for the application for proceedings;
(ii) The order to pay within twenty days the amount of the debt and the costs, or, when the proceedings are for security, to supply it within this time;
(iii) Notification to the debtor that he has ten days from the date of the order to object, if he intends to contest all or part of the debt or the right of the creditor to institute proceedings;
(iv) The warning that, if the debtor fails to comply with the order to pay or to object, the proceedings will take their course.

Article 70

1. The order to pay is drawn up in duplicate. One copy is sent to the debtor, the other to the creditor. If they are not the same, the debtor's copy is deemed to be the true copy.

2. When co-debtors are sued simultaneously, each must receive notice of the order to pay, unless several of them are represented by the same person.

Article 71

1. The order to pay is given to the debtor at the latest on the day after the application for proceedings is made.

2. A debt enforcement office which receives several claims against the same debtor must give notice of all orders to pay at the same time.

3. No new application may be executed before the first application has been executed.

Article 72

1. Notice is given by the superintendent or an employee of the debt enforcement office, or through the post in the way prescribed in the regulations for the service of judicial documents.

2. The person giving notice certifies on each copy the day on which it was given and the person to whom it was given.

Article 73

1. At the request of the debtor, the creditor will be invited, before expiry of the period for objection, to file at the debt enforcement office the original or a certified copy of his claim.

2. Failure on the part of the creditor to do this does not prolong the period for objection; but the judge will take this into account if appropriate, in determining the costs of the case.

Article 74

1. A debtor who wishes to oppose the order must notify the debt enforcement office accordingly orally or in writing within ten days of receipt of the order to pay.

2. A debtor who objects to only part of the debt must indicate the exact amount contested. If he fails to do this, his objection is null and void.

3. At the request of the debtor the debt enforcement office will give him a free copy of the objection.

Article 75

A person who has given grounds for his objection is not later restricted to those grounds.

Article 76

1. The objection is recorded on the copy of the order to pay sent to the creditor; if there is no objection this is also stated.

2. This copy is sent to the creditor immediately after the objection or on expiry of the period allowed for objection.

Article 77

1. A debtor who, without fault on his part, has been prevented from objecting within the legal time limit is nevertheless allowed to object until realisation of the assets or declaration of bankruptcy.

2. In this case, the debtor will declare his objection to the judge within three days of cessation of the event which prevented him from objecting and giving grounds for the late objection.

3. The judge seized with this objection may order a stay of the proceedings; he will rule on its admissibility after hearing the parties.

Article 78

1. Objection suspends the proceedings.

2. If the debtor contests only part of the debt, the proceedings may continue in respect of the sum admitted.

Article 79

A creditor in contested proceedings follows the ordinary procedure in order to establish his claim.

Article 80

1. However, anyone benefiting from an executory judgment may petition the judge for withdrawal of the objection.

2. Matters which have been finally determined at law or acknowledgements made before the court constitute executory judgments, as are also, within the limits of cantonal territory, the rulings and decisions of the administrative authority concerning obligations in public law (taxes, etc) to which the canton has accorded enforceable status.

Article 81

1. When the proceedings are founded on an executory judgment given by an authority of the Confederation or the canton in which the proceedings are taking place, the judge will order the withdrawal of the objection, unless the person objecting establishes the fact that the debt has been paid off or that he has obtained a stay of execution after the judgment, or that the judgment does not apply to him.

2. If the executory judgment was given in another canton the person who objects may also dispute the competence of the judge who gave it or assert to his advantage that he was not properly summoned or legally represented.

3. If the judgment was given in a foreign country with which there is a convention for reciprocal enforcement of judgments, the person who objects may take advantage of the grounds for objection set out in that convention.

Article 82

1. A creditor in proceedings founded on an acknowledgement of debt established by an authenticated document or in simple contract may apply for provisional withdrawal of the objection.

2. The judge will order provisional withdrawal if the defendant is unable to establish at the hearing that he has been released from the debt.

Article 83

1. When provisional withdrawal has been granted, the creditor may, if the period for payment has elapsed and depending on the means of the debtor, apply for provisional distraint or ask the judge to order an inventory of assets to be drawn up in application of article 162.

2. On his part, the debtor may, within ten days of the order withdrawing objection, commence an action for discharge of the debt in the court where the proceedings were first instituted; the action proceeds in the normal way.

3. If he does not avail himself of this right, or his action is dismissed, the withdrawal as well as the distraint become final.

Article 84

The judge will give his ruling on the demand for withdrawal within five days after hearing the parties.

Article 85

The debtor may at any time apply to the judge to cancel or suspend the proceedings if he establishes the fact that the debt, costs and interest have been paid off or that the creditor has granted him a stay.

Article 86

1. Anyone who has paid a sum he did not owe by reason of unopposed legal proceedings or a judgment withdrawing objection, has the right to claim it back within one year by means of the normal procedure.

2. Proceedings are instituted at the court where the proceedings were first instituted or at the defendant's local court, as chosen by the applicant.

3. By way of exception to article 72 of the federal code of obligations, the only fact which the applicant must prove is that the sum was not due.

Article 87

As regards the realisation of security, the order to pay is governed by the special provisions of articles 151–153; the order to pay, and any objection to the order to pay, in proceedings relating to bills of exchange, are governed by the special provisions of articles 178–189.

CHAPTER III. PROCEEDINGS FOR DISTRAINT

I: Distraint

Article 88

1. After expiry of a period of twenty days from the notice of the order to pay, the creditor may apply for distraint.

2. The right to apply for distraint lapses one year from the date of the notice of the order to pay. If it is opposed, time does not run between commencement of the action and judgment.

3. On request a creditor is entitled to receive free of charge a receipt for his application for distraint.

Article 89

The debt enforcement office will proceed with the distraint within three days of the application or will arrange for it to be executed through the debt enforcement office of the district where the goods to be seized are situated.

Article 90

The debtor must be notified of the distraint at least the day before it is executed. The notice will repeat the provisions of article 91.

Article 91

1. The debtor is bound by law to be present or to be represented at the distraint, and to indicate in so far as is agreed all the assets which belong to him even those not in his actual possession, and including, debts owed to him and other claims.

2. At the request of the official, the debtor is obliged to open his premises and unlock furniture. The police will be called to assist if the need arises.

Article 92

The following are not available for distraint:

(i) Clothes and necessary personal effects of the debtor and his family, kitchen utensils, cleaning utensils and furniture in so far as they are indispensable to the debtor and his family or in so far as the proceeds of their immediate sale would be so little that the increase in costs due to their seizure is not justified; in the latter case, these objects and their values must be noted in the record of the distraint proceedings;
(ii) Religious books and objects;
(iii) Tools, instruments and books in so far as they are necessary to the debtor and his family for the exercise of their trade or profession or in so far as the proceeds of their immediate sale would be so little that the increase in costs due to their seizure is not justified; in the latter case these objects and their values must be noted in the record of the distraint proceedings;
(iv) Either two dairy cows or heifers, or four goats or sheep, at the choice of the debtor as well as small domestic animals with fodder and litter for four months, in so far as these animals are indispensable to the upkeep of the debtor and his family or to the operation of his trade;
(v) The foodstuffs and necessary fuel of the debtor and his family for two consecutive months from the distraint, or the cash or credit needed to acquire them;
(vi) The debtor's uniform, equipment, arms, horse and army pay;
(vii) Life annuities which are non-distrainable under Article 521 of the federal code of obligations;
(viii) Disablement allowances for those injured in military service or while in service with the national police force; allowances for the family of citizens who have died in either of those services;
(ix) Grants awarded by a pension fund or a benevolent society in case of sickness, poverty, death, etc;
(x) Allowances or capital due or awarded to the victim or his family, as compensation for personal injury or for damage to health;
(xi) Income under article 20 of the Federal Law of 20th December 1946 arising from old age and life insurance policies;
(xii) Family allowances; and
(xiii) Entitlements to personal allowances not yet due from a social security agency.

Article 93

Wages, salaries and other income deriving from employment, usufructs and their products, alimony, retirement pensions, allowances paid through insurance or retirement funds, allowances for loss of wages in favour of persons obliged to do military service or civil protection service, payments arising from unemployment insurance and unemployment benefit, emergency allowances, military assistance and other similar allowances may only be attached in so far as they exceed the amount which is estimated as indispensable for the debtor and his family.

Article 94

1. The following standing crops may not be distrained:

(i) Produce from meadows, before 1st April;
(ii) Produce from fields, before 1st June;
(iii) Produce from vineyards, before 20th August.

2. Disposal of these crops by the debtor before or on those dates will not defeat a claim made by the distrainer.

3. The rights of secured creditors of standing crops are reserved on condition that the creditor has himself applied for realisation of his security before the crops under distraint have been harvested.

Article 95

1. Distraint attaches first to moveable property including debts owed to the debtor; items capable of being readily sold must be seized first, those which the debtor could easily do without rather than those which he would have difficulty in doing without.

2. Real estate will only be distrained in the absence of sufficient moveable assets to cover the debt or when the creditor and debtor agree to its seizure.

3. Last to be distrained are sequestrated assets, those designated by the debtor as belonging to a third party and those claimed by third parties.

4. A debtor whose fodder is distrained may demand that a corresponding number of livestock be distrained at the same time.

5. In general the official who performs the distraint shall as far as possible reconcile the interests of the creditor with those of the debtor.

Article 95(a)

Loans between husband and wife are only attached when there are insufficient assets to cover the debt.

Article 96

1. The debtor is forbidden at law to dispose of distrained assets without the consent of the superintendent. The distraining official will inform the debtor of this provision.

2. Any disposal of assets by the debtor is void in so far as such disposals prejudice the rights of the creditors except where goods are acquired by third parties who acted in good faith.

Article 97

1. The distraining official will estimate the value of the objects distrained. He may appoint experts for that purpose.

2. The official will only distrain assets necessary to cover the debt together with interest and costs due to the creditor.

Article 98

1. When the assets distrained are cash, bank notes, bearer bonds, bills of exchange or other documents of title transferable by endorsement, gold or silver items or other valuable items, the debt enforcement office will take them into its custody.

2. Other assets may be provisionally left with the debtor or a third party in possession, who will present them on demand.

3. However these items will be taken into custody by the official or a third party if the superintendent considers such action to be appropriate or if the creditor shows that such action is necessary in order to protect his rights under the distraint.

4. The debt enforcement office may also take custody of assets over which a third party has security; it will restore the assets to the person entitled if realisation of the security does not take place.

Article 99

When the asset distrained is a debt or other right not established by bearer bond or transferable by endorsement, the superintendent will give notice to the third party debtor that in the future he will no longer be able to settle the debt other than through the debt enforcement office.

Article 100

The debt enforcement office is responsible for the conservation of distrained property and for the collection of debts as they fall due.

Article 101

1. Distraint of real estate takes effect as a restriction on further disposal; the debt enforcement office will notify the Land Registry of the distraint and the amount in respect of which the distraint was made. Notification is also given when new creditors join in the distraint and when the distraint has terminated.

2. Notice of the distraint of real estate property is deleted if no application for realisation is made within two years of the distraint.

Article 102

1. Distraint of real estate property includes fruit and other products, without prejudice to the rights of secured creditors.

2. The debt enforcement office will notify the secured creditors of the distraint and, if appropriate, tenants and farmers.

3. The debt enforcement office is responsible for the management and cultivation of any land subject to distraint.

Article 103

1. The debt enforcement office is responsible for the harvesting of fruit crops (arts. 94 and 102).

2. If the debtor has no means, resources necessary for the upkeep of the debtor and his family will be set aside.

Article 104

When the asset distrained is a usufruct or a share in an undivided inheritance, or in a company or an association the office will notify any third party interests.

Article 105

If requested the creditor is obliged to make an advance to cover the costs of the conservation of the distrained assets.

Article 106

1. If the debtor claims that an asset found in his possession belongs to or is charged to a third party, or when a third party claims an interest in the property or a charge over it, the debt enforcement office will refer to such claims at the distraint hearing; the debt enforcement office will inform the parties of these claims if notice of the distraint has already been given.

2. At the same time the office will allow the creditor and debtor a period of ten days in which to reach a decision over any claim made by a third party.

3. If no decision is made, the debtor and creditor are deemed to have admitted the claim.

Article 107

1. If the creditor or the debtor contests the claim, the debt enforcement office will invite the third party to defend its claim within the ten days.

2. The judge seized with the action will postpone final judgment for as long as the proceedings relate to an item subject to litigation. The time limits provided under article 116 do not run while the action continues.

3. A third party who does not defend his claim within the fixed period is deemed to have waived his claim.

4. If the third party has not been informed of his right to defend his claim, he can claim the distrained asset or its sale proceeds before these are distributed.

Article 108

Claims for stolen or lost goods remain regulated by articles 206 and 207 of the federal code of obligations. Agreed private sale under the supervision of the debt enforcement office takes effect as a public sale under article 206 of the code.

Article 109

When a distrained asset is not found in possession of the debtor, but in possession of a third party who claims to be the owner or asserts a security interest in it, the debt enforcement office will give the creditor a period of ten days to institute action. If the creditor does not use this period to institute action, he is deemed to have recognised the right of the third party.

Article 110

1. Creditors who apply for distraint within the thirty days following the first distraint share in the first distraint. The debt enforcement office will take such action as is necessary to complete the distraint from time to time according to the number of applications, so long as such action is necessary to meet the claims of the creditors in the same series.

2. Applications made after the thirty days constitute successive series of demands in the same way, and for which new distraint actions are commenced.

3. Distrained items may be included in a subsequent distraint action so long as payment of their sale proceeds to creditors belonging to the previous series is not prejudiced.

Article 111

1. The spouse, children and wards of the debtor, as well as the persons placed under his trusteeship, have the right to share in the distraint without prior legal proceedings for a period of forty days by virtue of any claims arising from marriage, parental or guardianship authority. However this right can only be exercised if the distraint has been made during the period of guardianship, parental authority or marriage, or in the following year. The duration of an action or legal proceedings is not taken into account. Adult children of the the debtor may, at any time and without taking prior proceedings, share in the distraint for claims founded under article 334 of the Swiss Civil Code. Guardians may also share in the distraint under the names of infant children, wards and persons placed under trusteeship.

2. The debt enforcement office will give notice to the debtor and the creditors of any application to share in the distraint; the debt enforcement office will give them ten days to oppose any such applications.

3. If an application by a person claiming a share in the distraint is opposed, he will join in the action only on a temporary basis and must institute his own action within ten days or risk exclusion. The proceedings are instituted in summary form.

Article 112

1. Distraint is recorded in a written statement. The written statement is signed by the official or employee who conducts the distraint; he will note the names of the creditor and debtor, the amount of the debt, the date and the time of the distraint, the assets distrained and their estimated values, and also the claims of third parties.

2. If the goods distrained are found to be subject to sequestration, the sequestrator's right to share (art. 281) is noted in the written statement.

3. If the distrained assets are insufficient or are wholly unsatisfactory to meet the debt, the official will make a note of this fact.

Article 113

A copy of the written statement of distraint is delivered to the creditor and debtor within three days of the distraint.

Article 114

1. The participation of further creditors and supplementary distraints are noted at the foot of the written statement.

2. A complete copy of the written statement is sent to any further creditors; the previous distraining parties and the debtor will receive a copy of the supplementary statement.

Article 115

1. If there are no assets available for distraint, the written statement shall take effect as a deed of insufficiency of assets within the meaning of article 149.

2. When the estimated value of distrained assets is insufficient, a provisional insufficiency of assets will arise and the creditors are accorded the rights referred to in article 271, paragraph 5 and article 285.

II: Realisation

1. Application for sale

Article 116

1. A creditor may apply for the sale of assets which have been distrained at the earliest one month and at the latest one year after the distraint, if the assets are moveable property, including claims; and at the earliest six months and at the latest two years after the distraint if the assets are real estate.

2. Where several creditors have an interest in the distraint, time starts to run from the last application for distraint.

Article 117

1. As regards the series to which he belongs, any creditor may apply for the sale of assets.

2. The creditors may also apply for the sale of assets which have been distrained to the extent of their appreciation in value (art. 110, 3rd paragraph).

Article 118

Where his distraint is only provisional, the creditor may not apply for sale. Time does not begin to run under article 116 with regard to such a creditor.

Article 119

1. Realisation will take place in accordance with articles 122–143.

2. Realisation will be suspended as soon as the proceeds reach the total amount of the claims for which the distraint was established. Realisation of objects distrained on a temporary basis may only occur in the cases referred to in article 124, 2nd paragraph.

Article 120

The debt enforcement office will inform the debtor of the application for sale within three days.

Article 121

The proceedings fail if the application is not made within the legal time limit or, if withdrawn, the proceedings are not restored within this time limit.

2. Sale of moveable property

Article 122

1. Moveable property including claims owed to the debtor will be sold by the debt enforcement office at the earliest ten days and at the latest one month after the application for sale.

2. Standing crops may not be sold before maturity without the consent of the debtor.

Article 123

1. If the debtor is able to show that he is in financial difficulties without fault on his part and if he undertakes to pay regular instalments to the debt enforcement office and immediately effects the first payment, the superintendent may postpone the sale by up to seven months.

2. This period may be extended if necessary by any period during which proceedings are stayed. The instalments and their due date must be rescheduled on expiry of the stay of proceedings.

3. The superintendent will determine the amount and date of the instalments; in so doing he must take into account the position of both the debtor and the creditor.

4. In proceedings applied for on the grounds either of debts which rank under article 219 as first class debts or of periodic contributions to maintenance, the sale may be postponed by a maximum of three months.

5. The postponement is null and void by operation of law if an instalment is not made punctually. At the instigation of the creditor and after having heard the debtor, the supervisory authority may also at any time revoke the postponement or make it dependent on the making of larger instalments if the creditor is able to show that the debtor is in a position to discharge the whole debt or to make greater instalments.

Article 124

1. On application of the debtor, the sale may take place even before the creditor has the right to apply for sale.

2. The superintendent may at any time proceed with the sale of objects which depreciate rapidly or which are costly to maintain.

Article 125

1. The sale will be by public auction. It will be preceded by an announcement giving the place, date and time of the sale.

2. The publicity given to this announcement and the method, time and place of the sale will be arranged by the superintendent in the manner he considers most favourable to the interested parties. It is not necessary to place the announcement in the official gazette.

3. If the debtor, the creditor and interested third parties have a known residence or representative in Switzerland they will be informed at least three days in advance of the day, time and place of the sale.

Article 126

1. The item to be sold will be auctioned after three calls to the person making the highest bid provided the bid is greater than the sum of the secured claims of the plaintiff.

2. If no sufficient offers are made the proceedings will be abandoned in relation to the item to be sold.

Article 127

If it is immediately clear that a sale in accordance with article 126 will not be possible, the superintendent may abandon the sale at the request of the plaintiff and draw up a deed of insufficiency of assets.

Article 128

Gold and silver objects may not be auctioned for a price which is less than the value of the metal.

Article 129

1. The sale will be completed on a cash basis.

2. However, the superintendent may allow a period of twenty days at the most for payment. In all cases delivery will only be made against payment.

3. If payment is not made within the time limit, the debt enforcement office will order a new public auction under article 126.

4. The previous bidder and his guarantors shall be liable for any reduction from the price at the first sale and for all other loss. Interest lost is calculated at a rate of 5 per cent.

Article 130

An agreed private sale may take place in the following cases:

(i) If all interested parties so request;
(ii) In the case of a security or commodity quoted in the market or on the stock exchange and for which an offer is made equal to the market price;
(iii) In the case of gold or silver objects which did not reach the market value of the metal in auction and for which the market price is offered;
(iv) In the case provided under article 124, 2nd paragraph.

Article 131

1. If all the distraining creditors so require, the claims owing to the debtor which are not quoted on the stock exchange or in the market will be paid to them in settlement, or to one of them for their account, at a full nominal value. In this case, the creditors are subrogated to the rights of the debtor to the extent of their claims.

2. Under the same conditions the distraining creditors or one of them may undertake to assert a claim, or claim for distraint against a third party debtor, at the risk and peril of the distraining creditors and without prejudice to their rights. In this event, any sum recovered will be applied first towards their own debts and costs.

Article 132

1. In the case of assets which are not specified in the preceeding articles such as usufructs, a share in an undivided inheritance, or in a company or other association, the superintendent will apply to the supervisory authority to determine the method of realisation.

2. The same rule applies to the sale of inventions, patent rights, industrial drawings and models, trademarks and copyrights.

3. After consulting the interested parties the authority may order a sale by public auction, delegate responsibility to an agent or take any other measure.

3. Sale of real estate

Article 133

1. Real estate will be sold by the debt enforcement office at public auction during the second month after the application for sale.

2. Article 123 will apply.

Article 134

1. The debt enforcement office will determine the conditions of sale according to the custom of the area and in the most advantageous manner.

2. At least ten days before the auction the conditions will be filed at the debt enforcement office where they will be available for inspection by the public.

Article 135

1. The conditions of sale will provide that the real estate is to be sold with all encumbrances (easements, land charges, mortgages, mortgage certificates, land charge notes) and that the personal obligations of the debtor will be assigned to the purchaser. The original obligor of a debt which has been assigned is only relieved of liability, in the case of a mortgage and a mortgage certificate, if the creditor fails to declare to him within a year of the sale that he does not intend to waive his rights against him (article 832 CC). Debts which have accrued due and which are secured on real estate will not be assigned, but are paid in priority out of the proceeds of sale.

2. The conditions of sale will specify the costs to be borne by the successful bidder.

Article 136

1. The sale shall be for cash or on credit. The period of credit shall not exceed six months.

2. [Repealed]

Article 136(a)

Acquisition of the property by the successful bidder may not be challenged except by way of petition for annulment of the sale.

Article 137

Where a period of time has been granted for payment the real estate will be managed by the debt enforcement office at the cost, risk and peril of the successful bidder until the purchase price is paid. No entry may be made on the land register in the intervening period without the authorisation of the debt enforcement office. Moreover, the debt enforcement office may require special security to guarantee the purchase price.

Article 138

1. The sale will be announced at least one month in advance.

2. The announcement will contain:

(i) the place, day and time of sale;
(ii) the date on which the conditions of sale will be filed;
(iii) the formal notice to the mortgage creditors and other interested parties to produce at the debt enforcement office within twenty days their title to the real estate, and in particular their title to any claim for interest and costs; failing which they will be excluded from the distribution of sale proceeds to the extent that their rights are not recorded in the public register.

3. This notice shall also be addressed to those who have easements if cantonal legislation is still applicable.

Article 139

A copy of the announcement shall be sent to the creditor, the debtor, any third party owner of the real estate and to all interested parties appearing in the public registers, provided they have a known residence or a legal representative.

Article 140

1. Before proceeding with the sale, the superintendent will draw up a statement of the charges encumbering the property (mortgages and liens, ground rents and rentals, usefructs, easements etc.) on the basis of the land register or copies of the land register (register of mortgages, record of charges on real estate etc.).

2. The debt enforcement office will provide the distraining creditors and the debtor with a copy of this statement giving them ten days within which to dispute the statement. Articles 106 and 107 apply.

3. The debt enforcement office will also proceed with a valuation of the real estate and provide the mortgage creditors with a copy.

Article 141

Articles 126 and 127 also apply to the realisation of real estate.

Article 142

If the real estate has been encumbered with an easement or a land charge without the agreement of a prior ranking creditor, this creditor will have the right to require the real estate to be auctioned with or without this charge. If the price offered for the real estate sold with the charge is not sufficient to pay the creditor he may require the charge to be struck from the land register as soon as the real estate thus unencumbered becomes realisable for a higher price. Any surplus proceeds of sale after the creditor has been satisfied is available to compensate the owner of the right to the extent of the value of the charge.

Article 143

1. If the successful bidder fails to pay within the time limit the transfer is revoked and the debt enforcement office will immediately order another auction to be held. Article 126 will also apply under these circumstances.

2. The first bidder and his guarantors are liable for any reduction from the price of the first sale and all other loss. Interest lost is calculated at a rate of 5 per cent.

Article 143a

In the event of conflict the provisions of the Swiss civil code and the supplementary cantonal legislation relating to the family home will prevail.

4. Distribution of the proceeds of sale

Article 144

1. Distribution of the proceeds of sale will take place as soon as all the assets included in the distraint have been sold.
2. Provisional distributions may be made at any time.
3. The costs of sale and distribution will be deducted from the proceeds of sale.
4. The net proceeds will be distributed to the creditors to the extent of their claims, including interest and the costs of the proceedings.
5. Any proceeds relating to provisional distraint will be deposited at the public trustees' office pending further instructions.

Article 145

If the proceeds of sale are insufficient to satisfy the creditors, the debt enforcement office will immediately complete the distraint without prejudice to any further distraints. Assets recently seized will be sold without further formality and as rapidly as possible. Compliance with time limits is not compulsory.

Article 146

1. If the proceeds of sale are not sufficient to pay all the creditors in full, the debt enforcement office will draw up an order of priority ranking among creditors.
2. The creditors will rank in the positions they would have been in under bankruptcy proceedings in accordance with article 219. The relevant date for the ranking of creditors in the first three classes is the demand for sale.

Article 147

The order of priority ranking among creditors will be filed at the debt enforcement office which will provide an abstract to each interested party.

Article 148

1. Within ten days of receipt of the abstract, any creditor may challenge the order of priority ranking by way of summons addressed to the interested parties before the judge in the district where the proceedings are taking place.
2. The action will take the form of summary proceedings.

Article 149

1. A distraining creditor who has not been fully paid will receive a deed of insufficiency of assets for the amount outstanding.
2. This deed constitutes an acknowledgement of debt as described in article 82 and confers the rights referred to in articles 271, paragraph 5, and 285.
3. The creditor is exempt from the requirement to issue an order to pay if he continues proceedings within six months of receipt of the deed.

4. The creditor may not claim interest from the debtor for the debt stated in the deed of insufficiency of assets. Any guarantors, joint debtors and other persons standing surety who are liable for subsequent interest may not demand reimbursement of interest from the debtor.

5. With regard to the debtor, the debt is free of any limitation period. His heirs may plead limitation if the creditor has not asserted his rights within the year of their acceding to the estate.

Article 150

1. A creditor who has been fully paid is required to deliver his deed of receipt for the debtor at the debt enforcement office.

2. If the claim is only partially paid, the creditor retains his deed of title to the claim, but the debt enforcement office will affix to it, or require to be affixed thereto by the competent authority, a memorandum indicating the amount for which it remains valid.

3. The debt enforcement office which has effected the sale of any real estate will provide for the deletion and transfer of easements, land charges and mortgages from the land register.

CHAPTER IV. PROCEEDINGS FOR THE REALISATION OF SECURITY

Article 151

1. An application for proceedings instituted on the grounds of a claim secured by a charge over moveables or by mortgage must, in addition to the information required by article 67, identify the item charged and the name of any third party who might have granted its security or become proprietor of the item charged.

2. A creditor who applies for proceedings to realise a charge over moveables is required, if appropriate, to notify any subsequent secured creditors (art. 217 of the federal code of obligations).

Article 152

1. Upon receipt of the application for proceedings, the debt enforcement office will draw up the order to pay in accordance with article 69, with the following modifications:

(i) the period for payment shall be one month in the case of a charge over moveables and six months in the case of a mortgage;
(ii) the notice will indicate that the security will be sold if the debtor does not comply with the order to pay or does not dispute it.

2. In the case of rented or leased property the debt enforcement office will advise the tenants or leaseholders of the proceedings.

Article 153

1. The order to pay will be drawn up in accordance with article 70.

2. If the security was granted by a third party or where a third party has become the owner of the item charged, a copy of the order to pay shall be addressed to him if his domicile is known.

3. If proceedings for redemption of a mortgage have been started under articles 828 and 829 of the Swiss civil code, the property may not be sold unless, at the end of the redemption proceedings, the plaintiff provides the debt enforcement office with proof that he still possesses a mortgage over the property as security for the claim which is subject to the proceedings.

4. The provisions of articles 71–86 concerning the order to pay and any disputed claim will also apply.

Article 154

1. A creditor may apply for the sale of moveable property subject to a charge at the earliest one month and at the latest one year after notification of the order to pay; and in the case of real estate subject to a mortgage at the earliest six months and at the latest three years after notification of the order to pay. If the application is opposed, time between commencement of proceedings and final judgment shall not count.

2. The proceedings will fail if the application is not made within the legal time limit or, if withdrawn, proceedings are not restored during that time limit.

Article 155

1. Articles 97, 1st paragraph, 102, 2nd paragraph, 103, 106, 107, 108 and 109 will apply to any property subject to a charge and in respect of which an application for sale has been made.

2. The debt enforcement office will inform the debtor of the application for sale within three days.

Article 156

The sale of any property subject to a charge will take place in accordance with articles 122 to 143. However, article 135 shall apply to the extent that such part of the sale price which relates to the plaintiff's claim must be paid in cash and the registry entry which relates to it must be deleted unless otherwise agreed.

Article 157

1. The costs of realisation and distribution will be deducted from the proceeds of sale.

2. The net proceeds will be distributed to the secured creditors to the extent of their claims including interest and the costs of the proceedings.

3. If the proceeds do not suffice to satisfy the creditors in full, the superintendent will determine the ranking and dividend for each person after taking account of the provisions of article 219, 2nd and 3rd paragraphs.

4. Articles 147, 148 and 150 apply.

Article 158

1. If the sale of the item charged does not take place due to lack of sufficient offers (articles 126 and 127) or if the proceeds of sale are insufficient to pay the plaintiff creditor in full, the creditor will be issued with a deed of insufficiency of assets.

2. An unsuccessful creditor may proceed by way of distraint or bankruptcy according to the means of the debtor so long as his right does not arise from a land charge note

or from some other form of land charge. The creditor is exempt from the requirement to issue an order to pay if he acts within one month.

CHAPTER V. PROCEEDINGS IN BANKRUPTCY

I: Ordinary proceedings in bankruptcy

Article 159

On expiry of the period twenty days from notification of the order to pay, the creditor may apply to the superintendent to give the debtor due notice of threat of bankruptcy proceedings.

Article 160

1. The notice of threat of bankruptcy will state:

(i) The particulars of the application for bankruptcy proceedings;
(ii) The date of the order to pay;
(iii) The warning that the creditor will be able to apply for bankruptcy proceedings within twenty days;
(iv) Notice that, under article 17, the debtor may within the next ten days petition the supervisory authority if he considers that he should not be subjected to bankruptcy proceedings.

2. The debtor will be reminded *inter alia* that the law allows him to propose a scheme of arrangement with creditors.

Article 161

1. The debtor is notified of the notice of threat of bankruptcy within three days of the application.
2. The bankruptcy office will send a copy of the notice of threat to the creditor immediately afterwards.
3. The notification is carried out in accordance with article 72.

Article 162

At the request of the creditor, the bankruptcy judge may, if he considers this measure necessary, decide that an inventory of the debtor's assets be drawn up.

Article 163

1. The inventory is drawn up by the bankruptcy office. It cannot be drawn up before notification of the notice of warning of bankruptcy.
2. The provisions of articles 90, 91 and 92 will likewise apply.

Article 164

1. The debtor is obliged on risk of prosecution to produce at any time the listed assets either in kind or their equivalent value except those which the superintendent may have released to him for his upkeep and the upkeep of his family.

2. The superintendent will draw the debtor's attention to this provision.

Article 165

1. The drawing-up of an inventory will be revoked by the superintendent if all the plaintiff creditors consent.

2. The effect of taking an inventory will cease to have effect at law four months after its date.

Article 166

1. On expiry of the period of twenty days from the notice of warning, the creditor may apply to the judge for a declaration of bankruptcy. He will attach to his application the order to pay and the notice of warning.

2. The right to apply for bankruptcy expires one year from the date of notification of the order to pay. If it is opposed, time running from commencement of proceedings to final judgment is not counted.

Article 167

A creditor who has withdrawn an application for bankruptcy may not renew it for one month.

Article 168

A judge seized with an application for bankruptcy will notify the parties of the time and date of the hearing at least three days in advance. They may appear in person or be represented.

Article 169

1. A creditor who applies for bankruptcy is responsible for costs up to the first creditor's meeting (art. 235).

2. The judge may require him to advance these costs.

Article 170

The judge may order any conservatory measures he deems necessary in the interests of the creditors.

Article 171

The judge will issue his decision during the hearing even in the absence of the parties. He must declare bankruptcy except in those cases referred to in articles 172 and 173.

Article 172

The judge will reject the application for bankruptcy in the following cases:

(i) If the supervisory authority has cancelled the notice of warning;

(ii) If the judge grants a debtor who has not opposed the proceedings within the time limits the benefit of article 77;
(iii) If the debtor gives documentary proof that the claim has been discharged as to capital, interest and costs or that the creditor has granted him a stay.

Article 173

1. If the supervisory authority, upon receipt of a petition, orders suspension of the proceedings the judge will adjourn his decision on the application for bankruptcy.

2. If he himself considers that the debtor is not subject to bankruptcy proceedings or that a debtor who does not have civil capacity has been sued unlawfully, the judge will also adjourn his decision and remit the case to the supervisory authority.

3. He will issue his decision on the application for bankruptcy after receiving the decision of the authority.

Article 173(a)

If the debtor proves he has made an application for a scheme of arrangement or for a stay of proceedings on exceptional grounds the court may adjourn the bankruptcy judgment.

Article 174

1. The decision in which the judge declares or refuses to declare bankruptcy may be referred to a superior judicial authority within ten days of its issue.

2. If that authority suspends execution of the judgment of first instance, it will, if appropriate, order the conservatory measures provided under article 170.

Article 175

1. The bankruptcy commences upon issue of the judgment declaring bankruptcy.

2. Issue of the judgment determines this moment.

Article 176

As soon as the declaration of bankruptcy becomes executory it is notified to the bankruptcy office, to the keeper of the land register and to the superintendent at the commercial registry. Termination and revocation of bankruptcy will also be notified to them.

II: Proceedings relating to bills of exchange

Article 177

1. A creditor who sues on a bill of exchange or cheque may apply for proceedings on a bill of exchange when the debtor is subject to bankruptcy even though the debt is secured.

2. The creditor will attach the bill of exchange or cheque to his application.

Article 178

1. When the bankruptcy office is satisfied regarding the existence of the following conditions it will immediately give notice of the order to pay.

2. This document sets out:

(i) The particulars of the applications for proceedings;
(ii) The demand to pay within five days the total amount of the claim with costs;
(iii) Notice that the debtor may dispute the claim within the same period by giving the bankruptcy office in writing his grounds for disputing the claim, and that, by virtue of articles 17 and 20, he also has five days in which to petition the supervisory board, if he considers the document contravenes the provisions of this law;
(iv) Notice that the debtor will incur the consequences provided under article 188 if he does not comply with the order to pay.

3. Articles 70 and 72 apply.

Article 179

At the debtor's request, he will be given the document disputing the claim free of charge.

Article 180

1. The document disputing the claim is attached to the creditor's copy of the order to pay; if this does not occur, the fact that it has not occurred is also noted.

2. The bankruptcy office will send this copy to the creditor immediately following issue of the document disputing the claim or upon expiry of the time limit for disputing the claim.

Article 181

The bankruptcy office will submit the document disputing the claim immediately to the judge who will decide on its admissibility at the latest within five days. The judge is entitled to hear the parties.

Article 182

The judge will declare the dispute of a claim admissible:

(i) If the debtor provides documentary proof that the bearer of the bill or cheque has been paid, or has consented to remission of the debt or has granted a stay;
(ii) If he alleges fraudulent title and this appears likely;
(iii) If the debtor raises an admissible exception to the rules regarding bills of exchange which appears well founded;
(iv) If he alleges another ground for disputing the claim founded on article 1007 of the code of obligations and his submissions are credible; in this case the

defendant must deposit in advance the amount of the bill in money or its equivalent value.

Article 183

1. If the judge rejects the dispute of a claim, he may order any necessary conservatory measures, in particular he may order an inventory of assets to be drawn up in accordance with articles 162–165.

2. He may also require the creditor to provide security.

Article 184

1. The decision on the admissibility of the dispute of a claim will be immediately communicated to the parties.

2. If the dispute of a claim is only admitted against deposit, the creditor will be requested to commence his action for payment within ten days. If he fails to comply within this period, the deposit is returned.

Article 185

The parties may appeal to the cantonal high court against the decision relating to the dispute of a claim within five days of communication of the decision.

Article 186

If the dispute of a claim is declared admissible, the proceedings are suspended and the creditor will assert his rights in ordinary proceedings.

Article 187

Whoever pays a sum in undefended proceedings which he did not owe has the right to reclaim it in accordance with article 86. This right arises even if he pays it after his dispute of a claim has been declared inadmissible.

Article 188

1. If a debtor who does not dispute the claim or whose dispute of claim has been rejected does not comply with the order to pay, the creditor may apply for bankruptcy simply on the production of title to his claim, the order to pay and, if appropriate, the judgment rejecting the dispute of claim.

2. The right to apply for bankruptcy expires one month from the date of notification of the order to pay. If the claim is disputed, any time up to judgment or, if appropriate, from the commencement of proceedings to final judgment, is not counted.

Article 189

1. Within three days of the application the judge will declare bankruptcy without hearing the parties.

2. Articles 169, 170, 173, 175 and 176 apply.

III: Bankruptcy without preliminary proceedings

Article 190

1. A creditor may apply for bankruptcy without preliminary proceedings:

(i) If the debtor has no known residence, if he has disappeared with the intention of evading his obligations, if he has defrauded or attempted to defraud his creditors or has concealed his assets in the course of proceedings for restraint against him;
(ii) if a debtor subject to bankruptcy proceedings has suspended payments;
(iii) In the case provided under article 309.

2. A debtor who has a residence or representative in Switzerland will be summoned to be heard before the judge within a short period.

Article 191

A debtor may petition for his own bankruptcy by declaring himself insolvent at law.

Article 192

Bankruptcy of limited companies and co-operative societies may be declared without preliminary proceedings in the cases provided under arts. 657 and 704 of the federal code of obligations.

Article 193

1. Renounced inheritances will be liquidated by the bankruptcy office. The provisions of chapter seven apply.
2. In this event, the general rules of the law of succession relating to official liquidation will prevail.

Article 194

Articles 169, 170, 174, 175 and 176 apply to bankruptcies without preliminary proceedings. In all cases, notification to the registry of commerce (art. 176) does not arise if the debtor is not subject to bankruptcy proceedings.

IV: Revocation of bankruptcy

Article 195

1. The judge will declare revocation of bankruptcy and the restoration of the debtor to unrestricted control over his assets when the debtor is presented with a declaration by all the creditors attesting that they withdraw their proofs of debt and also when a scheme of arrangement has been agreed.
2. Revocation may be declared upon the expiry of the period for proof of debts and up to termination of bankruptcy.
3. Revocation will be announced in public.

Article 196

If an inheritance is under liquidation in accordance with article 193, and before termination a person entitled presents himself and declares his acceptance of the succession, the judge will stop the liquidation provided that the heir provides security for the payment of debts.

CHAPTER VI. THE LEGAL EFFECT OF BANKRUPTCY

I: The effect of bankruptcy on the debtor's assets

Article 197

1. All assets which are capable of being distrained at the moment when bankruptcy proceedings commence form a single estate wherever they are located and are appropriated for the payment of creditors.

2. Assets entering into the ownership of the bankrupt person up to the termination of bankruptcy will become part of the bankrupt estate.

Article 198

Assets subject to a charge are likewise within the bankruptcy estate, subject to the preferential rights of the chargee.

Article 199

1. Unrealised assets distrained at the time of the commencement of bankruptcy proceedings and sequestrated assets are within the bankruptcy estate.

2. The proceeds of assets which have been realised are distributed in accordance with articles 144–150 and any surplus is added to the bankruptcy estate.

Article 200

The bankruptcy estate also includes anything which might be the subject of avoidance proceedings under articles 214 and 285–292.

Article 201

Bearer bonds and negotiable instruments transferred to the bankrupt for collection purposes only or as cover for specially designated future payments may be claimed back by the party entitled.

Article 202

If the bankrupt has sold an item belonging to another and has not been paid the price before the commencement of the bankruptcy proceedings, the owner has the right to demand transfer of the claim against the purchaser or the return of the price paid, if it has been added to the bankruptcy estate, against reimbursement of anything owing to the estate for the item.

Article 203

1. Items which have been sold and dispatched and of which the debtor has not taken possession before the commencement of bankruptcy proceedings may be recovered by the seller unless the bankruptcy estate pays him the price.

2. The claim for recovery may not lie if, before the announcement of bankruptcy, the items have been sold or charged to a third party in good faith, or are subject to a consignment note, bill of lading or waybill.

Article 204

1. After the commencement of bankruptcy proceedings a disposal by the debtor of assets forming part of the estate is void.

2. However, if before the announcement of bankruptcy was published, the debtor has paid on maturity a bill of exchange underwritten by him or a bill of exchange drawn on him, the payment is valid, provided the bearer of the bill knew nothing of the bankruptcy and could, if payment had been refused, have had recourse against a third party which would have been valid under the law on bills of exchange.

Article 205

1. From the date of commencement of bankruptcy proceedings, the debtor is unable to give valid receipt for any payments made to him. Anyone making a payment to him is not discharged as regards the creditors of the bankrupt person except to the extent of any sum or equivalent value received by the bankrupt estate.

2. Nevertheless, a debtor of the bankrupt person who has discharged his debt to the bankrupt before announcement of the bankruptcy is discharged unless he had actual knowledge of the bankruptcy.

Article 206

Proceedings against the debtor are discontinued. No proceedings may be commenced during the liquidation in bankruptcy.

Article 207

1. Except in an emergency, civil actions initiated by or against the debtor are suspended and cannot be continued until ten days following the second creditors' meeting (art. 252).

2. This provision does not apply to personal injury claims for damages and interest or to matrimonial, family or maintenance disputes.

3. Prescriptive and forfeiture periods are interrupted during the periods when proceedings are suspended.

II: The effect of bankruptcy on creditors' rights

Article 208

1. On the commencement of bankruptcy proceedings all the bankrupt's debts become due and payable with the exception however of those debts which are secured by

charges over the debtor's real estate. Interest accrued up to the date of the institution of bankruptcy proceedings and costs are added to the principal sum.

2. Debts which have not matured and which do not bear interest are discounted at the rate of 5 per cent.

Article 209

So far as the bankrupt is concerned commencement of bankruptcy proceedings stops interest running on all unsecured debts.

Article 210

1. If a claim is subject to a condition precedent or to term of uncertain duration, the creditor may nevertheless claim in the bankruptcy but he will only be entitled to the proceeds upon fulfilment of the condition precedent or completion of the term.

2. A claim under an annuity contract is governed by article 522 of the federal code of obligations.

Article 211

1. Any claim which is not for money is transformed into a claim for an equivalent amount of money.

2. However, the administrators of the bankrupt's estate may discharge the claim in kind, provided that they grant any security requested by the creditor.

3. Obligations relating to leaseholds are governed by the provisions of article 315 of the federal code of obligations.

Article 212

A person who has sold and delivered goods to the debtor prior to the commencement of bankruptcy proceedings may neither rescind the contract nor demand the return of the goods even though he may have expressly reserved this right.

Article 213

1. A creditor has the right to set off his claim against any claim the bankrupt may have against him.

2. Set-off is not permitted:

(i) If the debtor of the bankrupt became his creditor after the commencement of bankruptcy proceedings;
(ii) If the creditor of the bankrupt became his or his estate's debtor after the commencement of bankruptcy proceedings;
(iii) [Repealed].

3. A claim for set-off under a negotiable instrument is permissible if and to the extent that the creditor is able to establish that he acquired the negotiable instrument in good faith prior to the commencement of bankruptcy proceedings.

4. If a limited company or a co-operative society becomes bankrupt, arrears due on shares or on capital contributions may not be set off against what is owed by the company.

Article 214

Set-off may be contested if, before the commencement of bankruptcy proceedings, the debtor of the bankrupt with actual knowledge of the insolvency of his creditor acquired a claim against him with the intention of procuring for himself or for a third party by means of set-off an advantage to the prejudice of the bankruptcy estate.

Article 215

1. Guarantees given by the bankrupt are admitted as liabilities even though the debt may not have matured.

2. The bankruptcy estate is subrogated to the rights of the creditor against the principal debtor and those jointly liable with the debtor to the extent of the dividend paid by the estate (art. 504 of the federal code of obligations). In the case of bankruptcy of the principal debtor or of a joint debtor, articles 216 and 217 apply.

Article 216

1. Where several persons liable for the same debt are simultaneously bankrupt, the creditor may prove for his whole claim in each of the bankruptcies.

2. If the dividends taken together exceed the amount of the claim, the excess is distributed among those bankruptcy estates which paid an amount over and above the bankrupt's proportion on behalf of those jointly liable with him.

3. The several bankruptcy estates do not have recourse among one another for the dividends they have paid if the total of these dividends does not exceed the sum due to the creditor.

Article 217

1. Where a person jointly liable with the bankrupt has paid an instalment towards the debt, the debt is nonetheless admitted as a liability. for the original sum due even though the joint debtor does not have recourse against the bankrupt.

2. The creditor and the co-debtor have the right to prove in the bankruptcy.

3. The creditor will collect a dividend to the extent of his claim; the excess is returned to the co-debtor as the dividend relating to his right of recourse, and to the estate as regarding any surplus.

Article 218

1. When a partnership and a partner are simultaneously made bankrupt, the creditors of the partnership may only claim in the bankruptcy of the partner for the sum they are unable to recover from the partnership. Articles 216 and 217 apply to payment of this sum by the individual partners.

2. If one of the partners becomes bankrupt without the partnership becoming bankrupt, the creditors of the partnership may claim for the whole sum of the debts and the estate of the partner is subrogated as provided in article 215.

Article 219

1. The secured creditors have priority in the proceeds of sale of the security.

2. If a claim is secured by several charges the proceeds are apportioned in proportion to the amount of the debt.

3. The order of priority in claims secured by mortgages, regardless of the extension of such security to interest and other incidents, is governed by the provisions relating to mortgages.

4. Unsecured claims as well as guaranteed claims not covered by security rank as follows in the proceeds of sale of the assets in the estate:

First Class

(a) Claims which workers and outworkers may claim under a contract of employment and which arise in the six months immediately preceding the commencement of bankruptcy, claims arising from the anticipatory breach of contracts of employment caused by the bankruptcy of the employer and also claims arising from the enforcement of security.

(b) Pecuniary claims for family maintenance arising in the twelve months immediately preceding commencement of bankruptcy.

(c) Burial expenses.

Second Class

(a) Claims by persons whose estate has been placed in the administration of the debtor by virtue of guardianship or paternal authority for the sum which is thereby due to them; these claims only have priority if the bankruptcy was declared during the exercise of guardianship or paternal authority or in the year following. Time running during a trial or civil proceedings is not counted. Claims arising from the debtor's responsibility as a member of a guardianship authority (articles 426–430 of the Civil Code) are treated as claims arising from the responsibility of the debtor as a guardian or holder of paternal authority; likewise the above mentioned period is not taken into account;

(b) The claims of workers' funds for the sum due by the employer.

(c) Bonuses and benefits in accordance with the federal law of accident insurance;

(d) Claims arising under letters of guarantee generally and in particular those issued by institutions for loans granted to their members (under article 11, paragraph 1 of the federal law of 25th June 1930 on the issue of letters of guarantee) in the sum which, at the same time of commencement of bankruptcy, is in excess of the cover to which the creditor is entitled (arts. 14, 19 and 25 of the federal law on the issue of letters of guarantee); on the other hand, this priority does not exist for any under-value below the cover to which the creditor is entitled if the security is realised;

(e) Debts of an employer owed to funds intended to create and maintain welfare institutions for the benefit of employees and workers of the business as well as the claims of funds created in favour of partners to the extent that legal personality has been conferred on these funds;

(f) Claims for premiums for old age and life insurance in accordance with the federal law of 20th December 1946;

(g) Premiums and contributions payable to compensation funds for allocation to families;

(h) Claims for premiums for mandatory unemployment insurance;

(i) Claims for premiums for the scheme of benefits for loss of earnings in favour of those liable for military service or civil defence subscriptions in accordance with the Federal Law of 21st September 1952;

(k) Claims for subscriptions for health insurance in accordance with the Federal Law of 19th June 1959;
(l) Claims for premiums for sickness funds recognised by the Confederation;
(m) Any charge to withholding tax transferred by the debtor before commencement of bankruptcy or before distraint (art. 46 paragraph 2 of the Federal Law of 13th October 1965 on withholding tax).

Third Class
(a) Claims of doctors recognised by the state, claims of chemists and midwives, as well as expenses incurred in caring for the debtor and his family arising in the year preceding commencement of bankruptcy;
(b) Any deposit at a bank not benefiting from a cantonal guarantee and having a name including the word 'savings' up to 5000 francs per depositor; one bank book in any number of names only giving one entitlement to 5000 francs;
(c) Claims of an agent under a contract of agency for the twelve months preceding commencement of bankruptcy;
(d) Claims of a buyer arising under a sale on payment in advance terms (art. 277, paragraph 3 of the code of obligations);
(e) Claims of review bodies under article 22, and the claims of the observer of the banking commission under article 23 (fourth paragraph), of the Federal Law of 8th November 1934 on banks and savings banks.

Fourth Class
(a) [Repealed];
(b) Any deposit at a bank not benefiting from a cantonal guarantee and having a name including the word 'savings', up to 5000 francs per depositor, where the deposit exceeds 5000 francs, one bank book in any number of names only giving one entitlement to 5000 francs.

Fifth Class
All other debts.

Article 220

1. Creditors ranking in the same class have equal rights.
2. As long as creditors in a preceding class are not completely satisfied the following classes receive nothing.

CHAPTER VII. LIQUIDATION OF THE BANKRUPTCY ESTATE

I: Calculation of the bankruptcy assets

Article 221

1. As soon as the bankruptcy office has received notification of the commencement of bankruptcy proceedings it will draw up an inventory of the assets of the bankrupt person and take measures necessary to preserve the assets.
2. If some of these assets are situated in another district the bankruptcy office situated in that area will assist.

Article 222

1. The bankrupt is obliged on risk of prosecution to provide details of all his assets to the bankruptcy office and to make the assets available to the bankruptcy office.

2. If the bankrupt is dead or has absconded, this obligation is incumbent on all adult persons who lived with him.

3. The bankruptcy office will inform all interested parties of this obligation.

Article 223

1. The bankruptcy office will arrange to close and seal up all shops, warehouses and retail outlets belonging to the bankrupt, unless it is possible to administer these establishments under the supervision of the bankruptcy office up to the time of the first meeting of the creditors.

2. The bankruptcy office will take control of all ready cash, shares, accounting books, business records and contracts of any value.

3. The bankruptcy office will seal up any other property until production of the inventory of assets. The seals may remain for as long as the bankruptcy office considers necessary.

4. The bankruptcy office will also take control of any items which are outside the premises used by the bankrupt.

Article 224

The bankruptcy office will allow the bankrupt to retain control over the assets set out in article 92. These assets will nevertheless be included in the inventory.

Article 225

Items shown as belonging to third parties or claimed by third parties will also be included in the inventory. The inventory will set out these claims.

Article 226

Registered third party rights over real estate belonging to the bankrupt will be noted as a matter of course on the inventory.

Article 227

Every asset included in the inventory will be valued.

Article 228

1. The bankruptcy office will send the inventory to the bankrupt and ask him to declare the inventory accurate and complete.

2. This declaration is written on the inventory and signed by the bankrupt.

Article 229

1. The bankrupt is obliged on risk of prosecution to make himself available to the administrators of the bankruptcy estate during the liquidation unless he is expressly

excused. If necessary the bankrupt will be compelled by the authorities charged with public order to appear before the administrators.

2. The administrators may provide appropriate support to the bankrupt particularly if the bankrupt continues to make himself available to them.

3. The administrators will decide the time period during which the bankrupt and his family are able to continue to stay in their dwelling house.

Article 230

1. If the bankrupt has no assets, the bankruptcy office will report accordingly to the judge who has ordered the bankruptcy and the judge will declare suspension of the liquidation.

2. The bankruptcy office will publish any such suspension of liquidation. Publication of this measure means that the bankruptcy proceedings are closed unless within ten days the creditors demand continuation of the bankruptcy proceedings and make a payment of costs on account.

3. For two years after the suspension of the liquidation the creditors may still bring actions for distraint against the bankrupt.

II: Announcements to creditors

Article 231

1. If the bankruptcy office calculates that the total of the value of goods contained in the inventory will not be sufficient to cover the costs of the liquidation, it will notify the judge who declared the bankruptcy accordingly.

2. If the judge agrees, he will order the bankruptcy office to proceed with summary liquidation, unless a creditor requests ordinary liquidation before the assets have been distributed and makes a payment of costs on account.

3. In the case of summary liquidation the bankruptcy office will publish a notice inviting creditors to submit their demands within twenty days. The bankruptcy office will sell the assets for the best price available and distribute the proceeds without further formality. Termination of the liquidation is then announced in public.

4. In other cases the bankruptcy office proceeds with an ordinary liquidation in accordance with the requirements of the following articles.

Article 232

1. If the liquidation is an ordinary liquidation the bankruptcy office will publish an announcement declaring the commencement of bankruptcy.

2. The announcement will contain:

(i) The name and address of the bankrupt and the date of commencement of bankruptcy proceedings;

(ii) Instructions to creditors or to those having claims against the bankrupt to send details of their claims to the bankruptcy office within one month of the published notice and to send to the bankruptcy office all evidence of proof of those claims (documents of title, accounting entries etc.) in original or certified copies. In the case of creditors living outside Europe the bankruptcy office may extend this time period;

(iii) Instructions to the bankrupt's debtors to declare their debt within the same time period on risk of prosecution;

(iv) Instructions to those who maintain a lien over any assets of the bankrupt, on whatever grounds, to place their assets at the disposal of the bankruptcy office within the same time period and with all rights reserved. Failure to comply invokes the penalties set down by law and deprives them of their preferential right in the absence of sufficient excuse;

(v) The summons to the first meeting of creditors. This meeting will be convened at the latest within ten days of the announcement. The summons will make clear that co-debtors, sureties and other guarantors of the bankrupt are entitled to be present at the meeting.

Article 233

The bankruptcy office will send a copy of the announcement to all known creditors by ordinary post.

Article 234

If the liquidation involves a renounced inheritance and renunciation by the heirs was preceded by a notice to creditors under the law of succession, the period for proof of claims is reduced to ten days and creditors who have already proved their claims are not required to do so again under the liquidation.

III: Administration of the bankruptcy estate

Article 235

1. The first meeting of creditors is presided over by an official from the bankruptcy office, assisted by two creditors who together with him form the creditors' secretariat.

2. If persons attend the meeting who were not summoned, the secretariat will decide whether they may participate in the meeting.

3. The meeting is validly constituted if creditors representing at least one quarter of all known creditors are present. If there are only four or fewer, these must represent half the creditors.

4. Decisions of the meeting are taken by absolute majority. In the case of deadlock, the chairman of the meeting has a casting vote. The secretariat will arbitrate on disputes involving the counting of votes.

Article 236

If the meeting cannot be validly constituted, this will be duly recorded. In this event the bankruptcy office will administer the bankruptcy estate and continue the liquidation until the second meeting of creditors.

Article 237

1. If the meeting is validly constituted the bankruptcy office will report to it on the inventory of assets and on the bankruptcy estate.

2. The meeting will decide if the liquidation will be managed by the bankruptcy

office or by a special administration consisting of one or more persons chosen by the creditors.

3. In either of these cases, the meeting may appoint from its members a supervisory committee and grant to this committee such powers as the meeting considers necessary, in particular the following:

- (i) To supervise the administration of the bankruptcy and to give advice to the administrators when required and to oppose every measure which appears to be detrimental to the interests of creditors;
- (ii) To authorise the continuation of commercial or industrial activity and to regulate trading conditions;
- (iii) To ratify the settlement of accounts and to authorise the administrators to negotiate, settle or compromise claims;
- (iv) To oppose claims accepted by the administrators;
- (v) To authorise the distribution of dividends during liquidation.

Article 238

1. The meeting may make emergency resolutions particularly regulating continuation of the bankrupt's commercial or industrial activity, the opening of workshops, shops or other retail outlets, pending legal actions and private sales.

2. If the bankrupt proposes a scheme of arrangement, the creditors may order suspension of the liquidation.

Article 239

1. Decisions taken by the meeting may be referred by any creditor to the supervisory committee within five days.

2. The supervisory committee will issue its decision within a short period after hearing representations made by the bankruptcy office, and if appropriate, representations of the opposing creditor and the creditors proposing the decision.

Article 240

The administrators are responsible for the bankruptcy estate and its liquidation. They represent the bankruptcy estate at law.

Article 241

The provisions of articles 5, 8, first and second paragraphs, 9, 11, 13, 17 and 19 relating to the bankruptcy office also apply to a special administration.

Article 242

1. The administrators will decide if items claimed by third parties should be handed over to them.

2. The administrators will allow any person whose claim they dispute a period of ten days to commence proceedings. Any third party who allows this time period to expire will be deemed to have renounced the claim.

Article 243

1. The administrators will realise liquid credits belonging to the bankruptcy estate, if necessary by legal process.

2. Items which depreciate or are expensive to preserve will be sold without delay. Shares or other assets quoted on the stock exchange or in the market may be realised immediately.

3. Other assets will not be sold until after the second meeting of creditors.

IV: Verification of claims; priorities

Article 244

After expiry of the period allowed for proof of claims, the administrators will examine the claims and make the necessary verifications. The administrators will consult the bankrupt on each proof of claim.

Article 245

The administrators will decide which liabilities will be accepted. The administrators are not bound by the bankrupt's declarations.

Article 246

Claims entered in the register of mortgages or land charges are accepted with interest, even if not proven.

Article 247

1. Within twenty days after expiry of the period for proof of claims, the administrators will draw up a list of priorities in accordance with articles 219 and 220. If there is a supervisory committee the list will be submitted to it and the committee has three days to amend it.

2. If necessary these periods may be extended by the supervisory committee.

Article 248

The list of priorities will indicate the claims which have been rejected and the grounds for rejection.

Article 249

1. The list of priorities will be filed at the bankruptcy office.

2. The administrators will notify creditors of the list by public announcement.

3. Creditors whose claims have been rejected in whole or partially, or creditors who have not been accepted at the level of priority which they claimed are informed directly.

Article 250

1. A creditor objecting to the list must commence proceedings before the judge who ordered the bankruptcy within ten days of announcement of the filing of the list.

2. If the creditor alleges that his claim has been wrongfully rejected or reduced or that his claim has not been accorded the level of priority he claims, proceedings are brought against the bankruptcy estate. If the objecting creditor objects to another claim or the priority accorded to it, the proceedings are brought against the relevant creditor.

3. As soon as proceedings for the striking out of a claim or for modification of the rank of a claim are accepted as well-founded, the dividend relating to that claim is transferred to the opposing creditor up to the amount claimed including all costs incurred in the action, and the surplus is distributed in accordance with the corrected list of priorities.

4. The proceedings will be in summary form.

Article 251

1. A creditor who is late in proving his claim will be admitted up to termination of the bankruptcy.

2. Any costs caused by the delay are to be paid by the creditor who may be required to make a payment of costs on account.

3. The creditor has no right to distributions ordered prior to making his claim.

4. If the administrators allow the claim, they will amend the list of priorities and advise creditors by publishing the amendment.

5. Article 250 will apply.

V: Liquidation of the estate

Article 252

1. After the verification of claims the administrators will convene a second meeting of creditors. All creditors are invited to attend whether their claims are accepted in full or in part. The notice convening the meeting must be sent at least twenty days prior to the date of the meeting.

2. If an application for a scheme of arrangement is to be discussed, the notice convening the meeting must state this.

3. The meeting will be chaired by an administrator. Article 235, 3rd and 4th paragraphs, will apply by analogy.

Article 253

1. The administrators will present to the meeting a complete report on the progress of the liquidation and on the current state of the assets and liabilities of the bankrupt.

2. The meeting will decide whether it will confirm the terms of reference of the administrators and the members of the supervisory committee. The meeting has the right to take all decisions which it considers necessary to preserve the assets.

Article 254

If the meeting cannot be validly constituted, this will be duly recorded; the administrators and the committee will remain responsible until termination of the liquidation.

Article 255

Additional meetings may be called if the majority of creditors or the supervisory committee require or the administrators consider this to be necessary.

Article 256

1. Assets within the estate will be sold at the instigation of the administrators by public auction or by private sale if the creditors prefer.
2. Items over which security has been granted may only be sold privately with the consent of the secured creditors.

Article 257

1. The announcement of the sale will set out the time, place and date of the auction.
2. If real estate is involved, the announcement will be made at least one month in advance and will indicate the date after which the conditions of sale will be deposited at the bankruptcy office.
3. Each mortgagee creditor will receive a copy of the announcement and will be advised of the estimated sale price at the same time.

Article 258

The item for sale will be sold after three calls to the highest bidder. In the case of the sale of real estate article 142 applies.

Article 259

Articles 128, 129, 134, 135, 136, 136(A), 137 and 143 apply to the conditions of sale. The duties of the bankruptcy office are performed by the administrators of the bankruptcy.

Article 260

1. If the bankruptcy estate declines to assert a claim, the claim is transferred to those creditors who wish to assert it.
2. The proceeds of the claim after deduction of costs incurred will go towards satisfaction of the claims of the transferees in the order of their priority, and any excess will be transferred to the bankruptcy estate.

Article 260(a)

The provisions of the Swiss Civil Code and the complementary cantonal regulations relating to the family home remain valid.

VI: Distribution of the proceeds of sale

Article 261

When the proceeds of sale of the assets have been collected and the list of priorities has been finally established, the administrators will draw up a statement setting out the allocation of the sale proceeds and produce the final account.

Article 262

1. The costs incurred as a result of the commencement of bankruptcy proceedings and the liquidation are deducted.

2. The sale proceeds of assets subject to a charge will only bear the costs of administering and realising the security.

Article 263

1. The allocation statement and the final account will be kept open for inspection at the bankruptcy office for ten days.

2. This will be brought to the attention of the creditors, and each creditor is sent the abstract relating to his dividend.

Article 264

1. On expiry of the time for inspection the administrators will proceed with the distribution of monies.

2. The provisions of article 150 apply.

3. Dividends relating to claims subject to a condition precedent or an uncertain maturity date are deposited in the public trustees treasury office.

Article 265

1. On commencement of the distribution the administrators will send to each creditor who has not been fully paid a deed of insufficiency of assets in the unpaid sum. The document states whether the bankrupt has recognised or contested the claim. In the former case the document takes effect as a recognition of debt as defined in article 82.

2. The deed of insufficiency of assets confers the rights referred to in article 149. However further proceedings may not be commenced unless the debtor's financial position improves.

3. In the event of dispute the judge will issue his decision in summary accelerated proceedings.

Article 266

A provisional distribution of the proceeds may be made as soon as the time limit for opposition has expired.

Article 267

Claims which have not participated in the liquidation are treated as deeds of insufficiency of assets.

VII: Termination of bankruptcy

Article 268

1. After the distribution, the administrators will present a final report to the judge who declared the bankruptcy.

2. The judge will declare termination of bankruptcy if he is satisfied the liquidation has finished.

3. If the judge has any comments on the administration of the bankruptcy he will make them to the supervisory committee.

4. The bankruptcy office will announce in public the termination of bankruptcy proceedings.

Article 269

1. If, after termination of bankruptcy, assets are discovered which have escaped liquidation, the bankruptcy office will take possession of the assets, sell them and distribute the proceeds without other formality amongst the unpaid creditors in accordance with their rank.

2. The same arises when deposits mature.

3. If any rights are in doubt the bankruptcy office will notify the creditors by public announcement or by letter and proceed in accordance with the provisions of article 260.

Article 270

1. The bankruptcy must be liquidated within six months from commencement.

2. If necessary the supervisory committee may extend this period.

CHAPTER VIII. SEQUESTRATION

Article 271

1. The creditor of an unsecured mature debt may apply for sequestration of the debtor's assets in the following cases:

- (i) If the debtor has no fixed domicile;
- (ii) If the debtor, with the intention of avoiding his obligations, conceals his assets, absconds or makes ready to abscond;
- (iii) If the debtor is a transient or belongs to the category of persons who frequent fairs and markets, provided the claim is by its nature immediately realisable;
- (iv) If the debtor is not resident in Switzerland.
- (v) If the creditor has obtained a declaration of bankruptcy against the debtor whether provisional or definitive.

2. Sequestration may be requested under paragraphs (i) and (ii) above for a debt which has not matured. Sequestration renders the claim repayable on demand.

3. The provisions of treaties are reserved.

Article 272

Sequestration is authorised by the competent authority at the place where the assets are situated. The creditor must establish the claim and the grounds under which he is claiming sequestration.

Article 273

1. The creditor is liable for any damage or loss caused by the sequestration; he may be compelled to put up security;

2. Any action for damages with interest is commenced in the place of execution of the sequestration.

Article 274

1. The authority will appoint the superintendent or other official or employee for the purpose of executing the sequestration order and, to this end, will provide him with the order.

2. The order will state:

(i) The name and domicile of the creditor or his representative, if appropriate, and of the debtor;
(ii) The claim to which the order relates;
(iii) The grounds under which sequestration is requested;
(iv) The items to be sequestrated;
(v) That the creditor is liable for any loss occasioned and such security, if any, as the creditor is to provide.

Article 275

The sequestration is executed in the manner provided for distraint under articles 91–109.

Article 276

1. The official record of the sequestion will be entered at the foot of the order. The record will show details of the items and their value. It will be transmitted immediately to the debt enforcement office.

2. This office will provide a copy to both the creditor and the debtor within three days.

Article 277

The sequestrated assets are left in the possession of the debtor who must provide their equivalent value in cash or in kind and to this end obtain security either by deposit or joint and several guarantee from a person domiciled in the same district.

Article 278

1. A creditor who effects a sequestration without instituting any proceedings or preliminary action must apply for enforcement within ten days of receipt of the sequestration record.

2. If the sequestration is opposed, the creditor will, within ten days of receipt of notice of opposition, commence either an action withdrawing the claim or an action on the debt. If the withdrawal is declared inadmissible, the creditor must begin proceedings within ten days of communication of this decision.

3. If the action on the debt was already pending at the time of the sequestration, the creditor must apply for enforcement within ten days of communication of the judgment.

4. The sequestration ceases to have effect if the creditor allows the time limits to which he is entitled to pass, if he withdraws or allows to lapse either his action or the proceedings under it, and if his action is dismissed.

Article 279

1. A sequestration order is not open to appeal.

2. A debtor who contests the grounds for sequestration must commence an action in the court where the sequestration proceedings were initiated within five days of receipt of the official record of the sequestration. The proceedings are in summary form and, during such time, the time limits referred to in article 278 are suspended.

Article 280

If the sequestration is not opposed or is dismissed, enforcement continues by way of distraint or bankruptcy, according to the means of the debtor.

Article 281

1. If the sequestrated items have been distrained by another creditor before the sequestrating creditor is able to bring himself within the time limits for effecting the sequestration, the latter may participate as of right in the distraint on a provisional basis.

2. The expenses of the sequestration are paid out of the sale proceeds.

3. The sequestration creates no other preferential rights.

CHAPTER IX. SPECIAL PROVISIONS RELATING TO RENT AND FARM RENT

Article 282

1. Where the object of the proceedings is rent or farm rent, the order to pay will contain, if the creditor so requests, the penalty clause provided by articles 287 and 312 of the federal code of obligations and a warning that, once the legal time limit has expired, the debtor may be evicted by application made to the competent authority.

2. In the cases where article 287 authorises the lessor to terminate the lease after the expiry of six days, the time limit during which opposition may be made is reduced to three days.

Article 283

1. The lessor may apply provisionally to the enforcement office, even without preliminary proceedings, in order to protect his right of lien (articles 294, 295 and 297 of the federal code of obligations).

2. If a delay would involve risk, he may also request assistance from the police or the communal authorities.

3. The enforcement office will draw up an inventory of the items open to lien and will give the lessor time within which he may apply for proceedings to realise his security.

Article 284

Items removed secretly or with force may be returned with the assistance of the police within ten days of their removal. The rights of third parties acting in good faith are reserved. If opposition is made, the judge shall decide the case in summary proceedings.

CHAPTER X. ACTIONS TO SET ASIDE

Article 285

1. The purpose of an action to set aside is to declare void the transactions listed in articles 286 to 288.

2. The action may be commenced by:

(i) Any creditor holding a provisional or definitive deed of insufficiency of assets;
(ii) The administrators of the bankruptcy or the creditors, individually, in the cases listed in articles 260 and 269, paragraph 3.

Article 286

1. All gifts and gratuitous dispositions, except ordinary gifts, are void if made within six months before the distraint or declaration of bankruptcy.

2. The following are deemed to be gifts:

(i) Transactions for which the debtor has accepted a price which is notably less than the value of his consideration;
(ii) Transactions by virtue of which the debtor has constituted an annuity or usufructuary right in his own favour or in favour of a third party.

Article 287

1. The following transactions are similarly void, if made by a debtor who has become insolvent within six months before the distraint or the commencement of bankruptcy proceedings:

(i) Any security for an existing debt, unless the debtor undertook to provide the security before the debt came into existence;
(ii) Any payment made otherwise than in cash or other usual form of payment;
(iii) Any payment of a debt which is not due.

2. The action to set aside is not admissible when the beneficiary of the transaction proves that he was unaware of the debtor's situation.

Article 288

All transactions, whatever their date, made by the debtor with the intention of prejudicing his creditors or preferring certain creditors with their knowledge to the detriment of other creditors, are void.

Article 289

Disputes arising under articles 286–288 will be decided at the discretion of the judge, after taking into account all the circumstances of the case.

Article 290

Actions to set aside may be brought against persons who have contracted with, or have been paid by, the debtor, or against their heirs and third parties acting in bad faith. The rights of third parties acting in good faith are not open to challenge.

Article 291

1. A person who has benefited from a void transaction is obliged to make restitution. Any sum paid by him shall be returned to him, to the extent that the item still remains in the hands of the debtor or by which the debtor has been enriched. Any surplus may only be recovered from the debtor as a claim due.

2. Full rights are restored to a creditor who has repaid that which was paid to him by virtue of a void transaction.

3. A donee acting in good faith is only obliged to make restitution up to the amount by which he has been enriched.

Article 292

An action to set aside will be time-barred five years from the date of the unlawful transaction.

CHAPTER XI. SCHEMES OF ARRANGEMENT

I: Ordinary schemes of arrangement

Article 293

1. A debtor who intends to obtain the benefit of a scheme of arrangement must send to the competent authority a draft scheme, to which he will attach a detailed balance sheet and a report of his accounts, if he is obliged to keep accounts (article 877 of the federal code of obligations).

[Paragraphs 2 and 3 are repealed]

Article 294

1. Having heard the debtor, the authority will decide whether to accept his application, taking account of his situation, the state of his accounts, whether he conducts business in a fair manner and the reasons which prevent him from performing his obligations.

2. In cantons where proceedings relating to schemes of arrangement may be brought before two levels of authority, the decision may be appealed to the superior authority within ten days of its issue.

Article 295

1. If the application is accepted, the authority will grant the debtor a stay of execution for up to a maximum of four months ('scheme suspension period') and will appoint a commissioner. The superintendent or an official appointed in relation to the bankruptcy may be appointed for this purpose.

2. The commissioner will monitor the transactions of the debtor and perform the functions specified in article 298 and the following articles.

3. Articles 8, 11 and 17 apply to the commissioner.

4. On his recommendation, the scheme suspension period may be extended by a maximum of two months.

Article 296

The scheme suspension period is announced in public and is communicated to the debt enforcement office and the registrar of the charges registry.

Article 297

1. No proceedings may be brought against the debtor during the scheme suspension period, and any prescriptive period or time limit which would be interrupted by the bringing of proceedings is suspended.

2. However, even during the scheme suspension period, the charges, pay and salary which rank in the first class of priority under article 219 and periodical maintenance contributions may be the object of attachment proceedings, and proceedings may be brought to realise security for claims guaranteed by a mortgage over real estate; on the other hand, enforcement of such security may not take place.

Article 298

1. The debtor may carry on his affairs under the supervision of the commissioner. However, from the moment of public announcement of the scheme suspension period, and at risk of any such act being declared void, the debtor is not permitted to assign or mortgage real estate, grant security, act as guarantor or make disposals by way of gift.

2. If the debtor contravenes this provision or any requirement of the commissioner, the competent authority may, on the recommendation of the commissioner and having heard the debtor, revoke the scheme suspension period. Articles 307 and 308 will apply.

Article 299

Within the shortest possible time after his appointment, the commissioner will prepare an inventory of the assets of the debtor and value them.

Article 300

1. The commissioner will invite the creditors by means of public announcement to provide him with details of their claims within twenty days, at risk of exclusion from meetings relating to the scheme of arrangement.

2. At the same time, the commissioner will call a meeting of the creditors to discuss the scheme of arrangement and will give them notice that the documents will be available for inspection for a period of ten days before the meeting. The meeting may not take place until at least one month has elapsed since the public announcement.

Article 301

The commissioner will invite the debtor to comment on the claims submitted.

Article 301(a)

1. At the request of the debtor the authority responsible for the scheme of arrangement may, for a maximum period of one year from approval of the scheme of arrangement, suspend the sale of real estate encumbered with a charge by reason of a claim which came into existence before the commencement of scheme of arrangement proceedings, provided that interest on the mortgage debt is not more than one year in

arrears. The debtor must nevertheless show that the real estate is necessary to him for the carrying on of his business and that its sale would be likely to jeopardise his financial situation.

2. Creditors with an interest are invited to provide their written comments before the discussions leading to approval of the scheme of arrangement; they are called individually to the meeting of creditors and to the discussions held in the presence of the authority responsible for the scheme of arrangement.

Article 301(b)

1. The decision of the commissioner relating to the value of security is made available to creditors who may inspect it, and is communicated in written form to the debtor and to mortgage creditors, before the creditors meeting.

2. By applying to the authority responsible for the scheme of arrangement within the time limit for petitioning the authority, and paying the costs in advance, any interested person has the right to demand that a new valuation be made by experts. When a new valuation has been demanded by a creditor, he may only claim repayment of his expenses from the debtor if the first valuation is modified.

3. The cantonal supervisory authorities shall have the final decision on any dispute concerning the amount of the valuation.

Article 301(c)

The suspension of realisation proceedings provided under article 301(a) is null and void if the debtor makes a gratuitous disposal of the security, if he is declared bankrupt, or if he dies.

Article 301(d)

On the application of an interested creditor, and after having heard the debtor, the authority responsible for the scheme of arrangement will revoke the suspension of realisation proceedings ordered under article 301(a), if the creditor is able to show:

(i) That the debtor obtained the order by giving incorrect information to the authority, or
(ii) That his means or income have improved and that he is able to repay the debt without jeopardising his financial situation, or
(iii) That the realisation of the mortgaged real estate is not likely to jeopardise the debtor's financial situation.

Article 302

1. The commissioner will preside at the creditors' meeting and present a report on the debtor's financial position.

2. The debtor must attend the meeting in order to provide the necessary information.

3. The scheme of arrangement will be signed during the meeting.

4. Consent may still be given to the scheme during the following ten days.

Article 303

1. A creditor who has not consented to the scheme of arrangment retains all his rights against all joint obligors and guarantors of the debtor.

2. The same applies to a creditor who consents provided that, at least ten days in advance, he has informed the above persons of the date and place of the meeting and offers to surrender his rights in return for payment.

3. Without prejudice to his right of appeal, the creditor may also authorise such persons to take part themselves in the deliberations and may submit to their decision.

Article 304

1. At the end of the tenth day after the meeting, the commissioner will transmit to the competent authority all the documents relating to the scheme of arrangement, together with a reasoned opinion on whether the scheme of arrangement is acceptable and whether it should be approved.

2. The authority shall make its decision within a short period.

3. The date of the hearing is announced in public. Any person who opposes the scheme is advised that they may attend to make known their reasons for opposition.

Article 305

1. The scheme of arrangement is accepted when the majority of creditors representing at least two thirds of the amount of the claims under consideration has agreed to it.

2. Preferred creditors, and the wife of the debtor, are not taken into account, either in their personal capacity or as creditors; debts guaranteed by security count to the extent only of the unsecured amount as estimated by the commissioner.

3. The authority will decide if and to what extent the contested claims, or claims subordinated to a condition precedent, or having an uncertain maturity, will be taken into account; all these decisions of the authority are without prejudice to the judgment of any superior court.

Article 306

1. The authority responsible for the scheme of arrangement may refuse to approve the agreement if the debtor has committed an unfair or reckless act to the detriment of his creditors.

2. Approval is furthermore subject to the following conditions:

(i) The sum offered must be proportional to the resources of the debtor. Assets to which the debtor may become entitled by way of inheritance may be taken into consideration by the authority responsible for the scheme of arrangement;

(ii) Performance of the scheme of arrangement and payment in full of the recognised preferred creditors must be sufficiently guaranteed, except where the creditors expressly renounce this right.

Article 307

In cantons where proceedings relating to scheme of arrangement may be brought before two levels of authority, the decision approving the scheme may be appealed to the superior authority within ten days of its issue.

Article 308

1. The decision is made public and communicated, as soon as it has come into effect, to the debt enforcement office and to the registrar of the charges registry.

2. With effect from public announcement the scheme suspension period ceases to have effect.

Article 309

If the scheme of arrangement is not approved or where the scheme suspension period is revoked, a debtor who is subject to bankruptcy proceedings must immediately be declared bankrupt, if a creditor so requests within ten days.

Article 310

On approval of the scheme of arrangement the authority will grant a strict time period for commencing action to creditors whose claims are contested.

Article 311

Once approved the scheme of arrangement is binding on all creditors with the exception of secured creditors up to the value of their security.

Article 312

Once the scheme of arrangement has been approved distraints relating to items unsold before the scheme of arrangement will lapse.

Article 313

If the competent authority so orders, interest accruing on contested claims will be paid by the debtor into the public trustees treasury office until final judgment.

Article 314

Any promise made by the debtor to one of his creditors outside the stipulations of the scheme of arrangement is void as of right.

Article 315

1. Any creditor, who is not a party to the scheme of arrangement, may request the competent authority to revoke it as far as it affects him, whilst retaining all new rights acquired by virtue of the arrangement.

2. Article 307 applies by analogy.

Article 316

1. Similarly, any creditor may demand revocation of the scheme of arrangement where it has been vitiated by bad faith.

2. Articles 307, 308 and 309 apply by analogy.

II: Schemes of arrangement by way of renunciation of the debtor's assets

Article 316(a)

1. A scheme of arrangement by way of renunciation of the debtor's assets can only confer on the creditors the right to dispose of the assets of the debtor, including the right to demand that entries be made in the charges register. Creditors will exercise these rights by the intermediary of liquidators who cannot be creditors.

2. Claims which are within the scheme arrangement may not be the subject of compulsory execution proceedings.

Article 316(b)

1. The scheme of arrangement must contain provisions concerning:

(i) The renunciation by creditors of that part of their claim which is not satisfied out of the proceeds of the liquidation, or the precise regulation of the reservation of rights on such unsatisfied claims;
(ii) The number of liquidators and of members of the creditors' committee to be nominated by the creditors meeting;
(iii) The division of functions between the liquidator and the creditors' committee;
(iv) The manner of liquidation, in so far as this is not governed by law;
(v) The means, other than the official gazette, by which announcements intended for creditors must be made.

2. If the provisions of the scheme of arrangement are incomplete, the authority responsible for the scheme of arrangement may complete them.

3. If the scheme of arrangement does not make provision for all the assets of the debtor, it must specify the assets to which it relates.

Article 316(c)

1. A scheme of arrangement by way of renunciation of the debtor's assets applies to all debts which came into existence before the public announcement of the scheme suspension period, as well as those which come into existence after such date and up to final approval of the scheme of arrangement (but without the consent of the commissioner).

2. Debts incurred during the scheme suspension period with the consent of the commissioner constitute debts of the estate, even in a subsequent bankruptcy.

Article 316(d)

1. Once approval of the scheme of arrangement by way of renunciation of the debtor's assets has become final, the debtor no longer has the right to dispose of his assets and the signatory power of the previously entitled parties is extinguished.

2. If the debtor is registered on the commercial registry, the words 'in liquidation under scheme of arrangement' shall appear after the name of the business. The estate may be sued in this name for the debts which are not included in the scheme of arrangement.

3. The liquidators will do all acts necessary to conserve and realise the debtor's estate and will act on its behalf in law.

Article 316(e)

1. The liquidators will be the under supervision and control of the creditors' committee.

2. Decisions of the liquidators concerning realisation of the assets may be contested before the creditors' committee and the decisions of this committee may be referred to the supervisory authority within ten days of their issue.

Article 316(f)

1. The liquidators and the members of the creditors' committee are responsible, in the same manner as the persons mentioned in article 5, as regards each creditor, for any loss caused by their fault; in this regard, proceedings may be brought against them.

2. The limitation period for such action is one year beginning with the day on which those authorised under the scheme made the final account available to the creditors.

Article 316(g)

In order to determine the persons participating in the distribution of the proceeds of the liquidation and to establish their ranking, the liquidators will draw up – without further consultation with the creditors and by reference only to the books and documents produced – an order of priority which will be made available to the creditors.

Article 316(h)

1. As a general rule, the assets are realised either separately or as a whole. Realisation of the assets is made, in the case of claims owed to the debtor, either by way of collection or by sale and, in the case of other assets, by sale by private contract or at public auction.

2. The liquidators will choose the manner and time of realisation, in agreement with the creditors' committee.

Article 316(i)

Mortgaged real estate may not be sold by private sale by the liquidators without the agreement of those of the mortgagees whose claims would remain unsatisfied by the sale price; failing which, the real estate may not be sold except by public auction, which is regulated by articles 134 to 137, 142, 143, 257 and 258. In accordance with article 316(g) the order of priority governs the existence and rank of the mortgagees' rights and rights of easement.

Article 316(k)

Creditors secured by charges over moveables are not bound to transfer these charges for the account of the liquidators. Unless there is any contrary provision in the scheme of arrangement which provides for a stay, the creditors may realise their security at any moment which appears to them convenient, either by way of proceedings for realisation of the security, or, if the document constituting the security so permits, by means of a private sale or by sale on the stock market.

Article 316(l)

If the liquidators or the creditors' committee renounce a contested claim or a claim which is difficult to recover, in particular an action to set aside or an action seeking to establish liability against the agents or employees of the debtor, they will inform the creditors by circular or by official public announcement and offer them the surrender of such claims in accordance with article 260 of this law.

Article 316(m)

Compensation is governed by articles 213 and 214. Public announcement of the scheme suspension period and, if appropriate, of adjournment in advance of bankruptcy, are substituted for the commencement of the bankruptcy proceedings, in accordance with article 725, 817 and 903 of the code of obligations.

Article 316(n)

Before any distribution, including any provisional distribution, the liquidators will draw up a distribution schedule and provide it to the creditors or make it available to them for a period of twenty days. During this period, the schedule is open to challenge by the supervisory authority.

Article 316(o)

1. Secured creditors whose security has already been realised at the time of filing of the provisional distribution schedule will participate in the provisional distribution up to the amount of the effective deficit. This amount is determined by the liquidators, whose decision may only be contested under the procedure contained in article 316(n).

2. If, at the time of filing of the provisional distribution schedule, the security has not yet been realised, the secured creditor will participate in the distribution up to the estimated amount of the deficit, according to the commissioner's valuation. If the secured creditor shows that the proceeds of realisation of the security are less than the valuation, he has the right to participate in the dividend and the corresponding instalments.

3. If the proceeds of realisation of the security, added to provisional dividends already received, exceed the amount of the claim, the secured creditor is obliged to repay any surplus.

Article 316(p)

The liquidators will file a final account including a list of expenses together with the final distribution schedule.

Article 316(q)

1. Dividends which have not been collected within the period of time determined by the liquidators will be deposited with the public trustees' treasury office.

2. Dividends which have not been collected within a period of ten years will be distributed by the bankruptcy office; article 269 applies by analogy.

Article 316(r)

If the liquidation continues for more than one year, the liquidators will be obliged to provide, on the 31st December of each year, a statement of the estate liquidated so far and the assets which have not yet been realised, as well as a report on their activities. In the two first months of the following year, they will distribute the statement and report to the authority responsible for the scheme of arrangement by way of the creditors' committee and will make these documents available to the creditors.

Article 316(s)

1. Any transaction in law performed by the debtor before approval of the scheme of arrangement may be revoked in accordance with the principles of articles 285–292. The remedy provided under articles 286 and 287 extends to all transactions carried out within the six months preceding the scheme suspension period.

2. If the scheme suspension period was preceded by an adjournment of bankruptcy proceedings, in accordance with articles 725, 817 or 903 of the code of legal obligations, transactions carried out validly during this period are also subject to revocation according to article 288 and the remedy provided under articles 286 and 287 will extend to transactions carried out in the six months preceding the adjournment of bankruptcy proceedings.

3. As against the creditors, the liquidators can and must raise all the objections which the debtors' estate could make against the creditors by virtue of the provisions relating to actions to set aside.

Article 316(t)

Insofar as articles 316(a)–316(s) do not contain any contrary provision, and in so far as any derogations which do exist do not result from the particular nature of the procedure, the general provisions in relation to schemes of arrangement also apply to schemes of arrangement for the renunciation of the debtor's assets.

III: Schemes of arrangement within bankruptcy proceedings

Article 317

1. If a debtor who has been declared bankrupt proposes a scheme of arrangement the administrators of the bankruptcy will submit it with their recommendations to the creditors, who will discuss it at the earliest at their second meeting.

2. Articles 302 to 307 and 310 to 316 apply by analogy. The administrators will perform the functions of the commissioner.

3. The order relating to the scheme of arrangement is communicated to the administrators; if the scheme of arrangement is approved, the administrators will apply for revocation of the bankruptcy from the judge who ordered it.

CHAPTER XII. STAY OF PROCEEDINGS ON EXCEPTIONAL GROUNDS

Article 317(a)

In exceptional circumstances, in particular in the event of persistent economic crisis, the cantonal government may, with the consent of the Federal Council, declare that the provisions of this chapter will apply for a fixed period of time to debtors in a certain area who are affected by such circumstances.

Article 317(b)

1. It is possible for a debtor who, as a result of the exceptional circumstances provided under article 317(a), finds himself through no fault of his own unable to honour his commitments, to apply to the authority competent in matters relating to schemes of arrangement for a stay of proceedings on exceptional grounds for a period not exceedings six months, if circumstances suggest that, once the period of the stay ends, he would be able to reimburse his creditors in full.

2. He must submit with his application proof of his financial means and a list of his creditors; he must supply all the information required by the authority and produce all documents required from him.

3. If proceedings in bankruptcy have been brought against the debtor, he must also provide his balance sheet and his accounts books with his application.

4. Once the application is filed, the president of the authority may, as a provisional measure, suspend any proceedings already in hand, with the exception of matters concerning the claims referred to in article 317(c). The authority will decide if and to what extent the length of the suspension period should be added to any stay granted on exceptional grounds.

Article 317(c)

1. The authority will carry out any investigations it considers necessary, and thereafter, if the application for the stay does not immediately seem to be without grounds, the authority will arrange a hearing to which all the creditors are summoned by public announcement; it may also call upon experts to assist as necessary.

2. If the list of creditors produced by the debtor indicates that a relatively small number of creditors is involved, and the authority considers the list reliable, the public meeting of creditors, guarantors and co-debtors may be changed to a private meeting.

3. The creditors may refer to the case file before the hearing; they may also submit in writing their objections to the application for the stay.

4. The authority will issue its decision promptly. It may, in granting the stay, require the debtor to pay one or more instalments of the debt.

Article 317(d)

1. In cantons where proceedings relating to schemes of arrangement may be brought before two levels of authority, the decision may be referred to the higher cantonal authority by the debtor and each of his creditors up to ten days after it was issued.

2. The debtor and creditors who were present or represented at the initial proceedings will be summoned to attend the proceedings of the higher authority.

3. The stay on exceptional grounds awarded in the initial proceedings is effective until the final decision is made by the higher authority.

Article 317(e)

1. The authority will order an inventory of assets to be drawn up, at the latest upon granting the stay. The authority may take such other action as it thinks fit in order to protect the rights of the creditors.

2. In granting the stay, the authority may appoint a commissioner to supervise the management of the debtor's affairs.

Article 317(f)

The decision granting the stay is passed to the debt enforcement office and, if the debtor is subject to bankruptcy proceedings, to the bankruptcy judge. It is announced in public as soon as it becomes final.

Article 317(g)

1. During the period of stay, action may be brought against the debtor and continued up to distraint or the formal threat of bankruptcy. Salaries which have been attached will also be paid into the bankruptcy estate during the period of stay. The same rules apply to rents and farm rents as long as they are included in the guarantee *in rem* established as a result of proceedings brought before or during the period of stay. Orders for sale or bankruptcy on the other hand are unenforceable.

2. The time limits provided under articles 116, 154, 166 and 188 are extended by the length of the period of stay. The guarantee in rem securing interest payments on claims secured by a mortgage on (art. 818 ch.3,CC) is also extended by the length of the period of stay.

3. If the debtor is subject to proceedings in bankruptcy, the period of a year provided under article 219 in favour of creditors belonging to the second and third classes and the period of six months provided under articles 286 and 287 are also extended by the length of the period of stay.

Article 317(h)

The debtor is authorised to continue with his business, but he is forbidden during the period of stay to enter into enforceable contracts which would prejudice the legitimate interests of the creditors or which would favour some of them to the detriment of others.

Article 317(i)

1. In granting the stay, the authority may decide that, without the consent of the commissioner, or in cases where there is no commissioner, the authority itself, the debtor will have no legal right to dispose of or mortgage real estate, grant security or, stand surety, make gratuitous disposals, or discharge debts accrued before the stay.

However, consent is not required for the discharge of debts belonging to the second and third classes as defined in article 219 and for the payment of instalments as provided under article 317(c), 3rd paragraph.

2. If the authority makes these reservations upon granting the stay, this will be noted

in the announcement of the decision and the stay will be entered in the property register as a restriction of the right to make disposals.

Article 317(k)

1. The stay does not apply to claims under 50 francs, to periodical maintenance claims, or to claims for wages, salaries or other emoluments having first class rank as defined in article 219.

2. These claims however may only give rise during the period of stay to proceedings for distraint or for realisation of security, even if the debtor is already subject to bankruptcy proceedings.

Article 317(l)

1. Within the period determined in accordance with article 317(a), the authority may, on the application of the debtor, award an extension of the stay granted to the debtor for a maximum of four months if the need for the award is not the debtor's own fault.

2. The debtor must submit with his application a supplementary list of creditors and, if he is subject to proceedings in bankruptcy, a supplementary balance sheet.

3. The authority will notify the creditors of the application for extension by public announcement and will give them a time limit in which to submit their objections in writing. If a commissioner has been appointed, he will be asked to present a report.

4. Upon expiry of the time limit, the authority will issue its decision. The decision is subject to appeal on the same grounds and must be published under the same conditions as the stay itself.

5. The superior authority will issue its decision on appeal after considering the case as filed.

Article 317(m)

1. The authority must order revocation of the stay on the application of a creditor or the commissioner:

(i) If the debtor fails to make due payment of the amounts required of him;
(ii) If he contravenes the instructions of the commissioner, prejudices the legitimate interests of creditors or favours certain of them to the detriment of others;
(iii) If a creditor proves that the information given to the authority by the debtor is false, or if the debtor is in a position to meet all of his obligations.

2. The debtor will be given a hearing or invited to submit his remarks in writing. The authority will issue its decision on the matter after considering, if appropriate, any supplementary information; in the case of an appeal, the superior authority will likewise issue its decision. Any revocation will be announced in public on the same conditions as the grant of a stay.

3. If the stay is revoked under paragraphs 2 or 3 above, no stay under a scheme of arrangement and no further stay on exceptional grounds may be granted.

Article 317(n)

1. If the debtor decides to apply for a scheme of arrangement during a period of stay on exceptional grounds, the draft scheme of arrangement supported by the relevant

documents and the commissioner's notice must be filed before expiry of the period of stay.

2. In the six months following expiry of the period of stay, no stay under a scheme of arrangement and no further stay on exceptional grounds may be granted.

3. A debtor who has withdrawn an application for a stay on exceptional grounds or whose application is refused may not submit a new application for the next six months.

Article 317(o)

1. If a limited company has been granted a stay on exceptional grounds, no postponement of declaration of bankruptcy may be granted under article 725 of the code of obligations within one year from the end of the stay.

2. When a judge has postponed the declaration of bankruptcy of a limited company under article 725 of the code of obligations, a stay on exceptional grounds may not be granted within one year from the date of postponement.

3. These provisions also apply to postponement of the declaration of bankruptcy of a limited liability company or a co-operative society (articles 817 and 903 of the code of obligations).

CHAPTER XIII. TRANSITIONAL PROVISIONS

Article 318

1. This law comes into effect on 1st January 1892.

2. However, article 333 will only be effective following consolidation of this law within the laws of the Confederation.

3. As of the entry into force of this law, provisions contrary to the federal law, cantonal legislation and schemes of arrangement are repealed, save for the exceptions referred to in the following articles.

[Article 319 to 334 are transitional provisions]

Article 335

In accordance with the Federal Law of 17th June 1874 relating to a public referendum on federal laws and decrees, the Federal Council is responsible for the promulgation of this law.

THE FEDERAL LAW RELATING TO THE CONSEQUENCES IN PUBLIC LAW OF UNSATISFIED DISTRAINT AND BANKRUPTCY, 29TH APRIL 1920

The Federal Assembly of the Swiss Confederation, in accordance with articles 66, 64 and 74, 2nd paragraph, of the Federal Constitution; and the memorandum of the Federal Council of 1st December, 1916, decrees:

Article 1

1. Unsatisfied distraint and bankruptcy in themselves do not entail the removal of voting rights.

[paragraphs 2 and 3 repealed]

Article 2

1. Subject to article 1 and unless any other provisions of federal law are thereby contravened, the cantons may specify that persons subject to unsatisfied distraint and bankruptcy are not able to hold public office, or carry out a licensed profession, and that unsatisfied distraint and bankruptcy have other consequences in public law.

2. All such consequences in public law must however cease to take effect as soon as the bankruptcy is revoked or all creditors are paid or agree to the recovery of civil rights by the debtor.

Article 2(a)

There are no consequences in public law of unsatisfied distraint and bankruptcy arising out of losses suffered by one spouse on behalf of the other.

Article 3

1. Any disenfranchisement in contravention of the provisions of this law will cease to apply when this law comes into effect.

2. All provisions contrary to federal or cantonal law, in particular article 26 of the Federal Law of 11th April 1889 concerning proceedings in debt and bankruptcy will be repealed at the same time.

Article 4

The Federal Council will determine the date when this law will come into effect.

Date of entry into force: 1st August 1921

JAPAN

The Japanese insolvency laws are contained in the Bankruptcy Law of 25th April 1922 and the Corporate Reorganisation Law of 7th June 1952, in both cases as amended. This translation is of the law as it was on 1st January 1993.

As its title suggests, Book I of the 1922 law sets out the substantive provisions and is followed by Book II, which deals with procedure, a very much shorter Book III which contains the provisions for discharge and rehabilitation, and finally Book IV which sets out the criminal offences in bankruptcy and the penal provisions relating to these offences. The 1952 law sets out detailed provisions for corporate recovery when this is appropriate in the interest of creditors, shareholders and what the law describes as 'other persons'.

CHAPTER EIGHT

Japanese Insolvency Laws

TABLE OF CONTENTS

BANKRUPTCY LAW
LAW NO 71, 25TH APRIL 1922

BOOK I. SUBSTANTIVE PROVISIONS

Chapter I: General provisions

Article 1 (Bankruptcy, when effective)

Bankruptcy shall become effective from the time of adjudication.

Article 2 (Status of aliens)

An alien or foreign corporation shall have the same status as a Japanese national or Japanese corporation in regard to bankruptcy, provided however, that this shall apply only when Japanese nationals or Japanese corporations have the same status under the native laws of the alien or the foreign corporation.

Article 3 (Principle of territoriality)

1. A bankruptcy adjudged in Japan shall be effective only with respect to the bankrupt's properties which exist in Japan.
2. A bankruptcy adjudged in a foreign country shall not be effective with respect to properties existing in Japan.
3. Obligations, of which demand may be made by way of judicial proceedings under the Code of Civil Procedure, shall be deemed to exist in Japan.

Article 4 (Continuation of corporate capacity)

A corporation which has been dissolved shall be deemed to continue to exist for purposes of bankruptcy.

Article 5 (Bankruptcy, and qualified acceptance and separation of property)

The adjudication of bankruptcy of a successor or of properties succeeded to shall not preclude the qualified acceptance or separation of property; provided however, that the procedures thereof shall be suspended until the ruling of annulment of bankruptcy or of discontinuance of the bankruptcy procedure shall have become final and conclusive or until the time of the ruling of termination of the bankruptcy procedure.

Chapter II: Bankrupt estate

Article 6 (Scope of bankrupt estate)

1. Any and all properties held by the bankrupt at the time of adjudication of bankruptcy shall constitute the bankrupt estate.
2. Claims which the bankrupt may enforce in the future on causes arising prior to the adjudication of bankruptcy shall belong to the bankrupt estate.
3. Properties which cannot be attached shall not belong to the bankrupt estate; provided however, that this shall not apply to the properties mentioned in Article 131

items (4) and (5) of the Civil Execution Law (Law No. 4, of 1974), to those properties of which attachment has been permitted pursuant to the provision of Article 132 paragraph 1 of said Law, as well as to those properties which have become capable of being attached after the adjudication of bankruptcy.

Article 7 (Management and disposal of bankrupt estate)

The right to manage and dispose of the bankrupt estate shall vest exclusively in the administrator in bankruptcy.

Article 8 (Bankruptcy and absolute acceptance)

In cases where succession has commenced in favour of the bankrupt prior to the adjudication of bankruptcy, the absolute acceptance made by the bankrupt subsequent to the adjudication of bankruptcy shall have the effect of qualified acceptance so far as the bankrupt estate is concerned.

Article 9 (Bankruptcy and renunciation of succession)

1. In cases where succession has commenced in favour of the bankrupt prior to the adjudication of bankruptcy, even if the renunciation of succession has been effected by the bankrupt subsequent to the adjudication of bankruptcy, it shall have the effect of qualified acceptance so far as the bankrupt estate is concerned.

2. Notwithstanding the provisions of the preceding paragraph, the administrator in bankruptcy may assert the effect of renunciation. In such cases, he shall make statement to that effect to the Court within three months after having become aware that there has been renunciation.

Article 10 (Bankruptcy and testamentary gift by universal title)

The provisions of the preceding two Articles shall apply mutatis mutandis to testamentary gifts by a universal title.

Article 11 (Bankruptcy and testamentary gift by specific title)

1. If, in cases where there has been a specific testamentary gift in favour of the bankrupt prior to the adjudication of bankruptcy, the bankrupt failed to effect either acceptance or renunciation at the time of adjudication of bankruptcy, the administrator in bankruptcy may effect acceptance or renunciation thereof in place of the bankrupt.

2. The provisions of Article 987 (Interested person's right of peremptory notice) of the Civil Code shall apply mutatis mutandis in the case mentioned in the preceding paragraph.

Article 12 (Bankruptcy of properties to be succeeded to)

1. In cases where bankruptcy has been adjudged of properties to be succeeded to, any and all properties pertaining to the estate shall constitute the bankrupt estate.

2. The rights possessed by the person succeeded to against the successor and by the successor against the person succeeded to shall be deemed not to have been extinguished.

Article 13

[Deleted.]

Article 14 (Disposal of property by successor)

1. In cases where bankruptcy has been adjudged of properties succeeded to, after a successor has disposed of the whole or part of the properties succeeded to, the right which the successor possesses with respect to the counter-performance shall belong to the bankrupt estate.

2. In cases where the successor has already taken the counter-performance, he shall restore it to the bankrupt estate; provided however, that in case the successor was not, at the time, aware of the facts comprising causes of bankruptcy or that the petition for bankruptcy had been filed, it shall be sufficient to return the benefits actually enjoyed.

Chapter III: Claims in bankruptcy

Article 15 (Claims in bankruptcy, definition)

Claims on property rights against the bankrupt which have arisen out of causes existent prior to the adjudication of bankruptcy shall be claims in bankruptcy.

Article 16 (Enforcement of claim in bankruptcy)

Claims in bankruptcy may not be enforced except through the bankruptcy procedure.

Article 17 (Acceleration of due date)

Obligations subject to a time limit shall be deemed to have become due at the time of adjudication of bankruptcy.

Articles 18 to 21 inclusive

[Deleted.]

Article 22 (Amount of obligations of which subject is not money and of indefinite obligations on funds payable at regular intervals)

In cases where the subject-matter of an obligation is not money, or though it is money, indefinite in amount, or where the amount is specified in a foreign currency, the value appraised at the time of adjudication of bankruptcy shall be the amount of such claims in bankruptcy. The same shall also apply in cases where a claim on funds payable at regular intervals is indefinite in amount or the period of duration.

Article 23 (Amount of obligations subject to condition and of future claims)

With regard to obligations subject to conditions, the whole amount thereof or its value appraised pursuant to the provisions of the preceding Article shall be the amount of claims in bankruptcy.

2. The provisions of the preceding paragraph shall apply mutatis mutandis to future claims which may be enforced against the bankrupt.

Article 24 (Bankruptcy in case several persons are each liable in toto)

In cases where several persons are each liable to perform *in toto*, if all or some of them have been adjudged bankrupt, the creditor may enforce his claim as bankruptcy creditor against each of the bankrupt estates with respect to the whole amount of obligation held at the time of adjudication of bankruptcy.

Article 25 (Claims in bankruptcy in case of bankruptcy of guarantor)

In cases where a guarantor has been adjudged bankrupt, the creditor may exercise his rights as bankruptcy creditor with respect to the whole amount obligation held at the time of adjudication of bankruptcy.

Article 26 (Holder of right of indemnity to be exercised in future)

1. In cases where several persons are liable to perform *in toto* if all of them or some or a single one of them have been adjudged bankrupt, a person possessing a right of indemnity to be exercised in the future against the bankrupt may exercise his rights as bankruptcy creditor with respect to the whole amount thereof; provided however, that this shall not apply if the creditor has exercised his rights as bankruptcy creditor with respect to the whole amount of such obligations.

2. In the case mentioned in the proviso to the preceding paragraph, if the person possessing the right of indemnity mentioned in the preceding paragraph has effected performance, he shall acquire the right of the creditor in proportion to such performance.

3. The provisions of the preceding two paragraphs shall apply mutatis mutandis to the right of indemnity which may be enforced in the future against the bankrupt by a third person who has furnished securities.

Article 27 (Where part of obligation is guaranteed)

The provisions of Article 24 (Bankruptcy in case several persons are each liable *in toto*), Article 25 (Claims in bankruptcy in case of bankruptcy of guarantor), and paragraphs 1 and 2 (Rights of indemnity) of the preceding Article shall apply mutatis mutandis to portions of obligation shared by each guarantor in cases where several guarantors are each liable to guarantee a part of the obligation.

Article 28 (Bankruptcy of partner with unlimited liability and creditors of corporation)

If a person who owes unlimited liability to creditors with respect to obligations of a corporation has been adjudged bankrupt, creditors of the corporation may exercise their rights as creditor in bankruptcy with respect to the whole amount of obligations held at the time of adjudication of bankruptcy.

Article 29 (Indirect liability of partners with limited liability)

In cases where bankruptcy has been adjudged of a person owing limited liability to creditors with respect to obligations of a corporation, or of the corporation, creditors of the corporation may not exercise their rights against the person owing limited liability;

provided however, that the corporation shall not be precluded from exercising its rights as creditor in bankruptcy with respect to demand for contributions.

Article 30 (Bankruptcy of successor and obligees of person succeeded to)

In cases where a successor has been adjudged bankrupt, obligees of the person succeeded to and testamentary donees may exercise their rights as creditor in bankruptcy with respect to the whole amount of their claims, even in cases where there has been separation of property.

Article 31 (Bankruptcy of properties to be succeeded to as well as of successor, and obligees of person succeeded to)

In cases where bankruptcy has been adjudged of properties to be succeeded to as well as of a successor, obligees of the person succeeded to and testamentary donees may exercise their rights as creditor in bankruptcy against each of the bankrupt estates with respect to the whole amount of their claims.

Article 32 (Qualified acceptance and obligees of person succeeded to)

In the cases provided for in the preceding two Articles, if the successor who was adjudged bankrupt has effected qualified acceptance, obligees of the person succeeded to and testamentary donees may not exercise their rights as creditor in bankruptcy against the successor's own properties. The same shall also apply in cases where the effect of qualified acceptance is recognised by virtue of the provisions of Article 8 and of Article 9 paragraph 1.

Article 33 (Bankruptcy of properties to be succeeded to and successors' claims)

When there has been adjudication of bankruptcy with respect to properties to be succeeded to, the successor shall possess the same right as obligees of the person succeeded to with regard to the obligations against the person succeeded to and defrayal made for extinguishing claims against the person succeeded to.

Article 34 (Bankruptcy of properties to be succeeded to and obligees of person succeeded to)

When there has been adjudication of bankruptcy with respect to properties to be succeeded to, obligees of the person succeeded to may not exercise their rights as creditor in bankruptcy.

Articles 35–37 inclusive

[Deleted.]

Article 38 (Costs of participating in procedure)

Costs required for participating in the procedure of bankruptcy shall constitute claims in bankruptcy.

Article 39 (Preferred claims in bankruptcy)

Claims in bankruptcy having the general preferential right and other general priority rights with respect to properties pertaining to the bankrupt estate shall be preferred to other claims.

Article 40 (Equality among claims of same rank)

Obligations which are to be performed as in the same rank of priority shall each be paid in proportion to the amount of respective claims.

Article 41 (Calculation of period of priority rights)

In cases where the right of priority exists with respect to the amount of claim for a specified period, the period shall be computed retroactively from the time of adjudication of bankruptcy.

Article 42 (Priority of obligees of person succeeded to in case of bankruptcy of properties succeeded to)

In cases where there has been adjudication of bankruptcy with respect to properties to be succeeded to, the claim of obligees of the person succeeded to shall be preferred to the claim of testamentary donees.

Article 43 (Rank of priority between obligees of person succeeded to and successor's creditors, in case on bankruptcy of successor)

In cases where a successor has been adjudged bankrupt upon petition being filed within the period during which petition may be filed for bankruptcy of the properties to be succeeded to, the claim of the successor's creditors shall be preferred to that of obligees of the person succeeded to and of testamentary donees shall be preferred to that of the successor's creditors.

Article 44 (Successor's creditors preferred)

In cases where there has been adjudication of bankruptcy with respect to properties to be succeeded to as well as of a successor, the claim of the successor's creditors shall, with respect to the bankrupt estate of the successor, be preferred to that of obligees of the person succeeded to and of testamentary donees.

Article 45

Deleted.

Article 46 (Deferred claims in bankruptcy)

The claims set forth below shall be deferred to other claims in bankruptcy:

(1) Interest accruing after adjudication of bankruptcy;
(2) Damages and penalties for failure of performance after adjudication of bankruptcy;
(3) Costs of participating in the bankruptcy procedure;
(4) Fines, minor fines, costs of criminal action, value collected in place of confiscation, and administration fines;
(5) In case the obligation bears no interest and is to become due after adjudication of bankruptcy, a portion thereof which corresponds to the amount of interest computed in a manner of calculation whereunder the total of the principal and the interest calculated at the legal rate of interest for the

period from the time of adjudication of bankruptcy to the due date will equal to the amount of obligation;

(6) In cases where the obligation bears no interest and its due date is indefinite, a portion thereof which corresponds to the difference between the amount of the obligation and the value thereof appraised at the time of adjudication of bankruptcy;

(7) In cases where the obligation is a claim on funds payable at regular intervals, of which the amount and the period of duration are to be definite, a portion thereof which corresponds to the total of interest on each of the funds paid at regular intervals, calculated in a manner similar to that mentioned under item (5); and, if the total of the principal amounts calculated in a manner similar to that provided for in the same item with respect to each of the instalment payments is in excess of the amount of the principal which is to bear such interest as will correspond to the instalment payment at the legal rate of interest, a portion of the obligation which corresponds to such amount in excess.

Chapter IV: Claims appertaining to bankrupt estate

Article 47 (Scope of claims appertaining to bankrupt estate)

The following claims shall be claims appertaining to the bankrupt estate:

(1) Costs of judicial proceedings defrayed for the common benefits of creditors in bankruptcy;

(2) Claims which can be collected under the National Tax Collection Law or after the manner of collecting national taxes; provided however, that as for claims arising out of causes which arose subsequent to the adjudication of bankruptcy, those only which have arisen with respect to the bankrupt estate;

(3) Expenses required for the management, realisation, or dividends distribution of the bankrupt estate;

(4) Claims arising because of acts done by the administrator in bankruptcy with respect to the bankrupt estate;

(5) Claims which have arisen against the bankrupt estate because of the management of affairs without mandate (negotiorum gestio) or unjust enrichment;

(6) Claims which have arisen against the bankrupt estate because of acts done for urgent necessity subsequent to the termination of mandate or extinction of agent's powers;

(7) Claims held by the other party, in cases where by virtue of the provisions of Article 59 paragraph 1, the administrator in bankruptcy effects performance of obligations;

(8) Claims which have arisen prior to the termination of bilateral contract, in cases where offer for cancellation of such contract has been made because of the adjudication of bankruptcy;

(9) Allowance in aid payable to the bankrupt and his dependants.

Article 48 (Claims on charge under testamentary gift subject to charge)

In cases where the administrator in bankruptcy has taken performance of a testamentary gift subject to a charge, the claim to receive benefits of the charge shall constitute claims appertaining to the bankrupt estate to the extent not exceeding the value of the subject-matter of testamentary gift.

Article 49 (Payment of claims appertaining to bankrupt estate)

Claims appertaining to the bankrupt estate shall, from time to time, be paid outside of the bankruptcy procedure.

Article 50 (Priority of claims appertaining to bankrupt estate)

Claims appertaining to the bankrupt estate shall first be paid out of the bankrupt estate.

Article 51 (Method of payment in case of insufficiency of bankruptcy estate)

1. When it has become clear that the bankrupt estate is insufficient to pay the total amount of claims appertaining thereto, claims appertaining to the bankrupt estate shall, notwithstanding the rights of priority prescribed in laws and ordinances, be paid in proportion to the amount of claims not yet paid; provided however, that this shall not preclude the effect of the right of retention, the special preferential right, the right of pledge, and the right of hypothec, which subsists with respect to claims appertaining to the bankrupt estate.

2. The claims appertaining to the bankrupt estate mentioned in Article 47 items (1) to (7) inclusive shall be preferred to other claims appertaining to the bankrupt estate.

Article 52 (Application mutatis mutandis of provisions relative to bankruptcy claims)

1. The provisions of Article 17 (Acceleration of due date), Article 22 (Amount of obligations of which subject is not money and of indefinite obligations on funds payable at regular intervals), and Article 23 paragraph 1 (Amount of obligations subject to conditions) shall apply mutatis mutandis to the claims appertaining to the bankrupt estate mentioned in Article 47 item (7) and Article 48.

2. In cases where the claim appertaining to the bankrupt estate mentioned in the preceding paragraph is an obligation bearing no interest or a claim on funds payable at regular intervals, the amount thereof shall be the amount remaining after deducting the sum corresponding to a portion thereof which if it were a claim in bankruptcy, is to be deferred to other claims in bankruptcy by virtue of the provisions of Article 46 items (5) to (7) inclusive.

Chapter V: Effect of bankruptcy on juristic acts

Article 53 (Juristic acts done by bankrupt after adjudication)

1. A juristic act done by the bankrupt after adjudication of bankruptcy with respect to a property pertaining to the bankrupt estate may not be set up against creditors in bankruptcy.

2. A juristic act done by the bankrupt on the day of adjudication of bankruptcy shall be presumed to have been done subsequent to the adjudication of bankruptcy.

Article 54 (Acquisition of rights after adjudication)

1. Even if a right is acquired, after adjudication of bankruptcy, with respect to a property pertaining to the bankrupt estate, not by virtue of the bankrupt's juristic act, such acquisition may not be set up against creditors in bankruptcy.

2. The provisions of paragraph 2 of the preceding Article shall apply mutatis mutandis to the acquisition mentioned in the preceding paragraph.

Article 55 (Registration and recordation effected after adjudication)

1. Any registration, or provisional registration under Article 2 item (1) of the Immovable Property Registration Law, of immovable properties or of vessels, effected subsequent to the adjudication of bankruptcy on causes of registration arising prior to the adjudication of bankruptcy may not be set up against creditors in bankruptcy; provided however, that this shall not apply to any registration or provisional registration effected by the person entitled to demand registration without knowledge of the facts of adjudication of bankruptcy.

2. The provisions of the preceding paragraph shall apply mutatis mutandis to the recordation or provisional recordation of the creation, transfer, or alteration of a right.

3. The provisions of paragraph 1 shall apply mutatis mutandis to the registration of creation, assignment, or alteration of the right of enterprise hypothecation.

Article 56 (Payment to bankrupt after adjudication)

1. Payment to the bankrupt made after adjudication of bankruptcy without knowledge of the facts thereof may be set up against creditors in bankruptcy.

2. Payment to the bankrupt made after adjudication of bankruptcy with knowledge of the facts thereof may be set up against creditors in bankruptcy to the extent the bankrupt estate has thereby been benefited.

Article 57 (Acceptance or payment of bills after adjudication)

1. If, in cases where the drawer or endorser of a bill of exchange has been adjudged bankrupt, the drawee or the person designated to accept or pay in case of need has accepted or paid without knowing the facts, he may exercise his rights as a creditor in bankruptcy with respect to obligations which have arisen thereby.

2. The provisions of the preceding paragraph shall apply mutatis mutandis to a cheque or valuable instrument which has for its object the delivery of moneys and other things, or of valuable instruments.

Article 58 (Presumption of bona fide and mala fide)

For purposes of application of the provisions of the preceding three Articles, it shall be presumed that prior to public notice of the adjudication of bankruptcy, the facts were not known, and that subsequent to the public notice, the facts were not known.

Article 59 (Bilateral contracts)

1. If the bankrupt and the other party have not yet both completed performance of a bilateral contract at the time of adjudication of bankruptcy, the administrator in bankruptcy may, at his option, either rescind the contract, or perform obligations of the bankrupt and demand of the other party performance of obligations.

2. In the case mentioned in the preceding paragraph, the other party may give peremptory notice to the administrator in bankruptcy, designating a reasonable period of time and demanding that a definite answer be given within the period as to whether he rescinds the contract or demands performance of obligations. If the administrator in bankruptcy fails to respond with a definite answer within the given period, it shall be deemed that he has rescinded the contract.

Article 60 (Rescission by administrator and rights of other party)

1. In cases where the contract has been rescinded pursuant to the provisions of the preceding Article, the other party may, with regard to the compensation to losses, exercise his rights as a creditor in bankruptcy.

2. In cases where what the bankrupt gained by counter-performance still actually remains in the bankrupt estate, the other party may demand return thereof, and if it no longer actually exists, the other party may, with respect to the value thereof, exercise his rights as a holder of claims appertaining to the bankrupt estate.

Article 61 (Sale of merchandise having exchange quotations)

1. In cases where, with respect to a merchandise of which there exist exchange quotations, it is impossible to attain the object for which the contract has been entered into unless performance is effected at a specified time or within a specified period, if such time is to arrive after the adjudication of bankruptcy, the contract shall be deemed to have been rescinded. In such cases, the amount of damages shall be determined according to the difference between the quotation for a transaction of the same type to be performed at the same time either at the place of performance or at another place which is to serve as the standard to the quotation at the former place and the price of the sale.

2. The provisions at paragraph 1 of the preceding Article shall apply mutatis mutandis to the damages mentioned in the preceding paragraph.

3. In the case mentioned in the first paragraph, if provisions have been made otherwise at the exchange, such provisions shall govern.

Article 62 (Cases where right of rescission is provided for in the Civil Code)

The provisions of Article 59 paragraph 2 (Other party's right to issue peremptory notice for definite answer) shall apply mutatis mutandis to the exercise of the right of rescission possessed by the other party or by the administrator in bankruptcy mentioned in Article 621, Article 631, or Article 642 paragraph 1 of the Civil Code.

Article 63 (Contract of lease)

1. In cases where a lessor has been adjudged bankrupt, the advance payment of rental or disposition of claims on rental may not be set up against creditors in bankruptcy,

except with respect to rentals for the current period at the time of adjudication of bankruptcy or for the next following period.

2. Any person, who has suffered losses because of being unable, by virtue of the provisions of the preceding paragraph, to set up against creditors in bankruptcy, may exercise his rights as a creditor in bankruptcy with respect to the compensation of such losses.

3. The provisions of the preceding two paragraphs shall apply mutatis mutandis to the right of superficies or the right is emphyteusis.

Article 64 (Contract of work)

1. In cases where the bankrupt owes duties to carry out work under a contract of work, the administrator in bankruptcy may furnish necessary materials and cause the bankrupt to carry out the work. If the work need not be carried out by the bankrupt himself, a third party may be caused to carry it out.

2. In the case mentioned in the preceding paragraph, the remuneration which the bankrupt is to receive from the other party shall belong to the bankrupt estate.

Article 65 (Contract of mandate)

In cases where the mandator has been adjudged bankrupt, if the mandatory has managed the affairs entrusted to him without receiving notice of the adjudication of bankruptcy and without knowing the facts that there has been adjudication of bankruptcy, he may exercise his rights as a creditor in bankruptcy with respect to obligations that have arisen thereby.

Article 66 (Account current)

1. An account current shall terminate when one of the parties has been adjudged bankrupt. In such cases, each party may close the account and demand payment of the balance.

2. The right to demand pursuant to the provisions of the preceding paragraph shall belong to the bankrupt estate if held by the bankrupt and shall be a claim in bankruptcy if held by the other party.

Article 67 (Bankruptcy of owners in common)

1. In cases where several persons hold a property right in common, if some one among the owners in common is adjudged bankrupt, the partition thereof may be effected without resorting to the bankruptcy procedure, even if there exist stipulations against partition.

2. In the case mentioned in the preceding paragraph, other owners in common may acquire the bankrupt's share upon payment of reasonable compensation.

Article 68 (Management of property by spouse or by parent)

1. The provisions of Article 758 paragraphs 2 and 3 (Mismanagement by spouse managing under contract of matrimonial property) and of Article 759 (Change of managing spouse; requisites for setting up partition) of the Civil Code shall apply mutatis mutandis in cases where the person managing property of a spouse has been adjudged bankrupt, and the provisions of Article 835 (Mismanagement by holder of

parental power) of the same Code shall apply mutatis mutandis in cases where the person who is to exercise the parental power has been adjudged bankrupt.

2. For purposes of application of the Domestic Affairs Trial Law, measures taken for the change of person managing property and the partition of community property under the provisions of Article 758 paragraphs 2 and 3 of the Civil Code, which provisions apply mutatis mutandis under the preceding paragraph, shall be deemed to be a matter coming under Class B of Article 9 paragraph 1 of the Domestic Affairs Trial Law; and, the declaration of forfeiture of the right of management under the provisions of Article 835 of the Civil Code, which apply mutatis mutandis by virtue of the preceding paragraph, shall be deemed to be a matter coming under Class A of Article 9 paragraph 1 of the Domestic Affairs Trial Law.

Article 69 (Taking over of suit relative to properties appertaining to bankrupt estate)

1. An action pending at the time of adjudication of bankruptcy relative to a property appertaining to the bankrupt estate may be taken over by the administrator in bankruptcy or by the opponent party. The same shall also apply to an action concerning the claims mentioned under item (7) of Article 47.

2. In cases mentioned in the preceding paragraph, the costs of litigation shall be a claim appertaining to the bankrupt estate.

Article 70 (Effect on compulsory execution and measures for preservation of rights)

1. Compulsory execution, provisional attachment, or provisional disposition or the enforcement procedures of the right of enterprise hypothecation levied on or ordered with respect to properties appertaining to the bankrupt estate by virtue of claims in bankruptcy shall cease to be effective as against the bankrupt estate; provided however, that with regard to compulsory execution, the administrator in bankruptcy may continue the proceedings on behalf of the bankrupt estate.

2. In cases where the administrator in bankruptcy continues the proceedings pursuant to the provisions of the proviso to the preceding paragraph, the costs shall constitute a claim appertaining to the bankrupt estate, and with regard to an action for objection to compulsory execution instituted by a third person, the administrator in bankruptcy shall be the defendant.

3. The provisions of the preceding two paragraphs shall apply mutatis mutandis to the procedure of official auction sale levied on a property appertaining to the bankrupt estate by a holder of the general preferential right.

Article 71 (Effect on tax delinquency measures and cases administrative affairs)

1. In cases where measures against tax delinquency under the National Tax Collection Law or after the manner of collecting national taxes have been taken on properties appertaining to the bankrupt estate, the adjudication of bankruptcy shall not preclude the continuation of such measures.

2. In cases where there exists, at the time of adjudication of bankruptcy, a case pending at an administrative government office with respect to properties appertaining to the bankrupt estate, the proceedings of such cases shall be suspended until it is taken over or until closing of the bankruptcy procedure.

3. The provisions of Article 69 (Taking over of proceedings) shall apply mutatis mutandis in the case mentioned in the preceding paragraph.

Chapter VI: Right of avoidance

Article 72 (Acts which can be avoided)

The following acts may be avoided in favour of the bankrupt estate:

(1) Any act done by the bankrupt with the knowledge that it would prejudice creditors in bankruptcy; provided however, that this shall not apply in cases where the person benefited by the act did not know at the time of the act the facts that it would prejudice creditors in bankruptcy;

(2) Any act relative to furnishing of securities or extinction of obligations, and any other act prejudicial to creditors in bankruptcy, done by the bankrupt subsequent to suspension of payment or after petition for bankruptcy has been filed; provided however, that this shall apply only in cases where the person benefited by the act knew at the time of the act that there had been suspension of payment or that petition for bankruptcy had been filed;

(3) Any of the acts mentioned under the preceding item, of which the other party is a relative of the bankrupt or a person sharing livelihood with the bankrupt; provided however, that this shall not apply in cases where the other party did not know at the time of the act that there had been suspension of payment or that petition for bankruptcy had been filed;

(4) Any act relative to furnishing of securities or extinction of obligations done by the bankrupt subsequent to suspension of payment or after petition for bankruptcy has been filed, or within thirty days prior thereto, which does not appertain to the duties of the bankrupt, or which in its method or time, does not appertain to the duties of the bankrupt; provided however, that this shall not apply in cases where creditors did not know at the time of the act the facts that there had been suspension of payment or that petition for bankruptcy had been filed, or that it would prejudice creditors in bankruptcy;

(5) Any gratuitous act, or non-gratuitous act which should nevertheless be deemed to be the same as a gratuitous act, done by the bankrupt subsequent to suspension of payment or filing of petition for bankruptcy, or within six months prior thereto.

Article 73 (Exception as to payment of bills or notes)

1. The provisions of the preceding Article shall not apply, in cases where a person, to whom the bankrupt has paid a bill or note, is to lose his rights on the bill or note against one or more of the obligators, if he fails to receive such payment.

2. In the case mentioned in the preceding paragraph, if the last of the persons who have to make payment in recourse, or the person who has commissioned to have the bill or note to be drawn, knew or did not know by negligence at the time the bill or note was drawn that there had been suspension of payment or that petition for bankruptcy had been filed, the administrator in bankruptcy may cause such person to reimburse the sum paid by the bankrupt.

Article 74 (Avoidance of acts done for setting up change of rights against third persons)

1. In cases where an act has been done which is necessary for setting up against third persons creation or transfer of, or change in, a right subsequent to suspension of

payment or filing of petition for bankruptcy, if the act has been done mala fide after fifteen days have elapsed since the date of the creation or transfer of, or the change in, the right, such act may be avoided; provided however, that as for registration or recordation, this shall not apply in cases where the formal registration or the formal recordation, as the case may be, has been effected after provisional registration or provisional recordation.

2. The provisions of the preceding paragraph shall apply mutatis mutandis to those recordation whereby the effect of acquisition of a right arises.

Article 75 (Avoidance of act of execution)

The right of avoidance shall not be precluded from being exercised, even when there exists the title for execution with respect to the act which is to be avoided, or the act in question is one based on the act of execution.

Article 76 (Manner of exercising right of avoidance)

The right of avoidance shall be exercised by the administrator in bankruptcy by way of an action or plea.

Article 77 (Effect of exercise of right of avoidance)

1. The exercise of the right of avoidance restores the bankrupt estate to its original state.

2. In cases where any of the acts mentioned under item (5) of Article 72 has been avoided, if the other party were in good faith at the time of the act, it shall be sufficient if he reimburses the benefits which he is actually enjoying.

Article 78 (Rights of other party)

1. If, in cases where an act of the bankrupt has been avoided, what he gained by counter-performance still actually remains in the bankrupt estate, the other party may demand return thereof, and in case the benefits arising from the counter-performance still actually exist, may exercise his rights as a holder of claims appertaining to the bankrupt estate to the extent of the remaining benefits.

2. In cases where the benefits arising from the counter-performance exist no more, the other party may, for purposes of reimbursement of value thereof, exercise his rights as a holder of claims appertaining to the bankrupt estate. In case the value of counter-performance exceeds the benefits actually existing, the same shall also apply to the difference.

Article 79 (Restoration of claims of other party)

If, in cases where an act of the bankrupt has been avoided, the other party has returned what he had gained by performance or reimbursed the value thereof, the claim of the other party shall thereby be restored to its original condition.

Article 80 (Right of avoidance in case of bankruptcy of properties to be succeeded to)

The provisions of Article 72 (Acts which can be avoided), Article 73 (Execution as to payment of bills or notes), and the preceding two Articles (Rights of other party; restoration of claims of other party) shall apply mutatis mutandis to acts done by the person succeeded to, the successor, the administrator of properties to be succeeded to, and the executor with respect to properties to be succeeded to, in cases where there has been adjudication of bankruptcy with respect to properties to be succeeded to.

Article 81 (Avoidance of payment to testamentary donees)

If, in cases where there has been adjudication of bankruptcy with respect to properties to be succeeded to, the payment to testamentary donees or other acts relative to extinction of obligations are prejudicial to bankruptcy creditors whose claims have preference over those obligations, such acts may be avoided.

Article 82 (Avoidance under Article 80 and distribution of surplus assets)

If, in cases where there has been adjudication of bankruptcy with respect to properties to be succeeded to, the act mentioned in Article 80 has been avoided, the remainder of the properties succeeded to shall be distributed to the other party to the act avoided, in proportion to the value of the right in question, after payments have been made to obligees of the person succeeded to.

Article 83 (Right of avoidance against sub-acquirers)

1. The right of avoidance may also be exercised against sub-acquirers in any of the following cases:

(1) When the sub-acquirer knew at the time of sub-acquisition that there were causes for avoidance against each or his predecessors;
(2) When the sub-acquirer is a relative of the bankrupt or a person sharing livelihood with him; provided however, that this shall not apply in cases where the sub-acquirer did not know at the time of sub-acquisition that there were causes for avoidance against each of his predecessors;
(3) When there exist causes for avoidance against each of the predecessors, in case the sub-acquirer acquired through a gratuitous act or non-gratuitous act which should nevertheless be deemed to be the same as a gratuitous act.

2. The provisions of Article 77 paragraph 2 (Duty to reimburse of bona fide party) shall apply mutatis mutandis in cases where the right of avoidance has been exercised under the provisions of item (3) of the preceding paragraph.

Article 84 (Restriction on avoidance by reason of knowledge of suspension of payment)

Any act done one year or more prior to the date of adjudication of bankruptcy may not be avoided on the ground that the facts of suspension of payment have become known.

Article 85 (Extinctive prescription of right of avoidance)

The right of avoidance shall be extinguished by prescription when it is not exercised for two years from the date of adjudication of bankruptcy. The same shall also apply when twenty years shall have elapsed since the day on which the act has been done.

Article 86 (Suspension and taking over of action for avoidance)

1. In case an action instituted by a creditor in bankruptcy under Article 424 of the Civil Code is pending at the time of adjudication of bankruptcy, the proceedings of such action shall be suspended until it is taken over or until closing of the bankruptcy procedure.

2. The provisions of Article 69 (Taking over of proceedings) shall apply mutatis mutandis in the case mentioned in the preceding paragraph.

Chapter VII: Right to redeem

Article 87 (Redemption of properties not belonging to bankrupt)

The adjudication of bankruptcy shall not affect the right to redeem from the bankrupt estate properties not belonging to the bankrupt.

Article 88: (Prohibition of redemption of property transferred for security)

Any person, who transferred a property to the bankrupt prior to the adjudication of bankruptcy, may not redeem the property on the ground that the transfer has been made for the purpose of security.

Article 89 (Redemption of sold goods in transit)

1. In cases where the seller has sent out to the purchaser goods which are the subject-matter of a sale, if the purchaser has been adjudged bankrupt while he has not yet paid the entire sum of the purchase price and not yet received the goods at the destination, the seller may redeem the goods; provided however, that this shall not preclude the administrator in bankruptcy from demanding delivery of the goods upon payment of the entire sum of the purchase price.

2. The provisions of the preceding paragraph shall not preclude the application of the provisions of Article 59.

Article 90 (Commission agent's right to redeem)

The provisions of paragraph 1 of the preceding Article shall apply mutatis mutandis in cases where a commission agent who has been commissioned to purchase goods has sent out the goods to the principal.

Article 91 (Right to redeem by way of compensation)

1. In cases where the bankrupt has transferred the property forming the subject-matter of the right to redeem prior to the adjudication of bankruptcy, the holder of the right to redeem may demand transfer of the right to demand counter-performance. The same shall also apply where the administrator in bankruptcy has transferred a property which is the subject-matter of the right to redeem.

2. In the case mentioned in the preceding paragraph, if the administrator in bankruptcy has received counter-performance, the holder of the right to redeem may

demand delivery of the property which the administrator in bankruptcy took by way of counter-performance.

Chapter VIII: Right of separation

Article 92 (Persons entitled to separation)

Persons who possess the special preferential right, right of pledge, or right of hypothec subsisting on properties pertaining to the bankrupt estate shall have the right of separation on properties forming the subject-matter of these rights.

Article 93 (Person possessing right of retention)

1. Those rights of retention subsisting on properties pertaining to the bankrupt estate which exist by virtue of the provisions of the Commercial Code shall be deemed to be the special preferential rights shall be deferred to other special preferential rights.

2. Except those mentioned in the preceding paragraph, the right of retention shall lose its effect as against the bankrupt estate.

Article 94 (Co-owner's right of separation)

In cases where a property right is held in common by several persons, if one of them has been adjudged bankrupt, other co-owners who possess against such person claims relative to the co-ownership shall have the right of separation on that part of the property held in common which is to accrue to the bankrupt by partition.

Article 95 (Exercise of right of separation)

The right of separation shall be exercised without resorting to the bankruptcy procedure.

Article 96 (Persons possessing right of separation, enforcing claims in bankruptcy)

Persons possessing the right of separation may exercise their rights as creditor in bankruptcy, only with respect to that amount of their claims of which they cannot obtain payment through exercise of their right of separation; provided however, that this shall not preclude them from exercising their rights as creditor in bankruptcy with respect to their claims of which they have relinquished the right of separation.

Article 97 (Persons treated similarly as those entitled to right of separation)

1. Persons who possess the special preferential right, right of pledge, or right of hypothec on the bankrupt's properties not belonging to the bankrupt estate, may exercise their rights as creditor in bankruptcy, only with respect to that amount of their claims of which they cannot obtain payment through exercise of these rights. The same shall also apply to persons who, in case the bankrupt has again been adjudged bankrupt, possess claims in bankruptcy in connection with the previous bankruptcy.

2. Those provisions of Book 2 which relate to the right of separation shall apply mutatis mutandis to persons who possess the rights mentioned in the preceding paragraph.

Chapter IX: Right of setoff

Article 98 (Right of setoff)

In cases where a creditor in bankruptcy owes, at the time of adjudication of bankruptcy, obligations due to the bankrupt, setoff may be effected without resorting to the bankruptcy procedure.

Article 99 (Setoff of claims and debts subject to time limit or condition subsequent)

Even in cases where the claim of creditor in bankruptcy is, at the time of adjudication of bankruptcy, subject to a time limit or condition subsequent, or where it is one mentioned in Article 22, setoff shall not thereby be precluded. The same shall also apply in cases where the debt is subject to a time limit or condition or where it relates to a future claim.

Article 100 (Creditor's rights as to obligation subject to condition precedent)

In cases where a person possessing a claim subject to a condition precedent or a future claim performs his obligation, he may demand deposit of the amount of performance to the extent of the claim in question, in order to provide for effecting setoff at a later date.

Article 101 (Creditor's rights as to obligation subject to condition subsequent)

In cases where a person possessing a claim subject to a condition subsequent effects setoff, he shall furnish security for or make deposit of the amount of setoff.

Article 102 (Extent of setoff; amount of creditor's claims)

1. In cases where the claim possessed by a creditor in bankruptcy is one bearing no interest or a claim on funds payable at regular intervals, setoff may be effected to the extent only of such an amount as will remain after deduction of the portion mentioned under items (5) to (7) inclusive of Article 46.

2. The provisions of Article 22 (Amount of claims of which subject is not money and of indefinite claims on funds payable at regular intervals) and Article 23 (Amount of claims subject to conditions and of future claims) shall apply mutatis mutandis to claims possessed by creditors in bankruptcy.

Article 103 (Scope of setoff permissible with regard to rents, land rents and farm rents)

1. If the creditor in bankruptcy is a lessee, setoff may be effected with respect to rentals of the current term at the time of adjudication of bankruptcy, as well as of the next following term. The same shall also apply to rentals of later terms in cases where caution-money has been deposited.

2. The provisions of the preceding paragraph shall apply mutatis mutandis to land rentals and farm rentals.

Article 104 (Prohibition of setoff)

Setoff shall not be effected in any of the following cases:

(1) Where a creditor in bankruptcy has assumed obligation due to the bankrupt estate subsequent to the adjudication of bankruptcy;

(2) Where a creditor in bankruptcy has assumed obligation due to the bankrupt with the knowledge that there has been suspension of payment or that petition for bankruptcy has been filed; provided however, that this shall not apply if the assumption is based on causes provided for in laws, or if it is based on causes which had arisen prior to the time the creditor in bankruptcy had become aware of suspension of payment or of suspension of payment or of petition for bankruptcy having been filed, or on causes which had arisen one year or more prior to the time of adjudication of bankruptcy;

(3) Where a obligor of the bankrupt has acquired other person's claims in bankruptcy after adjudication of bankruptcy;

(4) Where an obligor of the bankrupt has acquired a claim in bankruptcy with the knowledge that there has been suspension of payment or that petition for bankruptcy has been filed; provided however, that this shall not apply in cases where the acquisition is based on causes provided for in laws, or on causes which had arisen prior to the time the obligor had become aware of suspension of payment or of petition for bankruptcy having been filed, or on causes which had arisen one year or more prior to the time of adjudication of bankruptcy.

BOOK II. PROCEDURAL PROVISIONS

Chapter I: General provisions

Article 105 (Complaint against decisions under bankruptcy procedure)

Bankruptcy cases shall come under the exclusive jurisdiction of the District Court having jurisdiction over the location of the principal place of business, or of the principal place of business in Japan if the principal place of business is in a foreign country, in case the debtor is a person engaged in business, and in case he is not a person engaged in business, or in case he has no place of business, of the District Court having jurisdiction over the locality wherein exists his ordinary court jurisdiction.

Article 106 (Jurisdiction of bankruptcy of properties to be succeeded to)

Cases of bankruptcy of properties to be succeeded to shall come under the exclusive jurisdiction of the District Court which has jurisdiction over the locality in which the succession has commenced.

Article 107 (Jurisdiction of situs of res)

1. In cases where there is no Court having jurisdiction pursuant to the provisions of the preceding two Articles, the Court having jurisdiction over the location of property shall have the exclusive jurisdiction.

2. The location of an obligation shall be deemed to be in the locality wherein claim thereof by way of judicial proceedings may be prosecuted.

3. In cases where two or more Courts have jurisdiction in accordance with the provisions of the preceding two paragraphs, the Court with which petition for bankruptcy has first been filed shall have the exclusive jurisdiction.

Article 108 (Code of Civil procedure, applicable mutatis mutandis)

Unless it is provided otherwise in this Law, the Code of Civil Procedure shall apply mutatis mutandis to the bankruptcy procedure.

Article 109 (Mutual assistance between Courts)

With regard to bankruptcy cases, the Courts may request assistance on legal matters to each other.

Article 110 (Oral proceedings not compulsory; suo sponte *investigation by Court)*

1. In the bankruptcy procedure, decisions may be given without going through oral proceedings.

2. The Court may, of its own motion, make necessary investigations in bankruptcy cases.

Article 111 (Decisions to be served suo sponte*)*

Decisions under the bankruptcy procedure shall be served by the Court of its own motion.

Article 112 (Complaint against decisions under bankruptcy procedure)

Except where it is provided otherwise in this Book, any person having interests in the decision under the bankruptcy procedure may file immediate complaint to such decision. The period within which the complaint may be filed shall be, in case public notice has been given of the decision, two weeks computed from the day the public notice has been given.

Article 113

[Deleted.]

Article 114 (Forms of application, statements, and complaint)

Applications, statements, and complaints under the bankruptcy procedure may be submitted either in writing or by word of mouth.

Article 115 (Manner and time of becoming effective of public notice)

1. Public notices to be given pursuant to the provisions of the present Book shall be given in the Official Gazette as well as in the newspapers which are to carry the public notice of matters required to be registered.

2. A public notice shall become effective on the day next following the day it has been carried for the last time.

Article 116 (Public notice given by putting up on bulletin board)

In case none of the newspapers mentioned in paragraph 1 of the preceding Article exists within the locality over which the Court has jurisdiction, the public notice shall be given by putting it up on the bulletin board of the court and of the Summary Court having jurisdiction over the locality where the bankrupt's place of business or residence is situated, or of the office of the city, town, or village, or of government offices similar thereto, located within the bounds of said jurisdiction. In such cases, the public notice shall become effective when three days shall have elapsed from the day it has been so put up.

Article 117 (Public notice taking place of service)

In cases where service is required by virtue of the provisions in the present Book, public notice may be substituted for service.

Article 118 (Cases where service is required in addition to public notice)

1. In cases where the provisions in the present Book require service in addition to public notice, the service may be effected by mailing the documents.

2. In the case mentioned in the preceding paragraph, the public notice shall have the effect of service upon any and all persons concerned.

Article 119 (Official request for registration of bankruptcy of corporation)

When adjudication of bankruptcy has been given of a corporation, the Court shall, of its own motion, request without delay the registration offices of the localities wherein is situate each of its places of business or each of its offices, to effect registration of bankruptcy, attaching to the written request a certified copy of the ruling of bankruptcy.

Article 120 (Official request for registration of bankruptcy)

When the Court has become aware that there exists registration relative to the person adjudged bankrupt, it shall, of its own motion, request without delay the registration office to effect registration of bankruptcy, attaching to the written request a certified copy of the ruling of bankruptcy. The same shall also apply in cases where it has become known that there exists a right pertaining to the bankrupt estate which has been registered.

Article 120-2

The provision of the preceding Article shall apply mutatis mutandis in cases where, in relation to a right pertaining to the bankrupt estate which has been registered, there was make a measure under the provision of Article 155 paragraph 1 or where there was made alteration or cancellation of the measure.

Article 121 (Application mutatis mutandis to other registrations relative to bankruptcy)

The provisions of Article 119 and Article 120 shall apply mutatis mutandis in cases where the ruling has become final and conclusive for annulment of bankruptcy, discontinuance or bankruptcy, or annulment of compulsory composition, or where there has been the ruling for termination of bankruptcy. The same shall also apply in cases where application has been filed for the official request for registration in case the administrator in bankruptcy has waived and released out of the bankrupt estate a right, of which registration of bankruptcy had been effected.

Article 122 (Duties of registration office; exemption of registration tax)

1. When the official request for registration has been made pursuant to the provisions of the preceding four Articles, the registration office shall, without delay, effect registration as requested.

2. No registration licence tax shall be imposed on the registration mentioned in the preceding paragraph.

Article 123 (Registration of avoidance)

1. In cases where an act forming the cause of registration has been avoided, the administrator in bankruptcy shall effect registration of avoidance. The same shall also apply when registration has been avoided.

2. The provisions of Article 121 (Registration in case of annulment, discontinuance, termination, etc.) and of paragraph 2 (Exemption of registration tax) of the preceding Article shall apply mutatis mutandis to the case mentioned in the preceding paragraph.

Article 124 (Application mutatis mutandis to recordation)

The provisions of the preceding five Articles (Official request for registration; cases where registrations are effected; duties of registration office; registration of avoidance) shall apply mutatis mutandis to those rights appertaining to the bankrupt estate which have been recorded.

Article 125 (Notice to government offices of bankruptcy of corporations)

1. In cases where a corporation has been adjudged bankrupt, if there has been permission by a government office with respect to the formation of the corporation or the enterprise forming its object, the Court shall notify the competent government office or the administrative agency to which the powers of the competent government office are delegated that there has been adjudication of bankruptcy.

2. The provisions of the preceding paragraph shall apply mutatis mutandis in cases where the ruling has become final and conclusive for annulment of bankruptcy, discontinuance of bankruptcy, or annulment of compulsory composition, or where there has been the ruling for termination of bankruptcy.

Article 125-2

If the ruling of annulment is made with respect to the liability restricting procedure having been commenced for the bankrupt, the bankruptcy procedures shall be suspended until said ruling becomes final and conclusive.

Chapter 2: Adjudication of bankruptcy

Article 126 (Causes of bankruptcy, in general)

1. When the debtor is unable to pay, the Court shall, upon application, adjudge him bankrupt by way of ruling.

2. When the debtor has suspended payment, he shall be deemed to be unable to pay.

Article 127 (Causes of bankruptcy of corporations)

1. A corporation may also be adjudged bankrupt, even when it is unable fully to perform its obligations with its assets.
2. The provision of the preceding paragraph shall not apply, so long as a commercial partnership (*gomei-kaisha*) or limited partnership (*goshi-kaisha*) continues to exist.

Article 128 (Petition for bankruptcy of corporation subsequent to dissolution)

Petition for bankruptcy of a corporation may be filed even after its dissolution, so long as delivery or distribution of the surplus assets has not yet been completed.

Article 129 (Causes of bankruptcy of properties to be succeeded to)

In cases where full performance of obligations due to obligees of the person succeeded to or testamentary donees is impossible with the properties to be succeeded to, the Court shall, upon application, declare bankruptcy by way of ruling.

Article 130 (Succession taking place subsequent to filing of petition or adjudication of bankruptcy)

In cases where succession has commenced subsequent to the filing of petition for bankruptcy or the adjudication of bankruptcy, the bankruptcy procedure shall be continued with respect to the properties to be succeeded to.

Article 131 (Period for filing petition for bankruptcy of properties to be succeeded to)

With respect to properties to be succeeded to, petition for bankruptcy may be filed only within the period during which separation of property may be applied for pursuant to the provisions of Article 941 of the Civil Code. In cases where there has been, in the meantime, qualified acceptance or separation of property, the same shall also apply, so long as performance to obligees of the person succeeded to and testamentary donees has not yet been completed.

Article 132 (Persons who can file petition for bankruptcy)

1. Either creditors or the debtor may file petition for bankruptcy.
2. In cases where a creditor files petition for bankruptcy, prima facie proof shall be given of the existence of his claim and the facts comprising causes of bankruptcy.

Article 133 (Persons who can file petition for bankruptcy of corporations)

1. Petition for bankruptcy may be filed by directors (*riji*) with respect to juristic persons created under the Civil Code, by partners with unlimited liability with respect to commercial partnerships (*gomei-kaisha*) or limited partnerships (*goshi-kaisha*),

by directors (*torishimariyaku*) with respect to limited companies (*kabushiki-kaisha*) or mutual companies (*sogo-kaisha*).

2. With respect to the incorporated bodies mentioned in the preceding paragraph, liquidators may also file petition for bankruptcy.

Article 134 (Petition filed by not all of directors, etc.)

In cases where petition for bankruptcy is not filed by all of the directors (*riji*), partners with unlimited liability, directors (*torishimariyaku*), or of the liquidators, prima facie proof shall be given of the facts comprising causes of bankruptcy.

Article 135 (Application mutatis mutandis to other corporations)

The provisions of the preceding two Articles shall apply mutatis mutandis to incorporated bodies other than those mentioned in Article 133.

Article 136 (Persons who can file petition for bankruptcy of properties to be succeeded to)

1. Besides obligees of the person succeeded to and testamentary donees, the successor, the administrator of properties to be succeeded to, and the executor may file petition for bankruptcy of properties to be succeeded to.

2. The administrator of properties to be succeeded to, the executor, or the successor in case there has been qualified acceptance or separation of property, shall file petition for bankruptcy, immediately upon finding out that it is impossible fully to perform obligations due to obligees of the person succeeded to and testamentary donees with the properties to be succeeded to.

3. When filing petition for bankruptcy, the successor, the administrator of properties to be succeeded to, or the executor shall give prima facie proof of the facts comprising causes of bankruptcy.

Article 137 (When there has been adjudication of bankruptcy abroad)

In cases where there has been adjudication of bankruptcy in a foreign country already at the time of filing petition for bankruptcy, the person filing petition for bankruptcy need not give prima facie proof of the facts comprising causes of bankruptcy.

Article 138 (When petition is filed by persons other than creditors)

In cases where the person filing petition for bankruptcy is not a creditor, he shall, at the same time with the filing of petition, submit a document showing the outline of the state of properties and a list of creditors and debtors. When it is impossible to submit them at the same time with the filing or petition, they shall thereafter be submitted without delay.

Article 139 (Advance payment of costs)

1. When a creditor files petition for bankruptcy, a sum which the Court considers reasonable as costs of the bankruptcy procedure shall be paid in advance. Upon failure of advance payment, the Court may dismiss the petition.

2. No complaint may be filed against the ruling relative to the advance payment of costs.

Article 140 (Costs provisionally defrayed out of national treasury)

In cases where the person filing petition for bankruptcy is not a creditor, costs of the bankruptcy procedure shall provisionally be defrayed from the national treasury. The same shall also apply in cases where the Court has granted adjudication of bankruptcy in case the person filing petition for costs, or where the sum paid in has become insufficient, or bankruptcy is a creditor, despite failure of advance payment of costs, or where the sum paid in has become insufficient, or where the Court has granted adjudication of bankruptcy of its own motion.

Article 141 (Entry of hour and day of adjudication)

The hour and date of adjudication of bankruptcy shall be entered on the written ruling of adjudication of bankruptcy.

Article 142 (Measures to be taken at same time with adjudication of bankruptcy)

1. The Court shall, at the same time with the adjudication of bankruptcy, appoint the administrator in bankruptcy, and specify the following particulars:

(1) The period for report of claims; provided, however, that the period shall be not less than two weeks and not exceeding four months from the date of adjudication of bankruptcy;
(2) The date of the first meeting of creditors; provided, however, that the date shall be within one month of the date of adjudication of bankruptcy;
(3) The date of investigation of claims; provided, however, that between the date and the last day of the period for report, there shall be an interval of not less than one week and not exceeding one month.

2. The dates mentioned under items (2) and (3) of preceding paragraph may be consolidated.

Article 143 (Public notice of adjudication of bankruptcy)

1. The Court shall, immediately upon adjudication of bankruptcy, give public notice of the following particulars:

(1) The principal text of the ruling of adjudication of bankruptcy;
(2) The full name and address of the administrator of bankruptcy;
(3) The periods and the dates specified pursuant to the provisions of the preceding Article;
(4) The orders that persons who owe debts to the bankrupt and persons who are possessed of properties appertaining to the bankrupt estate shall not pay or surrender such properties to the bankrupt, and that they shall, within a specified period, report to the administrator in bankruptcy that they owe debts or are possessed of properties, and in case the persons possessing properties have the right of separation, that they have obligations.

2. A document containing the particulars mentioned in the preceding paragraph shall be served upon known creditors, debtors, and persons possessing properties.

3. The provisions of the preceding two paragraphs shall apply mutatis mutandis in

cases where a change has taken place in any of the particulars mentioned under items (2) to (4) inclusive of the first paragraph.

4. Any person who failed to file the report mentioned under item (4) of the first paragraph shall compensate losses thereby inflicted upon the bankrupt estate.

Article 144 (Notice to public procurators)

When the Court has granted adjudication of bankruptcy, it shall notify the public procurator to that effect without delay.

Article 145 (Discontinuance ruled at same time with adjudication)

1. When the Court finds that the bankrupt estate is not sufficient to pay costs of the bankruptcy procedure, it shall rule for discontinuance of bankruptcy at the same time with the adjudication of bankruptcy. In such cases, the Court shall give public notice of the principal text of the ruling of adjudication of bankruptcy, as well as of the principal text, together with the tenor of the reasons therefor, of the ruling for discontinuance of bankruptcy.

2. In the case mentioned in the preceding paragraph, if the cancellation of the ruling for discontinuance of bankruptcy has become final and conclusive, the provisions of the preceding three Articles (Measures to be taken at same time with adjudication; public notice; notice to public procurator) shall apply mutatis mutandis.

Article 146 (Exception to discontinuance ruled at same time with adjudication)

The provisions of the preceding Article shall not apply in cases where there has been advance payment of the sum which is sufficient to pay costs of the bankruptcy procedure.

Article 147 (Restriction on bankrupt's residence)

Unless permission of the Court is obtained, the bankrupt may not depart from his dwelling place.

Article 148 (Arrest of bankrupt)

1. When deemed necessary, the Court may order that the bankrupt be brought before the Court.

2. In order to bring the bankrupt before the Court, the warrant for appearance shall be issued.

3. The provisions of the Code of Criminal Procedure relative to taking in custody shall apply mutatis mutandis to bringing the bankrupt before the Court.

Article 149 (Putting bankrupt under surveillance)

1. In cases where there is likelihood of the bankrupt's absconding, or concealing or destroying his properties, the Court may order him to be put under surveillance.

2. In the case mentioned in the preceding paragraph, the Court shall send the

authentic copy of the ruling to the public procurator, who shall order the police officer or junior police officer of the police station, which has jurisdiction over the locality where the bankrupt resides, to carry out surveillance.

Article 150 (Prohibition of interview and communication)

The bankrupt, who has been ordered to be kept under surveillance, may not interview or communicate with outsiders, unless permission of the Court is obtained.

Article 151 (Cancellation of order for surveillance)

1. When the need for putting the bankrupt under surveillance has ceased to exist, the Court shall, upon the application of the bankrupt or the administrator in bankruptcy, or of its own motion, annul the ruling for surveillance.

2. In the Case mentioned in the preceding paragraph, the Court shall forward the authentic copy of the ruling to the public procurator, who shall order the police officer or junior police officer to release the bankrupt from surveillance.

Article 152 (Provisions applicable mutatis mutandis to persons to be treated similar to bankrupt)

The provisions of the preceding five Articles (Restrictions on freedom of bankrupt) shall apply mutatis mutandis to the bankrupt's legal representative, a director (*riji*) or persons similar thereto, and a manager. The same shall also apply to the successor, his legal representative, and a manager, in the case of bankruptcy of properties to be succeeded to.

Article 153 (Duty to explain)

1. The bankrupt, his agent, director (*riji*) and persons similar thereto shall, upon demand by the administrator in bankruptcy, inspection commissioners or the meeting of creditors, give necessary explanations concerning bankruptcy. The same shall also apply to the successor, his agent, the administrator of properties to be succeeded to, and the executor, in the case of bankruptcy of properties to be succeeded to.

2. The provisions of the preceding paragraph shall apply mutatis mutandis to persons who have had any of the capacities mentioned in the preceding paragraph.

Article 154 (Bringing to Court or surveillance prior to adjudication)

When petition for bankruptcy has been filed, the Court may order the debtor or any of the persons mentioned in Article 152 to be brought before the Court or be put under surveillance, even prior to the adjudication of bankruptcy.

Article 155 (Preservation measures on estate prior to adjudication)

1. When petition for bankruptcy has been filed, the Court may, upon the application of persons interested or of its own motion, order provisional attachment, provisional disposition, or any other necessary measures for preservation of the bankrupt estate, ever prior to the adjudication of bankruptcy.

2. The Court may either change or annul any of the measures ordered pursuant to the provisions of the preceding paragraph.

3. The decision under the provisions of the preceding two paragraphs shall be given by way of a ruling.

4. The immediate complaint against the trial in accordance with the provision of paragraph 1 or paragraph 2 shall not have the effect of suspension of execution.

Article 155-2 (Suspension of liability limitation procedure)

1. The court may, if recognised necessary in the case where a petition for bankruptcy was filed, order to suspend the liability limitation procedure until there is made the decision to the petition for bankruptcy, due to the petition from an interested person or ex officio. Provided that this shall not apply if there made the decision of commencing the liability limitation procedure.

2. The court may cancel the decision of suspension under the provision of the preceding paragraph.

3. No complaint can be raised against the decision under the preceding two paragraphs.

Article 156 (Publication of annulment of bankruptcy)

1. When the ruling for annulment of bankruptcy has become final and conclusive, the Court shall immediately give public notice of its principal text.

2. The provisions of Article 143 paragraph 2 (Necessity of service), Article 144 (Notice to public procurator), Article 151 paragraph 2 (Release of surveillance), Article 152 (Persons to be treated similar to bankrupt), and Article 355 (Payment of claims appertaining to bankrupt estate) shall apply mutatis mutandis to the case mentioned in the preceding paragraph.

Article 156-2 (Decision of abolition of liability limitation procedure)

1. The court shall, in the case where the decision of abolishing the liability limitation procedure commenced for the bankrupt became conclusive, fix the following matters for the limitation claimants:

(1) The period for reporting claims; provided that the period need be one week or more but two months or less from the day on which the decision of abolishing the liability limitation procedure became conclusive;

(2) The date of investigating claims; provided that there shall be a period of one week or more but one month or less between said date and the last day of the period for reporting claims.

2. The court shall give a public notice of the period and date fixed in accordance with the provision of the preceding paragraph.

3. The document stating the matters mentioned in Article 143 paragraph 1 item (1), item (2), and the preceding paragraph shall need be served to the known limitation claimants.

4. The document stating the matters mentioned in paragraph 2 shall need to be served to the bankruptcy administrator, the bankrupt, and the bankrupt creditors having made the report. Provided that, if the date fixed in accordance with the provision of paragraph 1 item (2) is the same as the date fixed in accordance with the provision of Article 142 paragraph 1 item (3), this shall not apply to the bankrupt creditors having made the report.

5. The provisions of paragraph 2, paragraph 3 and the main clause of the preceding paragraph shall apply mutatis mutandis in the case where the matters mentioned in paragraph 2 were changed.

Chapter III: Administrator in bankruptcy

Article 157 (Appointment by Court)

The administrator in bankruptcy shall be appointed by the Court.

Article 158 (Number)

The administrator in bankruptcy shall be one in number; provided however, that when deemed necessary, the Court may appoint more than one.

Article 159 (Certificate of appointment)

1. The Court shall issue to the administrator in bankruptcy a document certifying his appointment.

2. When performing his duties, the administrator in bankruptcy shall produce the certificate mentioned in the preceding paragraph, whenever requested by any person interested.

Article 160 (Resignation)

1. The administrator in bankruptcy may not resign from his office unless there exist just causes.

2. When the administrator in bankruptcy intends to resign from the office, application therefor shall be filed with the Court.

Article 161 (Supervision by Court)

The administrator in bankruptcy shall be subject to supervision by the Court.

Article 162 (Capacity to sue or be sued)

In a suit connected with the bankrupt estate, the administrator in bankruptcy shall be the plaintiff or the defendant, as the case may be.

Article 163 (Discharge of duties by several administrators)

1. When there is more than one administrator in bankruptcy, they shall perform their duties conjointly; provided however, that they may, with permission of the Court, take charge of duties as divided among them.

2. In cases where there is more than one administrator in bankruptcy, the manifestation of intention by a third person shall be sufficient if effected to one of them.

Article 164 (Duty to use care)

1. The administrator in bankruptcy shall discharge his duties with the care of a good manager.

2. When the administrator in bankruptcy has failed to use care as provided for in the preceding paragraph, such administrator in bankruptcy shall, jointly and severally, be liable to compensate losses to the person interested.

Article 165 (Appointment of agent)

1. The administrator in bankruptcy may appoint in advance his agent on his own responsibility in order to cause such agent to perform his duties in case he is temporarily unable to act.

2. The approval of the Court shall be obtained for appointing an agent pursuant to the provisions of the preceding paragraph.

Article 166 (Advance payment of expenses; remuneration)

The administrator in bankruptcy may receive advance payment of expenses, as well as remuneration. The amount thereof shall be determined by the Court.

Article 167 (Removal)

The Court may, upon resolution adopted at the creditor's meeting or upon the application of inspection commissioners, or of its own motion, remove the administrator in bankruptcy from his office. In such cases, the Court shall question the administrator in bankruptcy.

Article 168 (Duty to account)

1. Upon termination of the office of the administrator in bankruptcy, the administrator in bankruptcy or his successor in office shall, without delay, file a report of account with the creditor's meeting.

2. In cases where the bankrupt, creditors in bankruptcy, or the substituted administrator in bankruptcy have not raised objection to the account at the creditor's meeting, it shall be deemed that the account has been approved.

3. the administrator in bankruptcy shall submit to the Court the report of account and the written opinion of inspection commissioners three days prior to the date of creditors' meeting, for inspection by persons interested.

Article 169 (Emergency measures upon termination of office)

If, upon termination of the office of the administrator in bankruptcy, there exist urgent circumstances, the administrator in bankruptcy or his successor in office shall take necessary measures until the substituted administrator in bankruptcy or the bankrupt becomes able to manage the properties.

Chapter IV: Inspection commissioners

Article 170 (Resolution as to having or not having inspection commissioners)

Whether or not inspection commissioners are to be appointed shall be resolved upon at the first meeting of creditors; provided however, that the resolution may be altered in the subsequent meeting of creditors.

Article 171 (Appointment)

1. Inspection commissioners shall be three or more in number, and appointed at the creditors' meeting.
2. The approval of the Court shall be obtained for resolutions on the appointment of inspection commissioners.

Article 172 (Manner of discharging duties)

1. The discharge of the duties of inspection commissioners shall be decided upon by the majority of their votes.
2. Any of them who has special interests may not exercise the vote.

Article 173 (Right to examine estate)

Inspection commissioners may each demand, at any time, of the administrator in bankruptcy the report on the bankrupt estate or investigate the state of the bankrupt estate.

Article 174 (Removal)

1. Inspection commissioners may, at any time, be removed from office upon resolution adopted at the creditors' meeting.
2. In cases where there exists any important ground, the Court may, upon the application of the person interested, remove inspection commissioners from office.

Article 175 (Provisions applicable mutatis mutandis)

The provisions of Article 164 (Administrator's duty to use care) and Article 166 (Advance payment of expenses remuneration) shall apply mutatis mutandis to inspection commissioners.

Chapter V: Meeting of creditors

Article 176 (Convention of meeting)

The Court shall, upon the application of the administrator in bankruptcy or inspection commissioners, or of its own motion, convene the meeting of creditors. The same shall also apply in cases where application has been filed by bankruptcy creditors who represent one-fifth or more of the value as appraised by the Court of the total amount of the claims which have been reported.

Article 177 (Publication of date and object of meeting)

1. The court shall give public notice of the date of the creditors' meeting, as well as matters forming the object of the meeting.
2. In cases where there has been rendition of the ruling on postponement or continuation of the creditors' meeting, service or public notice thereof may be dispensed with.

Article 178 (Command by Court)

The meeting of creditors shall be subject to command of the Court.

Article 179 (Requisites for adopting resolution)

1. In order to adopt a resolution at the creditors' meeting, there shall be consent thereto given by the majority of the bankruptcy creditors present, capable of exercising the right of vote, of whom the amount of claims exceed one half of the total amount of their claims.

2. Those who have special interests in the resolution to be adopted at the creditors' meeting may not exercise their right of vote.

Article 180 (Cases where resolution may, by virtue of Court's decision, be deemed to have been adopted)

1. Even in cases where a resolution cannot be adopted pursuant to the provisions of the preceding Article, if the amount of claims held by those who have given consent to the matter to be resolved upon exceeds one half of the total amount of claims held by the bankruptcy creditors present capable of exercising the right of vote, the Court may rule that the resolution shall be deemed to have been adopted.

2. The Court shall give public notice of the ruling mentioned in the preceding paragraph. No complaint shall be filed against such ruling.

Article 181 (Exercise by proxy of right to vote)

Creditors in bankruptcy may exercise their right of vote by proxy. In such cases, the proxy shall submit a document evidencing his authority.

Article 182 (Amount of claims on which right of vote is exercised)

1. Bankruptcy creditors may exercise their right of vote in proportion to the amount of claims which are definite.

2. In cases where the administrator in bankruptcy or bankruptcy creditors have raised objection to indefinite claims, claims subject to condition precedent, future claims, or the amount of claims of which payment cannot be obtained through exercise of the right of separation, the Court shall determine whether the right of vote is to be exercised or not and also on what amount it is to be exercised.

3. The Court may, upon the application of persons interested, modify at any time the ruling granted pursuant to the provisions of the preceding paragraph.

4. In cases where there has been rendition of the ruling granted pursuant to the provisions of the preceding two paragraphs, service thereof may be dispensed with. No complaint shall be filed against such rulings.

5. Creditors in bankruptcy may not exercise their right of vote with respect to the claims mentioned in Article 46.

Article 183 (Resolution effective taking place of consent by inspection commissioners)

1. A resolution adopted at the creditors' meeting may be substituted for the consent of inspection commissioners.

2. In case a resolution adopted at the creditors' meeting differs from the opinion of inspection commissioners, the resolution shall govern.

Article 184 (Prohibition of execution of resolution)

1. In cases where a resolution adopted at the creditors' meeting runs counter to the general interests of creditors in bankruptcy, the Court may, upon the application of the administrator in bankruptcy, inspection commissioners or creditors in bankruptcy, or of its own motion, prohibit the resolution from being carried into effect.

2. For filing the application mentioned in the preceding paragraph, a bankruptcy creditor who has not had the right of vote shall give prima facie proof that he is a creditor in bankruptcy.

3. In cases where there has been rendition of the ruling for prohibition granted pursuant to the provision of the first paragraph, service thereof may be dispensed with.

Chapter VI: Administration and realisation of bankrupt estate

Article 185 (Taking possession, and management, of bankrupt's property)

The administrator in bankruptcy shall, immediately upon assuming his office, proceed to take possession of, and manage, properties appertaining to the bankrupt estate.

Article 186 (Affixing seals)

1. When deemed necessary, the administrator in bankruptcy may cause the clerk of the Court, a bailiff, or a notary public to seal up properties appertaining to the bankrupt estate. In such cases, the person who affixed seals shall prepare the record thereof.

2. The provisions of the preceding paragraph shall apply mutatis mutandis in the case of unsealing.

Article 187 (Closing property ledgers)

The clerk of the Court shall, immediately upon adjudication of bankruptcy, close books of the bankrupt's assets, sign and affix his seal thereto, and prepare the record wherein he shall enter the present state of the books; provided, however, that name-writing and seal-impression may be substituted for signature and seal-affixing.

Article 188 (Appraisal of assets)

The administrator in bankruptcy shall, without delay, appraise the value of any and all properties appertaining to the bankrupt estate, in the presence of the clerk of the Court, a bailiff, or a notary public. In such cases, the bankrupt shall be requested to be present, except in cases where there is likelihood of delay.

Article 189 (Preparation of inventory and balance sheet)

1. The administrator in bankruptcy shall prepare the inventory and the balance sheet.

2. The administrator in bankruptcy shall sign and affix his seal to certified copies of the inventory and of the balance sheet and submit them to the Court. The same shall also apply to the record of sealing up of properties.

3. Name-writing and seal-impression may be substituted for the signature and seal-affixing under the preceding paragraph.

4. The person interested may demand inspection of the documents mentioned in paragraph 2.

Article 190 (Management of mails)

1. The Court shall request the government office in charge of communication or other public communication agencies to deliver to the administrator in bankruptcy mails and telegrams addressed to the bankrupt.

2. The administrator in bankruptcy may open the mails and telegrams mentioned in the preceding paragraph which he has received.

3. The bankrupt may demand inspection of the mails and telegrams mentioned in the preceding paragraph, and also demand surrender of those which do not concern the bankrupt estate.

Article 191 (Release of control of mails)

1. The Court may, upon the application of the bankrupt, revoke or restrict the request mentioned in paragraph 1 of the preceding Article, after consulting the opinion of the administrator in bankruptcy.

2. When the ruling for annulment or discontinuance of bankruptcy has become final and conclusive, or when there has been the ruling for termination of bankruptcy, the Court shall revoke the request mentioned in paragraph 1 of the preceding Article.

Article 192 (Granting allowance in aid; continuation of business; custody of valuables)

1. Prior to the first meeting of creditors, the administrator in bankruptcy may, upon obtaining permission of the Court, grant allowances in aid to the bankrupt and his dependants, or continue the bankrupt's business.

2. The manner of keeping in custody moneys, valuable instruments, and other valuables shall be determined by the Court.

Article 193 (Report on progress of bankruptcy)

1. The administrator in bankruptcy shall report to the first meeting of creditors the circumstances which led to the adjudication of bankruptcy, and the progress as to, and the present state of, the bankrupt and the bankrupt estate.

Article 194 (Matters required to be resolved upon at first meeting)

At the first meeting of creditors, resolution shall be adopted upon granting of allowances in aid, discontinuance or continuation of the business, and the manner of keeping in custody of valuables.

Article 195 (Presentation of subject-matter of right of separation)

1. The administrator in bankruptcy may demand of persons possessing the right of separation the presentation of properties forming the subject-matter of the right.

2. In case the administrator in bankruptcy intends to appraise the properties mentioned in the preceding paragraph, the person possessing the right of separation may not refuse it.

Article 196 (Restriction on time of realisation)

1. Prior to the completion of the investigation of general claims, the administrator in bankruptcy may not carry out realisation of the bankrupt estate. When there has been proposal for compulsory composition prior to the completion of the investigation of general claims, the same shall also apply until the matter shall have been settled.

2. Those properties appertaining to the bankrupt estate, which are likely to inflict losses on the bankrupt estate unless they are realised without delay, may, notwithstanding the provisions of the preceding paragraph, be realised by the administrator in bankruptcy with consent of inspection commissioners, and in the absence of inspection commissioners, upon obtaining permission of the Court.

Article 197 (Acts requiring consent of inspection commissioners)

In order to do any of the following acts, the administrator in bankruptcy shall obtain consent of inspection commissioners; provided however, that this shall not apply to those acts mentioned under items (7) to (14) inclusive, of which the value is not less than one hundred thousand yen:

(1) Voluntary sale of real rights on immoveable property, Japanese vessels of which registration is required, and foreign vessels;
(2) Voluntary sale of mining right, fishery right, patent right, design right, right of utility model, circuit layout right, copyrights, and neighbouring right thereof;
(3) Assignment of business;
(4) Sale *in bloc* of merchandises;
(5) Obtaining loans;
(6) Approval of the renunciation of succession under the provisions of Article 9 paragraph 2, approval of the renunciation of testamentary gifts by a universal title under the provision is Article 10, and renunciation of specific testamentary gifts under the provisions of Article 11 paragraph 1;
(7) Voluntary sale of moveables;
(8) Assignment of obligations and of valuable instruments;
(9) Demand for performance under the provisions of Article 59 paragraph 1;
(10) Institution of an action;
(11) Agreement of compromise and of arbitration;
(12) Relinquishment of a right;
(13) Admittance of claims appertaining to the bankrupt estate, of the right to redeem; and of the right of separation;
(14) Redemption of the subject-matter of the right of separation.

Article 198 (Permission of Court to be substituted for consent)

1. In cases where it is necessary to do, prior to the first meeting of inspection commissioners by virtue of the provisions of the preceding Article, the administrator in bankruptcy shall obtain permission of the Court.

2. In cases where inspection commissioners have not been appointed, the administrator in bankruptcy shall obtain resolution of the creditors' meeting; provided however, that in case of urgent necessity, it shall be sufficient to obtain permission of the Court.

Article 199 (Consulting bankrupt's opinion)

In the cases mentioned in the preceding two Articles, the administrator in bankruptcy shall consult opinion of the bankrupt, except in cases where there is likelihood of delay.

Article 200 (Order of Court for suspension of execution)

Even in cases where the administrator in bankruptcy has obtained consent of inspection commissioners for doing any of the acts mentioned in Article 197, the Court may, upon the application of the bankrupt, order suspension of the carrying out of the act in question and convene the creditors' meeting to cause it to adopt a resolution concerning the act in question.

Article 201 (Protection of bona fide third party)

Even if the administrator in bankruptcy contravened the provisions of Articles 196 to 198 inclusive on the order for suspension of execution provided for in the preceding Article, such facts may not be set up against bona fide third persons.

Article 202 (Manner of realisation)

The properties and rights mentioned under items (1) and (2) of Article 197 shall be realised in accordance with the provisions of the Civil Execution Law and those of other law or ordinance concerning the proceedings for compulsory execution.

Article 203 (Realisation of subject of right of separation) (14)

1. The administrator in bankruptcy may realise properties forming the subject-matter of the right of separation in accordance with the provisions of the Civil Execution Law and those of other law or ordinance concerning the proceedings of compulsory execution. In such cases, the person possessing the right of separation may not refuse it.

2. In the case mentioned in the preceding paragraph, if the sum payable to the person possessing the right of separation is not yet definite, the administrator in bankruptcy shall separately deposit the price. In such cases, the right of separation shall subsist on the price.

Article 204 (Designation of period for disposal by person holding right of separation)

1. In cases where a person possessing the right of separation has the right of disposal of the subject-matter of the right of separation without resorting to the method pre-

scribed in law, the Court shall, upon the application of the administrator in bankruptcy, designate the period for such disposal by the person possessing the right of separation.

2. If the person possessing the right of separation fails to make disposal within the period mentioned in the preceding paragraph, he shall forfeit the right mentioned in the preceding paragraph.

Article 205 (Administrator's report on state of affairs)

The administrator in bankruptcy shall report to the creditors' meeting or inspection commissioners the state of the bankrupt estate in accordance with what is prescribed by the creditors' meeting.

Article 206 (Demand for return of things deposited)

1. In order to demand return of moneys, valuable instruments and other valuables which the administrator in bankruptcy has deposited, he shall obtain consent of inspection commissioners, and in the absence of inspection commissioners, permission of the Court; provided however, that if the creditors' meeting has otherwise resolved upon, such resolution shall govern.

2. If, in cases where the administrator in bankruptcy has contravened the provisions of the preceding paragraph, the person with whom the deposit was made is in good faith and without negligence, his performance of obligation shall be valid.

3. The provisions of the preceding two paragraphs shall apply mutatis mutandis, in cases where the administrator in bankruptcy issues securities in order to cause the person with whom the deposit has been made to make payment and other performances.

Article 207 (Materialising of partner's duty to make contribution)

The provisions of Article 126 (Partner's duty to make contribution in case of impossibility to make full performance of obligations) of the Commercial Code shall apply mutatis mutandis in cases where a corporation has been adjudged bankrupt.

Articles 208–224

[Deleted.]

Articles 225

In cases where a contract of undisclosed association has terminated because of bankruptcy of the proprietor of business, the administrator in bankruptcy may demand contribution to the extent of the amount of losses to be borne by the parties to the undisclosed association.

Article 226 (Bankruptcy of successor and disposal of properties to be succeeded to)

1. In cases where a successor has made qualified acceptance, or where there has been separation of property, after the successor had been adjudged bankrupt, the disposal of

properties to be succeeded to shall be effected by the administrator in bankruptcy. The same shall also apply in cases where the successor has been adjudged bankrupt after there has been qualified acceptance or separation of property.

2. When the administrator in bankruptcy has completed the disposal mentioned in the preceding paragraph, the inventory and the balance sheet of the bankrupt estate shall be supplemented with respect to the surplus assets.

3. The provisions of the preceding two paragraphs shall apply mutatis mutandis in cases where a testamentary donee under a universal title has been adjudged bankrupt.

Article 227 (Provisions applicable mutatis mutandis)

The provisions of the preceding Article shall apply mutatis mutandis in cases where the effect of qualified acceptance is recognised by virtue of the provisions of Article 8 or Article 9 paragraph 1.

Chapter VII: Report and investigation of claims in bankruptcy

Article 228 (Manner of reporting claims)

1. Bankruptcy creditors shall, within the period designated by the Court, report to the Court the amount and causes of their claims, the general preferential right or other general right of priority, if any, and if any of the claims mentioned in Article 46 is included, the distinction thereof, and also submit evidential documents, or certified copies or extract copies thereof.

2. A person possessing the right of separation shall report, in addition to the particulars mentioned in the preceding paragraph, the subject-matter of the right of separation and the amount of claim of which performance could not be had through exercise of the right.

3. In cases where an action is pending with respect to a bankruptcy claim at the time of adjudication of bankruptcy, the Court in which the action is pending, the title of the case and the case number shall also be reported in addition to the particulars mentioned in the first paragraph.

Article 229 (Preparation of list of claims)

1. The clerk of the Court shall prepare the list of claims and enter therein the following particulars;

(1) The full name and address of creditors;
(2) The amount and causes of claims;
(3) If it is a claim of which there exists a right of priority, such right; if any of the claims mentioned in Article 46 is included, the distinction thereof;
(4) The amount of claim which persons possessing the right of separation have reported pursuant to the provisions of paragraph 2 of the preceding Article.

2. The clerk of the Court shall deliver to the administrator in bankruptcy a certified copy of the list of claims.

Article 230 (Keeping documents of report and list of claims)

Documents relative to the report of claims and the list of claims shall be kept at the Court for inspection by persons interested.

Article 231 (Particulars to be investigated regarding claims)

On the day for investigation of claims, the particulars mentioned in Article 229 paragraph 1 shall be investigated with respect to each claim.

Article 232 (Appearance of persons concerned)

1. The bankrupt shall appear and state his opinions on the day for investigation of claims, provided however, that he may cause his agent to appear, when there exist just causes.

2. Those creditors in bankruptcy who have filed the report and their agents may appear and state their opinions on the day for investigation of claims. The agents shall submit a document which proves their authority.

Article 233 (Necessity of appearance of administrator)

The investigation of claims shall not be conducted unless the administrator in bankruptcy appears.

Article 234 (Investigation of claims reported after expiry of period)

1. Claims, of which the report has been filed after expiration of the period for report, may be investigated on the day for general investigation of claims, except in cases where objection is raised by the administrator in bankruptcy and creditors in bankruptcy.

2. In cases where objection has been raised by the administrator in bankruptcy or creditors in bankruptcy, the court shall set a special day for investigation of the claims mentioned in the preceding paragraph. In such cases, the costs shall be borne by the creditors who filed the report after expiration of the period for report.

Article 235 (Provisions applicable mutatis mutandis to cases of change in matters reported)

The provisions of the preceding Article shall apply mutatis mutandis in cases where after expiration of the period for report, such changes have been made in the matters reported by creditors in bankruptcy as will adversely affect the interests of other creditors in bankruptcy.

Article 236 (Report after day for general investigation and special day)

The provisions of Article 234 paragraph 2 (Special day) shall apply mutatis mutandis in cases where a creditor in bankruptcy has reported his claim after the day for general investigation of claims.

Article 237 (Special day for investigation of claims)

The ruling which sets a special day for investigation of claims shall be given public notice, and served upon the administrator in bankruptcy, the bankrupt, and those bankruptcy creditors who have filed the report.

Article 238 (Change of day; postponement and continuation)

The provisions of the preceding Article shall apply mutatis mutandis to changes of the day for investigation of claims and also to the postponement and continuation of the investigation of claims; provided however, that public notice and service may be dispensed with, if there has been rendition of the ruling.

Article 239 (Prohibition of complaint)

No complaint may be filed against the rulings granted pursuant to the provisions of the preceding two Articles.

Article 240 (Becoming final and conclusive of claims)

1. If, on the day for investigation of claims, no objection has been raised by the administrator in bankruptcy and creditors in bankruptcy, the amount of claims, the right of priority, and the distinction as to the claims mentioned in Article 46 shall thereupon become final and conclusive.

2. In cases where an action is pending at the time of adjudication of bankruptcy with respect to a claim objected to by the bankrupt, the creditor may take over such action against the bankrupt as the opponent party.

Article 241 (Entry on list of claims)

1. The Court shall enter the results of investigation of claims on the list of claims. The same shall also apply to objections raised by the bankrupt.

2. The clerk of the court shall enter on the deed of claim which has become final and conclusive a statement that it has become final and conclusive, and affix thereto the seal of the Court.

Article 242 (Effect of entry on list of claims)

With regard to those claims which have become final and conclusive, the entries on the list of claims shall have the same effect as a judgment which has become final and conclusive, as against all of the bankruptcy creditors.

Article 243 (Notice of objection)

1. In cases where a bankruptcy creditor fails to appear on the day for investigation of claims, if objection has been raised to his claim, the Court shall give notice thereof to the creditor.

2. The provisions of Article 118 paragraph 1 (Service by mail) shall apply mutatis mutandis to the notice mentioned in the preceding paragraph.

Article 244 (Action for confirmation of claim)

1. With regard to a claim objected to, the creditor may seek confirmation of the claim through instituting an action against the person who raised objection.

2. Where there are several persons who raised objection, they shall be co-defendants. The same shall also apply in cases where the bankrupt is one of the objecting persons.

3. The Court shall deliver to the creditor an extract copy of the list of claims bearing on his claim.

Article 245 (Jurisdiction of action for confirmation of claim)

The action for confirmation of claim shall come under the exclusive jurisdiction of the court of bankruptcy.

Article 246 (Taking over of action on claims objected to)

1. In cases where an action is pending at the time of adjudication of bankruptcy with respect to a claim of which objection has been raised, if the creditor intends to seek confirmation of his claim, he shall take over the action against the objecting person as the opponent party.

2. The provisions of Article 244 paragraph 2 (More than one person objecting) shall apply mutatis mutandis to the case mentioned in the preceding paragraph.

Article 247 (Causes of action restricted)

A creditor in bankruptcy may institute the action for confirmation of his claim, or take over the action pursuant to the provisions of Article 240 paragraph 2 or of the preceding Article, only with respect to the matters entered on the list of claims.

Article 248 (Manner of asserting objection against claims with title for execution)

1. With regard to a claim of which there exists title for execution or a final judgment, the person objecting may assert his objection only through judicial proceedings which can be prosecuted by the bankrupt.

2. The provisions of Article 244 paragraphs 2 and 3 (More than one person objecting; delivery of extract copy of list of claims), Article 246 (Taking over of proceedings), and the preceding Article shall apply mutatis mutandis to the case mentioned in the preceding paragraph.

Article 249 (Entry of results of action for confirmation of claim)

The Court shall, upon the application of the administrator in bankruptcy or of creditors in bankruptcy, enter on the list of claims the results of the action for confirmation of claim.

Article 250 (Effect of judgment on action for confirmation of claim)

A judgment given in the action for confirmation of claim shall be effective as against all of the creditors in bankruptcy.

Article 251 (Reimbursement of costs)

In cases where the bankrupt estate has been benefited because of the action for confirmation of claim, those bankruptcy creditors who have asserted objections may demand reimbursement of costs of litigation as holder of claims appertaining to the bankrupt estate, to the extent of the benefits so received.

Article 252 (Amount of controversy in action for confirmation of claim)

The value of the subject-matter of an action for confirmation of claim shall be determined by the Court, in which the action has been instituted, in the light of the estimated amount of dividend distribution taken as the standard.

Article 253

[Deleted.]

Article 254 (Report on fines, minor fines, etc.)

1. With regard to the claims mentioned under item (4) of Article 46, the State or the public body concerned shall report to the Court without delay the amount and causes thereof.

2. The provisions of Article 241 paragraph 1 (Entry on list of claims) shall apply mutatis mutandis to those claims which have been reported pursuant to the provisions of the preceding paragraph.

Article 255 (Where matter amenable to petition or suit is involved)

1. In cases where the cause of the claim reported pursuant to the provisions of paragraph 1 of the preceding Article is an administrative action of which a motion for complaint, such as investigation demand, or a suit may be brought, the Court shall notify the administrator in bankruptcy of the amount and causes of the claim without delay.

2. The provisions of Article 248–250 inclusive (Manner of asserting objection against claims with title for execution; entry of results of action on list of claims; effect of judgment) shall apply mutatis mutandis in cases where the administrator in bankruptcy asserts objection.

Chapter VIII: Distribution of dividends

Article 256 (Time of distribution)

After completion of the investigation of general claims, dividends shall be distributed without delay, each time the administrator in bankruptcy considers there exist moneys fit for distribution.

Article 257 (Consent or permission required for distribution)

In order to distribute dividends, the administrator in bankruptcy shall obtain consent of inspection commissioner, and in the absence of inspection commissioners, permission of the Court.

Article 258 (Preparation of, and entries on, list of dividends)

1. The administrator in bankruptcy shall prepare a list of dividends and enter thereon the following particulars:

(1) The full name and address of creditors whom dividends are to be distributed;
(2) The amount of claims of which dividends are to be distributed;
(3) The amount which can be distributed as dividends.

2. Claims of which dividends are to be distributed shall be distinguished depending on whether or not the right of priority exists: those having priority rights shall be entered in accordance with the rank or priority, and as for those which are devoid of priority rights, entries shall be made, making distinction between those deferred by virtue of the provisions of Article 46 and others.

Article 259 (Submission of list of dividends)

The administrator in bankruptcy shall submit to the Court the list of dividends for inspection by persons interested.

Article 260 (Publication of amount of dividends)

The administrator in bankruptcy shall give public notice of the total amount of claims of which dividends are to be distributed, as well as of the amount of money which can be distributed as dividends.

Article 261 (Exclusion of claims objected to)

With regard to claims of which objection is raised, if the creditor fails to prove to the administrator in bankruptcy, within two weeks computed form the day the public notice of dividends has been given, that an action has been instituted seeking confirmation of the claim or that the action has been taken over, the claim shall be excluded from the distribution of dividends.

Article 262 (Exclusion of person possessing right of separation)

If a person possessing the right of separation fails to give to the administrator in bankruptcy within the period for exclusion prescribed in the preceding Article prima facie proof of the fact that he has commenced disposal of the subject-matter of the right as well as of the amount of claim of which payment could not be had by such disposal, he shall be excluded from the distribution of dividends.

Article 263 (Revision of list of dividends)

The administrator in bankruptcy shall immediately revise the list of dividends in any of the following cases:

(1) When the cause for revision of the list of dividends has arisen within the period for exclusion;
(2) When proof or prima facie proof has been given of the matters provided for in the preceding two Articles;

(3) When a person possessing the right of separation has, within the period for exclusion, manifested to the administrator in bankruptcy his intention to relinquish his right, or has proved the amount of claim of which he could not obtain payment through exercise of his right.

Article 264 (Objection to list of dividends)

1. Creditors may file with the Court their objection to the list of dividends, only within one week after expiration of the period for exclusion.

2. In cases where the Court has ordered revision of the list of dividends, it shall keep the written ruling for inspection by persons interested. In such cases, the period for filing complaint shall be computed from the day on which the Court commenced to keep for inspection the written ruling.

Article 265 (Determination of rate of distribution and notice thereof)

1. In cases where objection has been raised after expiration of the period prescribed in paragraph 1 of the preceding Article, the administrator in bankruptcy shall, without delay after ruling has been granted thereon, determine the rate of distribution and give notice thereof to each of the creditors.

2. In order to determine the rate of distribution, it shall be necessary to obtain consent of inspection commissioners, and in the absence of inspection commissioners, permission of the Court.

Article 266 (Receipt of dividends by creditor holding claim subject to condition subsequent)

Any person possessing a claim subject to condition subsequent may not receive dividends, unless he furnishes reasonable security.

Article 267 (Compulsory composition and suspension of distribution)

When there has been proposal for compulsory composition, the Court may, upon the application of the person making the proposal, order suspension of the distribution of dividends, only when the administrator in bankruptcy has not yet issued notice of the rate of distribution. In such cases, public notice shall be given to that effect.

Article 268 (Continuation of distribution proceedings)

In cases where suspension of distribution has been ordered pursuant to the provisions of the preceding Article, if the ruling of dismissal or disapproval of the proposal for compulsory composition has become final and conclusive, or where the creditors' meeting has adopted a resolution disapproving the compulsory composition, the Court shall order that the distribution proceedings shall be continued. In such cases, public notice shall be given to that effect.

Article 269 (Manner of distributing dividends)

1. Creditors shall receive dividends from the administrator in bankruptcy.

2. When the administrator in bankruptcy has distributed dividends, he shall enter the amount of dividends distributed on the list of dividends and the deed of obligation, and sign and affix his seal thereto.

Article 270 (Preference given to those excluded in previous distribution)

In cases where a creditor, who was excluded from distribution because of having failed to prove, or to give prima facie proof of, the particulars mentioned in Article 261 or Article 262, has proved or given prima facie proof within the period of exclusion for later distribution, he may receive dividends in preference to other creditors of the same rank of priority, with respect to such sum as he should have received in the previous distribution.

Article 271 (Deposit of dividends)

The administrator in bankruptcy shall deposit the amount of dividends to be distributed for any of the following claims:

(1) Claims objected to pursuant to the provisions of Articles 244, 246, or 248, of which an action has been instituted or the action has been taken over;
(2) Claims, of which the proceeding of a motion for complaint, such as investigation demand, or a suit has not been settled before the notice of the rate of distribution is issued;
(3) The amount of claim, of which a person possessing the right of separation has given prima facie proof pursuant to the provisions of Article 262;
(4) Claims subject to condition precedent and future claims;
(5) Claims subject to condition subsequent, in cases where security is not furnished pursuant to the provisions of Article 266.

Article 272 (Permission of last distribution)

In order to effect the last distribution of dividends, the administrator in bankruptcy shall obtain permission of the Court, even if inspection commissioners have given consent thereto.

Article 273 (Period of exclusion for last distribution)

The period of exclusion for the last distribution of dividends shall be determined by the Court within the range of not less than two weeks and not exceeding one month computed from the date of public notice of dividends. No complaint shall be filed against this ruling.

Article 274 (Determination of amount of last distribution and notice)

With respect to the last distribution of dividends, the administrator in bankruptcy shall determine the amount of dividends to be distributed to each of the creditors and issue notice thereof without delay upon settlement of objections to the list of dividends.

Article 275 (Exclusion of creditors possessing claim subject to condition precedent)

In cases where a claim subject to condition precedent or a future claim has not become capable of being exercised within the period of exclusion for the last distribution, the creditor shall be excluded from the distribution of dividends.

Article 276 (Unconditional payment to creditors possessing claim subject to condition subsequent)

In cases where the condition of a claim subject to condition subsequent fails to materialise within the period of exclusion for the last distribution, the security furnished pursuant to the provisions of Article 266 shall lose its effect, and the sum deposited pursuant to the provisions of Article 271 item (5) shall be paid to the creditor. The same shall also apply to the security furnished or the sum deposited under the provisions of Article 101.

Article 277 (Exclusion of persons possessing right of separation)

In cases where a person possessing the right of separation fails, within the period of exclusion for the last distribution, to manifest his intention to the administrator in bankruptcy to relinquish his right, or to prove the amount of claim of which he could not obtain payment through exercise of his right, he shall be excluded from the distribution of dividends.

Article 278 (Distribution of sums deposited)

The sums deposited on behalf of the creditors who have been excluded pursuant to the provisions of Article 275 or of the preceding Article shall be distributed to other creditors. The same shall also apply to the sum deposited under the provisions of Article 100.

Article 279 (Revision of list of dividends)

In cases where, prior to issuing notice of amounts to be distributed as dividends, there has come up anew a property to be appropriated to the distribution of dividends, the administrator in bankruptcy shall revise the list of dividends without delay.

Article 280 (Deposit of dividends)

The administrator in bankruptcy shall deposit the following dividends on behalf of creditors:

(1) The dividends deposited pursuant to the provisions of Article 271 item (1) or item (2);
(2) The dividends to be distributed for the claim, of which a suit or petition is not settled prior to the issue of notice of the amount of dividends;
(3) The dividends not taken by creditors.

Article 281 (Creditors' meeting for report of account)

At the meeting of creditors convened for the report of account, a resolution shall be adopted concerning the disposal of properties which, being destitute of value, have not been realised by the administrator in bankruptcy.

Article 282 (Ruling for termination of bankruptcy procedure)

1. Upon termination of the meeting of creditors, the Court shall rule for termination of the bankruptcy procedure and give public notice of the principal text of the ruling as well as of the tenor of reasons thereof.

2. No complaint shall be filed against the ruling mentioned in the preceding paragraph.

Article 283 (Additional distribution of dividends)

1. In cases where, after the notice of amounts to be distributed as dividends has been issued, there has come up anew a property to be appropriated to the distribution of dividends, the administrator in bankruptcy shall, upon obtaining permission of the Court, distribute additional dividends. The same shall apply, even after the ruling has been granted for termination of the bankruptcy procedure.

2. Upon obtaining permission for the distribution of additional dividends, the administrator in bankruptcy shall, without delay, give public notice of the sum which can be distributed as dividends, determine the amount of dividends to be distributed to each of the creditors, and issue notice thereof.

Article 284 (Basis for additional distribution of dividends)

Additional dividends shall be distributed in accordance with the list of dividends prepared for the last distribution of dividends.

Article 285 (Report of account)

Upon distributing additional dividends, the administrator in bankruptcy shall, without delay, prepare the report of account, file it with the court, and apply for approval thereof.

Article 286 (Creditors holding claims appertaining to bankrupt estate who are unknown to administrator)

Those creditors possessing claims appertaining to the bankrupt estate who are not known to the administrator in bankruptcy prior to issuing the notice of the rate of distribution or of the amount to be distributed as dividends, shall not obtain payment in accordance with the sums which are to be distributed in each of the distributions.

Article 287 (Effect of entries of definite claim on list of claims)

1. With regard to a definite claim, the entries on the list of claims shall have the same effect as a judgment which has become final and conclusive only in cases where the bankrupt did not object to the claim on the day for investigation of claims.

2. The creditors may, after termination of the bankruptcy procedure, levy compulsory execution by virtue of entries on the list of claims.

Article 288 (Supplementation of bankrupt's objections)

1. In cases where the bankrupt was unable to appear on the day of investigation of claims because of causes for which he should not be held responsible, he may file with the Court of bankruptcy an application for restoration of the original condition for the purpose of supplementing his objections, only within one week of the day said causes shall have ceased to exist.

2. The Court shall, of its own motion, serve the application for restoration of original condition upon persons who possess claims, to which the bankrupt has raised objection.

3. When the Court has granted restoration of the original condition, there shall be recognised the same effect as if the bankrupt had raised objection on the day of investigation of claims. In such cases, the Court shall enter objections on the list of claims.

Article 289 (Surplus assets of properties to be succeeded to)

In cases where bankruptcy has been adjudged of properties to be succeeded to, those obligees of the person succeeded to and testamentary donees who have been excluded from the last distribution of dividends may exercise their rights with respect to the surplus assets.

Chapter IX: Compulsory composition

Article 290 (Right to propose composition)

The bankrupt may, at any time, propose for compulsory composition.

Article 291 (Proposal of composition by corporation)

In the case of a juristic person, in order to make proposal for compulsory composition, there shall be agreement among its directors (*riji*) or persons similar thereto.

Article 292 (Proposal of composition with respect to properties to be succeeded to)

In the case of properties to be succeeded to, the proposal for compulsory composition shall be made by the successor, and of there exist several successors, they shall agree in making such proposal.

Article 293 (Composition and persons possessing general priority rights)

Persons who possess general preferential right and other general priority rights shall not be deemed to be creditors in bankruptcy for purposes of compulsory composition.

Article 294 (Presentation of terms of composition)

When making proposal for compulsory composition, the person proposing shall present to the Court the manner of payment, the security if he intends to furnish security, and other terms of compulsory composition.

Article 295 (Cases where composition is impossible)

There shall be no compulsory composition, in cases where the whereabouts of the person proposing compulsory composition is unknown, or where public prosecution against fraudulent bankruptcy is pending. The same shall also apply when judgment of conviction of fraudulent bankruptcy has become final and conclusive.

Article 296 (Cases where proposal of composition can be dismissed)

The Court may upon consulting opinions of the administrator in bankruptcy and of inspection commissioners, dismiss proposal for compulsory composition in any of the following cases:

(1) When resolution disapproving compulsory composition has ever been adopted at the meeting of creditors;

(2) When the proposal has ever been retracted subsequent to the public notice of the date of creditors' meeting to be convened for compulsory composition;

(3) When there has ever been granted the ruling disapproving compulsory composition;

(4) When the ruling for annulment of compulsory composition has ever been granted.

Article 297 (Submission of written opinion of inspection commissioners)

In cases where the Court does not dismiss the proposal for compulsory composition, if there exist inspection commissioners, they shall be caused to submit their written opinion.

Article 298 (Keeping documents)

Documents relative to the proposal for compulsory composition and the written opinion of inspection commissioners shall be kept at the Court for inspection by persons interested.

Article 299 (Date of creditors' meeting for composition)

1. The date of the creditors' meeting for compulsory composition shall be set on a day falling within one month of the day of public notice of the ruling thereof.

2. On the date, those creditors in bankruptcy who have filed the report, the person proposing compulsory composition, persons who become a guarantor for purposes of compulsory composition, or otherwise assume debts together with the bankrupt or furnish security on behalf of bankruptcy creditors, the administrator in bankruptcy, and inspection commissioners shall be summoned.

3. A document containing the terms of compulsory composition as well as the tenor of the opinion of inspection commissioners shall be served upon the persons mentioned in the preceding paragraph.

Article 300 (Consolidation of dates)

The Court may, upon the application of the person proposing compulsory composition and of inspection commissioners, consolidate the date of the creditors' meeting for compulsory composition with that of investigation of general claims.

Article 301 (Composition to be applied for at hearing)

1. The person proposing compulsory composition shall appear on the day of hearing and apply for compulsory composition; provided however, that when there exist just causes, he may cause his agent to appear in his place.

2. The agent shall submit a document proving his authority.

3. In cases where the person proposing compulsory composition or his agent fails to appear on the day and to apply for compulsory composition, he shall be deemed to have retracted the proposal.

Article 302 (Change of terms of composition)

The person proposing compulsory composition may change the terms thereof at the meeting of creditors only when the bankruptcy creditors are thereby benefited.

Article 303 (Time of resolution on composition)

Compulsory composition shall not be resolved upon, prior to the completion of investigation of general claims, or after there has been permission of the last distribution of dividends.

Article 304 (Principal of equality of terms of composition)

The terms of compulsory composition shall be equal with respect to each of the bankruptcy creditors; provided however, that this shall not apply in cases where persons who are to suffer disadvantages have consented thereto.

Article 305 (Nullity of act of providing with special benefits)

Any act, whereby the person proposing compulsory composition or a third person provides a bankruptcy creditor with special benefits not by virtue of the terms of compulsory composition, shall be null and void.

Article 306 (Requisites for resolution approving composition)

1. In order to adopt resolution approving compulsory composition, there shall be consent of persons who represent the majority of the bankruptcy creditors present who are capable of exercising the right of vote and whose claims represent in amount three-quarters or more of the total claims of those bankruptcy creditors who have filed the report.

2. For purposes of computation of the amount of claims and the total claims mentioned in the preceding paragraph, with respect to definite claims, the amount thereof shall govern, and with respect to other claims, what the Court has determined pursuant to the provisions of Article 182 paragraph 2 shall govern.

Article 307 (Designation of date for continuation)

In cases where any of the conditions prescribed in the preceding Article has materialised, or where persons, who represent the majority of the bankruptcy creditors present who are capable of exercising the right of vote and whose claims exceed in amount one half of their total claims, have given consent to continuation of the day, the Court shall, upon the application of the person proposing compulsory composition or of its own motion, set the date of continuation and give rendition thereof.

Article 308 (Ruling on approval or disapproval of composition)

1. When resolution has been adopted approving compulsory composition, the Court shall rule as to approval or disapproval of compulsory composition on the date of resolution or another date immediately set.

2. The persons mentioned in Article 299 paragraph 2 may state their opinions as to whether or not approval shall be given of compulsory composition.

Article 309 (Provisions applicable mutatis mutandis)

The provisions of the proviso to Article 238 (Public notice and service unnecessary because of rendition) and of Article 239 (Prohibition on filing complaint) shall apply mutatis mutandis to the ruling setting dates pursuant to the provisions of the preceding two Articles.

Article 310 (Ruling disapproving composition)

1. The Court may, upon the application of bankruptcy creditors or of its own motion, grant the ruling of disapproval of compulsory composition, only in the following cases:

(1) If, in cases where the procedure of compulsory composition or resolution connected therewith is in contravention of the provisions of laws, the deficiency is irremediable;
(2) If the causes mentioned in Article 295 have arisen after resolution has been adopted on compulsory composition;
(3) If the resolution on compulsory composition has come to be adopted in an unjust manner;
(4) If the resolution on compulsory composition is against the general interests of bankruptcy creditors.

2. In order that bankruptcy creditors who have not possessed the right of vote may file the application mentioned in the preceding paragraph, they shall give prima facie proof that they are bankruptcy creditors.

3. The applicant shall give prima facie proof of the facts comprising causes for application.

Article 311 (Resolution approving composition and continuation of corporate capacity)

1. In cases where a juristic person has been adjudged bankrupt, if resolution has been adopted approving compulsory composition, the corporate existence may be continued in accordance with the provisions relative to change of the article of incorporation in the case of an incorporated association, and upon obtaining approval of the competent authorities in the case of an incorporated foundation.

2. The powers of the competent government official provided for in the preceding paragraph may be delegated in whole or part to the administrative agencies.

Article 312 (Approval or disapproval of composition of juristic person)

1. In cases where it has been determined whether or not a juristic person is to be continued in existence, or where the procedure therefor is not taken without delay, the Court shall, upon the application of the director (*riji*) or persons similar thereto of the juristic person, or of its own motion, set a date and give public notice thereof, for the purpose of granting ruling as to whether compulsory composition is approved or not.

2. No complaint may be filed against the ruling setting the date mentioned in the preceding paragraph.

3. In cases where the juristic person is not to be continued in existence, or where the procedure therefor is not taken without delay, the Court shall grant the ruling of disapproval of compulsory composition.

Article 313 (Persons eligible to right of vote in composition of properties to be succeeded to)

In cases where properties to be succeeded to have been adjudged bankrupt, only obligees of the persons succeeded to may participate in adopting resolution on compulsory composition.

Article 314 (Persons eligible to right of vote in composition of successor)

In cases where a successor has been adjudged bankrupt, if there has been qualified acceptance or separation of property, the successor's creditors only may participate in adopting resolution on compulsory composition.

Article 315 (Persons eligible to right of vote in composition of successor, in case of bankruptcy of properties to be succeeded to and successor)

In cases where properties to be succeeded to and a successor have been adjudged bankrupt, the successor's creditors only may participate in adopting resolution on the compulsory composition of the successor.

Article 316 (Deduction of amount of claims not eligible to participation in resolution)

In the cases mentioned in the preceding three Articles, the claim of a creditor who cannot participate in adopting resolution on compulsory composition shall not be computed in the total claims mentioned in Article 306 paragraph 1.

Article 317 (Protection of creditors who cannot participate in resolution)

1. In cases where compulsory composition is to injure the just and proper interest of the creditors in bankruptcy mentioned in the preceding Article, the Court shall, upon the application of such creditors, grant the ruling of disapproval of compulsory composition.

2. The provisions of paragraph 2 (Prima facie proof of being bankruptcy creditor) and paragraph 3 (Prima facie proof of causes for application) of Article 310 shall apply mutatis mutandis to the application mentioned in the preceding paragraph.

Article 318 (Rendition and public notice or ruling as to approval or disapproval of composition)

The ruling as to whether or not compulsory composition is to be approved shall be given rendition as well as public notice; provided however, that service thereof may be dispensed with.

Article 319 (Filing complaint by creditors not having right of vote)

In order that those bankruptcy creditors who have not had the right to vote may file complaint against the ruling as to whether or not compulsory composition is to be approved, prima facie proof shall be given of their being creditors in bankruptcy.

Article 320 (Restrictions on persons complaining against ruling of disapproval)

Those creditors in bankruptcy who cannot participate in the adoption of resolution on compulsory composition may not file complaint against the ruling of disapproval of compulsory composition.

Article 321 (Becoming effective of composition)

The compulsory composition shall become effective when the ruling of approval thereof becomes final and conclusive.

Article 322 (Entries on list of claims)

When the ruling of approval of compulsory composition has become final and conclusive, the clerk of the Court shall enter the terms of compulsory composition on the list of claims.

Article 323 (Payment of claims appertaining to bankrupt estate and definite claims having priority right)

1. When the ruling of approval of compulsory composition has become final and conclusive, the administrator in bankruptcy shall make payment of definite claims held by creditors appertaining to the bankrupt estate and by persons possessing the general preferential right or other general priority rights.

2. With regard to those claims appertaining to the bankrupt estate and claims having general priority right which have been objected to, the administrator in bankruptcy shall make deposits on behalf of creditors. The same shall also apply to those claims having general priority rights of which prima facie proof has been given to the administrator in bankruptcy.

Article 324 (Provisions applicable mutatis mutandis)

The provisions of Article 282 (Public notice of ruling for termination; prohibition on filing complaint) shall apply mutatis mutandis in cases where the ruling of approval of compulsory composition has become final and conclusive.

Article 325 (Restrictions on management and disposal by bankrupt)

With regard to the management and disposal of the bankrupt estate, the bankrupt shall comply with restrictions prescribed in compulsory composition.

Article 326 (Scope of effect of composition)

1. The compulsory composition shall have its effect in favour of, as well as against, all the creditors in bankruptcy.

2. The compulsory composition shall not affect the rights which creditors in bankruptcy possess against the bankrupt's guarantor and other persons who assume

debts together with the bankrupt, nor security furnished on behalf of bankruptcy creditors.

Article 327 (Composition and liability of partnership members)

Partners who are liable for debts of an incorporated partnership (*gomei-kaisha*) shall be liable to bankruptcy creditors to the extent prescribed in compulsory composition; provided however, that in cases where compulsory composition provides otherwise, such provisions shall govern.

Article 328 (Compulsory execution levied on basis of list of claims)

Bankruptcy creditors who possess definite claims may, only in cases where the bankrupt has not raised objection to the claims on the day for investigation of claims, levy compulsory execution by virtue of entries on the list of claims after termination of the bankruptcy procedure as against the bankrupt and persons who become a guarantor for purposes of compulsory composition or otherwise assume debts together with the bankrupt or furnish security on behalf of bankruptcy creditors; provided however, that this shall not preclude the application of Articles 452 and 453 of the Civil Code.

Article 329 (Annulment of concession by unjust composition)

1. In cases where compulsory composition has come to be accomplished through unjust contrivance, each of the bankruptcy creditors may annul concessions prescribed in the compulsory composition; provided however, that this shall not apply to any creditor in bankruptcy who has by negligence failed to apply for the ruling of disapproval of compulsory composition.

2. The right to annul concession shall be extinguished if the creditor in bankruptcy fails to exercise it for one month from the time he has become aware of the cause for annulment. The same shall also apply when two years have elapsed since the time the ruling of approval of compulsory composition has become final and conclusive.

Article 330 (Annulment of concession by reason of non-performance)

In cases where the bankrupt has failed to perform as prescribed in compulsory composition, the creditor in bankruptcy for whom the performance failed may annul concession prescribed in the compulsory composition.

Article 331 (Effect of annulment of concession)

1. The annulment of concession shall not affect the rights which bankruptcy creditors have acquired by compulsory composition.

2. With regard to the claims restored by annulment of concession, bankruptcy creditors may not exercise their rights until after the completion of performance under the compulsory composition.

Article 332 (Annulment of composition by reason of non-performance)

1. If, in cases where the bankrupt has failed to perform as prescribed in compulsory composition, there has been application by persons who represent the majority of those

bankruptcy creditors who have filed the report and of whom the amount of claims corresponds to three-quarters or more of their claims, the Court shall grant the ruling for annulment of compulsory composition.

2. Bankruptcy creditors who have received the entire performance as prescribed in compulsory composition shall not be computed in the number of persons required for filing application mentioned in the preceding paragraph. With respect to those who have received the whole or part of the performance, the amount of their claims shall be the amount of bankruptcy claims as it had been therefore minus the amount they have received.

3. The provisions of Article 306 paragraph 2 (Computation of amount of claims as at time of resolution approving composition) shall apply mutatis mutandis to the computation of the amount of claims and the total claims mentioned in the first paragraph.

Article 333 (Annulment of composition by reason of fraudulent bankruptcy)

1. In cases where the judgment of conviction of fraudulent bankruptcy has become final and conclusive, the Court may, upon the application of bankruptcy creditors or of its own motion, grant the ruling for annulment of compulsory composition.

2. The Court may order the measures mentioned in Articles 154 and 155, even prior to the becoming final and conclusive of the judgment of conviction.

Article 334 (Provisions applicable mutatis mutandis)

The provisions of Article 331 paragraph 1 (Effect of annulment of concession) shall apply mutatis mutandis to the annulment of compulsory composition.

Article 335 (Continuation of bankruptcy procedure by reason of annulment of composition)

When the ruling for annulment of compulsory composition has become final and conclusive, the bankruptcy procedure shall be continued.

Article 336 (Annulment of composition and adjudication of bankruptcy)

For purposes of application of the provisions of Book 1, the annulment of compulsory composition shall be deemed to be the adjudication of bankruptcy, and the application for annulment of compulsory composition in the case of Article 332 and the institution of public prosecution in the case of Article 333 shall be deemed to be suspension of payment or petition for bankruptcy, if there has therefore been no suspension of payment or petition for bankruptcy.

Article 337 (Provisions applicable mutatis mutandis)

1. The provisions of Articles 141 inclusive (Measures to be taken at time of adjudication of bankruptcy) and Articles 154–156 inclusive (Measures prior to adjudication; publication of annulment) shall apply mutatis mutandis to the annulment of compulsory composition.

2. The costs of continuation of bankruptcy procedure shall be provisionally defrayed out of the national treasury.

Article 338 (Amount of claims in revived bankruptcy)

As for creditors who have been subjected to the effect of compulsory composition, the amount of claims in bankruptcy shall be what remains of the amount of claims in the previous bankruptcy after deduction therefrom of the amount received in accordance with what is prescribed in the compulsory composition.

Article 339 (Scope of investigation of claims)

With respect to definite claims therefore ascertained, the amount only which bankruptcy creditors have received in accordance with what is prescribed in compulsory composition shall be investigated.

Article 340 (Treatment of sums received according to what is prescribed in compulsory composition)

In cases where there exists anything received by creditors who have been subjected to the effect of compulsory composition in accordance with what is prescribed in the compulsory composition, the amount of claim in the previous bankruptcy shall be deemed to be the amount of claim of which dividends are to be distributed, and the standard for the rate of distribution shall be determined by adding to the bankrupt estate what the creditor has so received; provided however, that such creditor may not receive dividends until other bankruptcy creditors receive dividends at the same rate as he himself has received.

Article 341 (Furnishing of security ceasing to be effective)

The furnishing of security effected by the bankrupt after termination of the bankruptcy procedure to those creditors who have been subjected to the effect of compulsory composition shall cease to be effective by annulment of the compulsory composition.

Article 342 (Prohibition of application for new bankruptcy by composition creditors)

Creditors who have been subjected to the effect of compulsory composition may not file petition for bankruptcy with respect to former claims.

Article 343 (Concurrence of annulment of composition and new bankruptcy)

1. In cases where applications have been filed for annulment of compulsory composition as well as for bankruptcy, if the Court has, in regard to one of them, granted the ruling for annulment of compulsory composition or adjudication of bankruptcy, the other application shall be dismissed.

2. No complaint may be filed against the ruling of dismissal granted pursuant to the provisions of the preceding paragraph.

Article 344 (New bankruptcy prior to performance under composition)

The provisions of Article 331 paragraph 1 (Effect of annulment of concession), and Article 338–341 inclusive (Computation of amount of claims; scope of investigation; furnishing of security ceasing to be effective) shall apply mutatis mutandis in cases where there has been adjudication of bankruptcy in cases where the ruling for annulment of compulsory composition may be granted pursuant to the provisions of Article 333.

Article 345 (Composition relative to properties to be succeeded to and successor's duty to manage)

1. In cases where there has been adjudication of bankruptcy with respect to properties to be succeeded to, the successor shall continue the management of the properties to be succeeded to until the completion of performance under compulsory composition with the same degree of care as given to his own properties; provided however, that in case the compulsory composition provides otherwise, such provisions shall govern.

2. The provisions of Article 645 (Duty to report of mandatory), Article 646 (Mandatory's duty to deliver and transfer), Article 650 paragraphs 1 and 2 (Right to demand reimbursement of defrayals), and Article 918 paragraphs 2 and 3 (Measures necessary for preservation of properties to be succeeded to) of the Civil Code shall apply mutatis mutandis in the case mentioned in the preceding paragraph.

3. The measures relative to the preservation and management of properties to be succeeded to mentioned in Article 918 paragraphs 2 and 3 of the Civil Code which apply mutatis mutandis by virtue of the preceding paragraph shall, for purposes of application of the Domestic Affairs Trial Law, be deemed to be the matters mentioned under Class A of Article 9 paragraph 1 of the same Law.

Article 346 (Provisions applicable mutatis mutandis)

The provisions of Article 131 (Period for filing petition for bankruptcy of properties to be succeeded to) shall apply mutatis mutandis to application for the annulment of compulsory composition relative to properties to be succeeded to.

Chapter X: Discontinuance of bankruptcy

Article 347 (Discontinuance by reason of waiver of bankruptcy)

1. The bankrupt may apply for discontinuance of bankruptcy, in cases where consent has been obtained from all the creditors in bankruptcy who have filed the report within the period for reporting claims, or where security has been furnished, with consent of other creditors in bankruptcy, from the bankrupt estate on behalf of bankruptcy creditors of whom consent is not obtained.

2. The Court shall determine whether or not the creditor's consent is to be required with respect to claims which are not yet definite. The same shall also apply as to whether the security to be furnished to bankruptcy creditors is adequate or not.

3. No complaint shall be filed against the ruling granted pursuant to the provisions of the preceding paragraph.

Article 348 (Application for discontinuance and continuation of corporate capacity)

In cases where a corporation has been adjudged bankrupt, procedures of continuation of its corporate existence shall be taken, in order to apply for the discontinuance of bankruptcy. The provisions of Article 311 (Resolution approving composition and continuation of corporate capacity) shall apply mutatis mutandis in such cases.

Article 349 (Submission of documents for proof)

In order to apply for the discontinuance of bankruptcy, documents proving that conditions necessary for the application are met shall be submitted.

Article 350 (Public notice of application for discontinuance)

The Court shall give public notice that the application for discontinuance of bankruptcy has been filed, and keep documents relative to the application for inspection by persons interested.

Article 351 (Statement of objection by creditors)

1. Bankruptcy creditors may file with the Court objections to the application for discontinuance of bankruptcy, within two weeks computed from the day of the public notice mentioned in the preceding Article.
2. Bankruptcy creditors who filed the report prior to the expiration of the period mentioned in the preceding paragraph may also file objection.

Article 352 (Consulting opinions of persons concerned)

The Court shall, after expiration of the period mentioned in paragraph 1 of the preceding Article, consult opinions of the bankrupt, the administrator in bankruptcy, and those bankruptcy creditors who filed objection, as to whether or not conditions necessary for granting the ruling for discontinuance of bankruptcy are fulfilled.

Article 353 (Discontinuance by reason of insufficiency of costs)

1. In cases where after the adjudication of bankruptcy, the Court has found the bankrupt estate insufficient to cover the costs of the bankruptcy procedure, the Court shall, upon the application of the administrator in bankruptcy or of its own motion, grant the ruling for discontinuance of bankruptcy. In such cases, the Court shall consult the opinion of the creditor's meeting.
2. The provisions of the preceding paragraph shall not apply in cases where there has been advance payment of a sum which is sufficient to cover the costs of the bankruptcy procedure.

Article 354 (Public notice of ruling for discontinuance)

When the Court has granted the ruling for discontinuance of bankruptcy, public notice shall be given of its principal text as well as the tenor of reasons thereof.

Article 355 (Payment of obligations appertaining to bankrupt estate)

When the ruling for discontinuance of bankruptcy has become final and conclusive, the administrator in bankruptcy shall pay obligations appertaining to the bankrupt estate, and with respect to those to which objections have been raised, shall make deposit on behalf of the creditors.

Article 356 (Provisions applicable mutatis mutandis)

The provisions of Article 291 (Persons proposing composition of corporation) and Article 292 (Persons proposing composition of properties to be succeeded to) shall apply mutatis mutandis to the application for discontinuance of bankruptcy.

Article 357

The provisions of Article 287 (List of claims as title for execution) shall apply mutatis mutandis in cases where the ruling for discontinuance of bankruptcy has become final and conclusive.

Chapter XI: Petty bankruptcy

Article 358 (Requisites of petty bankruptcy)

1. In cases where it is found that the amount of properties belonging to the bankrupt estate does not amount to one million yen, the Court shall grant the ruling of petty bankruptcy at the same time with the adjudication of bankruptcy.

2. In the case mentioned in the preceding paragraph, the Court shall give public notice of the principal text of the ruling of petty bankruptcy, in addition to the particulars mentioned in Article 143 paragraph 1, and also enter it on the document mentioned in paragraph 2 of the same Article.

Article 359 (Ruling of petty bankruptcy given during bankruptcy procedure)

1. In case the Court has found out, in the course of bankruptcy proceedings, that the amount of properties belonging to the bankrupt estate does not amount to one million yen, it may grant the ruling of petty bankruptcy.

2. In cases where the ruling of petty bankruptcy has been granted pursuant to the provisions of the preceding paragraph, the Court shall give public notice of the principal text of the ruling and also serve a document stating to that effect upon the administrator in bankruptcy, and inspection commissioners, as well as upon known creditors and debtors.

Article 360 (Annulment of petty bankruptcy)

In case the Court has found out, in the course of bankruptcy proceedings, that the properties belonging to the bankrupt estate exceeds one million yen, it may grant the ruling annulling petty bankruptcy. The provisions of paragraph 2 of the preceding Article shall apply mutatis mutandis in such cases.

Article 361 (Filing of complaint prohibited)

No complaint may be filed against the ruling of petty bankruptcy and the ruling of annulment of petty bankruptcy.

Article 362 (Consolidation of dates of creditors' meeting and investigation of claims)

The date of the first meeting of creditors and that of investigation of claims shall be consolidated, except in cases where there exist unavoidable reasons.

Article 363 (No committee of inspection)

There shall be no inspection commissioners.

Article 364 (Ruling substituted for resolution of creditors' meeting)

1. Except for the first meeting of creditors, the first meeting of creditors after annulment of compulsory composition, and the creditors' meeting convened for investigation of claims, report of account, and compulsory composition, rulings of the Court shall be substituted for resolution adopted at the meeting of creditors.

2. No complaint may be filed against the ruling granted under the preceding paragraph.

Article 365 (Single distribution)

There shall be only a single distribution of dividends, and the provisions as to the last distribution shall govern; provided however, that this shall not preclude the distribution of additional dividends.

Article 366 (Mode of public notice)

Public notices connected with the proceedings of petty bankruptcy shall be sufficient if given by being put up on the bulletin board in accordance with the provisions of Article 116.

BOOK III. DISCHARGE AND REHABILITATION

Chapter I: Discharge

Article 366-2 (Application for discharge)

1. The bankrupt may, at any time, file application for discharge until closing of the bankruptcy procedure. In cases where the ruling for discontinuance of bankruptcy has been granted at the same time with the adjudication of bankruptcy, application for discharge may be filed if it is within one month even after the ruling has become final and conclusive.

2. When application for discharges has been filed, no proposal for compulsory composition nor application for discontinuance of bankruptcy under the provisions of Article 347 may be filed.

3. When there has been proposal for compulsory composition, application for discharge may not be filed until after the ruling for dismissal or disapproval thereof has become final and conclusive, or until after resolution of disapproval of compulsory composition has been adopted at the creditors' meeting.

4. When application for discontinuance of bankruptcy has been filed pursuant to the provisions of Article 347, application for discharge may not be filed until after the ruling of dismissal thereof has become final and conclusive.

5. In cases where the bankrupt was unable to apply for discharge pursuant to the provisions of the first paragraph because of causes for which he shall not be held responsible, belated application for discharge may be filed if it is within one month after the causes have ceased to exist.

Article 366-3 (Submission of register of creditors)

The bankrupt shall, at the same time with the application for discharge, submit the register of creditors containing the full name and address of bankruptcy creditors, the amount and causes of bankruptcy claims, and in case the right of separation exists, the subject-matter thereof as well as the amount of claim of which payment could not be obtained through exercise of the right. In cases where it cannot be submitted at the same time with the application, it shall thereafter be submitted without delay.

Article 366-4 (Questioning bankrupt)

1. When application for discharge has been filed, the Court shall set a date of hearing and question the bankrupt.

2. The ruling which sets the date of hearing mentioned in the preceding paragraph shall be given public notice, and served upon the public procurator, the administrator in bankruptcy, and known creditors in bankruptcy who are to be subjected to the effect of discharge.

3. The provisions of the preceding paragraph shall apply mutatis mutandis to changes of the date of hearing mentioned in the first paragraph as well as postponement and continuation of the questioning.

4. The provisions of the proviso to Article 238 (Public notice and service, not necessary, of rulings of which there was rendition) and Article 239 (Prohibition of complaint) shall apply mutatis mutandis to the ruling granted pursuant to the provisions of the preceding two paragraphs.

5. The date of hearing mentioned in the first paragraph may be consolidated with that of the creditors' meeting or of investigation of claims.

Article 366-5 (Investigation and report by administrator)

The Court may cause the administrator in bankruptcy to investigate as to existence or non-existence of causes for refusal of discharge, and to report the results on the date of questioning mentioned in the preceding Article.

Article 366-6 (Keeping documents)

The Court shall keep documents relative to the application for discharge and also records of the investigation by the administrator in bankruptcy mentioned in the preceding Article for inspection by persons interested.

Article 366-7 (Objection to application for discharge)

1. The public procurator, the administrator in bankruptcy, or bankruptcy creditors who are to be subjected to the effect of discharge may file with the Court objection to the application for discharge on the date of questioning mentioned in Article 366-4 or within the period of not less than one month which the Court specifies on that date.

2. In cases where there has been rendition of the ruling specifying the period mentioned in the preceding paragraph, service thereof may be dispensed with.

Article 366-8 (Opinions to be consulted)

When objection has been filed, the Court shall consult opinions of the bankrupt and of the person who filed objection.

Article 366-9 (Causes for refusal of discharge)

The Court may grant the ruling of refusal of discharge only in the following cases:

(1) When it is considered that there exist on the part of the bankrupt acts corresponding to any of the offences mentioned in Articles 374, 375, 377, or 382;

(2) When the bankrupt has, notwithstanding that there exist facts comprising causes of bankruptcy, ever acquired properties by credit transactions within one year prior to the adjudication of bankruptcy, through employing fraudulent means in order to let other people believe that there exist no such facts;
(3) When the bankrupt has submitted false register of creditors, or made false statements to the Court with respect to the state of his properties;
(4) When the bankrupt has ever obtained discharge within ten years prior to the application for discharge;
(5) When the bankrupt has acted in contravention of the bankrupt's duties prescribed in the Law.

Article 366-10 (Dismissal of application for discharge)

1. In cases where the bankrupt has failed to appear without just cause on the day for trial of discharge, or though appearing, refused to make statements, the Court may dismiss the application for discharge.
2. In the case mentioned in the preceding paragraph, the bankrupt may not again apply for discharge with respect to the same bankruptcy.

Article 366-11 (Ruling for discharge, when effective)

The ruling for discharge shall not become effective until after it has become final and conclusive.

Article 366-12 (Effect of discharge)

The bankrupt who has been granted discharge shall be exempt of all the obligations due to the bankruptcy creditors, except the dividends to be distributed under the bankruptcy procedure; provided however, that this shall not apply to the following claims:

(1) Taxes;
(2) Damages arising out of torts which the bankrupt has inflicted with malicious intent;
(3) Salaries of employees; provided however, that this shall be restricted to the portion of which the general preferential right exists;
(4) Moneys taken for custody from employees and moneys deposited as guaranty for good behaviour of employees;
(5) Claims which the bankrupt did not enter in the register of creditors, despite his being aware thereof, excepting, however, cases where the creditor was aware of the adjudication of bankruptcy having been granted;
(6) Fines, minor fines, costs of criminal action, value collected in place of confiscation, and administrative fines.

Article 366-13 (Effect against guarantors, etc.)

Discharge shall not affect the rights which bankruptcy creditors possess against the bankrupt's guarantors and other persons who assume obligations together with the bankrupt, and the security which has been furnished on behalf of creditors in bankruptcy.

Article 366-14 (Public notice and entry on list of claims)

When the ruling of discharge has become final and conclusive, the Court shall give public notice of its principal text, and if there exists the list of claims, enter thereon the statement that the ruling of discharge has become final and conclusive.

Article 366-15 (Annulment of discharge)

When the judgment pronouncing the bankrupt guilty of fraudulent bankruptcy has become final and conclusive, the Court may, upon the application of bankruptcy creditors or of its own motion, grant the ruling for annulment of discharge. The same shall also apply if, in cases where discharge has been procured by unjust methods of the bankrupt, creditors in bankruptcy have filed application for annulment of discharge within one year after discharge.

Article 366-16 (Opinions to be consulted)

Prior to deciding upon annulment of discharge, the Court shall consult opinions of the bankrupt and of the applicant.

Article 366-17 (Annulment of discharge, when effective)

The ruling for annulment of discharge shall not become effective until after it has become final and conclusive.

Article 366-18 (Priority of new creditors)

When there has been annulment of discharge, persons who come to possess claims against the bankrupt because of causes which have arisen subsequent to discharge and not later than the annulment thereof shall be entitled to obtain payment in preference to other creditors.

Article 366-19 (Public notice and entry on list of claims)

When the ruling for annulment of discharge has become final and conclusive, the Court shall give public notice of its principal text, and if there exists the list of claims, enter thereon the statement that the ruling for annulment of discharge has become final and conclusive.

Article 366-20 (Provisions applicable mutatis mutandis)

The provisions of Articles 108 to 112 inclusive (Code of civil procedure, applicable mutatis mutandis; mutual assistance; oral proceedings not compulsory; *suo sponte* investigation by Court; service made of Court's own motion; complaint) and Article 114 to 118 inclusive (Forms of application, etc.; method of public notice; public notice substituted for service; service in addition to public notice) shall apply mutatis mutandis to the proceedings for discharge and annulment thereof.

Chapter II: Rehabilitation

Article 366-21 (Rehabilitation ipso jure)

1. The bankrupt shall be rehabilitated in the following cases:

(1) When the ruling of discharge has become final and conclusive;
(2) When the ruling approving compulsory composition has become final and conclusive;
(3) When the ruling for discontinuance of bankruptcy granted upon application pursuant to the provisions of Article 347 has become final and conclusive;

(4) When ten years have elapsed after adjudication of bankruptcy without the judgment pronouncing the bankrupt guilty of the offence of fraudulent bankruptcy.

2. In cases where the ruling for annulment of discharge or for annulment of compulsory composition has become final and conclusive, the rehabilitation under item (1) or (2) of the preceding paragraph shall cease to be effective for the future.

Article 367 (Rehabilitation upon application)

1. In cases where the bankrupt who has not been rehabilitated under the provisions of the preceding Article has been relieved of his liability to all the obligations due to bankruptcy creditors by performance of his obligations or otherwise, the Court of bankruptcy shall, upon the application of the bankrupt, grant the ruling of rehabilitation.
2. The applicant shall submit documents showing that he has been relieved of his liability.

Article 368 (Ruling of rehabilitation, when effective)

The ruling of rehabilitation shall not become effective until after it has become final and conclusive.

Article 369 (Public notice of application for rehabilitation)

The Court shall give public notice to the effect that the application for rehabilitation has been filed and keep documents relative to the application for inspection by persons interested.

Article 370 (Objection by creditors)

Bankruptcy creditors may file with the Court objection against the application for rehabilitation within three months computed from the day the public notice has been given pursuant to the preceding Article.

Article 371 (Opinions to be consulted)

When objection has been filed, the court shall consult opinions of the bankrupt as well as of bankruptcy creditors who filed objection.

Article 372 (Public notice of ruling of rehabilitation)

When the ruling of rehabilitation has become final and conclusive, the Court shall give public notice of its principal text.

Article 373 (Provisions applicable mutatis mutandis)

The provisions of Articles 108–112 inclusive (Code of civil procedure, applicable mutatis mutandis; mutual assistance; oral proceedings not compulsory; *suo sponte* investigation by Court; service made of Court's own motion; complaint) and Articles 114–117 inclusive (Application; method of public notice) shall apply mutatis mutandis to the proceedings for rehabilitation.

BOOK IV. PENAL PROVISIONS

Article 374 (Offence of fraudulent bankruptcy)

If a debtor perpetrates any of the acts mentioned below, regardless of whether the act is done prior to or subsequent to the adjudication of bankruptcy, for the purpose of benefiting himself or other persons, or injuring creditors, and when the adjudication has become final and conclusive, it shall constitute the offence of fraudulent bankruptcy, and the debtor shall be punished with imprisonment with hard labour for a term not exceeding ten years:

(1) To conceal or destroy properties appertaining to the bankrupt estate, or dispose of them in a way disadvantageous to creditors;
(2) To increase the burden of the bankrupt estate in a false way;
(3) To fail to prepare commercial books which should be prepared as required in the provisions of the law, to fail to make in such books entries whereby the present state of properties is sufficiently known or to make false entries therein, or to conceal or destroy such books;
(4) To make changes in, to conceal or destroy, the books which the clerk of the Court has closed pursuant to the provisions of Article 187.

Article 375 (Offence of negligent bankruptcy)

If a debtor perpetrates any of the acts mentioned below, regardless of whether the act is done prior to or subsequent to the adjudication of bankruptcy, and when the adjudication has become final and conclusive, the debtor shall be punished with imprisonment with hard labour for a term not exceeding five years or a fine not exceeding three hundred thousand yen.

(1) To reduce assets unduly or to assume excessive debts through extravagance, gambling or other speculative undertakings;
(2) To assume obligations under unduly disadvantageous terms for the purpose of delaying the adjudication of bankruptcy, or to purchase merchandises on credit and dispose of them under unduly disadvantageous terms;
(3) Any acts relative to furnishing security or to extinguishment of obligations effected for the purpose of bestowing special benefits to some creditors, despite being aware of the existence of facts comprising causes of bankruptcy, which do not pertain to the duty of the debtor, or of which the manner or time does not pertain to the duty of the debtor;
(4) To fail to prepare commercial books which should be prepared as required in the provisions of the law, to fail to make in such books entries whereby the present state of properties is sufficiently known or to make false entries therein, or to conceal or destroy such books;
(5) To make changes in, to conceal or destroy such books; which the clerk of the Court has closed pursuant to the provisions of Article 187.

Article 376 (Offence of fraudulent bankruptcy of persons similar to bankrupt)

If the legal representative of a debtor, director (*riji*) or persons similar thereto or manager has perpetrated any of the acts specified in the preceding two Articles, and when the adjudication of bankruptcy of the debtor has become final and conclusive, the provisions of the preceding two Articles shall be complied with. The same shall also apply in cases of bankruptcy of properties to be succeeded to, with respect to the successor, as well as his legal representative and manager.

Article 377 (Offence of breach of surveillance)

1. In cases where a person who was ordered to be put under surveillance under this Law, absconds, or interviews or communicates with outsiders without obtaining permission of the Court, he shall be punished with imprisonment with hard labour for a term not exceeding one year or a fine not exceeding fifty thousand yen.

2. When the bankrupt has departed from his dwelling place without obtaining permission of the Court, the punishment shall be the same as provided for in the preceding paragraph.

Article 378 (Offences of fraudulent bankruptcy by third persons)

Any person, other than the debtor and the persons mentioned in Article 376, who has perpetrated any of the acts mentioned in Article 374, or any person who has exercised a false right as bankruptcy creditor for the purpose of benefiting himself or other persons, shall be punished with imprisonment with hard labour for a term not exceeding ten years, when the adjudication of bankruptcy of the debtor has become final and conclusive.

Article 379 (Annulment of compulsory composition and application of penal provisions)

For purposes of application of the provisions of Articles 374 and 375 as well as of the preceding Article, the annulment of compulsory composition shall be deemed to be the adjudication of bankruptcy.

Article 380 (Offence of taking bribes)

1. If the administrator in bankruptcy or an inspection commissioner has taken or demanded, or promised bribes in connection with his duties, he shall be punished with imprisonment with hard labour for a term not exceeding three years or a fine not exceeding two hundred thousand yen. The same shall also apply, if a bankruptcy creditor, his agent or director (*riji*) or persons similar thereto has taken or demanded, or promised bribes in connection with resolutions to be adopted at the creditors' meeting.

2. In the case mentioned in the preceding paragraph, bribes which have been taken shall be confiscated. In case it is impossible to confiscate the whole part thereof, the value thereof shall be collected.

Article 381 (Offence of offering bribes)

1. Any person, who has given or offered, or promised bribes to the administrator in bankruptcy, an inspection commissioner, or a bankruptcy creditor, his agent, director (*riji*) or persons similar thereto, shall be punished with imprisonment with hard labour for a term not exceeding three years or a fine not exceeding two hundred thousand yen.

2. When a person who has committed the offence provided in the preceding paragraph, has denounced himself to the authorities, the punishment may either be reduced or remitted.

Article 382 (Offence of breach of duty to explain)

1. If any person, who has the duty to give explanations under the provisions of Article 153, has failed to explain without cause or has given false explanation, he shall be punished with imprisonment with hard labour for a term not exceeding one year or a fine not exceeding fifty thousand yen.

2. When a person, who has committed the offence provided in the preceding paragraph, has reported the facts to the Court of bankruptcy, the punishment may either be reduced or remitted.

SUPPLEMENTARY PROVISIONS (LAW NO 70, 24TH APRIL 1926)

The enforcement date of this Law shall be prescribed by Imperial Ordinance (enforced as from 1 October 1929 by Imperial Ordinance No 105 of 1929).

SUPPLEMENTARY PROVISIONS (LAW NO 68, 5TH APRIL 1939)

The enforcement date of this Law shall be prescribed by Imperial Ordinance (enforced as from 1 January 1940 Imperial Ordinance No 510 of 1939)

SUPPLEMENTARY PROVISIONS (LAW NO 61, 16TH APRIL 1947)

Article 33

This Law shall come into force as from the enforcement date of the Constitution of Japan (enforced as from 3 May 1947).

SUPPLEMENTARY PROVISIONS (EXTRACTS) (LAW NO 223, 22ND DECEMBER 1947)

Article 29

This Law shall come into force from 1 January 1948.

Article 31

1. With regard to the bankruptcy in cases to which apply the provisions of Article 25 paragraph 1 of the Supplementary Provisions to the Law for Partial Amendment of the Civil Code (hereinafter to be referred to as the new law) which comes into force on the same day as this Law in connection with succession, what has heretofore been done shall be followed as before, notwithstanding the provisions of Article 19 (Partial amendments to the bankruptcy law).

2. In cases where there has been, prior to the coming into force of this Law, the adjudication of bankruptcy of properties succeeded to involved in the succession provided for in Article 25 paragraph 2 of the Supplementary Provisions to the new law, it shall also be the same as provided in the preceding paragraph.

SUPPLEMENTARY PROVISIONS (LAW NO 173, JUNE 1952)

1. This Law shall come into force from 1 August 1952.

2. With regard to cases wherein there has been adjudication of bankruptcy prior to the coming into force of this Law, what has heretofore been done shall be followed as before, notwithstanding the revised provisions of Articles 18 to 22 inclusive, Articles 38, 46, 52, 102, 182, 228, 229 240, 254, and 258 of the Bankruptcy Law (with regard to the revised provisions of Article 229 of the same Law, except the part thereof which 'the clerk (*shoki*) of the Court' is amended 'the clerk (*shoki-kan*) of the Court').

3. In a case wherein there has been closing of the bankruptcy procedure prior to the coming into force of this Law, the bankrupt may, except in the cases mentioned under items (2) and (3) of Article 366-21 paragraph 1 of the Bankruptcy Law, file application for discharge if it is within one year from the date of coming into effect of this Law, notwithstanding the provisions of Article 366-2 paragraph 1 of the same Law. The same shall also apply to the bankrupt in a bankruptcy case which is pending in the Court at the time of coming into force of this Law.

4. The Provisions of Article 366-2 paragraph 5 of the Bankruptcy Law shall apply mutatis mutandis in cases where the bankrupt mentioned in the preceding paragraph has been unable to file application for discharge within the period prescribed in the same paragraph because of causes for which he should not be held responsible.

5. The bankrupt, of whom there have been the causes mentioned under items (2) to (4) inclusive of Article 266-21 paragraph 1, shall be rehabilitated at the time of coming into force of this Law.

6. When the ruling for annulment of compulsory composition has become final and conclusive subsequent to rehabilitation granted because of the ruling approving compulsory composition having become final and conclusive by virtue of the provisions of the preceding paragraph, the rehabilitation shall cease to be effective for the future.

7. The provisions of paragraph 5 shall apply mutatis mutandis to persons who have been adjudged financial wreck (*shindai-kagiri*) or of whom there has been declaration of insolvency (*kashi-bunsan*).

SUPPLEMENTARY PROVISIONS (LAW NO 106, 30TH APRIL 1968)

(Enforcement date)

1. This Law shall come into force as from 1 July 1958.

CORPORATE REORGANISATION LAW
LAW NO 172, 7TH JUNE 1952

Chapter 1: General provisions

Article 1 (Purpose)

The purpose of this Law shall consist in bringing about sustenance and regeneration of the business of a limited company (*kabushiki-kaisha*) (hereinafter referred to as the 'company'), of which, despite its financial difficulty, there is a prospect of rehabilitation, through adjustment of the interests of its creditors, shareholders, and other persons interested.

Article 2 (Reorganisation proceedings, when effective)

The reorganisation proceedings shall become effective from the time of the ruling for its commencement.

Article 3 (Status of aliens)

Aliens or foreign companies shall have the same status as Japanese nationals or Japanese companies in regard to corporate reorganisation.

Article 4 (Principle of territoriality)

1. Reorganisation proceedings commenced in Japan shall be effective with respect to only the company's properties existing in Japan.

2. Reorganisation proceedings commenced in a foreign country shall not be effective with respect to properties situated in Japan.

3. Obligations, of which demand may be made by way of judicial proceedings under the Code of Civil Procedure (Law No. 29 of 1980), shall be deemed to exist in Japan.

Article 5 (Interruption of prescription)

Participation in reorganisation proceedings shall have the effect of interrupting prescription. Provided that this shall not apply in the case where the reorganisation creditors or reorganisation secured creditors have withdrawn a report on their participation or where such report has been dismissed.

Article 6 (Jurisdiction for reorganisation case)

Cases of reorganisation shall come under the exclusive jurisdiction of the District Court having jurisdiction over the location of the head office of the company, or, if the head office is abroad, the location of its principal place of business in Japan.

Article 7 (Transfer of reorganisation case)

The Court mentioned in the preceding Article may, of its own motion, transfer a case of reorganisation to the District Court having jurisdiction over the location where another business place of the company or its property is situated, when deemed necessary for avoiding marked losses or delay.

Article 8 (Code of Civil Procedure applicable mutatis mutandis)

In case there is no special provision in this Law, the Code of Civil Procedure shall apply mutatis mutandis to reorganisation proceedings.

Article 9 (Voluntary oral proceedings and investigation of authority's own motion)

1. The decision concerning reorganisation proceedings may be given without oral proceedings.

2. The Court may, of its own motion, make necessary investigation relating to reorganisation cases.

Article 10 (Decision served of Court's own motion)

The Court shall, of its own motion, serve its decision concerning reorganisation proceedings.

Article 11 (Complaint)

Only when there is any special provision in this Law, a person having interests in the decision of the Court concerning reorganisation proceedings may file an immediate complaint against such decision. In the case where the public notice of the decision has been given, the period for filing a complaint shall be two weeks counting from the day on which the public notice has been given.

Article 12 (Public notice)

1. Public notice given under this Law shall be inserted in the Official Gazette as well as in a newspaper designated by the Court.

2. A public notice shall become effective on the day next following the day on which it has been inserted last.

Article 13 (Public notice given by posting up on notice board)

1. In case the company's debt amounts to twenty million yen or less, the public notice may, notwithstanding the provision or paragraph 1 of the preceding Article, be given, in place of having it inserted in a newspaper, by posting it up on the notice boards of the Court and the Summary Court having jurisdiction over the location where the head office of the company (the principal business place in Japan, if the head office is in a foreign country) is situated, or the notice board of the office of a city, town, or village located within the bounds of said jurisdiction of the public office similar thereto. In such cases, is shall be deemed to have been inserted in a newspaper on the day after the lapse of three days from the date of publication on the notice board.

2. The provision of the preceding paragraph shall not apply in the case where the company has issued uninscribed debenture certificates, share certificates, or fractional share certificates.

Article 14 (Service upon debenture holders, etc.)

1. The service of documents made in accordance with the provisions of this Law upon the debenture holders of the company may be made by ordinary mail to the addresses if the debenture holders have filed their addresses in accordance with the provision of this Law, and if they failed to do so, to the addresses appearing on the register of debentures or the addresses notified to the company by the debenture holders.

2. The service of documents upon the reorganisation secured creditors whose security rights have been registered may be made by ordinary mail to the addresses of the reorganisation secured creditors if the reorganisation secured creditors have filed their addresses in accordance with the provisions of this Law, and if they failed to do so, to the addresses appearing on the official registry book.

3. The service of documents under the provisions of this Law upon the shareholders of the company may be made by ordinary mail to the addresses appearing on the register of shareholders or the ledger of fractional shares to the addresses notified to

the company by the shareholders, or to the addresses notified to the receiver by the shareholders in accordance with the provision of Article 131.

4. In the case where documents have been sent by mail in accordance with the provision of the preceding three paragraphs, the service shall be deemed to have been made at the time when the mailed documents shall have ordinarily arrived.

5. In the cases mentioned in paragraphs 1 through 3, the clerk of the Court shall prepare the documents, enter therein the full name of the person upon whom the service is to be made, his address and the hour and date of mailing the documents, and also sign his name and affix his seal thereto. Provided that such name-writing and seal-impression may be replaced by affixing name and seal.

Article 15 (Cases where public notice is given and documents are served)

1. In the case where the public notice and service are required in accordance with the provisions of this Law, the service of documents may be made by ordinary mail.

2. In the case mentioned in the preceding paragraph, the public notice shall have the effect of service made upon all the persons interested.

3. The provision of paragraph 5 of the preceding Article shall apply mutatis mutandis in the case mentioned in paragraph 1.

Article 16 (Public notice given in place of service)

In the case where it is difficult to know the address, the place of residence, or other places where the service is to be made, of the person upon whom the service is to be made in accordance with the provisions of this Law, the Court may order the public notice shall be substituted for the service.

Article 17 (Official request for registration)

1. If the Court has ruled for commencement of reorganisation proceedings, it shall, of its own motion, without delay request the registry office of the locality where the head office or branch office of the company (the business place in Japan, if the head office is in a foreign country) is situated, to register the commencement of reorganisation proceedings, attaching to the request a certified copy or extract copy of the ruling.

2. In the registration mentioned in the preceding paragraph, the full name or appellation of the receiver shall also be registered.

3. The provision of paragraph 1 shall apply mutatis mutandis in the case where a change has taken place in the matters mentioned in the preceding paragraph, and where any matter required to be registered has taken place with regard to the company or a new company because of carrying out of the plan of reorganisation or by virtue of the provisions of this Law prior to the termination of reorganisation proceedings.

Article 18 (Official request for registration)

1. If found out that there exists a right, which has been registered, appertaining to the assets of the company, the Court shall, of its own motion, without delay request the registry office to register the commencement of reorganisation proceedings, attaching to the request a certified copy or extract copy of the ruling for the commencement of reorganisation proceedings.

2. The provision of the preceding paragraph shall apply mutatis mutandis in the case where there has taken place the acquisition or loss of, or a change in, the right whose

registration has been effected, because of carrying out of the reorganisation plan or by virtue of the provisions of this Law prior to the termination of reorganisation proceedings. Provided that this shall not apply to registration of which the person entitled to demand registration is a person other than the company, reorganisation creditor, reorganisation secured creditor, shareholder, and new company.

Article 18-2 (Official request for registration)

1. If the Court has taken the measures under the provision of the latter clause of Article 39 paragraph 1, it shall, without delay of its own motion, request the registry office of the locality where the head office or branch office of the company (the business place in Japan, if the head office is in a foreign country) is situated, to register said measures, attaching to the request a certified copy or extract copy of the ruling.

2. The provision of the preceding paragraph shall apply mutatis mutandis in the case where a change has taken place in the matters to be registered, and where the measures under the provision of the latter clause of Article 39 paragraph 1 were reversed.

3. The provision of paragraph 1 of the preceding Article shall apply mutatis mutandis in cases where the measures, under the provision of the former clause of Article 39 paragraph 1 or the provision of Article 72 paragraph 1 item (2) or paragraph 2, were taken concerning rights of which registration is effected, and where such measures were changed or reversed.

Article 18-3 (Official request for registration)

1. If the right to manage the business of the company as well as to administer and dispose the property thereof was granted to the director in accordance with the provision of Article 211 paragraph 3 or Article 248-2 paragraph 1, the Court shall, of its own motion, without delay request the registry office of the locality where the head office of the company (the business place in Japan, if the head office is in a foreign country) is situated, to register to that effect, attaching to the request a certified copy or extract copy of the ruling of approval of reorganisation plan or the ruling of granting the right under the provision of said paragraph.

2. The provision of the preceding paragraph shall apply mutatis mutandis in cases where the stipulation of reorganisation plan under the provision of Article 211 paragraph 3 or the decision under the provision of Article 248-2 paragraph 1 was reversed.

Article 19 (Official request for registration)

The provisions of Article 17 paragraph 1 and Article 18 paragraph 1 shall apply mutatis mutandis in cases where the ruling has become final and conclusive for annulment of the ruling for the commencement of reorganisation proceedings, for discontinuance of the reorganisation proceedings, or for disapproval of the reorganisation plan, and where the ruling for approval of the reorganisation plan or for termination of the reorganisation proceedings has been rendered.

Article 20 (Function of registry office)

1. If the request for registration has been made under the provisions of Article 17 through the preceding Article, the registry office shall so register without delay.

2. When registering the commencement of reorganisation proceedings, the registry office shall, of its own motion, delete registration for the commencement of composi-

tion, the commencement of arrangement, or the commencement of special liquidation, if there exists such registration with respect to the company.

3. When registering the annulment of the ruling for the commencement of reorganisation proceedings, the registry office shall, of its own motion, restore registration, if there exists such registration as has been deleted in accordance with the provision of the preceding paragraph.

4. The provisions of the preceding two paragraphs shall apply mutatis mutandis to the registration of bankruptcy, when the approval of the reorganisation plan or cancellation of such approval is registered.

Article 21 (Registration of avoidance)

1. In the case where an act forming the cause of registration has been avoided, the receiver shall apply for registration of such avoidance. The same shall apply in the case where a registration has been avoided.

2. The provision of Article 19 shall apply mutatis mutandis in the case mentioned in the preceding paragraph.

Article 22 (Application mutatis mutandis to recordation)

The provisions of Article 18, Article 18-2 paragraph 3 and the preceding three Articles shall apply mutatis mutandis to the rights for which recordation has been effected.

Article 23 (Transition into bankruptcy procedure)

1. In the case where the ruling has become final and conclusive for dismissal of the application for commencement of the reorganisation proceedings, or for discontinuance of the reorganisation proceedings, or for disapproval of the reorganisation plan with respect to the company before adjudication of bankruptcy, if it is found that there exist facts comprising causes of bankruptcy with respect to the company, the Court may, of its own motion, declare bankruptcy in accordance with the Bankruptcy Law (Law No. 71 of 1922).

2. In the case mentioned in the preceding paragraph, the request for registration under the provision of Article 19 or for recordation under the provision of Article 19 as applied mutatis mutandis by virtue of the preceding Article shall be made together with the request for registration or recordation of bankruptcy.

Article 24 (Transition into bankruptcy procedure)

If an adjudication of bankruptcy has been rendered in accordance with the provision of paragraph 1 of the preceding Article, in respect of applying the provisions of Book I of the Bankruptcy Law, the ruling for commencement of the reorganisation proceedings, the order for commencement of proceedings in arrangement or special liquidation procedure which ceased to be effective by commencing the reorganisation proceedings, the application for commencement of composition in composition procedure, or the acts of directors or similar officers of the company showing the offence of fraudulent bankruptcy shall be deemed to be suspension of payment or petition for bankruptcy unless suspension of payment or petition for bankruptcy was made therefore, the claims for common benefits shall be the claims appertaining to the bankrupt's estate.

Article 25 (Transition into bankruptcy procedure)

If the bankruptcy procedure has, with respect to the company after adjudication of bankruptcy, been continued because of the ruling for dismissal of the application for commencement of the reorganisation proceedings, for discontinuance of the reorganisation proceedings under the provisions of Article 273 through Article 274, or for disapproval of the reorganisation plan having become final and conclusive, the claims for common benefits shall constitute the claims appertaining to the bankrupt's estate.

Article 26 (Transition into bankruptcy procedure)

1. If the ruling for discontinuance of reorganisation proceedings under the provision of Article 277 has, with respect to the company after adjudication of bankruptcy, become final and conclusive after the bankruptcy procedure, ceased to be effective because of the ruling for approval of the reorganisation plan, the Court shall, of its own motion, declare bankruptcy.

2. In the case mentioned in the preceding paragraph, it shall, in respect of applying the provisions of Book 1 of the Bankruptcy Law, be deemed that the petition for bankruptcy has been filed at the time of petition for bankruptcy in the bankruptcy procedure which ceased to be effective because of the ruling for approval of the reorganisation plan, and the claims for common benefits shall constitute the claims appertaining to the bankrupt's estate.

3. The provision of Article 23 paragraph 2 shall apply mutatis mutandis in the case mentioned in paragraph 1.

Article 27 (Transition into composition procedure)

1. If, in the case where there has been granted the ruling mentioned in Article 23 paragraph 1, it is recognised to be reasonable to do so, the Court may give approval to file application for composition even prior to becoming final and conclusive of such ruling.

2. If the approval mentioned in the preceding paragraph has been granted by the Court, the composition procedure shall be taken in accordance with the Composition Law (Law No. 72 of 1922).

Article 28 (Transition into composition procedure)

1. In the case where the composition procedure has been commenced upon application as provided for in the preceding Article after the composition procedure ceased to be effective because of the ruling for commencement for the reorganisation proceedings, the application for commencement of composition shall, in respect of applying the provisions of Articles 10 and 33 of the Composition Law, be deemed to have been filed at the time when the commencement of composition has been applied for in the composition procedure which ceased to be effective.

2. In the case where the composition procedure has been commenced upon application as provided for in the preceding Article, the claims for common benefits shall, in respect of applying the provision of Article 56 of the Composition Law, be deemed to be the claims arising because of the composition or the costs of the composition procedure.

Article 29 (Duty to file petition of bankruptcy, etc. and application for commencement of reorganisation proceedings)

Even when a liquidator of the company files a petition of bankruptcy or applies for commencement of special liquidation procedure by virtue of other laws, it shall not preclude to apply for the commencement of reorganisation proceedings.

Chapter II: Commencement of reorganisation proceedings

Article 30 (Commencement of proceedings)

1. In the case where a company is unable to pay its obligations that are due without exceedingly impeding continuation of its business, the company may file with the Court an application for commencement of reorganisation proceedings. The same shall also apply in the case where the facts comprising causes of bankruptcy are likely to take place with respect to the company.

2. In the case mentioned in the latter clause of the preceding paragraph, the creditors having claims corresponding to one-tenth or more of the amount of the capital, or the shareholders having shares corresponding to one-tenth or more of the total number of shares issued, may also file the application.

Article 31 (Application subsequent to dissolution)

In order that a company during liquidation or special liquidation, or a company after bankruptcy adjudication may apply for commencement of reorganisation proceedings, it shall resort to a resolution as provided for in Article 343 of the Commercial Code (Law No. 48 of 1899).

Article 32 (Application)

1. An application for the commencement of reorganisation proceedings shall be made in writing.

2. The following particulars shall be stated in the application:

(1) The full names and addresses of the applicant and his legal representative;
(2) The corporate name and the location of the head office of the company, as well as the full name of its representative; if the head office is in a foreign country, the location of its principal business place in Japan, as well as the full name of its representative in Japan;
(3) The tenor of application;
(4) The facts comprising causes of the commencement of reorganisation proceedings;
(5) The objects of the company and the state of its business;
(6) The total number of shares issued by the company, the amount of capital, as well as the assets, debts, and other aspects of its financial state;
(7) Any other procedure or disposition pending with respect to the assets of the company, which is known to the applicant;
(8) The applicant's opinion, if any, as to the plan of reorganisation.

3. The application shall contain, in addition to the particulars mentioned in the preceding paragraph, the amount and causes of claims in the case where the applica-

tion is filed by creditors, and the number of shares held in the case where the application is filed by shareholders.

Article 33 (Prima facie evidence)

1. When applying for the commencement of reorganisation proceedings, prima facie evidence shall be given of the facts comprising the causes of the commencement of reorganisation proceedings.

2. If the application mentioned in the preceding paragraph is filed by the creditors or shareholders, they shall give prima facie evidence also of the amount of claims or the number of shares held by them.

Article 34 (Advance payment of costs)

1. When applying for the commencement of reorganisation proceedings, the sum specified by the Court as the costs of the proceedings shall be paid in advance.

2. The sum mentioned in the preceding paragraph shall be determined by the Court, taking into consideration the size of the case and other factors. When the application has been filed by persons other than the company, the costs to be incurred subsequent to the commencement of the reorganisation proceedings shall be determined, taking into consideration the sum which can be paid out of the assets of the company.

3. Immediate complaint may be filed against the ruling on the advance payment of costs.

Article 35 (Notice, etc. to supervisory administrative agency)

1. When an application for commencement of reorganisation proceedings has been filed, the Court shall give notice to that effect to the administrative government agency supervising the business of the company, the chief of the taxation office of the company (if the head office is in a foreign country, the principal business office in Japan; hereinafter the same in this Article) is situated, and the chief of To, Do, Fu or prefecture, or of the city, town, or village, or public bodies similar thereto, in which the head office of the company is situated.

2. The Court may, if deemed necessary, demand the statement of opinion concerning the reorganisation proceedings of the company from the administrative government agent having jurisdiction over the business of the company, the person having power to collect the claims mentioned in Article 122 paragraph 1, or other person deemed to be proper by the Court.

3. The agency or person mentioned in the preceding paragraph may state to the Court their opinions concerning the reorganisation proceedings of the company.

Article 36 (Questioning)

When an application has been filed for the commencement of reorganisation proceedings by creditors or shareholders, the Court shall question the representative of the company (if the head office is in a foreign country, the representative in Japan; hereinafter the same).

Article 37 (Order for suspension of other procedures)

1. In the case where the application for commencement of reorganisation proceedings, if deemed necessary, the Court may, upon application of the person interested or of its own motion, for the time until the ruling is given of application for commence-

ment of reorganisation proceedings, order suspension of bankruptcy procedure: composition procedure; arrangement procedure; special liquidation procedure; procedure of compulsory execution, of provisional attachment, of provisional disposition already done against the company's assets under their reorganisation claims or reorganisation security rights; procedure of official auction sale as enforcement of security right (hereinafter simply referred to as 'auction sale') or procedure of execution of enterprise hypothecation right; procedure of a suit connected with the company's assets; or procedure for the case pending in an administrative government agency in connection with the company's assets. Provided that, this shall not apply to the procedure of compulsory execution, of provisional attachment, of provisional disposition, or of auction sale in the case where there is a likelihood of inflicting unreasonable losses on the creditors or applicant for official auction sale.

2. If it is deemed necessary in the case where an application has been filed for commencement of reorganisation proceedings, the Court may order suspension of the disposition for tax delinquency under the National Tax Collection Law (Law No. 147 of 1959), disposition for tax delinquency after the manner of national tax collection, or disposition of properties furnished as security for tax liabilities. In such cases, the opinions of the person who has power to collect shall be consulted in advance.

3. The ruling for suspension mentioned in the preceding paragraph shall cease to be effective when ruling has been given on the application for commencement of the reorganisation proceedings, or when two months have elapsed from the date of the ruling for suspension.

4. During the period of suspension of the disposal under the provision of paragraph 2, prescription shall not run.

5. The Court may amend or annul the ruling for suspension granted pursuant to the provisions of paragraphs 1 and 2.

Article 38 (Prerequisites for commencement of proceedings)

The Court shall dismiss the application for commencement of the reorganisation proceedings in any of the following cases:

(1) Where the costs of the proceedings are not paid in advance;
(2) Where the creditors or shareholders have acquired the claims or shares with a view to applying for commencement of the reorganisation proceedings;
(3) Where the application has been made for the purpose of avoiding bankruptcy or avoiding enforcement of the enterprise hypothecation right;
(4) Where the bankruptcy procedure, composition procedure, arrangement procedure, or special liquidation procedure is pending in the Court and it is in the general interests of creditors to resort to such procedures;
(5) Where there is no prospect of rehabilitation;
(6) Where an application has been filed, making it its principal purpose to avoid performance of tax liabilities, or otherwise to gain benefits in the performance of tax liabilities;
(7) Where an application has been filed in any other ways which are not faithful.

Article 39 (Measures for preservation of rights)

1. Even prior to granting the ruling for commencement of reorganisation proceedings, the Court may, upon the application of persons interested or of its own motion, order provisional attachment, provisional disposition, or any other necessary preserva-

tive measures concerning the business or property of a company. The same shall also apply to the administration by a preservation administrator or to the disposition ordering supervision by an overseer.

2. The Court may amend or annul the orders granted pursuant to the provision of the preceding paragraph.

3. The decision made pursuant to the provisions of the preceding two paragraphs shall be given by way of a ruling. Immediate complaint may be filed against such rulings.

4. The immediate complaint of the preceding paragraph shall have no effectiveness to suspend the execution.

5. The Court shall, if it has made the disposition under the provision of the latter clause of paragraph 1, give public notice to that effect. The same shall also apply in the cases where any change occurred in the matters of public notice or where said disposition was cancelled.

6. The provision of Article 15 shall not apply in the case of the preceding paragraph.

Article 40 (Preservation administrator)

1. If the order of administration by a preservation administrator was made in accordance with the provision of the latter clause of paragraph 1 of the preceding Article, the rights of managing the business of the company as well as of administering and disposing the property of the company shall vest in the exclusive jurisdiction of the preservation administrator appointed by the Court. Provided that, the permission of the Court shall be obtained by the preservation administrator for his effecting any action not belonging to ordinary affairs of the company.

2. Any action effected not obtaining the permission under the proviso to the preceding paragraph shall be null and void. Provided that, it cannot be set up against a third party in good faith.

Article 41 (Deputy preservation administrator)

1. A preservation administrator may, if necessary, appoint a deputy preservation administrator on his own responsibility for effecting his duties.

2. The appointment of the deputy preservation administrator under the preceding paragraph shall be made on obtaining the permission of the Court.

Article 42 (Overseer)

If the order of supervision by an overseer was made in accordance with the provision of the latter clause of Article 39 paragraph 1, the consent of the overseer appointed by the Court shall be obtained by the company for its effecting any action designated by the Court.

Article 43 (Application mutatis mutandis of provisions etc. concerning receiver)

1. The provisions of Articles 54 through 55, Article 94, Article 95, Article 96 paragraph 1, Article 97, and Article 98-2 through 100 shall apply mutatis mutandis to the preservation administrator.

2. The provisions of Articles 68 through 70 shall apply mutatis mutandis in the case where the disposition of ordering administration by a preservation administrator was

made in accordance with the provision of the latter clause of Article 39 paragraph 1 and where said disposition was cancelled.

3. The provisions of paragraph 1 and 2 Article 98-2, and Articles 98-3 through 98-5 apply mutatis mutandis to the overseer.

Article 44 (Restriction to withdrawal of application for commencement of proceedings)

After the disposition under the provision of Article 39 paragraph 1 was made, the application for commencement of reorganisation proceedings cannot be withdrawn without obtaining the permission of the Court.

Article 45 (Written ruling for commencement)

The date and hour of the ruling shall be given in the written ruling for the commencement of reorganisation proceedings.

Article 46 (Particulars to be specified at the same time with commencement)

The Court shall, at the same time with the ruling for the commencement of reorganisation proceedings, appoint a receiver or receivers, and specify the following particulars:

(1) The period for report of reorganisation claims and reorganisation security rights. Provided that, the period shall be not less than two weeks and not exceeding four months from the date of the ruling;
(2) The date of the first meeting of persons concerned. Provided that, the date shall be within two months from the date of the ruling;
(3) The date of investigation of reorganisation claims and reorganisation security rights. Provided that, between the date and the last day of the period for report, there shall be an interval of not less than one week and not exceeding two months.

Article 47 (Public notice and service of commencement)

1. When the Court has granted the ruling for the commencement of reorganisation proceedings, it shall immediately give public notice of the following particulars:

(1) The principal text of the ruling for the commencement of reorganisation proceedings;
(2) The full name or corporate name of the receiver;
(3) The period and the date specified pursuant to the provision of the preceding Article;
(4) The orders to the effect that the persons owing debts to the company and the persons possessing properties of the company shall not pay the debts or surrender the properties to the company, and that they shall, within a specified period, report to the receiver that they owe debts or possess properties.

2. Papers containing the particulars mentioned in the preceding paragraph and the tenor of the opinions of the investigation commissioners on the fitness for commencement of reorganisation proceedings shall be served to the receiver, company, as well as

known reorganisation creditors, reorganisation secured creditors, and the shareholders; and papers containing the particulars mentioned in the preceding paragraph, to the investigation commissioners and known persons owing debts to the company and possessing properties of the company.

3. The provisions of the preceding two paragraphs shall apply mutatis mutandis in the case where a change has taken place in any of the particulars mentioned in paragraph 1 items (2) through (4). Provided that, public notice need not be given as to the change of the date of investigation of reorganisation claims and reorganisation security rights.

4. Any persons who failed to file the report mentioned in paragraph 1 item (4) shall compensate damages thereby inflicted upon the assets of the company.

Article 48 (Notice of commencement)

1. The particulars mentioned in paragraph 1 of the preceding Article and the tenor of the opinion of the investigation commissioner under paragraph 2 of said Article shall be notified to the administrative government agency supervising the business of the company, the Minister of Justice, and the Minister of Finance.

2. The provisions of the preceding paragraph shall apply mutatis mutandis in the case where a change has taken place in any of the particulars mentioned in paragraph 1 items (2) and (3) of the preceding Article.

Article 49 (Keeping documents)

The documents relative to the application for the commencement of reorganisation proceedings shall be kept at the Court for inspection by persons interested.

Article 50 (Complaint)

1. Immediate complaint may be filed against the decision on the application for commencement of the reorganisation proceedings.

2. The provision of Article 37 shall apply mutatis mutandis in the case where an immediate complaint has been filed against the ruling for dismissal of the application for commencement of the reorganisation proceedings.

Article 51 (Annulment of ruling for commencement)

1. If the ruling for annulment of the ruling for commencement of the reorganisation proceedings has become final and conclusive, a public notice shall immediately be given of the principal text of such ruling.

2. The provisions of Article 47 paragraph 2 and Article 48 paragraph 1 shall apply mutatis mutandis in the case mentioned in the preceding paragraph.

3. In the case mentioned in paragraph 1, the receiver shall make payment of the claims for the common benefits, and shall, with respect to those claims of which objection has been raised, make deposit on behalf of the creditors thereof.

Article 52 (Reduction, etc. of capital after commencement)

1. For the time after commencement of the reorganisation proceedings till its termination, the reduction of capital, issuance of new shares or debentures, amalgamation, dissolution, change of organisation or continuation of the company, divi-

dend of profits or interests, or distribution of money under Article 293-5 paragraph 1 of the Commercial Code shall not be effected, otherwise than by the reorganisation proceedings.

2. Permission of the Court shall be obtained in order to amend the articles of incorporation of the company otherwise than by the reorganisation proceedings, for the time after commencement of the reorganisation proceedings till its termination.

Article 53 (Business and management of assets after commencement)

If the ruling for commencement of the reorganisation proceedings has been granted, the right to administer the business as well as to manage and dispose of the assets of the company shall vest exclusively in the receiver. Provided that, this shall not apply if said right has been given to the director in accordance with the provision of Article 211 paragraph 3 or Article 248-2 paragraph 1.

Article 54 (Acts requiring permission of Court)

The Court may, if deemed necessary, prescribe that the receiver shall obtain permission of the Court to do any of the following acts:

(1) Disposal of the assets of the company;
(2) Getting transfer of property;
(3) Obtaining loans;
(4) Rescission of the contract mentioned in Article 103;
(5) Institution of lawsuit;
(6) Compromise and arbitration agreement;
(7) Relinquishment of rights;
(8) Approval of claims for common benefits and of right to redeem;
(9) Request for extinguishment for retention right under the provision of Article 161-2, and conversion of security pertaining to reorganisation security rights;
(10) Any other acts designated by the Court.

Article 54-2 (Transaction of receiver on his own account)

A receiver cannot, without obtaining permission of the Court, take over the company's products or other properties, transfer his own products or other properties to the company, or otherwise transact with the company on behalf of himself or of a third person.

Article 55 (Transaction of receiver on his own account)

Any act done without obtaining the permission mentioned in the preceding two Articles shall be null and void. Provided that, the nullity may not be set up against a bona fide third person.

Article 56 (Acts done by company after commencement)

1. The validity of any juristic act effected by the company with regard to the assets of the company after commencement of the reorganisation proceedings shall not be asserted, in so far as the reorganisation proceedings are concerned.

2. Any juristic act done by the company on the date of commencement of the reorganisation proceedings shall be presumed to have been done after commencement of the reorganisation proceedings.

Article 57 (Acquisition of rights after commencement)

1. Even if a right is acquired, otherwise than by the act of the company, on the assets of the company in connection with reorganisation claims or reorganisation security rights after commencement of the reorganisation proceedings, the validity of such acquisition shall not be asserted, in so far as the reorganisation proceedings are concerned.

2. The provision of paragraph 2 of the preceding Article shall apply mutatis mutandis to the acquisition mentioned in the preceding paragraph.

Article 58 (Registration and recordation after commencement)

1. The validity of any registration, or of provisional registration provided for in Article 2 item (1) (Where necessary procedural requisites are not met for application for registration) of the Immoveable Property Registration Law (Law No. 24 of 1899) of immoveable properties or vessels, effected subsequent to the commencement of the reorganisation proceedings on the causes of registration arising prior to the commencement of the reorganisation proceedings shall not be asserted, in so far as the reorganisation proceedings are concerned. Provided that, this shall not apply to any registration or provisional registration effected by a person entitled to demand registration or provisional registration without knowing the fact of commencement of the reorganisation proceedings.

2. The provision of the preceding paragraph shall apply mutatis mutandis to the recordation or provisional recordation of creation, transfer, or alteration of a right.

3. The provision of paragraph 1 shall apply mutatis mutandis to the registration of creation, transfer, or alteration of an enterprise hypothecation right.

Article 59 (Payment to company after commencement)

1. The validity of payment made to the company subsequent to the commencement of reorganisation proceedings may, without knowing the facts thereof, be asserted, even in so far as the reorganisation proceedings are concerned.

2. The validity of payment made to the company subsequent to the commencement of reorganisation proceedings with knowledge of the facts may be asserted only to the extent the assets of the company have thereby been benefited, in so far as the reorganisation proceedings are concerned.

Article 60 (Presumption of bona fide and mala fide)

It shall, for the purpose of applying the provisions of the preceding two Articles, be presumed that the facts were not known prior to the public notice of the commencement of reorganisation proceedings, and that the facts were known subsequent to the public notice thereof.

Article 61 (Co-ownership)

1. If, in the case where the company holds any property right in co-ownership with other person, the reorganisation proceedings have been commenced, the

receiver may demand partition, even if it had been stipulated that there shall be no partition.

2. In the case mentioned in the preceding paragraph, the other co-owner may acquire the share held by the company upon paying reasonable compensation.

Article 62 (Right to redeem)

The commencement of reorganisation proceedings shall not affect the right to redeem from the company the properties not belonging to the company.

Article 63 (Security by way of transfer)

Any person who transferred a property to the company prior to the commencement of reorganisation proceedings may not redeem the property on the ground that the transfer has been made for the purpose of security.

Article 64 (Redemption of sold goods in transit)

1. If, in the case where the seller has sent out to the buyer the goods which are the subject-matter of sale, the reorganisation proceedings have been commenced with respect to the buyer while the buyer has not yet paid the purchase money in full, and further, not yet received the goods at the destination, the seller may redeem the goods. Provided that, this shall not preclude the receiver from demanding delivery of the goods after obtaining the permission of the Court and paying the purchase money in full.

2. The provision of the preceding paragraph shall not preclude the application of the provision of Article 103.

Article 65 (Commission agent's right to redeem)

The provision of paragraph 1 of the preceding Article shall apply mutatis mutandis in the case where a commission agent having commissioned to purchase goods has sent out the goods to the assignor.

Article 66 (Right to redeem by way of compensation)

1. In the case where the company has transferred the property forming the subject-matter of the right to redeem prior to the commencement of reorganisation proceedings, the holder of the right to redeem may demand transfer of the right of demanding counter-performance. The same shall apply in the case where the receiver has transferred the property which is the subject-matter of the right to redeem.

2. If, in the case mentioned in the preceding paragraph, the counter-performance has been given to the receiver, the holder of the right to redeem may demand delivery of the property given to the receiver as counter-performance.

Article 67 (Suspension, etc. of other procedures)

1. If the ruling for commencement of the reorganisation proceedings has been granted, the petition for bankruptcy, the application for commencement of composition, for commencement of reorganisation proceedings, for commencement of arrangement, for commencement of special liquidation as well as the compulsory

execution, provisional attachment, provisional disposition, official auction sale, and enforcement of the right of enterprise hypothecation against the assets of the company under reorganisation claims or reorganisation security rights shall not be done; the bankruptcy procedure as well as the procedures for compulsory execution, provisional attachment, provisional disposition, official auction sale, and enforcement of the right of enterprise hypothecation, which have already been done against the assets of the company under the reorganisation claims or reorganisation security rights, shall be suspended; and the composition procedure, arrangement procedure, or special liquidation procedure shall lose its effect.

2. If the ruling for commencement of the reorganisation proceedings has been granted, the disposition for tax delinquency under the National Collection Law against the assets of the company under reorganisation claims or reorganisation security rights, disposition for tax delinquency after the manner of national tax collection, and disposition of properties furnished as security for tax liabilities shall not be carried out, and these dispositions which have already commenced shall be suspended for the period from the date of the ruling to the time of approval of the reorganisation proceedings, or for the period of one year from the date of the ruling.

3. If deemed necessary, the Court may, upon application of the receiver or of its own motion, extend the one-year period mentioned in the preceding paragraph. In such case, the Court shall obtain in advance the consent of the person who has power to collect.

4. The person who has power to collect may give the consent mentioned in the preceding paragraph.

5. For the period during which the measures or disposals are prohibited or suspended under the provisions of paragraphs 2 and 3, prescription shall not run.

6. If the Court deems that there is no impediment to reorganisation, it may, upon application of the receiver or the person having power to collect the claims mentioned in Article 122 paragraph 1, or of its own motion, order continuation of the suspended procedure or disposition; and if deemed necessary for the purpose of reorganisation, the Court may, upon application of the receiver or of its own motion, order annulment of the suspended procedure or disposition by having or not having securities furnished. Provided that, this shall not apply to the bankruptcy procedure.

7. The claims which have arisen as against the company by reason of those procedures which have lost effect by virtue of the provision of paragraph 1, the right against the company to claim expenses relative to such procedures, and the right against the company to claim expenses relative to the procedure or disposition continued pursuant to the provision of the preceding paragraph shall be the claims for common benefits.

Article 68 (Interruption or stay of lawsuit)

If there is the ruling for commencement of reorganisation proceedings, the lawsuit procedures relative to the assets of the company shall be interrupted or stayed.

Article 69 (Taking over suits)

1. Of the suits which have been suspended pursuant to the provision of the preceding Article, any suit which has no bearing on reorganisation claims or reorganisation security rights may be taken over by the receiver or by the other party thereto. In such cases, the right to claim costs of litigation against the company shall constitute the claims for common benefits.

2. In the case where the reorganisation proceedings have come to an end before the suit is taken over under the provision of the preceding paragraph, the company shall take over the suit ipso jure.

3. In the case where the reorganisation proceedings have terminated after the taking over was done under the provision of paragraph 1, the suit shall be suspended. In such cases, the company shall take over the suit.

4. In the case mentioned in the preceding paragraph, the other party may also take over the suit.

Article 70 (Cases pending in administrative government agency)

The provisions of the preceding two Articles shall apply mutatis mutandis in those cases relative to the properties of the company which are pending in an administrative government agency at the time of commencement of the reorganisation proceedings.

Article 71 (Transfer of cases)

1. In the case where a suit relative to the properties of the company is pending in another Court at the time of commencement of the reorganisation proceedings, the reorganisation Court may, by way of a ruling, request transfer of the case. The same shall also apply to those suits which have come to be pending in another Court subsequent to commencement of the reorganisation proceedings.

2. If the ruling mentioned in the preceding paragraph has been granted, the Court which has been requested to make the transfer shall transfer the suit to the reorganisation Court.

3. The transfer mentioned in the preceding paragraph may be made, even in the case where the suit is being suspended or has been discontinued.

4. The provisions of the preceding three paragraphs shall not apply to the suits pending in a superior Court.

Article 72 (Dispositions to be made by Court)

1. If the ruling for commencement of the reorganisation proceedings has been granted, the Court may, upon application of the receiver or of its own motion, take the following measures, if deemed necessary:

(1) Assessment of the right against promoters or directors demanding payment on shares or payment of the total amount or non-paid amount of, the assets which are the object of investment by assets or the assets which were agreed to be obtained by the company after the company has been established, or the right demanding compensation for damages on the ground of liabilities of promoters, directors, statutory auditors or liquidators;

(2) Preservative measures to be taken on properties belonging to promoters, directors, auditors, or liquidators, by virtue of the right to demand payment on shares, payment of the total amount of non-paid amount of the assets, or the right to demand compensation for damages mentioned in the preceding item.

2. If it is found that there exists urgent necessity, the Court may take the measures mentioned in item (2) of the preceding paragraph, even prior to granting the ruling for commencement of the reorganisation proceedings, upon application of the preservation administrator or of its own motion.

3. The provisions of Article 39 paragraphs 2 through 4 shall apply mutatis mutandis to the measures mentioned in the provisions of paragraph 1 item (2) and the preceding paragraph.

Article 73 (Commencement of assessment procedure of right to demand payment on shares, etc.)

1. In applying for the assessment mentioned in the provision of paragraph 1 item (1) of the preceding Article, it shall be necessary to give prima facie evidence of the facts comprising thereof.

2. In the case where the Court commences, of its own motion, the assessment procedure, it shall give a ruling to that effect.

Article 74 (Decision on assessment)

1. The decision on assessment or the decision dismissing the application for assessment shall be given by way of a ruling containing statement of the reasons.

2. The Court shall question the persons interested before the ruling is granted.

Article 75 (Action for objection)

1. Any person who is discontented with the decision on assessment may institute an action for objection within the peremptory period of one month of the date of service of the ruling.

2. A judgment of approval of, or alteration in, the assessment shall, so far as compulsory execution is concerned, have the same effect as a judgment ordering performance.

3. The action mentioned in paragraph 1 shall come under the exclusive jurisdiction of the reorganisation Court, and the oral proceedings shall not be commenced until after the period mentioned in said paragraph shall have expired.

4. In the case where several actions are pending at the same time, the oral proceedings as well as the decision shall be consolidated.

Article 76 (Effect of assessment)

If no action is instituted within the period mentioned in paragraph 1 of the preceding Article, the assessment shall have the same effect as a final and conclusive judgment ordering performance. The same shall also apply when the action has been dismissed.

Article 77 (Interruption of prescription)

The application for assessment shall be deemed to be a judicial demand so far as interruption of prescription is concerned. The same shall also apply where the Court has, of its own motion, commenced the assessment procedure.

Article 78 (Right of avoidance)

1. Any of the acts set forth below may be avoided in favour of the company's assets subsequent to the commencement of reorganisation proceedings:

(1) Any action done by the company with the knowledge that it would prejudice reorganisation creditors or reorganisation secured creditors (hereinafter in this Article referred to as the 'reorganisation creditors, etc.'). Provided that,

this shall not apply in the case where the person benefited by the act did not know at the time of the act the fact that it would prejudice the reorganisation creditors, etc.;

(2) Any act prejudicial to reorganisation creditors, etc. done by the company after suspension of payment or after petition for bankruptcy, application for commencement of composition, commencement of reorganisation proceedings, commencement of arrangement, or commencement of special liquidation (hereinafter referred to as 'suspension of payment, etc.' in this Article), and any act connected with furnishing of securities or extinction of obligations. Provided that, this shall apply only in the case where the person benefited by the act knew at the time of the act that there has been suspension of payment, etc. or the fact that it is prejudicial to reorganisation creditors, etc:

(3) Any act concerning furnishing of securities or extinction of obligations done by the company subsequent to suspension of payment, etc. or within thirty days prior thereto, which does not appertain to the duties of the company, or which does not appertain to the duties of the company in its method or time. Provided that, this shall not apply in the cases where the creditor did not know at the time of the act the fact that the company did it in knowing that it would prejudice equality with respect to other reorganisation creditors, etc., and where the creditor did not also know such fact when it is subsequent to suspension of payment, etc.

(4) Any gratuitous act, or non-gratuitous act assimilated to a gratuitous act, which the company has done subsequent to suspension of payment, etc. or within six months prior thereto.

2. The provision of the preceding paragraph shall not apply to the acts relative to furnishing of securities or extinction of obligations done by the company, with respect to the claims mentioned in Article 121 paragraph 1 item (5) and Article 122 paragraph 1, as against the person who has power to collect the same.

Article 79 (Exception in case obligations of bills or notes are paid)

1. The provision of paragraph 1 of the preceding Article shall not apply in the case where a person who has received the payment on bill or note from the company is to lose the right on bill or note against one or more obligors, if he fails to receive such payment.

2. In the case mentioned in the preceding paragraph, if the last of the persons bound to pay on recourse or the person having commissioned drawing of bill or note knew or did not know by negligence at the time of drawing that there has been suspension of payment, petition for bankruptcy, application for commencement of reorganisation proceedings, for commencement of arrangement, or for commencement of special liquidation, the receiver may cause such persons to reimburse the sum paid by the company.

Article 80 (Avoidance of acts done for setting up change of rights against third persons)

1. In the case where an act has been done, which is necessary for setting up creation or transfer of, or change in, a right against third persons subsequent to suspension of payment, or petition for bankruptcy, application for commencement of composition, commencement of reorganisation proceedings, commencement of arrangement, or

commencement of special liquidation, if the act has been done mala fide after fifteen days have elapsed since the date of the creation or transfer of, or change in, the right, such act may be avoided. Provided that, this shall not apply to registration or recordation, if the formal registration or formal recordation has been effected after the provisional registration or provisional recordation was made.

2. The provision of the preceding paragraph shall apply mutatis mutandis to those recordations whereby the effect of acquisition of a right arises.

Article 81 (Avoidance of act of execution)

The right of avoidance shall not be precluded from being exercised, even when there exists executory obligatory title with respect to the act which is to be avoided, or when such act is based on the act of execution.

Article 82 (Exercise of right of avoidance)

1. The right of avoidance shall be exercised by the receiver by way of a lawsuit, demand for avoidance, or plea.

2. Cases of the lawsuit and of demand for avoidance mentioned in the preceding paragraph shall come under the exclusion jurisdiction of the reorganisation Court.

Article 83 (Prima facie evidence of causes of demand for avoidance)

On demanding avoidance, the facts comprising causes thereof shall be given prima facie evidence.

Article 84 (Decision on demand for avoidance)

1. The decision approving or dismissing demand for avoidance shall be given by way of a ruling containing statement of the reason.

2. The Court shall question the opponent party or the sub-acquirer before the ruling is granted.

Article 85 (Lawsuit for objection)

1. Any person who is discontented with the ruling approving demand for avoidance may institute a lawsuit for objection within a peremptory period of one month from the date of service of the ruling.

2. The lawsuit mentioned in the preceding paragraph shall come under the exclusive jurisdiction of the reorganisation Court.

Article 86 (Lawsuit for objection)

If the judgment approving the ruling of demand for avoidance has become final and conclusive, the ruling shall have the same effect as a judgment which has become final and conclusive. The same shall also apply in the case where a lawsuit is not instituted within the period prescribed in paragraph 1 of the preceding Article or where the lawsuit has been dismissed.

Article 87 (Effect of exercise of right of avoidance)

1. The exercise of a right of avoidance restores properties of the company to the original condition.

2. If, in the case where any of the acts mentioned under item (4) of Article 78 para-

graph 1 has been avoided, the opponent party has been bona fide at the time of the act, it shall be sufficient if he reimburses the benefits which he is actually enjoying.

Article 88 (Rights of other party)

1. In the case where an act of the company has been avoided, if the counter-performance gained thereby still actually remains in the assets of the company, the other party may demand return thereof, and if the benefits arising from the counter-performance still exist actually, the other party may exercise his right as a holder of claims for the common benefits to the extent of the remaining benefits.

2. In the case where the benefits arising from the counter-performance exist no more, the other party may, with respect to reimbursement of value thereof, exercise his right as a reorganisation creditor. In the case where the value of counter-performance is in excess of the benefits actually existing, the same shall also apply to the difference.

Article 89 (Restoration of claims of other party)

If, in the case where an act of the company has been avoided, the other party has returned what he gained by performance or has reimbursed the value thereof, the claim of the other party shall be thereby restored to its original condition.

Article 90 (Right of avoidance against subsequent acquirers)

1. The right of avoidance may also be exercised against subsequent acquirers in any of the following cases:

(1) Where the subsequent acquirer knows at the time of acquisition that there are causes for avoidance against his respective predecessors;
(2) Where there exist causes for avoidance against his respective predecessors, if the subsequent acquirer made acquisition by a gratuitous act or non-gratuitous act assimilated to a gratuitous act.

2. The provision of Article 87 paragraph 2 shall apply mutatis mutandis in the case where the right of avoidance has been exercised pursuant to the provision of item (2) of the preceding paragraph.

Article 91 (Restriction to avoidance because of knowledge of suspension of payment)

Any act done one year prior to the date of application for commencement of reorganisation proceedings may not be avoided on the ground that the facts of suspension of payment have become known.

Article 92 (Period for exercise of right of avoidance)

The right of avoidance shall not be exercised when two years have elapsed since the date of commencement of reorganisation proceedings. The same shall also apply where twenty years have elapsed from the date of the act.

Article 93 (Lawsuit, etc. for avoidance of fraudulent acts)

1. In the case where a lawsuit is instituted by a reorganisation creditor under Article 424 (Right of avoidance of fraudulent act) of the Civil Code (Law No. 89

of 1986) or a lawsuit for avoidance under the Bankruptcy Law is pending at the time of commencement of the reorganisation proceedings, the lawsuit shall be suspended or discontinued.

2. The provision of Article 69 shall apply mutatis mutandis in the case mentioned in the preceding paragraph. In such cases, the word 'company' appearing in paragraphs 2 and 3 of said Article shall read as 'the reorganisation creditor or the administrator in bankruptcy'.

Chapter III: Receiver and investigation commissioner

Article 94 (Appointment of receiver)

The receiver shall be appointed from among persons suitable for discharging his duties.

Article 95 (Appointment of receiver)

1. A trust company, bank and other corporation shall be eligible as a receiver.

2. In the case where a corporation has been appointed the receiver, the corporation shall designate from among the representatives a person who is to perform the duties of the receiver, and report it to the Court.

Article 96 (Capacity to sue or be sued)

1. In a suit relative to the assets of the company, the receiver shall be the plaintiff or the defendant.

2. The provision of the preceding paragraph shall not, in the case where the rights of managing the business of the company as well as of administering and disposing the assets of the company were granted to the director of the company, apply to the lawsuit instituted thereafter.

3. The provisions of Article 68 and Article 69 shall apply mutatis mutandis to the lawsuit of the preceding paragraph in the case where the stipulation of reorganisation plan under the provision of Article 211 paragraph 3 or the decision under the provision of Article 248-2 paragraph 1 was cancelled.

Article 97 (Discharge of duties by several receivers)

1. In the case where there are several receivers, they shall perform their duties conjointly. Provided that, this may, with permission of the Court, take charge of the duties as divided among them.

2. In the case where there are several receivers, the manifestation of intention by a third person shall be sufficient if effected to one of them.

Article 98 (Agent of receiver)

1. The receiver may, if necessary, appoint his agent on his own responsibility in order to cause such agent to perform his duties.

2. The permission of the Court shall be obtained for appointing the receiver's agent as provided for in the preceding paragraph.

Article 98-2 (Investigation by receiver)

1. The receiver may request the employee, such as a director, auditor or a manager, of the company to make report on the circumstances of business and assets of the company, and to inspect the articles, such as books and documents, of the company.

2. The receiver may, if necessary, appoint an appraiser on obtaining approval of the Court.

3. The receiver may, in making investigation, demand assistance of a bailiff on obtaining approval of the Court.

Article 98-3 (Supervision, etc. to receiver)

1. The receiver is under the supervision of the Court.

2. The Court shall deliver to the receiver the document validating its appointment.

3. The receiver shall, if requested by an interested person in performing his duties, present the document of the preceding paragraph.

Article 98-4 (Duty of care by receiver)

1. The receiver shall perform his duty with the care of a good manager.

2. If the receivers neglected to make the care under the provision of the preceding paragraph, they shall be jointly and severally responsible to make compensation for damage to the interested persons.

Article 98-5 (Dismissal of receiver)

If there are important reasons, the Court may, on application by interested persons or of its own motion, dismiss the receiver. In this case, the Court shall interrogate the receiver.

Article 99 (Duty to report account)

Upon termination of the office of a receiver, the receiver or his successor in office shall, without delay, file a report of account with the Court.

Article 100 (Emergency measures upon termination of office)

If, upon termination of the office of a receiver, there exist urgent circumstances, the receiver or his successor in office shall take necessary measures, until the succeeding receiver or the company becomes able to manage the assets.

Article 101 (Investigation commissioner)

1. The Court may, if deemed necessary, appoint one or several investigation commissioners.

2. The investigation commissioner shall, according to the order of the Court, investigate the following matters and report the results thereof to the court, or state his opinion to the Court:

(1) The facts comprising the cause of the commencement of reorganisation proceedings, existence or non-existence of the conditions mentioned in

Article 38 items (2) through (7), circumstances of business and assets of the company, and other necessary matters for commencement of the reorganisation proceedings as well as the propriety of commencing the reorganisation proceedings;

(2) Existence or non-existence of the circumstances needing the disposition as prescribed in Article 39 paragraph 1 or 2, or in Article 72;

(3) Propriety of the inventory and balance sheet prepared by the receiver concerning administration circumstances of the business and assets of the company, and other matters ordered by the Court;

(4) Propriety of the reorganisation plan draft or the reorganisation plan;

(5) Other matters needing the investigation report or the statement of opinions by the investigation commissioners concerning reorganisation case.

3. The investigation commissioners shall be appointed from among persons who are suitable for performing their duties and have no beneficial interests in the case.

Article 101-2 (Investigation commissioner)

The report of the investigation commissioners and the documents concerning the opinion thereof shall be kept at the Court for perusal by persons interested.

Article 101-3 (Investigation commissioner)

The provisions of Article 95, Article 97 paragraph 1, and Articles 98-2 through 98-5 shall apply mutatis mutandis to investigation commissioners.

Chapter IV: Reorganisation creditors, reorganisation secured creditors, and shareholders

Article 102 (Reorganisation claims)

Claims on property which have arisen against the company out of the causes existent prior to the commencement of reorganisation proceedings shall be reorganisation claims.

Article 103 (Bilateral contracts)

1. If the company and the other party have not yet both completed performance of a bilateral contract at the time of commencement of the reorganisation proceedings, the receiver may either rescind the contract or perform obligations of the company and demand of the other party's performance of obligations.

2. In the case mentioned in the preceding paragraph, the other party may give peremptory notice to the receiver demanding a definite answer as to whether he rescinds the contract or demands performance of obligations. If the receiver fails to respond with a definite answer within thirty days of the receipt of such notice, the receiver shall be deemed to have relinquished the right of rescission mentioned in the preceding paragraph.

3. The Court may, upon application of the receiver or the other party, or of its own motion, either extend or shorten the period provided for in the preceding paragraph.

4. The provisions of the preceding three paragraphs shall not apply to labour conventions.

Article 104 (Bilateral contracts)

1. If the contract has been rescinded pursuant to the provision of the preceding Article, the other party may, with regard to the compensation for damages, exercise his right as reorganisation creditor.

2. If what the company gained by counter-performance still actually remains in the assets of the company, the other party may demand return thereof, and if it no longer exists, the other party may, with respect to the value thereof, exercise his right as a holder of claims for common benefits.

Article 104-2 (Bilateral contract aiming at continuous performance)

1. The other party of bilateral contract liable for continuous performance to the company cannot, after commencement of the reorganisation proceedings, refuse to perform his duty by the reason that payment has not yet been made with respect to the reorganisation claim or reorganisation security right pertaining to the performance before the application of commencement of reorganisation proceedings.

2. The claim (with respect to the continuous performance calculating the amount of claim for a certain period, the claim pertaining to the performance for the period covering the day of application shall be included) pertaining to the performance made by the other party of bilateral contract before the commencement of reorganisation proceedings after the application for commencement of reorganisation proceedings shall be the claims for common benefits.

3. The provisions of the preceding two paragraphs shall not apply to labour contracts.

Article 105 (Acceptance of bills, etc. after commencement)

1. If, in the case where the reorganisation proceedings have been commenced with respect to a company which is the drawer or endorser of a bill of exchange, the drawee or the referee in case of need has accepted or paid without knowing the facts, such drawee or referee in case of need may exercise his right as a reorganisation creditor with respect to obligations which have arisen thereby.

2. The provision of the preceding paragraph shall apply mutatis mutandis to a cheque or valuable instrument which has for its object the delivery of money, other things, or valuable instruments.

3. The provision of Article 60 shall apply mutatis mutandis in applying the provisions of the preceding two paragraphs.

Article 106 (Contract of lease, etc.)

1. In the case where the reorganisation proceedings have been commenced with respect to a company which is a lessor, the validity of advance payment of rental or of disposition of claims on rental may not be asserted in so far as the reorganisation proceedings are concerned, except with respect to the rental for the current term as at the time of commencement of the reorganisation proceedings or for the next following term.

2. Any person who has incurred damages because of his inability, by virtue of the provision of the preceding paragraph, to assert the validity in connection with the reorganisation proceedings may exercise his right as reorganisation creditor with respect to the compensation for such damages.

3. The provisions of the preceding two paragraphs shall apply mutatis mutandis to the right of superficies or the right of emphyteusis.

Article 107 (Account current)

1. An account current shall terminate, when the reorganisation proceedings have been commenced with respect to one of the parties. In such case, each party may close the account and demand payment of the balance.

2. The right to demand pursuant to the provision of the preceding paragraph shall be a reorganisation claim, if held by the other party.

Article 108 (Where company is liable in all together with other persons)

If, in the case where several persons are liable each to perform all of the obligation, the reorganisation proceedings have been commenced with regard to all or several of them, the creditor may exercise his right as reorganisation creditor in each of the reorganisation proceedings with respect to the entire amount of obligation held at the time of commencement of the reorganisation proceedings.

Article 109 (Where company is liable to guarantee)

In the case where the reorganisation proceedings have been commenced with regard to a company which is a guarantor, the creditor may exercise his right as reorganisation creditor with respect to the entire amount of obligation held at the time of commencement of the reorganisation proceedings.

Article 110 (Right of indemnity to be exercised in future)

1. If, in the case where several persons are liable each to perform all of the obligation, the reorganisation proceedings have been commenced with regard to all or several of them or a single one of them, any person possessing the right of indemnity to be exercised in the future as against such person or persons may exercise his right as a reorganisation creditor with respect to the entire amount; provided however, that this shall not apply if the creditor has exercised his right as a reorganisation creditor with respect to the entire amount of obligation.

2. If, in the case mentioned in the proviso to the preceding paragraph, the person possessing the right of indemnity mentioned in said paragraph has performed the obligation, he shall acquire the right of the creditor in proportion to such payment.

3. The provisions of the preceding two paragraphs shall apply mutatis mutandis to the right of indemnity which a third person furnishing security might exercise in the future as against the company.

Article 111 (Where part of obligation is guaranteed)

The provisions of Articles 108 and 109, as well as paragraphs 1 and 2 of the preceding Article shall apply mutatis mutandis to a part of obligation shared by each guarantor, in the case where several guarantors should each guarantee a part of obligation.

Article 112 (Prohibition of performance of reorganisation obligations)

With respect to reorganisation claims, no one shall effect performance, receive performance, or do any other acts which will extinguish them (except exemption) otherwise than through the reorganisation proceedings. Provided that, with respect to the claims mentioned in paragraphs 1 and 4 of next Article, the above shall not apply in the case where the receiver effects payment on obtaining permission of the Court; with respect to the claims mentioned in Article 122 paragraph 1, the above shall not apply in the cases where the disposition for tax delinquency or disposition of the subject-matter of security, or the continuation thereof is permissible, where the company's claim, as has been attached by disposition for tax delinquency (inclusive of claims to which the effect of attachment extends), is performed voluntarily by the garnishee in favour of the person who has power to collect the claims while the disposition for tax delinquency is suspended, where a person who has power of collection effects appropriation with refundment money or overpaid tax, and where the receiver effects performance with permission of the Court.

Article 112-2 (Permission to pay reorganisation claims)

1. If a medium and small entrepreneur for whom the company is a main customer is feared to be seriously impeded in continuing his enterprise unless the reorganisation claim owned by him is paid, the Court may, ever prior to the ruling to approve the reorganisation plan, permit the whole or partial payment thereof, on application by the receiver or of its own motion.

2. The Court shall, for granting the permission under the provision of the preceding paragraph, take in consideration the circumstances of transaction between the company and the medium and small entrepreneur under said paragraph, financial conditions of the company, interests of the interested persons and all other circumstances.

3. The receiver shall, if he is requested to make application under paragraph 1 by a reorganisation creditor, report immediately to the Court to that effect, and he shall, if he intends not to make said application, without delay report the circumstances to the Court.

4. If the reorganisation proceedings could be progressed smoothly by means of early payment of a small amount of the reorganisation claims, the Court may, even prior to the ruling to approve the reorganisation plan, permit payment thereof on application by the receiver.

Article 113 (Rights of reorganisation creditors)

1. A reorganisation creditor may participate in the reorganisation proceedings with reorganisation claims possessed by him.

2. Reorganisation creditors shall have the right of vote, with respect to the claims mentioned in next Article through Article 118, in proportion to the sum calculated in accordance with those provisions, and with respect to other claims, in proportion to the amount thereof.

Article 114 (Claims subject to time limit, bearing no interest)

In the case where a claim subject to time limit is one which bears no interest and of which the time limit is to arrive after the commencement of reorganisation proceedings, the amount of legal interest accruing on the claim from the commencement of reorganisation proceedings to the arrival of the time limit shall be deducted from the amount of the claim.

Article 115 (Claims on funds payable at regular interval)

The provision of the preceding Article shall apply mutatis mutandis to claims on funds payable at regular intervals of which the amount and the period of duration are definite. Provided that, in the case where the total amount thereof exceeds the amount of principal on which interest is to accrue at the legal rate of interest corresponding in amount to the funds payable at regular intervals, such amount of principal shall govern.

Article 116 (Claims with indefinite time limit, etc.)

If, in the case provided for in Article 114, the time limit is indefinite, the amount of appraisal as at the time of the commencement of reorganisation proceedings shall govern. The same shall also apply in the case where the amount of the claim on funds payable at regular intervals or the period of duration thereof is indefinite.

Article 117 (Claims with indefinite time limit, etc.)

In the case where the subject-matter of a claim is not money, or where although it is money, the amount thereof is indefinite, or where the amount is represented in foreign currency, the amount of appraisal as at the time of commencement of the reorganisation proceedings shall govern.

Article 118 (Claims subject to conditions and future claims)

1. With regard to conditional claims, the amount of appraisal as at the time of commencement of the reorganisation proceedings shall govern.

2. The provision of the preceding paragraph shall apply mutatis mutandis to future claims which may be enforced against the company.

Article 119 (Income tax collectible at source of payment, etc.)

Of reorganisation claims, the income tax collectable at the source of payment; securities transaction tax; liquor tax; tobacco tax; consumption tax; gasoline tax; local road tax; petroleum gas tax; petroleum tax; Do-Fu-prefecture tobacco tax (including To tobacco tax) and city-town-village tobacco tax (including the special ward tobacco tax) to be collected by the method of payment by self-assessment; and the local taxes to be collected and paid in by special collecting agents, which are not yet due at the time of commencement of reorganisation proceedings, may be claimed as claims for common benefits. The same shall also apply to the wages and salaries of the company employees for the six-month period preceding the commencement of the reorganisation proceedings, and also to the claims for the refund of moneys deposited as securities for good behaviour of the company employees, arising out of causes existent prior to the commencement of the reorganisation proceedings.

Article 119-2 (Claims for retirement allowance of employees)

1. The claim for retirement allowance of an employee of the company who retired from the company prior to the ruling to approve the reorganisation plan shall be a claim for common benefits, within the limit of whichever the larger amount either of the amount equivalent to the total sum of the salaries for six-month period prior to retirement or the amount equivalent to one-third of the amount of his retirement allowance.

2. The claim for retirement allowance under the preceding paragraph which is periodical claim shall, notwithstanding the provision of said paragraph, be a claim for common benefits in the amount equivalent to one-third of the periodical money for each period.

3. The provisions of the preceding two paragraphs shall not apply to the claims for retirement allowance which shall be the claims for common benefits by virtue of the provision of Article 208.

Article 119-3 (Borrowed money, etc. before commencement)

If a director of the company or the preservation administrator has, before the commencement of reorganisation proceedings after the application for commencement of reorganisation proceedings, borrowed funds, purchased raw and finished materials, or otherwise done acts inevitable for continuing the business of company on obtaining the permission of the Court, the claims arising by such acts shall be the claims for common benefits.

Article 120 (Computation of period of priority rights)

In the case where a right of priority exists with respect to the amount of claims for a certain prescribed period, such period shall be computed retroactively from the time of commencement of the reorganisation proceedings.

Article 121 (Deferred reorganisation claims)

1. The claims set forth below shall be reorganisation claims:

(1) Interest accruing subsequent to the commencement of reorganisation proceedings;
(2) Damages and penalties for failure of performance subsequent to the commencement of reorganisation proceedings;
(3) Expenses for participation in the reorganisation proceedings;
(4) In addition to the expenses mentioned under the preceding item, those claims on property right arising out of causes existent after commencement of the reorganisation proceedings which are not claims for the common benefits;
(5) Fines, minor fines, costs of criminal action, value collected in place of confiscation, and administrative fines, accruing prior to the commencement of reorganisation proceedings;
(6) Of taxes accruing prior to the commencement of reorganisation proceedings, the amount of tax not reported, of which evasion, attempt at evasion, refund, or payment has not been effected, in the case where the imprisonment with hard labour has been meted out or a fine imposed on the charges of evasion, attempt at evasion, refund procured by unjust act, or failure to pay what should be collected and paid in, or where there has been performance of what had been ordered by way of notification under Article 14 paragraph 1 (inclusive of the cases being applied mutatis mutandis in Local Tax Law (Law No. 226 of 1950) (Notification disposition) of the National Tax Violation Control Law (Law No. 67 of 1900).

2. The claims mentioned in the preceding paragraph shall be deferred to other reorganisation claims. Provided that, this shall not apply to those claims collectible after the manner of national tax collection which are other than those mentioned under item (6) of said paragraph.

3. With respect to the claims mentioned under item (5) of paragraph 1, the reorgani-

sation plan shall not provide for reduction or exemption thereof nor contain any other provisions whereby the claims are affected.

Article 122 (Claims on tax, etc.)

1. In order to provide in the organisation plan for the postponement of tax payment for a period of three years or less or the postponement of conversion of property due to disposition for tax delinquency with respect to those claims which can be collected in accordance with National Tax Collection Law or after the manner of national tax collection, the opinion of the person who has power to collect shall be referred, and in order to provide the reduction or exemption, postponement of collection for a period of exceeding three years or the postponement of conversion of property due to disposition for tax delinquency, transmission of obligations, or any other provisions whereby the claims are affected, the consent of the person who has power to collect shall be obtained.

2. In order to provide for needing the consent of the person who has power to collect in accordance with the provision of the preceding paragraph with respect to the delinquency tax, interest tax, or the arrears arising for the time till the day of lapse of one year from the day of ruling for commencement of the reorganisation proceedings (if the ruling to approve the reorganisation plan was made before said day, it shall be the day of the ruling), the opinion of said person shall, notwithstanding the provision of said paragraph, be referred. The same shall, in the case of providing the postponement of tax payment or the postponement of conversion of property due to delinquency measures, also apply to the delinquency tax or the arrears pertaining to said postponement period.

3. The person who has power to collect may give the consent mentioned in paragraph 1.

4. For the period during which the postponement of tax payment or the postponement of conversion of property due to tax delinquency measures is effected pursuant to the provision of paragraph 1 or paragraph 2, the prescription shall not run.

Article 123 (Reorganisation security rights)

1. Reorganisation claims, or claims on property right against persons other than the company arising out of causes existent prior to the commencement of reorganisation proceedings, which fall within the scope secured by the special preferential right, pledge, hypothec, or the right of retention under the Commercial Code, subsisting on the assets of the company at the time of commencement of the reorganisation proceedings, shall be the reorganisation claims. Provided that, the claims for interests, or for compensation for damages or penalty money due to non-performance shall be limited to those having arisen until the expiration of one year after the commencement of reorganisation proceedings (if the ruling to approve the reorganisation plan up to said time, it shall be the time of said ruling).

2. The provision of the proviso to the preceding paragraph shall not apply to debentures.

3. The provisions of Article 108 through Article 112-2 shall apply mutatis mutandis to reorganisation security rights.

Article 124 (Rights of reorganisation secured creditors)

1. A reorganisation secured creditor may participate in the reorganisation proceedings with reorganisation security right held by him.

2. A reorganisation secured creditor may participate in the reorganisation proceedings as a reorganisation creditor with respect to the portion of the amount of his claims which exceeds the value of the subject-matter of the security right (if there exists security right of a prior rank, the value of the subject-matter of the security right minus the amount of claim secured by such security right; hereinafter the same in this Article).

3. A reorganisation secured creditor shall have the right to vote in proportion to the amount of the value of the subject-matter of the security right, and if the amount of the secured claim is less than the value of the subject-matter of the security right, in proportion to the amount of the secured claim. Provided that, the amounts of interest after the commencement of reorganisation proceedings as well as of compensation for damages and penalty money due to non-performance shall not be counted in computing the amount of the secured claim.

4. The provisions of Article 113 paragraph 2 and Article 114 through 118 shall apply mutatis mutandis to the right of vote of reorganisation secured creditors.

Article 124-2 (Value of subject-matter of security right pertaining to reorganisation security right)

The value of the subject-matter of security right pertaining to reorganisation security right shall be value at the time of the commencement of reorganisation proceedings appraised by deeming that the business of the company is continued.

Article 125 (Report of reorganisation claims)

1. A reorganisation creditor desiring to participate in the reorganisation proceedings shall, within the period designated by the Court, report to the Court his full name and address, the contents and causes of each of the claims, the amount as to the right to vote, and if the claim has general rights of priority or it is the claim mentioned in Article 121 paragraph 1 (hereinafter referred to as 'deferred claims'), the statement to that effect, and also shall submit to the Court evidential documents, or certified copies or extract copies thereof.

2. Of each claim, a certain portion of which has general priority rights or certain portion of which pertains to deferred claims, shall separately be reported.

3. In the case where an action is pending with respect to a reorganisation claim at the time of commencement of the reorganisation proceedings, the Court in which the action is pending, the parties thereto, and the title of the case and the case number shall also be reported, in addition to the particulars mentioned in paragraph 1.

4. If extinguishment of reorganisation claim or other change which does not injure the interest of another reorganisation creditor with respect to the matters which were reported has occurred, the reorganisation creditor or the receiver shall without delay report to the Court to that effect, and further shall submit the evidential documents or certified copies or extract copies thereof to the Court.

Article 126 (Report of reorganisation security rights)

1. A reorganisation secured creditor who intends to participate in the reorganisation proceedings shall, within the period designated by the Court, report to the Court his full name, address, the contents and causes of each of the reorganisation security rights, the subject-matter and value of the security rights, the amount as the right of vote, and if a person other than the company is the obligor, his full name and address, and also shall submit to the Court evidential documents, or certified copies or extract copies thereof.

2. The provisions of paragraph 3 and paragraph 4 of the preceding Article shall apply mutatis mutandis to reorganisation security rights.

Article 127 (Delayed filing of reports, etc.)

1. In the case where a reorganisation creditor or a reorganisation secured creditor was unable to file the report within the period designated by the Court due to causes for which he is not responsible, delayed filing of the report shall be permissible, only if it is done within one month of the time when the causes have ceased to exist. The provision of Article 158 paragraph 1 (Extension or shortening of period) of the Code of Civil Procedure shall not apply mutatis mutandis to such period.

2. With regard to reorganisation claims or reorganisation security rights which have arisen after expiration of the period for report, the report shall be filed within the peremptory period of one month after the rights have arisen.

3. The reports referred to in the preceding two paragraphs may not be filed after closing of the meeting of persons interested for examination of the draft plan or reorganisation.

4. The provisions of paragraph 1 and the preceding paragraph shall apply mutatis mutandis in the case where a reorganisation creditor or a reorganisation secured creditor makes such changes in the matters reported as will affect the interests of other reorganisation creditors or reorganisation secured creditors, due to causes for which he is not responsible.

Article 127-2 (Special exception for report of claim for retirement allowance)

1. The report of the claim for retirement allowance of an employee of the company shall be made after he retired.

2. If an employee of the company retired before the ruling to approve the reorganisation plan after the expiration of the period for report as determined by the Court, it shall be sufficient if the report of the claim for retirement is done within the peremptory period of one month after retirement.

3. The provisions of the preceding two paragraphs shall apply mutatis mutandis to the claim for retirement allowance of the director, representing director, or the auditor. In theses cases, 'retired' in the preceding paragraph shall be changed to read as 'retired or dismissed in accordance with the provision of Article 252 paragraph 3'.

Article 128 (Change of name of person reported)

1. Any person who has acquired reorganisation claims or reorganisation security rights which were reported, may change the name in which the report was filed, even after expiration of the period for report.

2. Any person who intends to have the reporter's name changed shall report to the Court his full name and address, the right he acquired, and the hour and day as well as causes of acquisition, and also shall submit evidential documents, or certified copies or extract copies thereof.

Article 129 (Rights of shareholders)

1. A shareholder may participate in the reorganisation proceedings with the shares held by him.

2. Shareholders shall have the right of vote in proportion to the number of shares held by them.

3. Shareholders shall not have the right of vote, in the case where there exist the facts comprising causes of bankruptcy with respect to the company.

Article 130 (Rights of shareholders)

1. The persons who can participate in the reorganisation proceedings as the shareholders possessing inscribed shares shall be determined by statement in the register of shareholders or the ledger of fractional shares.

2. The Court may, if necessary for determining the persons who can participate in the reorganisation proceedings in accordance with the provision of the preceding paragraph, order the company not to change the statement of the register of shareholders or not to issue the fractional share certificates by fixing the period of not exceeding two months.

3. The Court must make public notice of the period under the preceding paragraph before two weeks thereof.

Article 131 (Rights of shareholders)

The persons who possess uninscribed share certificates or fractional share certificates shall, for participating in the reorganisation proceedings, deposit the share certificates or fractional share certificates with the receiver, and report the full name and addresses thereof.

Article 131-2 (Permission of participation to shareholders)

1. The Court may, on application by the shareholders who are not stated in the register of shareholders or the ledger of fractional shares or by the shareholders who cannot deposit the share certificates or fractional share certificates under the provision of the preceding Article, permit said shareholders to participate in the reorganisation proceedings. In this case, with respect to the share certificates pertaining to said permission, persons other than those having obtained the permission cannot participate in the reorganisation proceedings as the shareholders, notwithstanding the provisions of the preceding two Articles.

2. The Court may, on application from the shareholders or of its own motion, change or cancel the determination under the provisions of the preceding two paragraphs.

3. An immediate complaint may be raised against the determination under the provisions of the preceding two paragraphs.

Article 132 (List of reorganisation creditors, or reorganisation secured creditors)

The clerk of the Court shall prepare the list of reorganisation creditors and the list of reorganisation secured creditors and enter therein the particulars mentioned below, classifying the rights in an appropriate manner according to their nature.

List of reorganisation creditors:

(1) The full names and addresses of reorganisation creditors;
(2) The contents and causes of reorganisation claims;
(3) The amount as to the right to vote;

(4) If it is a claim having a right of priority, or it is a deferred claim, a statement to that effect.

List of reorganisation secured creditors:

(1) The full names and addresses of reorganisation secured creditors;
(2) The contents and causes of reorganisation security rights, the subject-matter of security rights and the value thereof, and if persons other than the company are the obligors, their full names and addresses;
(3) The amount as to the right of vote.

Article 133 (Delivery of certified copy)

The clerk of the Court shall deliver to the receiver certified copies of the list of reorganisation creditors and the list of reorganisation secured creditors.

Article 134 (Keeping, etc. of documents of reports)

1. Documents relative to the reports of reorganisation claims and reorganisation security rights, as well as the list of reorganisation secured creditors shall be kept at the Court for inspection by persons interested.

2. The receiver shall, if requested by persons interested, have the documents concerning report of shares under the provision of Article 131 perused.

Article 135 (Date for investigation of reorganisation claims and reorganisation security rights)

At the date for investigation of reorganisation claims and reorganisation security rights, the particulars mentioned in Article 132 shall be investigated with respect to those reorganisation claims and reorganisation security rights which have been reported.

Article 136 (Appearance of persons concerned)

1. The representative of the company shall appear and state his opinion on the day for investigation of reorganisation claims and reorganisation security rights. Provided that, he may cause his agent to appear, if there exist just causes.

2. The reorganisation creditors and the reorganisation secured creditors who have filed the report, as well as the shareholders, and their agents may appear at the date of investigation mentioned in the preceding paragraph and raise objection with respect to other reorganisation claims or reorganisation security rights.

3. Agents shall submit a document which proves their authority.

Article 137 (Appearance of receiver)

The investigation of reorganisation claims and reorganisation security rights shall not be conducted unless the receiver appears.

Article 138 (Investigation of reorganisation claims, etc. reported after expiry of period)

1. Reorganisation claims and reorganisation security rights reported pursuant to the provision of Article 127 may be investigated on the day for general investigation of reorganisation claims and reorganisation security rights, only when reorganisation creditors, reorganisation secured creditors, and shareholders do not object thereto. The same shall also apply to other reorganisation claims and reorganisation security rights, of which the report has been filed after expiration of the period of report.

2. In the case where an objection has been raised by the persons mentioned in the preceding paragraph, the Court shall set a special day for investigation of the reorganisation claims and reorganisation security rights of which the reports have been filed pursuant to the provision of Article 127. In such cases, the costs shall be borne by the reorganisation creditors and reorganisation secured creditors.

Article 139 (Change in matters reported)

The provision of the preceding Article shall apply mutatis mutandis in the case where, with regard to the matters reported by reorganisation creditors or reorganisation secured creditors, any change has been made after expiration of the period for report which affects the interests of other reorganisation creditors or reorganisation secured creditors.

Article 140 (Investigation of reorganisation claims, etc. of which delayed report has been filed after date for general investigation)

The provision of Article 138 paragraph 2 shall apply mutatis mutandis in the case where any change has been made in particulars which reorganisation creditors or reorganisation secured creditors report, or have reported, pursuant to the provision of Article 127 after the date for general investigation of reorganisation claims and reorganisation security rights.

Article 141 (Special day for investigation of reorganisation claims and reorganisation security rights)

1. The ruling which sets a special day for investigation of reorganisation claims and reorganisation security rights shall be served upon the receiver, company, the reorganisation creditors and the reorganisation secured creditors who have filed the report, as well as upon the shareholders.

2. The service mentioned in the preceding paragraph may be made by mailing the documents by ordinary mail.

3. The provisions of Article 14 paragraphs 4 and 5 shall apply mutatis mutandis in the case mentioned in the preceding paragraph.

4. If the company has issued uninscribed share certificates or fractional share certificates, the Court shall make public notice of the date under paragraph 1. In this case, the provision of Article 15 paragraph 2 shall not apply.

Article 142 (Change of day; postponement and continuation of investigation)

The provision of the preceding Article shall apply mutatis mutandis to the change of the day for investigation of reorganisation claims and reorganisation security rights, and also to the postponement and continuation of the investigation of reorganisation claims and reorganisation security rights. Provided that, the service need not be made, if a pronouncement has been made.

Article 143 (Becoming final and conclusive of reorganisation claims and reorganisation security rights, etc.)

When no objection has been raised by the receiver, reorganisation creditors, reorganisation secured creditors, and shareholders at the date of investigation of reorganisation claims and reorganisation security rights, the contents of reorganisation claims and reorganisation security rights, the amount as to the right to vote, and as to the claims having priority right or the deferred claims, that they have priority or are deferred, shall become final and conclusive.

Article 143-2 (Investigation of claims for retirement allowance and special exception for determination)

1. The Court shall, in the case where the report under the provision of Article 127-2 paragraph 2 (including the case of applying mutatis mutandis in paragraph 3 of said Article) was made, immediately notice, without effecting the investigation under the provision of Articles 135 through 142 with respect to the claims for retirement allowance thus reported, the receiver and the company to the effect that such report has been made. The same shall also apply in the case where any change which would prejudice the interests of another reorganisation creditor or reorganisation secured creditor in respect of the matters thus reported.

2. The provision of the preceding Article shall apply mutatis mutandis in the case where no objection has, within three days from the day on which the notice of the preceding paragraph was made, been raised by the receiver.

Article 144 (Entry in lists of reorganisation creditors and of reorganisation secured creditors)

1. The Court shall enter the results of investigation of reorganisation claims and reorganisation security rights in the list of reorganisation creditors and in the list of reorganisation secured creditors. The same shall also apply to the objections raised by the company.

2. The clerk of the Court shall enter in the deed of any reorganisation claim or reorganisation security right which has become final and conclusive, a statement that it has become final and conclusive, and affix the seal of the Court thereto.

Article 145 (Effect of entry)

With regard to those reorganisation claims and reorganisation security rights which have become final and conclusive, the entries in the list of reorganisation creditors and the list of reorganisation secured creditors shall have the same effect as a judgment which has become conclusive, as against all of the reorganisation creditors, reorganisation secured creditors, and shareholders.

Article 146 (Notice of objection)

If, in the case where reorganisation creditors or reorganisation secured creditors do not appear at the date of investigation of reorganisation claims and reorganisation security rights, an objection has been raised respecting their rights, the Court shall give notice thereof to the holder of right. The same shall also apply in the case where an objection has, with respect to the claims for retirement allowance of Article 143-2 paragraph 1, been raised within three days from the day on which the notice under the provision of said paragraph was made.

Article 147 (Action for confirmation of reorganisation claims or reorganisation security rights)

1. With regard to reorganisation claims or reorganisation security rights, of which objections (exclusive of those raised by the company) have been raised, the holder of

such claims or security rights may, through instituting an action, seek confirmation of the right in question as against the person who raised the objection.

2. The action mentioned in the preceding paragraph shall be instituted within one month from the day on which the investigation (in the case of the latter clause of the preceding Article, it shall be the notice under the provision of the latter clause of said Article) was made on the right.

3. In the case where there are several persons who raised objection, they shall be co-defendants.

4. The Court shall, upon demand by the reorganisation creditor or reorganisation secured creditor, deliver an extract copy of the list of reorganisation creditors or of reorganisation secured creditors relative to the rights in question.

Article 148 (Jurisdiction of action for confirmation of reorganisation claims or reorganisation security rights)

The reorganisation Court shall have exclusive jurisdiction of the action for confirmation of reorganisation claims or reorganisation security rights.

Article 149 (Taking over of action on reorganisation claim or reorganisation security right of which objection was raised)

1. If, in the case where an action is pending, at the time of commencement of the reorganisation proceedings, with regard to the reorganisation claim or reorganisation security right mentioned in Article 147 paragraph 1, a reorganisation creditor or reorganisation secured creditor intends to seek confirmation of his right, he shall take over the action as against the person who raised the objection.

2. The provisions of Article 147 paragraphs 2 and 4 shall apply mutatis mutandis to the case mentioned in the preceding paragraph.

Article 150 (Causes of action limited)

A reorganisation creditor or reorganisation secured creditor may institute the action for confirmation of his right, or take over the action pursuant to the provision of the preceding Article, only with respect to the matters entered in the list of reorganisation creditors or the list of reorganisation secured creditors pursuant to the provision of Article 144 paragraph 1.

Article 151 (Objection raised solely by reorganisation creditor, etc.)

1. Of the reorganisation claims or reorganisation security rights mentioned in article 147 paragraph 1, with regard to those of which objection is raised solely by a reorganisation creditor, reorganisation secured creditor, or shareholder, the objecting person may raise his objection only through instituting an action.

2. The provisions of Article 147 paragraphs 2 and 4 and of Article 148 through the preceding Article shall apply mutatis mutandis to the case mentioned in the preceding paragraph.

Article 152 (Objections against claims with title, etc.)

1. Of the reorganisation claims or reorganisation security rights mentioned in Article 147 paragraph 1, with regard to those of which there exists executable title of

obligation or a final judgment, the objecting person may raise his objection only through judicial proceedings which can be prosecuted by the company.

2. The provisions of Article 147 paragraphs 2 through 4 and of Articles 149 and 150 shall apply mutatis mutandis to the case mentioned in the preceding paragraph.

Article 153 (Entry of results of action for confirmation of reorganisation claims or reorganisation security rights)

The Court shall, upon application of the receiver, a reorganisation creditor, reorganisation secured creditor, or a shareholder, enter in the list of reorganisation creditors or the list reorganisation secured creditors the results of the action for confirmation of a reorganisation claim or reorganisation security right.

Article 154 (Effect of judgment on action for confirmation of reorganisation claims or reorganisation security rights)

A judgment given in the action for confirmation of a reorganisation claim or reorganisation security right shall be effective as against all of the reorganisation creditors, reorganisation secured creditors, and the shareholders.

Article 155 (Reimbursement of costs of litigation)

In the case where the assets of the company have been benefit through the action for confirmation of a reorganisation claim or reorganisation security right, the reorganisation creditor, reorganisation secured creditor, or the shareholder who raised the objection may demand, as a holder of claims for the common benefits, reimbursement of the costs of litigation to the extent of the benefits so received.

Article 156 (Value of subject-matter of action for confirmation of reorganisation claims or reorganisation security rights)

The value of the subject-matter of the action for confirmation of reorganisation claims or reorganisation security rights shall be determined by the reorganisation Court, taking as the standard the estimated amount of benefits to be received under the reorganisation plan.

Article 157 (Report of fines, taxes, etc.)

1. With regard to the claims mentioned in Article 121 paragraph 1 item (5) and Article 122 paragraph 1, the State or the public body concerned shall report to the Court without delay the amount and causes of such claims as well as the contents of security rights.

2. The provision of Article 144 paragraph 1 shall apply mutatis mutandis to the claims which have been reported pursuant to the provision of the preceding paragraph.

Article 158 (Case where filing of complaint is permissible)

1. If the cause of the claims reported pursuant to the provision of paragraph 1 of the preceding Article is a demand for investigation, litigation, or other measures of which filing of complaint is permissible, the receiver may file a complaint in such manner as the company is permitted to do so.

2. The provisions of Article 149, Article 153 and Article 154 shall apply mutatis mutandis to the filing of complaint mentioned in the preceding paragraph.

Article 159 (Classification of reorganisation creditors, etc.)

1. The reorganisation creditors, reorganisation secured creditors, and the shareholders shall be classified into groups as set forth below for preparing and adopting resolution on the draft plan of reorganisation. Provided that, this shall not apply to the person who possess the claims mentioned in Article 121 paragraph 1 item (5) and Article 122 paragraph 1:

(1) Reorganisation secured creditors;
(2) Reorganisation creditors possessing claims of which have the general preferential right or other general priority rights;
(3) Reorganisation creditors other than the reorganisation creditors mentioned in the preceding item and next item;
(4) Reorganisation creditors possessing deferred claims;
(5) Shareholders holding shares of a type having preferential contents with regard to distribution of the surplus assets;
(6) Shareholders other than the shareholders mentioned under the preceding item.

2. The Court may, taking into consideration the nature of rights held by the persons mentioned under each of the items in the preceding paragraph as well as the relationship of their interests, effect classification, either by forming a single group with persons coming under two or more groups or by forming two or more groups with persons coming under a single group. Provided that, reorganisation creditors, reorganisation secured creditors and shareholders shall respectively form a separate group.

3. The receiver, company, the reorganisation creditors and the reorganisation secured creditors who have filed the report, as well as the shareholders may state their opinions on the classification made pursuant to the preceding paragraph.

4. The Court may at any time make alteration in the classification until resolution is adopted on the draft plan of reorganisation.

5. The provisions of Article 141 paragraphs 1 through 3 shall apply mutatis mutandis to the service of the ruling granted pursuant to the provisions of paragraph 2 or the preceding paragraph. Provided that, the service may be dispensed with, in the case where a pronouncement has been made at the meeting of persons interested or at the date for investigation of reorganisation claims and reorganisation security rights.

Article 160 (Agent commissioners)

1. Reorganisation creditors, reorganisation secured creditors, or shareholders may, with permission of the Court, either conjointly or separately, appoint one or several agent commissioners.

2. The authority of agent commissioners shall be proved in writing.

3. Agent commissioner shall be able to do any and all acts relative to the reorganisation proceedings on behalf of the reorganisation creditors, reorganisation secured creditors, or shareholders who have appointed him.

4. In the case where there are two or more agent commissioners, they shall exercise their power conjointly. Provided that, manifestation of intention by a third party shall be sufficient if made to one of them.

5. If the exercise by an agent commissioner of his power is considered exceedingly improper and unjust, the Court may cancel the permission granted under paragraph 1.

6. If reorganisation creditors, reorganisation secured creditors, or shareholders have removed agent commissioners, they shall file with the Court a report to that effect without delay.

Article 161 (Deleted in 1991)

Article 161-2 (Demand for extinction of retention right under the Commercial Code)

1. The receiver may demand a person having the retention right under the Commercial Code on the company's property at the time of commencement of the reorganisation proceedings, to extinguish the retention right by depositing with competent authority the amount of claims which are secured by retention right, or the money, if such amount of claims exceeds the value of the subject-matter of the retention right, equivalent to the value of the subject-matter.

2. If the retention right is extinguishing by virtue of the provision of the preceding paragraph, the person having had said retention right shall have the same right as the pledgee on the deposit money under said paragraph.

Article 162 (Setoff)

1. If, in the case where a reorganisation creditor or reorganisation secured creditor owes obligation to the company at the time of commencement of the reorganisation proceedings, his claim and the obligation have both become fit for setoff prior to the expiration of the period for report of reorganisation claims and reorganisation security rights, the reorganisation creditor or reorganisation secured creditor may effect setoff, otherwise than through the reorganisation proceedings, only within said period. The same shall also apply in the case where the obligation is subject to a time limit.

2. The setoff under the provision of the preceding paragraph may, with regard to the rent obligation of the reorganisation creditor or reorganisation secured creditor accruing after commencement of the reorganisation proceedings, be effected only for the rent in the current term or next ensuing term. Provided that, in the case where caution-money has been deposited, the setoff may be effected with respect to the rent obligation accruing subsequent thereto.

3. The provision of the preceding paragraph shall apply mutatis mutandis to land rent and farm rent.

Article 163 (Prohibition of setoff)

Setoff shall not be effected in any of the following cases:

(1) Where a reorganisation creditor or reorganisation secured creditor has assumed obligation against the company after commencement of the reorganisation proceedings;
(2) Where a reorganisation creditor or reorganisation secured creditor has assumed obligation against the company with knowledge of there having been suspension of payment, petition for bankruptcy, application for commencement of composition, commencement of reorganisation proceedings, commencement of arrangement, or commencement of special

liquidation. Provided that, this shall not apply if the assuming is based on a legal cause, on a cause which occurred before the reorganisation creditor or reorganisation secured creditor has come to know that there has been suspension of payment or petition for bankruptcy, application for commencement of composition, commencement of reorganisation proceedings, commencement of arrangement, or commencement of special liquidation, or on a cause which occurred before one year or more before the time of any of bankruptcy adjudication, commencement of composition, commencement of reorganisation proceedings, commencement of arrangement, or commencement of special liquidation;

(3) Where an obligor of the company has acquired other person's reorganisation claim or reorganisation security right after commencement of the reorganisation proceedings;

(4) Where a company obligor has acquired a reorganisation claim or reorganisation security right with knowledge of there having been suspension of payment or petition for bankruptcy, application for commencement of composition, commencement of reorganisation proceedings, commencement of arrangement, or commencement of special liquidation. Provided that, this shall not apply in the case where the acquisition is based on the causes provided for in laws, on the causes which arose prior to the time when the obligor has become aware of suspension of payment or petition for bankruptcy, application for commencement of composition, commencement of reorganisation proceedings, commencement of arrangement, or commencement of special liquidation, or on the causes which arose one year or more prior to the time of any of bankruptcy adjudication, commencement of composition, commencement of reorganisation proceedings, commencement of arrangement, or commencement of special liquidation.

Chapter V: Meeting of interested persons

Article 164 (Summons to meeting)

1. On the day of the meeting of interested persons, the receiver, company, the reorganisation creditors and the reorganisation secured creditors who have filed the report, the shareholders, as well as the persons who assume obligations or furnish securities for the purpose of reorganisations, if any, shall be summoned.

2. Notwithstanding the provision of the preceding paragraph, the reorganisation creditors, reorganisation secured creditors, and the shareholders who cannot exercise the right of vote may not be summoned. As for the first meeting or interested persons, the same shall apply to the persons who have been served upon pursuant to the provision of Article 47 paragraph 2.

Article 165 (Notice of meeting)

The date of the meeting of interested persons shall be noticed to the administrative government agency which supervises the business of the company, the Minister of Justice, and the Minister of Finance.

Article 166 (Command by Court)

The meeting of the interested persons shall be subject to command of the Court.

Article 167 (Public notice of date and object of meeting)

1. The Court shall give public notice of the date of the meeting of interested persons, as well as the matters forming the object of the meeting.

2. In the case where there has been a pronouncement on postponement or continuation of the meeting of interested persons, a service or public notice thereof may be dispensed with.

Article 168 (Consolidation of dates of meetings)

If deemed reasonable, the Court may, upon the application of the receiver or of its own motion, consolidate the date of the meeting of interested persons and that of investigation of reorganisation claims and reorganisation security rights.

Article 169 (Objection to right of vote)

The receiver, the reorganisation creditors, and the reorganisation secured creditors who have filed the report, as well as the shareholders may raise objection to the right of vote of reorganisation creditors, reorganisation secured creditors, and the shareholders. Provided that, this shall not apply to the right to vote of those reorganisation creditors and reorganisation secured creditors who possess those reorganisation claims and reorganisation security rights which have become final and conclusive under the investigation procedure provided for in the preceding chapter.

Article 170 (Exercise of right to vote)

1. The reorganisation creditors, reorganisation secured creditors, and the shareholders, who hold reorganisation claims and reorganisation security rights which have become final and conclusive as well as the rights to vote to which no objection has been raised, may exercise their rights to vote in proportion to the amount which has become final and conclusive or to the amount or number which has been reported.

2. With regard to the rights to which objection has been raised, the Court shall rule as to whether or not to permit the exercise of the right to vote and also as to for what amount or number the right to vote is to be exercised.

3. The Court may, upon the application of persons interested or its own motion, alter at any time the ruling granted pursuant to the provision of the preceding paragraph.

4. The ruling granted pursuant to the provisions of the preceding two paragraphs need not be served if its pronouncement has been made.

Article 171 (Exclusion of improper voters)

1. If, viewed in the light of the time of acquisition of the right, the value paid, and other reorganisation circumstances, it is found that a reorganisation creditor, reorganisation secured creditor or a shareholder possessing the right to vote has acquired the right for the purpose of receiving unjust benefits, such as taking a bribe, in connection with resolutions to be adopted at the meeting of persons interested, the Court may prevent these persons from exercising their right to vote.

2. The Court shall, before making disposition under the preceding paragraph, examine the said person entitled to vote.

Article 172 (Persons incapable of exercising right of vote)

Besides those persons who cannot exercise the right to vote in accordance with the provisions of the preceding two Articles, the following persons shall not exercise the right to vote:

(1) Persons whose rights are not affected by the plan of reorganisation;
(2) Persons holding the claims mentioned in Article 121 paragraph 1 item (5) and Article 122 paragraph 1;
(3) Persons whose protection is provided for by virtue of the provision of Article 234 paragraph 2.

Article 173 (Exercise by proxy of right to vote)

The reorganisation creditors, reorganisation secured creditors, and shareholders may exercise their rights to vote by proxy. In such cases, the proxy shall submit a document certifying his authority.

Chapter VI: Proceedings after commencement of reorganisation proceedings

Article 174 (Management of business and assets of company)

The receiver shall, upon assuming his office, immediately proceed to manage the business and assets of the company.

Article 175 (Management of mails)

1. The Court may request the government agency or other persons in charge of affairs of communication to deliver to the receiver mails and telegrams addressed to the company.

2. The receiver may open and inspect the mails and telegrams mentioned in the preceding paragraph which he has received.

3. The company may demand inspection of the mails and telegrams mentioned in the preceding paragraph, and also demand surrender of those which do not concern the assets of the company.

Article 176 (Management of mails)

1. The Court may, upon application of the company or of its own motion, cancel or change the request mentioned in paragraph 1 of the preceding Article, upon referring to the opinion of the receiver.

2. Upon termination of the reorganisation proceedings, the Court shall cancel the request mentioned in paragraph 1 of the preceding Article. The same shall also apply if the rights of managing the business of the company, as well as of administering and disposing the assets were granted to the director in accordance with the provisions of Article 211 paragraph 3 or Article 248-2 paragraph 1.

Article 177 (Appraisal of value of assets)

1. The receiver shall, without delay after commencement of the reorganisation proceedings, appraise the value as at the time of commencement of the proceedings of all

assets of the company in the presence of a clerk of the Court, bailiff or a notary public. In such cases, the company shall be requested to be present, except in the case where there is likelihood of delay.

2. The appraisal under the provision of the preceding paragraph shall be done on the assumption that the business of the company is continued.

Article 178 (Preparation of inventory and balance sheet)

1. The receiver shall, immediately after completing the appraisal under the provision of the preceding Article, prepare the inventory and the balance sheet as at the time of commencement of the proceedings.

2. The Court may, if it recognises to be necessary before completion of the appraisal under the provision of the preceding paragraph, order the receiver to prepare the inventory and the balance sheet as at the time of commencement of the reorganisation proceedings by attaching the value under the provisions of Article 34 item (2), Article 285-2, and Article 285-4 through Article 285-7 (Value of assets) of the Commercial Code with respect to the assets whose appraisal has not yet been completed.

3. The receiver shall sign his name and affix his seal to certified copies of the inventory and the balance sheet mentioned in the preceding two paragraph, and submit them to the Court. Provided that name-writing and seal-impression may be substituted for signature and seal-impression.

Article 179 (Receiver's report of investigation)

The receiver shall, without delay after assuming his office, investigate and report to the Court the following matters:

(1) Circumstances which led to the commencement of reorganisation proceedings;
(2) Process and present state as to the business and assets of the company;
(3) Existence or non-existence of the circumstances which require the measures mentioned in Article 72;
(4) Any other matters necessary for the purpose of reorganisation.

Article 180 (Investigation of reorganisation creditors, etc.)

The receiver shall investigate and report to the Court the particulars mentioned in the following, within the period specified by the Court:

(1) The full names and addresses of the reorganisation creditors, the contents and causes of reorganisation claims, the amount as to the right to vote, and if the claims are those having priority rights or deferred claims, such facts;
(2) The full names and addresses of the reorganisation secured creditors, the contents and causes of reorganisation security rights, the subject-matter and value of security rights, the amount as to the right to vote, and if persons other than the company are obligors, their full names and addresses.

Article 181 (Reports, etc. to be made subsequent to above)

In addition to those provided for in the preceding four Article, the receiver shall, as prescribed by the Court, report to the Court the conditions of management of the business and assets of the company, and any other matters as ordered by the Court, and also prepare the inventory and the balance sheet as at the time of approval of the reorganisation plan and as at the time by the Court, and submit to the Court certified copies thereof.

Article 182 (Reports, etc. to be made subsequent to above)

1. With respect to the valuation of the assets to be stated in the inventory and the balance sheet of the preceding Article, the value appraised in accordance with the provision of Article 177 shall be deemed as the acquisition value, and the provisions of Article 34 item (2), Article 285-2, and Article 285-4 through Article 285-7 (Valuation of assets) of the Commercial Code shall apply mutatis mutandis.

2. With respect to the assets determined to be transferred in the draft plan of reorganisation or the reorganisation plan, the disposition price may be attached, notwithstanding the provision of the preceding paragraph. Provided that, the permission of the Court shall be obtained before determination of the approval of reorganisation plan.

3. In the case where the permission of the Court is granted for preparing the draft plan containing liquidation, the disposition prices shall, notwithstanding the provision of paragraph 1, be attached to all assets.

Article 183 (Keeping documents)

The documents submitted to the Court pursuant to the provisions of Article 178 through Article 181 shall be kept at the Court for inspection by the persons interested.

Article 184 (Suspension of business)

If, in the case where, with respect to a company which is continuing its business, there exist special circumstances making it unsuitable to continue the business, it is intended to suspend its business, the receiver shall obtain the permission of the Court.

Article 185 (Method of custody of assets, etc.)

The Court may make necessary directions as to the method of custody of money and other assets and also as receipt and disbursement of money.

Article 186 (Legal adviser)

If necessary, the receiver may appoint a legal adviser with permission of the Court.

Article 187 (First meeting of interested persons)

The receiver shall report to the first meeting of interested persons a summary of the particulars mentioned in Article 179 or Article 180.

Article 188 (First meeting of interested persons)

At the first meeting of interested persons, the Court shall hear the opinions of the receiver, company, the reorganisation creditors and reorganisation secured creditors who have filed the report, as well as the shareholders, on the appointment of the receiver and the management of business and assets of the company.

Article 189 (Preparation and filing of draft plan of reorganisation)

1. After expiration of the period for report of reorganisation claims and reorganisation security rights, the receiver shall, within the period specified by the Court, prepare a draft plan of reorganisation, and submit it to the Court.

2. The Court may, upon application or of its own motion, extend the period mentioned in the preceding paragraph.

3. In the case where the draft plan cannot be prepared, the receiver shall, within the periods prescribed in the preceding two paragraphs, file a report to that effect with the Court.

Article 190 (Preparation and filing of draft plan of reorganisation)

1. The company, the reorganisation creditors and the reorganisation secured creditors who have filed the report, as well as the shareholders may prepare a draft plan of reorganisation within the period specified by the Court, and submit it to the Court.

2. The provision of paragraph 2 of the preceding Article shall apply mutatis mutandis in the case mentioned in the preceding paragraph.

Article 191 (Draft plan whose contents are liquidation)

1. If it has become clear after commencement of the reorganisation proceedings that it is difficult to prepare a draft plan of reorganisation whose contents are to cause the company to continue to exist or to continue the business through amalgamation, formation of a new company, or transfer of business, the Court may, upon application of the person who is to prepare the draft plan, permit preparation of a draft plan whose contents are liquidation. Provided that, this shall not apply if it prejudices the general interests of the creditors.

2. The Court may cancel the permission mentioned in the preceding paragraph at any time until the draft plan is referred to a resolution.

3. The provision of Article 159 paragraph 3 shall apply mutatis mutandis to the permission under paragraph 1.

Article 192 (Meeting of interested persons for examination of draft plan of reorganisation)

When a draft plan of reorganisation has been submitted, the Court shall convene a meeting of interested persons for examination of the draft plan, designating the date thereof.

Article 193 (Meeting of interested persons for examination of draft plan of reorganisation)

At the meeting of interested persons mentioned in the preceding Article, the Court shall, after hearing explanation as to the draft plan from the person who submitted it, hear the opinions on the draft plan of the receiver, company, the reorganisation creditors who have filed the report, as well as the shareholders.

Article 194 (Opinion of supervising government office, etc.)

1. If deemed necessary, the Court may demand the administrative government agency having jurisdiction over the business of the company, the Minister of Justice,

the Minister of Finance, and other persons recognised adequate by the Court, to make statement of opinions on the draft plan of reorganisation.

2. With regard to a draft plan which specifies the matters requiring the permission, approval, licence, or other actions of an administrative government agency, the Court shall hear the opinion on such matters of the administrative government agency concerned.

3. The administrative government agency having jurisdiction over the business of the company, the Minister of Justice or the Minister of Finance may at any time present their opinions on the draft plan to the Court.

Article 195 (Opinion of labour union of company, etc.)

The Court shall, with respect to the draft plan of reorganisation, hear the opinion of the labour union if there is a labour union organised by the majority of employees of the company, or hear the opinions of the person representing the majority of employees of the company, if there is no labour union organised by the majority of employees of the company.

Article 196 (Amendments to draft plan of reorganisation)

The person who submitted a draft plan of reorganisation may, with permission of the Court, amend the draft plan until the date of the meeting of interested persons convened for examination of the draft plan.

Article 197 (Order for amendments to draft plan of reorganisation)

1. The Court may, upon the application of persons interested or of its own motion, order the persons who submitted the draft plan of reorganisation to amend the draft plan.

2. If the Court issued the order mentioned in the preceding paragraph, the person who submitted the draft plan shall amend the draft plan within the period specified by the Court.

Article 198 (Reconvention of meeting of interested persons)

1. In the case where the amendments have been made pursuant to the provision of the preceding Article after the date of the meeting of interested persons convened for examination of the draft plan of reorganisation, the Court may reconvene further meeting of interested persons for examination of the draft amendments, designating the date thereof.

2. The provision of Article 193 shall apply mutatis mutandis to the meeting of interested persons under the preceding paragraph.

Article 199 (Exclusion of draft plan of reorganisation)

If the draft plan of reorganisation is considered to contravene provisions of laws, or not to be a fair and equitable plan, or to be impossible of execution, the Court may not refer the draft plan to the meeting of interested persons for examination or resolution.

Article 200 (Meeting of interested persons for adopting resolution on draft plan)

1. If an order for amendments is not issued on a draft plan of reorganisation which has been examined by the meeting of interested persons pursuant to the provision of Article 192 or Article 198, the Court shall convene a meeting of interested persons for adopting a resolution on the draft plan, designating the date thereof.

2. In the case mentioned in the preceding paragraph, the Court shall serve in advance a copy of the draft plan or a summary thereof to the receiver, company, the reorganisation creditors and reorganisation secured creditors who have filed the report, shareholders, the persons who assume obligations or furnish securities for reorganisation, the administrative government agency which supervises the business of the company, the Minister of Justice, and the Minister of Finance. Provided that, this shall not apply creditors, and the shareholders who are ineligible for exercising the voting rights.

3. The provisions of Article 141 paragraphs 2 and 3 shall apply mutatis mutandis to the service under the preceding paragraph.

Article 201 (Appearance of persons who assume obligations for reorganisation)

1. The persons who assume obligations or furnish securities for the purposes of reorganisation shall appear and make statement to that effect at the date of paragraph 1 of the preceding Article. Provided that, if there exist justifiable reasons, they may cause their agents to appear.

2. The agents shall submit documents certifying their authority.

Article 202 (Change of draft plan of reorganisation)

The person who submitted a draft plan of reorganisation may, with permission of the Court, change the draft plan at the meeting of interested persons of Article 200 paragraph 1, only in the case where the change does not affect adversely the interests of the reorganisation creditors, reorganisation secured creditors, and the shareholders.

Article 203 (Time of resolution)

The draft plan of reorganisation shall not be referred for resolution, prior to the completion of investigation of general reorganisation claims or reorganisation security rights.

Article 204 (Method of resolution)

At the meeting of interested persons under Article 200 paragraph 1, the reorganisation creditors, reorganisation secured creditors and the shareholders shall adopt the resolution, divided into groups as classified pursuant to the provision of Article 159.

Article 205 (Requisites for resolution of approval)

In order to adopt the resolution approving the draft plan of reorganisation at the meeting of the interested persons, the consent shall be obtained, in the group of reorganisation creditors, from those who possess the right to vote corresponding to two-thirds or more of the total amount of the votes of reorganisation creditors who can exercise the vote; and in the group of reorganisation secured creditors, with regard to the draft plan which provides for the postponement of the time limit of reorganisation security rights, from those who possess the right to vote corresponding to three-fourths or more of the total amount of the votes of reorganisation secured creditors who can exercise the vote, with regard to the draft plan which provides for the reduction or exemption of reorganisation security rights or otherwise contains the provisions affecting the security rights in manners other than postponement of the time limit of reorganisation security rights, from those who possess the right to vote corresponding to four-fifths or more of the total amount of the votes of reorganisation secured creditors who can exercise the vote, and with regard to the draft plan as provided for in Article 191, from all the reorganisation secured creditors who can exercise the vote; and in the group of shareholders, from those who possess the right to vote corresponding to the majority of the total amount of the right to vote of shareholders who can exercise the vote.

Article 206 (Setting another day for continuation of meeting)

Even in the case where the resolution approving the draft plan of reorganisation has not been adopted at the meeting of the interested persons, if adjournment of the meeting to another day has been consented respectively by those, in the group of reorganisation creditors, who possess the right to vote corresponding to a majority of the total amount of votes of reorganisation creditors who can exercise the vote; by those, in the group of reorganisation secured creditors, who possess the right to vote corresponding to two-thirds or more of the total amount of the votes of reorganisation secured creditors who can exercise the vote; by those, in the group of shareholders, who possess the right to vote corresponding to one-third or more of the total amount of the votes of shareholders who can exercise the vote, the Court shall, upon application of the receiver, the company, or those reorganisation creditors, reorganisation secured creditors, or shareholders who can exercise the vote, or of its own motion, set another day for continuation of the meeting and pronounce it.

Article 207 (Time of resolution for approval)

1. The resolution approving the draft plan of reorganisation shall be adopted within two months of the first day of the meeting of interested persons mentioned in Article 200 paragraph 1.

2. If deemed necessary, the Court may, upon the application of the person who submitted the draft plan, or of its own motion, extend the period mentioned in the preceding paragraph. Provided that, the period so extended shall not exceed one month.

Article 208 (Claims for common benefits)

The following claims shall be the claims for common benefits:

(1) Costs of judicial proceedings defrayed for the common benefits of reorganisation creditors, reorganisation secured creditors, and shareholders;
(2) Costs of management and disposal of the assets of the company defrayed after commencement of the reorganisation proceedings;
(3) Costs required for execution of the plan of reorganisation. Provided that, those accruing after termination of the reorganisation proceedings shall be excluded;
(4) Remuneration, expenses, and reward payable under the provisions of Article 285 and Article 287;

(5) Claims arising out of borrowing of funds and other acts done after commencement of the reorganisation proceedings by the receiver or a director of the company on his authority in connection with the business and assets of the company;
(6) Claims which have arisen against the company because of the management of affairs without mandate (negotiorum gestio) or unjust enrichment after commencement of the reorganisation proceedings;
(7) Claims held by the other party in the case where the receiver performs obligation pursuant to the provision of Article 103 paragraph 1;
(8) Unavoidable expenses to be defrayed on behalf of the company, other than those mentioned in the preceding respective items.

Article 209 (Payment of claims for common benefits)

1. The claims for common benefits shall be paid from time to time, otherwise through the reorganisation proceedings.

2. The claims for common benefits shall be paid in preference to reorganisation claims and reorganisation security rights.

Article 210 (Method of payment in case of insufficiency of company assets)

If it has become clear that the assets of the company are insufficient to pay the total amount of the claims for common benefits, the claims for common benefits shall, notwithstanding the priority rights prescribed in laws and ordinances, be paid in proportion to the amounts of claims not yet paid. Provided that, this shall not preclude the effect of the retention right, special preferential right, pledge, and hypothec right, which subsists with respect to the claims for common benefits.

Article 210-2 (Suspension, etc. of compulsory execution based on claims for common benefits)

1. If, in the case where the compulsory execution or provisions attachment had been done to a property of the company based on the claims for common benefits, said compulsory execution or provisional attachment should seriously impede the reorganisation of the company and further the company is in possession of any property which could easily be converted into money, the Court may, on application of the receiver or ex officio, order suspension or cancellation of said compulsory execution or provisional attachment, by having or not having securities furnished.

2. The Court may change or cancel the ruling of suspension under the provision of the preceding paragraph.

3. The Court may, if it has become clear that the properties of the company are insufficient to pay the whole amount of the claims for common benefits, order to cancel the compulsory execution or provisional attachment under paragraph 1, on application of the receiver or ex officio.

4. Immediate complaint may be filed against the ruling under the provisions of the preceding three paragraphs.

Chapter VII: Terms of reorganisation plan

Article 211 (Terms of reorganisation plan)

1. The reorganisation plan shall stipulate the terms for modifying the rights of all or some of the reorganisation creditors, reorganisation secured creditors, or shareholders,

and the terms concerning payment of the claims for common benefits. The same shall also apply to the terms concerning the method of raising the funds for payment of the obligations, and concerning the purposes for which income in excess of the amount estimated in the plan is to be expended.

2. The plan may stipulate the terms concerning the assignment of business or of assets, contributions, or leasing-out of property, commissioning of operation of the enterprise, amendment of the articles of incorporation, change of directors, representing directors, or auditors, reduction of capital, issuance of new shares or of debentures, amalgamation, dissolution, or formation of a new company, and any other terms necessary for the purposes of reorganisation.

3. The plan may stipulate that the rights of managing the business of the company as well as of administering and disposing the properties thereof are granted to the director.

Article 212 (Rights of reorganisation creditors, etc.)

1. When modifying the rights of reorganisation creditors, reorganisation secured creditors, or shareholders, the right to be modified shall clearly be specified, and the contents of the right as they are after the modification shall be stipulated.

2. If there are reorganisation creditors, reorganisation secured creditors, or shareholders whose rights are not affected by the reorganisation plan, the rights of such persons shall clearly be specified.

Article 213 (Due date of obligations)

If the obligations are assumed or the due date of obligations is postponed under the reorganisation plan, the period for maturity of such obligations shall not exceed the durable period of the subject-matter of security if there exists security, and twenty years if there is no security or if the durable period of the subject-matter of security can not be determined.

Article 214 (Furnishing of securities and assumption of obligations)

1. If the company or any person other than the company furnishes securities for the purpose of reorganisation, the person furnishing securities shall clearly be specified and the contents of such security rights shall be stipulated.

2. If any person other than the company takes over obligations, or is such person assumes obligations through becoming a guarantor or otherwise for the purpose of reorganisation, such person shall clearly be specified and the contents of such obligations shall be stipulated.

Article 215 (Reorganisation claims, etc. not yet final and conclusive)

If there exist reorganisation claims or reorganisation security rights to which objection has been raised and of which the procedure for their becoming final and conclusive has not yet been settled, the possibility of becoming final and conclusive of such rights shall be considered, and appropriate and proper measures therefor shall be determined upon.

Article 215-2 (Reorganisation claims, etc. already paid)

With respect to the reorganisation claims and the reorganisation security rights, those which have been already paid by obtaining the permission of the Court in accordance with the provision of Article 112-2 paragraph 1 or 4 (including the case applied mutatis mutandis in Article 123 paragraph 3) shall be clearly stated.

Article 216 (Claims for common benefits)

As regards the claims for common benefits, those which have already been paid shall clearly be indicated, and there shall be reasonable stipulations as to those to be paid in the future.

Article 217 (Assignment of business or assets, etc.)

If the whole or a part of the business or assets of the company is to be assigned; contributions are to be made; properties are to be leased out; the whole or a part of operation of the company's enterprise is to be commissioned; a contract whereunder profits and losses of the business are shared with another person or any other contract similar thereto is to be concluded, modified, or cancelled; or the assignment of the whole or a part of another person's business or assets is to be taken, there shall be the stipulations as to the subject-matter, the value thereof, the other party, and other particulars, and if the value is to be distributed among reorganisation creditors, reorganisation secured creditors, or shareholders, the stipulations shall be made of the method of such distribution.

Article 218 (Right in dispute)

If there exists a right pertaining to the company of which a controversy is not yet settled, there shall be the stipulations for compromise or conciliation thereof, or for prosecution of an action by the receiver or other secure methods of exercising such right.

Article 219 (Change of articles of incorporation)

If changes are to be made in the articles of incorporation of the company, the contents of such changes shall be specified.

Article 220 (Change of directors, etc.)

1. If directors or auditors of the company are to be appointed, or representing directors of the company are to be elected, either the person to be appointed or elected and the term of office, or the method of appointment or election and the term of office shall be specified.

2. If any of the directors, representing directors, of auditors of the company is to remain in office, such person and his term of office shall be specified.

3. In the cases provided for in the preceding two paragraphs, if two or more representing directors are to represent the company jointly, there shall be stipulations to that effect.

4. The terms of office mentioned in paragraph 1 and paragraph 2 shall not exceed one year.

Article 221 (Reduction of capital)

If the capital of the company is to be reduced, the following particulars shall be specified:

(1) The amount of capital to be reduced;

(2) Method of reduction of capital.

Article 222 (Issuance of new shares)

1. If the company is to issue new shares without causing reorganisation creditors, reorganisation secured creditors, or shareholders to pay in or to effect contributions in kind anew, the following particulars shall be specified:

(1) The distinction as to whether the new shares have par value or not, as well as the types and number thereof;
(2) Matters relating to the allotment of new shares;
(3) The amount of capital and reserve funds to be increased through issuance of new shares.

2. If the company is to issue new shares through causing reorganisation creditors, reorganisation secured creditors, or shareholders to pay in or to effect contribution in kind anew, the following particulars shall be specified:

(1) The particulars mentioned under items (1) and (3) of the preceding paragraph;
(2) The amount to be paid in and other matters relative to the allotment of new shares and the date or payment on new shares (this date shall fall on a day subsequent to the expiration of three months or more after the date of ruling approving the reorganisation plan);
(3) If there are persons who effect contribution in kind anew, such persons, properties forming the subject-matter of contribution, the value thereof, as well as the distinction as to whether the shares allotted against contribution have par value or not, as well as the type and number of such shares.

3. Except in the cases mentioned in the preceding two paragraphs, the following particulars shall be specified, when the company is to issue new shares:

(1) The particulars mentioned in paragraph 1 item (1);
(2) The particulars mentioned under item (3) of the preceding paragraph;
(3) The value at which new shares are issued, and the date of payment on such shares (this date shall fall on a day subsequent to the expiration of three months or more after the date of ruling approving the reorganisation plan);
(4) The amount not credited to the capital out of the value at which new shares are issued.

Article 223 (Issuance of debentures)

If the company is to issue debentures, the following particulars shall be specified:

(1) The total amount of debentures;
(2) The amount of each debenture, the rate of interest payable on the debentures, the method and time of redemption of debentures and of payment of interest, and other contents of debentures;
(3) The method of issuing debentures; and, if debentures are to be issued, causing or without causing reorganisation creditors, reorganisation secured creditors, or shareholders to pay in anew, the particulars of allotment thereof;

(4) If the debentures are secured debentures, the contents of the securities.

Article 224 (Amalgamation by absorption)

If the company is to amalgamate with another company and one of them continues to exist after amalgamation, the following particulars shall be specified:

(1) The corporate name of the other company;
(2) If the company which continues to exist is to increase, in consequence of amalgamation, the total number of shares to be issued, the distinction as to whether the shares to be increased have par value or not, the type and number of such shares:
(3) The distinction as to whether the shares to be issued to reorganisation creditors, reorganisation secured creditors, or shareholders of the company which is to cease to exist in consequence of amalgamation have par value or not, the types and number of such shares, as well as particulars relative to allotment thereof;
(4) The amount of capital and the matters concerning reserves to be increased on the part of the company which continues to exist;
(5) If it is stipulated that money is to be paid, or debentures are to be allotted to shareholders of the company which is to cease to exist in consequence of amalgamation, such stipulations;
(6) The hour and day of the other company's general meeting of shareholders to be convened for adopting a resolution approving the agreement of amalgamation;
(7) If the time of amalgamation is specified, the stipulation thereof.

Article 225 (Amalgamation whereby new company comes into existence)

If the company is to amalgamate with another company and a new company is thereby to come into existence, the following particulars shall be specified:

(1) The corporate name of the other company;
(2) The corporate name, the object, the location of the head office and branch offices, and the manner in which public notices are given, of a new company;
(3) The distinction as to whether the shares to be issued by the new company have par value or not, as well as the types and number of such shares;
(4) Deleted;
(5) The distinction as to whether the shares to be issued to reorganisation creditors, reorganisation secured creditors, or to shareholders of each company have par value or not, as well as the types and number of such shares, and the particulars as the allotment thereof;
(6) The amount of capital and the matters concerning reserves of the new company;
(7) If it is stipulated that money is to be paid, or debentures are to be allotted to shareholders of each company, such stipulations;
(8) The particulars mentioned under items (6) and (7) of the preceding Article.

Article 226 (Formation of new company)

1. If a new company is to be formed by causing reorganisation creditors, reorganisation secured creditors, or shareholders to subscribe to shares, without their being re-

quired to pay in or to effect contribution in kind anew, the following particulars shall be specified:

(1) The corporate name, the object, the location of the head office and branch offices, and the manner in which public notices are given, of the new company;
(2) The total number of shares to be issued by the new company;
(3) The amount of each share, if shares having par value are to be issued;
(4) Deleted;
(5) The distinction as to whether the shares to be issued to reorganisation creditors, reorganisation secured creditors, or shareholders have par value or not, as well as the types and number of such shares, and the particulars as to allotment thereof;
(6) Any other matters to be stated in the articles of incorporation of the new company;
(7) The amounts of capital and reserve funds of the new company;
(8) Properties to be transferred from the company to the new company, and the value thereof;
(9) Persons who are to be directors, representing directors, and auditors of the new company, as well as the method of appointing or electing them, and the term of office (provided that the term shall not exceed one year);
(10) If the new company is to issue debentures, the particulars mentioned in Article 223.

2. Except in the case as provided for in the preceding paragraph, if a new company is to be formed otherwise that through amalgamation, the following particulars shall be specified:

(1) The particulars mentioned under items (1) through (3), item (6), and items (8) through (10) of the preceding paragraph;
(2) The distinction as to whether the shares to be issued upon formation of the new company have par value or not; the types and number of such shares, the value at which they are issued and the amount not credited to the capital out of such value; and, if shares are to be subscribed to by reorganisation creditors, reorganisation secured creditors, or shareholders by causing or not causing them to pay in or to effect contribution in kind anew, particulars mentioned under item (5) of the preceding paragraph;
(3) If there exist persons who effect contribution in kind anew, such persons, properties forming the subject-matter of contribution, the value thereof, and the distinction as to whether shares allotted against contribution have par value or not, as well as the types and number of such shares.

Article 227 (Dissolution)

If the company is to dissolve otherwise than through amalgamation, there shall be stipulations to that effect, and the time of dissolution shall also be specified.

Article 228 (Differentiation in terms and conditions)

1. The reorganisation plan shall establish fair and equitable gradation in its terms and conditions, taking into consideration the rank of priority of the following rights:

(1) Reorganisation security rights;
(2) Reorganisation claims having the general preferential rights and other general priority rights;
(3) Reorganisation claims other than those mentioned under the preceding item and the next item;
(4) Deferred reorganisation claims;
(5) Rights of shareholders of the type having preferential contents with respect to the distribution of surplus assets;
(6) Rights of shareholders other than those mentioned under the preceding item.

2. The provision of the preceding paragraph shall not apply to the claims mentioned in Article 121 paragraph 1 item (5) and Article 122 paragraph 1.

Article 229 (Principle of equality)

The terms and conditions of the reorganisation plan shall be equal as among the persons who possess the right of the same nature. Provided that, with regard to reorganisation creditors and reorganisation secured creditors, this shall not apply in the case where equity is not impaired even if special stipulations be made in respect of those claims of which the amount is small, and if discriminative stipulations be otherwise made among such persons.

Article 230 (Stipulations as to appointment, etc. of directors, etc.)

The stipulations in the reorganisation plan concerning appointment, election, or remaining in office of directors, representing directors, or auditors of the company or of the new company (exclusive of the new company which is formed by way of amalgamation), or the manner in which they are appointed or elected, shall be equitable and in accord with the general interests of reorganisation creditors, reorganisation security holders, and shareholders.

Article 231 (Voidance of giving of special benefits)

Any act which the company or a third person, being not subject to the terms and conditions of the reorganisation plan, gives special benefits to certain reorganisation creditors, reorganisation secured creditors, or shareholders shall be void.

Chapter VIII: Approval or disapproval and execution of reorganisation plan

Article 232 (Approval or disapproval of reorganisation plan)

1. If the resolution approving the reorganisation plan has been adopted at the meeting of interested persons, the Court shall rule as to whether or not it approves the plan, either on the day of the meeting or on another day which it has set immediately.

2. The persons mentioned in Articles 164 and 165 may state their opinions on whether the plan is to be approved or not.

3. Public notice of the ruling which sets the day on which the plan is to be approved or disapproved need not be given nor be served, if there has been a pronouncement thereof.

Article 233 (Requisites for approval of reorganisation plan)

1. The Court may grant the ruling approving the reorganisation plan, only in the case where the following requisites are met:

(1) The reorganisation proceedings or the plan are in accord with the provisions of laws;
(2) That the plan is fair, equitable, and feasible;
(3) That the resolution has been adopted in honest and just manner;
(4) With regard to the plan, the contents of which is amalgamation, that the resolution has been adopted for approval of the agreement of amalgamation at the general meeting of shareholders of the other company;
(5) With regard to the plan which stipulates the matters requiring permission, approval, licence, and other actions of an administrative government agency, that it does not contravene in important aspects the opinion of an administrative government agency under the provision of Article 194 paragraph 2.

2. Even in the case where the reorganisation proceedings are in contravention of the provisions of laws, if it is considered inappropriate not to approve the plan, taking into consideration the degree of such contravention, the present state of the company, and all the other circumstances of the case, the Court may grant the ruling for approval of the plan.

Article 234 (Approval in case there exists group dissenting)

1. Even in the case where, with respect to the draft plan of reorganisation, there are groups, of which it was impossible to obtain consent of the persons who possess the right to vote exceeding the amount or number as prescribed by laws at the meeting of interested persons, the Court may grant the ruling for approval of the plan, through modifying the draft plan and stipulating in favour of the reorganisation creditors, reorganisation secured creditors, or shareholders of the group the terms which protect the rights of such persons through resorting to any of the following methods:

(1) With regard to reorganisation secured creditors, to transfer to the new company, to assign to others or to preserve in the company, the properties forming the subject-matter of security rights, allowing the holders' rights to subsist as they are;
(2) To sell the properties forming the subject-matter of the right with respect to the reorganisation secured creditors, to sell the properties of the company to be appropriated to payment of claims with respect to reorganisation creditors, or to sell the properties of the company to be appropriated to distribution of the surplus assets with respect to the shareholders, at a price not less than the fair price set by the Court (with regard to the properties forming the subject-matter of the security right, the appraisal shall be made as if there were no encumbrance because of the right), and thus to make payment with, or to distribute or make deposit of, the balance of the proceeds of such sale after deducting therefrom the expenses of the sale;
(3) To pay a fair price set by the Court to the holder of the right;
(4) To give fair and equitable protection to the holder of the right in other ways similar to the preceding respective items.

2. If there exist groups, of which it is evident, with respect to the draft plan, that it is impossible to obtain, at the meeting of interested persons, the consent of persons who possess the right to vote exceeding the amount or number as prescribed by laws, the Court may, upon the application of the person who is to prepare the draft plan, permit the preparation fo the draft plan through stipulating in advance the terms which protect the rights by resorting to any of the methods mentioned in the preceding paragraph, on behalf of the reorganisation creditors, reorganisation secured creditors, or shareholders of the group.

3. If the application mentioned in the preceding paragraph has been filed, the Court shall consult the opinions of the applicant or of one or more of the holders of the rights of the group mentioned in said paragraph.

Article 235 (Pronouncement, etc. of ruling on approval or disapproval of reorganisation plan)

1. There shall be pronouncement of the ruling as to approval or disapproval of the reorganisation plan, and public notice shall be given of its principal text, the tenor or reasons thereof, and the plan or a summary thereof. Provided that the service thereof may be dispensed with.

2. The provision of Article 35 paragraph 1 shall apply mutatis mutandis in the case where the ruling mentioned in the preceding paragraph has been granted.

Article 236 (Time of becoming effective of reorganisation plan)

The organisation plan shall become effective from the time the ruling for approval thereof is granted.

Article 237 (Complaint)

1. Immediate complaint may be filed against the ruling approving or disapproving the reorganisation plan. Provided that this shall not apply to those reorganisation creditors or reorganisation secured creditors who failed to file the report.

2. In order that the reorganisation creditors, reorganisation secured creditors, or shareholders who have not possessed the right to vote may file the complaint mentioned in the preceding paragraph, prima facie proof shall be given that they are reorganisation creditors, reorganisation secured creditors, or shareholders.

3. The complaint mentioned in paragraph 1 shall not affect the execution of the plan. Provided that the Court with which the complaint has been filed or the reorganisation Court may, upon application, suspend the execution of the whole or a part of the plan or take any other necessary measures, with or without requiring to put up guaranty, until the ruling on the complaint is rendered, if the complaint appears legally justifiable, there is urgent necessity in order to avoid irreparable losses which are to be inflicted through execution of the plan, and the facts have been given prima facie proof.

4. The provisions of the preceding three paragraphs shall apply mutatis mutandis to the complaint under the provision of Article 419-2 (Special complaint) of the Code of Civil Procedure which is applied mutatis mutandis in Article 8 of this Law.

Article 238 (Case where ruling disapproving reorganisation plan has become final and conclusive)

The provisions of Article 282 and Article 283 shall apply mutatis mutandis in the case where the ruling disapproving the reorganisation plan has become final and conclusive.

Article 239 (Entries on list of reorganisation creditors, etc.)

If the ruling approving the reorganisation plan has become final and conclusive, the clerk of the Court shall enter the terms and conditions of the plan on the list of reorganisation creditors and the list of reorganisation secured creditors.

Article 240 (Scope of effect of reorganisation plan)

1. The reorganisation plan shall have its effect on behalf of, and against, the company, all the reorganisation creditors, reorganisation secured creditors, and shareholders, as well as the persons who assume obligations or furnish securities for the purpose of reorganisation, and the new company (exclusive of new companies which are formed in consequence of amalgamation).

2. The plan shall not affect the rights which reorganisation creditors or reorganisation secured creditors possess against the company's guarantor or any other persons who assume obligations conjointly with the company, nor shall it affect the securities which persons other than the company have furnished on behalf of reorganisation creditors or reorganisation secured creditors.

Article 241 (Exemption of liability, etc. for reorganisation claims, etc.)

If the ruling has been granted for approval of the reorganisation plan, except for the rights recognised in the stipulations of the plan or the provisions of this Law, the company shall be exempt from the liabilities for all the reorganisation claims and reorganisation security rights, and the security rights which subsisted on the shareholders' rights and the properties of the company shall be extinguished. Provided that this shall not apply to the claims for retirement allowance of the person who was director, representing director, auditor or an employee of the company after commencement of the reorganisation proceedings and was continuously in the post of director, representing director, auditor, or an employee of the company after the ruling of approving the reorganisation plan, and to the claims mentioned under Article 121 paragraph 1 item (5) and item (6).

Article 242 (Rights modified)

1. If the ruling has been granted for approval of the reorganisation plan, the rights of reorganisation creditors, reorganisation secured creditors, and shareholders shall be modified in accordance with the provisions of the plan.

2. The provisions of Article 208 (Effect of pledge) and Article 209 paragraph 3 (Delivery of share certificates) of the Commercial Code shall apply mutatis mutandis to those money or other things, shares, obligations or other rights, share certificates, and fractional share certificates, which are to be received by shareholders because of the modification of rights provided for in the preceding paragraph.

Article 243 (Rights of reorganisation creditors and reorganisation secured creditors)

In the case where the rights have been recognised by virtue of the provisions of the reorganisation plan as against the reorganisation creditors or the reorganisation secured creditors, the rights shall be deemed to have been recognised only against the holders of the reorganisation claims or reorganisation security rights which have become final and conclusive.

Article 244 (Rights of shareholders not participated in reorganisation proceedings)

In the case where the rights have been recognised against the shareholders by virtue of the provisions of the reorganisation plan, the rights shall be recognised even against the persons who failed to participate in the reorganisation proceedings.

Article 245 (Effect of entries on list of reorganisation creditors, etc.)

1. If the ruling for approval of the reorganisation plan has become final and conclusive, with respect to the rights which have been recognised by virtue of the provisions of the plan on the basis of reorganisation claims or reorganisation security rights, the entries on the list of reorganisation creditors or the list of reorganisation secured creditors shall have the same effect as a judgment which has become final and conclusive as against the company, the new company (exclusive of new companies which are formed in consequence of amalgamation), the reorganisation creditors, the reorganisation secured creditors, the shareholders of the company and the persons who assume obligations or furnish security for the purpose of reorganisation.

2. The persons, who possess the rights provided for in the preceding paragraph, the contents of which consists of the claims on payment of money or other performance of obligation, may, subsequent to termination of the reorganisation proceedings, levy compulsory execution against the company and the persons who assumed obligations for the purpose of reorganisation, as entered on the list of reorganisation creditors or the list of reorganisation secured creditors. Provided that this shall not prejudice application of the provisions of Article 452 (Beneficial excuse for notice) and Article 453 (Beneficial excuse for execution) of the Civil Code.

Article 246 (Suspended procedures ceasing to be effective)

1. If the ruling approving the reorganisation plan has been granted, the bankruptcy procedure, compulsory execution, provisional attachment, provisional disposition, procedure of official auction sale, and the enforcement procedures of the right of enterprise hypothecation, which have been suspended under the provisions of Article 67 paragraph 1, shall cease to be effective. Provided that, this shall not apply to the measures or disposals which have been continued under the provision of paragraph 6 of said Article.

2. The claims appertaining to the bankruptcy's estate under the bankruptcy procedure which have ceased to be effective by virtue of the provision of the preceding paragraph (exclusive of those mentioned in item (2) (Claims which can be collected under the National Tax Collection Law or after the manner of collection national taxes) and item (9) (Allowance in aid payable to bankrupt and his dependants) of Article 47 of the Bankruptcy Law)) shall constitute the claims for common benefits.

Article 247 (Execution of reorganisation plan)

1. If the ruling approving the reorganisation plan has been granted, the receiver shall promptly carry out the plan.

2. In the case where the rights of managing the business of the company as well as of administering and disposing the properties thereof are granted to the director in accordance with the provisions of Article 211 paragraph 3 or Article 248-2 paragraph 1, the receiver shall supervise the director in carrying out of the plan by the director.

3. In the case where a new company is to be formed as provided for in the plan, the duties of promoters or of commissioners for formation shall be discharged by the receiver.

4. The provision of paragraph 2 shall apply mutatis mutandis to supervision by the receiver on the carrying out of the plan of the new company (excluding the new company incorporated due to amalgamation; hereinafter the same in this paragraph), and the provision of Article 98-2 shall apply mutatis mutandis to investigation of the new company by the receiver.

Article 248 (Order of Court on execution of reorganisation plan)

1. The Court may issue orders necessary for executing the reorganisation plan to the persons mentioned in Article 240 paragraph 1 as well as to the receiver.

2. If deemed necessary for making sure the execution of the plan, the Court may cause appropriate securities to be furnished on behalf of the person who possesses the claims under the stipulations of the plan or the provisions of this Law, or of the person who possesses the reorganisation claims or reorganisation security rights which have been objected to and of which no settlement is yet attained of the procedure whereby such claims or security rights are to become final and conclusive.

3. The provisions of Article 112 (Method of offering security), Article 113 (Defendant's right over security), Article 115 (Cancellation of security), and Article 116 (Substitution of object offered for security) of the Code of Civil Procedure shall apply mutatis mutandis to the security under the provision of the preceding paragraph.

Article 248-2 (Granting of rights to director after approving reorganisation plan)

1. The Court may, even in the case where no stipulation has been made in the reorganisation plan under the provision of Article 211 paragraph 3, grant the rights of managing the business of the company as well as of administering and disposing the properties thereof to the director on application of the receiver or ex officio, if the Court recognises to be adequate.

2. The Court may, on application of the receiver or ex officio, cancel the ruling under the provision of the preceding paragraph.

3. The Court shall, if it has granted the ruling under the provisions of the preceding two paragraphs, give public notice to that effect. In this case, the provision of Article 15 shall not apply.

Article 249 (Exclusion of statutory provisions, etc. relative to resolution of general meeting of shareholders, etc.)

With regard to execution of the reorganisation plan, the resolution need not be adopted at the constituent general meeting, the general meeting of shareholders (inclusive of certain types of general meeting shareholders), or the meeting of the board of directors, notwithstanding the provisions of laws and ordinances or of the articles of incorporation.

Article 250 (Exception to provisions of Commercial Code relative to assignment of business, etc)

1. If, by virtue of the provision of Article 217, the reorganisation plan has provided that the whole or a part of the business or properties of the company is to be assigned; contributions are to be made or the properties are to be leased out; the whole or a part

of operation of the company's enterprise is to be commissioned; a contract whereunder profits and losses of the business are shared with another person or any other contract similar thereto is to be concluded, modified, or cancelled; or the assignment of the whole or part of the business or properties of another person is to be taken, these acts may be effected pursuant to the stipulations of the plan.

2. In the cases mentioned in the preceding paragraph, the provisions of Articles 245-2 through 245-4 (Demand by opposing shareholders for buying shares) of the Commercial Code shall not apply.

Article 251 (Exception to provisions of Commercial Code relative to change of articles of incorporation)

If, by virtue of the provision of Article 219, the reorganisation plan may stipulate for the modification of the articles of incorporation of the company, the articles of incorporation shall be modified by the stipulations of the plan at the time of the ruling approving the plan.

Article 252 (Exception to provisions of Commercial Code relative to change of directors)

1. If, by virtue of the provision of Article 220, the reorganisation plan has provided for the appointment of directors or auditors or the election of representing directors, these officers shall be appointed or elected at the time of the ruling approving the plan.

2. In the case where the plan contains, by virtue of the provision of Article 220, the provisions as to the method of appointment of directors, the appointment or election of these officers may be made in the method as provided for in the plan. In such cases, the provisions of Article 254 paragraph 1 (inclusive of the cases where the provision applies mutatis mutandis under Article 280 of the Code) (Appointment of directors and auditors) and Article 261 paragraph 1 (Election of representing directors) of the Commercial Code shall not apply.

3. The directors, representing directors, or auditors whose remaining in office has not been stipulated in the plan shall be removed from the office at the time of the ruling approving the plan.

4. The term of office of those directors, representing directors, or auditors who have been appointed or elected under the provisions of paragraphs 1 and 2, or who have remained in office pursuant to the stipulations of the plan as well as the method of representation by such representing directors, shall be governed by what is provided for in the plan.

5. In the case of paragraph 2, in addition to a certified copy or extract copy of the ruling approving the plan, the documents concerning appointment or election shall be attached to the official request or the application for registration of change due to appointment of directors or auditors, or election of representing directors.

Article 253 (Exception to provisions of Commercial Code, etc. relative to reduction of capital)

1. If, by virtue of the provision of Article 221, the reorganisation plan has provided for the reduction of capital, the capital may be reduced in accordance with the provisions of the plan.

2. In the case mentioned in the preceding paragraph, the provisions of Article 212 paragraph 2 (Procedure for retirement of shares), Article 376 paragraphs 2 and 3 (Procedure for reduction of capital), and Article 380 (Action for nullity of reduction of state capital) of the Commercial Code shall not apply; and the cases, as provided for in

Article 217 paragraph 2 (Permission for sale of odd number of shares otherwise than by auction sale) of said Code which applies mutatis mutandis in Article 377 paragraph 1 of said Code, shall come under the jurisdiction of the reorganisation Court.

3. In the case mentioned in paragraph 1, a certified copy or extract copy of the ruling approving the plan shall be attached to the application for registration of change by reason of the reduction of capital of the company.

Article 254 (Exception to provisions of Commercial Code etc. relative to issue of new shares)

1. If, by virtue of the provision of Article 222 paragraph 1, the reorganisation plan has stipulated that the company is to issue new shares without causing the reorganisation creditors, reorganisation secured creditors or the shareholders to pay in or to effect contribution in kind anew, theses persons shall become shareholders at the time of the ruling approving the plan, or at the time specially fixed in the plan.

2. The provisions in Article 280-5-2 of the Commercial Code (a shareholders' right to subscribe new shares) shall not apply if the preceding paragraph applies.

3. In the case mentioned in paragraph 2 of this Article, the provisions of the articles of incorporation relative to the pre-emptive right shall not be binding.

4. The provisions of Article 215 paragraphs 1 and 2 of the Commercial Code, Article 216, and Article 217 (Consolidation of shares) thereof shall apply mutatis mutandis in the case where allotment of shares to shareholders begets odd number of shares. In such cases, the cases shall come under the jurisdiction of the reorganisation Court, and the provisions of Article 132-3 (Application for permission for sale of odd number of shares otherwise than auction sale) of the Law concerning Procedures for Non-contentious Matters (Law No. 14 of 1898) shall apply mutatis mutandis.

Article 255 (Exception to provisions of Commercial Code etc. relative to issue of new shares)

1. If, by virtue of the provision of Article 222 paragraph 2 or paragraph 3, the reorganisation plan has provided that the company is to issue new shares, the new shares may be issued in accordance with the provisions of the plan.

2. In the case mentioned in the preceding paragraph, the provisions of Article 280-3 (Uniformity of issuance conditions), Article 280-5-2, Article 280-8 (Investigation of contributions other than money), Article 280-10 (Demand for suspension of issuance), Article 280-11 (Liability of subscriber at unfair price), Article 280-13 (Directors' liability to secure subscription), Article 280-13-2 (Directors' liability to indemnity loss), and Articles 280-15 through 280-18 (Action for nullifying issuance of new shares) of the Commercial Code shall not apply.

3. In the case mentioned in paragraph 1, the provisions of the articles of incorporation relative to the pre-emptive right shall not be binding; and the cases provided for in Article 178 (Changing of bank, etc. of receiving payment) of the Commercial Code which applies mutatis mutandis in Article 280-14 paragraph 1 (Application mutatis mutandis of provisions on incorporation of company in case of issuance of new shares) of said Code shall come under the jurisdiction of the reorganisation Court.

4. In the case mentioned in paragraph 1, the provision of Article 280-5 (Execution of pre-emptive right) of the Commercial Code shall apply mutatis mutandis. In such cases, the phrase 'shareholder' appearing in paragraph 1 of said Article shall read as 'reorganisation creditor, reorganisation secured creditors, or shareholder', and the phrase 'if there is a provision in the articles of association granting the holders of an odd-lot share certificate a right to subscribe the new share where odd-lot share certifi-

cates were issued' appearing in paragraph 2 of said Article shall read as if share certificates or bond certificates in bearer form, or odd-lot share certificates are issued.

5. In the case where new shares are to be issued, causing the reorganisation creditors, reorganisation secured creditors, or the shareholders to pay in or to effect contribution in kind anew, it shall be sufficient for these persons to pay in the sum prescribed in the plan, or to effect contribution in kind as being provided for in the plan.

6. The provision of paragraph 3 of the preceding Article shall apply mutatis mutandis in the cases where allotment of shares, made through causing the shareholders to pay in or to effect contribution in kind anew, begets odd number of shares. Provided that, in such cases, the sum to be paid in for shares in odd numbers or the amount corresponding to the contribution in kind to be effected shall be deducted from the proceeds to be surrendered to the former shareholders.

7. In the case mentioned in paragraph 1, in addition to a certified copy or extract copy of the ruling approving the plan, the documents evidencing subscription to and taking of shares, as well as the certificate of custody of money paid in the bank or trust company dealing the payment on shares shall be attached to the official request, or the application, for the registration of change by reason of issuance of new shares by the company.

Article 256 (Exception to provision of Commercial Code, etc. relative to issuance of debentures)

1. If, by virtue of the provision of Article 223, the reorganisation plan has provided that the company is to issue debentures without causing the reorganisation creditors, reorganisation secured creditors, or the shareholders to pay in anew, these persons shall become debenture holders at the time of the ruling approving the plan.

2. In the case mentioned in the preceding paragraph, the provision of Article 298 (Restriction to invite subscription for new debentures in case there exist debentures not yet paid in) of the Commercial Code shall not apply.

3. In the case mentioned in paragraph 1, the amount of debentures issued to the reorganisation creditors or the reorganisation secured creditors pursuant to the provisions of the plan shall not be computed in the total amount of debentures with respect to application of the provision of Article 297 (Restriction of total amount of debentures) of the Commercial Code.

Article 257 (Exception to provision of Commercial Code, etc. relative to issuance of debentures)

1. Except for the case as provided for in the preceding Article, if, by virtue of the provision of Article 223, the reorganisation plan has provided that the company is to issue debentures, the debentures may be issued in accordance with the provisions of the plan.

2. In the case where the debentures are to be issued, causing the reorganisation creditors, reorganisation secured creditors, or the shareholders to pay in anew, it shall be sufficient for these persons to pay in the sum specified in the plan.

3. The provisions of Article 255 paragraph 4 as well as of paragraph 2 and 3 of the preceding Article shall apply mutatis mutandis in the case mentioned paragraph 1.

4. In the case mentioned in paragraph 1, in addition to a certified copy or extract copy of the ruling approving the plan, the documents evidencing subscription to and taking of convertible debentures or debentures with pre-emptive right, and the documents evidencing payment on each convertible debenture or each debenture with pre-

emptive right shall be attached to the official request, or the application, for the registration of convertible debentures or debentures with pre-emptive right.

Article 258 (Exception to provisions of Commercial Code, etc. relative to amalgamation)

1. If, by virtue of the provision of Article 224 or Article 225, the reorganisation plan has stipulated that the company is to amalgamate with another company, the amalgamation may be effected in accordance with the stipulations of the plan.

2. In the case mentioned in the preceding paragraph, the reorganisation creditors or reorganisation secured creditors, who have been allotted the shares of the company which continues to exist after the amalgamation or of a new company which is formed in consequence of the amalgamation, shall become the subscribers to shares at the time of the ruling approving the plan, and become the shareholders at the time when the amalgamation has become effective.

3. In the case mentioned in paragraph 1, the provisions of Article 408-2 (Keeping of balance sheets), Article 408-3 (Demand by opposing shareholders for buying shares) and Article 415 (Persons entitled to institute action for nullification of amalgamation) of the Commercial Code shall not apply; and the cases provided for in Article 217 paragraph 2 thereof which applies mutatis mutandis in Article 416 paragraph 3 (Application mutatis mutandis of provisions relative to consolidation of shares in case of amalgamation) thereof shall come under the jurisdiction of the reorganisation Court.

4. In the case mentioned in paragraph 1, notwithstanding the provisions of Article 416 paragraphs 1 and 2 (Application mutatis mutandis of provisions relative to amalgamation, etc. of *gomei-kaisha*) of the Commercial Code, the provisions of Article 100 (Procedure for protection of creditors), Article 104 paragraphs 1 and 3 (Action for nullification of amalgamation), Article 105 (Procedure for action for nullification of amalgamation), Article 106 (Order to creditors to furnish security), Articles 108 through 111 (Registration of nullity of amalgamation, effect of judgment, over third persons, non-retroactive effect of judgment, liability for payment of obligations as well as vesting of properties subsequent to amalgamation), and Article 376 paragraph 3 (Objection by debenture holders) of said Code shall not apply mutatis mutandis.

5. The provisions of the preceding four paragraphs shall not preclude application of the provisions of the Commercial Code to another company which is the party to amalgamation.

6. The provision of Article 256 shall apply mutatis mutandis in the case where debentures have been allotted to the shareholders pursuant to the provision of Article 224 item (5) or Article 225 item (7). In such cases, the shareholders shall become debenture holders at the time when the amalgamation has become effective.

7. In the case mentioned in paragraph 1, the documents mentioned in Article 90 (Registration of amalgamation) of the Commercial Registration Law (Law No. 125 of 1963) (excluding the documents mentioned in Article 67 item (2) of said Law concerning company) shall be attached to the official request, or the application, for the registration of change of the company by reason of amalgamation, in addition to a certified company or extract copy of the ruling approving the plan.

8. In the case mentioned in paragraph 1, the minutes of the meeting of the board of directors relative to representing directors, and the documents mentioned in Article 91 (Registration of amalgamation) of the Commercial Registration Law (excluding the documents mentioned in Article 67 item (2), Article 68 paragraph 1 item (3) and Article 90 item (2) of said Law concerning company) shall be attached to the official request, or the application, for the registration of formation of the company in consequence of

amalgamation, in addition to a certified copy or extract copy of the ruling approving the plan.

9. When the Court officially requests the registration of the preceding two paragraphs, the Court shall also officially request the registration of dissolution due to amalgamation of the company being the other party to the amalgamation.

10. If, in the case mentioned in paragraph 1, the company being the other party to the amalgamation continues to exist after the amalgamation, the provision of Article 17 paragraph 3 shall not apply.

11. A certified copy or extract copy of the ruling approving the plan, the minutes of the general meeting of shareholders of the company being the other party, as well as the documents mentioned in Article 90 item (1), item (3) and item (4) of the Commercial Registration Law (excluding the documents mentioned in Article 67 item (2) of said Law concerning the company) shall be attached to the application of registration of change due to amalgamation of the company being the other party to the amalgamation in the case of the preceding paragraph.

Article 259 (Exception to provisions of Commercial Code, etc. relative to formation of new company)

1. If, by virtue of the provision of Article 226, the reorganisation plan has stipulated that a new company is to be formed through causing the reorganisation creditors, reorganisation secured creditors, or the shareholders to take shares, without causing them to pay in or to effect contribution in kind anew, the new company shall be formed at the time when the registration of formation has been effected, after having prepared the articles of incorporation and having obtained attestation thereof from the reorganisation Court.

2. In the case mentioned in the preceding paragraph, the assets of the company to be transferred to the new company pursuant to the stipulations of the plan shall be transferred to the new company at the time of formation of the new company, and those reorganisation creditors, reorganisation secured creditors, or shareholders who have been allotted the shares or debentures of the new company shall become the shareholders or debenture holders at the time of formation of the new company.

3. The provisions of Article 252 paragraphs 1, 2 and 4, Article 254 paragraph 4, Article 256 paragraph 3, and Article 257 shall apply mutatis mutandis in the cases mentioned in the preceding two paragraphs.

4. In the case mentioned in paragraph 1, if the method of appointing directors or auditors, or electing representing directors is stipulated in the articles of incorporation as well as the plan, the documents relative to such appointment or election, or if the transfer agent or agent for recordation is appointed, the documents evidencing thereof shall be attached to the official request for registration of the formation of a new company, in addition to a certified copy or extract copy of the ruling approving the plan.

Article 260 (Exception to provisions of Commercial Code, etc. relative to formation of new company)

1. Except the cases provided for in the preceding Article, if, by virtue of the provision of Article 226, the reorganisation has stipulated that a new company is to be formed otherwise that through amalgamation, the new company may be formed in accordance with the stipulations of the plan.

2. In the case mentioned in the preceding paragraph, the provisions of Article 167 (Attestation of articles of incorporation), Article 168-2 (Determination of matters in respect of issuance of shares at the time of incorporation), Article 169 (Promoters' taking of shares), Article 170 (Payment and appointment in promotive incorporation), Article 173 (Investigation by inspector, measures taken by Court), Article 173-2 (Investigation and notification of establishment procedures), Article 175 paragraph 2 item (9) (Entries on application for subscription relative to shares taken by promoters), Article 181 (Investigation by inspectors), Article 183 (Appointment of directors and auditors at constituent general meeting), Article 184 (other than the part in relation to the matters concerning Article 173-2 paragraph 1 item (2) and (3) in paragraph 1) (Investigation and report on procedure of formation), Article 185 (Alteration of anomalous matters on procedure of formation), Article 186 (Claim for damage against promoters), Article 192 (Promoters' liability to secure taking of a payment on shares etc.), Article 192-2 (Promoters' liability to indemnify the non-paid amount of assets), Article 193 (Promoters' liability in damages), Article 195 (Joint and several liability of directors, etc.), Article 196 (Release of promoters' liability, representative suit by shareholders), Article 198 (Liability of self-styled promoters), the latter part of paragraph 2 of Article 222-2 (Determination of conditions to convert convertible shares), and Article 428 (Action for nullity of incorporation) of the Commercial Code shall not apply.

3. In the case mentioned in paragraph 1, the articles of incorporation shall be attested by the reorganisation Court; the case mentioned in Article 178 of the Commercial Code shall come under the jurisdiction of the reorganisation Court; the articles of incorporation shall not be modified contrary to the tenor of the plan at the constituent general meeting; and the promoters' liability specified in Article 194 (Promoters' liability in cases where the company fails to come into existence) of said Code shall be borne by the company.

4. In the case mentioned in paragraph 1, if the reorganisation creditors, reorganisation secured creditors, or the shareholders are to take shares without being required to pay in or to effect contribution in kind anew, or are to take debentures without being required to pay in anew, these persons shall become shareholders or debenture holders at the time of formation of the new company.

5. In the case mentioned in paragraph 1, if the reorganisation creditors, reorganisation secured creditors, or the shareholders are to take shares, being required to pay in or to effect contribution in kind anew, with regard to shares not to be taken among the shares to be issued for these persons, further invitation for subscription to shares may be dispensed with, and the number of such shares may be deducted from the total number of shares to be issued upon formation of the new company unless it contravenes the provision of Article 166 paragraph 3 (Total number of shares to be issued upon formation of company) of the Commercial Code.

6. The provisions of Article 252 paragraphs 1, 2 and 4, Article 254 paragraph 4, Article 255 paragraphs 4 through 6, Article 256 paragraph 3, and Article 257 shall apply mutatis mutandis in the cases mentioned in the preceding five paragraphs.

7. In the case mentioned in paragraph 1, the documents evidencing the application for subscription to and taking of shares, the reports of investigation by directors and auditors together with the accompanying papers, the minutes of the constituent general meeting, and the certificate relative to the custody of money paid in the bank or trust company dealing the payment on shares, shall be attached to the official request, or the application, for the registration of formation of the new company, in addition to the documents mentioned in paragraph 4 of the preceding Article.

Article 261 (Exception to provisions of Commercial Code, etc. relative to dissolution)

1. If, by virtue of the provision of Article 227, the reorganisation plan has provided that the company is to be dissolved otherwise than through amalgamation, the company shall dissolve at the time specified in the plan.

2. In the case mentioned in the preceding paragraph, a certified copy or extract copy of the ruling approving the plan shall be attached to the application for the registration of dissolution.

Article 262 (Forfeiture of rights of new shareholders, etc.)

1. In the case where the reorganisation creditors, reorganisation secured creditors, or the shareholders have become the shareholders or debenture holders of the company anew or those of the new company by virtue of the provisions of Article 254 paragraph 1, Article 256 paragraph 1, Article 258 paragraphs 2 and 6, Article 259 paragraph 2, or Article 260 paragraph 4, except where the share certificates or fractional share certificates have been surrendered pursuant to the provision of Article 254 paragraph 4 (inclusive of the case where the provision applies mutatis mutandis in Article 259 paragraph 3 and Article 260 paragraph 6) or to the provision of Article 416 paragraph 3 of the Commercial Code, the company or the new company shall, on behalf of these persons, without delay give public notice to the effect that the delivery of share certificates or debenture certificates (if the person is a holder of fractional shares, delivery of fractional shares or confirmation that he is a shareholder; the same in paragraph 4 and next Article) shall be demanded, and that if the demand be not made within three years after becoming shareholders or debenture holders, they are to forfeit their rights, and further, it shall give notice to that effect individually to the persons entitled who are known.

2. In order to make the demand as provided for in the preceding paragraph, the persons who have been the shareholders or debenture holders shall surrender to the company or the new company the former share certificates, fractional share certificates, or debenture certificates (referred to as the 'former share certificates, etc.' in next paragraph and next Article).

3. The former share certificates, etc. may be made null and void by means of a public peremptory notice. In such cases, the provision of the preceding paragraph shall not apply to the person who has obtained decision of nullification.

4. If, notwithstanding the public notice having been given by the company or the new company mentioned in paragraph 1, delivery of share certificates or debenture certificates is not demanded within the period specified in said paragraph, the shareholders or debenture holders as provided for in said paragraph shall forfeit their rights.

5. If the shareholders have forfeited their rights in accordance with the provision of the preceding paragraph, the company or the new company may acquire the shares, notwithstanding the provision of Article 210 (Prohibition to acquire own shares) of the Commercial Code. In such cases, the company or the new company shall dispose of such shares at an appropriate time.

Article 263 (Forfeiture of rights of new shareholders, etc.)

In the case where the persons who have been shareholders or debenture-holders are unable to surrender the former share certificates, etc. within the period mentioned in paragraph 1 of the preceding Article, if the demand is made by them within said period and no one else makes the demand within such period, the company or the new company may, notwithstanding the provision of said Article, deliver the share certificates or debenture certificates to those persons who have made the demand.

Article 264 (Assignment of right to subscribe to shares, etc.)

If the reorganisation creditors, reorganisation secured creditors, or the shareholders possess the right to subscribe for shares or debentures of the company or the new company by virtue of the stipulations of the reorganisation plan, they may assign such right to others.

Article 265 (Exception to Law Relating to Prohibition of Private Monopoly and Methods of Preserving Fair Trade)

In the case where the reorganisation creditors, reorganisation secured creditors, or the shareholders acquire shares of the company or the new company by virtue of the stipulations of the reorganisation plan, such acquisition shall be deemed to be acquisition as a result of the receipt of payment in kind, with respect to application for the provision of Article 9-2 (Restriction on possessing stocks by great scale company) and Article 11 (Restriction on possessing stocks by financial company) of the Law Relating to Prohibition of Private Monopoly and Methods of Preserving Fair Trade (Law No. 54 of 1974).

Article 266 (Exception to Securities and Exchange Law)

If, by virtue of the stipulations of the reorganisation plan, shares or debentures of the company or of the new company are to be issued to the reorganisation creditors, reorganisation secured creditors, or the shareholders, the provision of Article 4 paragraph 1 (Notification of invitation of subscription or of public sale of valuable instruments) of the Securities and Exchange Law (Law No. 25 of 1948) shall not apply.

Article 267 (Exception to restriction on disposal of estate)

In the case where the assets of the company are disposed or pursuant to the stipulations of the reorganisation plan, the provisions of laws and ordinances relative to restrictions on the disposal of factory's estate and other estate, or of assets belonging to such estate shall not apply.

Article 268 (Transmission of rights arising out of permission, approval, etc.)

In the case where, by virtue of the provisions of the reorganisation plan, the rights and duties arising out of permission, approval, licence and other actions of administrative government agencies procured by the company are to be transferred to the new company, the new company shall, notwithstanding the provisions of other laws and ordinances, take over such rights and duties.

Article 269 (Exception to Corporation Tax Law, etc.)

1. In the case where the reorganisation plan has provided that the new company is to succeed to tax liabilities of the company, the new company shall be liable to pay such taxes, and the tax liabilities of the company shall be extinguished.

2. If there has been the ruling for commencement of the reorganisation proceedings, the accounting period of the company shall terminate at the time of such commencement, and the next following accounting period shall terminate at the time of the ruling approving the plan or on the day of termination of the

reorganisation proceedings. Provided that this shall not preclude the application of the provision of the proviso to Article 13 paragraph 1 (Case where period of accounting exceeds one year) of the Corporation Tax Law (Law No. 34 of 1965), and the provision of Article 72-13 paragraph 4 (Cases where period of accounting exceeds one year) of the Local Tax Law.

3. Sums of gains, as arising due to re-appraisal of the company's assets and extinction of obligations under the reorganisation proceedings, coming up to the deficit amounts under the provision of Article 2 (Definitions) item 20 of the Corporation Tax Law (excluding those applicable of the provisions of Article 57 paragraph 1 (Bringing forward of deficit for accounting period having filed blue return) or Article 58 paragraph 1 (Bringing forward of damage money due to disaster for accounting period having not filed blue return) of said Law) which were brought forward from before the commencement of the reorganisation proceedings shall not be counted in the amount of gains, for the purpose of computing the amount of income under said Law for each of the accounting periods during which the re-appraisal of the assets or the extinction of obligations has taken place.

4. With regard to the corporation tax and the enterprise tax for the accounting period of the company which ensues the time of commencement of the reorganisation proceedings, the provisions of Article 71 (Interim return) (including the cases applicable mutatis mutandis in Article 145 paragraph 1 (Application mutatis mutandis to foreign corporation) of the Corporation Tax Law) of said Law and of Article 72–26 (Interim return payment of corporation whose accounting period exceeds six months) of the Local Tax Law shall not apply.

5. No registration licence tax shall be imposed on registrations effected pursuant to the provisions of Article 17 paragraphs 1 and 2 and the former clause of paragraph 3, Article 18 paragraph 1, Article 18-2 through 19, Article 20 paragraphs 2 through 4, and Article 21 (inclusive of the cases where these provisions apply mutatis mutandis in Article 22).

6. The tax rate of the registration licence tax for registration of increase of capital in the case where the plan stipulated that the company issues new shares (excluding the case falling under next paragraph) shall, notwithstanding the provision of Article 9 (Taxable basis and tax rate) of the Registration License Tax Law (Law No. 35 of 1967), be 1/1,000 (it shall be 3.5/1,000 with respect to the part, in the increased amount of capital, corresponding to the amount other than the amount equivalent to the part issuing the new shares without having the reorganisation creditors, reorganisation secured creditors, or the shareholders newly pay money or contribute in kind).

7. The tax rate of the registration license tax for registration of increase of capital due to incorporation or amalgamation of a new company in the case where the plan stipulated that the company consolidates with another company shall, notwithstanding the provision of Article 9 of the Registration License Tax Law, be 1/1,000 (it shall be 3.5/1,000 with respect to the part, respectively in the amount of capital or the increased amount of capital due to amalgamation, corresponding to the amount other than the amount equivalent to the part corresponding to the amount of capital just before said amalgamation of the company extinguished due to the amalgamation and the amount equivalent to the part of allocating the shares to the reorganisation creditors or the reorganisation secured creditors).

8. The tax rate of the registration licence tax for registration of incorporation of a new company in the case where the plan stipulated that a new company is incorporated not by amalgamation shall, notwithstanding the provision of Article 9 of the Registration Licence Tax Law, be 1/1,000 (it shall be 3.5/1,000 with respect to the part corresponding to the amount other than the amount equivalent to the part of issuing

the shares without having the reorganisation creditors, reorganisation secured creditors, or the shareholders newly pay money or contribute in kind).

9. The tax rate of the registration license tax for registration of assignment or creation in the case where the plan stipulated that a new company accepts assignment or creation of a right relating to immoveables or vessel from the company shall, notwithstanding the provision of Article 9 of the Registration Licence Tax Law, be 4/1,000. Provided that this shall not apply if the amount of the registration license tax computed by applying said tax rate as to said registration exceeds the amount of the registration tax licence computed by applying the provision of said Article.

Article 270 (Retirement allowance)

1. Any person who had been a director, representing director, auditor, or employee of the company after commencement of the reorganisation proceedings and who has continuously been a director, representing director, auditor, or employee of the new company ever since, cannot receive from the company a retirement allowance on the ground that he retired from the company.

2. The length of service in the company of the person mentioned in the preceding paragraph shall be deemed to be the length of service in the new company, for the purpose of computing the retirement allowance.

Article 271 (Modification of reorganisation plan)

1. If, because of unavoidable causes, need arose after the ruling approving the reorganisation plan for modifying the matters provided for in the plan, the Court may, upon the application of the receiver, company, reorganisation creditors, reorganisation secured creditors, or the shareholders who have filed the report, modify the plan only if it is prior to termination of the reorganisation proceedings.

2. In the case where, pursuant to the provision of the preceding paragraph, an application has been filed for modification of the plan which is considered to affect adversely the reorganisation creditors, reorganisation secured creditors, or the shareholders, the provisions relative to the procedure for the case where the draft plan of reorganisation has been submitted shall apply mutatis mutandis. Provided that it shall not be necessary to cause those persons who are not adversely affected by modification of the plan to participate in the procedure, and those who consented to the former plan and who do not attend the meeting of interested persons for adopting resolution on the draft for modified plan shall be deemed to have consented to the draft for modified plan.

3. If the stipulation under the provision of Article 211 paragraph 3 was cancelled due to modification of the plan, the Court shall make public notice to that effect. In this case, the provision of Article 15 shall not apply.

4. The provisions of Article 236 and Article 237 shall apply mutatis mutandis in the case where there has been the ruling for modification of the plan.

Article 272 (Termination of reorganisation proceedings)

1. In the case where the reorganisation plan has been carried out, or where it has come to be considered certain that the plan will be carried out, the Court shall, upon application of the receiver or of its own motion, rule for termination of the reorganisation proceedings and give public notice of the principal text of such ruling and the tenor of the reasons therefor. Provided that the service thereof need not be given.

2. The provision of Article 35 paragraph 1 shall apply mutatis mutandis in the case where there has been the ruling mentioned in the preceding paragraph.

Chapter IX: Discontinuance of reorganisation proceedings

Article 273 (Discontinuance before approval of reorganisation plan)

The Court shall, of its own motion, rule for discontinuance of the reorganisation proceedings in any of the following cases:

(1) In the case where the draft plan of reorganisation is not submitted within the period specified by the Court or within extension thereof, or where all the draft plans submitted within such period are not sufficient for referring them to the meeting of interested persons for examination or resolution;

(2) In the case where the resolution disapproving the draft plan has been adopted, or where the resolution approving the draft plan is not adopted within two months of the first day of the meeting of interested persons convened for resolution, or within extension thereof.

Article 273-2 (discontinuance before approval of reorganisation plan)

If it has become clear before the ruling of approval of reorganisation plan that the reorganisation is hopeless, the Court shall, on application of the receiver or of its own motion, make the ruling of discontinuance of reorganisation proceedings.

Article 274 (Discontinuance before approval of reorganisation plan)

1. If it has become clear that the company is able to make full payment of the obligations due to reorganisation creditors and reorganisation secured creditors of whom the report has been filed within the period for report, the Court shall, upon application of the receiver, company, or the reorganisation creditors or reorganisation secured creditors who filed the report, rule for discontinuance of the reorganisation proceedings.

2. The applicant shall give prima facie proof of the facts comprising the causes for discontinuance of the reorganisation proceedings provided for in the preceding paragraph.

Article 275 (Discontinuance before approval of reorganisation plan)

If the application has been filed as provided for in the preceding Article, the Court shall issue, to the company as well as to those reorganisation creditors and reorganisation secured creditors who have filed the reports, the notice to that effect and also that they shall present to the Court their opinions, if any, and keep documents relative to the application open for inspection by the persons interested.

Article 276 (Discontinuance before approval of reorganisation plan)

The Court shall not rule for discontinuance of the reorganisation proceedings unless one month has elapsed since the notice mentioned in the preceding Article was issued.

Article 277 (Discontinuance after approval of reorganisation plan)

If it has become clear subsequent to the ruling approving the reorganisation plan that there is no prospect of execution of the plan, the Court shall, upon application of the receiver or of its own motion, rule for discontinuance of the reorganisation proceedings.

Article 278 (Discontinuance after approval of reorganisation plan)

1. The Court shall hold a hearing and consult the opinions of interested persons prior to granting the ruling mentioned in the preceding Article.

2. The ruling which sets the date of hearing mentioned in the preceding paragraph shall be given public notice and served upon the persons known among those who possess the rights recognised in the stipulations of the reorganisation plan under the reorganisation claims or reorganisation security rights which became final and conclusive.

Article 279 (Discontinuance after approval of reorganisation plan)

The discontinuance of reorganisation proceedings under the provision of Article 277 shall not affect the execution of the reorganisation plan and the effect which has arisen by virtue of the provisions of this Law.

Article 280 (Public notice of ruling for discontinuance)

If the Court has granted the ruling for discontinuance of the reorganisation proceedings, the Court shall give public notice of its principal text as well as of the tenor of the reasons therefor. Provided that the service thereof may be dispensed with.

Article 281 (Complaint)

1. The provisions of Article 237 paragraphs 1 and 2 shall apply mutatis mutandis to the complaint against the ruling for discontinuance of reorganisation proceedings and also to the complaint provided for in Article 419-2 of the Code of Civil Procedure which applies mutatis mutandis by virtue of Article 8 of this Law.

2. The provision of Article 35 paragraph 1 shall apply mutatis mutandis in the case where the ruling for discontinuance of reorganisation proceedings has become final and conclusive.

Article 282 (Payment of claims for common benefits)

If the ruling for discontinuance of reorganisation proceedings has become final and conclusive, except in the case where the adjudication of bankruptcy or approval of application for composition is to be granted under the provision of Article 23 paragraph 1 or Article 27, the receiver shall pay the claims for common benefits, and as for those objected to, make deposits on behalf of the creditors concerned.

Article 283 (Effect of entries on list of reorganisation creditors, etc.)

1. If the ruling for discontinuance of reorganisation proceedings provided for in Articles 273 through 274 has become final and conclusive, with regard to the reorganisation claims or reorganisation security rights which have become final and conclusive, the entries on the list of reorganisation creditors or the list or reorganisation secured creditors shall have the same effect as a final and conclusive judgment, as against the company. Provided that this shall apply only in the case where the company did not

raise objection to the right on the day for investigation of reorganisation claims and reorganisation security rights.

2. The reorganisation creditors or reorganisation secured creditors may, after termination of the reorganisation proceedings, levy compulsory execution against the company, as entered on the list of reorganisation creditors or the list of reorganisation secured creditors.

Article 284 (Effect of entries on list of reorganisation creditors, etc.)

The provisions of Article 245 paragraph 2 shall apply mutatis mutandis in the case where the ruling for discontinuance of reorganisation proceedings under the provision of Article 277 has become final and conclusive.

Chapter X: Remuneration and reward

Article 285 (Remuneration, etc. payable to receiver, etc.)

1. Investigation commissioner, preservation administrator, overseer, and the receiver shall be entitled to advance payment of expenses, as well as to the remuneration as determined by the Court. The same shall apply to legal advisers, agents of preservation administrator, and agent of the receiver.

2. The amount of remuneration to be determined under the preceding paragraph shall be befitting the duties and responsibilities of the respective offices.

Article 286 (Remuneration, etc. payable to receiver, etc.)

In the case where the persons mentioned in the preceding Article have, after having acquired their official capacity taken assignment of, or have assigned, without obtaining permission of the Court, claims against the company or the new company or shares thereof, they shall not be entitled to payment of expenses and remuneration.

Article 287 (Reward, etc. to agent commissioners, etc.)

In the case where the reorganisation creditors, reorganisation secured creditors, shareholders or agent commissioners, or the agents thereof have contributed to reorganisation, the Court may permit these persons to redeem out of the assets of the company the expenses whose extent is appropriate, or to receive payment of reward. The amount thereof shall be determined by the Court.

Article 288 (Reward, etc. to agent commissioners, etc.)

In the case where there exist the facts that the reorganisation creditors, reorganisation secured creditors, or the shareholders have obtained benefits through taking assignment of, or through assigning, the claims against the company or the new company or shares thereof, subsequent to commencement of the reorganisation proceedings, the Court shall take into consideration such facts in granting permission in accordance with the provision of the preceding Article. The same shall also apply in the case where there exist the facts that the agent commissioners or agents, after having acquired their official capacity, have obtained benefits through taking assignment of, or assigning, claims against the company or the new company or the shares thereof.

Article 289 (Complaint)

Immediate complaint may be made against the ruling under the provisions of Article 285 and Article 287.

Chapter XI: Penal provisions

Article 290 (Offence of fraudulent reorganisation)

1. If a director or a person similar thereto, or a manager of the company commits any of the acts mentioned below, regardless of whether the act is done prior to or subsequent to commencement of the reorganisation proceedings, for the purpose of benefiting himself or other persons, or injuring creditors, those persons who possess on the company's assets the special preferential right, right of pledge, right of hypothec, or the right of retention under the Commercial Code (hereinafter referred to as 'secured creditors' in this Article), or shareholders, and if, with respect to the company, the ruling for commencement of the reorganisation proceedings has become final and conclusive, such person shall be liable to penal servitude not exceeding ten years or a fine not exceeding five hundred thousand yen:

(1) To conceal or destroy the assets of the company, or dispose of them in a way disadvantageous to the creditors, secured creditors, or shareholder;
(2) To increase the burden of the company in a false way;
(3) To fail to prepare commercial books which should be prepared as required by the provisions of the laws, to fail to make in such books entries whereby the state of assets is sufficiently known, or to make false entries therein, or to conceal or destroy such books.

2. The provision of the preceding paragraph shall not apply in the case where there exists the relevant Article in the Criminal Code (Law No. 45 of 1907)

Article 291 (Offence of fraudulent reorganisation by third persons)

1. Any person other than those mentioned in the preceding Article who has committed any of the acts mentioned in said Article, or any person who has exercised false rights as a reorganisation creditor, reorganisation secured creditor, or a shareholder for the purpose of benefiting himself or other persons, shall be liable to penal servitude not exceeding ten years or a fine not exceeding five hundred thousand yen, if the ruling for commencement of the reorganisation proceedings as to the company has become final and conclusive.

2. The provision of the preceding paragraph shall not apply in the case where there exists the relevant Article in the Criminal Code.

Article 292 (Offence of taking bribes)

1. If an investigation commissioner, preservation administrator, overseer, receiver, legal adviser, preservation administrator's agent, or a receiver's agent has taken or demanded, or promised bribes in connection with his duties, he shall be liable to penal servitude not exceeding three years or a fine not exceeding two hundred thousand yen. The same shall also apply, if a reorganisation creditor, reorganisation secured creditor, shareholder, agent commissioner, or agent of these persons, officer or employee has

taken or demanded, or promised bribes in connection with resolutions to be adopted at the meeting of interested persons.

2. If, in the case where the investigation commissioner, preservation administrator, or the receiver (hereinafter referred to as the 'receiver, etc.' in this Article) is a corporation, an officer or an employee who takes charge of duties of the receiver, etc. has taken or demanded, or promised bribes in connection with such duties, he shall be liable to penal servitude not exceeding three years or a fine not exceeding two hundred thousand yen. The same shall also apply, in the case where the receiver, etc. is a corporation, and if an officer or employee thereof caused the receiver, etc. to take or demand, or promise bribes in connection with the duties of the receiver, etc.

3. Bribes, which the offender or the receiver, etc. who is a corporation has taken, shall be confiscated. In the case of being impossible to confiscate the whole or a part thereof, the value thereof shall be collected.

Article 293 (Offences of offering bribes)

Any person who has given or offered, or promised the bribes provided for in paragraph 1 or paragraph 2 of the preceding Article shall be liable to penal servitude not exceeding three years or a fine not exceeding two hundred thousand yen.

Article 294 (Offence of refusing report or inspection)

If an employer, such as a director, auditor or a manager of the company or the new company (excluding the new company incorporated due to amalgamation) has refused to submit reports or to permit inspection under the provision of Article 98-2 paragraph 1 (including the case where the provision applies mutatis mutandis in Article 43 paragraph 1 or 3, Article 101-3 or Article 247 paragraph 4), or has made a false report, he shall be liable to penal servitude not exceeding one year or a fine not exceeding fifty thousand yen.

Article 295 (Where punishable with administrative fines)

A director or person similar thereto, or a manager of the company of which the reorganisation proceedings have been commenced, or of the new company, shall be liable to an administrative fine not exceeding three hundred thousand yen in any of the following cases:

(1) Where contravening the Court's order issued pursuant to the provision of Article 130 paragraph 2;
(2) Where contravening the Court's order issued pursuant to the provision of Article 248 paragraph 1 or paragraph 2;
(3) Where failing to give public notice or issue notice as required in the provision of Article 262 paragraph 1, or where failing to dispose of shares in contravention of the provision of paragraph 5 or said Article.

2. In the case where the person, who assumes obligations or furnishes securities, on behalf of reorganisation creditors, reorganisation secured creditors or shareholders, or for the purpose of reorganisation, has committed the act mentioned under item (2) of the preceding paragraph, the same shall apply as is provided for in said paragraph.

SUPPLEMENTARY PROVISIONS

This Law shall come into force as from 1 August 1952.

SPAIN

The most important provisions of Spanish insolvency law are contained in the Commercial and Civil Procedure Codes and in the Suspension of Payments Law of 26th July 1922. The translation starts with the eight sections of Chapter I, Book IV, of the Commercial Code. Section I sets out very briefly the general rules for suspension of payments. For traders or companies which are within section VIII, the full measures will be found in the Suspension of Payments Law of 26th July 1922. For certain other companies suspension of payments is governed by section VIII. Sections II to V contain the substantive Spanish bankruptcy laws: definitions and classification, the effect of bankruptcy on contracts, agreements with creditors and creditors' rights in general, and the position of partners and shareholders. The nine sections of Chapter XII of the Civil Procedure Code set out the procedural provisions of Spanish bankruptcy. Section I deals with moratoria, sections II and III with the declaration of bankruptcy, section IV with the administration of creditors and the appointment of receivers, sections V to VII with the three main applications: administration of the proceedings, admission of debts and the final classification of the proceedings. Section VIII governs settlements between creditors and the bankrupt and section IX governs the basic maintenance provisions. These procedural steps are amplified in the following six sections of Chapter XIII of the Civil Procedure Code.

Important procedural provisions regarding registration are contained in Chapter XIII of the Register of Companies, and, finally, Title XVII of the Civil Code deals with competition between creditors and priority issues.

CHAPTER NINE

Spanish Insolvency Laws

TABLE OF CONTENTS

COMMERCIAL CODE
BOOK IV

CHAPTER I. SUSPENSION OF PAYMENTS AND BANKRUPTCY

Section I: Suspension of payments and its effect

Article 870

A trader who, while possessing sufficient assets to cover all his debts, anticipates that it will be impossible to pay them on their respective due dates, may apply for a suspension of payments which shall be declared by the judge of first instance in the trader's district on the basis of the trader's statement.

Article 871

A trader who holds sufficient assets to cover all his liabilities may also apply for suspension of payments within 48 hours of the due date of an obligation which he has not settled.

Article 872

A trader who seeks a declaration of suspension of payments must attach to his petition a balance sheet showing his assets and liabilities and his proposal regarding the delay requested from his creditors, which may not be more than three years. If the purpose of this is to release or reduce the debts, the judge will refuse to proceed with the petition for suspension of payments.

Article 873

The suspension of payments proceedings will comply with the procedures set out in the relevant law. If the requested delay is refused by the committee of creditors, the proceedings will be terminated.

The provisions of articles 870 to 873 apply to the suspension of payments by companies and businesses not included in article 930.

Before a company not included in article 930 can suspend payments, the shareholders must pass a resolution in a general meeting convened for that express purpose following the period set out in article 871. The period of notice for that meeting, will be the shortest period allowed by the articles of association or other constitutional documents.

Section II: General bankruptcy provisions

Article 874

A trader who ceases to pay his debts as they fall due will be deemed to be bankrupt.

Article 875

A declaration of bankruptcy will be made:

1. When the bankrupt himself so requests.
2. On a reasoned petition submitted by a legitimate creditor.

Article 876

In order for a declaration of bankruptcy to be made at the request of a creditor, the petition must be based on the grounds on which an execution or enforcement order has been issued, and insufficient unencumbered assets must have been obtained from the attachment to satisfy the claim.

A declaration of bankruptcy will also be made at the request of creditors who, although they have not obtained an attachment order, are able to prove their claims and that the trader has generally ceased to pay his debts as they fall due, or, in the case of a suspension of payments, if the trader has not presented a proposal for a settlement with his creditors within the time limit stated in article 872.

Article 877

Where a trader absconds, or goes into hiding, at the same time closing his offices, warehouses or other buildings, and leaving no representative to manage and fulfil his obligations, there will be sufficient grounds for a creditor's declaration of bankruptcy if the creditor is able to prove his claim and offer proof of the circumstances referred to above to the judge or court.

Where the fact that the debtor has absconded is publicly acknowledged or confirmed, the court will, in addition, proceed on its own motion, to order occupation of the absconder's establishments and will prescribe the measures to be taken for their preservation while the creditors exercise their rights in relation to the declaration of bankruptcy.

Article 878

Once bankruptcy has been declared, the bankrupt will be disqualified from administering his assets.

All disposals and acts of administration by him retrospective to the effective time of the bankruptcy will be null and void.

Article 879

Amounts which the bankrupt has paid in cash, bills or credit bonds during the 15 days prior to the declaration of bankruptcy, in respect of debts and obligations due after the declaration of bankruptcy, will be returned in their entirety by the recipients of those amounts.

Any discounting of his own bills by the trader during the same period will be deemed to be a pre-payment.

Article 880

Contracts entered into by the bankrupt during the 30 days preceding his bankruptcy will be declared fraudulent and will be unenforceable by his creditors if they fall within any of the following categories:

1. Transfers of immoveable property for no consideration.
2. Creation of dowries for his daughters from his personal property.
3. Transfers and assignments of immoveable property in payment of debts not due at the time of the declaration of bankruptcy.

4. Ordinary charges granted over wrongfully pre-dated obligations or loans of money or merchandise not advanced or delivered at the time when the agreement was executed before a notary public and witnessed by those who were party to it.
5. Gifts inter vivos which do not appear to be made for consideration, effected after the date of the closing balance sheet prior to the bankruptcy, and which cause the bankrupt's liabilities to exceed his assets.

Article 881

The following will be declared void at the request of the creditors if they can prove that the bankrupt has acted with the intention of defrauding them of their rights:

1. Disposals of real property in the month prior to the declaration of bankruptcy.
2. The creation of dowries in the same period of time from the assets of the husband and wife for the benefit of their daughters, or any other transfer of these assets for no consideration.
3. Endowments or acknowledgements of debts effected by the trader in favour of his or her spouse during the six months prior to the bankruptcy, provided that these do not constitute immoveable property inherited or acquired from, or previously in possession of, the spouse in whose favour the endowment or acknowledgement was made.
4. All acknowledgements of receipt of money or bills or loans which, if made under a notarial document six months prior to the bankruptcy, were not authenticated by a notary public's certificate, or, if made under a private instrument, were not being properly recorded in the books of the contracting parties.
5. All contracts, obligations and trading operations of the bankrupt not made at least ten days prior to the declaration of bankruptcy.

Article 882

At the request of the creditors, all gifts or contracts made or entered into during the two years prior to the bankruptcy may be rescinded if any suspicion of fraud or attempt to defraud the creditors can be proved.

Article 883

By virtue of the declaration of bankruptcy, all outstanding debts of the bankrupt will be deemed to fall due on the date thereof.

If payment is made before the time specified in the relevant obligation, it will be discounted accordingly.

Article 884

Interest will cease to accrue on all the bankrupt's debts with effect from the date of declaration of bankruptcy, except in respect of mortgage debts and pledges up to the amount of their respective guarantees.

Article 885

A trader who succeeds in obtaining revocation of a declaration of bankruptcy at the petition of his creditors may bring an action for damages against them if they have acted out of malice or deceit, or unjustly.

Section III: Categories of bankruptcy and associated matters

Article 886

There are three types of bankruptcy:

1. Involuntary bankruptcy.
2. Culpable bankruptcy.
3. Fraudulent bankruptcy.

Article 887

Involuntary bankruptcy arises when a trader is subject to unexpected difficulties which, as chance events in the normal and prudent good administration of a business, reduce his capital to the extent that he is unable fully or in part to settle his debts.

Article 888

Culpable bankruptcy will be deemed to occur where a trader finds himself in one of the following situations:

1. If the domestic and personal expenses of the bankrupt have become excessive and disproportionate in relation to his liquid assets, bearing in mind his status and family.
2. If he has suffered any type of gaming losses which exceed the amount that a prudent head of family might spend on this type of recreation.
3. If the losses arise as a consequence of imprudent and substantial bets, or purchases and sales or other operations effected with intent to defer the bankruptcy.
4. If, in the six months prior to the declaration of bankruptcy, he sells at a loss, or for less than the market price, merchandise purchased on credit and on which payment is still outstanding.
5. If it is shown that, in the period from the last inventory up to the declaration of bankruptcy, there was a time when the bankrupt owed in the form of direct obligations double the amount of his liquid assets as disclosed by the inventory.

Article 889

The following will also be deemed to be culpable bankrupts save where there are exceptional circumstances which demonstrate that the bankrupt is free from blame:

1. Those who have not kept their books of account in the manner and in accordance with all the essential and indispensable requirements set out in

Chapter III of Book I and those who, while conforming to these requirements, have made errors which may have been prejudicial to third parties.

2. Those who have not made a declaration of bankruptcy in the terms and form prescribed in article 871.
3. Those who, being absent at the time of the declaration of bankruptcy or during the judicial proceedings, fail without legitimate excuse to attend in person in the circumstances where this is required by law.

Article 890

A trader to whom any of the following circumstances apply will be deemed a fraudulent bankrupt:

1. Absconding with all or part of his assets.
2. Including fictitious assets, credits, debts, losses or expenses in the balance sheet, annual report, books of account or other documents relating to his trade or business.
3. Failing to keep books of account, or including in whatever books have been kept, incorrectly dated items and entries in the wrong place to the prejudice of a third party.
4. Destroying, erasing or changing by any other method any of the contents of the books of account to the prejudice of a third party.
5. Failing to show in his accounts the outflow or existence of the assets comprising his most recent inventory, or of money, securities, goods and chattels of whatever kind, which are subsequently known or proved to have entered into the possession of the bankrupt.
6. Concealing in the balance sheet any sum of money, credits, merchandise or other types of assets or rights.
7. Using and applying for his own business, funds or instruments belonging to a third party which have been entrusted to him by way of deposit or agency or for his administration.
8. Without authorisation from the owner, seeking to discount bills of exchange belonging to third parties which are in the custody of the trader for collection, remittance or a non-trading purpose, and without accounting for their proceeds.
9. If, being commissioned to sell merchandise or to deal in commercial credits or securities, he conceals the transaction from their owner for any length of time.
10. Falsely simulating transfers of any type.
11. Granting, signing, consenting to or recognising fictitious debts, assuming unless proved to the contrary that they are all without quantifiable value and show no cause of action in debt.
12. Buying immoveable property, bills or credits and putting them in the name of a third party to the prejudice of his creditors.
13. Anticipating payments to the prejudice of his creditors.
14. Trading, after the last balance sheet, in bills of exchange drawn by him on a person who holds no funds or credit or any authorisation to do so.
15. If, after issue of the declaration of bankruptcy, he has collected and appropriated for his own personal use money, bills or credits from the bankruptcy estate or diverted any part of this for his own use.

Article 891

The bankruptcy of a trader, whose true situation may not be ascertained from his books of account, will be presumed to be fraudulent, unless proved to the contrary.

Article 892

The bankruptcy of official brokers will be deemed to be fraudulent when it is shown that they carried out any trade, operation or transaction for their own account, in their own name or that of others, even when the trading or dealing is not a primary cause of the bankruptcy.

If the bankruptcy arises through an official broker acting as guarantor of the operations in which he is involved, it will be presumed to be a fraudulent bankruptcy except where proved to the contrary.

Article 893

The following will be considered accessories to fraudulent bankruptcies:

1st Those who assist the bankrupt in concealing his assets.

2nd Those who, having conspired with the bankrupt to attribute debts to him or to increase the value of those which have in fact been set against his securities or assets, uphold this attribution in the hearing which investigates and determines the mandatory ranking of those debts, or in any other meeting of the creditors of the bankrupt estate.

3rd Those who, in order to obtain priority in the ranking of debts to the prejudice of the other creditors and, with the agreement of the bankrupt, alter the nature or the date of the debt, even when this has taken place before the declaration of bankruptcy is made.

4th Those who deliberately, and after the bankrupt has ceased to make payments, help him to conceal or steal any part of his assets or credits.

5th Those who, being holders of any property or asset of the bankrupt at the time when the bankruptcy is declared by a judge or court, and being aware of that fact, hand the property to the bankrupt and not to the legitimate administrators of the estate; unless this takes place in a country or province other than the domicile of the bankrupt, and they can prove that in the town of their residence there was no public notice of the bankruptcy.

6th Those who wrongfully deny to the administrators of the bankruptcy that they hold assets belonging to the bankrupt.

7th Those who accept endorsements by the bankrupt after the publication of the declaration of the bankruptcy.

8th Legitimate creditors who, to the prejudice of the majority and fraudulently, make private and secret agreements with the bankrupt.

9th Official brokers who take part in the same trading operations and transactions as the bankrupt trader.

Article 894

Without prejudice to the penalties they will incur under the criminal law accessories to a bankrupt will be ordered:

1st To lose any right they may have in the bankruptcy estate in respect of which they have been declared an accessory.

2nd To reinstate to the estate, with interest and indemnity for damage and prejudice, such assets, rights and shares on the basis of the theft of which the declaration of their complicity was issued.

Article 895

The assessment of the bankruptcy with a view to determining any criminal liability of the debtor, will always be handled under a separate court file and will be substantiated in proceedings between the Public Prosecutor's office, the receivers, and the bankrupt himself.

The creditors will have the right to be party to the proceedings and to apply for prosecution of the bankrupt; but they will do so at their own cost, and no action lies for recovery from the estate of the expenses or costs of the proceedings, whatever the results of their efforts.

Article 896

In no case, either at the request of a party or on the court's own motion, will proceedings be instituted for the crime of culpable or fraudulent bankruptcy without the judge or court first issuing the declaration of bankruptcy and having declared that there are grounds for the commencement of criminal proceedings.

Article 897

A determination of involuntary bankruptcy by way of final judgment will not prevent criminal proceedings when it appears from the proceedings pending on the creditors' agreement, on the admission of claims, or on any other matter, that there is evidence of acts open to indictment under the Penal Code and which will be communicated to the appropriate judge or court. In these cases the public prosecutor should first be heard.

Section IV: Agreements between bankrupts and their creditors

Article 898

At any time during the proceedings, once the debts have been acknowledged and the bankruptcy has been assessed, the bankrupt and his creditors may enter into an appropriate agreement.

Fraudulent bankrupts and those who abscond during the bankruptcy proceedings will not enjoy this right.

Article 899

Agreements between creditors and bankrupts must be reached in a duly constituted creditors' meeting.

Private transactions between the bankrupt and any of his creditors will be null and void: the creditor who is party to such a transaction will lose his rights in the bankruptcy proceedings and the bankrupt, for this reason alone, will be classified as culpable, unless he merits being considered as fraudulent.

Article 900

Preferred and mortgage creditors and those with special priority rights may abstain from taking part in the resolutions of the meeting drawing up the agreement; this abstention will not prejudice their respective rights.

If, on the other hand, they prefer to be heard and to vote on the proposed agreement, they will be subject to the payment delays or debt reductions agreed by the creditors' meeting without prejudice to the priority and ranking relating to the title to their claim.

Article 901

The proposed agreement will be discussed and put to the vote, which will be carried if agreed by more than half of the number of those present, provided that their interest in the bankruptcy covers three fifths of the total liabilities, less the amount of the debts of those creditors referred to in the first paragraph of the previous article, if they have made use of the right indicated in that paragraph.

Article 902

Within the eight days following the meeting in which the agreement is approved, the dissenting creditors and those who have not attended the meeting may oppose approval of the agreement.

Article 903

The only grounds of opposition to the agreement are:

1st Defects in the manner specified for the calling, or holding, of the meeting and the way in which discussions at the meeting are to take place.
2nd Failure of any of the voters to attend personally or to be represented, always provided that their vote would determine the majority in number or amount.
3rd Fraudulent collusion between the debtor and one or more of the creditors, or amongst the creditors themselves to vote in favour of the agreement.
4th Fraudulent exaggeration of the debts to achieve a majority of amount.
5th Deliberate inaccuracy in the general trading balance sheet of the bankrupt, or in the reports of the receivers, in order to facilitate acceptance of the debtor's proposals.

Article 904

Once it has been approved, and save as provided in article 900, the agreement will become binding both on the bankrupt and on all creditors whose debts date from the period before the declaration of bankruptcy, if they had been legally notified or if, having been notified of the approval of the agreement, they had not appealed against it in accordance with the provisions of the Civil Procedure Code, even though those debts were not included in the balance sheet or were not referred to in the proceedings.

Article 905

Assuming no express covenants to the contrary, debts will be cancelled under the agreement if waived in favour of the bankrupt, even though some assets of the bankruptcy may be left over or the fortunes of the bankrupt subsequently improve.

Article 906

If the debtor fails to perform under the agreement, any of his creditors may request the judge or the court dealing with the case to rescind the agreement and to continue the bankruptcy.

Article 907

Where no covenant has been expressly agreed as referred to in article 905, any creditors who have not been paid in full from what they perceive to be the assets of the bankrupt prior to completion of his liquidation, will retain a right of action for the outstanding amounts owed to them over any assets which the bankrupt acquires or might subsequently acquire.

Section V: Creditors' rights in bankruptcy and their classification

Article 908

Merchandise, commercial instruments and any other goods or assets which exist in the bankruptcy estate, the ownership of which has not been transferred to the bankrupt by legal and irrevocable title, will be deemed to be outside his control and will be made available to the legitimate owners subject to their right to them being recognised in a creditors' meeting or by final judgment. The bankrupt's estate will retain any rights which the bankrupt might have had in relation to his assets and is subrogated to him, provided always that any obligations attaching to those rights are complied with.

Article 909

The following are deemed to be included within the provisions of the preceding article for the purpose set out therein:

1st Unvalued and valued gifts by way of marriage in the hands of the husband if their receipt is recorded by notarial document registered according to articles 21 and 27 of this Code.

2nd The separate property of a married woman acquired by inheritance, legacy or gift whether it has been kept in the form in which it was acquired or has been replaced by or invested in others, as long as the investment or replacement has been registered in the Companies Register according to the articles mentioned in the previous paragraph.

3rd Assets and instruments which the bankrupt has deposited, or which are being administered on lease or rental on his behalf or which he has the right to use.

4th Merchandise which the bankrupt has in his custody on commission for purchase, sale, transit or delivery.

5th Bills of exchange or promissory notes which, without endorsement or indication of transfer of ownership, have been sent to the bankrupt for collection and any which he may have acquired on behalf of a third party, drawn or endorsed directly in favour of the principal.

6th Capital remitted other than by current account to the bankrupt, and which he holds for delivery to certain persons in the name and for the account of the principal, or in order to satisfy obligations which need to be settled in the former's domicile.

7th Amounts owed to the bankrupt for sales made for the account of a third party, or, similarly, bills of exchange or promissory notes which he holds even though they may not be made out in favour of the owner of the merchandise sold, provided it is proved that the obligation flows from those goods and that the goods are in the hands of the bankrupt on behalf of the owner so that he may sell them and send the proceeds to the owner in due course. This right will be presumed in favour of the bankrupt unless the transaction has been settled between them on current account.

8th Goods sold to the bankrupt for cash and not paid up in whole or in part, while they remain packed in the warehouse of the bankrupt, or in the same condition in which they were delivered, and in a state whereby they may be specifically distinguished by the marks or numbers of the bundles or packages.

9th Merchandise purchased by the bankrupt on trust, although not physically delivered to his warehouse or other agreed location, and merchandise in relation to which bills of lading or way bills have already been issued, after loading, by order of the buyer for the buyer's account and risk.

In the case of the previous paragraph and paragraph 8, the liquidators may arrest the goods purchased or reclaim them for the benefit of the bankruptcy estate by paying the price to the seller.

Article 910

Likewise the amount of the notes in circulation of issuing banks will be deemed to be included in the rule set out in article 908 for the purposes of that article in the event of the bankruptcy of these institutions.

Article 911

Once the deductions referred to in the previous articles have been made the creditors will be paid out of the proceeds of the assets of the bankruptcy in accordance with the terms of the following articles.

Article 912

The debts will be classified by dividing them into two categories: the first will include the debts which must be settled by the proceeds of the bankruptcy's moveable property; and the second, those which must be paid from the proceeds of the immoveable property.

Article 913

The order of preference of creditors within the first category will be as follows:

1st Specially preferred creditors in this order:
A) Creditors in respect of burial, funeral and executory expenses.
B) Maintenance creditors, i.e. those who may have supplied foodstuffs to the bankrupt or his family.
C) Employee creditors, meaning employees of the business during the six months prior to the bankruptcy.
D) Holders of creditors' rights derived from compulsory obligations for subsidies, social security payments, and mutual employment assurance payments during the period mentioned in the previous paragraph.

2nd Preferred creditors who hold a preferential right provided under this Code.

3rd Preferred creditors at law and legal mortgagees in the cases where, in accordance with the law, they have a prior ranking claim over moveable property.

4th Officially registered creditors and those who are creditors by virtue of commercial rights or commercial contracts in which an agent or broker has been involved.

5th Ordinary trade creditors.

6th Ordinary creditors under civil law.

Article 914

The order of preference in the payment of the creditors within the second section will be as follows:

1st Creditors with a right in rem according to the terms of and in the order set out in the Mortgages Law.

2nd The specially preferred creditors and the others listed in the previous article in the order set out therein.

Article 915

The amounts which the legal mortgage creditors should receive from the proceeds of sale of moveable property upon completion of the sale thereof will be paid on account of the proceeds to be received from the sale of immoveable property; and if they have received the total amount of their debt, they will be deemed to have been fully paid up and the next person in date order will thereafter be entitled to payment.

Article 916

The creditors will have their debts paid, regardless of date, on a pro-rata basis within each class and subject to the order set out in articles 913 and 914, except:

1st Mortgage creditors, who collect in the order of the registration dates of their mortgage documents.

2nd Notarial creditors and those who are creditors by virtue of commercial rights in which an official broker has been involved, who collect in the order of the notarisation dates of their contracts.

Notwithstanding the foregoing, but except as regards the order of preference for specific items set out in this Code, if several creditors in the same class are competing, the general rule will apply.

Article 917

The proceeds of sale will not be distributed amongst the creditors of a particular classification, letter or number as set out in articles 913 and 914 unless the debts in the prior ranking classification, letter or number as set out in those articles have been fully paid up.

Article 918

Creditors with a pledge created under a notarial document or by means of a contract arranged through the intervention of an official broker are not obliged to transfer to the bankruptcy estate the securities or objects which they received as security unless the representatives of the bankruptcy estate wish to recover them by settling the secured claim in full.

If the bankruptcy estate does not make use of this right, creditors with security quoted on the Stock Exchange may sell this security when the debt falls due, in accordance with the provisions of article 323 of this Code; and if the security is of some other type, it may be sold through an official broker, if such is available, or, if not, by public auction in the presence of a notary public.

Any surplus remaining after extinction of the claim will be transferred to the bankruptcy estate.

If, however a balance remains owing by the bankrupt, the creditor will be treated as a notarial creditor and classified according to the date of the contract.

Article 919

The ordinary or legal mortgage creditors, whose debts are not covered by the sale of the immoveable property on which they were secured, will be treated, as far as the balance of their debt is concerned, as notarial creditors along with the others of this type according to the date of their title documents.

Section VI: Reinstatement of the bankrupt

Article 920

Fraudulent bankrupts may not be reinstated.

Article 921

Bankrupts not included in the previous article may be reinstated by showing that the agreement made with their creditors has been performed in full.

If no agreement was made, they are obliged to show that all the claims proved in the bankruptcy proceedings have been satisfied from the assets of the bankruptcy or other monies subsequently received.

Article 922

On the reinstatement of the bankrupt all legal restraints arising from the bankruptcy will cease.

Section VII: General provisions relating to the bankruptcy of commercial undertakings

Article 923

The bankruptcy of a partnership or a limited partnership company includes the bankruptcy of those partners who have joint liability as set out in articles 127 and 148 of this Code and will have, in relation to all such partners, all the inherent effects of a declaration of bankruptcy, while keeping separate the liquidation of their individual estates.

Article 924

The bankruptcy of one or more of the partners does not of itself cause the bankruptcy of the partnership.

Article 925

If, at the time of the declaration of bankruptcy, the non-executive partners or the shareholders of a limited liability company do not hand over the full amounts they committed themselves to put into the company, the bankruptcy administrator or administrators will have the right to claim outstanding calls on capital up to the limits of their respective liability.

Article 926

Non-executive partners, shareholders of a limited liability company, and those joint account holders who, at the same time, are creditors of the bankruptcy, will not rank as claimants in the bankruptcy except to the extent that there is a surplus in their favour after the amounts which they are obliged to pay in their capacity as partners or shareholders, have been paid.

Article 927

In the case of partnerships, partners' private creditors whose debts were incurred prior to the constitution of the partnership will compete with the creditors of the partnership, being ranked and classified according to the nature of their respective debts and in accordance with the provisions of articles 913, 914 and 915 of this Code.

Subsequent creditors will only have the right to recover their debts out of the balance, if any, remaining, after the partnership debts have been paid, except for the preference given by law to the privileged debts and mortgage debts.

Article 928

In the event of the bankruptcy of limited companies which are not in voluntary liquidation, the agreement may provide for the continuation or transfer of the business, on conditions set out in the composition agreement.

Article 929

Companies will be represented during the process of bankruptcy as envisaged in such cases by their statutes and, failing that, by the Board of Directors; and they may at any stage of the bankruptcy process, put to the creditors such proposals for an agreement as they feel necessary, and these proposals should be decided on in accordance with the provisions of the next section.

Section VIII: Suspension of payments and bankruptcies of companies and railway and other public service undertakings

Article 930

Companies and railway and other general public, provincial or municipal service undertakings which are unable to meet their obligations may apply to a judge or court in the capacity of a business which has suspended payments.

A declaration of suspension of payments may also be made at the request of one or more legitimate creditors who, for the purposes of this article, are deemed to be those referred to in article 876.

Article 931

No judicial or administrative proceedings may interrupt the operation of a railway service or any other public service.

Article 932

A company or enterprise which submits an application in the capacity of a business which has suspended payments and requests an agreement with its creditors, must include a statement of its assets and liabilities with its application.

As regards the agreement, creditors and their claims are divided into three groups: the first includes debts owed to employees and those arising from the expropriation of works or materials; the second includes capital mortgage obligations represented by vouchers and redemptions due but not paid and calculated at their full value, and other credit obligations according to the type of issue, categorised in accordance with the number of mortgage obligation issues; and the third all other debts of whatever nature and however ranking amongst themselves and in relation to the previous groups.

Article 933

If the company or enterprise does not present its balance sheet in the form set out in the previous article, or if the declaration of suspension of payments has been requested by creditors who fulfil the conditions required in the second paragraph of article 930, the judge or court will order a balance sheet to be drawn up within a period of 15 days, after which time, if a balance sheet has still not been presented, it will be drawn up on the court's own motion under the same provisions and at the cost of the debtor company or enterprise.

Article 934

A declaration of suspension of payments made by the judge or court will have the following effects:

1st It will suspend executory proceedings and attachments.
2nd It will oblige the companies or enterprises to deposit in the Central Savings Bank or in banks authorised for such purpose any surplus remaining after deduction of, the administration, operating and reconstruction expenses.
3rd It will require the companies or enterprises to present to the judge or court, within a period of four months, a proposal for an agreement for payment of the creditors. If the debtor company or enterprise is constituted by shares the agreement will be approved in advance in ordinary or extraordinary shareholders' meeting.

Article 935

The agreement will be taken to be approved by the creditors if it is accepted by those representing three fifths of each one of the groups or sections referred to in article 932.

If a sufficient number of creditors to constitute the aforesaid majority has not been achieved within the specified period, the agreement will likewise be understood to have been approved by the creditors if it is accepted in a second meeting by creditors representing two fifths of the total of each of the two first groups and their sections, always provided that more than two fifths of any of these groups or sections or of the total liabilities do not oppose the agreement.

Article 936

Within the 15 days following the publication of the result of the votes, if this was in favour of the agreement, the dissenting creditors and those who did not attend may oppose the agreement by alleging defects in the calling of the creditors' meeting and in the membership of it, or for any of the reasons stated in paragraphs 2 to 5 of article 903.

Article 937

When the agreement has been approved without opposition or such opposition has been overruled by a final judgment, its terms will bind the debtor company or enterprise and all creditors whose debts dated from the time prior to the suspension of payments, if they have been legally cited or, if, having been notified of the agreement, they have not contested the agreement as provided for in the Civil Procedure Code.

Article 938

The declaration of bankruptcy of the companies or enterprises will follow when it is requested by them, or at the request of a legitimate creditor provided that any one or more of the following conditions is satisfied:

1st If four months have passed since the declaration of suspension of payments without a proposal for a creditors' agreement being presented to the judge or court.

2nd If the agreement was disallowed by a final judgment, or if it had not attracted sufficient support for it to be approved as provided in article 935.

3rd If, following approval of the agreement, the debtor company or enterprise does not comply with the agreement, provided that in this case the request is made by creditors representing at least a twentieth part of the liabilities.

Article 939

Once the bankruptcy has been declared, if this right still exists, the Government or the body which authorised the bankruptcy will be notified and an Administration Council will be constituted, consisting of a president appointed by the authorising body, two members appointed by the company or enterprise, one member for each group or section of creditors and three further members from any one of the above groups or sections.

Article 940

The Administration Council will provisionally organise the services of any public service undertaking; it will administer and operate it, and will also be obliged to:

1st Remit, by way of obligatory deposit, the revenue of the undertaking to the Central Savings Bank after deduction and payment of the administration and operating expenses.

2nd Hand over to the same savings bank, also by way of obligatory deposit, any cash in hand and securities which the company or enterprise held at the time when the Administration Council was appointed.

3rd Display the books and papers pertaining to the company or enterprise when appropriate and when so decreed by the judge or court.

Article 941

The classification and payment of the creditors will be carried out in accordance with the provisions of the fifth section of this chapter.

CIVIL PROCEDURE CODE
CHAPTER XII. CREDITORS' BANKRUPTCY PROCEEDINGS

Section I: Release and respite

Article 1.130

Prior to commencing bankruptcy proceedings, a debtor who is not a trader may apply to the court for release and respite, or for either of these, from his creditors.

The application must be accompanied by:

1. A list of the names of all the applicant's creditors, stating their addresses, the source and date of the debts and the amount of each debt.

2. A further detailed and precise list of his assets, together with their estimated sale value. The applicant may only exclude from this list those assets which, in accordance with article 1.449, are not open to attachment.

These lists will be signed by the debtor or by his representative under special power of attorney.

Article 1.131

The judge will decide upon the application, and immediately will order the creditors' meeting to be called, specifying a sufficient period of time not exceeding 30 days so that those residing within mainland Spain may attend, and stating the place, day and time at which the meeting will take place.

Article 1.132

Creditors residing outside mainland Spain may also be called by personal summons when so requested by the debtor and, in that event, this period of time will be extended by such time as the judge considers necessary to allow these creditors as to attend the meeting.

Article 1.133

Only those creditors included in the list submitted by the debtor may be summoned to the meeting and take part in it.

The summons will be made personally by court order to those whose address is known. Those whose address is not known will be summoned by public summons in the manner provided under article 269.

Article 1.134

As well as complying with the requirements of article 272, both the court summons and the public summons will require the creditors to appear at the meeting together with appropriate evidence of title to the debt, without which the debt will not be recognised.

Article 1.135

If enforcement proceedings are pending against the debtor, they will not be consolidated with these proceedings. However, any enforcement proceedings already in force will be suspended before any action is taken for the sale of assets on application by the debtor to the judge who is hearing the release and respite proceedings. The application will be officially communicated by the judge to those who are hearing such other proceedings.

Article 1.136

Enforcement proceedings against specially mortgaged assets are excepted from the above provisions.

Suspension granted pursuant to an order made under the previous article will be considered as cancelled and without any effect if two months elapse without an agreement for release or respite being granted or if such an agreement is refused.

Article 1.137

The creditors may be represented at the meeting by a third party under a valid power of attorney. This document must be submitted and form part of the record of the proceedings.

Those attorneys empowered to represent more than one party will only have one personal vote; however the debts they represent will be taken into account in calculating the weighted voting.

Article 1.138

In order to hold a creditors' meeting, the number of creditors present must represent at least three fifths of the liabilities.

Article 1.139

The meeting will be held on the appointed day before a judge assisted by a clerk of the court and in accordance with the following rules:

1. The clerk of the court will record the names of those present and their credits in the minutes of the proceedings, and the judge will thereupon examine the debt instruments and powers of attorney where appropriate. If those present have complied with such formalities and represent at least three fifths of the liabilities, the judge will consider the meeting duly constituted.
2. Immediately following the reading of the articles of this law referring to the objectives of the meeting, the debtor's application and the lists of debts and assets presented will be cited, and the discussion stage of the meeting will commence.
3. After two creditors have spoken in favour of the application, and two against, if so requested, and the debtor or his representative has answered these observations and clarified any uncertainties to the extent necessary, the judge will close the proceedings when he considers that the proposals have been sufficiently discussed.
4. The debtor may modify his proposal or proposals as a result of the discussion or may persist with those previously presented and with no further discussion the judge will put them to the vote, stating clearly and precisely which proposal is to be voted.
5. Voting will always be by poll and will be recorded in the minutes. All decisions are taken by majority vote.
6. The precise requirements for constituting a majority are:
   First. Two thirds of the votes of the creditors taking part in the ballot.
   Second. When the majority is smaller, the debts of those present who, by their votes, constitute a majority and which constitute at the least three fifths of the debtor's total liabilities.
7. When the results of the voting have been announced, objections against the majority vote will be admitted and recorded in the minutes and the meeting will be considered closed.
8. The minutes will be duly prepared, in the form of a concise account of all

that happened during the meeting, including the precise proposal or proposals voted upon and the count of votes taken. After the minutes have been read and approved, they will be signed by the judge, by all persons who voted, by a person present at the meeting on behalf of and at the request of those who are illiterate and by the clerk of the court.

Article 1.140

Creditors for personal services and maintenance, funeral expenses, the preparation of a last will and testament or the prevention of intestacy or administration proceedings, as well as holders of legal or voluntary mortgages may abstain from attending the meeting or taking part in the voting.

If they abstain from voting, they will not be under any obligation in respect of any agreement reached at the meeting.

If they take part in the voting, they will be bound by its terms together with the other creditors.

Article 1.141

The wife of the debtor may not take part in the discussion or the voting at the meeting relating to any release or respite.

Article 1.142

Any proposal for release or respite will be deemed to have been rejected if an insufficient number of creditors are present in order to constitute a valid meeting, or the two majorities in favour referred to in rule 6 of article 1.139 are not reached, notwithstanding that such majorities for a contrary vote are not attained either.

Article 1.143

If it is determined at the meeting to reject the requested release and respite, or no agreement is reached for lack of quorum, the proceedings are closed with no further action and the interested parties are at liberty to exercise any appropriate rights of action.

Article 1.144

If the agreement is favourable to the debtor, it may be challenged within ten days after the meeting by any creditor who was personally summoned but who has not attended the meeting or who, having attended, disagrees and objects to the majority vote.

For such purposes the creditors in this instance may examine the agreement reached at the meeting in the notary's office.

Article 1.145

Any creditors not personally summoned to the meeting will be notified of an agreement in favour if so requested by the debtor within three days of the conclusion of the meeting provided such debtor resides in any of the locations referred to in article 1.147.

Article 1.146

Upon notification such creditors will be warned (such warning to be included in the papers on sanction of nullity), to the effect that if no objections are made to the agreement at that moment or by appearance within three days thereafter, they will be bound by, and may not contest, the agreement.

Article 1.147

In respect of the cases referred to in the two preceding articles, the period for filing any objection will be: ten days for creditors who reside in mainland Spain, fifteen days for those residing in the Balearic Islands and Spanish possessions in Africa, and thirty days for those residing in the Canary Islands, in all cases commencing from the date of the notification.

Article 1.148

The provisions of the three preceding articles will not apply to creditors who reside overseas or abroad, whose rights against the debtor are not affected notwithstanding the agreement provided they have not attended the meeting.

Article 1.149

The release and respite agreement may only be challenged on the following grounds:

1. Defects in the manner of the convening and concluding of the meeting, and in the deliberations of the meeting.
2. Lack of legal status or due representation in respect of any of those who, with their vote, have constituted the majority.
3. Fraudulent collusion between one or more creditors and the debtor to vote in favour of release and respite.
4. Fraudulent overstatement of debts in order to obtain a quantitative majority.

Article 1.150

Any objection to the agreement will be filed in accordance with the requirements set out in article 524 and will be conducted in accordance with the procedure established for such matters. The debtor and any interested creditor who supports the agreement reached at the meeting will be considered as defendants.

Those who support the same cause will litigate jointly and under the same instructions.

The judgment as pronounced is subject to appeal with suspension of execution.

Article 1.151

Upon expiry of the ten-day period referred to in article 1.144 and, if applicable, the periods allowed under article 1.147, and provided no objection has been filed, the judge will, on his own motion, make an order whereby the agreement becomes effective and declaring the parties bound thereby.

The judge will also make an order in respect of the relevant provisions for enforcement, but always at the request of the party entitled.

Article 1.152

No appeal will be permitted against the order putting the agreement into effect referred to in the preceding article. The order binds all creditors specified in the debtor's list, excluding only those referred to in article 1.140 who abstained from voting and those who, not having been personally summoned to, nor attending, the meeting, did not receive the notification authorised in accordance with article 1.145.

Article 1.153

The right of action of all such creditors and those not specified in the debtor's list against the debtor is preserved intact in spite of the agreement unless they have expressly or impliedly adhered to it.

Article 1.154

All the costs of these proceedings will be for the account of the debtor who initiated them.

The costs of those objecting to the agreement reached at the creditors' meeting are for the account of whoever raised the objection without good cause.

Article 1.155

If the debtor fails to comply with the release and respite agreement in whole or in part, the rights of creditors existing prior to the agreement will be reinstated against the debtor.

In that event the debtor may be declared to be in compulsory bankruptcy on the application of any or all of the creditors, even though no enforcement proceedings are pending against the debtor.

Section II: Declaration of bankruptcy proceedings

Article 1.156

Bankruptcy proceedings may be voluntary or compulsory.

Bankruptcy proceedings will be considered to be voluntary when brought by the debtor himself and he surrenders all his assets to his creditors.

Bankruptcy proceedings will be considered to be compulsory when initiated on the application of all the creditors or any one of them.

Article 1.157

Any person who petitions for voluntary bankruptcy proceedings is required to attach the following documents to his application, without which the application will not be admitted:

1. A list of all his assets signed by the debtor, made separately and accurately and, indicating the estimated value. There may be excluded from the list

only those assets which, in accordance with article 1.449, may not be subject to attachment in enforcement proceedings.

2. A statement or list of the individual debts, stating date and source, and the names and addresses of the creditors.
3. A report stating the reasons for the petition for bankruptcy.

Article 1.158

Compulsory bankruptcy proceedings may only be declared upon the application of one or more lawful creditors who can satisfy the two following pre-conditions:

1. That there are two or more enforcement proceedings pending against the same debtor.
2. That following these enforcement proceedings there will be insufficient unencumbered assets to satisfy the amount claimed.

If article 1.155 applies, the satisfaction of these pre-conditions will not be required for the declaration of bankruptcy proceedings.

Article 1.159

A creditor who applies for declaration of bankruptcy must also justify his claim by attaching to his application his debt instrument and the enforcement order or evidence of such order issued at his request, unless a declaration of bankruptcy has already been requested in the enforcement order.

Article 1.160

If the judge considers that the requirements set out in the preceding two articles have been satisfied, he will make an order of declaration of bankruptcy and determine the measures set out in the following section.

Alternatively, the judge may reject the said declaration by way of an order open to appeal with suspension of execution.

Article 1.161

The order opening the declaration of bankruptcy proceedings will be immediately notified to the bankrupt who is thereby disqualified from administering his assets.

Article 1.162

The debtor may oppose a declaration of bankruptcy brought at the request of his creditors within three days from notification thereof.

If no such objection is made after three days, the declaration will remain legally binding.

Article 1.163

If the debtor opposes the declaration in due time, the order will be delivered to his court agent who has a period of four days which may not be extended in order to draw up the debtor's objections, and open a separate court file as required by the following article.

Article 1.164

Pending formulation and determination of the debtor's opposition, enforcement proceedings will continue together with the measures agreed therefor and any other appropriate measures for the seizure of the assets, books, papers and correspondence in accordance with the provisions of the following section.

In order to put this into effect a separate court file will be opened with a copy of the order for the declaration of bankruptcy together with any measures which may have been adopted for that purpose.

Article 1.165

The debtor's opposition will be formulated through the procedure established for such matters but the period for delivery allowed thereunder will be limited to four days for delivery of the orders to the creditor at whose request the proceedings were brought for the declaration of bankruptcy. A period of ten days which may not be extended is allowed for the production of evidence.

Article 1.166

Other creditors opposing the declaration of bankruptcy may also participate by bringing a joint action with the debtor under the same instructions. Those who wish to support the proceedings of the plaintiff creditor will likewise proceed with a joint action.

The judgment as pronounced is open to appeal with suspension of execution, but it will not suspend the proceedings under any separate action referred to in the preceding article.

Article 1.167

If the declaration of bankruptcy ceases to be valid, or if the judgment becomes final, a copy thereof will be attached to the other relevant bankruptcy applications, and when judicial intervention has ceased, the monies, assets, books, papers and correspondence which were under the supervision of the trustee and the clerk of the court will be returned to the debtor.

If the trustee performs administrative acts, he will provide accounts to the debtor.

Article 1.168

In the event that the bankruptcy declaration has been published, any judgment nullifying such declaration will also be published in the same manner if so requested by the bankrupt.

Article 1.169

If article 1.167 applies, the rights of the debtor are reserved and the debtor may claim from the creditor, at whose request the bankruptcy declaration was made, an indemnity for damages if the creditor has acted fraudulently or dishonestly.

This claim will be referred to in the order containing the judgment and will be formulated as ordinary proceedings by way of a claim for unliquidated damages.

Article 1.170

Any lawful creditor may oppose the declaration of bankruptcy, whether voluntary or compulsory, in order to render the action on behalf of all the creditors ineffective on the grounds of inadmissibility of the judgment or in order to substitute it by a declaration of insolvency pursuant to the procedure prescribed for under the law relating to commercial bankruptcy.

Article 1.171

This objection may only be presented within three days following the objector's summons and in the case where he has not been personally summoned, objection may be made by way of public summons of the creditors to the hearing. No objection will be admitted after expiry of these periods.

The objection will be formulated by the procedure established for such matters in a separate action which will be drawn up in accordance with the provisions of articles 747 and 748 but it will not cause the main hearing to be adjourned.

Article 1.172

By virtue of the declaration of bankruptcy all the bankrupt's outstanding debts will be deemed to have fallen due. Interest at legal rates will be discounted if payment should occur prior to the original due date.

Section III: Formalities following declaration of bankruptcy

Article 1.173

The court decision in which the declaration of bankruptcy is made will provide for the following matters:

1. The attachment and detention of all of the debtor's assets, the seizure of his books and papers and the retention of his correspondence.
2. The appointment of a trustee charged with the maintenance and administration of all the assets seized from the debtor.
3. The joinder to the bankruptcy proceedings of any execution proceedings pending against the bankrupt whether in that court or in others, save as otherwise provided in article 166.

Article 1.174

If the debtor has not absconded, he will be summoned to attend the seizure and attachment of his assets, books and papers which will be effected in the most appropriate and least expensive form, in accordance with the rules laid down for the supervision of an estate in intestacy proceedings.

Only those assets excluded from attachment under article 1.449 will be left at the bankrupt's disposal.

Article 1.175

The following rules will apply to the deposit of the assets:

1. Cash and bonds will be deposited in the designated public institution together with any precious objects and jewellery if the institution will accept them.
   A certified copy of the deposit receipt will be attached to the record of the proceedings, the original remaining in the custody of the trustee for delivery to the receivers in bankruptcy.
2. Products and other moveable property will be delivered into the custody of the trustee together with the relevant inventory.
3. Immoveable property will be placed under the trustee's administration with an interim notation relating to the attachment being recorded in the respective property registers.
4. An appropriate inventory will be drawn up from the accounting books and papers stating the condition in which they are found, and they will be kept in the court office until they are delivered to the receivers in bankruptcy unless the judge determines that they may be kept in their usual office without danger of misuse.

In every case any measures may be adopted which are considered necessary to avoid the occurrence of such misuse.

Article 1.176

The Postal Administrator will be given official notice of the retention of correspondence addressed to the debtor requiring him to place it at the disposal of the court.

Article 1.177

On the day and at the time designated the debtor will open the correspondence in the presence of the judge and the clerk of the court. Anything which may be relevant to the bankruptcy proceedings will remain in the custody of the latter, the remainder being given to the debtor.

If he should not appear or has absconded without appointing an attorney, the judge will open the correspondence in the presence of the clerk of the court, and this will be noted in the record of the court proceedings.

Article 1.178

If it transpires from the correspondence that it is necessary to take some urgent action in the interests of conservation of the assets, the judge will determine the action to be taken and inform the bankrupt accordingly.

Article 1.179

The person appointed as trustee-administrator of the bankruptcy proceedings must be a person of good reputation, responsibility and competence whether or not he is a creditor of the bankrupt.

It will not be necessary for him to provide a bond if the judge relieves him of this requirement at his own responsibility.

Article 1.180

When the trustee-administrator has accepted the office and been sworn in and, if the judge so requires has provided a bond, he will take up his duties and be given a certified copy of his appointment with the judge's approval thereof. He will inform those persons, named by him, of the appointment so that they may acknowledge him as such.

Article 1.181

The trustee-administrator will be the representative of the bankruptcy proceedings until the receivers in bankruptcy take up their duties.

In addition, his obligations and functions will be to:

1. Administer, safeguard and preserve the assets of the bankruptcy so that they suffer no impairment.
2. Collect the debts owing to the bankrupt.
3. Propose to the judge the sale of any moveable assets which cannot be preserved.

Article 1.182

In order to collect the debts the trustee will first obtain the permission of the court which will be recorded, under the signature of the judge and the clerk of the court, on the relevant debt instruments, if any, and if no such instruments exist, the court's permission will be verified by means of a certified copy of the order in which permission was granted.

The other matters referred to in the preceding article will be dealt with in accordance with the requirements applicable in similar cases to the administration of intestacy proceedings.

Article 1.183

The monies collected by the administrator of the bankruptcy will be deposited without delay, as specified by the court, in the public institution appointed for that purpose.

The judge, however, may leave in the hands of the administrator such amount as he considers necessary to cover the expenses of the proceedings.

Article 1.184

The judge may specify to the trustee daily fees in proportion to the nature and circumstances of the assets entrusted to his custody, and after taking into account the costs of the administration. In no case will these exceed fifty pesetas per day.

In any event the trustee-administrator will have the right to receive:

1. One half of one per cent. in respect of the debts collected.
2. One per cent. of the proceeds of sale of products and moveable property.
3. Five per cent. of the proceeds of the administration not arising from the circumstance mentioned in the previous paragraphs.

Article 1.185

The trustee's duties will cease on the same day that the receivers in bankruptcy take up their appointment, and he will hand over to them the administration and the assets given into his custody.

In the following fifteen days, he will render a verified account which must be approved by the court at a hearing at which the receivers in bankruptcy are present.

Article 1.186

In order to effect the joinder to the bankruptcy proceedings required pursuant to paragraph three of article 1.173, the following must be complied with:

1. If the enforcement proceedings are filed in the same court which is dealing with the bankruptcy proceedings, the judge will order the clerk of the court to consolidate these proceedings with the bankruptcy proceedings. The clerk will attach a certified copy of the order to the records of the enforcement proceedings and summon the executing party to attend the bankruptcy proceedings and to make use of his right of action.
2. If they are filed in other court offices under the jurisdiction of the same court, he will order the clerk of the court to obtain from his colleagues a certified copy of the order and require them to deliver to him the record of the enforcement proceedings so that it may be joined to the bankruptcy proceedings, and the executing party will be summoned for the aforementioned purpose.
3. In both cases, if the executing party opposes the joinder of the proceedings he will request in the enforcement proceedings within three days that the order in which this was required be reconsidered. After hearing the trustee-administrator of the bankruptcy during a further three days in which he will have had access to the record of the enforcement proceedings, the judge will resolve what he considers proper, his resolution being subject to appeal and open to stay of execution.
4. If the enforcements are being processed by other courts, the judge will send a certified copy of the order for the declaration of bankruptcy together with any other matters he considers to be necessary and will give official notice to them and will recover from them the record of the enforcement proceedings and will consolidate it with the main action proceedings on behalf of the creditors.

   In this case, the requirements set out in article 175 and the succeeding articles will apply, and if the judge from whom this is requested disallows the consolidation, a separate court file will be opened in the bankruptcy proceedings with a certified copy of all the requirements for further proceedings.

Article 1.187

The actions and litigation referred to in article 1.003 will also be consolidated with these actions.

Consolidation will be ordered in the usual way at the request of the trustee-administrator or the receivers in bankruptcy in the bankruptcy proceedings.

Article 1.188

When the declaration of bankruptcy has become final, and if the bankruptcy was compulsory, the judge will order the bankrupt to present within three days the list of his creditors and the report which are specified in paragraphs 2 and 3 of article 1.157.

Article 1.189

The judge may extend this period by the amount of time he believes necessary when it is apparent that the stated time is insufficient, and according to the importance and special circumstances of the bankruptcy proceedings.

Article 1.190

If the bankrupt does not comply with the provisions of the previous article within the prescribed period or is unable to comply with them because he has absconded, the proceedings will continue and this fact will be taken into account as an indication of his guilt when classifying the bankruptcy.

Article 1.191

Where the bankrupt is a legal person or a company which is not governed by the Commercial Code, if its director or manager does not comply with the provisions of article 1.188, the judge may appoint an expert to draw up a general balance sheet and a report on the causes which may have brought about the insolvency, providing him for this purpose with the books and papers of the insolvent company. The judge will determine the period of time he believes necessary for this purpose and which will not exceed thirty days.

Article 1.192

If the bankrupt absconds from the place of the hearing without leaving a person of sufficient authority to represent him in the bankruptcy proceedings, he will be called by means of public notice in the form prescribed in article 269 requiring him to appear at the court within nine days through an attorney, and if he does not comply with this, he will be declared to be in default, and the orders set out in article 281 will be carried out.

Section IV: Summoning of creditors and appointment of receivers in bankruptcy

Article 1.193

Without prejudice to the measures being taken as required by the previous section, as soon as the declaration of bankruptcy becomes final, the judge will order a formal public announcement of the bankruptcy together with the warning that no-one should make payments to the bankrupt on penalty of these being held to be unlawful, and that any such payments should be made to the trustee or to the receivers in bankruptcy once they have been appointed.

Article 1.194

At the same time, the judge will resolve to summon the creditors by means of the same announcements requiring them to present themselves at the court with the instruments of title evidencing their debts and to call them to a general meeting for the appointment of the receivers in bankruptcy on the day, and at the time and place appointed by the judge.

Article 1.195

There should be a period of at least twenty and not more than forty days with effect from publication of the announcements between the calling and holding of the meeting.

Article 1.196

The judge will appoint the day for the holding of the meeting, taking into account the number and place of residence of the creditors, so that all those who live in mainland Spain and the adjacent islands have time to attend the meeting or to authorise someone to represent them.

Article 1.197

The announcements referred to in article 1.193 and in the succeeding articles will be published and posted in the customary places in the locality of the court and the place of residence of the bankrupt and will be inserted in the list of public announcements if one exists and the official gazette of the province as well as the Madrid Gazette if the judge considers it to be advisable on the basis of the importance and circumstances of the bankruptcy.

Article 1.198

Without prejudice to the summons issued by public announcement, all creditors whose places of residence are known and who appear on the list presented by the bankrupt will be personally summoned by court order, and, for this purpose, the necessary court orders will be issued.

Article 1.199

The bankrupt will also be summoned by means of a court order to this first meeting and to any other meetings which are held during the bankruptcy proceedings so that he may appear in person or by means of an attorney if appropriate.

Article 1.200

The creditors will submit their debt instruments at the hearing either by appearing before the clerk of the court or in writing, at the election of the interested party.

Article 1.201

If submission is effected by personal appearance, the appropriate papers will be incorporated in the record of the proceedings and should include the surname, forename, marital status, profession and place of residence of the creditor, his home address, the nature of the document, its date and, if appropriate, the name of the notary public who authorised it, and the total amount of the debt claimed, also stating whether the interested party holds any security or if there is any other form of guarantee in his favour or in favour of a third party. This submission will be signed by the creditor and, failing that, by a witness at his request and by the clerk of the court.

Article 1.202

When submission is effected in writing, it will include the same details as mentioned above, using the appropriate stamped paper, and will be signed by the interested party or, failing that, by another person at his request.

If the creditor is represented by an attorney, the power of attorney will be added to the record of the proceedings together with the debt instruments.

Article 1.203

The clerk of the court will issue a receipt for any debt instrument submitted even though this may not be required by the interested party, recording the fact in the attendance note or the written submission.

Article 1.204

The debt instrument and the attendance notes or written submissions will form a separate section for which they will be kept in the order in which they are presented and the creditors will be given a number corresponding to the same order.

Article 1.205

In exceptional cases where the number of creditors is very high or due to the nature of the debts it is reasonably assumed that it will not be possible to carry out the provisions of the previous articles within the forty day period fixed by article 1.195 for the holding of the meeting, the judge may extend this period by such time as he considers necessary.

Article 1.206

Forty eight hours before the time appointed for the meeting, the submissions which creditors are required to make in order to be able to attend this meeting and take part in the election of the receivers in bankruptcy will be closed.

Those who make submissions after this time must do so in writing and they will thereupon be admitted only to subsequent proceedings.

Article 1.207

As the creditors present themselves with their debt instruments, the clerk of the court will draw up an individual statement or list of these, which must be complete by the time the meeting is held.

Article 1.208

This list will include the creditors' surnames and forenames, the amount of the debts claimed by each creditor, together with a number showing the order of submission and the page in the record of the proceedings where the respective documents are to be found, and will include in addition an indication of whether or not each one appears on the list presented by the bankrupt.

Article 1.209

The provisions of article 1.137 will apply to the meeting for the appointment of receivers in bankruptcy and any others which are held in relation to these hearings.

Article 1.210

Three receivers in bankruptcy will be appointed for any bankruptcy proceedings and this number may neither be increased nor decreased.

The exception to this is where all creditors attending the meeting agree to appoint one or two receivers in bankruptcy and the election is completely unanimous.

Article 1.211

Save in these circumstances, the three receivers in bankruptcy will be elected by two nominal "yea and nay" votes of the creditors attending the meeting, whatever their number or the amount of debt they represent.

Article 1.212

The appointment of the first and second receivers in bankruptcy will be made by means of the same type of vote, with the two who have won the support of voters representing the largest amount of capital or liabilities being elected, regardless of the number of voters concerned.

If there are more than two representing the same amount of capital, preference will be given to the one winning the largest number of votes, and if the number of votes is also the same, the winner will be selected by means of a lottery amongst those in the same position.

Article 1.213

The creditors whose votes, because they represented the majority of the capital, resulted in the appointment of the first two receivers in bankruptcy will not take part in the vote in respect of the third receiver in bankruptcy. Only the remaining creditors will take part in this second vote and the receiver in bankruptcy elected will be the one who has obtained the largest number of votes.

If there are two or more with the same number of votes, the third receiver in bankruptcy will be the one who has won the support of voters representing the larger capital sum and if this is also the same, lots will be drawn amongst those in the same position and the winner will be elected on the basis of chance.

Article 1.214

When it is necessary to replace any of the receivers in bankruptcy because of death or for any other reason the election of either of the first two will be by reference to the relative size of the capital, and that of the third by reference to the relative number of votes of the creditors who attend the meeting in accordance with the provisions of the preceding articles.

Article 1.215

Those elected as receivers in bankruptcy must, of necessity, be male creditors, of more than twenty five years of age, who attend the meeting in their own right and not as a representative of a third party, who have no known preference or claim to such preference and who reside in the locality of the bankruptcy proceedings.

Only when there are no creditors in their own right may representatives of third parties be elected.

If the only creditors are preferred creditors, or those who claim to be so, and representatives of others in a similar position, the election should apply to them.

Article 1.216

On the day and at the time appointed, the meeting will be held under the presidency of the judge and in the presence of the clerk of the court.

Once note has been taken of the creditors present and it is established that they are those included in the list drawn up by the clerk of the court, in accordance with article 1.207, the judge will hold the meeting to have been duly constituted, whatever the number of creditors present.

He will begin the session by reading the provisions of this law relating to the appointment of receivers in bankruptcy, following which the clerk of the court will provide a statement of the background to the declaration of bankruptcy, of the result of the steps taken to seize the assets, books and papers and of any other events which may have taken place.

When these formalities have been completed, the appointment of the receivers in bankruptcy will take place in the manner prescribed by article 1.210 and the succeeding articles.

An appropriate record of the result of the meeting will be drawn up giving a detailed statement of the nominal "yea and nay" votes and, if applicable, of any protests made, which, after it has been read and approved, will be signed by the judge, in the presence of the creditors, the debtor, if he attended, and the clerk of the court.

Article 1.217

Once the receivers in bankruptcy have been appointed, they will take up their appointment, subject to their having accepted the office and sworn to discharge their functions well and faithfully and, where necessary, subject to announcement of their appointment.

Their appointment will also be published by means of public announcements which will be posted in the usual places and inserted in the same official journals in which the notice of the meeting was published.

These public announcements will state that all matters relating to the bankrupt will be delivered to the receivers in bankruptcy.

Article 1.218

The functions of the receivers in bankruptcy are:

1. To represent the bankruptcy estate in the proceedings and at other times, defending its rights and pursuing and defending the actions in which they are competent to act.
2. To administer the assets of the bankruptcy estate, taking charge of them and of the books and papers.
3. To receive and collect all the debts, income and annuities belonging to the bankruptcy estate and pay the expenses of the same as necessary for the protection of its rights and for the preservation and benefit of the assets.
4. To procure the sale and realisation of all the assets, to pursue the rights and actions of the bankruptcy estate on the most favourable terms and in accordance with the due legal formalities.
5. To examine the certificates of title of the debts and propose to the creditors' meeting that they be recognised and classified.
6. To require the calling and holding of the creditors' meetings, in such cases and for such reasons as they consider necessary, in addition to the reasons specifically set out in this law.

Article 1.219

The receivers in bankruptcy will collectively have the right to the following remuneration, which will be divided amongst them in equal shares unless otherwise agreed.

In respect of the sale of public bonds, one half of one per cent. of the actual value.

In respect of the cash value realised from the sale of precious objects, moveable assets, goods and chattels or products which are not derived from their administration, two per cent.

In respect of the net proceeds from the sale of real estate and the realisation of debts or rights of the bankruptcy, one per cent.

In respect of the net proceeds from Government sources not arising from any of the matters referred to in the above paragraphs, five per cent.

If, in carrying out their duties, they are required to travel, their travel expenses will be paid at the judge's discretion and upon an order given to that effect.

Article 1.220

The election of the receivers in bankruptcy or any one of them may be challenged by the debtor or any one of the creditors in the proceedings who did not attend the meeting or who dissented from the majority and protested against the election at the time.

In order for the challenge to be admitted it must be presented within the three days following the meeting, if the debtor or the challenging creditor attended it, and in any other case within the same period of time commencing from the publication of the appointment of the receivers in bankruptcy.

Article 1.221

No cause for challenge will be admissible other than the following:

1. Legal defect which prevents the appointed person from exercising his office.
2. Procedural irregularity in the calling, holding and deliberations of the meeting.
3. Lack of legal capacity or legal representation of any of those making up a majority to the extent that, if his vote had not been counted, the same result, by reference either to number or capital amount, would not have been obtained.

Article 1.222

The challenge against the receiver in bankruptcy in question will be made in a separate application which will be drawn up by the challenger, with the writ in which it has been set out, a certified copy of the minutes of the meeting and any other particulars which the judge may require.

Article 1.223

When the separate application has been drawn up the challenger will be notified so that he may formalise it within four days whereupon it will be substantiated under the procedure established for such cases.

The judgment as pronounced is subject to appeal in any event.

Article 1.224

The trial of the bankruptcy proceedings will not be suspended as a result of opposition to the appointment of the receivers in bankruptcy.

Nor will it prevent the appointees from commencing the exercise of their functions, without prejudice to the outcome of such opposition.

Article 1.225

A receiver whose standing is not recognised in whole or in part by the creditors' meeting or by the judge, as the case may be, or who challenges some action against the bankruptcy assets, or disputes any of the agreements of the creditors' meetings, will be legally removed from the receivership and will be replaced in the manner prescribed in article 1.214.

Article 1.226

When, for the reasons stated in the preceding article, as a result of death or for any other cause, any of the receivers in bankruptcy has to be replaced, the election will take place in the first meeting to be held thereafter, whether it is the meeting dealing with the recognition, or with the ranking of the debts.

If the relevant event occurs after these meetings have been held and no further meeting has been called, the judge will agree to call a meeting so as to proceed with the replacement of the receiver in bankruptcy whose receivership has ended.

Meanwhile the receiver or receivers in bankruptcy who remain in office will continue to be the legal representatives of the bankruptcy estate.

Article 1.227

Once the receivers in bankruptcy have taken up their office, the proceedings will be divided into three separate court files.

The first, which will contain the previous proceedings, will be referred to as the "administration of the bankruptcy estate". In it, all matters relating to the administration itself will be tried, without prejudice to the formation of separate sections as and when necessary to avoid confusion in the proceedings.

The second will be directed towards the "recognition and ranking of debts".

The third, to the "classification of the bankruptcy".

Section V: First court file – Administration of the bankruptcy

Article 1.228

Once the appointment of the receivers has been published they will be handed an inventory of all assets, effects, books and papers relating to the bankruptcy.

The money will be kept at the disposal of the judge at the institution designated for that purpose, and the deposit voucher or vouchers will be handed to the receivers against a receipt made out under this court file.

Article 1.229

The receivers will be obliged, at their own responsibility, to preserve and administer the bankruptcy assets diligently, whilst endeavouring to produce the relevant income, yield or earnings until sale.

To that end the provisions set out in articles 1.016 to 1.029 for the administration of intestacy proceedings will apply to the administration of the bankruptcy proceedings without the requirement for the bankrupt to attend a hearing.

Article 1.230

The judge will allow the receivers such amount as he believes necessary to meet the ordinary expenses of the bankruptcy, and will order that it be taken out of the deposit if necessary.

These expenses will be considered to be the total of those required for the custody and preservation of the assets, the payment of any contributions and charges relating to the property, litigation and the general business of the bankruptcy.

Article 1.231

On the last day of each month the receivers will present an administrative statement or account unless the judge considers it necessary to extend this period after taking into consideration the income of the bankruptcy.

If cash amounts not required to cover the affairs of the bankruptcy proceedings have been advanced which have not been deposited by the receivers at the relevant public institution, the judge will order the receivers personally liable to account for such amounts and bind them over to account for such amounts at their own responsibility.

Article 1.232

The administrative statements or accounts will be placed in a separate folder within the first court file which, together with any other files which may be opened, will be held in the notary public's office at the disposal of the creditors and the debtor if they wish to examine them. No rights will accrue from the exhibition of these documents.

Article 1.233

The judge either himself, or at the request of the creditors or the bankrupt, may correct any breach which comes to light in the administration of the bankruptcy, adopting whatever measures he considers necessary including suspending the receiver or receivers who have committed such breach.

In such a case, the judge will immediately call a creditors' meeting to decide whatever they see fit. No appeal lies against the judge's decision.

If the agreement of the meeting is to suspend the receiver, he will be replaced at the same meeting in the manner set out in article 1.214.

In any other case, the suspension will be lifted with the agreement of the judge.

The provisions of this article are understood to be without prejudice to criminal proceedings if these are appropriate.

Article 1.234

Once the receivers have taken possession of the assets and the effects of the bankruptcy, they will proceed with the sale of these, either under the first court file or under separate files, save only for:

1. Assets in respect of which a claim for ownership is pending at the instigation of a third party, in which case final judgment will be reserved.
2. Property which, being the subject of a special mortgage, is under enforcement embargo and not included in the bankruptcy proceedings.

In this case, the judge presiding over the enforcement hearing will be formally requested to place at the disposal of the bankruptcy the balance, if any, after payment to the mortgage creditor.

Article 1.235

When the receivers believe the suspension or postponement of the sale of any of the assets to be in the interests of the bankruptcy, they will inform the judge who will allow it if he believes it to be appropriate, with the reservation that, at the first meeting to be held, the reasons for such suspension will be brought to the notice of the creditors so that a majority, as defined by rule 6 of article 1.139, may agree whatever measure is in their best interests.

Article 1.236

The sale will be carried out following the enforcement hearing according to the formalities established for each type of asset being lawfully collected.

Article 1.237

A valuation will be made by an assessor selected by the judge in accordance with article 616, and the provisions of article 617 and, where applicable, those following article 617.

At the request of the receivers, the judge may agree that three assessors be selected in the same way where, in his opinion, the size of the bankruptcy estate warrants such a measure.

Representatives of the receivers and the bankrupt will be called to the balloting and selection of the assessors, by way of a summons which will indicate the day and time of the hearing. If they appear and agree to the appointment of the assessor or assessors, those designated will be considered to have been appointed. If not, an election will be made in accordance with article 616.

Article 1.238

If there are no admissible bids, a second auction will be announced at a reduction of 25 per cent of the valuation.

If a bidder still does not come forward a creditors' meeting will be called in order to agree the manner in which the unsold assets will be adjudicated unless a third auction with no reserve is preferred.

If an adjudication is selected, this will take place at two thirds of the price which would have been used as the reserve in the second auction.

Article 1.239

It will also be possible to sell debts, rights and shares at public auction where they are either of a contentious nature, difficult to sell or of long term maturity, or because in order to claim them by judicial means it would be necessary to delay the termination of the bankruptcy for an indefinite period to realise their value.

In such cases and at the request of the receivers, the judge will declare the means which he considers to be the most appropriate to set the amount which, as a sale price, will serve as reserve in the auction.

Article 1.240

Once the sale by auction has been approved, the receivers will execute the relevant document in favour of the highest bidder who, having paid the sale price will place it on deposit at the disposal of the court as described above.

Article 1.241

The receivers may settle any pending litigation, either made on behalf of or brought against the bankruptcy estate and any other contentious matters in which the bankruptcy may have an interest, provided they are authorised to make any such settlement at the creditors' meeting.

If they do not have such authority, the matter once agreed will be submitted for the approval of the first meeting held or a meeting to be called for this purpose which will pass a majority resolution, such majority to be calculated in accordance with rule 6 of article 1.139.

In either case, the receivers will present the transaction as a separate item for judicial approval, without which it will not be valid. The judge will allow six days for a hearing with the bankrupt and, with no further proceedings, will resolve the matter in whatever manner he deems appropriate.

The order allowing or dismissing the transaction will be open to appeal.

Article 1.242

Once all the debts, or that part of them covered by the assets of the bankruptcy, have been paid, the receivers will submit a general account, fully substantiated, which will be attached to the accounts file and will be displayed at the notary's office for fifteen days at the disposal of the debtor and those creditors who have not been fully paid.

Article 1.243

After fifteen days and if no objection has been raised, the judge will approve the account and will order that the appropriate discharge be given to the receivers.

Article 1.244

Claims made against the account will be substantiated as regards the amount by the receivers in ordinary hearing.

Anyone making these claims will commence proceedings at his own expense and on his own responsibility without prejudice to any costs which may be ordered against the receivers if they lose the case.

Parties bringing the same suit will be joined in the action.

Article 1.245

If the receivers step down from office before the proceedings for liquidation of the bankruptcy are concluded, they will submit their general account within fifteen days which will be put to the examination and approval of the first creditors' meeting which is held prior to the report from the new receivers.

If no meeting is held, the judge will approve the account at a hearing with the new receivers and if any objections are raised, possibly by the creditors themselves, they will be substantiated under the procedure established for all such cases.

The decision or judgment made in relation to these objections will be open to appeal.

Article 1.246

Once the receivers' account has been approved, the debtor will be given his books, papers and any assets which remain after the debts and costs of the bankruptcy have been paid in full.

If they have not been paid in full, the current books and papers will be held in the notary's office for future use together with the judgment orders.

Article 1.247

The definitive outcome of the bankruptcy will be issued by court order personally to those creditors whose registered address is known and who have not been fully paid, and in all cases will be published by edict inserted in the journals in which the declaration of bankruptcy was first published.

Article 1.248

The discharge of the bankrupt will be declared in the judgment which orders publication of the final outcome of the bankruptcy without the need for a petition or a hearing with the receivers.

The discharge will be deemed to be without prejudice both to the rights of the creditors whose debts have not been fully paid and to the final verdict relating to the culpability of the bankrupt.

Section VI: Second court file – Admission, ranking and payment of debts

Article 1.249

Once the receivers have taken possession of the assets, books and papers of the bankruptcy proceedings, the second court file, which deals with the admission ranking and payment of debts, will be opened.

This file will comprise precise details of the statement or list of debts presented by the debtor and, at the same time, a separate division will be drawn up from the debt instruments presented by the creditors as required by article 1.204.

Part 1 – Admission of debts

Article 1.250

When the second court file has been prepared, the receivers will be informed accordingly within the period indicated by the judge depending on the circumstances of the bankruptcy proceedings but not exceeding 30 days. When the receivers have had sight of the matters presented and the debtor's books and papers, they will proceed with the examination and payment of debts and will give their opinion as to the admission of each debt.

Article 1.251

As a result of this examination and in order to report to the creditors' meeting, the receivers will draw up three statements to include, respectively:

1. All debts claimed in the order in which they were presented.

2. Those which, in their opinion, should be admitted.
3. Those which should not be admitted.

These statements will include all the debts claimed up to the date they were drawn up.

Article 1.252

The judge will formally require the receivers to verify the examination of the debts and the presentation of the statements within the time fixed by him, and will compel them, if necessary, to complete this task by means of a fine or any other appropriate measure.

Article 1.253

Once the receivers have presented these statements, the judge will agree to call a creditors' meeting for the admission of debts, stating the day, time and place where it is to be held.

The creditors will be summoned to the meeting personally, or by proxy, by means of a court order which will be delivered to their registered addresses, if any, or otherwise in the locality of the hearing where details have been provided. The remainder will be summoned by a notice in the manner required under article 1.197.

Article 1.254

Fifteen to thirty days should elapse between the calling and the holding of the meeting during which time the creditors and debtor may examine the receivers' opinion and the debt instruments which will be displayed in the court office for this purpose.

Article 1.255

When the meeting has been constituted under the presidency of the judge in the presence of the clerk of the court, those articles which relate to the admission of debts and the way in which resolutions relating to such admission should be challenged will be read, and the statements referred to in article 1.251 will be brought to the meeting's attention and discussed, point by point.

Each point will be voted upon separately, the debts being unanimously accepted or rejected and, if unanimity is not reached, by a majority decision which must be constituted in the manner required under rule 6 of article 1.139.

The minutes of this meeting which will include, if appropriate, the objections of those who disagree with the majority vote, will be signed by all the creditors present and by the debtor or his representative if present and by the judge and the clerk of the court.

Article 1.256

Debts relating to final judgments on enforcement proceedings consolidated with the bankruptcy proceedings may not be discussed.

These debts will be deemed to have been admitted although without any variation as regards their ranking, and without prejudice to the receivers' right to challenge them in respect of quantum in the full trial.

Article 1.257

If the majority votes and amounts are not attained, at the end of the meeting the judge will determine without any further procedural steps what he considers to be a lawful adjustment of the disputed debt.

This same procedure will be followed for all debts where the meeting has not been properly constituted due to insufficient creditors being present to reach agreement as required by article 1.138.

Article 1.258

It may be agreed at the meeting, or by the judge if appropriate, to leave pending the admission of any debt which has been presented with insufficient justification.

In this event, the interested party will give further evidence under the heading of a separate file during the period before the meeting dealing with the ranking of debts.

Article 1.259

Admitted creditors will be given a document, on ordinary paper, signed by the receivers and approved by the judge confirming the amount, source and admission of the debt.

Article 1.260

Creditors whose debts have not been admitted will be informed by the receivers of the decision of the meeting, or of the judge, by means of a circular letter which the clerk of the court will deliver to those who have their registered address or representative in the locality of the hearing in the manner prescribed for such notice and will send the remainder by post.

The appropriate document confirming that this has been carried out together with a copy of the circular letter will be included in the file relating to the application.

The clerk of the court will also return the debt instruments duly receipted and when these are presented for collection no requirement for a further decision of the court will be necessary.

Article 1.261

The resolutions of these meetings and the decisions made by the judge in the cases where the two majorities are not reached, may be challenged within eight days by the creditors not present at the meeting or by those who did attend but disputed and objected to the majority vote.

In the latter case, this period will start from the day following the meeting, and in the other cases, from the day following the day when the circular letter was delivered or sent.

Article 1.262

If after eight days no challenge has been made, the resolutions of the meeting or the decisions of the judge, where appropriate, will become final and no claim against them will be considered.

Article 1.263

Every challenge will be made under a separate file and will be substantiated by the receivers and, where appropriate, by the party interested in the challenged debt by means of the established procedure for these cases, the judgment thereon being open to appeal.

Article 1.264

The receivers are obliged to uphold the majority decision even when they have voted to the contrary; but are not obliged to uphold the resolutions issued by the judge.

The debtor may take part in any separate files which may be prepared. If the agreement is upheld, he will litigate with the receivers; if it is challenged, he will litigate with the creditor making the challenge; the parties will litigate jointly in both cases.

Article 1.265

The resolutions of the meeting may also be claimed to be null and void if the established procedure for the calling, holding and voting of the meeting has not been followed.

This claim may only be made by the debtor or the creditors who, having properly presented their debt instruments, did not attend the meeting or who, having attended, have disputed the validity of these by abstaining from the voting; this claim should be presented within the three days following the meeting after which time such claim will not be allowed.

Substantiation will be in accordance with the provisions of article 1.223, but without drawing up a separate file, and the principal action will be stayed.

Part 2 – Ranking

Article 1.266

Once a final judgment has been made on the case referred to in the previous article if the nullity claim has been overruled, or the eight days mentioned in article 1.261 for challenging the agreements reached in the meeting or by the judge have lapsed, a further meeting will be called of those creditors whose debts have been recognised for ranking, without prejudice to the continuation of any separate files prepared in accordance with the provisions of article 1.263.

The notice for this meeting will be in the form required by article 1.253.

Article 1.267

Fifteen to thirty days should elapse between issue of the notice and holding of this meeting.

When, in an exceptional case, the judge considers that this period is insufficient for the receivers to draw up the lists referred to in the following article, he may extend it by such time as he believes to be absolutely essential.

Article 1.268

In the intervening period, the receivers will draw up four lists to bring to the attention of the meeting. These will consist of:

First, creditors for personal services and maintenance.

If intestacy or proceedings in a bankrupt estate are involved, the first list will include creditors for funeral expenses appropriate to the circumstances of the deceased, and for expenses incurred in the preparation of his last will and testament and the drawing up of the inventory and legal matters, or for other obligations arising as a result of the intestacy and estate proceedings.

Secondly, mortgage creditors in the order of preference provided by law.

In addition to the creditors who hold in their favour legal mortgages found to be subsisting, those with voluntary mortgages will also be included in this list, with the proviso in relation to these that their priority will be limited to the specifically mortgaged assets; and if the value of the assets does not cover the total amount of the debt secured by the mortgage, these creditors will be considered to be unsecured for the difference.

Other creditors secured by a pledge will also be included in this list, but their preference will again be limited to the cash value of their security, any excess being returned to the credit of bankruptcy estate.

Thirdly, creditors by notarial document in date order.

Fourthly, ordinary creditors, including in this list all the debts not included in the three aforementioned lists.

Article 1.269

The receivers will draw up a separate note of assets of any type held by the bankrupt and belonging to third parties, stating the names of the owners of those assets.

If the owners have claimed these assets they will be handed over with the agreement of the receivers and the bankrupt. If any party does not agree, the claim will be substantiated under a separate file by means of a full trial corresponding to the amount of the claim.

Article 1.270

Before the day indicated for the meeting, the receivers should have given their opinion with respect to the separate files on any debts still awaiting recognition, or which may have been claimed after preparation of the statements required by article 1.251.

If the receivers believe these debts should be recognised, they will be included in the ranking lists, without prejudice to what may be agreed about their recognition at the meeting.

Article 1.271

When the meeting has been assembled in the prescribed manner, the session will begin by reading the articles of this law relating to the ranking of debts and to challenges to any agreements on this point.

Any debts awaiting recognition will then be discussed and the opinion of the receivers mentioned in the previous article will be put to the vote. The owners of recognised debts may take part in the discussions on ranking at the meeting.

Afterwards attention will be given to the ranking lists and the debts in the lists will be discussed.

When the discussion is ended, the opinion of the receivers on each debt will be put to the vote, being approved when there is a majority of votes and amounts, calculated as provided in rule 6 of article 1.139 unless the result is unanimous.

On conclusion of the meeting, the minutes will be drawn up by way of record of what has taken place and these will be signed by those present, the judge and the clerk of the court.

Article 1.272

If the two majorities are not reached, the judge will open court proceedings and will determine the issues on the debt or debts which have given rise to disagreement in accordance with his opinion of the law.

Article 1.273

The provisions of the previous article will also take effect if the meeting has not been properly constituted due to the absence of the number of creditors required for an agreement in accordance with the provisions of article 1.138.

In that event, the judge will make such decision as he considers just for each of the separate divisions relating to debts awaiting recognition, if there are any, and without delay he will give those debts within the second application their ranking by means of a ruling in which he will approve the lists drawn up by the receivers or make such rectifications as may be required by law.

Article 1.274

In the event that article 1.272 takes effect, the judge's decision will be notified to the receivers and the parties interested in the debts giving rise to the disagreement.

The decision on ranking in article 1.273 will be notified to the receivers and the recognised creditors or their representatives who have provided details of their address or have designated an address in the locality of the hearing.

If any admitted creditors are absent and have no legal representation in that place, they may be properly notified of this ruling by means of an edict which will be affixed in the usual public places.

Article 1.275

Within eight days following the holding of the meeting for the ranking of debts, the agreements may be challenged by recognised creditors who were not present at the meeting or who, having attended, disagreed with the majority vote and reserved their right of challenge.

The judge's decision may also be challenged within eight days of notification.

Once these periods have elapsed no further challenge will be admitted.

Article 1.276

All challenges to agreements reached at the meeting or decisions of the judge on the ranking of the debts, whether from one or several creditors, will be substantiated at the same time in the same second file according to the procedure established for incidental matters.

The receivers will always take part in these issues and will uphold the agreement of the meeting if appropriate.

The creditors whose debts are the object of a challenge will also be admitted as lawful participants as will the remainder who may wish to assist in upholding or challenging the agreements.

All those with similar claims should litigate jointly and under the same directions.

The bankrupt will not be admitted to take part in these proceedings.

Article 1.277

In order to enable opposition motions in these matters to be formalised, the civil proceedings will be handed over together with all the preceding records relative to the recognition and ranking of the debts to the challenger or challengers for a period of six days, and the same procedure will be applied to the response to this opposition.

When the judge considers such to be necessary, because there are many debts whose ranking is challenged he may increase the periods of notification to twelve days. In other cases he will have eight days to issue a judgment and thus comply with the procedure for such matters.

This judgment will be open to appeal with suspension of execution.

Part 3 – Default and its effects

Article 1.278

Creditors resident in Spanish territory on the Peninsula, in the Spanish possessions in Africa or in the Balearic Islands who did not appear before the court prior to the summons to the meeting for recognition of debt, will be considered to be in default if they appear later.

Article 1.279

The legal effects of default are:

1. That those in default pay for the recognition of their debt.
2. That they lose any preference which may be applicable to them, and are reduced to the level or ordinary creditor if they appear after the meeting for the ranking of debts has been held.
3. That they lose that proportion of their debt which would have related to them in any dividend paid before their presentation, with no right to participate except in any dividend paid in the future.

Article 1.280

If between presentation and recognition any dividend is paid, those in default will be included but the relevant amounts will be retained on deposit.

These amounts will be handed over when their debts are recognised; if they are not recognised, these sums will be returned to the bankruptcy estate.

Article 1.281

A separate file will be drawn up in order to recognise the debts of defaulting creditors; this will contain the appropriate application and documents presented for each debt and will include a statement evidenced by the clerk of the court as to whether the debt has or has not been included in the list of debts presented by the bankrupt.

If it has been included, the file will be handed to the receivers so that they may issue their opinion on the recognition of the debt.

If it has not been included, a hearing will be given to the bankrupt three days before handing the file to the receivers.

Article 1.282

When the defaulting creditor presents himself before the meeting for the ranking of debts has taken place, he will provide sufficient information at the meeting to resolve the recognition of the debt provided the debt has been checked sufficiently well beforehand in order to fulfil the requirements of the previous article.

If not, the judge will make a final decision on the admission, provided always that the receivers are in agreement.

If an agreement is not forthcoming, the interested party will retain the right to discuss it with the receivers in the definitive hearing relating to the amount, provided that the costs relating to that file shall be awarded against him.

Article 1.283

Creditors residing in the Canary Islands will not be in default until after the holding of the ranking meeting, irrespective of the manner in which they were summoned; the provisions of articles 1.279 and 1.280 will be applied to those who present themselves after this meeting.

Article 1.284

The creditors resident in overseas provinces or in any other country will not incur any penalty at all even after the meeting for the ranking of debts.

If they do subsequently present themselves, a separate file will be drawn up in which their debts should be admitted if they are lawful, and ranked by a ruling issued after the receivers and the bankrupt have been consulted. They will maintain the preference corresponding to their debts and they will be reinstated in the place indicated; but in no event will the other creditors be obliged to return what they have received.

If their debts are ranked as ordinary, they will be on equal footing with the others of their class, and when this has been done, they will join together with these on a pro-rata basis to participate in the assets of the bankruptcy which have still to be distributed.

Article 1.285

No audience will be given in this hearing to those creditors in default if they present themselves after all the assets of the bankruptcy have been distributed.

Part 4 – Payment of debts

Article 1.286

If the eight days mentioned in article 1.275 have passed without any challenge to the agreements reached in the meeting on the ranking or to the judge's decision, as appropriate, payment of the debts will proceed in the order established in the meeting up to the limit of the disposable funds of the bankruptcy.

Article 1.287

When the purpose of the challenge is to nullify the agreement reached in the meeting or refers to the whole ranking, payment will be suspended until final judgment is made.

If the ranking of only some debts is in question, payment will proceed and a separate file will be set up for this purpose which will include an affidavit of the statements and agreements reached in the meeting or the decision of the judge relating to the ranking of these debts.

Article 1.288

In the case of the second paragraph of the previous article, the amounts relating to the challenged debts will be kept on deposit until a final judgment is made on the challenge so that they may be appropriately applied.

The same will apply to the amounts relating to debts where recognition has been challenged, if no final judgment has yet been made on this point.

Article 1.289

The amounts relating to the creditors who, having had their debts recognised and ranked in the meeting, have been challenged by an individual creditor, will be handed over despite the challenge provided they offer a sufficient bond for the amount they have been given to the satisfaction and on the responsibility of the receivers.

Article 1.290

When payment of the debts included in the first three rankings has been made in the correct order, the remaining funds will be distributed on a pro-rata basis among the ordinary creditors by means of dividends, which will be repeated as the assets of the bankruptcy are realised and sufficient funds are raised to cover at least five per cent. of the debts pending.

If this should arise and the receivers delay making a proposal to the court for payment of a dividend, any one of the creditors may apply for such payment.

Article 1.291

In order to verify the payment, the judge will order the receivers to make the appropriate drawings in favour of each of the creditors who is to receive the full amount, agreeing at the same time that the necessary funds be put at their disposal and withdrawing such funds from the deposit.

On handing over the drawings to the creditor, the document recognising his debt will be collected and a cancellation note entered in it which will be signed by the interested party and the clerk of the court, and the latter will add this document to the separate file containing the title of the debt, making an appropriate note in the second court file.

The receivers, or the one who has been authorised by the others to do so, will pay out the funds against a receipt signed by the interested party which he will retain in support of his accounts.

Article 1.292

When payment is made by means of dividends to the ordinary creditors, these will be verified by the receivers, sufficient funds being placed at their disposal for this purpose.

The receivers, or the one who has been charged with so doing, will give each creditor or his lawful representative the amount due to him in the distribution of funds, noting the same on the recognition of debt document, without presentation of which no payment will be made, and the interested party will also give a separate receipt to the receivers.

Article 1.293

Once payment has been made, the receivers will present to the court a verified account, together with all the creditors' receipts, of the application of the funds received by them, placing whatever balance remains, if any, back on deposit together with the amounts relating to creditors who have not collected their payment.

This account will be added to the accounts file and the clerk of the court will issue the appropriate receipt to the receivers with the relevant details for safekeeping.

Article 1.294

When the ordinary creditors have been paid in full, on payment of the last dividend the recognition documentation will be collected and cancelled.

In this case or when all the funds of the bankruptcy have been exhausted, the hearing will be considered finished in accordance with the provisions of articles 1.242 et seq.

Section VII: Third court file – Classification of bankruptcy proceedings

Article 1.295

When the receivers have been appointed, they will be handed the first court file in the bankruptcy proceedings so that within thirty days, after examination of the books and papers of the debtor, they will issue in a reasoned and documented statement the opinion they have formed as to the bankruptcy and its causes, drawing such conclusions and making such declarations of intent as they consider appropriate.

Article 1.296

Together with precise evidence of the list, statement and report presented by the debtor, and the original statement of the receivers and accompanying documents, the third court file will be opened, and with the first court file provisionally attached to it, all the files will be passed to the Public Prosecutor so that he may also give his opinion.

Article 1.297

If the opinion of the Public Prosecutor agrees with the opinion of the receivers, and both are favourable to the bankrupt, the judge will re-open the court proceedings and may, if he considers such to be appropriate, declare that the bankrupt is not culpable.

Article 1.298

If the receivers' report and the report of the Public Prosecutor or either one of them is contrary to the report of the bankrupt, but are still favourable, and if the judge believes that he should not defer to them, he will allow the bankrupt a period of six days to give any explanation he believes to be appropriate and will hand the court proceedings file to him for that purpose.

The procedure for this will comply with the proceedings established for those persons who appear in ordinary hearings and the judgment given is open to appeal with suspension of execution.

Article 1.299

All the creditors have the right to present themselves under this court file and to take proceedings against the bankrupt.

If one or more of them do so and their actions have the same object as the receivers they should litigate jointly with the receivers and under common control.

If the purpose of their actions is different, they must litigate separately.

Article 1.300

When the bankrupt has been declared culpable by final judgment in relation to civil proceedings only, the judge will order criminal proceedings to commence under the third file. From then on, the substantiation will comply with the procedure established for criminal hearings.

Article 1.301

When a company, association or legal person is declared bankrupt, the receivers will state in the report required by article 1.295 the opinion they have formed on the criminal or civil responsibility which the administrators, directors or board members of the bankrupt company may have incurred through their part in acts, negotiations or agreements contrary to statutory or other law.

Article 1.302

In the case of the previous article, once the third file has been drawn up in accordance with the provisions of article 1.296 and substantiated in the manner required by that article and those which follow, a declaration will be made as to whether or not there is a basis on which to hold responsible all or some of those who have been involved in the running of the company.

If their liability is shown to be criminal, matters will proceed as ordered in article 1.300; and if their liability is only civil, the receivers may bring whatever action is appropriate.

Section VIII: Settlement between creditors and bankrupt

Article 1.303

At any stage during the bankruptcy proceedings, once the debts have been examined and recognised, and not before such time, the creditors and the bankrupt may come to whatever settlement they consider appropriate.

Article 1.304

Every application made by the debtor or any of the creditors to call a meeting for the purpose of the settlement must contain the following requirements, without which it will not be admitted:

1. That the settlement proposals are drawn up clearly and precisely.
2. That as many printed or manuscript copies of the settlement are attached as there are recognised creditors.
3. That the person who makes such proposals is obliged to pay the costs of calling and holding the meeting, even though he may plead poverty; he must also guarantee payment of these costs to the satisfaction of the judge.

Article 1.305

If in the third court file the receivers, the Public Prosecutor or any creditor has requested that the bankruptcy be declared culpable, the debtor may not agree a settlement with his creditors until a final judgment has been made discharging the bankruptcy declaration.

Article 1.306

The provisions of the previous article will not be applicable to companies or partnerships declared bankrupt if the administrators or managers are liable in law for the bankruptcy.

The criminal liability of any of these will not deprive the company from the benefits of a settlement with its creditors; but the culpable administrator may not make the settlement proposals nor may these be put forward by him in the meeting.

Article 1.307

If settlement proposals are presented when the meeting for the ranking of debts or any other later meeting is to be or has been called, preference will be given to bringing such proposals to the meeting's notice without the necessity of calling a meeting specially for this purpose.

If the proposals are presented before the holding of the recognition of debts meeting, they will also be brought to the attention of that meeting, but only after recognition has taken place; and only those creditors whose debts have been recognised may discuss the settlement.

In both cases, the proposals should be presented sufficiently in advance so that copies can be delivered to the creditors twenty-four hours before the date the meeting is to be held.

Article 1.308

Apart from the cases referred to in the previous article and in article 1.305, once the application with the requirements set out in article 1.304 has been presented, the judge will concur, and will order a creditors' meeting to be called to consider the settlement stating the date, time and place where it is to be held.

Article 1.309

A period of at least 15 days should elapse between calling and holding the meeting. The judge may increase this period to 30 days if the circumstances of the bankruptcy so require.

Article 1.310

The creditors whose debts have been recognised by the meeting or by the judge will be personally summoned to this meeting by means of a court order, together with those awaiting recognition, or their representatives if they have them, and, upon the service of the summons, each will be handed one of the copies presented in accordance with the provisions of paragraph 2 of article 1.304.

Those absent whose registered addresses are unknown, should there be any, will be summoned by edicts in the form prescribed by article 1.197.

The object of the meeting will be stated in the court orders and edicts together with the date, time and place at which it is to be held.

Article 1.311

The calling of the meeting to consider the settlement entails suspension of the second court file in the bankruptcy action as well as the first, in so far as the first relates to the disposal of assets, until the proposals presented have been discussed and agreed.

Article 1.312

The provisions of articles 1.137 to 1.154 for release and respite apply to settlements proposed after the declaration of bankruptcy with the following modifications:

1. Once the meeting has been constituted, it will begin with the reading of the provisions of this law relating to the settlement between the debtor and his creditors; afterwards all the records of the bankruptcy and its status, including any third court file, will be accounted for, and once the proposals for agreement have been read, a discussion will be opened on them.
2. If the settlement proposals are rejected as provided in article 1.143, the bankruptcy action will continue; this will also apply if there is a challenge, and the settlement is declared null and void.
3. The receivers must uphold any settlement agreed at the meeting and for that purpose they will take part in the hearing of any objection together with the other persons indicated in article 1.150.

4. The decision resulting from this hearing may be appealed by either party if the settlement is declared null and void. If not, only the losing party may appeal and the settlement will be enforced between the debtor and the creditors who accept it, without prejudice to anything resolved by the final judgment.

Article 1.313

Once the agreement of the meeting approving the settlement is final, it will be notified in a circular letter from the receivers to the creditors who have been recognised, or who are pending recognition and did not attend the meeting. The settlement will be published by edict in the same journals as were used for the declaration of bankruptcy, and by attaching a copy of it to the court proceedings.

Once this has been done, the hearing will be considered to have terminated, and the measures necessary to fulfil the agreement will be decided, which will be binding on all the creditors other than those who are excepted.

Section IX: Maintenance for the bankrupt

Article 1.314

If the bankrupt applies for maintenance, the judge will specify what he considers necessary in the circumstances, but only if, in his opinion, the assets are greater than the debts.

The ruling allowing or disallowing maintenance will be of an interim nature and will not be subject to appeal.

Article 1.315

The interim ruling made by the judge will be brought to the notice of the first creditors' meeting, which may approve, modify or abolish the maintenance, taking into consideration the requirements and circumstances of the bankrupt, but maintenance will be granted unless it can be clearly shown that there are insufficient assets to pay the debts.

Article 1.316

The agreement of the meeting allowing or disallowing maintenance may be challenged by the debtor or by the creditors who did not take part in it and by those who disagreed and protested against the majority vote at the time, providing they claim their right of action within eight days following the agreement.

The challenge will be substantiated by the procedure established for incidental matters and those who raise the same grounds should litigate jointly and under the same direction; the period for production of evidence may be increased to 30 days if the period allowed by article 753 is insufficient.

Article 1.317

While the hearing for maintenance is pending, the bankrupt will receive maintenance if the judge or the meeting has allowed it. Maintenance will not be allowed if the judge or the meeting have agreed to deny it.

When the amount fixed by the judge is different from that fixed by the meeting, the amount fixed by the meeting will be binding.

CHAPTER XIII. ON THE ORDER OF PROCEDURE FOR BANKRUPTCY

Article 1.318

According to the provisions of the 1st article of the Commercial Code, as amended by the law dated 30th July 1878, every trader, even though he may not have registered himself according to the nature of his trade, who considers himself to be in a state of bankruptcy will be subject to the procedures which have been established for such cases in the said Code and in this Chapter, and he may not subject himself to the ordinary rules for bankruptcy proceedings.

The judges will not allow any declaration of bankruptcy which may have been requested to take place and will decree the appropriate state of bankruptcy relating to those who find themselves in this situation.

Article 1.319

In all matters which are not provided for, or expressly decreed in the Commercial Code and in this Chapter in relation to the rules for procedure in bankruptcy, the decrees made for bankruptcy proceedings in the previous Chapter will apply, and the provisions therein will be considered as supplementary to those stated in this Chapter.

Article 1.320

In respect of the bankruptcy of railway companies, canal companies, and other similar public service companies subsidised by the state, the special proceedings decreed by the law of 12th November 1869 will be observed.

Article 1.321

The procedure for the bankruptcy of traders will be divided into five sections, dividing the legal proceedings under each one of these sections into their respective court files. These in turn will be subdivided into whatever files are necessary for the good order and clarity of the proceedings so that these may be carried out with all possible speed and with no hindrance from matters which cannot be substantiated at the same time.

Article 1.322

The first section will include matters relating to the declaration of bankruptcy, the steps to be taken consequent upon such declaration and their execution, the appointment of the receivers and matters incidental to their dismissal and replacement, and the agreement between the creditors and the bankrupt which will terminate the proceedings.

The second section will include the proceedings relating to the seizure of the bankrupt's assets and all matters relating to the administration of the bankruptcy up to full liquidation and the rendering of accounts by the receivers.

The third section will include the actions arising out of the retroactive effect of the bankruptcy proceedings on the contracts and administrative acts of the bankrupt which preceded the declaration of bankruptcy.

The fourth section will include the examination and recognition of the debts of the bankruptcy and the ranking of, and payment to, the creditors.

The fifth section will include the classification of the bankruptcy and the rehabilitation of the bankrupt.

Section I: Declaration of bankruptcy

Article 1.323

The formal declaration of bankruptcy may be requested by the bankrupt himself or by any lawful creditor whose rights arise out of commercial obligations.

Article 1.324

The trader's statement in support of his bankruptcy should be presented and duly formulated and documented in accordance with the provisions of articles 1.017, 1.018, 1.019, 1.020, 1.021 and 1.022 of the Commercial Code.

The request cannot be dealt with in any other form; the applicant for bankruptcy may not use presentation of the statement to his own advantage in order to make it appear that the requirements of article 1.017 of the Commercial Code have been complied with.

Article 1.325

A creditor who applies for a declaration of bankruptcy of his debtor will be obliged in the first place to prove his legal status either by means of a certificate in respect of the execution order made against the debtor at his request, or by an authenticated title document to his claim; upon fulfilment of these requirements the evidence he presents will be admitted in accordance with the terms of article 1.025 of the Commercial Code.

Once these have been adequately proved, the judge at first instance will issue the declaration of bankruptcy without summoning the bankrupt or giving him a hearing and will determine the relevant provisions applicable to the declaration.

Article 1.326

If the bankrupt contests the bankruptcy declaration order, a separate file will be drawn up within the period specified by article 1.028 of the Commercial Code, which will commence with the creditor's application, the grounds of his claim and the evidence set out above.

Following inspection of this file, the bankrupt may expand the grounds for his objection, and, for this purpose, and if the request was made in his statement contesting the declaration, the file will be transferred to the bankrupt for a period of three days.

Article 1.327

If the bankrupt makes an objection as provided above, and makes additional submissions in support of his objection, the file will be transferred to the creditor and under the same order the creditor will have conduct of the case for a non-extendible period of 20 days in order to submit a further proof. During this period the appropriate allegations and evidence of both parties will be admitted in accordance with article 1.031 of the Code.

Article 1.328

Creditors who support the objection to the discharge of the bankruptcy order may exercise their rights at the stage of the case when they appear at the civil proceedings but this will be without retrospective effect on such proceedings.

Article 1.329

If the creditor agrees to the bankrupt's request, the judge will authorise discharge of the declaration of bankruptcy order at the first hearing.

In accordance with article 1.032 of the Code the judge will also authorise discharge at the request of the bankrupt if no objection has been raised within eight days following transfer of the file to the creditor.

Article 1.330

After expiry of the period for production of evidence, the procedure will follow the provisions of article 755 and subsequent articles of this law.

The judgment is open to appeal in accordance with the provisions of article 1.031 of the Commercial Code.

Article 1.331

If the declaration of bankruptcy is annulled, the terms of article 1.167 of this law relating to the reinstatement of the debtor's assets, papers, freedom to trade and other rights will apply.

Article 1.332

The right of action for damages which, in accordance with the terms of article 1.034 of the Code, the bankrupt may bring against a creditor who fraudulently, falsely or with manifest injustice brings or upholds the declaration of bankruptcy will be dealt with under the same discharge file and will be substantiated in ordinary trial proceedings involving more than a certain sum of money.

Article 1.333

When issuing the declaration of bankruptcy order, the judge will appoint a registered trader as commissioner responsible for compliance with the other requirements of article 1.044 of the Code.

If there is no suitable registered trader in the locality of the hearing to act as commissioner, the judge at first instance will perform the relevant functions of that office in accordance with the terms of article 1.045 of the Code, except for those functions mentioned in paragraph four and those which apply to the receivers or to the trustee of the bankruptcy estate.

When the bankruptcy of an insurance undertaking is declared, whether it be an individual or a legal person and whatever the relevant category of insurance or reinsurance, the person appointed as a commissioner of that bankruptcy must be one of the inspectors or a provisional inspector of the Mercantile and Insurance Technical Inspectorate. The judge will officially inform the Central Commercial and Insurance Office recommending the appointment and advising the bankrupt party of his recommendation so that the appointment may be dispatched and communicated to him, as provided in the subsequent article.

In the case of bankruptcy of the persons referred to in the preceding paragraph, the person appointed as a trustee will be another inspector from the same body, but not the commissioner, similarly designated by the Central Office and appointed by the judge. This trustee will perform his duties without the necessity of providing a bond, it being understood that such a bond has already been provided by way of his office as inspector, and this also covers responsibilities contracted in his capacity as trustee.

Article 1.334

Without prejudice to any objection made by the bankrupt against the bankruptcy declaration order, and immediately upon issue of this order, the commissioner will be informed of his appointment by the judge at first instance, and he will proceed with the seizure of the assets and documents of the bankruptcy estate, its inventory and deposits in accordance with the requirements of articles 1.046, 1.047 and 1.048 of this Code.

Article 1.335

In order to procure the arrest of the bankrupt an order is required of one of the bailiffs of the court in accordance with the second paragraph of article 1.044 of the Commercial Code. Under this order the bankrupt is required in the presence of the Clerk of the Court to deposit forthwith a bond in an amount determined by the judge by way of bail. If this is done by a person making payment, or giving a secured guarantee or in cash, the bankrupt will be placed under house arrest; if not, he will be taken into custody and the relevant order will be issued to the mayor responsible for receiving the bankrupt into custody.

Article 1.336

In order to determine the amount and nature of the bond, the obligations of the surety and the means of effecting this where it is appropriate to do so, the provisions relating to such matters in the Criminal Procedure Law will be followed.

Article 1.337

Publication of the orders in which the bankruptcy is pronounced will be arranged by the clerk of the court and reference to this will be made in the records of the bankruptcy, stating the date and place of publication.

In order for these to take effect in the towns where the bankrupt has his place of business, the same orders will be sent with an official communication to the respective judicial authority of each town together with the request that the official communication be returned together with the appropriate documents confirming publication, and with the documents attached to the rulings.

In addition to the official journals of the locality or province in which the orders are to be published in accordance with provision no.5 of article 1.044 of the Code, the orders will also be published in the Madrid Gazette whenever the judge considers it prudent, and depending on the circumstances of the bankruptcy.

Article 1.338

For the purpose of retaining the bankrupt's correspondence an official communication will be sent to the Postal Services Administrator, alerting him to make this available to the court.

Article 1.339

The bankrupt, his attorney, if any, or the person in whose charge the management of the business has been left if he absconded before the declaration of bankruptcy, will be summoned in the same order to appear on a daily basis, or as often as determined, at the place and time appointed by the commissioner for the opening of the correspondence.

If no appearance is made at the time provided in the summons, the correspondence will be checked by the commissioner and the trustee.

Article 1.340

The request of the bankrupt for his release, or for discharge from arrest or the granting of a safe-conduct will not be admissible until the commissioner has informed the judge that he has concluded the work required in order to take possession of and examine all the accounting books, documents and papers relating to the business of the bankrupt.

Article 1.341

In that event the provisions of articles 1.060 and 1.061 of the Commercial Code will apply to the order.

Article 1.342

The commissioner will present the judge with a list of the bankrupts' creditors which will have been drawn up in the three days following the declaration of bankruptcy. Taking this list into account as well as the provisions of article 1.062 of the Code as amended by the law of 30th July 1878, the date of the first general meeting will be fixed and notified to the creditors in accordance with the terms of article 1.063 of the Code. If there are any creditors whose registered addresses are not known they will be summoned by orders in the manner set out in article 1.197 of this law.

Article 1.343

The bankrupt will be summoned to the meeting by an order drawn up under the relevant articles of this law.

Article 1.344

For the purposes of the general creditors' meeting, these orders will be passed to the commissioner together with all others, irrespective of how far they have been prepared or put into effect and these will be available during the meeting to provide an immediate explanation, when requested, of the results of the work carried out so far.

Article 1.345

The commissioner will examine the powers of attorney of those present at the meeting representing third parties and he will comply with the provisions of article 1.137 of this law for such cases and for those instances where more than one party is represented.

Article 1.346

The meeting at which the three receivers are appointed as provided in article 1.068 of the Code as amended by the law of 30th July 1878 will be held in the presence of the creditors who attend in accordance with the provisions of articles 1.067, 1.069 and 1.070 of the said Code as amended by that law.

Having held the two nominal ballots required pursuant to article 1.069, detailed minutes will be drawn up and read before the meeting is closed and the minutes are signed by the commissioner, the clerk of the court, the creditors present at the meeting and the bankrupt or his representative.

When a person or a legal entity which has been declared bankrupt is involved in insurance operations, as insurer or reinsurer, in whatever category of insurance or reinsurance such person or entity operates, three receivers will be elected of which at least one will be a member of the Mercantile and Insurance Technical Inspectorate.

Article 1.347

The appointment of receivers may be contested before the presiding judge on the grounds and in the manner set out in articles 1.220 to 1.224 of this law.

Article 1.348

When a creditor requests the removal of a receiver due to abuse in the conduct of his receivership, the judge will issue his decision after taking into account the grounds of such misconduct and the justification which accompanies the submission or the explanation given for the misconduct and after hearing the commissioner.

The judge will proceed in a similar fashion if the commissioner himself seeks the removal of a receiver. Based on the grounds on which the misconduct is founded, the judge will consider all the evidence he considers appropriate, and in the light of this evidence and taking into account the administrative application for removal, he will make such order as he considers relevant to the parties interested in the bankruptcy.

Article 1.349

The judgment ordering the removal of a receiver for reasons which do not constitute a criminal offence will be considered as administrative and will not prejudice the good standing or reputation of the receiver who has been removed, and becomes executory without being open to challenge.

Section II: Administration of the bankruptcy

Article 1.350

The court file relating to this section will commence with evidence of the judgment constituting the declaration of bankruptcy, with no previous records, and to which will be added the inventory of all the assets pertaining to the bankruptcy which are held in the bankrupt's home. This inventory will be drawn up in accordance with paragraphs numbered 3, 4 and 5 of article 1.046 of the Commercial Code.

Article 1.351

In order to take possession of, draw up the inventory of, and deposit the assets of the bankruptcy which are in different locations, the appropriate letters of requisition, endorsed with a note to the effect that they have been verified, will be issued to the respective judges. Any documents issued as a consequence of this should be original documents and upon receipt should be attached to the judgments.

Article 1.352

An official ruling of the commissioner is required before any withdrawal from warehouses or from the safe-deposit of bills of exchange, cash, drafts, promissory notes and other credit documents belonging to the bankruptcy estate can take place. Execution of the ruling will be officially registered and signed by the commissioner, the trustee and the clerk of the court.

Article 1.353

Property will be entered in the safe-deposit with due formality; this will only hold whatever is necessary to cover the requirements of the bankruptcy, the remaining cash and public instruments being deposited at the institution authorised by the government for this type of deposit.

Article 1.354

Any permission given by the commissioner for the urgent sale of assets of the bankruptcy or for unavoidable expenses required to preserve such assets must also be accounted for in an official ruling and as a consequence of a demand made by the trustees.

Article 1.355

Evidence of the appointment of the receivers, their acceptance and swearing in will be included in this application, together with their agreement with the drawing up of a general inventory subsequent to their appointment and to the delivery of the assets and papers relating to the bankruptcy to the receivers as provided for in articles 1.079, 1.080 and 1.081 of the Code.

Article 1.356

The procedure for examination and challenge of the accounts presented by the trustee will follow the order set out in the bankruptcy proceedings and following the commissioner's report.

Article 1.357

The findings of these proceedings will also be observed in relation to the exact expenses required to cover the needs of the bankruptcy. The judge will not authorise any extraordinary expenses proposed by the receivers unless officially assessed by the commissioner under a court order, following any extra judicial reports that he deems necessary. If such expenses do not exceed Ptas. 5000 the authorisation of the commissioner will be sufficient.

Article 1.358

Depending on the different mercantile instruments, moveable property of other types and real property involved, articles 1.084, 1.085, 1.086, 1.087 and 1.088 of the Code will be followed in evaluating and selling the assets of the bankruptcy.

Article 1.359

All the creditors of the bankruptcy and the bankrupt himself will be allowed to exercise the right of action permitted by articles 1.089 of the Code, against any receivers who purchase or have purchased the assets of the bankruptcy.

Claims of this type will be made under a separate file and will be substantiated by the procedures established for incidental matters, without prejudice to any criminal liability which the receivers may have incurred.

Article 1.360

All settlements which the receivers may have to make in connection with legal proceedings relating to the interests of the bankruptcy will be preceded by a ruling from the judge, proposed by the commissioner, setting out the guidelines for such transactions.

Article 1.361

The weekly deposits at the safe-deposit of funds which have been recovered will be recorded promptly in a separate note signed by the commissioner and the receivers, and the clerk of the court will confirm the deposit of such funds in the safe-deposit as an annex to this court file.

This same formality will be observed for the removal of funds withdrawn from the safe deposit as drawings by the commissioner, and for the removal of those which are deposited at the public institution.

Article 1.362

The comments made by the creditors on the monthly statements presented by the receivers on the state of the administration of the bankruptcy will be made known to the commissioner and, on the basis of his report, the judge will agree the procedure which he deems appropriate and beneficial for the bankruptcy estate.

Article 1.363

The procedure agreed by the commissioner for the administration of the bankruptcy in performance of his duties may be modified by the judge at the request of the receivers or any of the interested parties and he will then proceed to act having regard to the demands presented and the report made on the matter by the commissioner.

Article 1.364

The accounts provided by the receivers in respect of their administration will also be attached to this court file and an examination will be made of them in accordance with the provisions of articles 1.134 and 1.135 of the Code; and if discrepancies are inferred against these accounts either by agreement of the creditors' meeting or by the bankrupt or any particular creditor, the claim will be substantiated in proceedings by way of an ordinary hearing in this court file if the administration of the bankruptcy has been concluded, or, if this has not occurred, by opening a separate file.

Article 1.365

Claims by creditors of the bankrupt against the receivers for damage caused to the bankruptcy estate by fraud, misappropriation or culpable negligence will be extracted and substantiated in a separate division as part of these records, and in accordance with the procedure for an ordinary hearing.

Section III: Retroactive consequences of the bankruptcy

Article 1.366

The receivers in bankruptcy, as representatives of the creditors and legal administrators of the assets of the bankruptcy, have legal capacity to claim for avoidance in respect of acts which were carried out by the bankrupt to the prejudice of the bankruptcy estate whilst disqualified or which, because of their fraudulent nature, are open to avoidance even though they were carried out before disqualification.

Article 1.367

If the creditors observe any omission in this connection, they should apply to the commissioner who, after taking account of all the facts, will pass the resolutions necessary to secure that the rights of action of the creditors can be exercised, failing which the claimant may bring his complaint before the bankruptcy judge.

Article 1.368

Within 10 days of receipt of the books and papers of the bankruptcy, the receivers will compile the following lists:

A list relating to payments made by the bankrupt in the 15 days prior to the declaration of bankruptcy in respect of direct debts and obligations, the due date of which fell after the declaration.

A further list relating to contracts made during the 30 days prior to the declaration of bankruptcy which, being fraudulent, are void in law in accordance with article 1.039 of the Commercial Code; and also relating to gifts inter vivos which are covered by the provisions of article 1.040.

Article 1.369

Once the lists referred to in the preceding article have been checked and certified by the commissioner, the receivers will inform the interested parties of the extra-judicial claims required in order to reinstate to the bankruptcy estate all the assets which belong to it, and will notify them that if such claims should fail they will, with the prior approval of the commissioner, have recourse to the legal actions appropriate in each case to the objective of the claim.

Article 1.370

The receivers will also prepare another list of the contracts made by the bankrupt falling within any of the four cases referred to in article 1.041 of the Code, carrying out appropriate investigations to ascertain whether they were made fraudulently; and, if there is evidence of fraud in relation to any of them, they will make a statement to the commissioner who, in the light of this and of his own enquiries, will allow or disallow authorisation so that the receivers may file the claims proposed in the statement.

Article 1.371

The claims filed by the receivers in accordance with article 1.038 of the Commercial Code will be accompanied by documentary proof that payment was made during the period of disqualification and that the obligation did not fall due until after the declaration of bankruptcy. If necessary, the receivers may prepare their action by taking a legal deposition from the debtor.

Article 1.372

The receivers' claims and the accompanying documents will be made known to the defendant who will have three days within which to make such statement as he deems appropriate.

Article 1.373

If the debtor does not respond to the claim or if, following the response, the receivers' evidence is not dismissed, he will be ordered to make repayment.

Article 1.374

If it appears to the judge that the response of the debtor justifies requiring the production of evidence of the matter, he will allow for this within a non-extendible period of eight days, after which a judgment will be pronounced in respect of the matter in question in accordance with the procedures established in articles 755 to 758 of this law.

Article 1.375

In order to reinstate to the bankruptcy those assets which have been removed under contracts void in law by virtue of the provisions of article 1.039 of the Commercial Code, a recovery injunction will be sought by the receivers upon due justification by them on the grounds of the contents of the relevant contract, with a statement to the effect that it falls within this law.

Article 1.376

The orders issued for the application of articles 1.038, 1.039 and 1.040 of the Commercial Code take effect notwithstanding the filing of appeals.

Article 1.377

Claims for avoidance or revocation of contracts made by the bankrupt involving fraud against the creditors will be substantiated in the full trial relating to the relevant amount and in the competent court.

Section IV: Examination, ranking and payment of debts of the bankruptcy

Article 1.378

The general list of the creditors of the bankruptcy will be placed at the head of the court records relating to this section and, by way of continuation, the judge will issue an order fixing the term within which they must present to the receivers the documents evidencing the debts owed to them, and appointing the day on which the meeting for the examination and admission of their rights is to be held in accordance with the provisions of article 1.101 of the Commercial Code.

Details of these arrangements will be circulated to the creditors through the official rulings of the receivers as submitted to the commissioner and will be published in edicts and inserted in periodicals by the clerk of the court.

Article 1.379

The joinder to the bankruptcy hearing of the pending actions or of actions brought against the assets of the bankruptcy will follow in accordance with the rules established for such cases in the bankruptcy proceedings.

Article 1.380

When all the procedures set out in articles 1.102, 1.103, 1.104 and 1.105 of the Commercial Code for the proof and examination of debts have been carried out, if any of the creditors or the bankrupt consider they have suffered loss as a result of a resolution of the meeting, they may exercise their right to commence proceedings in the court which is dealing with the bankruptcy within a non-extendible period of 30 days.

Article 1.381

Creditors' claims relating either to the admission of debts or to the injustice of their ranking will comply with the procedure set out in the bankruptcy proceedings.

Section V: Classification of the bankruptcy and discharge of the bankrupt

Article 1.382

The court records relating to this section will begin with the report of the commissioner to the judge at first instance on the results of the admission of the bankrupt's books and papers under the relevant headings for the classification of the bankruptcy according to article 1.138 of the Commercial Code.

Article 1.383

Within 15 days of their appointment, the receivers will present the statement referred to in article 1.140 of the Code which, together with the rulings, will be passed to the Public Prosecutor.

The receivers in their declaration, together with the Public Prosecutor in the note of his opinion, will make a formal proposal for the classification of the bankruptcy; and, together with the rulings, will hand these to the bankrupt for a period of six days so that he may reply to this demand.

Article 1.384

If the bankrupt does not respond to the communication by him of the rulings or, in the event that he returns them without opposing the receivers or the Public Prosecutor's proposal, the judge will call for the rulings to be produced at the hearing and will make the classification he considers correct in law according to the records of the case and the declaration of bankruptcy which he will also have before him.

Article 1.385

If the bankrupt contests the receivers' or the Public Prosecutor's proposal, the rulings will be used as proof and their substantiation will continue to be used until judgment is given in accordance with the procedure established in this law for such events; the term of proof may be extended, if requested by the parties, up to the maximum of 40 days allowed in article 1.152 of the Code.

The judgment is open to appeal with suspension of execution but will nonetheless be enforced in relation to the liberty of the bankrupt, if such is decreed.

Article 1.386

The procedure set out in article 1.143 of the Code will be followed in respect of the judgment and its execution.

When the classification file shows grounds for qualifying the bankruptcy as one of fraud or concealment, the judge will request evidence to be produced to enable criminal proceedings to be instituted against the bankrupt.

No appeal lies against this decision.

Article 1.387

The receivers, as such, will take no part in the criminal case against bankrupts of the third, fourth or fifth class unless with the agreement of the general creditors' meeting.

Any creditor who uses his right of action in such a case in accordance with criminal law will do so at his own expense and with no recourse in any circumstances against the bankruptcy estate under any decision resulting from the case.

Article 1.388

Bankrupts' requests for discharge will be heard after the classification hearing but under the same application in which classification has been discussed, the procedure being as set out in chapter XI, book IV of the Commercial Code.

When the commissioner has issued the report ordered as provided under article 1.173 of that Code, the Public Prosecutor will be informed of the rulings so that he may issue his opinion on whether the discharge should proceed and with no further procedure the judge will issue the decision which he considers fit in accordance with the said article.

The resultant decision is open to appeal with suspension of execution.

Section VI: Agreement between creditors and bankrupt

Article 1.389

In accordance with the provisions of article 1.147 of the Commercial Code, as amended by the law of 30th July 1878, no consideration will be given to any proposal for agreement between the bankrupt and his creditors which is presented before the conclusion of the examination and admission of the debts and the classification of the bankruptcy has been made.

Article 1.390

When the hearing has reached the position indicated in the previous article, if the bankruptcy has not been classified as being of the third, fourth or fifth class, the judge will allow the bankrupt or any of the creditors to request the calling of a meeting to discuss the agreement.

This request should contain the requirements detailed in article 1.304 of this law.

Article 1.391

The provisions of articles 1.307 to 1.311 of this law may also be applied to this procedure.

Article 1.392

The provisions of article 1.152 and the subsequent articles of the Commercial Code will apply with respect to holding the extraordinary meeting for dealing with the agreement and any opposition to it.

Article 1.393

No opposition will be allowed on the part of creditors who consented to the agreement in the meeting.

Article 1.394

In the case of opposition made by dissenting creditors or by those who did not attend the meeting, a hearing and submission of evidence will be given to the bankrupt and receivers, within a non-extendible period of 30 days, during which time both the litigating parties and any other creditor who later presents himself to assist in the motion of opposition will invoke and prove by means of contrary summons any matter which they think fit.

Article 1.395

When the time allowed for producing evidence has expired, proceedings will be continued in accordance with article 755 and the subsequent articles of this law.

The judgment as issued is open to appeal without suspension of execution and will become enforceable between the debtor and creditors who accepted the agreement without prejudice to any decision on appeal and in accordance with article 1.158 of the Code as amended by the law of 30th July 1878.

Article 1.396

If the agreement is not opposed within the period of eight days provided under in article 1.157 of the Code the judge will call the rulings before him and, having regard to the declaration of bankruptcy application and its classification, will make the relevant decision in accordance with the provisions of article 1.159 of that Code.

SUSPENSION OF PAYMENTS LAW, 26TH JULY 1922

Article 1

Any files relating to the suspension of payments of traders and business partnerships which are not within article 930 of the Commercial Code will be subject to the provisions of this law.

Article 2

Any trader or business enterprise desiring to be declared in a state of suspension of payments will attach to the written application the following documents:

1st The detailed balance sheet of assets and liabilities, or at least a statement of the position of the business which shows, as precisely as possible, the state in which it is at the time of the request, the assets of the petitioner and the total amount of his liabilities. In this event, the judge will determine a period of no more than 30 days for presentation of the definitive balance sheet, which will be drawn up under the supervision of the inspectors.

If immoveable properties are involved, the deeds of the same or a detailed description of them should be attached.

2nd A list of names, with no exceptions, of all the creditors, showing their addresses and amounts owed, date of their respective debts and due dates.

When the petitioner declares that the number of his creditors is greater than one thousand, or due to the type of operation from which the debt emanates it is not possible to determine the amount of the same, it will be sufficient for him to state, with reference to the most recent balance sheet, the approximate number of creditors, the names of those known to him and the global amount of their debts.

3rd A report on the causes of the suspension and the means by which he will settle his debts.

4th A proposal for the payment of his debts.

5th When the enterprise which makes the application for suspension of payments is a limited company, the application will be accompanied by a certificate from the board of directors authorising such a request and justifying the calling of a meeting of shareholders for ratification of this agreement. If, within the period fixed by the articles of the company, a general meeting is not held, or this meeting does not ratify the decision of the Board, the suspension of payments file will be closed, and the creditors will be free to exercise their right of action.

In the agreement of the shareholders' meeting ratifying the decision of the board of directors, the persons or organisations who will represent the company for the purposes of the file will be noted therein, together with necessary powers for them to modify the agreement proposal drawn up and to participate in all matters or questions which might arise.

6th An indication of the branches, agencies or other direct representative establishments belonging to the petitioner, stating the locations at which these operate.

All these documents will be signed by the petitioner or his representative under special power.

Article 3

Together with the application and documents mentioned in the previous article, the accounting books will also be lodged at the court by the petitioner; not only those he is required to keep by the Commercial Code or special laws, but also those which he voluntarily believes it appropriate to authenticate as being a necessary part of the accounting system he has adopted. The papers as lodged will state that the clerk of the court, with the agreement of the inspectors, has placed, duly signed and sealed, a note of the suspension application following the last entry in each one of these books. In these notes, the clerk of the court will refer to any anomaly which he has observed in the books, particularly the corrections, erasures, and unfilled spaces or pages. The judge will add his approval and the term of the court secretary will immediately return the books to the suspended trader or enterprise to keep in his office so that he may continue entering transactions. The account books will be held at all times at the disposal of the judge, the inspectors and the creditors, in the manner prescribed by the court.

Article 4

The judge in charge of the file will examine the trader's application and if it has been produced in the correct form and the documents and books indicated in previous articles accompany it, he will consider that the declaration of suspension of payments has been officially requested, and that same day or, if not, the following day, he will issue his decision which will be communicated telegraphically to all the courts of the locations where the trader or enterprise referred to in the declaration has branches, agencies or direct representation. This decision, which will be published in any way the judge considers appropriate, will be noted in a special register kept in each court, in the Companies Register and in the property register where the immoveable property of the suspended trader or enterprise is recorded.

In the same decision the court will order all the operations of the debtor to be supervised. To this end, it will appoint three inspectors, two of which will be expert commercial accountant-assessors or practitioners who appear in the lists which the Chambers of Commerce and Industry and the regional representative of the Bankers' Association send annually to the court (or to the Court Secretariat if there are several courts in the locality). In making the appointment preference will be given to the list sent by the organisation to which the debtor is associated according to his type of business. The third inspector will be a creditor appointed by the judge from those amongst the top third, by order of importance, of the debts from the list presented when requesting the declaration of suspension of payments.

When the person or enterprise applying for the declaration of suspension of payments carries out any sort of insurance operations, either as insurer or reinsurer, two of the three inspectors should be civil servants from the Commercial and Insurance Inspectorate, appointed by the Director of Commerce and Insurance.

The inspectors, whose functions are obligatory, will commence those functions, if possible, on the day of their appointment prior to their being appropriately sworn in. If the third inspector should have any difficulty in taking up his functions, the other two will commence theirs. Until the inspectors begin to carry out their functions, the judge himself will do so.

If the debtor, or any of his creditors when they are known, opposes the appointment of the inspectors, the judge, having examined the justifications presented, will resolve the matter once and for all and with no further recourse; if he validates the opposition in his judgment, he will appoint the inspector who should replace the deposed one, using the same process.

The judges who have been telegraphically informed that an application has been made for a declaration of suspension of payments of a trader or business partnership which has branches, agencies or representatives within the territory covered by their jurisdiction, will immediately declare such branches, agencies or representative establishments under official supervision.

If the suspension is of little importance or its nature so indicates and the judge believes it to be appropriate, he may appoint a sole inspector who, in this case, will necessarily be a creditor appointed as indicated in the previous paragraphs.

Article 5

The inspectors under a suspension of payments file will:

1st Inspect the books of the suspended trader or enterprise and make sure that all operations carried out are duly entered into them following the lodging procedures mentioned in article 3.

2nd Supervise all operations which the suspended entity may carry out in accordance with the law and ensure that the cash balance is checked daily.

3rd Inform the judge of all important occurrences in relation to the suspended trader or enterprise and his business, and in connection with resolutions which may be required in defence of or for the protection of creditors' interests.

4th Advise the judge of the background to the claims in which the suspended trader or enterprise may wish to participate in defence of, or to claim in respect of, his rights over a third party.

The inspectors will also be required to propose the pursuit of the appropriate rights of action in the interests of the estate of the suspended trader or enterprise either at their own instigation or at the instigation of any other creditor, and they may, if so authorised by the judge, pursue such rights themselves if the majority interest requires it.

Article 6

Until the agreement proposal has been approved by the creditors in any of the ways set out in articles 14 and 18 of this law, the suspended trader or enterprise will retain the administration of his assets and the management of his business within whatever limits are set by the court, subject to a special report on this matter issued by the inspectors, who will take the relevant precautionary and security measures necessary to achieve the suspension and replacement of the trader, manager or board of directors. Until this has been decreed, the suspended trader or enterprise will operate within the following rules:

1st With the collaboration of the inspectors, he will check all payments due, whatever the amounts and source, including any acceptances, endorsements or protests of commercial drafts.

2nd At the same time, he will obtain the agreement of the inspectors for any obligation he may acquire, contract he may enter into and to check any payment made.

3rd Again with the agreement of the inspectors, he will continue with his ordinary operations, and may sell assets, goods, or merchandise which it may be necessary to dispose of by mutual agreement of the interested parties or because preservation is impossible, prejudical or costly.

The suspended trader or enterprise who carries out any of the operations indicated in this article without the collaboration or agreement of the inspectors or makes any payment without the express authorisation of the judge before the inspectors take up their appointments, will incur the liabilities defined in article 548 of the Penal Code and the administrative acts performed by him, or contracts into which he enters, will be null and void.

If any of the inspectors differs in opinion from his colleagues, the opinion of the majority will prevail. If, because of its nature, this opinion is not forthcoming, the matter will be decided by the judge.

Article 7

The inspectors will receive a remuneration fixed by the judge, according to the amount of the capital and the work such supervision requires, not exceeding an amount of Ptas. 100 per day.

Article 8

Within the terms fixed by the judge and in no less than 20 and no more than 60 days, the inspectors will draw up, subject to whatever report by the assessors as may be deemed necessary, a statement of opinion which will deal with the following:

1st The accuracy of assets and liabilities in the balance sheet with a list of the type of debts in each category.
2nd The state of the suspended trader or enterprise's accounting and the inaccuracies noted therein in accordance with this law.
3rd The accuracy or inaccuracy of the causes of the suspension as set out in the annual report lodged at the court.

Together with this statement, the definitive balance sheet and list of creditors will be lodged at the court if not already done so, together with a list of the debts according to their legal classification, stating which creditors have the right to abstain from the meeting according to the classification referred to in article 15, para 3 and article 22 of this law. The inspectors may obtain whatever legal advice they deem appropriate in respect of that article.

The inspectors' statement will be followed by a hearing for the suspended trader or enterprise within a non-extendible period of three days.

If the inspectors do not lodge their statement at the court within the fixed period, apart from the penal responsibility which they will incur, any creditor who is an inspector will lose title to his claim and the assessors will lose their right to practise during a period of two years. In this case, the clerk of the court will draw up, within a period of 15 days, a comprehensive court report of all the matters which should be contained in the inspectors' statement.

In connection with this, and after taking into special consideration the inspectors' statement or the clerk of the court's report to the court as the case may be, the judge will declare the petitioner to be in a state of suspension of payments.

In his ruling the judge will declare whether, due to the assets being higher or the same as the liabilities, the suspended trader or enterprise should be considered to be in a state of provisional insolvency or whether, due to the assets being less than the liabilities, the trader or enterprise should be considered as being in a state of definitive insolvency. In this latter case he will decide by what amount the liabilities are greater than the assets and will allow the debtor a period of 15 days within which he, or someone in his name, will deposit or guarantee the difference to the satisfaction of the judge, to the effect that the definitive insolvency becomes a provisional insolvency. If this period elapses with no deposit or guarantee being made, the judge will immediately proceed to the drawing up of a record of classification in order to determine exactly the liabilities incurred by the suspended trader or enterprise. In any event, he will fix the limits of the suspended trader or enterprise's business transactions while the trader or enterprise remains in this state.

Once the creditors' meeting has been held, this ruling, which will be executory and without prejudice, may be opposed by any of the creditors or the suspended trader or enterprise, in the manner or period of time set out in articles 16 and 17 of this law, all the courts being informed immediately that a request for suspension of payments has been recognised. It will also be given such publicity as the judge may think fit according to the amount of the liabilities and the number of creditors.

Article 9

With effect from the application for the suspension of payments, and while the file is being verified, the court will not allow any direct or indirect ancillary opposition contesting the source of the judicial declaration or postponing its immediate effect.

The judge will reject outright, with no further recourse, any claim with this intent, but the petitioner may reserve the right to repeat his application in the relevant declarative hearing.

Nor may the creditors apply for a declaration of bankruptcy while the suspension of payments file is pending.

The ordinary and executory hearings which do not relate to the attachment of specific mortgaged or pledged assets and which are in the process of being heard at the time of the declaration of suspension of payments will continue to be heard through to judgment, execution of which will remain suspended until the file has been closed.

With effect from the application for suspension of payments, all embargoes and receiverships, which might have been issued against the unmortgaged or unpledged assets, will be suspended and included in the inspecting auditors' activities for as long as these continue in accordance with the standards laid down by the courts. None of this will impair the rights of the privileged creditors or the title to their claims for the settlement of their debts.

Article 10

In provisional insolvency cases, the judge will agree to the convening of a creditors' meeting in the same ruling which declares the suspension of payments, as provided under article 8. In the event of definitive insolvency, the convening of such a meeting will not be agreed until after the period of 15 days provided under article 8 for depositing or guaranteeing the amount of the deficit. When this procedure has been completed, if the judge wishes to maintain the classification of definitive insolvency, he will convene the meeting immediately, unless within five days, the suspended trader or enterprise or creditors representing two fifths of the total liabilities either apply for the file to be dismissed or for a declaration of bankruptcy.

A period of not less than 30 days will elapse between the convening of the meeting and the time when it takes place. This period will be increased to 60 days if, in the opinion of the court, the number of, or place of residence of, the creditors so demands. The notice of the meeting will be issued by means of an order to those living within the district and by registered letter with acknowledgement of receipt, which should be attached to the file for those residing outside the district. The meeting will also be given such publicity as the judge may determine according to the circumstances of the case.

Until the day fixed for holding the meeting, the clerk of the court will hold the following documents at the disposal of the creditors or their representatives so that they may obtain copies or make notes as they see fit: the inspectors' statement, the statement of assets and liabilities, the annual report, the balance sheet, the list of creditors having the right of abstention referred to in articles 15 and 22 of this law, and the creditors' agreement submitted by the debtor.

Article 11

Up to 15 days before the meeting takes place, the debts listed by the debtor may be challenged, and applications may be made for inclusion or exclusion from the list of debts by those creditors having the right to abstain together with those mentioned in article 22. The debts which are not challenged within that period will be considered during the meeting. The objection may be made by any of the creditors in the suspension without the services of a lawyer or other attorney being required. The inspectors should also enter an objection if they suspect the legitimacy of a debt or the accuracy of its amount.

The objection should either be in writing addressed to the judge or by appearing before the clerk of the court and will be formulated in such a way so that either the debt is totally rejected or reduced to such amount as is considered to be accurate. The challenger, who may not use expert witnesses or evidence, will refer to the entries in the books or papers of the suspended trader or enterprise on which he will rely to justify his claim, or will present the documents he wishes to use.

Any creditor who has been omitted from the debtor's list or who appears as being owed less than he considers due may, in the same way and using the same procedure, request inclusion in the list, or that his debt be increased if he considers the omission unjust or the amount incorrect.

In order to exercise the rights granted to the creditors under this article, the commission of auditors is obliged to make available to the creditors all records and information they may request, particularly in relation to the books and papers of the suspended trader or enterprise.

Article 12

Eight days before the meeting is held the judge will receive the definitive list of creditors drawn up by the inspectors. This list will include the six following groups:

(A) those creditors named by the debtor whose debts have not been challenged;
(B) those creditors named by the debtor who request that the figure given be increased;
(C) those creditors who have been omitted by the debtor and who have requested that they be included;
(D) those creditors included by the debtor whose debts have been challenged as being excessive;
(E) those creditors included by the debtor whose debts have been conclusively challenged; and
(F) creditors having the right not to attend by virtue of articles 15 and 22.

In the list, the debts will be set out separately so as to show clearly those amounts which are undisputed and those which are the object of controversy. The judge will determine each claim with no further recourse; but on behalf of the creditors or the representatives of the estate under suspension he will reserve the right for the claim to be heard in the corresponding ordinary court. Commencement of proceedings in the ordinary court will not prevent execution of the judgment, except under the special circumstances set out in paragraph 6 of article 16. Once the list has been approved by the judge it will be transferred to the clerk of the court and, up to one hour prior to the time fixed for the meeting, the creditors may examine it in the clerk of the court's office.

Article 13

The meeting will be held on the day and at the time and place stated in the public announcement, and may continue for several days if necessary. It will be presided over by the judge, and all the creditors shown in the list mentioned in the previous article may attend personally or through duly accredited representatives, or their assignees by endorsement or transfer. The debtor and the inspectors will be required to attend the meeting, the former having the right to be represented by a lawyer in his defence who will speak on his behalf.

If the debtor does not attend either personally or through a special proxy, the judge will dismiss the proceedings.

When the hearing has been opened by the judge, the lists approved by him will be read out and there will be no discussion on the debts contained therein; but objections may be made by the interested parties, without prejudice to any later claim which in each case will proceed in accordance with the law.

If the debts of those creditors attending in person and by way of representatives amount to at least three fifths of the total liabilities of the debtor after deducting the amount of the debts of creditors who, having had their right to abstain recognised, have acted on it, the judge will declare the meeting legally constituted. If that number of creditors has not attended, the judge will adjourn the hearing, declaring the matter legally concluded.

This judgment, against which no appeal lies, will be communicated as a matter of course to the judges before whom all pending cases against the debtor will be heard, and it will be published and registered in the manner and according to the requirements set out in article 8.

The inspectors will not conclude their function until ten days after the date on which this agreement is communicated and published.

No claim will be admitted which might postpone the holding of the meeting.

Article 14

When the meeting has been legally constituted, the clerk of the court will read out the debtor's petition, the proposal for a creditors' agreement, the figures showing the assets and liabilities and the report referred to in paragraph 3 of article 8.

Once the discussion on the debtor's proposal has begun three creditors may speak for the proposal and three against. The debtor or his defending representative and the inspectors may speak as many times as they wish. The creditors may modify the proposal in the light of the discussion, freely consenting to such provisions as they consider necessary, either within or in addition to the debtor's proposal, provided that they obtain his approval and they fulfil the requirements set out in this article. Voting will be by poll and the creditors' agreement will be deemed to be approved if a simple majority of the creditors present vote in favour, provided always that the amount of their debt makes up three fifths of the total liabilities of the debtor, after deduction of the amount of debt of the creditors who may have used their right to abstain if the duration of the agreement is not more than three years.

If the duration of the creditors' agreement has no such limit, and in all cases of definitive insolvency, in order for approval to be given it will be necessary for a simple majority of the creditors present to vote in its favour representing three quarters of the total liabilities as set out in the previous paragraph.

If liabilities in that amount are not represented, the judge will convene a new meeting of creditors in which the agreement will be approved if those holding two thirds of the liabilities are in favour.

When the number of creditors on the list exceeds two hundred, it will be sufficient for one or other of the majorities approving the agreement set out in the previous paragraphs to be present and a poll will not be necessary.

When special advantages are set out in the creditors' agreement in favour of certain groups of creditors, their votes for their own benefit will not be taken into account.

In the event of definitive insolvency, the proposal agreed at the creditors' meeting may have as its objective the objective referred to in article 928 of the Commercial Code.

Article 15

The judge will only declare the vote in favour of the creditors' agreement, and will not give it his approval until the period stated in article 16 has lapsed. The inspectors' office will terminate unless the meeting agrees that they should continue their supervision in the same way, by appointing the same inspectors or others, and determines the method of substitution or reversal of appointments, and confers on them representation of the estate under suspension so that they may exercise the appropriate right of action in the interests of the estate.

If a majority vote is not reached as set out above the creditors' agreement as proposed will be deemed rejected.

Prior ranking and privileged creditors and mortgagees included in paragraphs 1, 2 and 3 of article 913 of the Commercial Code may choose not to attend the meeting; but if they do attend they will be bound in the same manner as the other creditors. Their debts will not be taken into account when calculating the majority referred to in the previous article.

The minutes of the meeting will be signed by the judge, the clerk of the court and the inspectors.

Article 16

Within eight days of the meeting the creditors who did not attend it or who having attended dissented from the majority vote or had been removed by the judge from the list referred to in article 12, may oppose approval of the creditors' agreement.

The only grounds for this objection are:

1st Defect in the process specified for the convening, holding and discussions of the meeting and for agreements made at the meeting.

2nd Lack of legal status or representation of any of the voters, provided that the contested vote has a decisive influence in forming a majority.

3rd Fraudulent collusion in relation to the vote as between the debtor and one or more of the creditors, or between the creditors themselves.

4th Fraudulent overstatement of debts in order to obtain the required majority.

5th Error in the estimated liabilities made by the judge in the ruling referred to in article 8, provided that this affects the classification of the insolvency proceedings.

6th Inadmissible declaration of the right not to attend, when the amount of the relevant debts of the non-attending creditors affects formation of the majority of the liabilities required for approval of the agreement.

7th Fraudulent mis-statement in the general balance sheet.

Article 17

At the end of the period mentioned in the previous article and if no objection has been raised, the judge will issue a ruling approving the creditors' agreement and ordering the interested parties to adhere to it, adopting the relevant judgments and issuing the relevant mandates to the companies and property registries.

If an objection has been raised to the creditors' agreement, the procedure set out in article 744 and the subsequent articles of the Law of Civil Procedure will be followed. The issues will be dealt with as between the debtor and creditors who appear therein, and they should join together in any litigation and be represented together when they are pursuing the same cause of action. If the objection was raised by several creditors, the judge will agree to the joinder of claims on his own motion, which will then be determined together.

The judgment made on an objection is open to appeal with suspension of execution and the following non-extendible time limits are fixed for this procedure: five days to appear before the court; a further five to draw up the court report; ten for the ordinary examination of all interested parties in the court secretary's office; five for examination of the writs of the opposing parties; ten for the convening and holding of the hearing, which may not be adjourned, and another ten to pass judgment. Only a petition for relief may be granted against this judgment.

If the debtor fails to fulfil the terms of the creditors' agreement, any one of his creditors may request the judge in charge of the suspension proceedings that it be rescinded and that a declaration of bankruptcy be made.

Article 18

When the number of creditors exceeds two hundred, the judge may agree to adjourn the meeting, and substitute therefor the written procedure as described in this article, provided the requirements and formalities set out below are also rigorously observed.

Up to eight days before the day appointed for the holding of the meeting, the debtor or any of the creditors may request the use of the procedure provided under this article. If this request is made, the judge will immediately inform the inspectors who should make a report within the non-extendible period of three days, the meeting meanwhile being adjourned. If the inspectors' report is unfavourable and the judge disallows the request no appeal lies from the judge's decision. If he agrees to it and regardless of the inspectors' report, the judge's decision is subject to appeal without suspension of proceedings.

In the ruling which deals with the request, the suspended trader or enterprise will be allowed a reasonable period of not less than one month and not more than four, in which he may present to the judge a proposal for a creditors' agreement supported by the creditors and submitted in the proper form.

Article 19

Within the period allowed, the suspended trader or enterprise will present to the court a proposal for a creditors' agreement together with each creditors' vote cast by individual appearance before the clerk of the court who is handling the proceedings or any related actions under a notarial document. This does not apply to creditors who are resident outside the area where the proceedings are taking place or in areas where no notary public resides. They may register their vote by presenting themselves to the clerk of the court for the municipality where they live. In all of these cases, several creditors may attend together to give their assent. Each vote, certified by the clerk of the court or notary public, will clearly and unequivocally express the approval or disapproval of the proposal for a creditors' agreement by those registering their vote, or will specify in full, where appropriate, the main changes which should be made to the debtor's proposal. On expressing his opinion, each voter may attach explanatory details and reasons in support of his vote.

If the votes received suggest changes to the proposal for a creditors' agreement, the judge is bound to listen to the report of the inspectors on such matters. This must be issued within the non-extendible period of 15 days.

The judge will approve the creditors' agreement – according to whether it is a moratorium or a definitive insolvency – if the votes in favour of the proposed provisions constitute either of the two majorities of liabilities provided under each case in article 14; but when changes are introduced to the debtor's proposal for a creditors' agreement because of the votes registered on the appearance before the clerk of the court or by notarial document, the debtor will be given the opportunity either to consent to them or to reject them within a period of five days after which the judge will either approve the creditors' agreement or dismiss the proceedings.

In the event that the creditors' agreement does not provide for a moratorium of less than three years and in all cases of definitive insolvency, if the creditors representing three quarters of the liabilities necessary for its approval do not meet within the appointed period, the judge will fix a new period of 30 days, and in this case it will be sufficient for its approval if representatives of only two thirds of the liabilities are present.

Once the proposal for a creditors' agreement has been approved, the judge will make the necessary arrangements for it to receive due publicity, according to the importance of the commercial entity and the number and residence of the creditors. Objections to the creditors' agreement will be regulated by the procedure set out in articles 16 and 17.

Article 20

Once the declaration of definitive insolvency has become final, separate proceedings will be drawn up with a view to the elimination of liabilities undertaken by the suspended trader or enterprise, or by the directors or managers of commercial companies who may have requested and obtained such a declaration.

This classification of insolvency is applicable to bankruptcy as defined in articles 886 to 894 inclusive of the Commercial Code. These proceedings will be based on the auditors' report referred to in article 8 and the testimony or certificate of the records which make up the basis of the considerations and conclusions of this report. Parties to these proceedings will be, on the one hand, the Public Prosecutor, the inspectors (who are themselves subject to legal process if an accusation is made against them), and the creditors, who, at their own expense, wish to take part. All those who seek the same classification of insolvency will be joined as a single party in the litigation. The other party in the proceedings will be the debtor or managers who will be required to undertake liability. The period for answering the claim will be the same for all the defendants.

This action for an undertaking to accept liability will be heard in accordance with due procedure and in the order of largest amount; but the issues heard at first instance, and on appeal, will not be subject to special procedure. Consequently all the issues will be resolved upon final judgment. If a party intends to rectify a defect in the procedure, the requested correction will be implemented if the other parties agree.

As well as the inspectors, both the creditors present and the Public Prosecutor may request at any moment in the proceedings that conservatory measures which they consider necessary be taken to protect assets affected by the liabilities in issue. The judge will agree to this request when the report and the records produced show clearly who is liable and why.

Decisions taken in these separate proceedings do not prevent or prejudice the commencement of criminal proceedings, and the decisions reached by the criminal courts will not affect the agreement unless the crime is committed within the creditors' agreement itself and has a decisive influence on it. In that event, and with respect to the creditors' agreement, the criminal judgment will give rise to the same retrospective effect and procedure as under final judgment in civil cases.

Article 21

When the suspension of payments is classified as a definitive insolvency, the retrospective rules of bankruptcy will be applicable to the suspension of payments as defined in articles 879, 880, 881 and 882 of the Commercial Code, but the questions raised about the case will be aired in separate proceedings without causing alteration or delay to any of the procedures in the suspension proceedings.

Articles 1366 and 1377 of the law of Civil Procedure will apply to these separate proceedings, but, in relation to the inspectors appointed by the judge or the creditors under the creditors' agreement, and depending upon the time when it becomes effective, the provisions set out in those articles will be attributable to the receivers and police officials dealing with the bankruptcy.

Article 22

Any creditors who rely on the rights recognised in articles 908 to 910 of the Commercial Code may abstain from attending the meeting without affecting their rights under the creditors' agreement. Creditors in this category whose debts have not been recognised in the relevant list referred to in the groups set out in article 12 may make their claims in other separate proceedings, which will be dealt with under the procedure established in articles 1532 and the subsequent articles of the law of Civil Procedure under third party claims to ownership. The claimant, the debtor and the auditors or the representative of the creditors will constitute the parties to those proceedings.

Article 23

The Public Prosecutor will be party to the proceedings from the moment when the suspension of payments proceedings are commenced until final completion of performance of the creditors' agreement.

Article 24

The time limits established in this law will be considered to have expired by the mere effluxion of time with no requirement for summons even in the proceedings for determination of the classification referred to in article 20.

Additional articles

1st The provisions of this law will be applied to suspension of payments proceedings current at the time they come into force. The proceedings are subject to the provisions of article 4 and the subsequent articles of this law.

2nd After four years of this law being in force, the Government may suspend its effect, reporting accordingly to Parliament.

In that event, suspension of payments proceedings which are being dealt with according to the provisions of this law will remain subject to this law until completion.

CORPORATE REGISTRATION
CHAPTER XIII. THE REGISTRATION OF SUSPENSIONS OF PAYMENTS, BANKRUPTCIES AND OTHER MEASURES OF SUPERVISION

Section I: The registration of suspensions of payments and of bankruptcies

Article 284 – Registration of suspensions of payments

On the page relating to each trader, company or registerable entity, the following entries will appear:

1. The resolution for admission to the procedure of requesting a declaration of suspension of payments.
2. The order for the declaration of suspension of payments and, if appropriate, the order for the declaration of definitive insolvency.
3. The decision of the judge stating that the action has been legally concluded on the grounds that the minimum number of creditors as set out in article 13 of the law of Suspension of Payments did not attend the meeting.
4. The order approving the suspension of payments agreement with the creditors or the court ruling evidencing a motion of opposition to its approval.
5. Any resolutions made in connection with the suspension of payments proceedings which may affect limitation of the powers of the debtor to own property, together with resolutions appointing and substituting the auditors.

Article 285 – Registration of bankruptcies

On the page opened for each trader, company or registerable entity, the following entries will appear:

1. The conservatory measures referred to in article 877 of the Commercial Code.
2. The order declaring the bankruptcy.
3. The judgment reversing the bankruptcy order.
4. The judicial ruling definitively fixing the backdating of the bankruptcy.
5. The judicial ruling relating to the receivership.

6. The judgment determining the classification of the bankruptcy, together with the judgment which, if appropriate, could result in subsequent penal action for criminal insolvency.

If the judgment determining the classification of the bankruptcy declares that a person entered in the Companies Registry is an accessory, the relevant entry will also be made on the page of the register applying to that person.

Article 286 – Suspension of payments or bankruptcy of an unregistered trader

1. If the name of the trader, whose request for a declaration of suspension of payments has been processed, has not been entered in the register, his name will first be entered by means of a judicial mandate which should contain the reasons for requiring that an entry be made. The same procedure will be followed if the conservatory measures set out in article 877 of the Commercial Code have been issued or a bankruptcy order has been issued.
2. In the case of irregular business partnerships, the same registration procedure will be carried out. In the absence of a certificate of incorporation, registration will be made by means of a judicial mandate stating, at least, the registered address of the partnership and the identity of the partners.

Article 287 – Registerable matters and the reasons for registration

1. The entries referred to in the previous articles will be made by means of a judicial mandate or by an affidavit of the relevant resolution which will, if necessary, state whether or not it is final. In circumstances where it is not final, it will be considered to be of a precautionary nature.
2. The provisions of the judicial ruling will be recorded in the register with the name of the judge or court and the date on which it was made.

Article 288 – Recording of insolvency proceedings

All cautionary annotations or entries relating to any trader or business partnership subject to a suspension of payments or bankruptcy order will record the suspension or bankruptcy.

Article 289 – Cancellation of entries

1. The entries referred to in article 284 may be cancelled by means of a judicial mandate, recording the provisions of the final judgment by which the suspension of payments is dismissed; alternatively, the approved creditors' agreement will be declared to have been fully performed.
2. The entries referred to in article 285 may be cancelled by means of judicial mandate recording the provisions of the final judicial ruling by which the bankruptcy is declared to be terminated, except in relation to disqualification of the bankrupt himself or those in charge of the bankrupt partnership. This may only be cancelled by means of a judicial mandate recording the provisions of the final judgment of reinstatement.

Section II: The registration of administrative measures in relation to financial entities

Article 290 – Registerable administrative measures

1. On the page opened for each financial entity the following entries will appear:
   (1) The measures for supervision of these entities and the temporary substitution of their administrative or management bodies as determined by the competent administrative authority.
   With particular reference to insurance entities, the conservatory measures will be registered which are referred to under items (c), (d), (e), (f), (h) and (j) of the second paragraph of article 42 of the law governing private insurance, and also in the fourth paragraph of this law.
   (2) The measures for supervision of the liquidated entity as determined by the competent administrative authority.
   (3) The penalty of suspension, removal from office, or removal with disqualification of those holding administrative or managerial positions in financial entities, stating the duration of such a penalty.
   When the accused individual is a trader, the penalty of removal from office with disqualification will also be entered on the page corresponding to that person.
   If the accused individual was not registered, an entry will be made in the name of that person.
   (4) Revocation of the authorisation permitting the entity to operate as a financial entity.
   (5) The dissolution of financial entities by agreement on their own motion, the appointment and dismissal of liquidators, together with the declaration of liquidation of the entity. In this latter case, the registrar will make a closing entry on the page for the liquidated entity.
2. With regard to the matters addressed in this section, financial entities will be considered to be financial institutions, credit institutions, insurance institutions and those entities which carry on business in the securities market which are registered in the relevant special registers of the Bank of Spain, the General Directorate of Insurance, and the National Commission for the Securities Market.

Article 291 – Registerable matters and the reasons for registration

1. The entries referred to in the previous article will be made by means of the relevant administrative resolution.
2. The provisions of the administrative resolution will be recorded in the entry together with the name of the authority and the date on which it was made.
   If appropriate, the Registrar will also enter the name and surname or firm/trading name of the persons or entities who should be carrying out the supervisory functions or who have been appointed provisional administrators, liquidators or director-liquidators, indicating whether these persons or entities should act individually or jointly and, if necessary, their functions and powers.

Article 292 – Registerable administrative measures with respect to financial entities which are holding companies

On the page opened for each financial entity which is the holding company for a group of companies and which does not have the status of a credit institution, the administrative resolution recording the compulsory dissolutions of that entity will be entered together with the date when the period of liquidation commences and the name, surname or trading name of the liquidators and an outline of their terms of reference.

CIVIL CODE

TITLE XVII. COMPETITION AND PREFERENCE OF DEBTS

Section I. General provisions

Article 1.911

In order to fulfil his obligations, a debtor is liable to the extent of all his present and future assets.

Article 1.912

A debtor may judicially request release and respite from his debts, or either of these, from his creditors; but the exercise of this right will have no legal effect except in the circumstances and manner prescribed in the Law of Civil Procedure.

Article 1.913

A debtor whose liabilities are greater than his assets and who has ceased to pay his current obligations, must present himself before the competent tribunal for bankruptcy proceedings as soon as he recognises this situation.

Article 1.914

A declaration of bankruptcy disqualifies the bankrupt from managing his assets or carrying out any other type of equivalent function in law which he would otherwise be entitled to perform.

Article 1.915

His rights will be reinstated upon termination of bankruptcy proceedings; unless these are classified in such a way as to prevent this.

When bankruptcy proceedings are declared, all the bankrupt's debts not yet due will then become due.

If debts are paid before their due date, they will be discounted at the corresponding legal interest rates.

Article 1.916

From the date of declaration of bankruptcy, interest will cease to accrue on all the bankrupt's debts, except for debts secured by mortgage or pledge up to the amount secured.

If any excess sum remains after payment of the principal amount of the debts, it will be used to pay interest at whichever is the lower of the legal rate and the contractual interest rate.

Article 1.917

Agreements between a debtor and his creditors which have been judicially concluded, with all the formalities required by law, relating to release and respite or under the bankruptcy proceedings, will be binding on all parties thereto and for those who, summoned and notified in due form, have not protested within the prescribed period. Creditors, who have the right to abstain, and having duly exercised such right, are excepted. The creditors referred to in Articles 1.922, 1.923 and 1.924 have the right to abstain.

Article 1.918

When an agreement of release and respite is made with creditors of the same class, a lawful agreement of the majority of such creditors will be binding on all such creditors without prejudice to the respective priority of each debt.

Article 1.919

If the debtor complies with the agreement, his obligations will be extinguished as provided in the terms of such agreement; but if he fails to comply with the terms of the agreement, in whole or in part, the rights of the creditors to the amounts they have not received of their original claim will be reinstated and any of them may apply for a declaration of bankruptcy or for continuation of the bankruptcy proceedings.

Article 1.920

Unless the debtor and his creditors expressly agree to the contrary, once the bankruptcy proceedings have ended the creditors will retain their rights to recover the unsatisfied part of their debts from any assets the debtor might subsequently acquire.

Section II. Classification of debts

Article 1.921

Debts will be classified for their rank and payment in the order and in the terms set out in this chapter.

Article 1.922

In relation to particular items of the debtor's moveable property, the following will have preference:

1st Debts for the construction, repair, conservation or purchase price of moveable property within the control of the debtor, up to the value of the same.
2nd Debts secured by a pledge which is within the control of the creditor, over the pledged item and up to the value of that item.
3rd Debts secured by the collateral of bonds or securities, issued by a public or commercial establishment, and up to the value of such bonds or securities.
4th Debts relating to transportation, secured against the goods transported, up to the value of those goods, including carriage and storage expenses and fees up to the time of delivery and for 30 days thereafter.
5th Debts for board and lodging expenses, secured by the debtor's furniture within the lodging.
6th Debts for the purchase of seeds, costs of cultivation and advance payments to the debtor, secured by the income of the harvest for which they were originally intended.
7th Debts for rental and annual leases, secured by the furniture of the lessee located in the leased property and on the income from the same.

If the moveable property securing the preference has been removed, the creditor may claim the property from whoever holds it within a period of 30 days from the date when the removal took place.

Article 1.923

In relation to particular immoveable property and rights in rem of the debtor, the following will have preference:

1st Debts in favour of the State, secured by assets in respect of which taxes have been incurred, for an amount of the last complete fiscal year due but not paid.
2nd Debts owed to insurers up to two years insurance premiums, secured against the assets insured; and, if the insurance is mutual, up to the last two dividends which may have been shared out.
3rd Mortgages and financial loans, noted and registered in the Property Register, over the mortgaged assets or over those assets which were the subject of the relevant financings.
4th Debts registered in the Property Register as a conservatory measure by means of a judicial order relating to attachments, seizures and the execution of a judgment against the assets referred to in the entry in the Register and only when it relates to subsequent debts.
5th Loans of money, which have not been noted or registered, over the property in respect of which the loan was made and only in respect of debts other than those referred to in the four preceding paragraphs of this article.

Article 1.924

In respect of the debtor's remaining moveable and immoveable property the following will enjoy preference:

1st Debts owed to the province or municipality for taxes in respect of the last complete fiscal year, due but not paid, and not covered under article 1.923, paragraph no. 1.
2nd Accrued debts for:

A. Legal and administrative expenses of the insolvency proceedings in the common interests of the creditors, incurred with due authorisation or approval.
B. The debtor's funeral, according to the custom of the locality, and also those of his or her spouse and children under paternal authority (patria potestes) if they do not possess their own assets.
C. Expenses of these persons' terminal illness arising during their final year, calculated until the date of death.
D. Wages and salaries of employees and domestic service relating to the debtor's final year.
E. Amounts due under the mandatory payment systems for state benefits, social security and mutual employment contributions for the same period of time referred to in the preceding paragraph, provided these have no greater degree of preference over the matters referred to in the previous article.
F. Advances made to the debtor for himself or the family for which he is responsible in respect of comestibles, clothing or footwear during the same period of time.
G. Living expenses incurred during the insolvency proceedings hearing, unless considered exorbitant.

3rd Debts without special privilege set out:
A. In a notarial instrument,
B. In a final judgment as debts awarded in litigation.

These debts will take preference as between themselves according to the date of the notarial instrument or judgment.

Article 1.925

Debts of any class or type other than those referred to in the preceding articles are not entitled to preference.

Section III. Preference of debts

Article 1.926

Preferential debts in respect of certain moveable property exclude all others to the extent of the value of the moveable property to which the preference relates.

If there are two or more competing debts in respect of certain moveable property, the following rules will apply as far as preference in payment is concerned:

1st The pledged debt excludes all others to the extent of the value of the item subject to the security.
2nd In the case of collateral, which has been legally constituted in favour of more than one creditor, the preference among creditors will be determined in accordance with the order of dates of the guarantee documents.
3rd Debts for advances on seed, cultivation and harvesting expenses will have preference over lease and rental debts secured on the income of the harvest in respect of which they were incurred.
4th In any other case, the proceeds of sale of moveable property will be distributed pro-rata amongst the debts having special preference in respect of such moveable property.

Article 1.927

Debts which enjoy preference with respect to certain immoveable property or rights in rem, will exclude the total amount of all others to the extent of the value of the immoveable property or right in rem to which the preference relates.

If two or more debts are in competition with respect to the same immoveable property or rights in rem, the following rules will apply with regard to their respective preference:

1st Those debts referred to in paragraphs 1 and 2 of article 1.923 will have preference, in their order, over debts referred to in the remaining paragraphs of that article.
2nd Noted and registered mortgages and financial loans referred to in paragraph 3 of article 1.923, and debts referred to in paragraph 4 of that article, will enjoy preference amongst themselves in accordance with the order of entry of the respective registration or annotation in the Property Register.
3rd Unnoted and unregistered financial loans not appearing in the Register and referred to in paragraph 5 of article 1.923, will enjoy preference amongst themselves in reverse order of their date of creation.

Article 1.928

The remainder of the debtor's capital, after payment of the preferential debts with respect to certain assets, whether moveable or immoveable property, will be aggregated with his other assets available for payment of the remaining debts.

In respect of those debts which, being preferential in relation to certain assets, whether moveable or immoveable property, and which have not been fully discharged from the sale proceeds of these assets, any shortfall will be fully discharged, in the relevant order and ranking in accordance with their respective category.

Article 1.929

Those debts which do not enjoy preference in respect of certain assets and debts which do enjoy preference for the unrealised amounts or debts in respect of which the right to preference has been prescribed, will be paid in accordance with the following rules:

1st The order referred to in article 1.924.
2nd Preferential debts by date order and those which have the same date, on a pro-rata basis.
3rd Ordinary debts referred to in article 1.925 and with no date order.

INDEX